ZIGGY'S
STAR
PERFORMANCES

ZIGGY'S STAR PERFORMANCES

by Tom Wilson

A collection of the creator's favorites
from ZIGGY's past ten years

Foreword by Gene Shalit

Andrews and McMeel
A Universal Press Syndicate Company
Kansas City • New York

ZIGGY® is syndicated internationally by Universal Press Syndicate.

 For information write Andrews and McMeel, a Universal Press Syndicate Company, 4900 Main Street, Kansas City, Missouri 64112.

ISBN: 0-8362-1859-0

Library of Congress Catalog Card Number: 89-84807

FOREWORD
by Gene Shalit

I don't have to urge you to pick up a copy of *Ziggy's Star Performances.* You already have. So you're joining the millions who Zig with Ziggy—the lovable character who's ambushed by life. Dear old Ziggy. Though not so old, considering that he leaped from Tom Wilson's brain in 1971. Ziggy has been bumping into the world's problems, anomalies, and Chef's Specials for almost two decades— every day of the week, every week of the year. From that plethora, Tom Wilson has chosen the best, the crème de la crème, the Ziggiest cartoons for this All Star reunion.

Ziggy leads a semisolitary life, going through the emotions with only a dog, a duck, a fish, a plant, and, occasionally, a psychiatrist who tends to nod off when Ziggy speaks.

Ziggy's idea of a night out is to go to Mom's Diner, where she's likely to offer to cut his food or admonish him to wear his scarf when he leaves. Sometimes he brings a mirror so he'll have company.

No matter where he is, Ziggy is a stranger, and stranger things happen to no one else. When Ziggy checks the fruit counter, navel oranges are separated into "innies" and "outies." If he consults a map that says "You are here," a notice in the corner taunts, "But everyone else is over here!" Mechanical contrivances lie in wait: A vending machine hits him in the face with a pie . . . his refrigerator shelves proclaim their calories . . . a toaster holds his toast hostage.

Wherever Ziggy turns, life turns on him, or turns him down, or turns away, or takes a bizarre turn. Ziggy is by turns confronted by redundancies, paranoia, or crafty used-car salesmen. It's remarkable how Tom Wilson has managed to keep up this high level of life's insights. He has a gift for turning every insight out.

And have you noticed how often Ziggy seems to be alone? There's poor Ziggy by himself, perplexed by a bewildering sign, a drooping plant, a Venetian blind lying tangled on the floor. But know what? Don't feel sorry for Ziggy. He's never alone. He's with you and some 44 million other women, men, and children every single day. He is greeted with love and smiles by the throngs who receive his greeting cards every year. Just think—more millions of people have been wished a happy birthday by Ziggy than by any other bald man in history.

And Ziggy is not alone because right there with him, every stroke of the way, is his nibs, Tom Wilson, who's been drawn to Ziggy ever since Ziggy's first brush with life's befuddlements.

Day after day, his graphic adventures are a sketch—reflecting our lives so keenly that he winds up on our refrigerator doors to remind us that there, but for the grace of Ziggy, go we.

Only one omission mars this grand collection: My all-time favorite has been left out (through an oversight, I'm sure). And to rectify this, let's put it here:

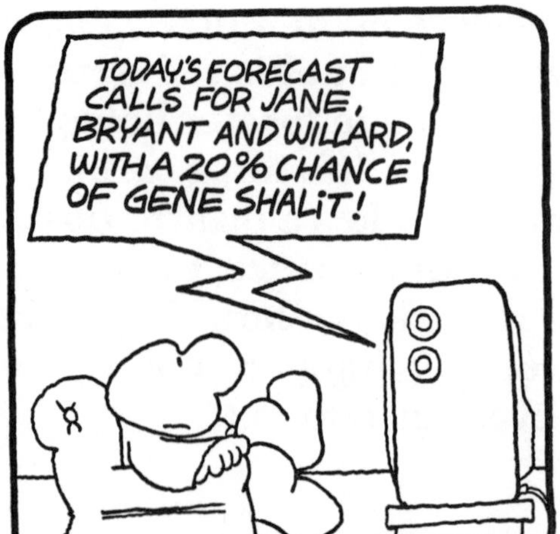
TODAY'S FORECAST CALLS FOR JANE, BRYANT AND WILLARD, WITH A 20% CHANCE OF GENE SHALIT!
TOM WILSON

for our Friends
Jim Andrews,
and
John Gibbons

...who live on within
our Memories,
within our hearts,
within these pages.

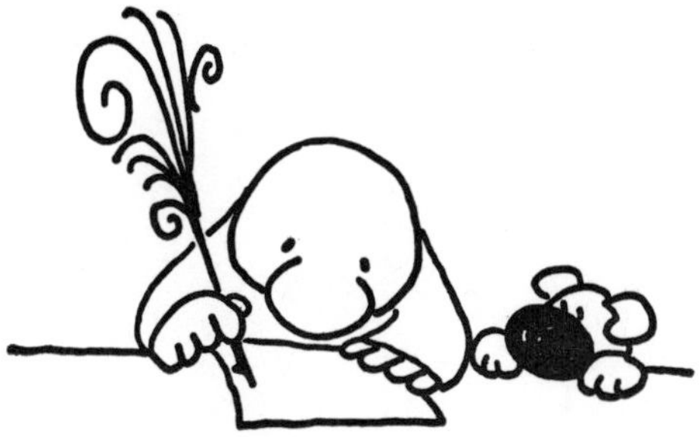

ZIGGY
and
Tom Wilson

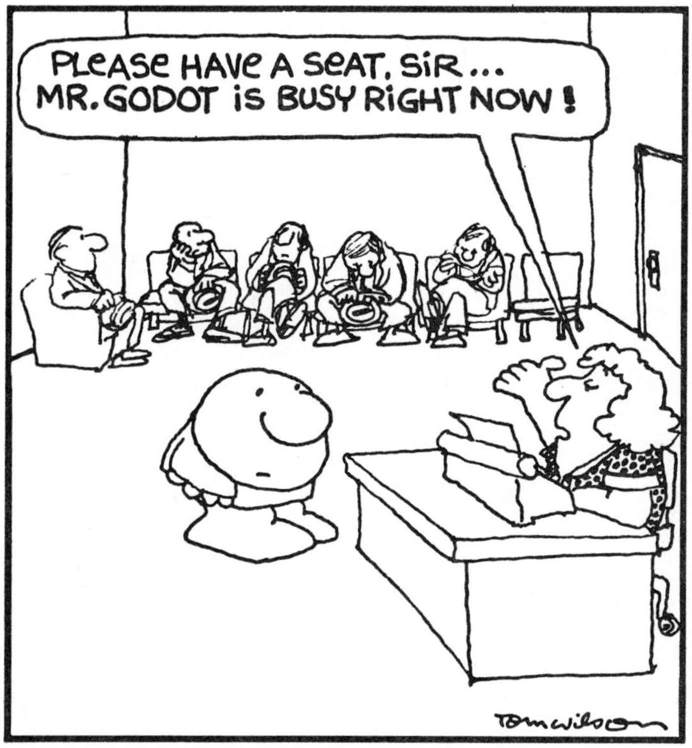
PLEASE HAVE A SEAT, SIR ...
MR. GODOT IS BUSY RIGHT NOW!
Tom Wilson

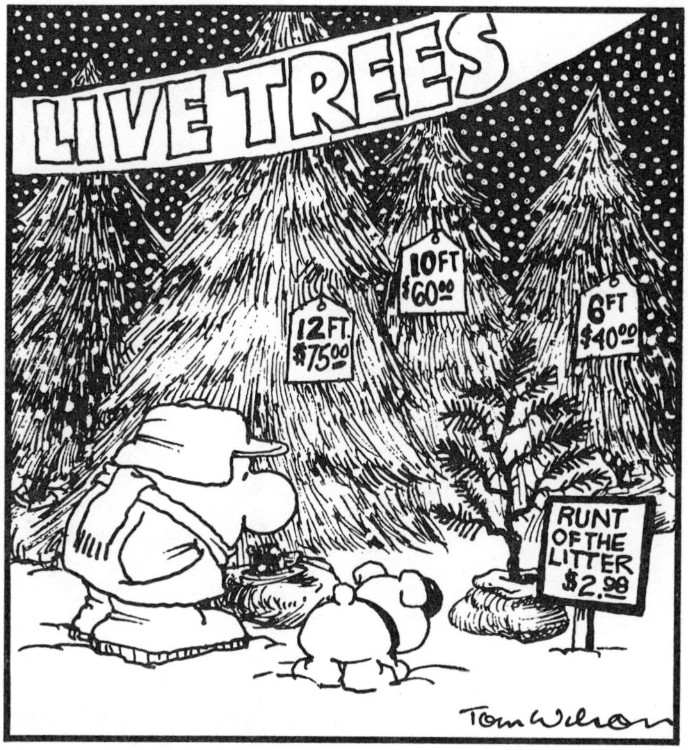
LIVE TREES
12 FT. $75.00
10 FT $60.00
6 FT $40.00
RUNT OF THE LITTER $2.98
Tom Wilson

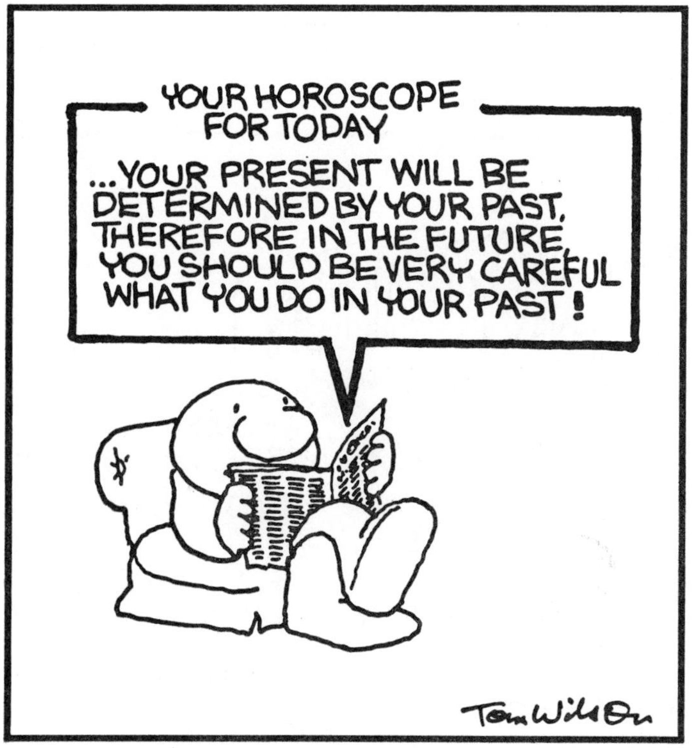
YOUR HOROSCOPE FOR TODAY
...YOUR PRESENT WILL BE DETERMINED BY YOUR PAST, THEREFORE IN THE FUTURE, YOU SHOULD BE VERY CAREFUL WHAT YOU DO IN YOUR PAST!
Tom Wilson

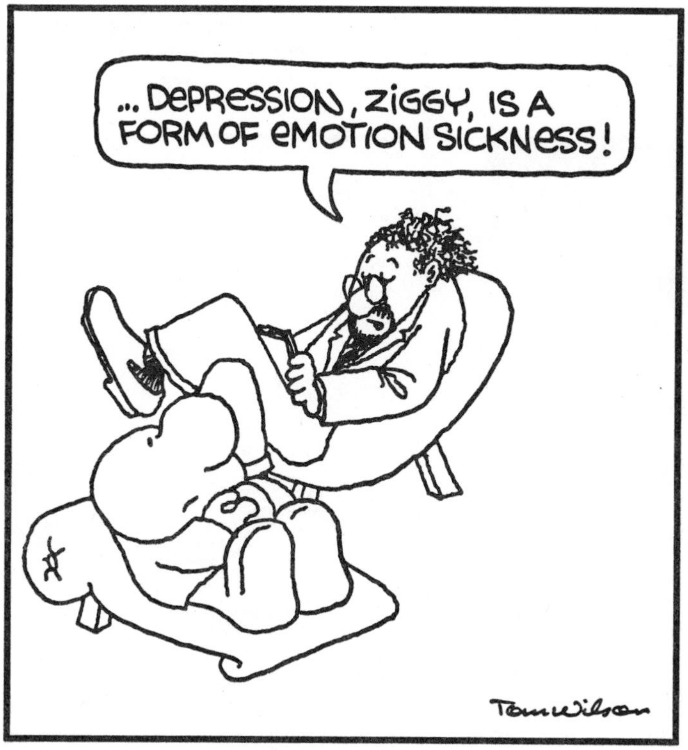
... DEPRESSION, ZIGGY, IS A FORM OF EMOTION SICKNESS!
Tom Wilson

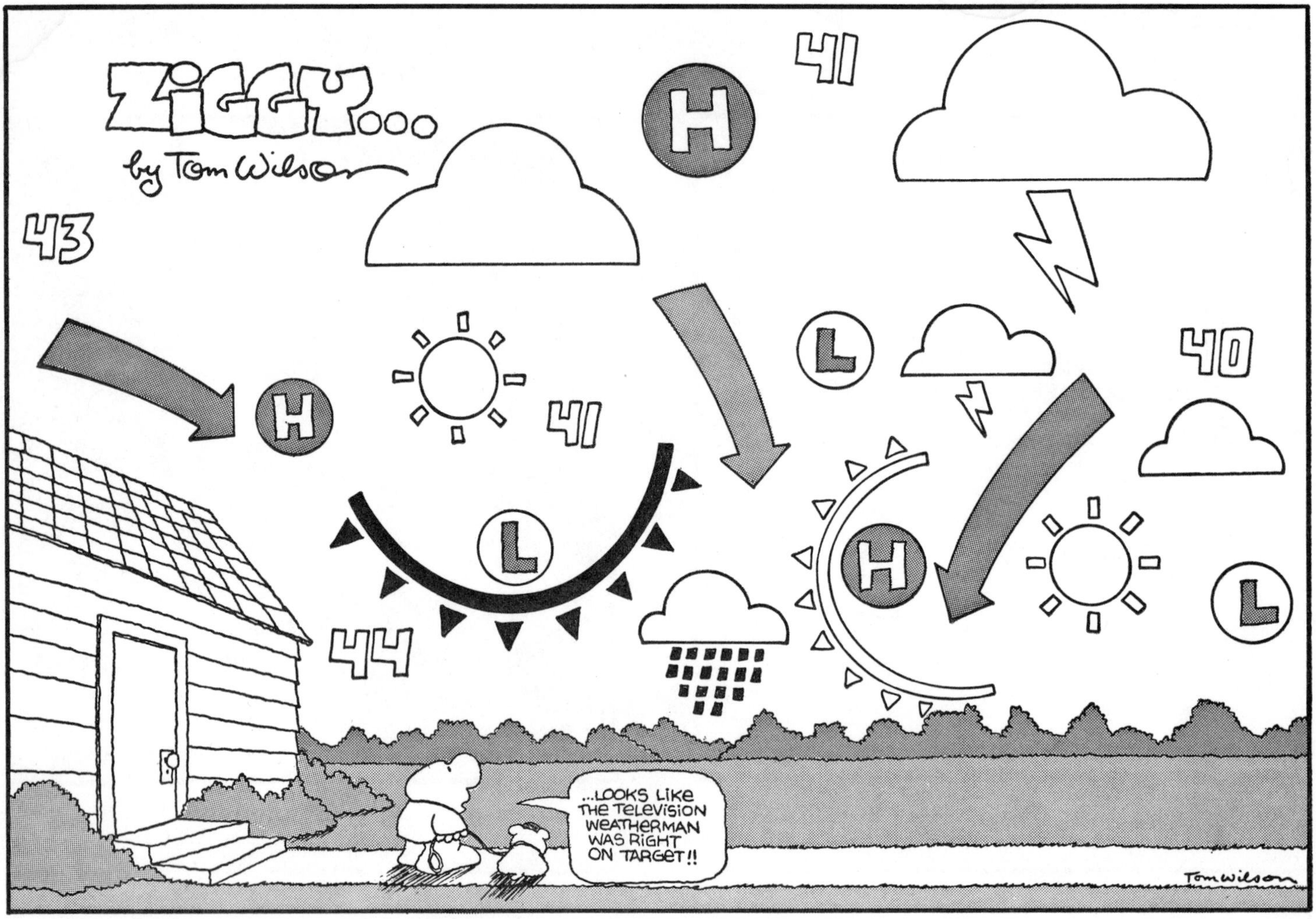
ZIGGY...
by Tom Wilson
43
41
41
40
44
H
H
H
L
L
L
L
...LOOKS LIKE THE TELEVISION WEATHERMAN WAS RIGHT ON TARGET!!
Tom Wilson

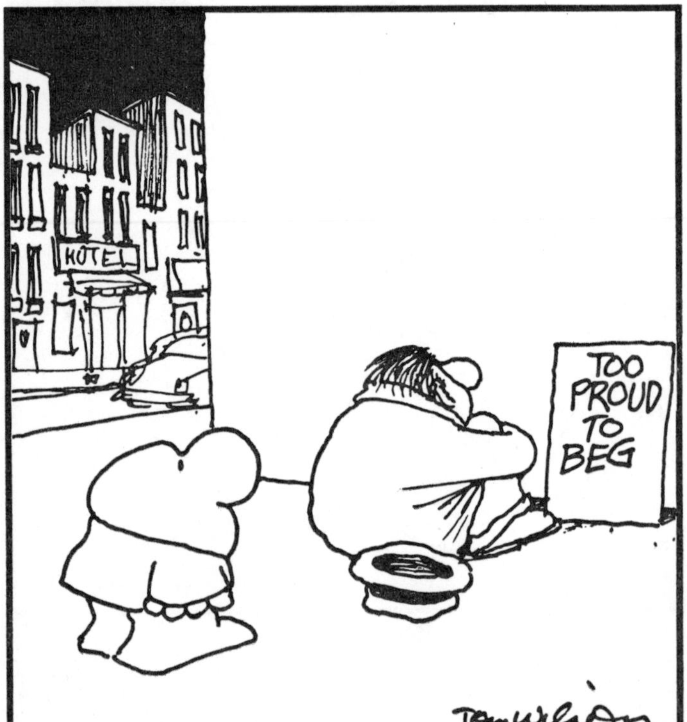
HOTEL
TOO PROUD TO BEG
Tom Wilson

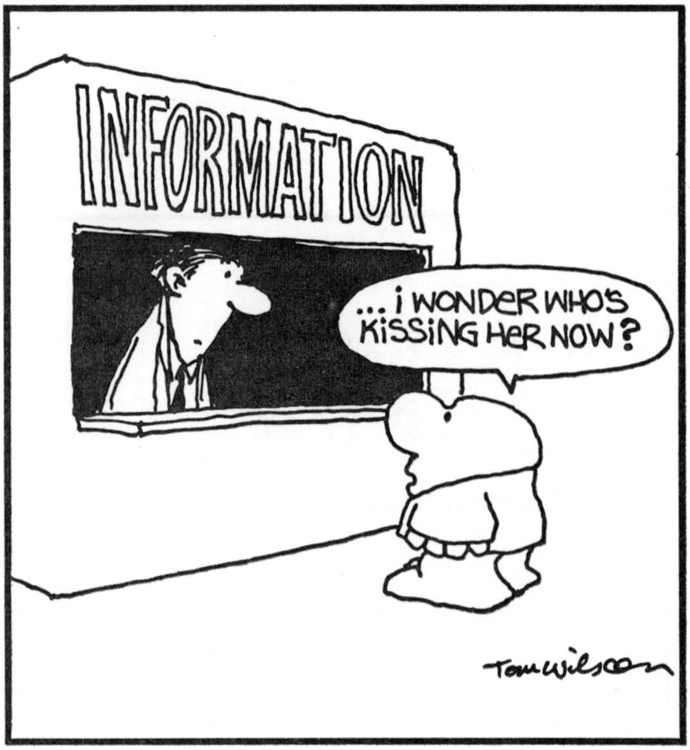
INFORMATION
...i WONDER WHO'S KISSING HER NOW?
Tom Wilson

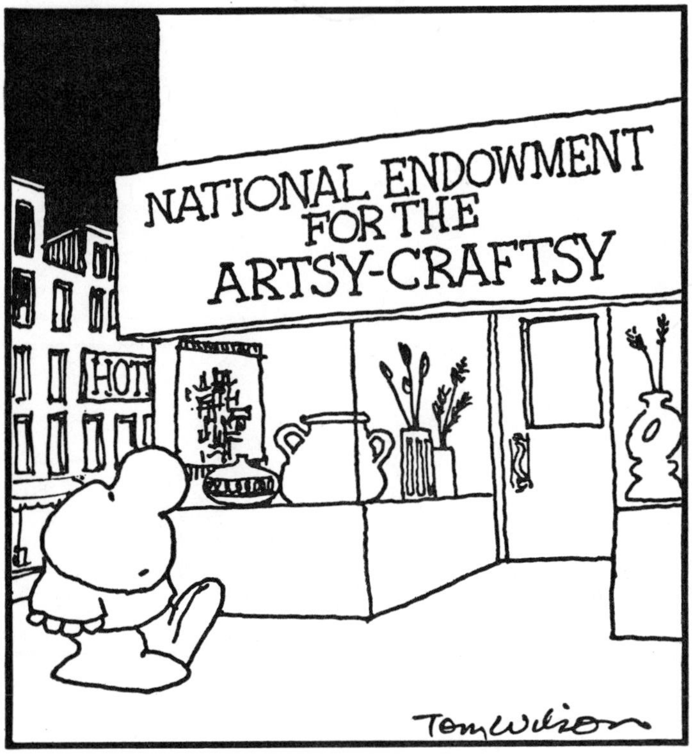
NATIONAL ENDOWMENT FOR THE ARTSY-CRAFTSY
HOT
Tom Wilson

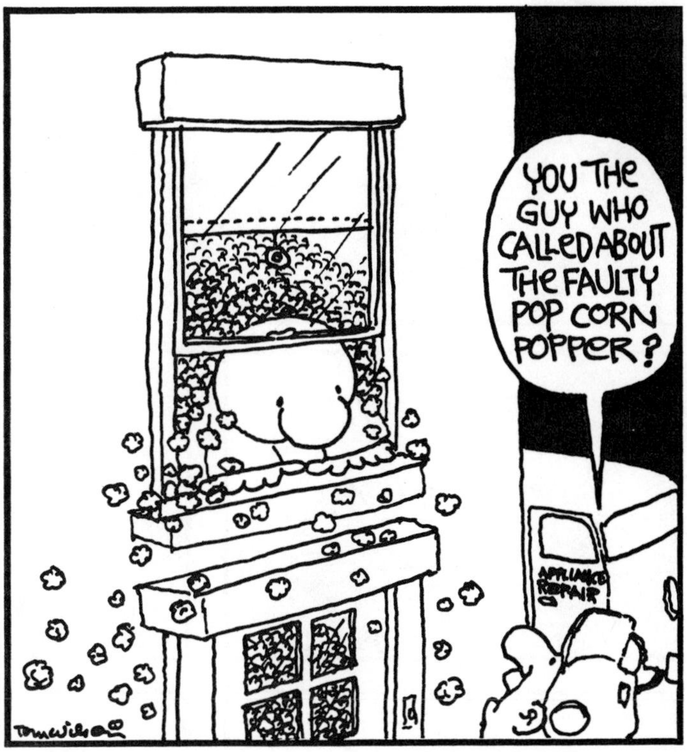
YOU THE GUY WHO CALLED ABOUT THE FAULTY POP CORN POPPER?
APPLIANCE REPAIR
Tom Wilson

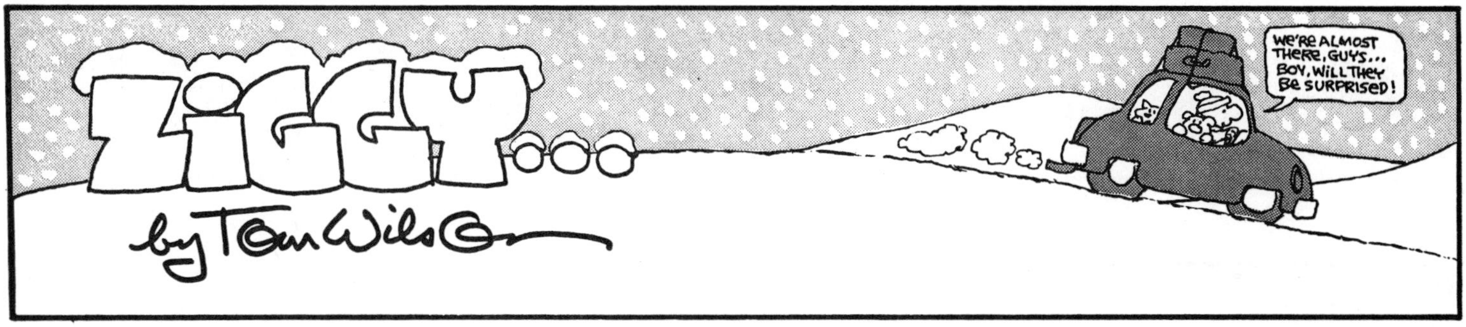
ZIGGY...
by Tom Wilson
WE'RE ALMOST THERE, GUYS... BOY, WILL THEY BE SURPRISED!

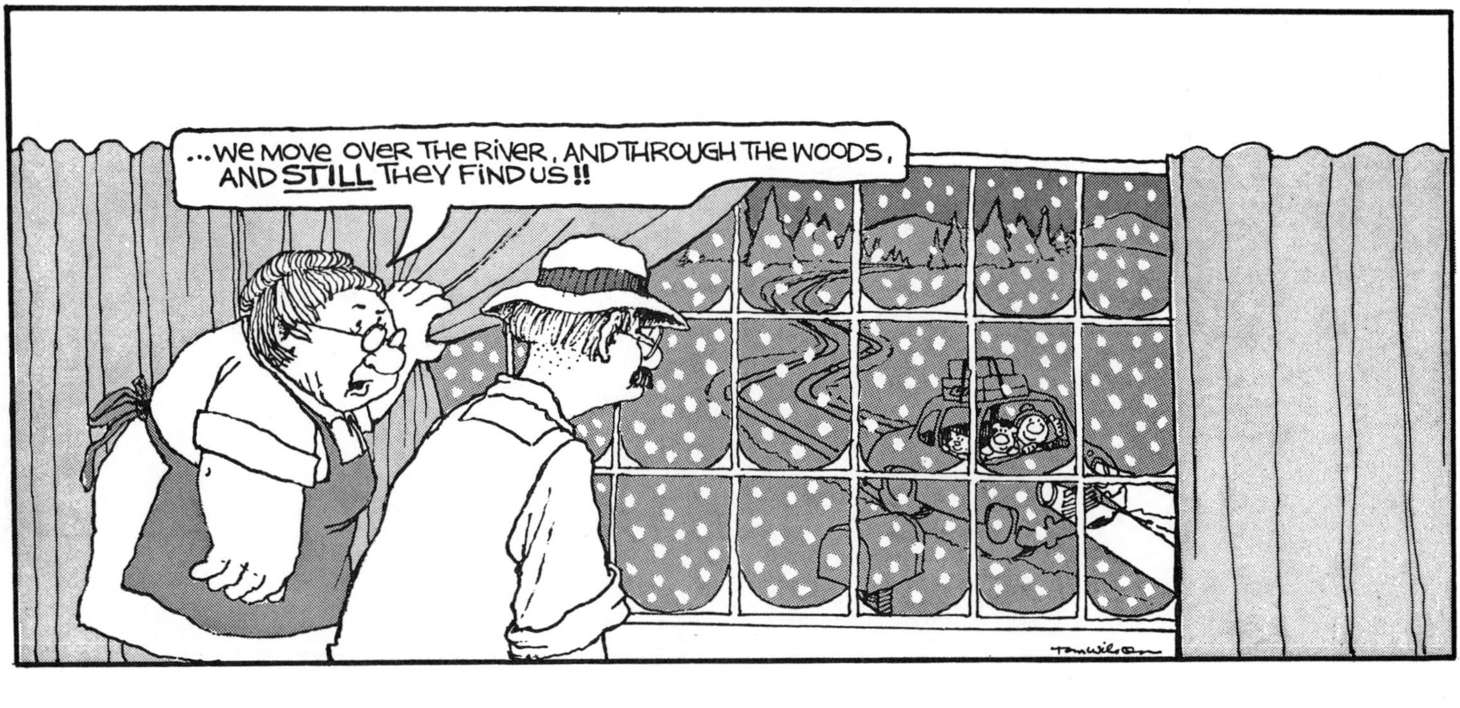
...WE MOVE OVER THE RIVER, AND THROUGH THE WOODS, AND STILL THEY FIND US!!
Tom Wilson

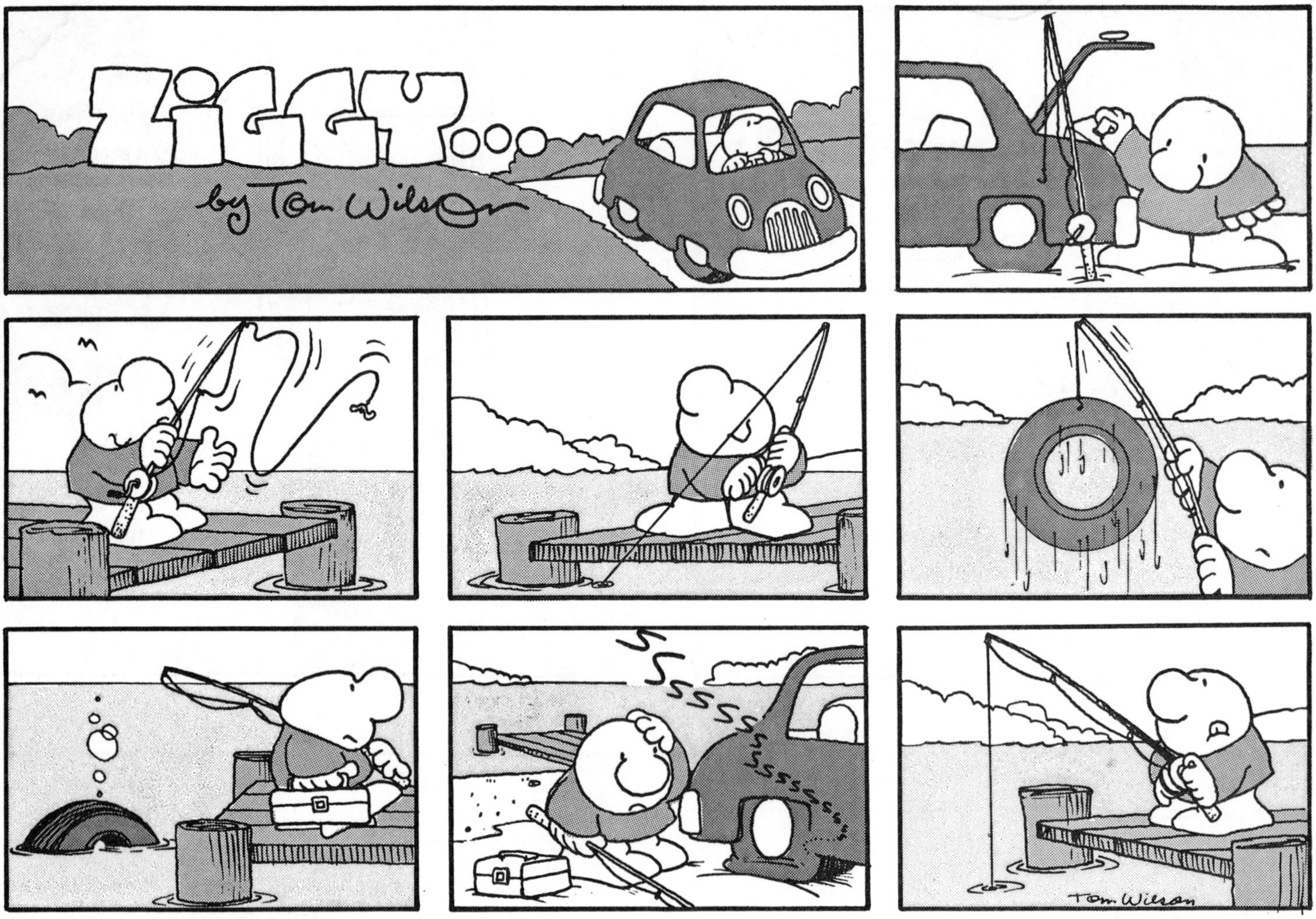
ZIGGY...
by Tom Wilson
Tom Wilson

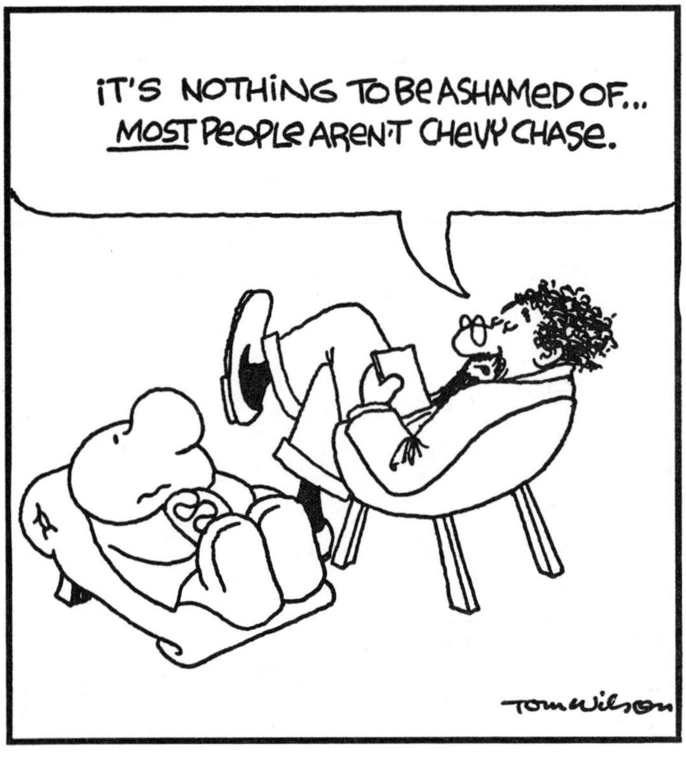
IT'S NOTHING TO BE ASHAMED OF...
MOST PEOPLE AREN'T CHEVY CHASE.
Tom Wilson

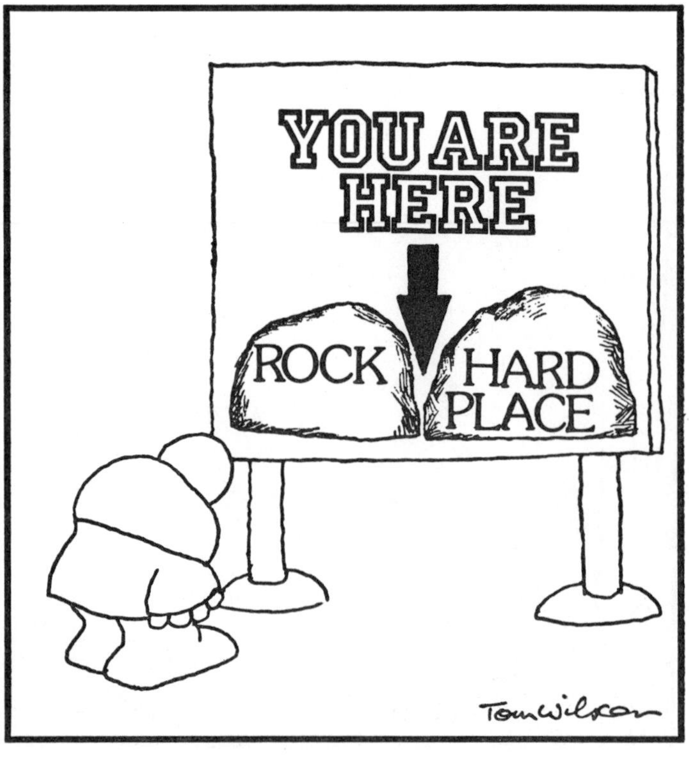
YOU ARE HERE
ROCK
HARD PLACE
Tom Wilson

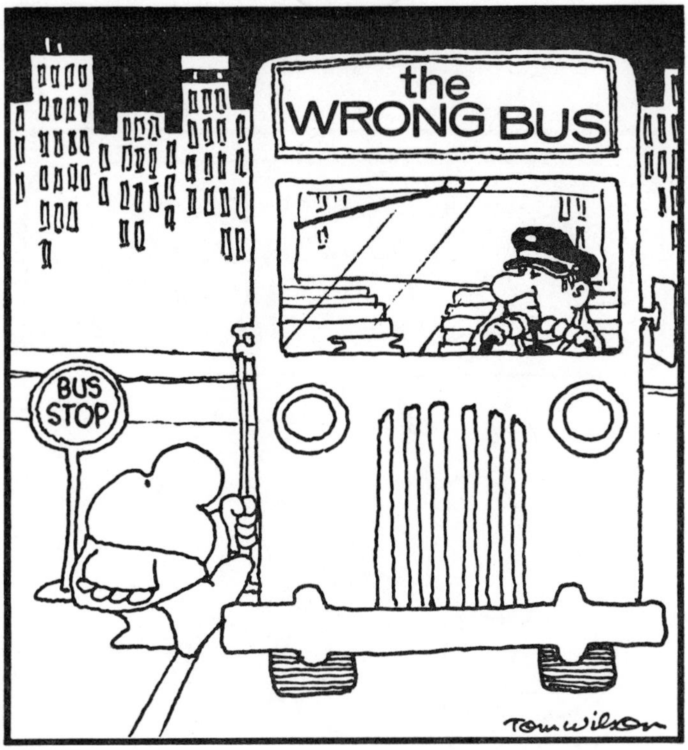
the WRONG BUS
BUS STOP
Tom Wilson

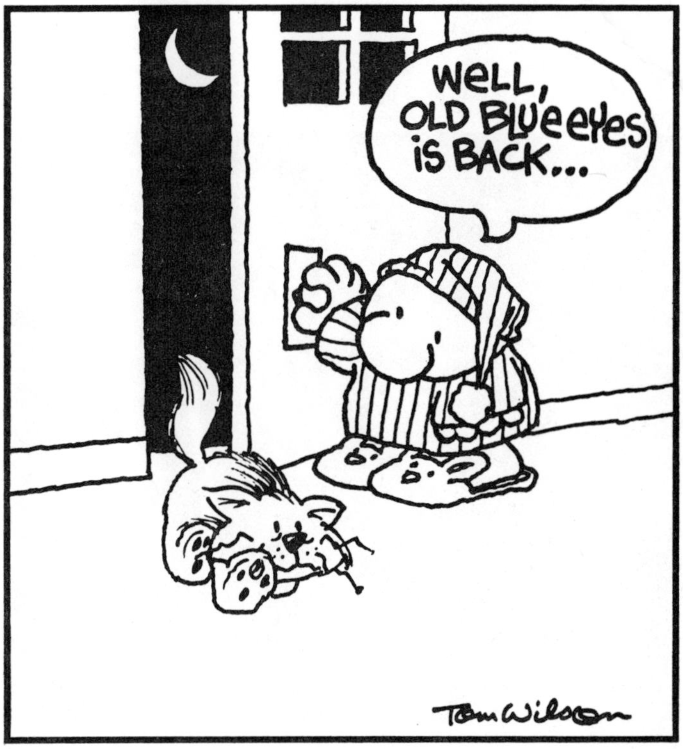
WELL, OLD BLUe eYeS IS BACK...
Tom Wilson

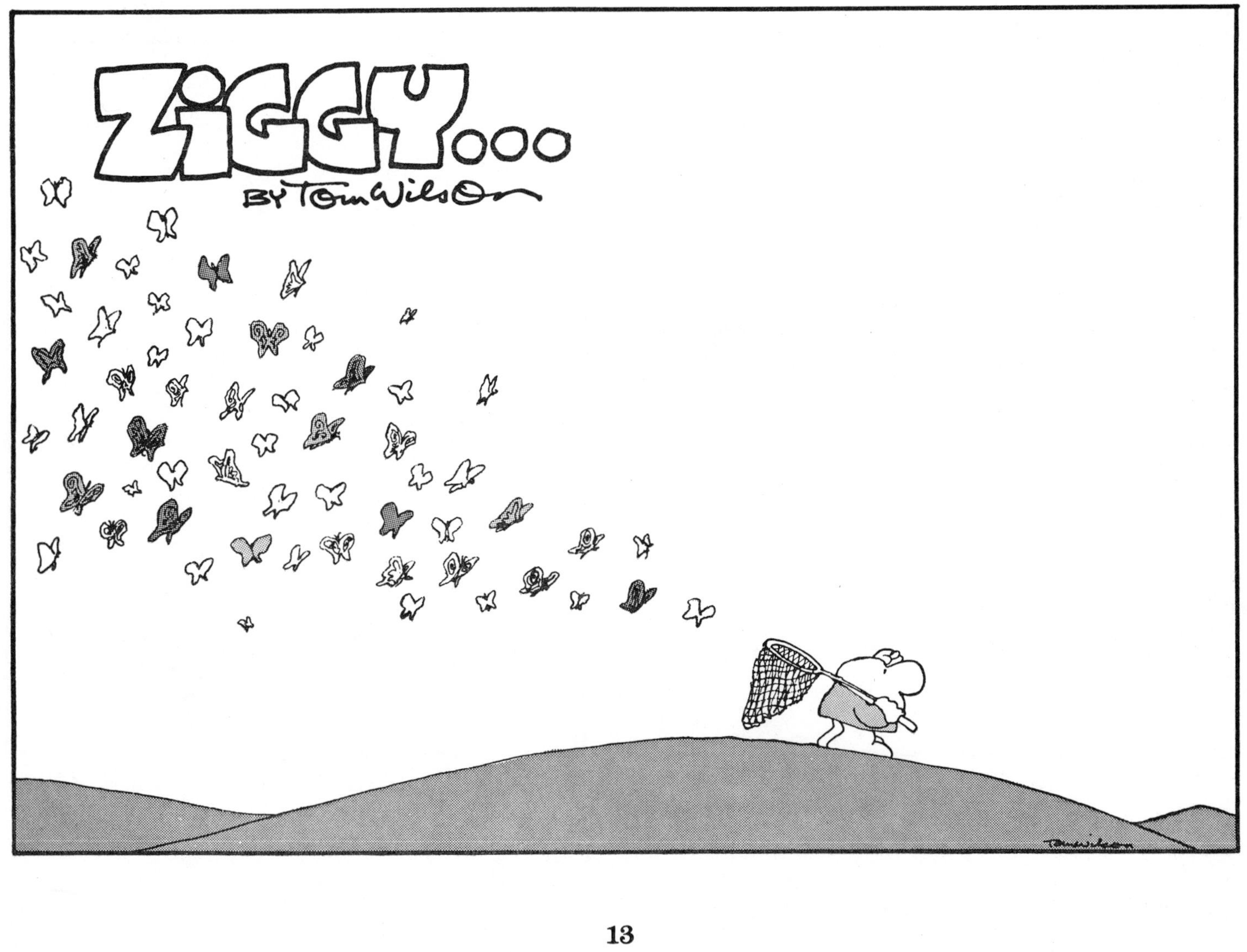
ZiGGY...
BY Tom Wilson

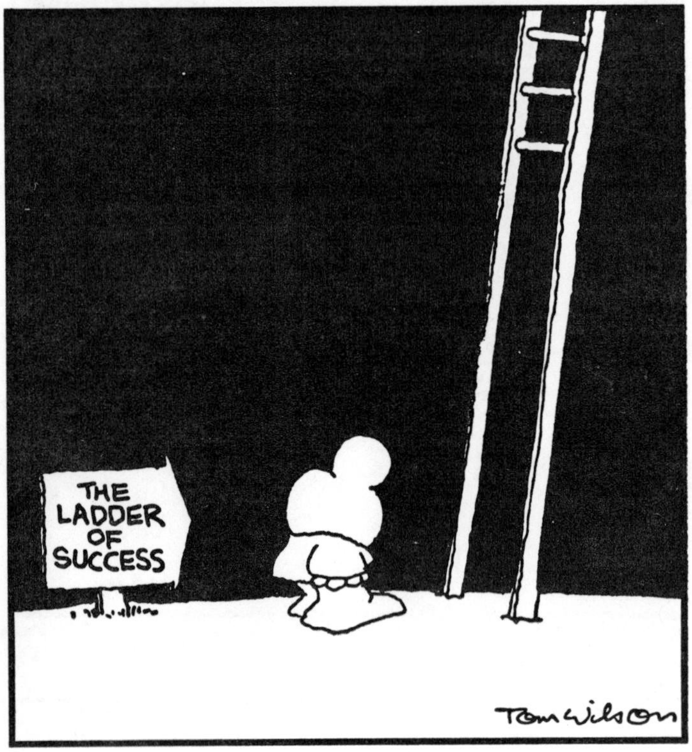
THE LADDER OF SUCCESS
Tom Wilson

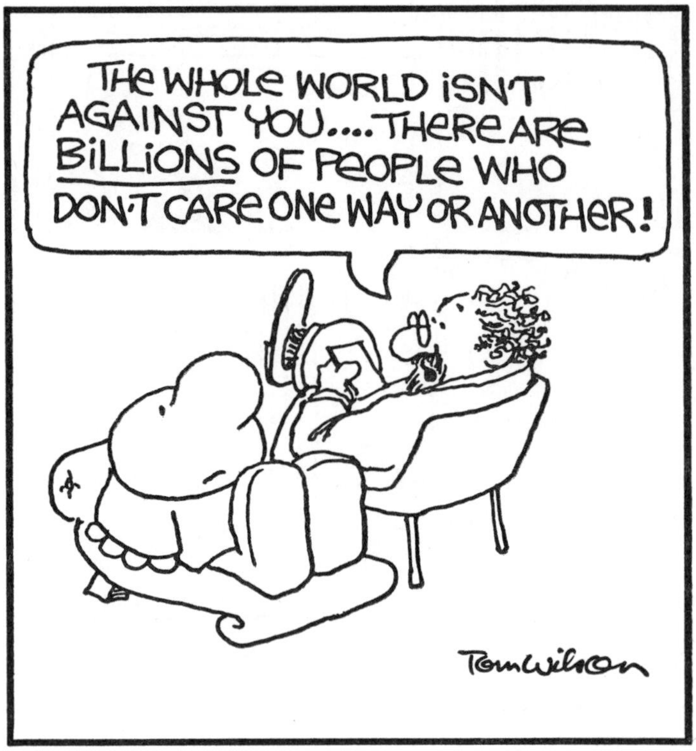
THE WHOLE WORLD ISN'T AGAINST YOU.... THERE ARE BILLIONS OF PEOPLE WHO DON'T CARE ONE WAY OR ANOTHER!
Tom Wilson

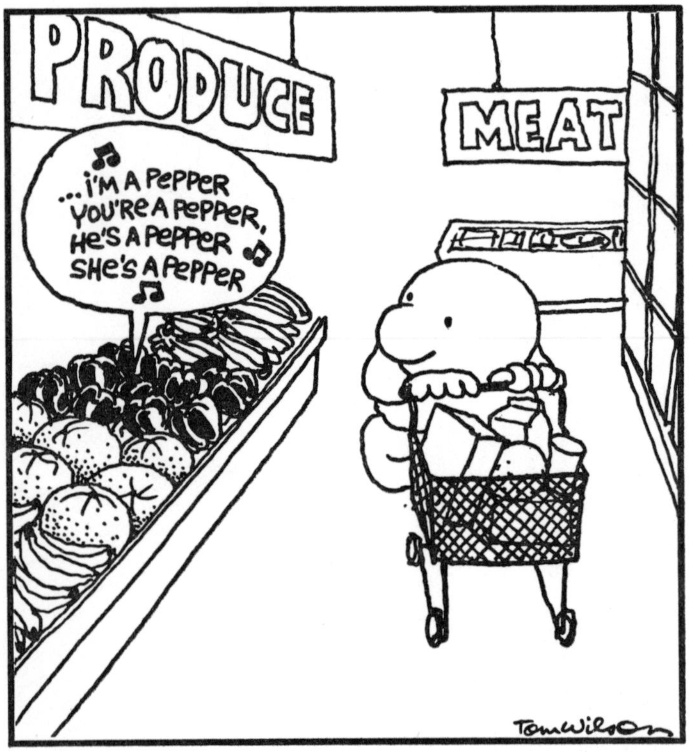
PRODUCE
MEAT
...I'M A PEPPER YOU'RE A PEPPER, HE'S A PEPPER SHE'S A PEPPER
Tom Wilson

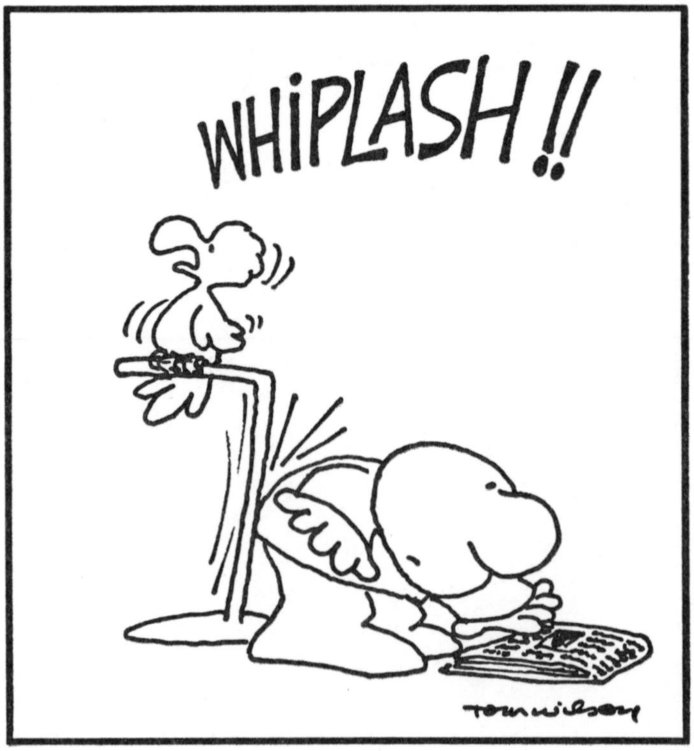
WHIPLASH!!
Tom Wilson

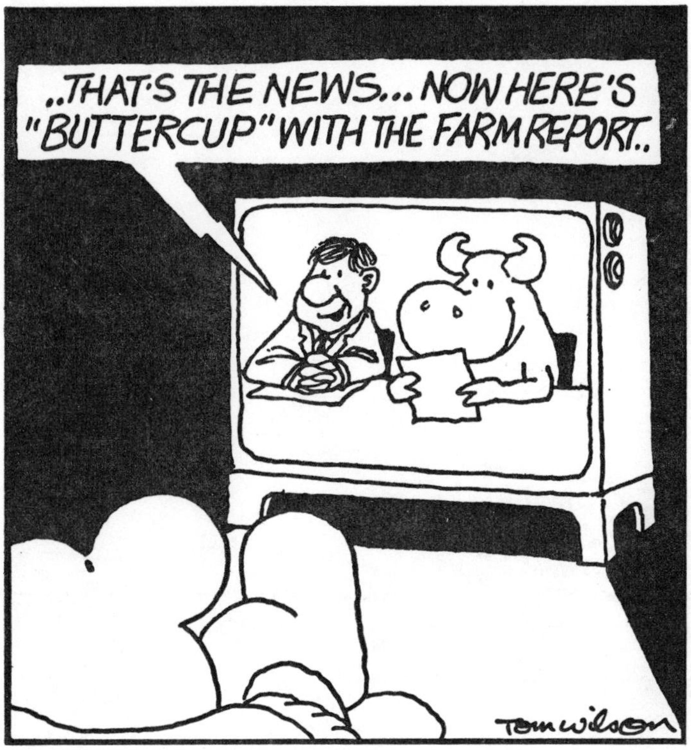
..THAT'S THE NEWS... NOW HERE'S "BUTTERCUP" WITH THE FARM REPORT..
TOM WILSON

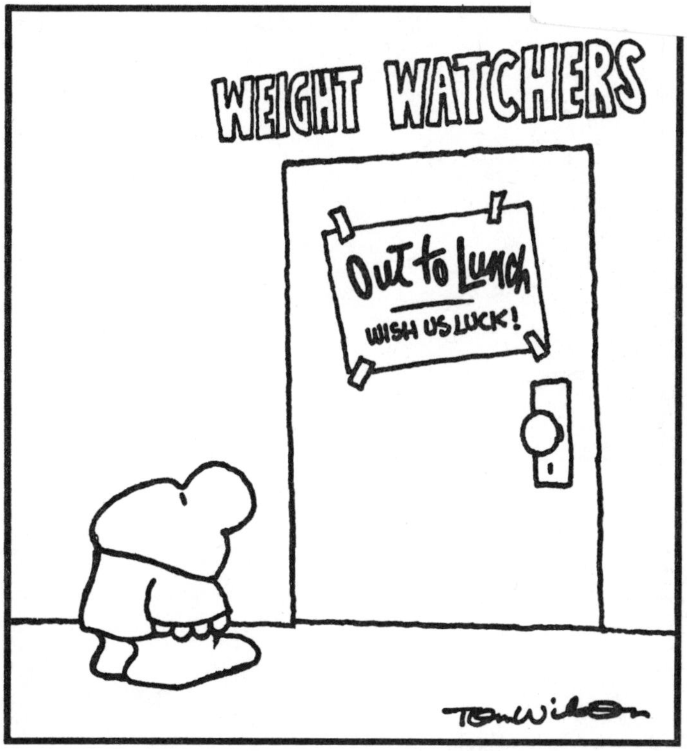
WEIGHT WATCHERS
Out to Lunch
WISH US LUCK!
TOM WILSON

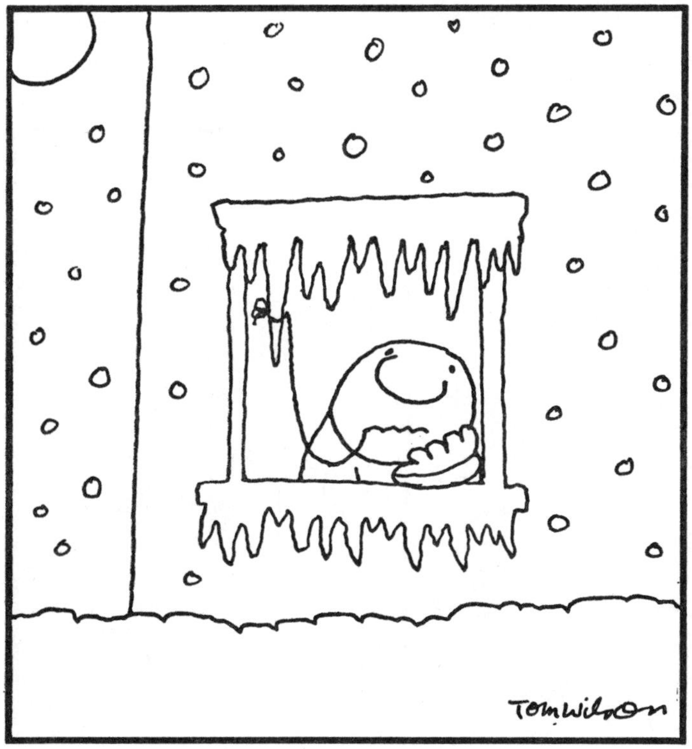
TOM WILSON

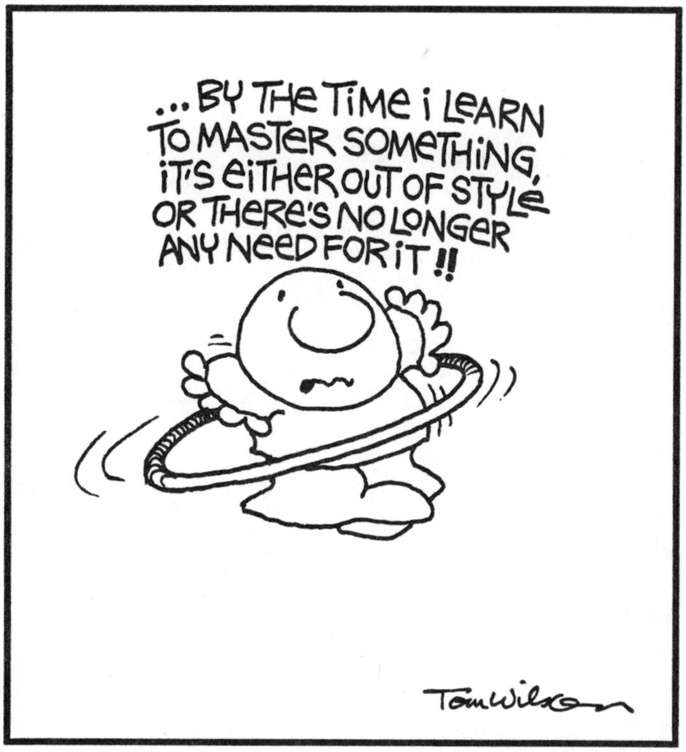
... BY THE TIME I LEARN TO MASTER SOMETHING, IT'S EITHER OUT OF STYLE OR THERE'S NO LONGER ANY NEED FOR IT!!
TOM WILSON

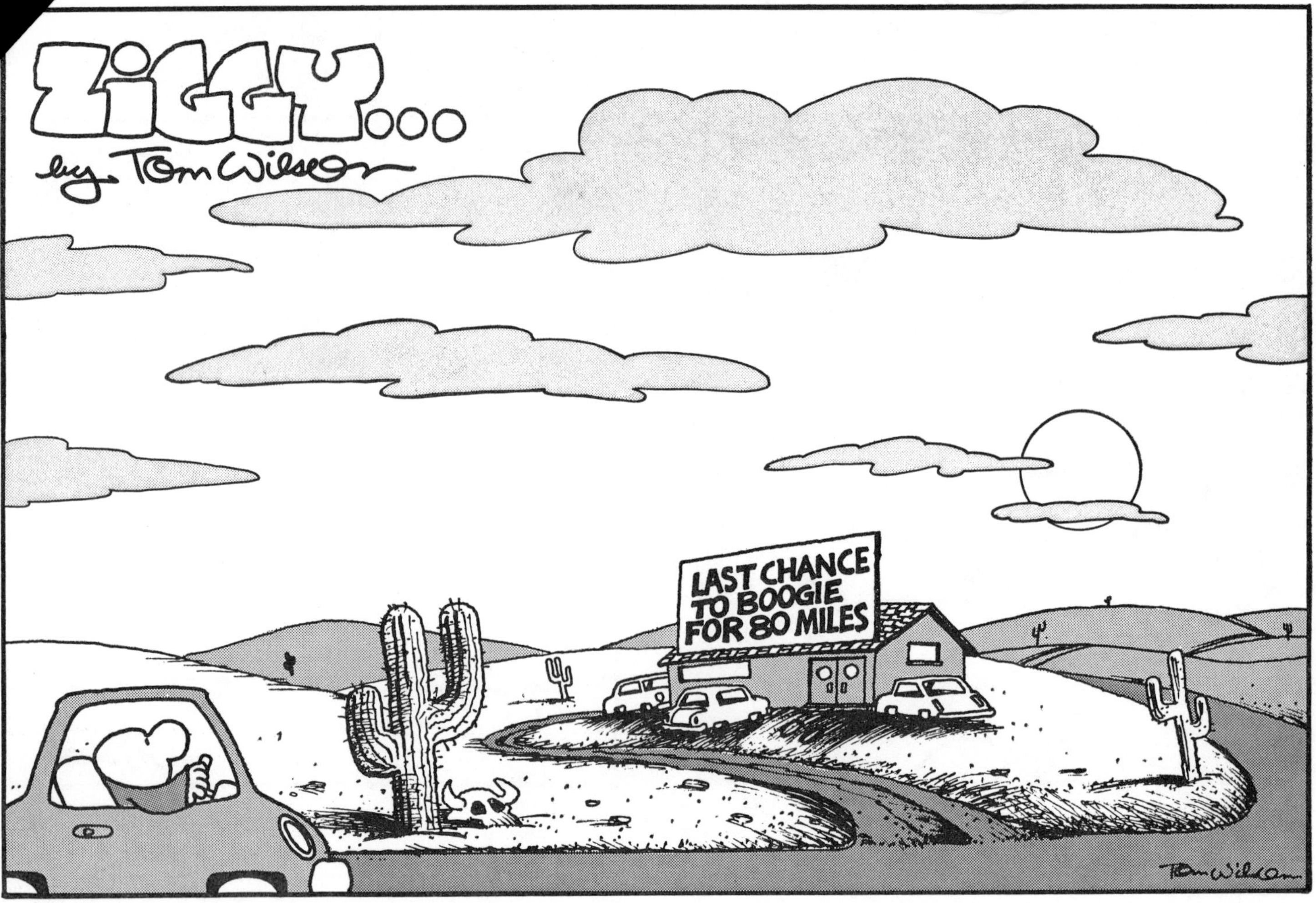
ZIGGY...
by Tom Wilson
LAST CHANCE TO BOOGIE FOR 80 MILES
Tom Wilson

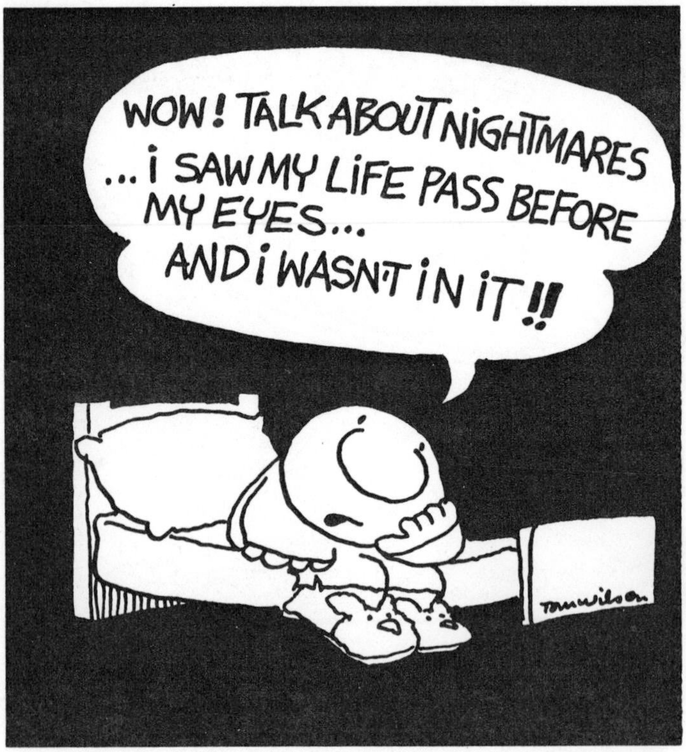
WOW! TALK ABOUT NIGHTMARES ...i SAW MY LiFE PASS BEFORE MY EYES... AND i WASN'T iN iT!!
tom wilson

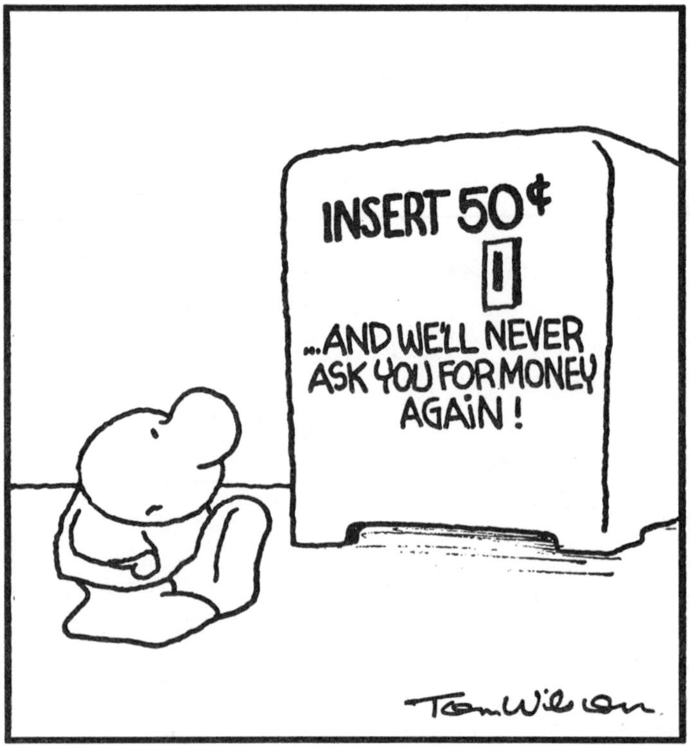
INSERT 50¢
...AND WE'LL NEVER ASK YOU FOR MONEY AGAiN!
Tom Wilson

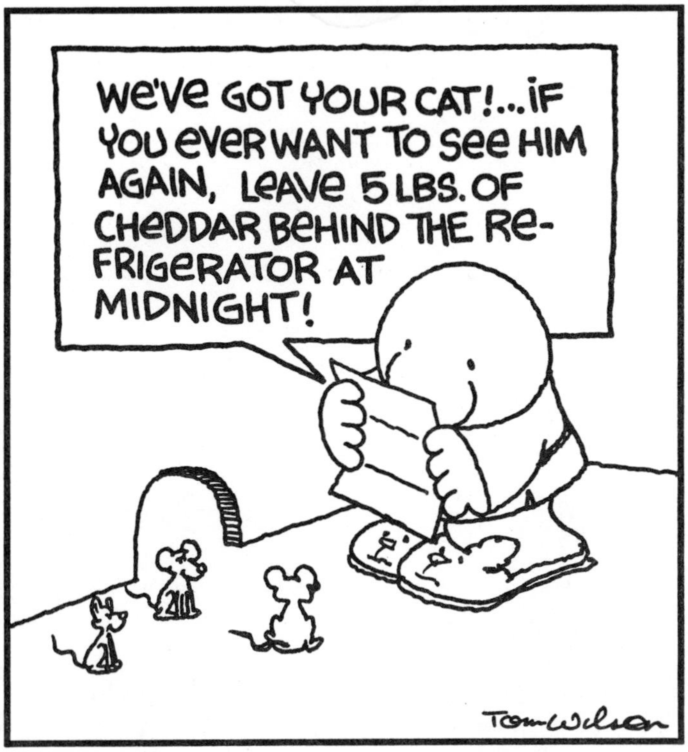
WE'VE GOT YOUR CAT!...IF YOU EVER WANT TO SEE HIM AGAIN, LEAVE 5 LBS. OF CHEDDAR BEHIND THE RE-FRIGERATOR AT MIDNIGHT!
Tom Wilson

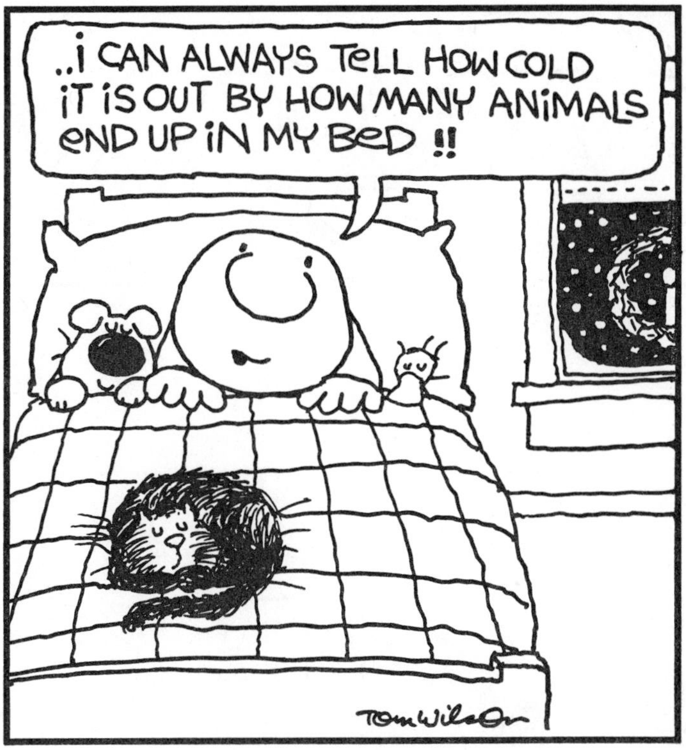
..I CAN ALWAYS TELL HOW COLD IT IS OUT BY HOW MANY ANIMALS END UP IN MY BED !!
Tom Wilson

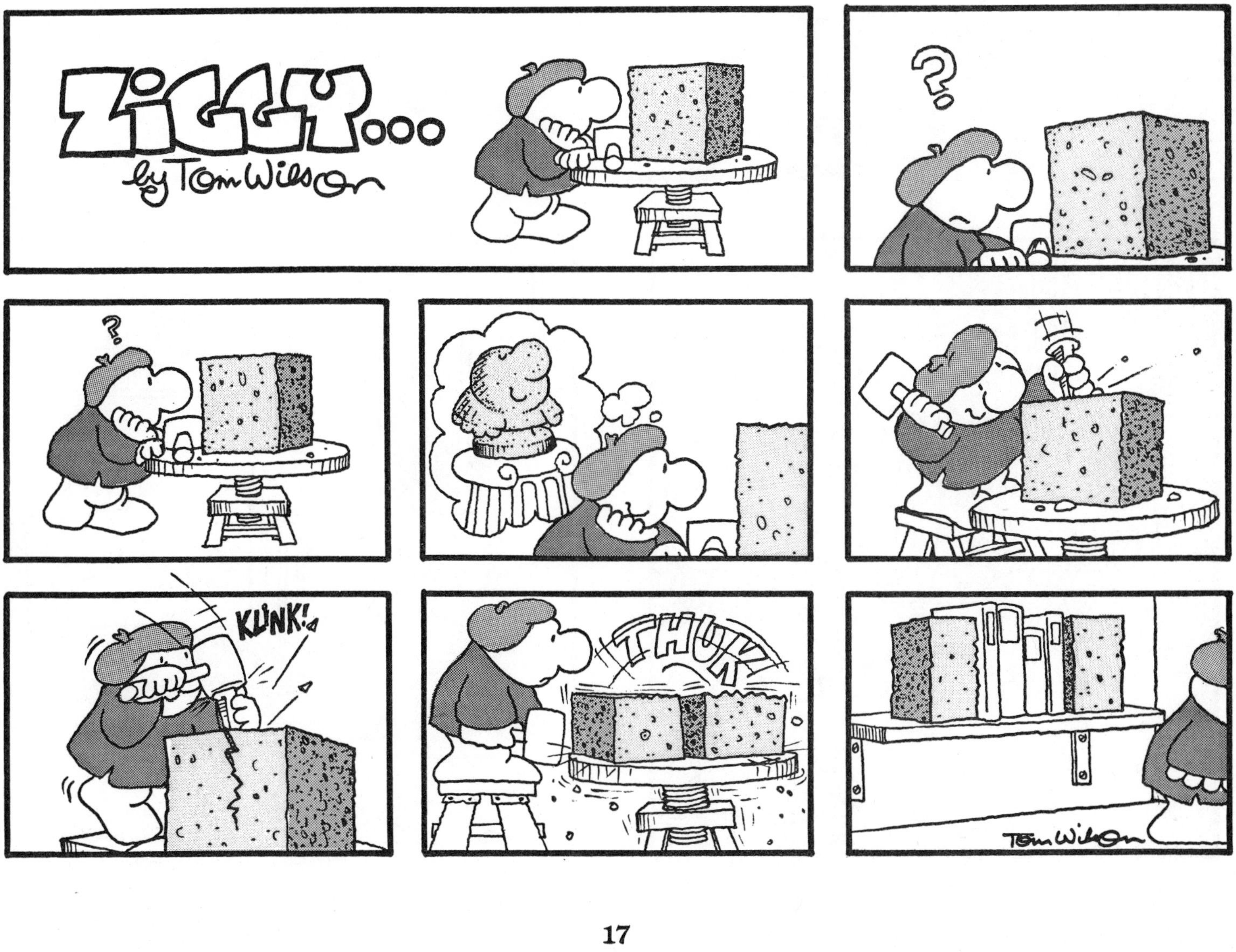
ZIGGY...
by Tom Wilson
?
?
KLINK!
THUNK
Tom Wilson

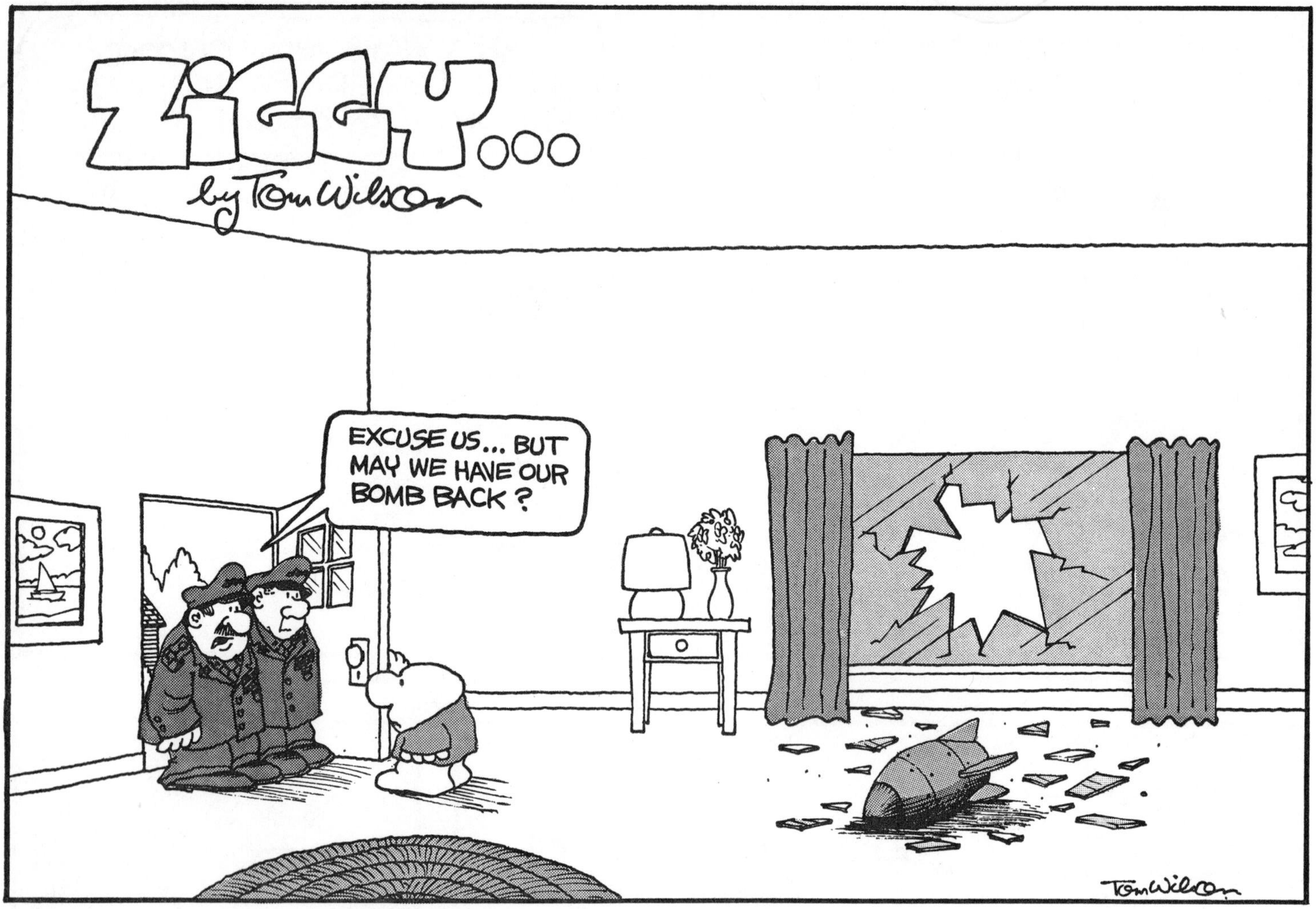
ZiGGY...
by Tom Wilson
EXCUSE US... BUT MAY WE HAVE OUR BOMB BACK?
Tom Wilson

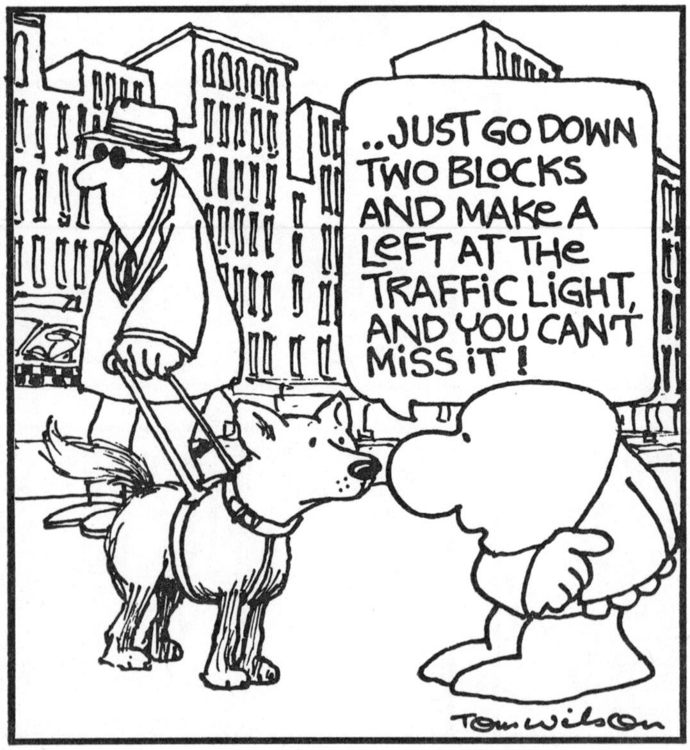
..JUST GO DOWN TWO BLOCKS AND MAKE A LEFT AT THE TRAFFIC LIGHT, AND YOU CAN'T MISS IT!
Tom Wilson

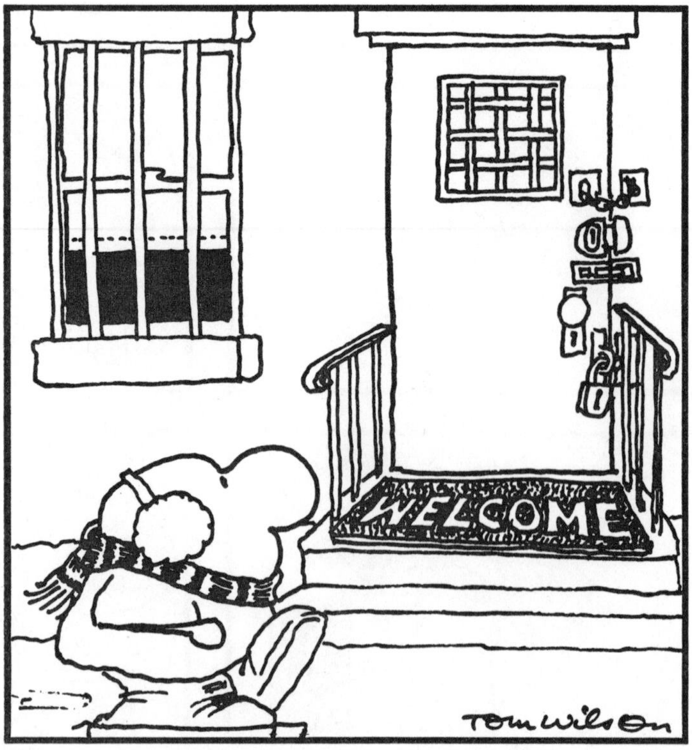
WELCOME
Tom Wilson

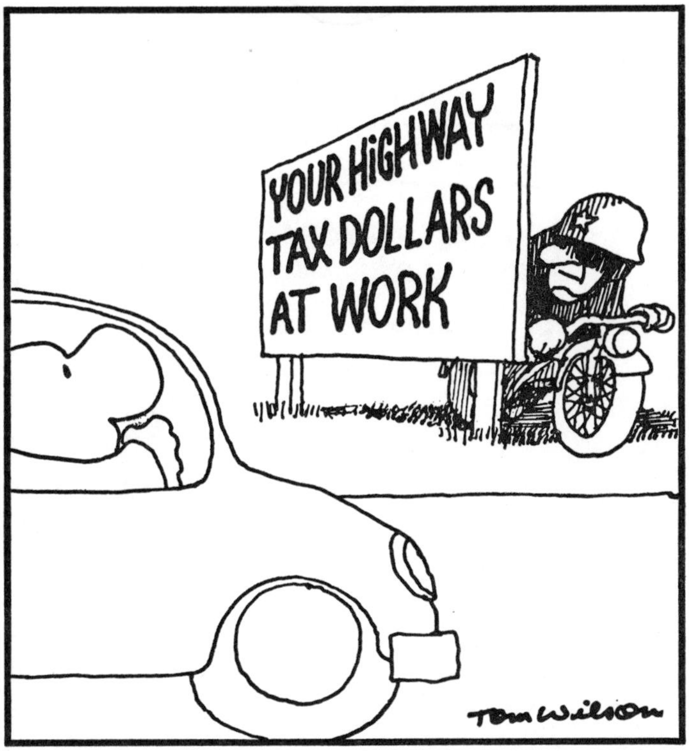
YOUR HIGHWAY TAX DOLLARS AT WORK
Tom Wilson

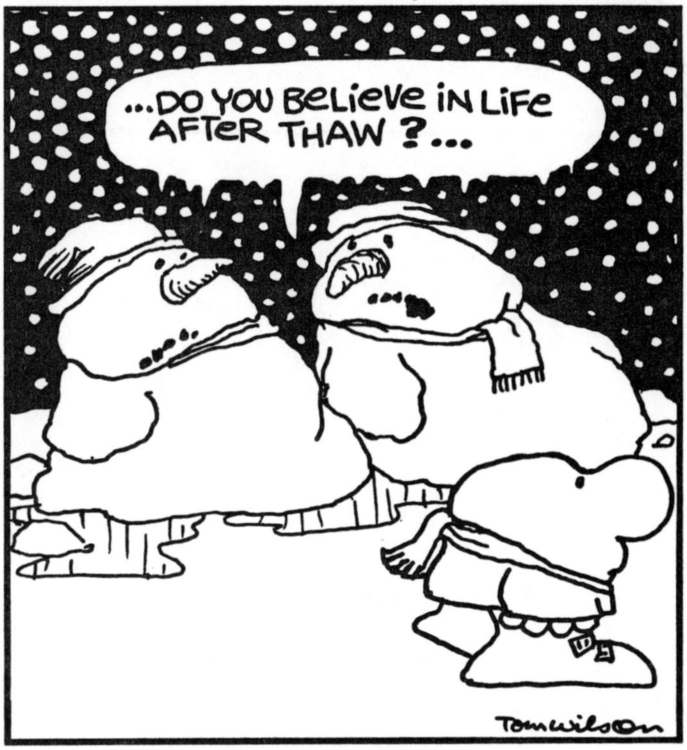
...DO YOU BELIEVE IN LIFE AFTER THAW ?...
Tom Wilson

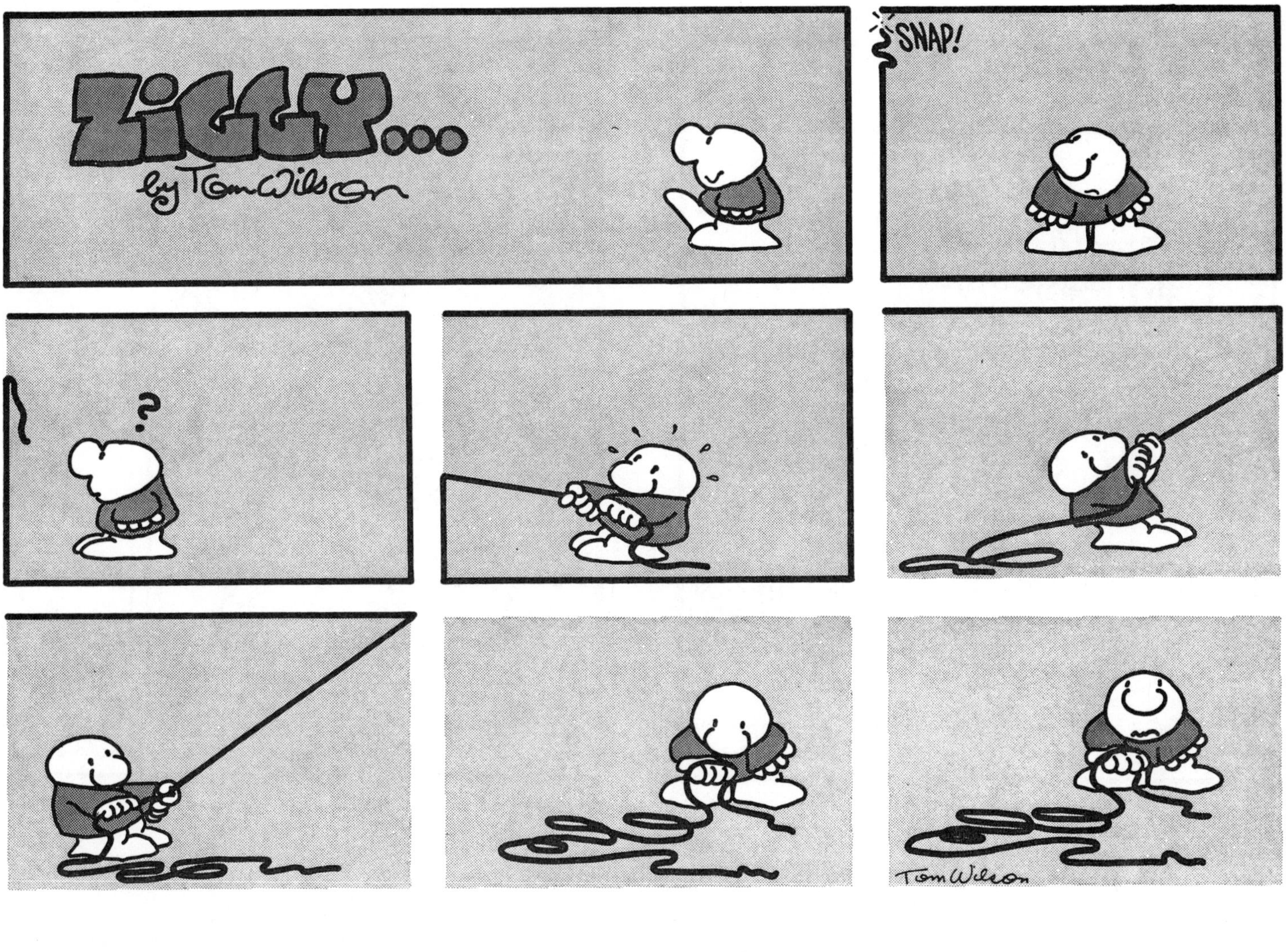
ZIGGY...
by Tom Wilson
SNAP!
?
Tom Wilson

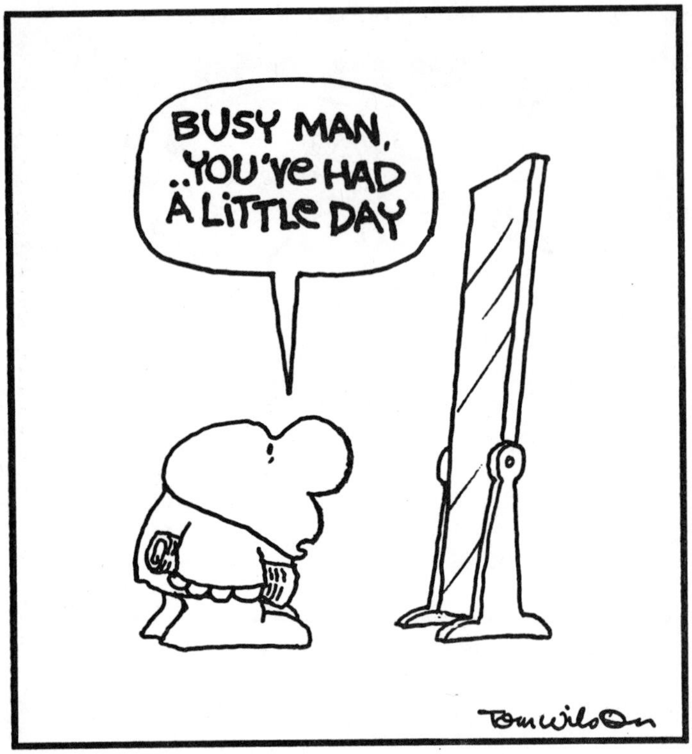
BUSY MAN, ..YOU'VE HAD A LITTLE DAY
Tom Wilson

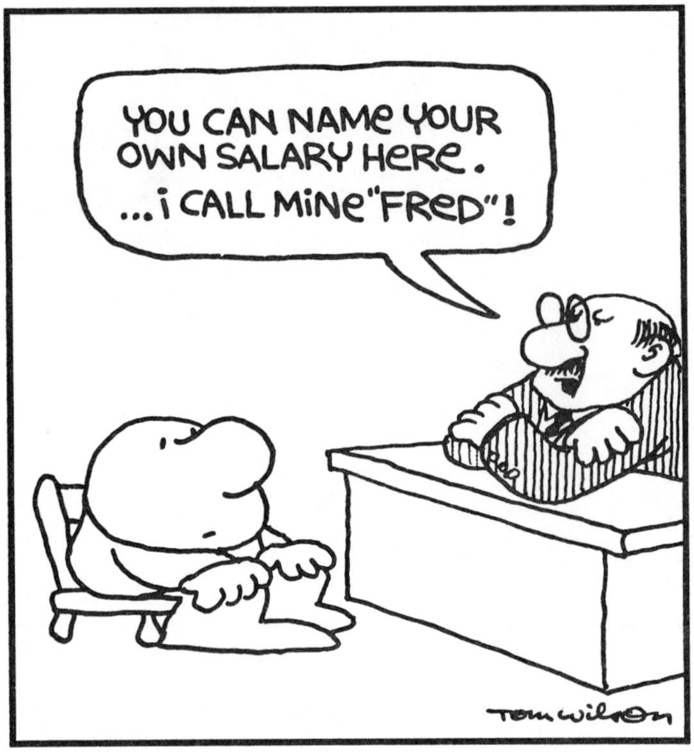
YOU CAN NAME YOUR OWN SALARY HERE. ...I CALL MINE "FRED"!
Tom Wilson

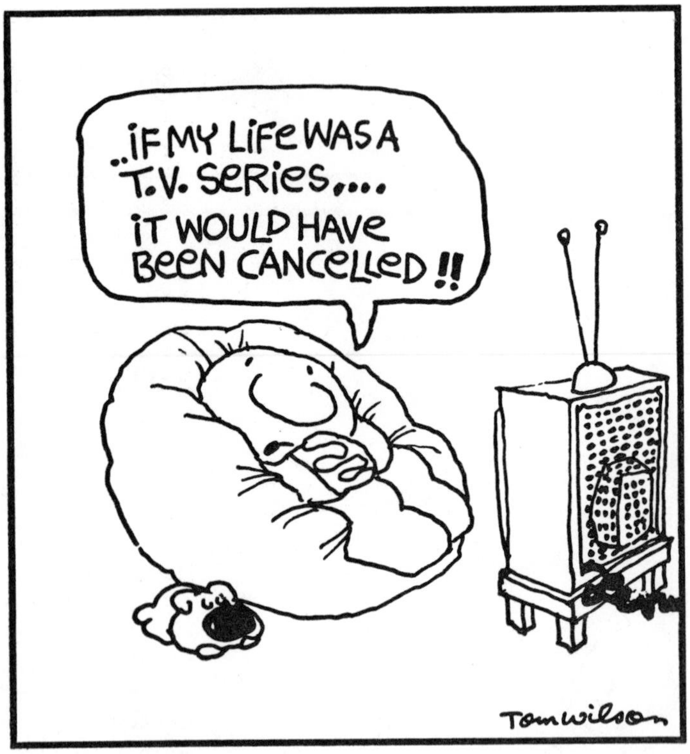
..IF MY LIFE WAS A T.V. SERIES,... IT WOULD HAVE BEEN CANCELLED !!
Tom Wilson

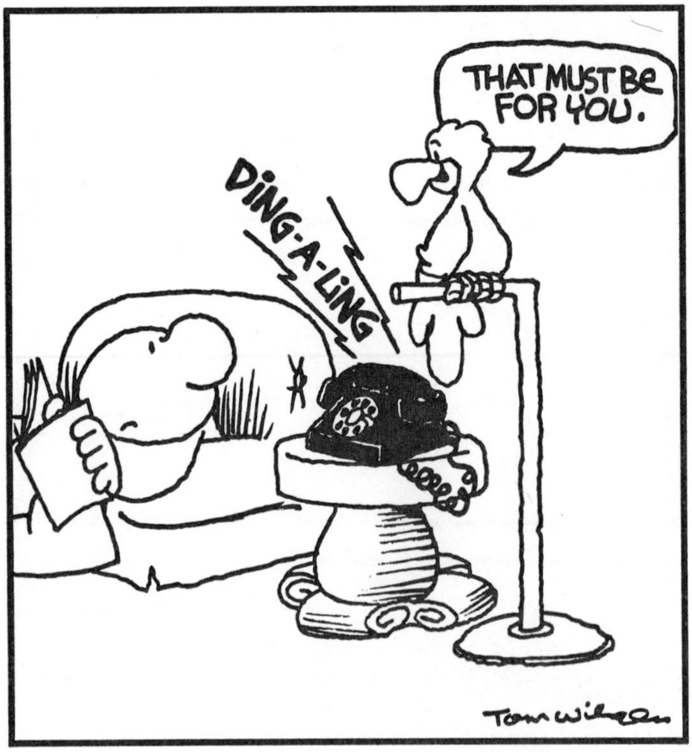
THAT MUST BE FOR YOU.
DING-A-LING
Tom Wilson

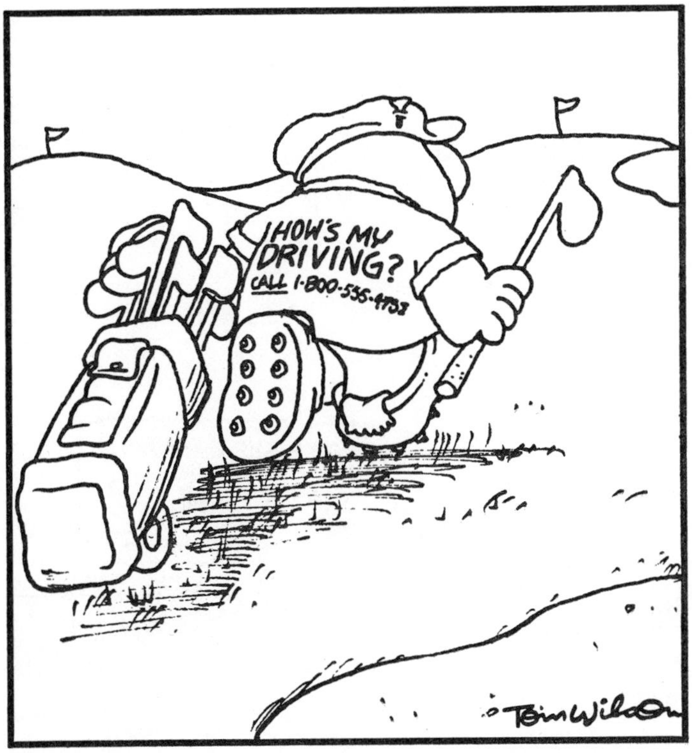
HOW'S MY DRIVING?
CALL 1-800-555-4753
TOM WILSON

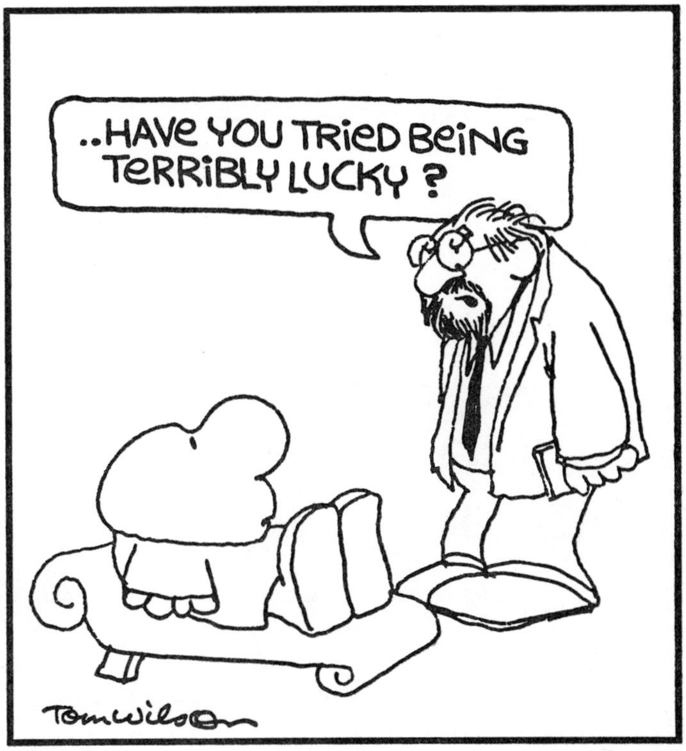
..HAVE YOU TRIED BEING TERRIBLY LUCKY ?
TOM WILSON

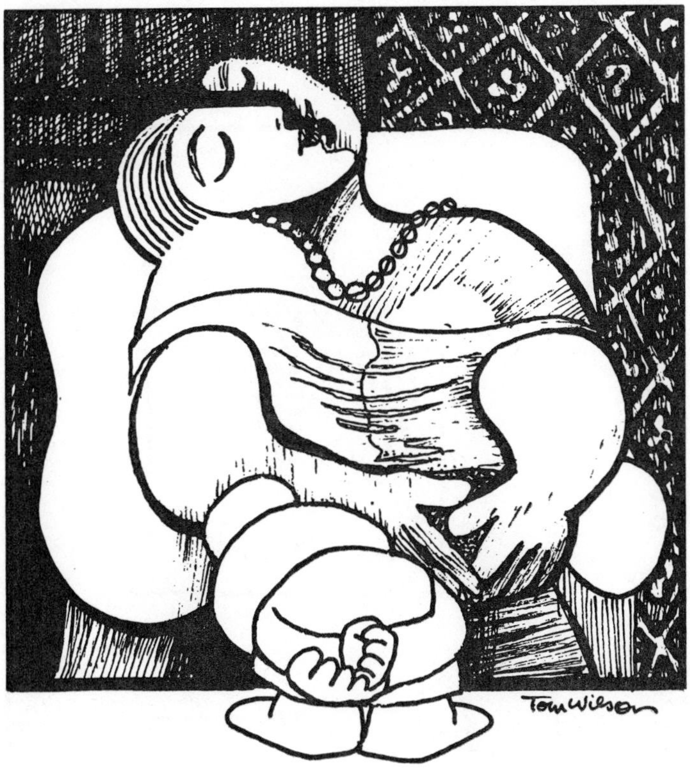
TOM WILSON

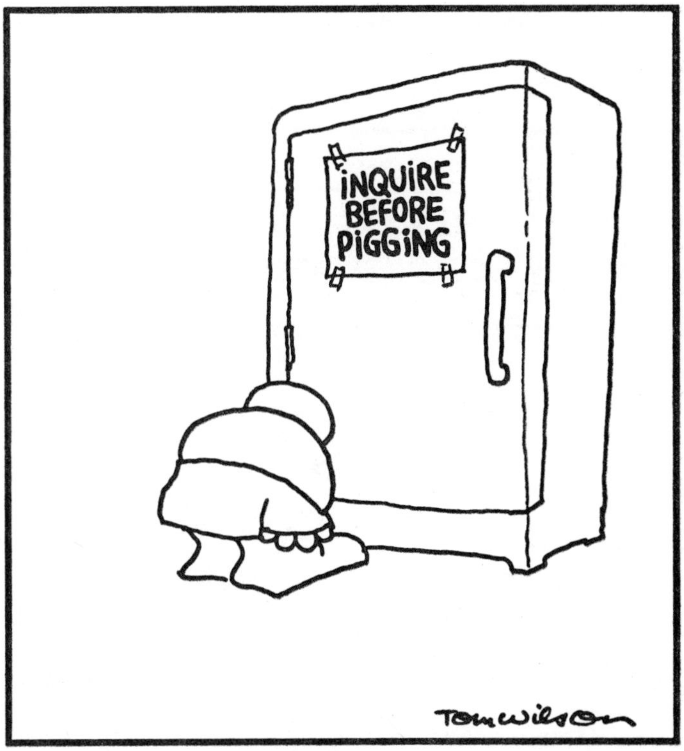
INQUIRE
BEFORE
PIGGING
TOM WILSON

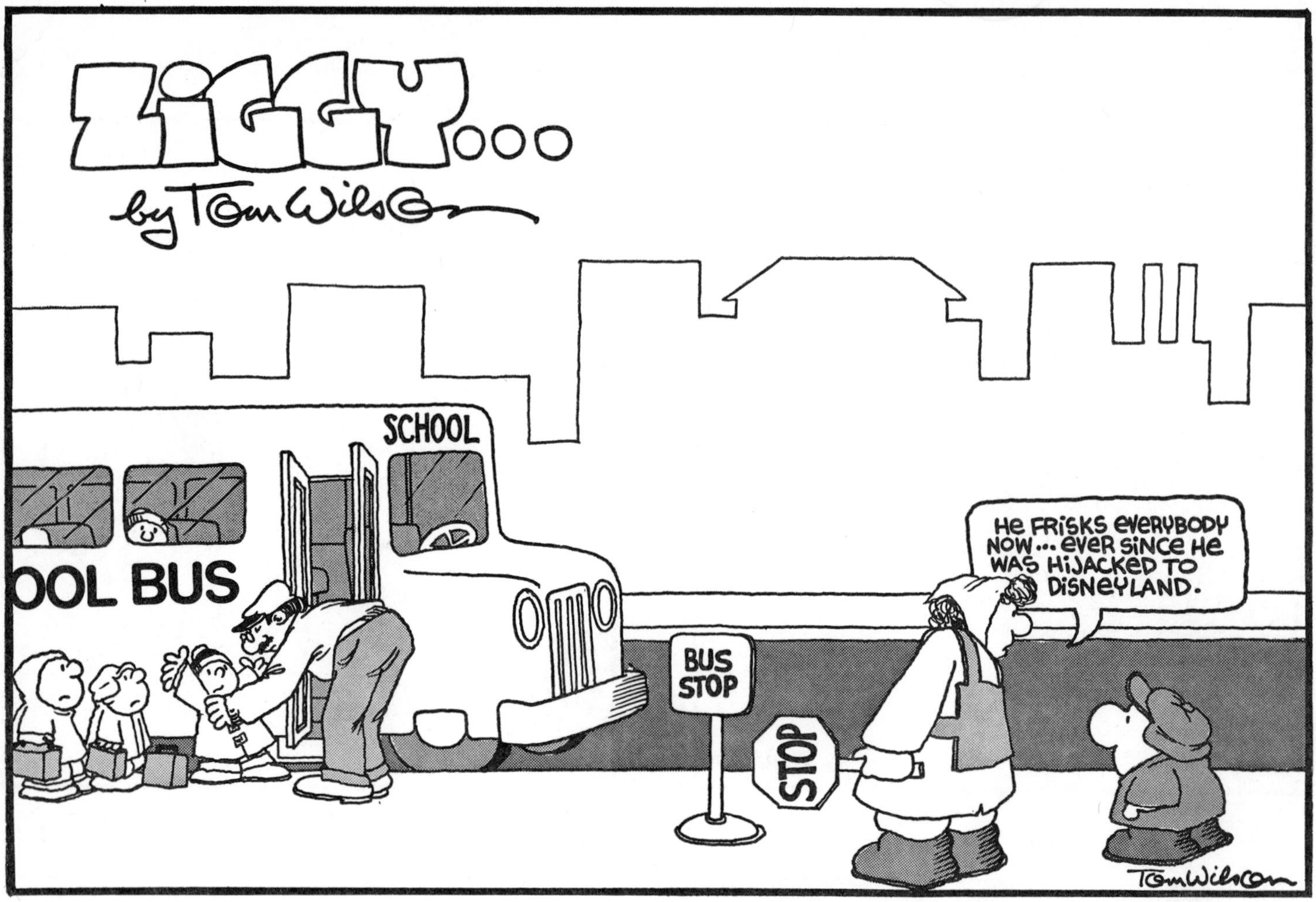
ZiGGY...
by Tom Wilson
SCHOOL
OOL BUS
HE FRISKS EVERYBODY NOW... EVER SINCE HE WAS HIJACKED TO DISNEYLAND.
BUS STOP
STOP
Tom Wilson

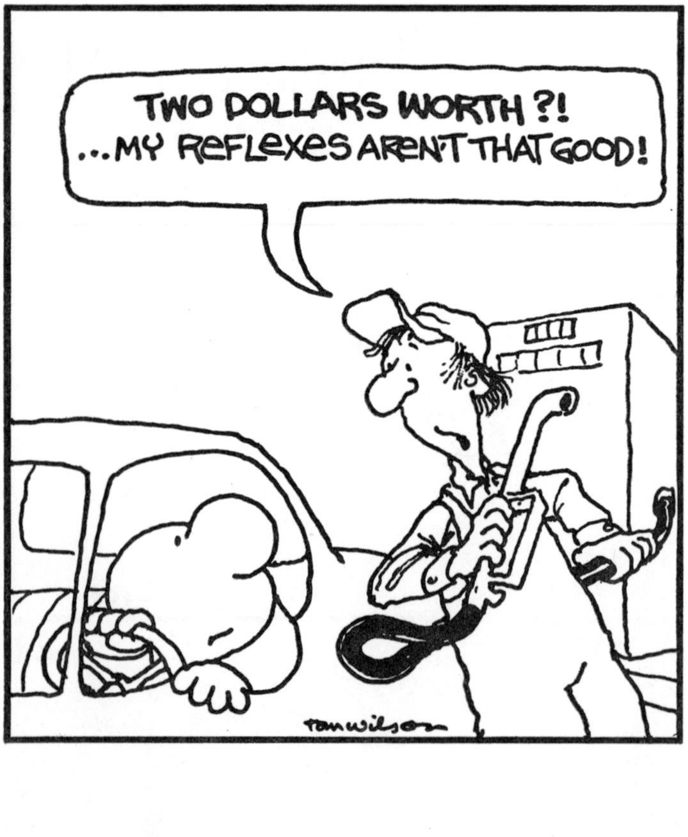
TWO DOLLARS WORTH ?! ...MY REFLEXES AREN'T THAT GOOD!
tom wilson

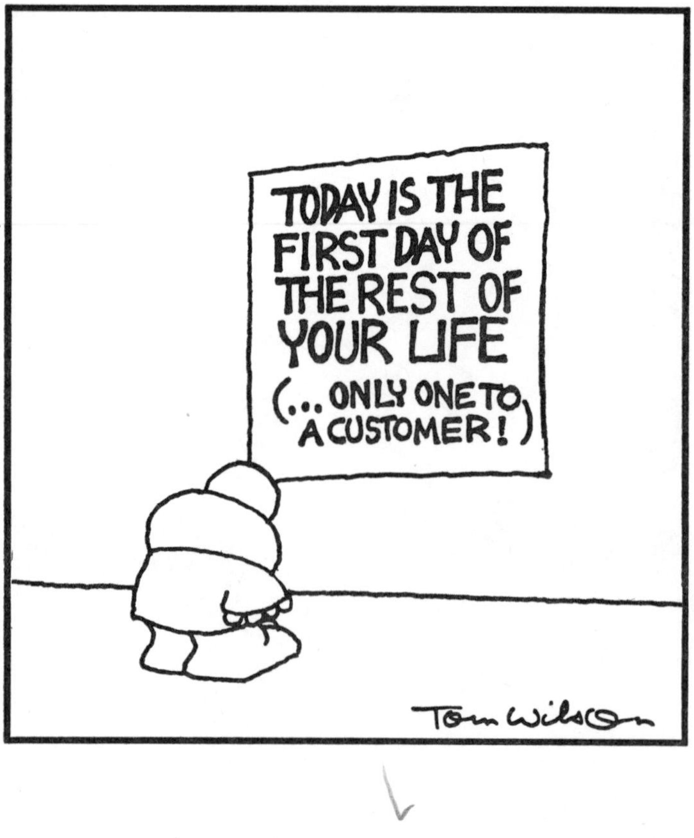
TODAY IS THE FIRST DAY OF THE REST OF YOUR LIFE (... ONLY ONE TO A CUSTOMER!)
Tom Wilson

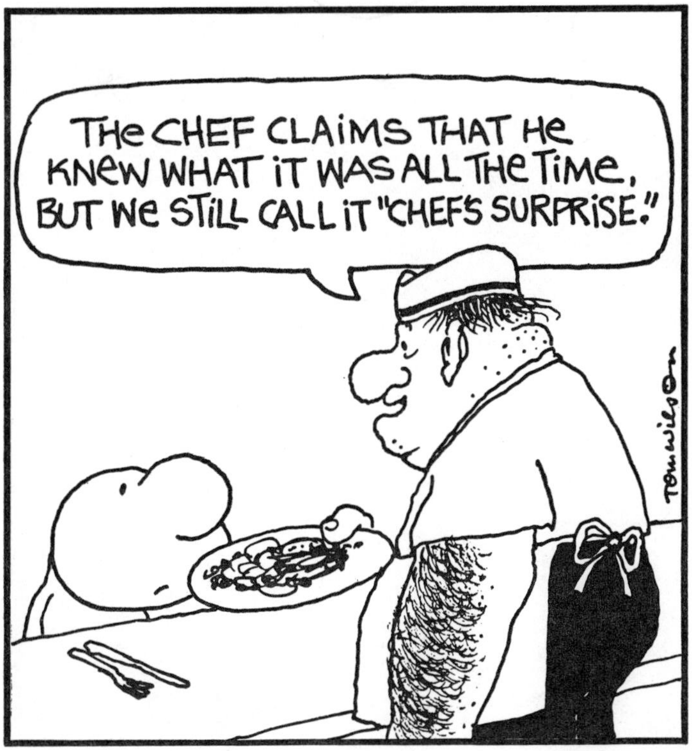
The CHEF CLAIMS THAT He KNEW WHAT IT WAS ALL The Time, BUT We STILL CALL IT "CHEF'S SURPRISE."
Tom Wilson

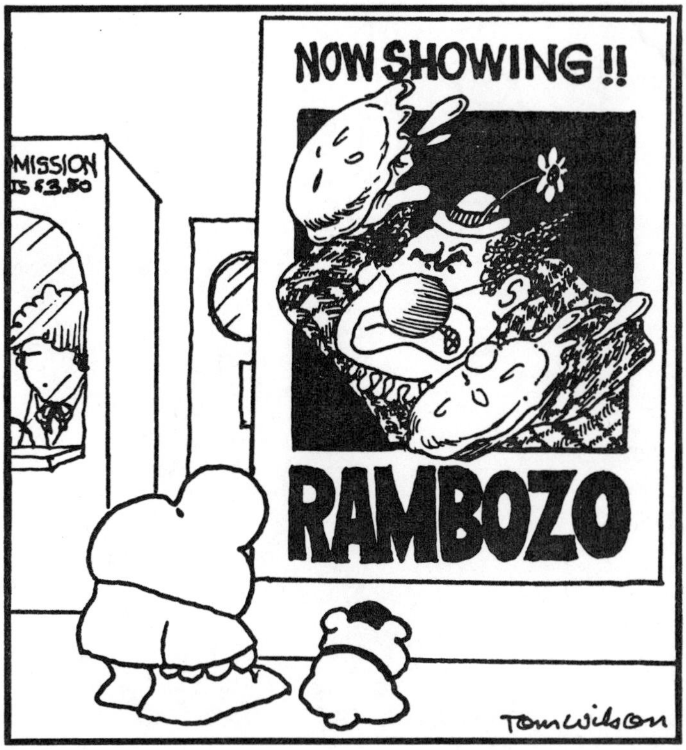
NOW SHOWING !!
RAMBOZO
MISSION
Tom Wilson

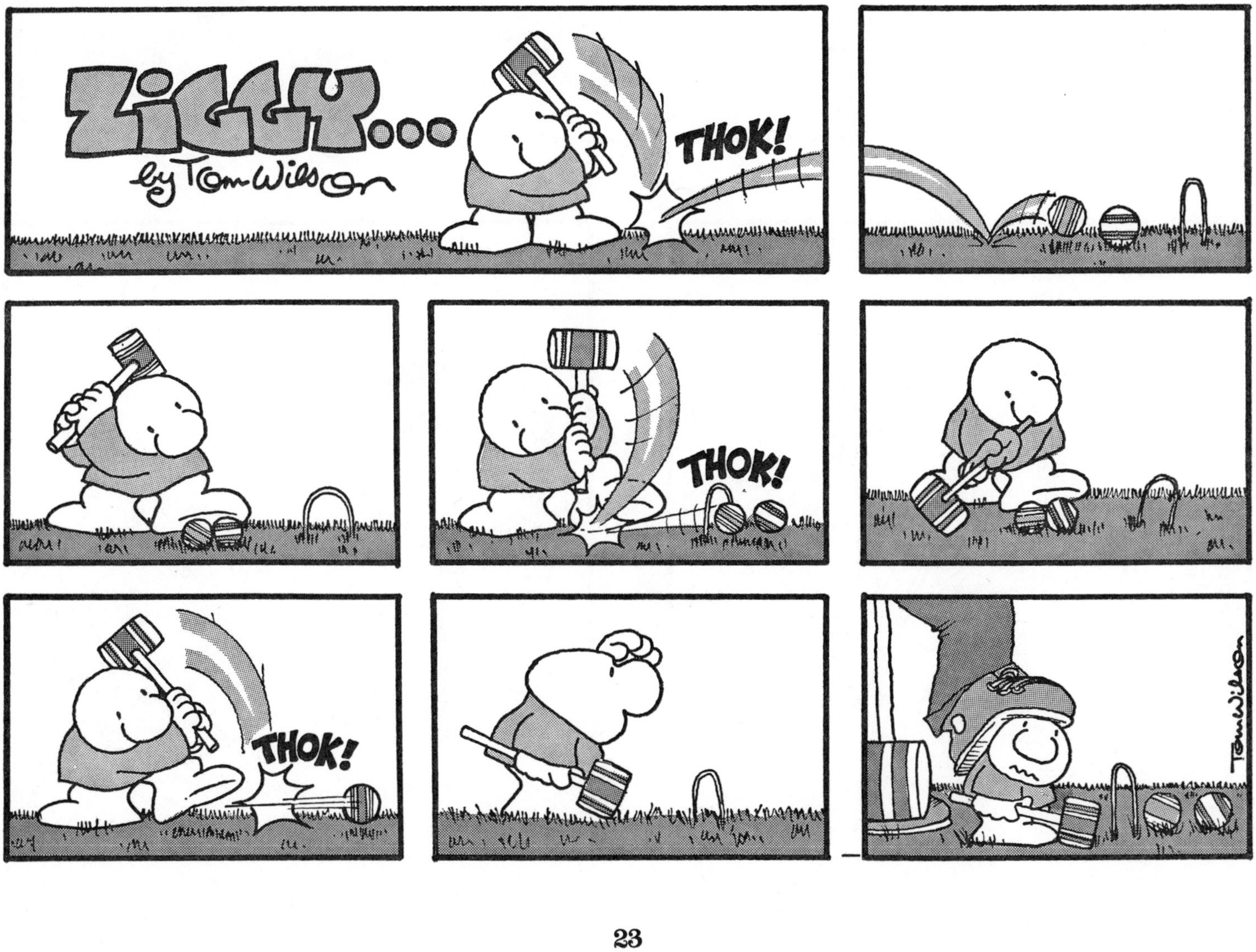
ZIGGY...
by Tom Wilson
THOK!
THOK!
THOK!
Tom Wilson

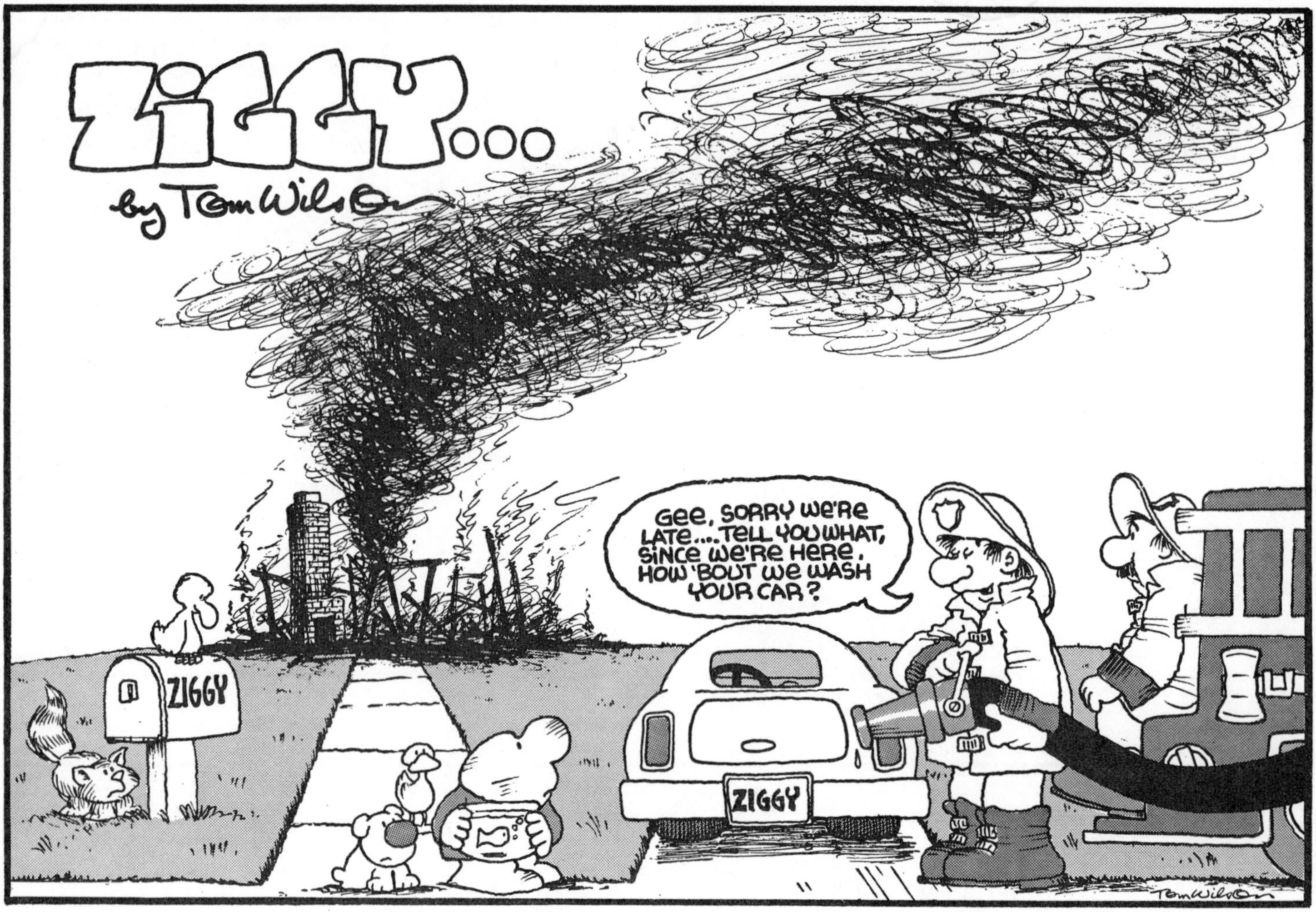
ZiGGY...
by Tom Wilson
GEE, SORRY WE'RE LATE.... TELL YOU WHAT, SINCE WE'RE HERE, HOW 'BOUT WE WASH YOUR CAR?
ZIGGY
ZIGGY
Tom Wilson

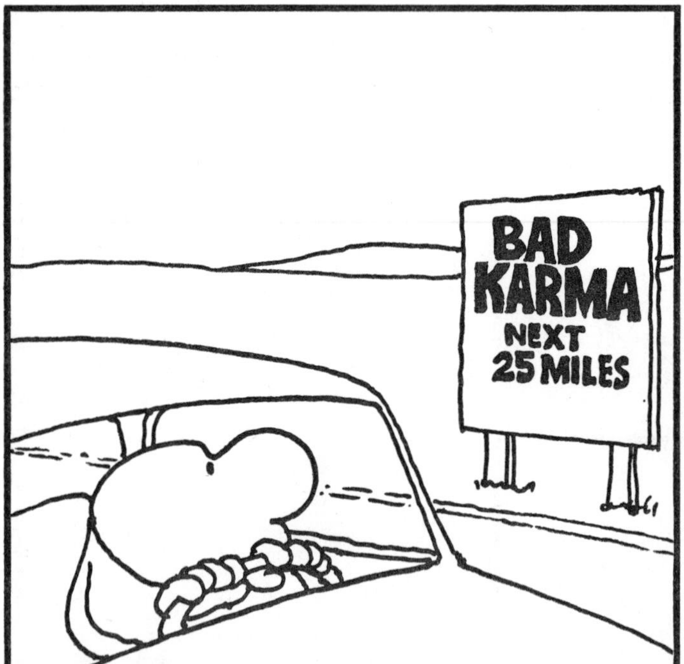
BAD KARMA NEXT 25 MILES
Tom Wilson

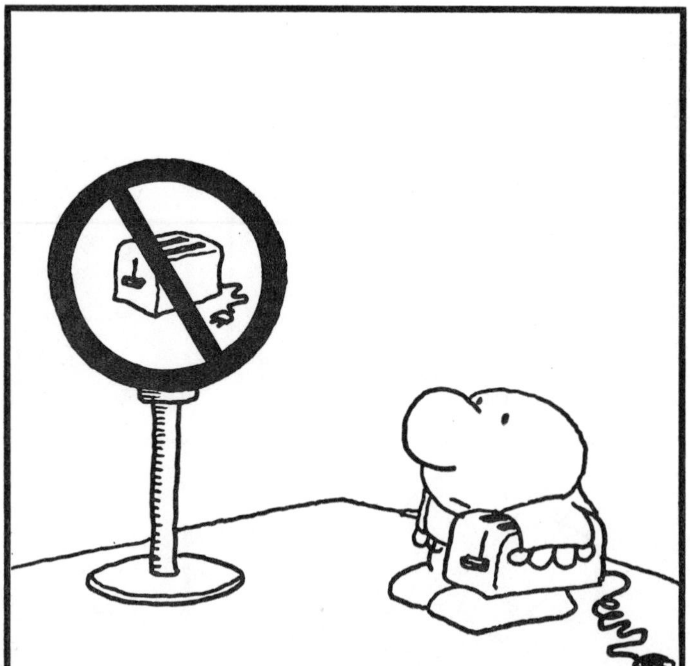
Tom Wilson

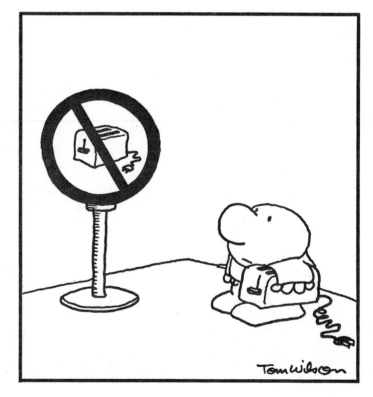

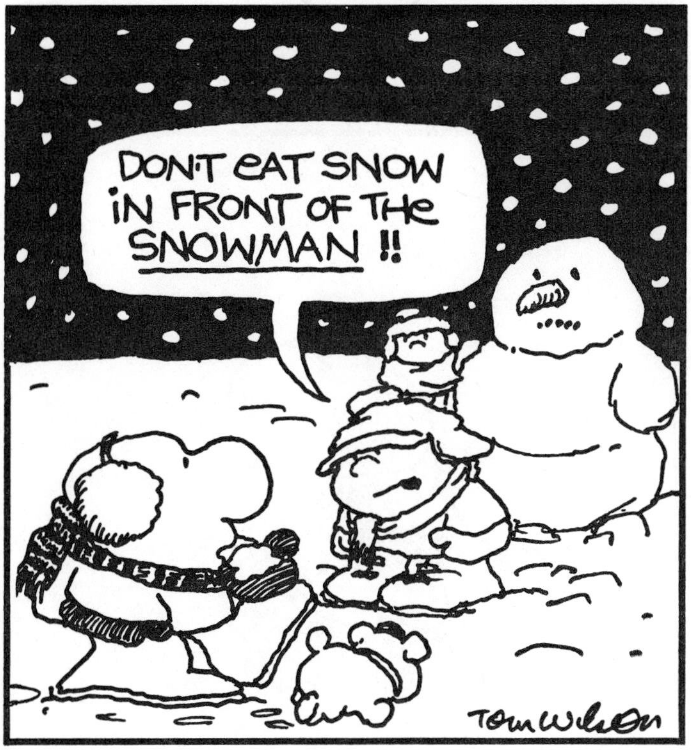
DON'T EAT SNOW IN FRONT OF THE SNOWMAN !!
TOM WILSON

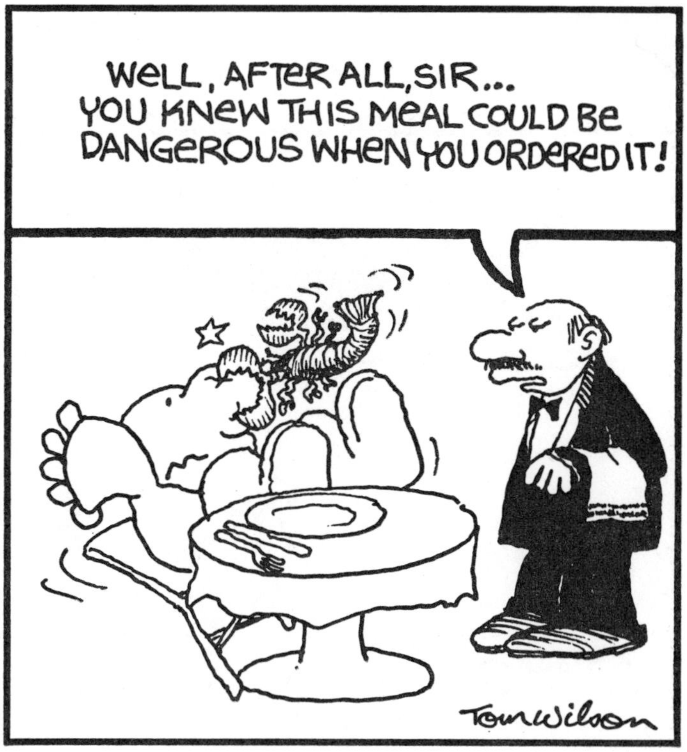
WELL, AFTER ALL, SIR... YOU KNEW THIS MEAL COULD BE DANGEROUS WHEN YOU ORDERED IT!
TOM WILSON

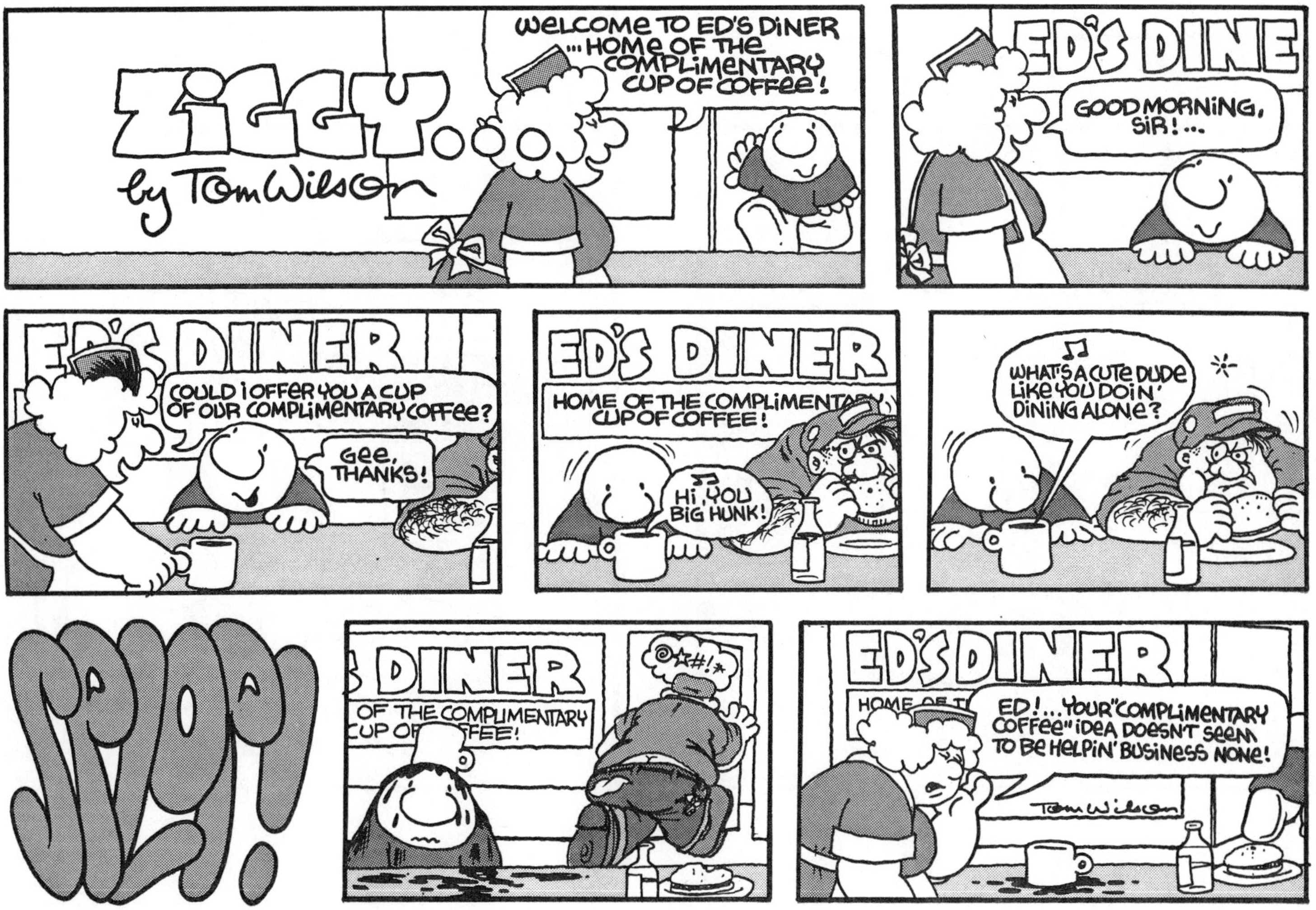
ZIGGY
by Tom Wilson
WELCOME TO ED'S DINER ...HOME OF THE COMPLIMENTARY CUP OF COFFEE!
ED'S DINE
GOOD MORNING, SIR!...
ED'S DINER
COULD I OFFER YOU A CUP OF OUR COMPLIMENTARY COFFEE?
GEE, THANKS!
ED'S DINER
HOME OF THE COMPLIMENTARY CUP OF COFFEE!
HI, YOU BIG HUNK!
WHAT'S A CUTE DUDE LIKE YOU DOIN' DINING ALONE?
SPLOP!
DINER
OF THE COMPLIMENTARY CUP OF FEE!
ED'S DINER
ED!...YOUR "COMPLIMENTARY COFFEE" IDEA DOESN'T SEEM TO BE HELPIN' BUSINESS NONE!
TOM WILSON

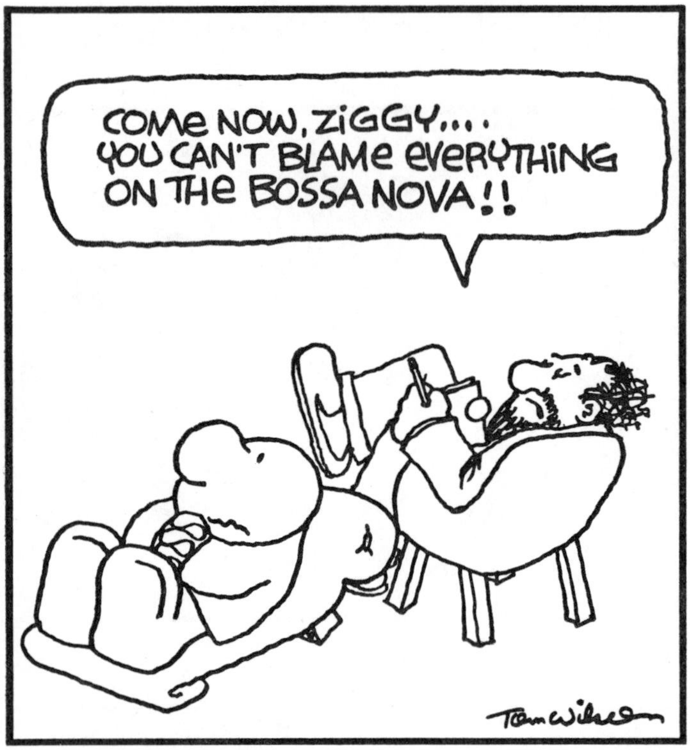
COME NOW, ZIGGY....
YOU CAN'T BLAME EVERYTHING
ON THE BOSSA NOVA!!
Tom Wilson

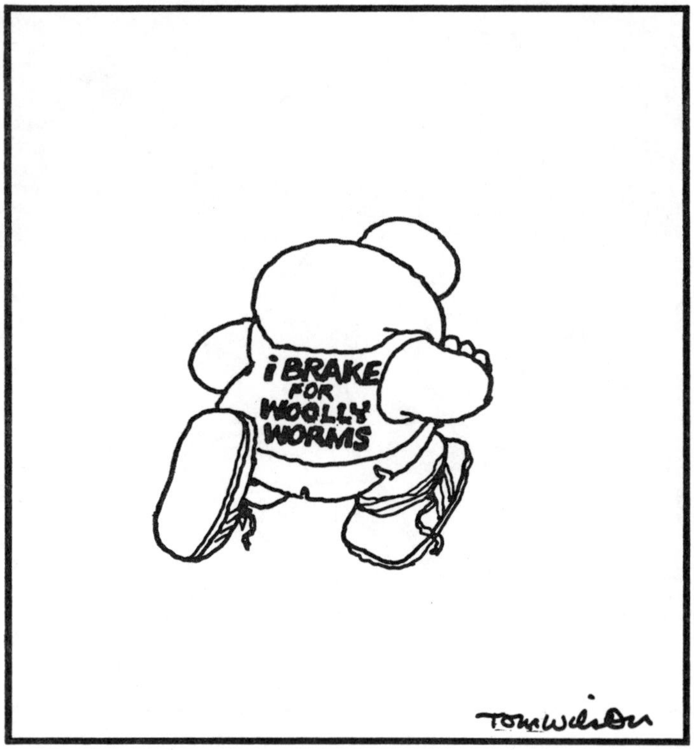
I BRAKE
FOR
WOOLLY
WORMS
Tom Wilson

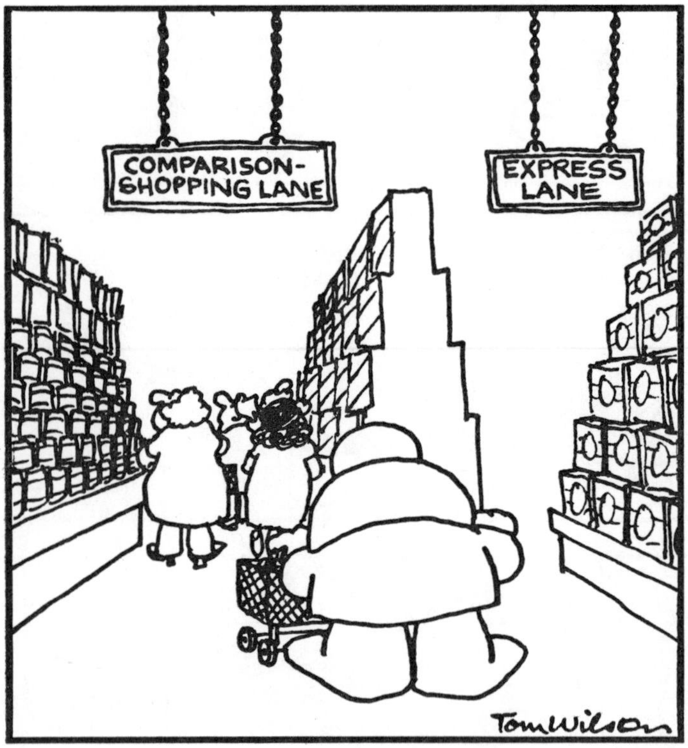
COMPARISON-
SHOPPING LANE
EXPRESS
LANE
Tom Wilson

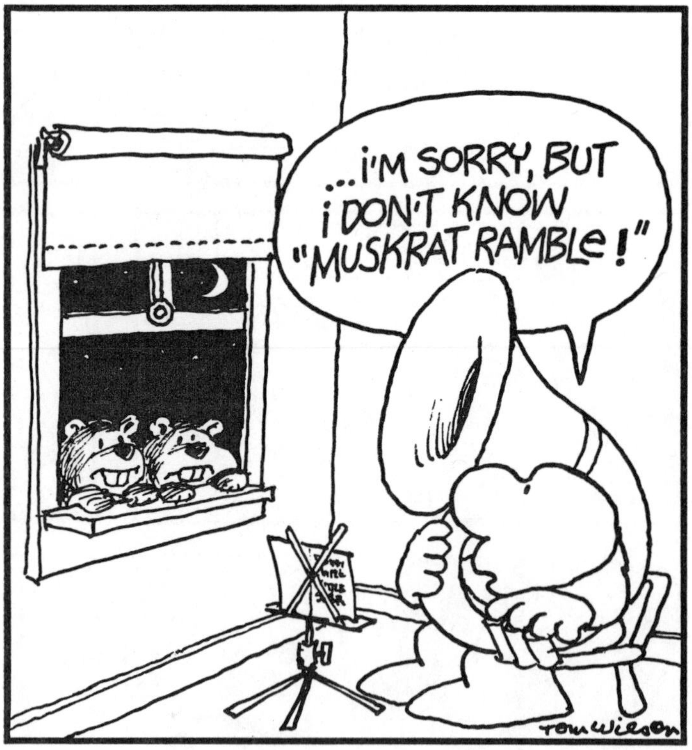
...I'M SORRY, BUT
I DON'T KNOW
"MUSKRAT RAMBLE!"
Tom Wilson

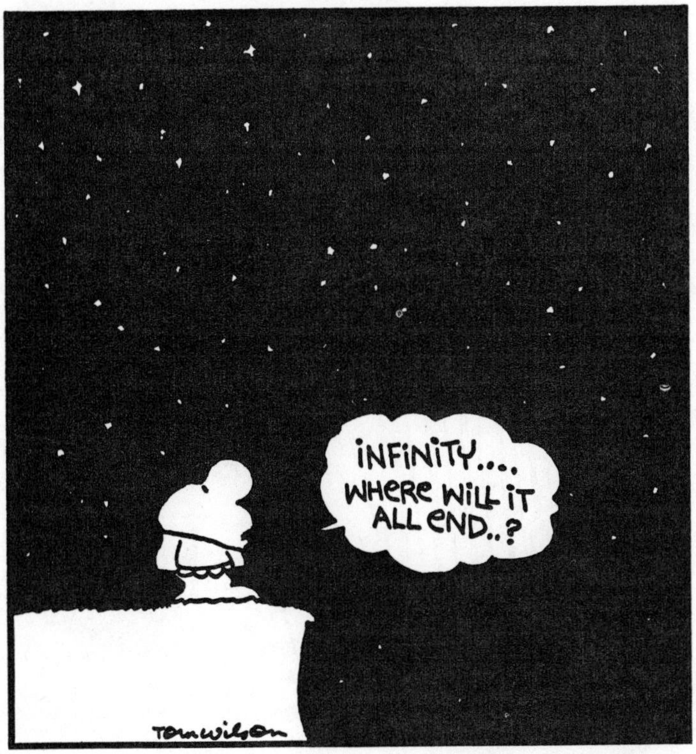
INFINITY....
WHERE WILL IT ALL END..?
Tom Wilson

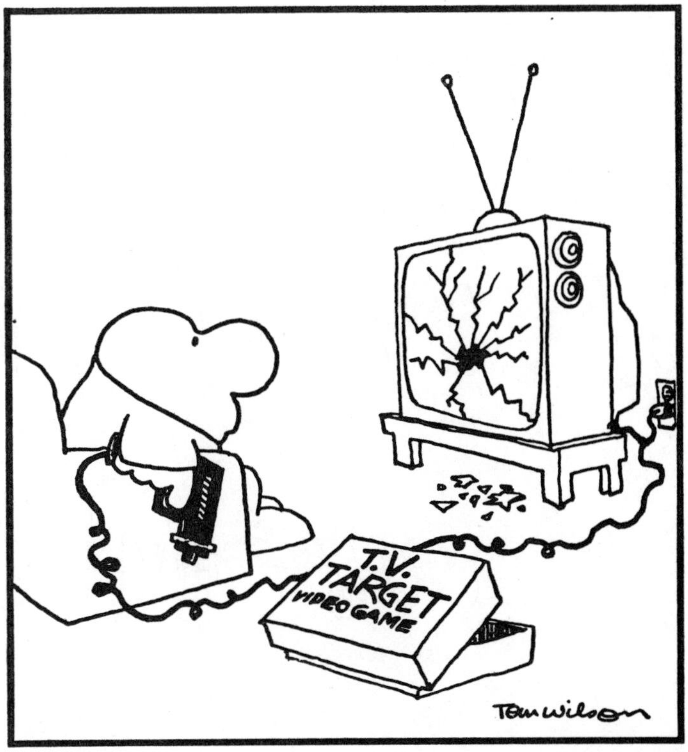
T.V. TARGET
VIDEO GAME
Tom Wilson

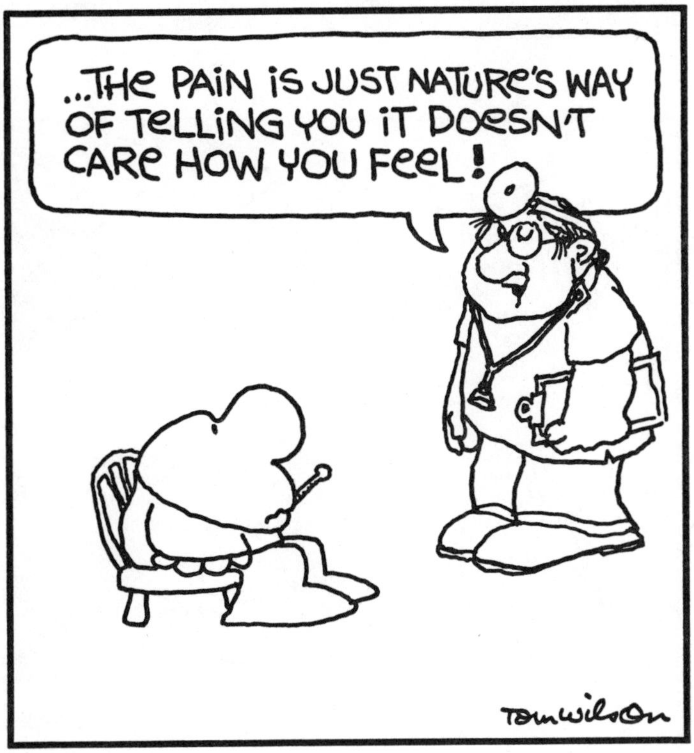
...THE PAIN IS JUST NATURE'S WAY OF TELLING YOU IT DOESN'T CARE HOW YOU FEEL!
Tom Wilson

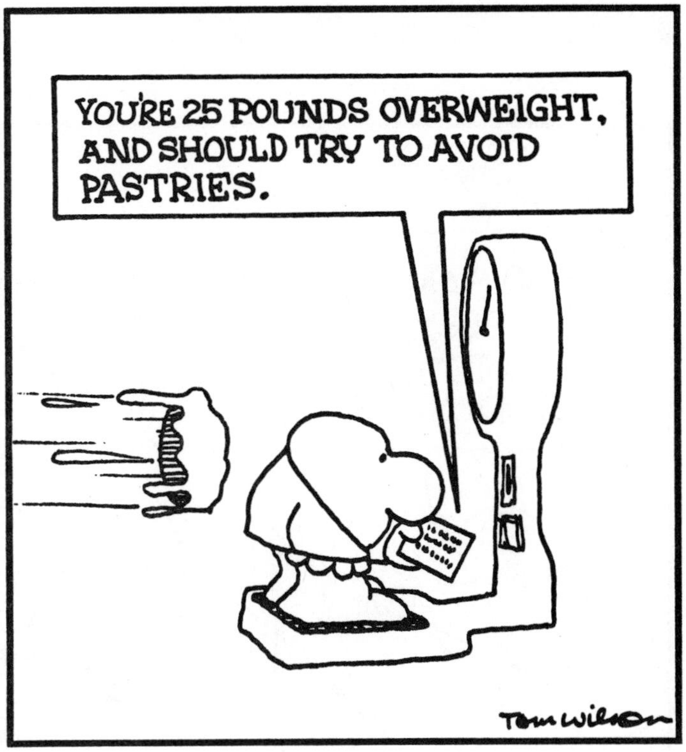
YOU'RE 25 POUNDS OVERWEIGHT, AND SHOULD TRY TO AVOID PASTRIES.
Tom Wilson

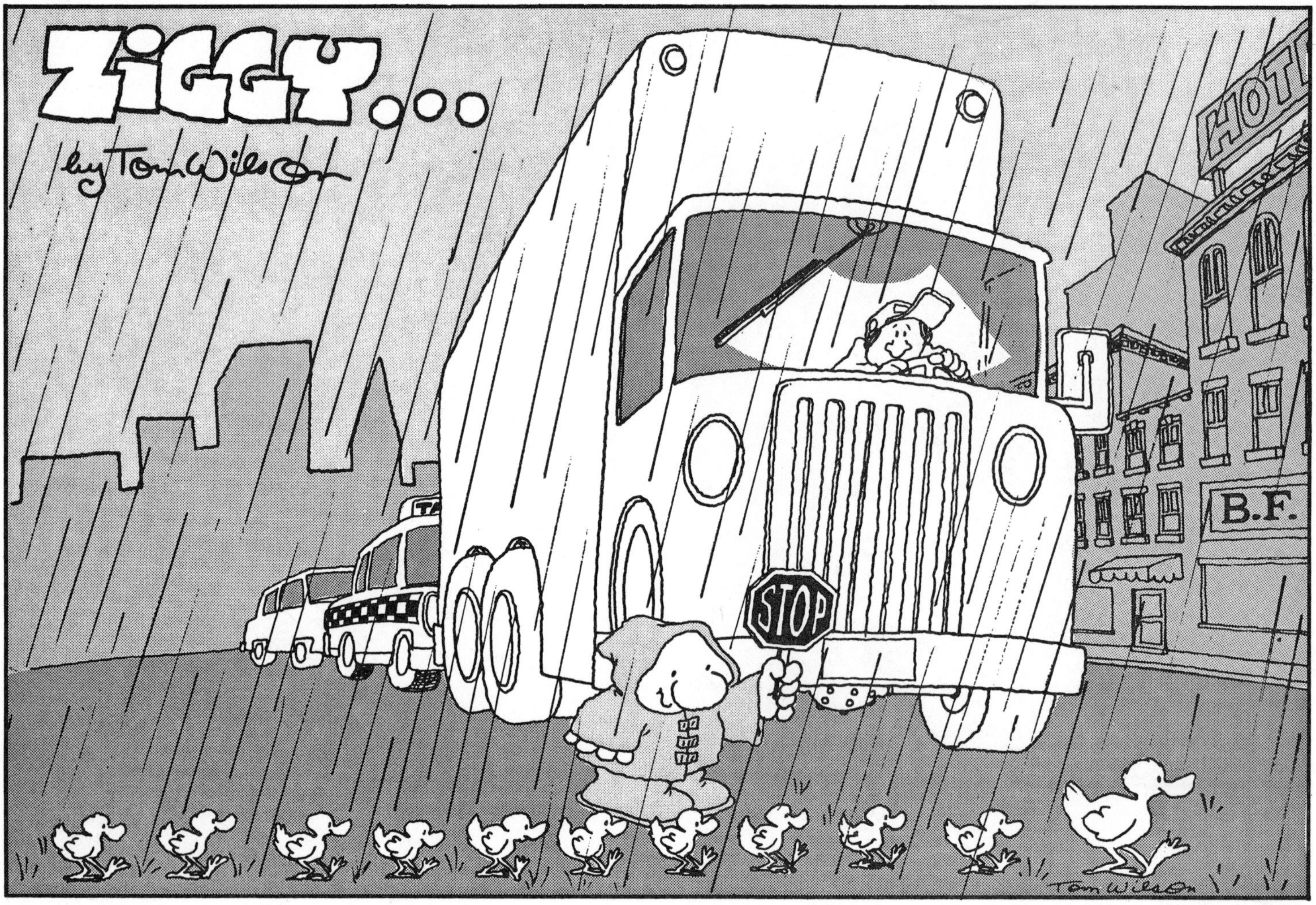
ZIGGY...
by Tom Wilson
HOTEL
TAXI
B.F.
STOP
Tom Wilson

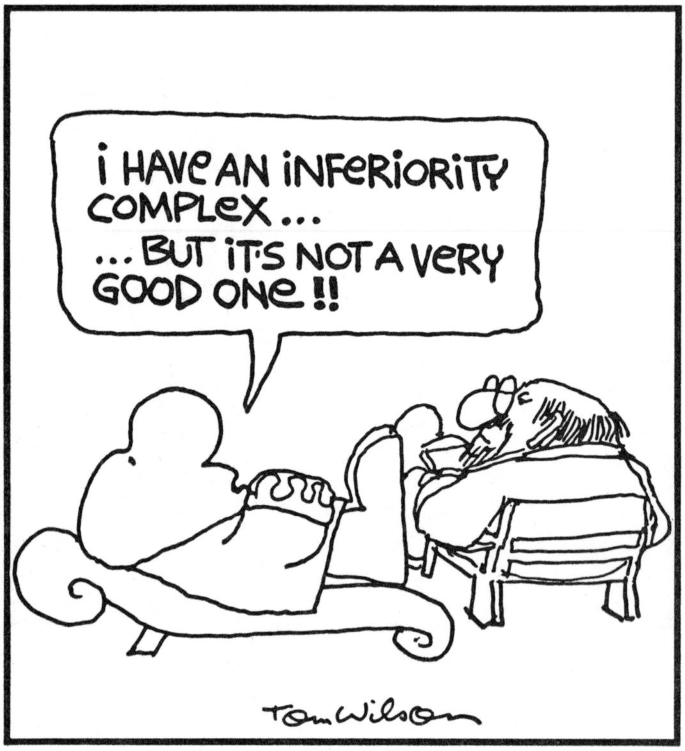
i HAVE AN iNFERiORiTY COMPLEX ...
... BUT iT'S NOT A VERY GOOD ONE !!
Tom Wilson

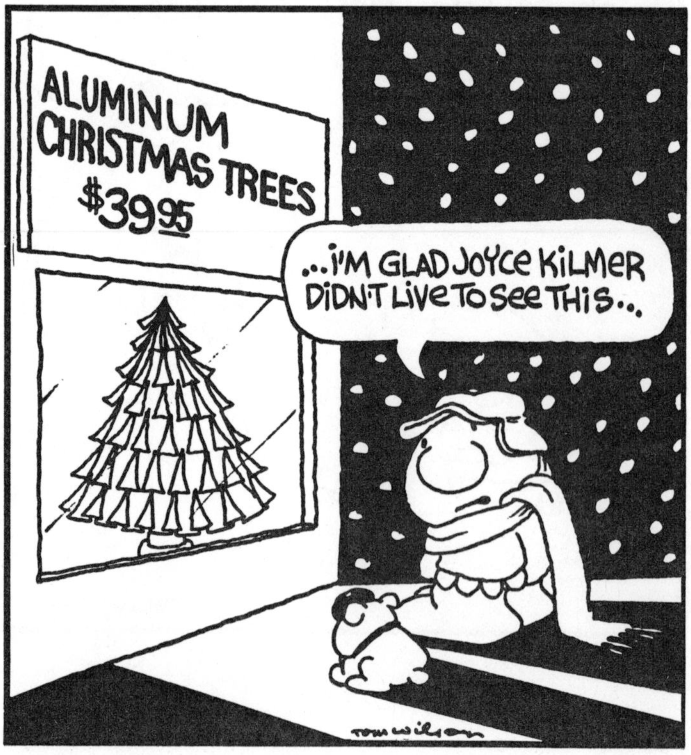
ALUMINUM CHRISTMAS TREES $39.95
...i'M GLAD JOYCE KiLMER DiDN'T LiVE TO SEE THIS...
Tom Wilson

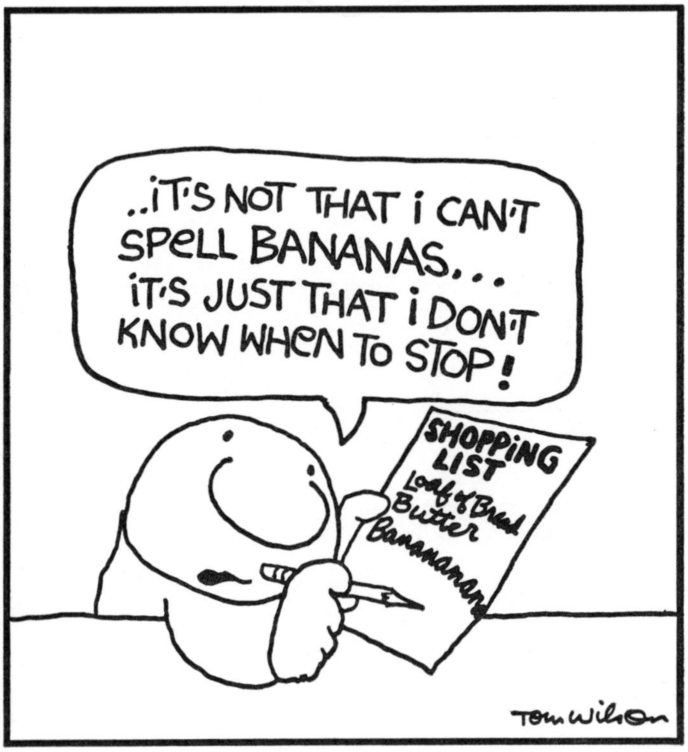
..IT'S NOT THAT I CAN'T SPELL BANANAS... IT'S JUST THAT I DON'T KNOW WHEN TO STOP!
SHOPPING LIST
Loaf of Bread
Butter
Banananananan
Tom Wilson

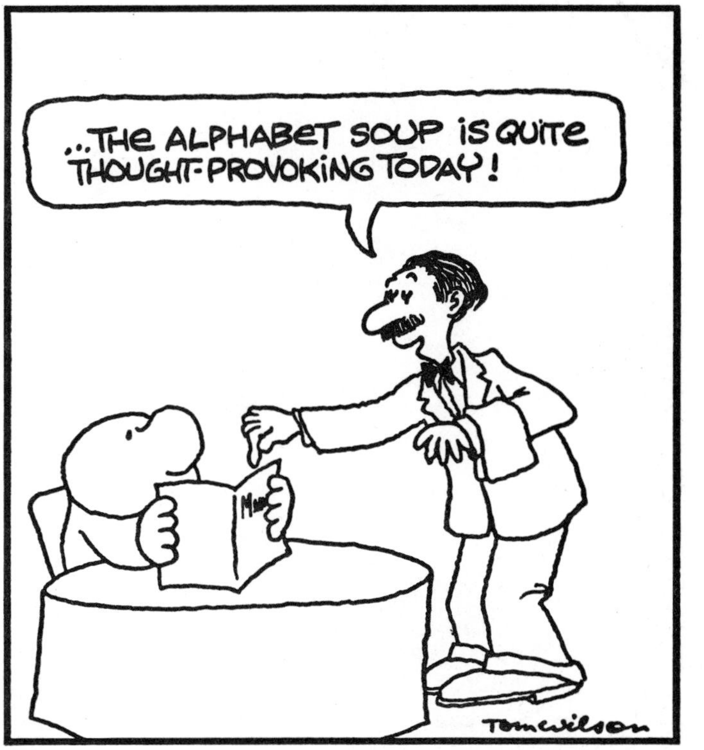
...THE ALPHABET SOUP IS QUITE THOUGHT-PROVOKING TODAY!
Tom Wilson

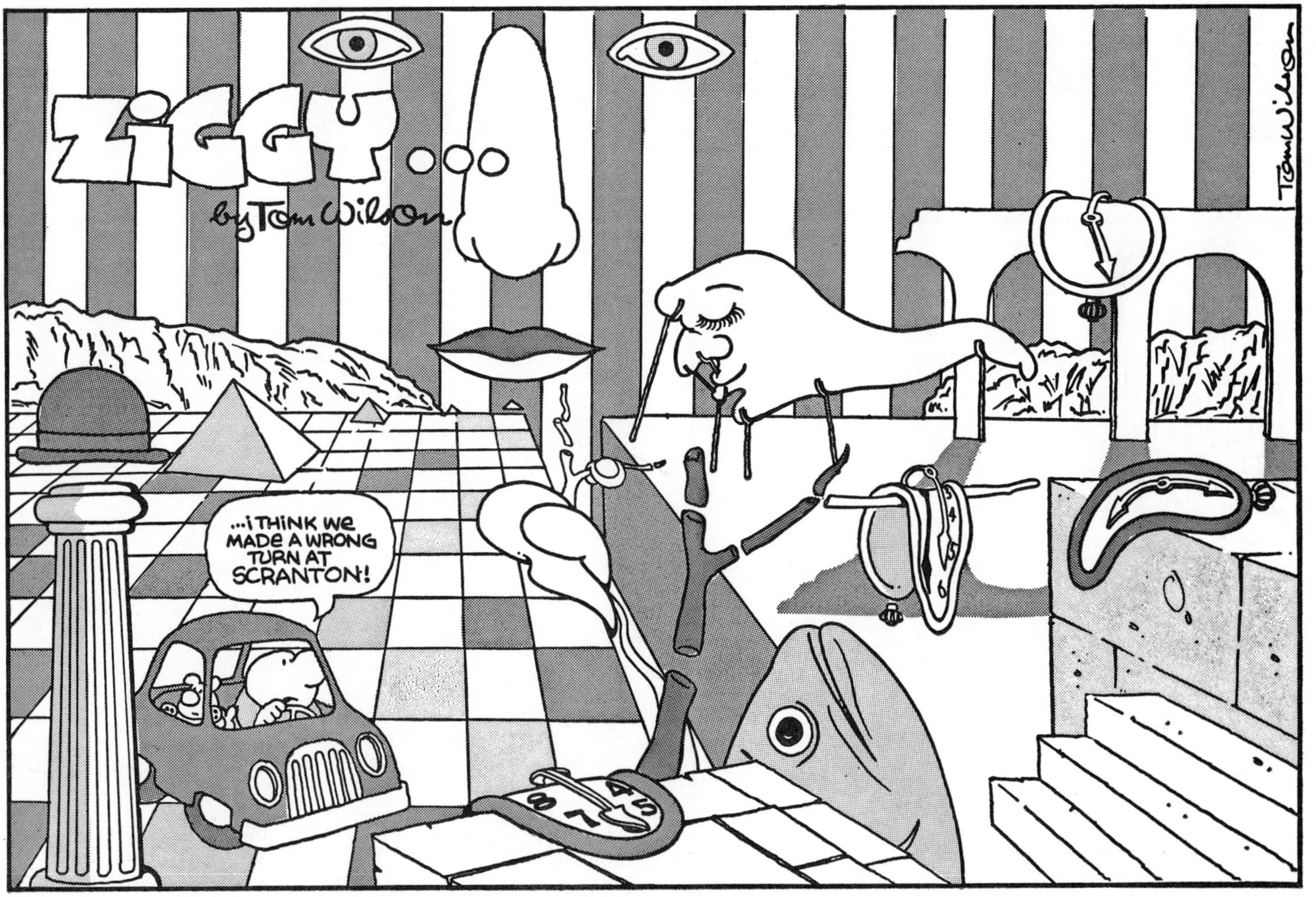
ZIGGY...
by Tom Wilson
...I THINK WE MADE A WRONG TURN AT SCRANTON!
Tom Wilson

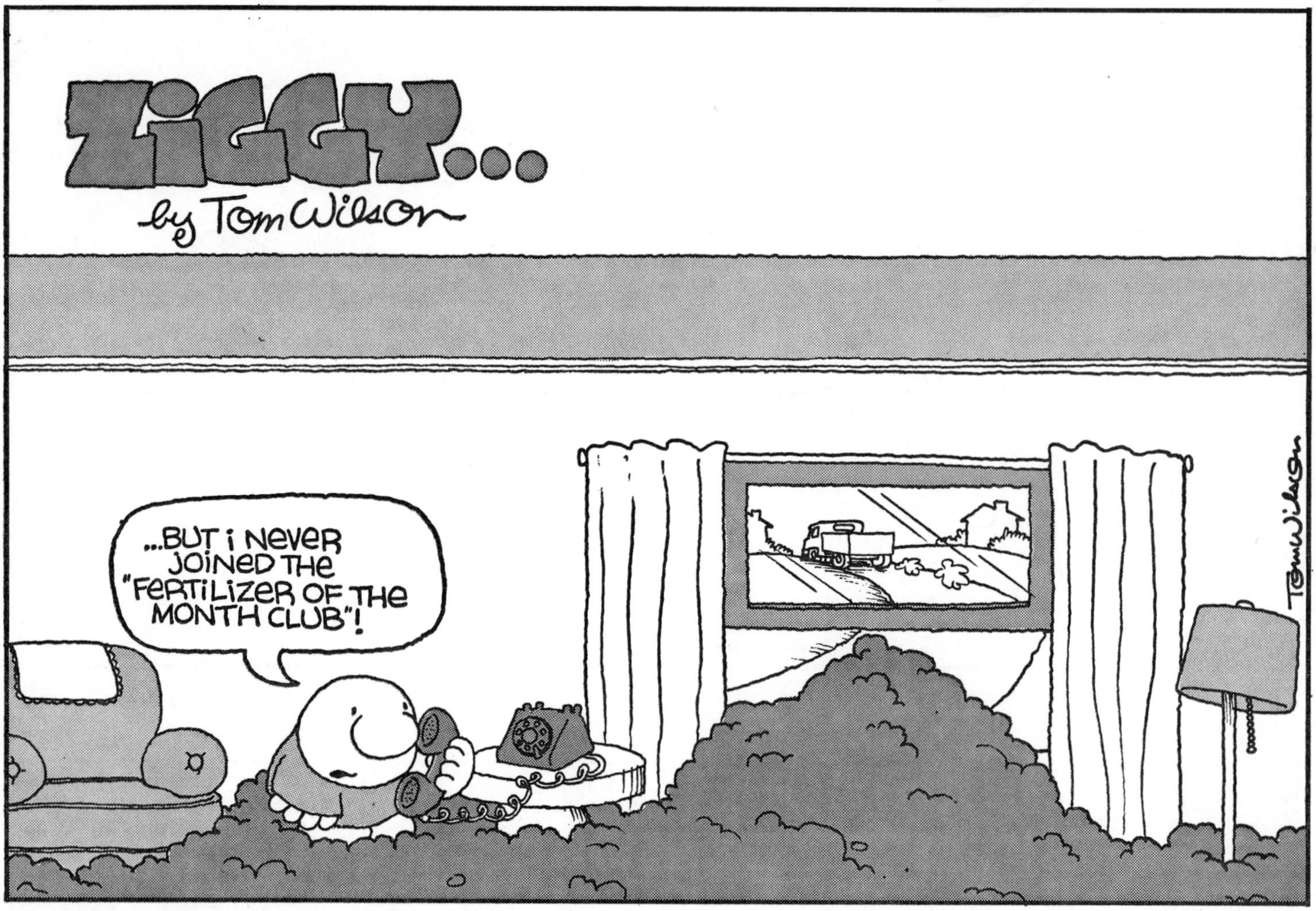
ZIGGY...
by Tom Wilson
...BUT i NEVER JOINED THE "FERTILIZER OF THE MONTH CLUB"!
Tom Wilson

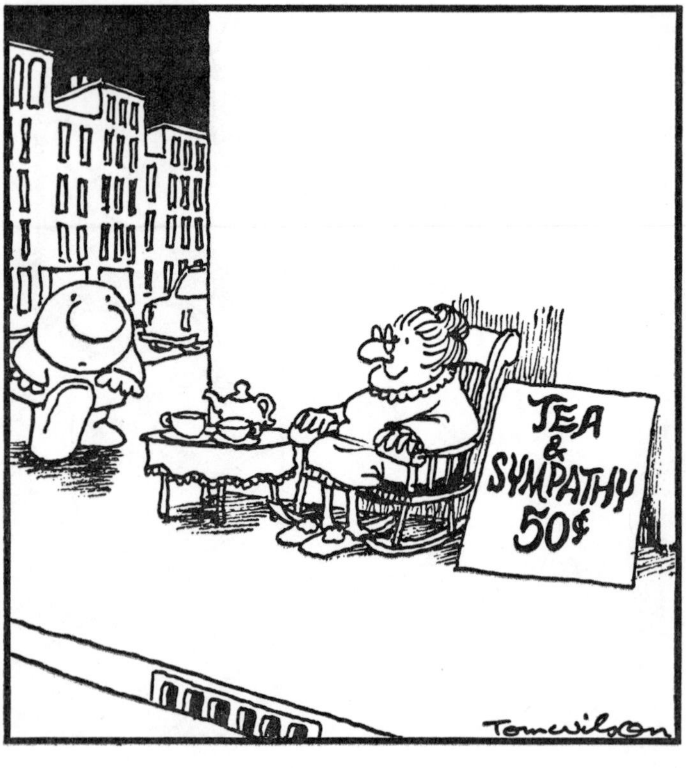
TEA & SYMPATHY 50¢
Tom Wilson

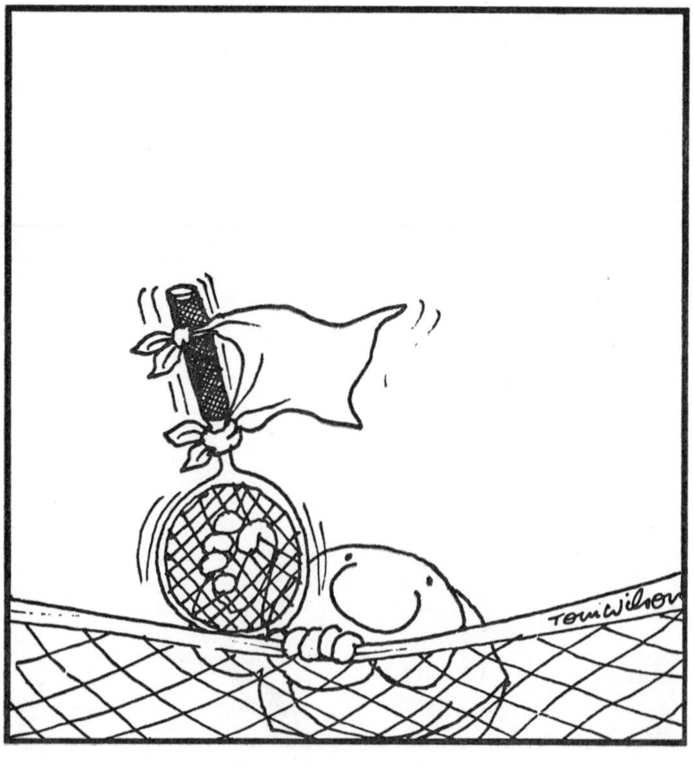
Tom Wilson

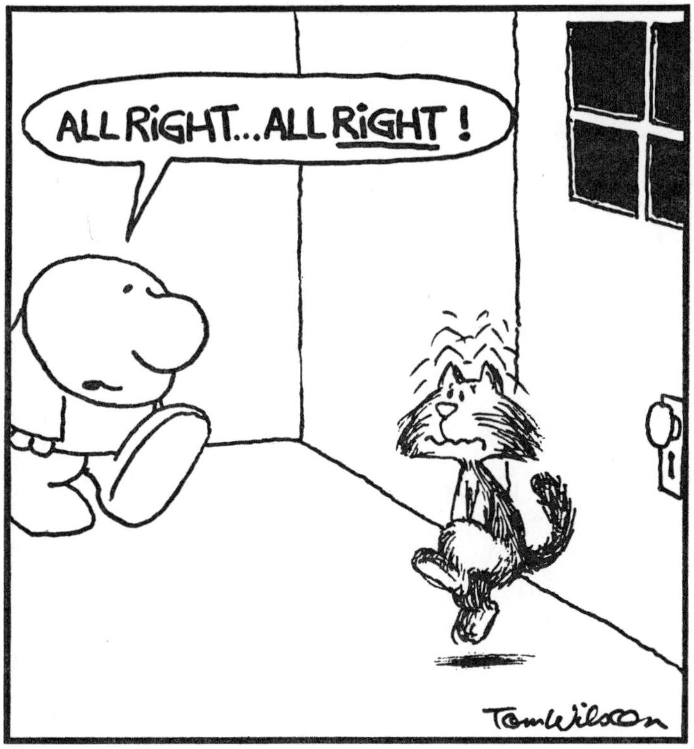
ALL RiGHT...ALL RiGHT !
Tom Wilson

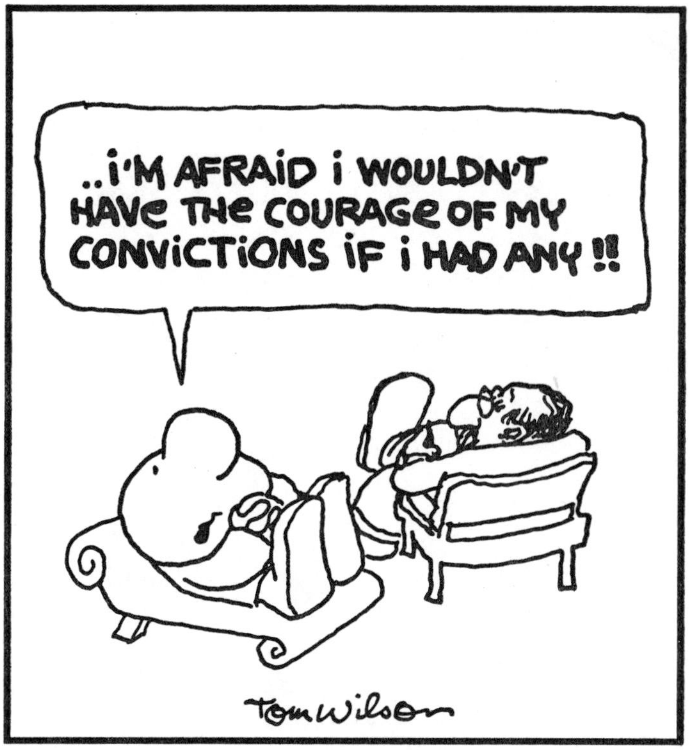
..i'M AFRAiD i WOULDN'T HAVE THE COURAGE OF MY CONViCTiONS iF i HAD ANY !!
Tom Wilson

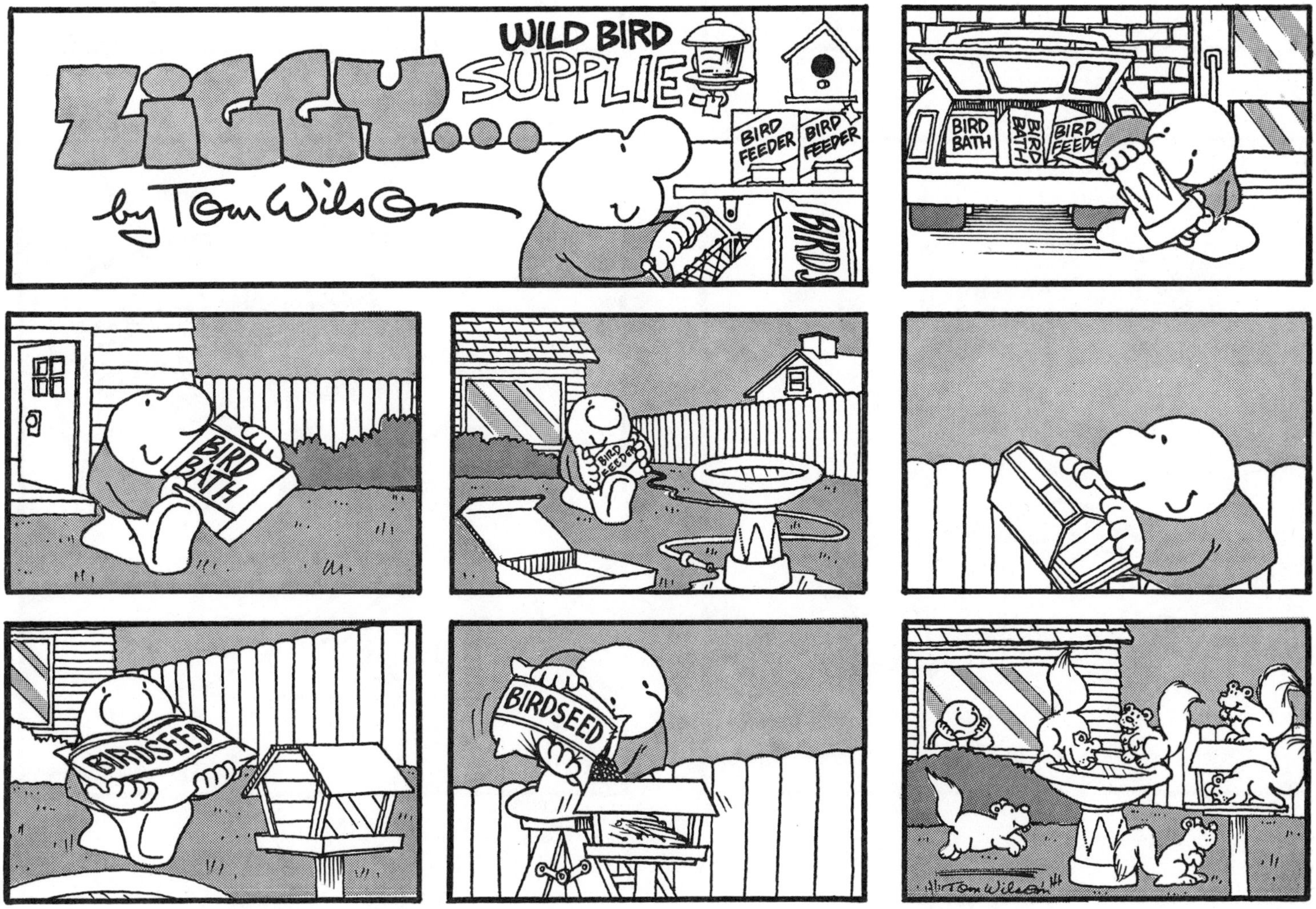
ZiGGY...
by Tom Wilson
WILD BIRD SUPPLIES
BIRD FEEDER
BIRD FEEDER
BIRD BATH
BIRD BATH
BIRD FEEDER
BIRD BATH
BIRD FEEDER
BIRDSEED
BIRDSEED
Tom Wilson

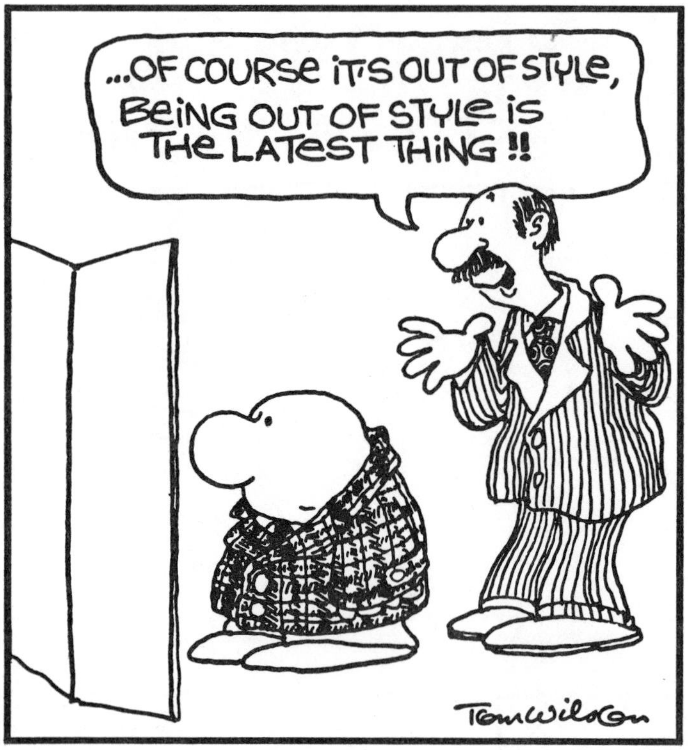
...OF COURSE IT'S OUT OF STYLE, BEING OUT OF STYLE IS THE LATEST THING !!
TOM WILSON

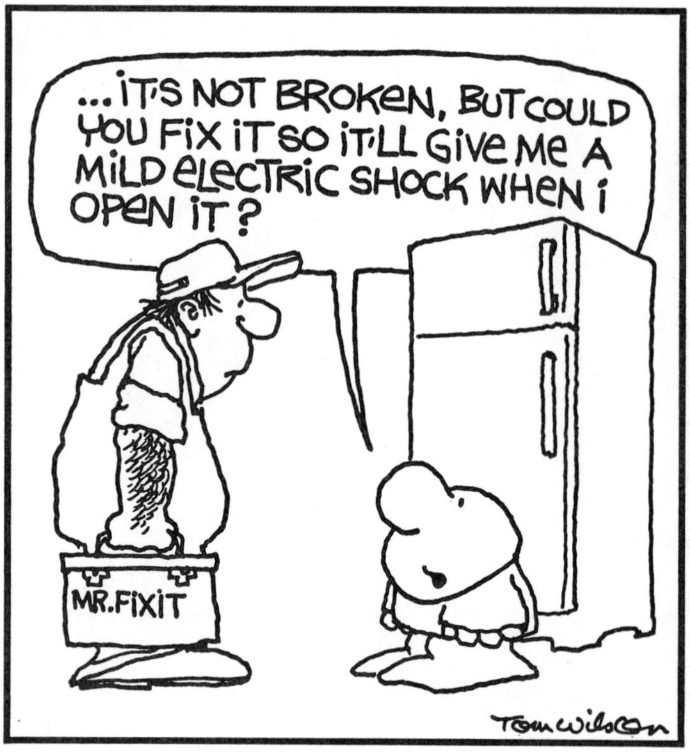
...IT'S NOT BROKEN, BUT COULD YOU FIX IT SO IT'LL GIVE ME A MILD ELECTRIC SHOCK WHEN I OPEN IT?
MR. FIXIT
TOM WILSON

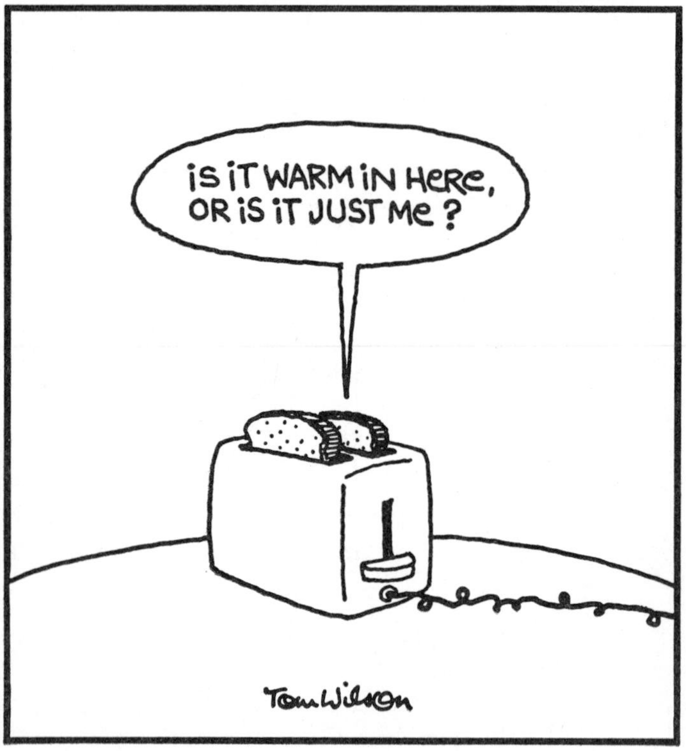
IS IT WARM IN HERE, OR IS IT JUST ME?
TOM WILSON

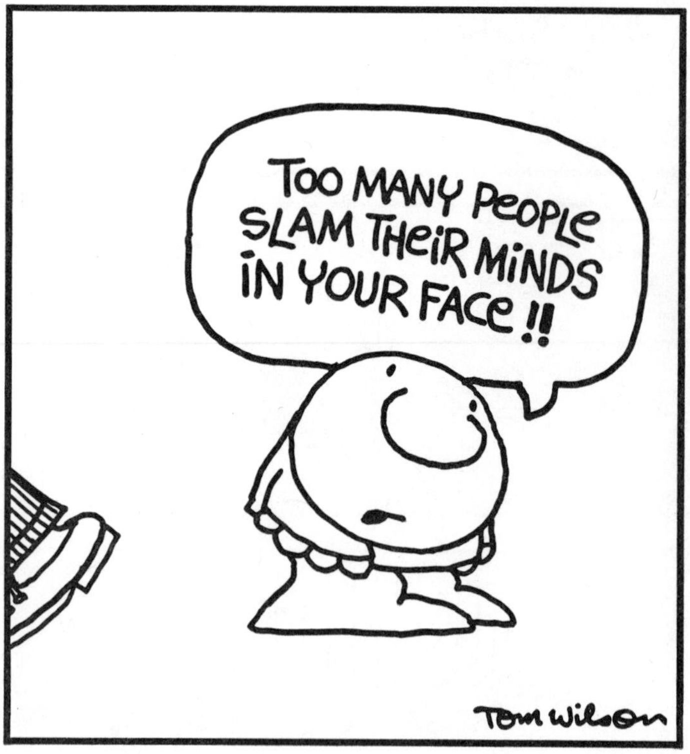
TOO MANY PEOPLE SLAM THEIR MINDS IN YOUR FACE !!
TOM WILSON

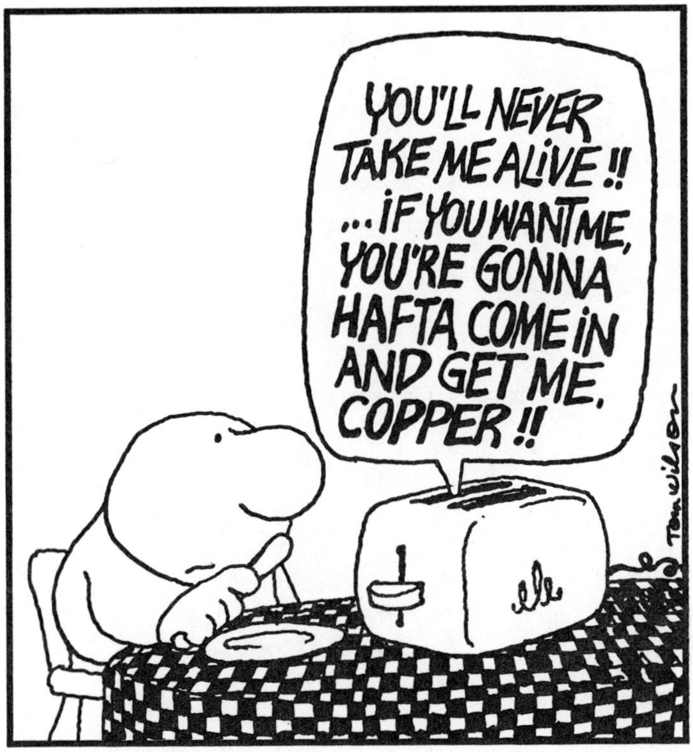
YOU'LL NEVER TAKE ME ALIVE !! ...IF YOU WANT ME, YOU'RE GONNA HAFTA COME IN AND GET ME, COPPER !!
Tom Wilson

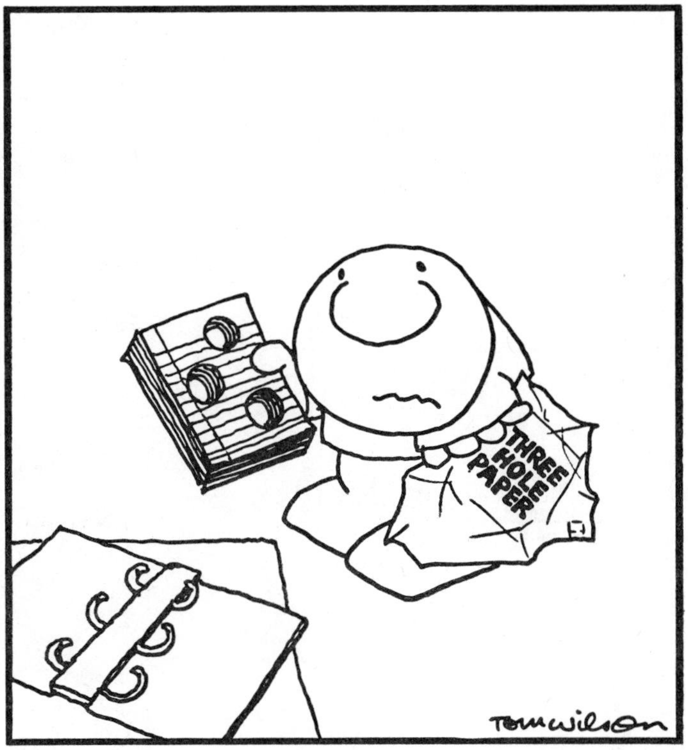
THREE HOLE PAPER
Tom Wilson

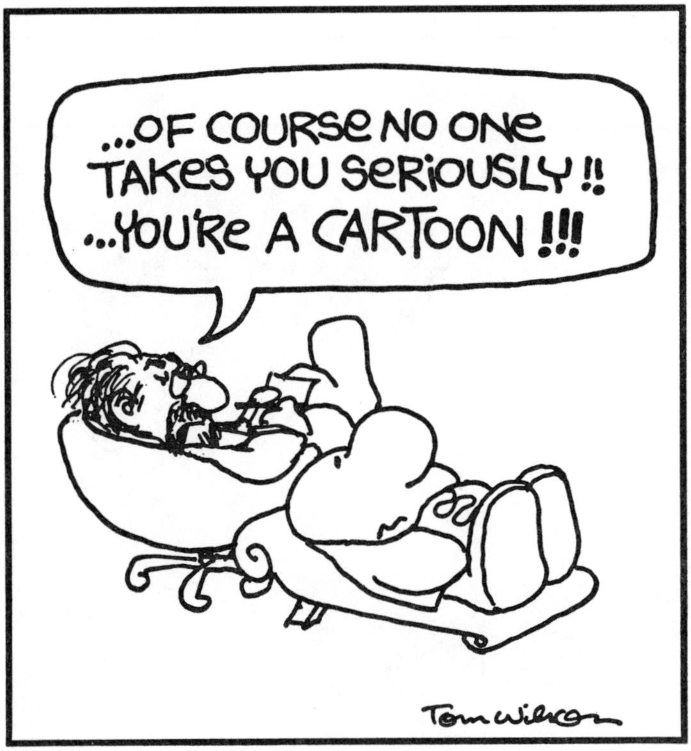
...OF COURSE NO ONE TAKES YOU SERIOUSLY !! ...YOU'RE A CARTOON !!!
Tom Wilson

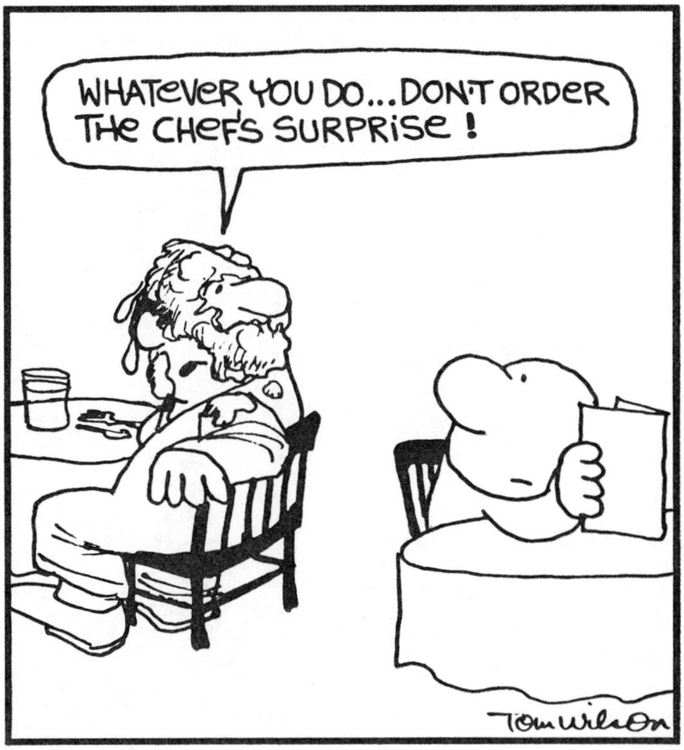
WHATEVER YOU DO...DON'T ORDER THE CHEF'S SURPRISE !
Tom Wilson

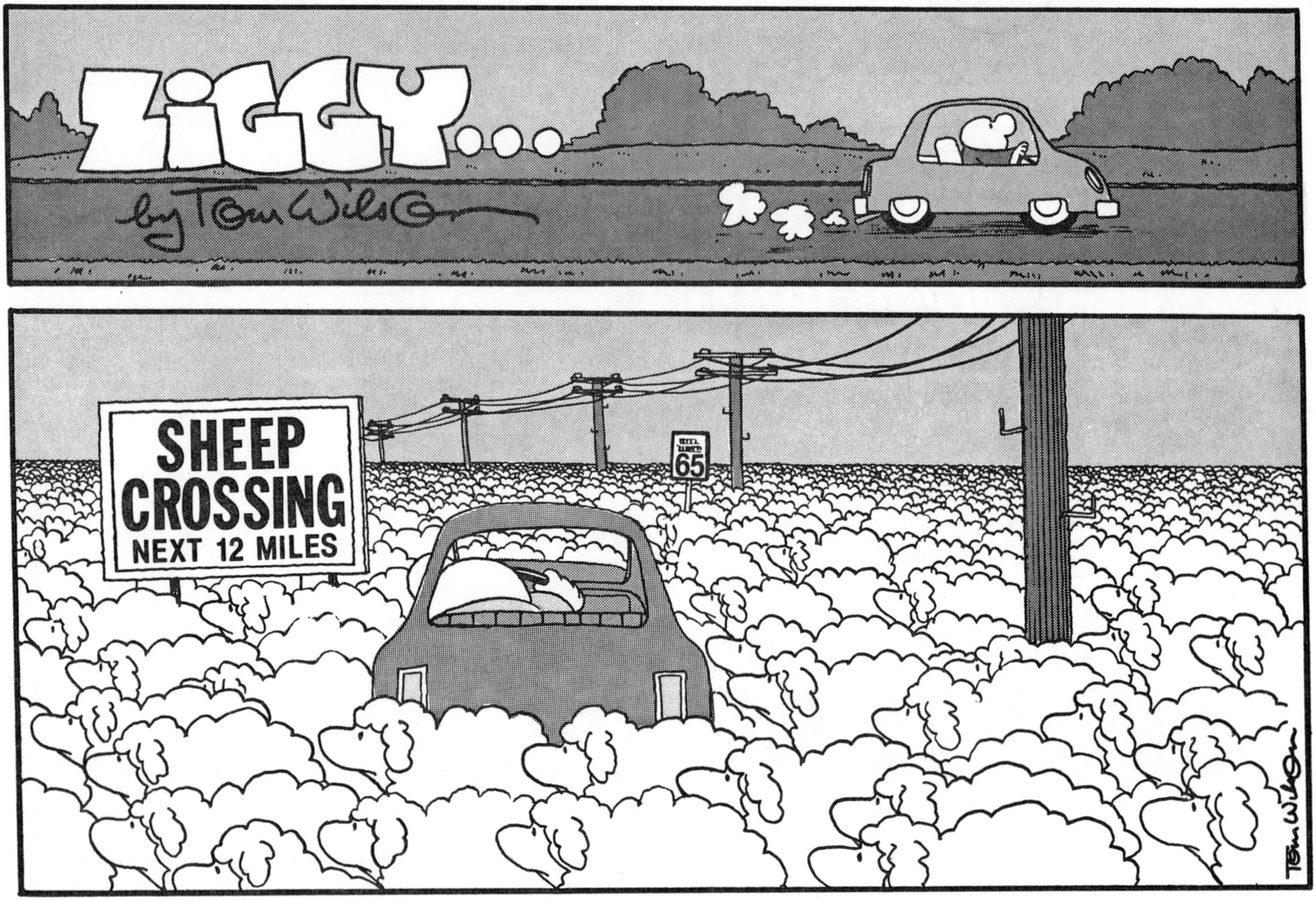
ZIGGY...
by Tom Wilson
SHEEP CROSSING NEXT 12 MILES
65
Tom Wilson

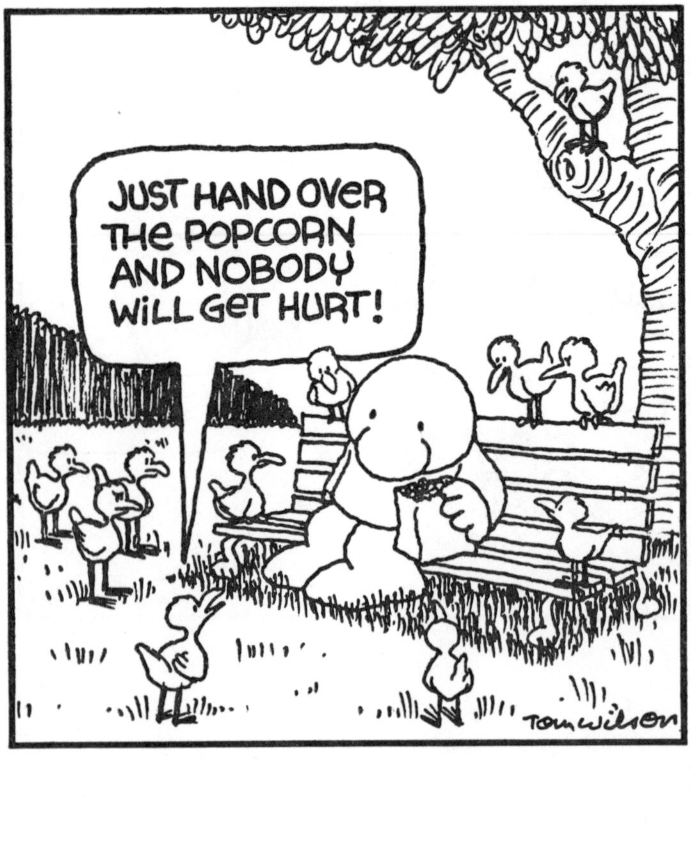
JUST HAND OVER THE POPCORN AND NOBODY WILL GET HURT!
Tom Wilson

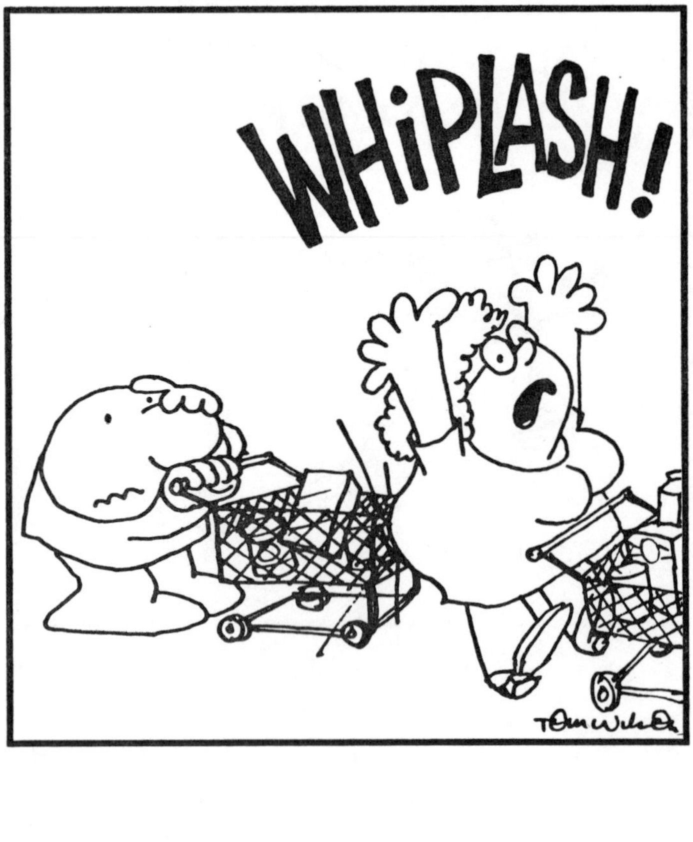
WHIPLASH!

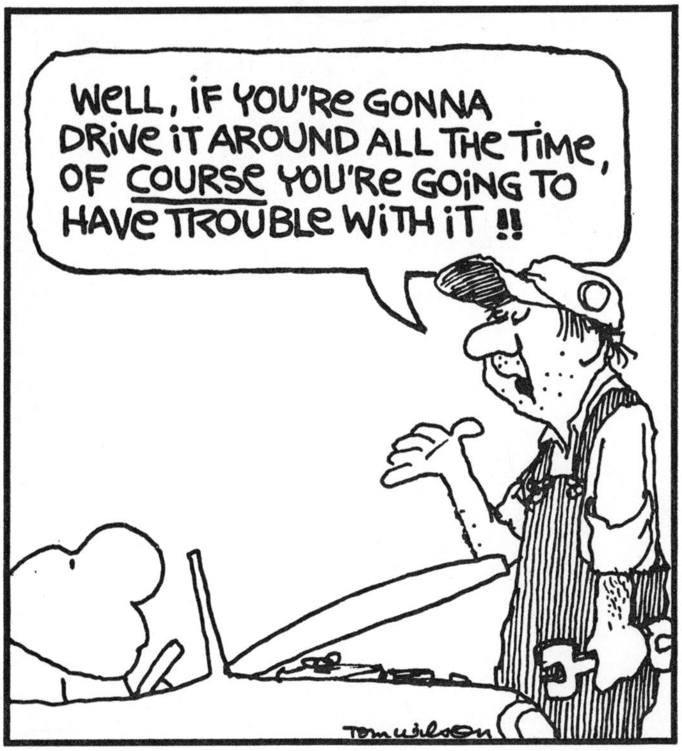
WELL, IF YOU'RE GONNA DRIVE IT AROUND ALL THE TIME, OF COURSE YOU'RE GOING TO HAVE TROUBLE WITH IT !!
TOM WILSON

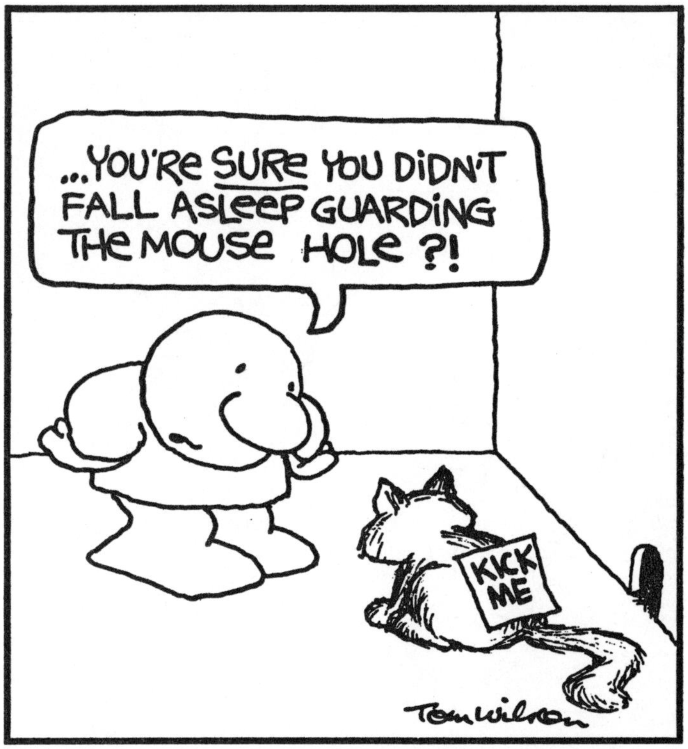
...YOU'RE SURE YOU DIDN'T FALL ASLEEP GUARDING THE MOUSE HOLE ?!
KICK ME
TOM WILSON

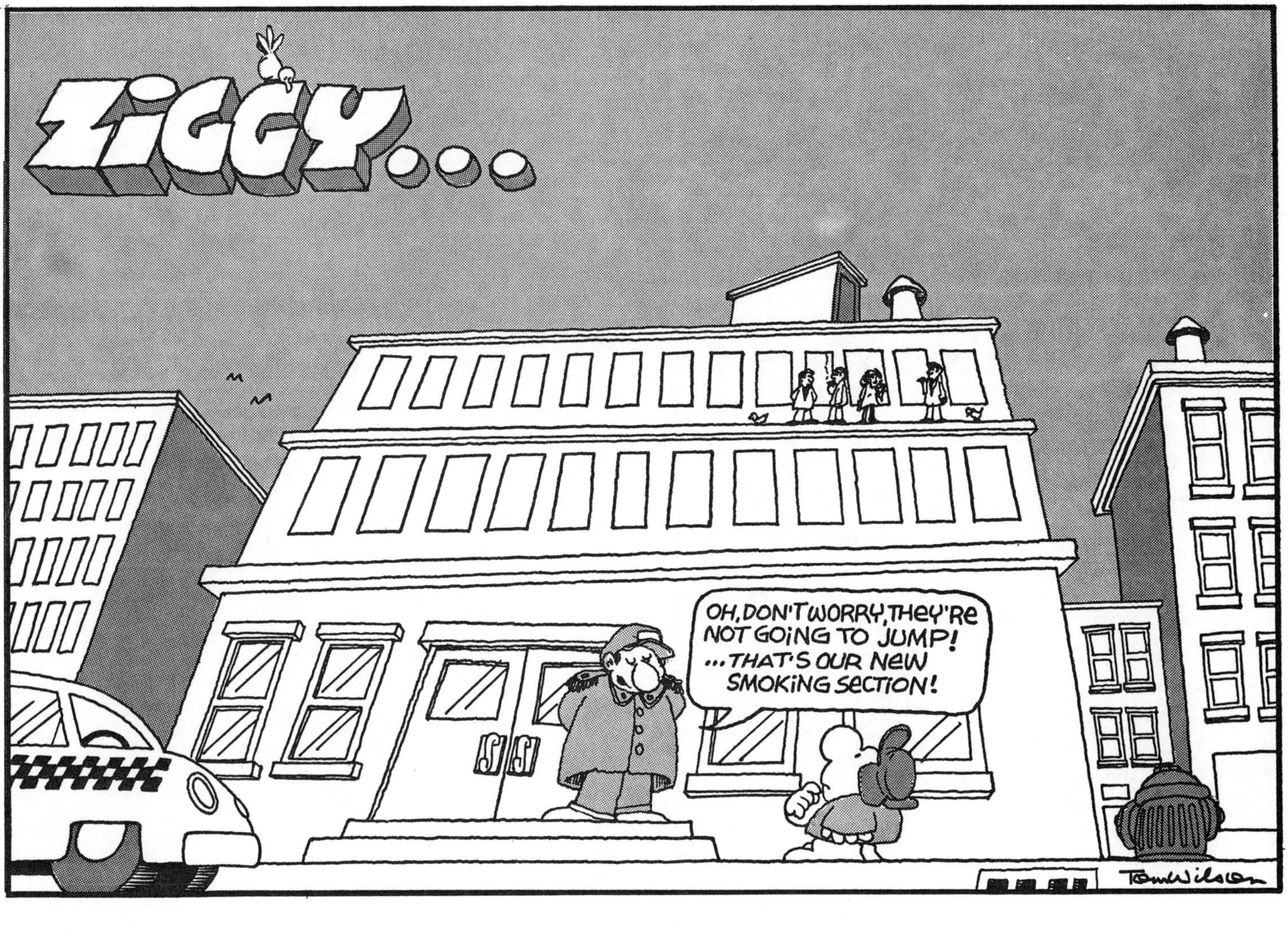
ZIGGY...
OH, DON'T WORRY, THEY'RE NOT GOING TO JUMP! ...THAT'S OUR NEW SMOKING SECTION!
TOM WILSON

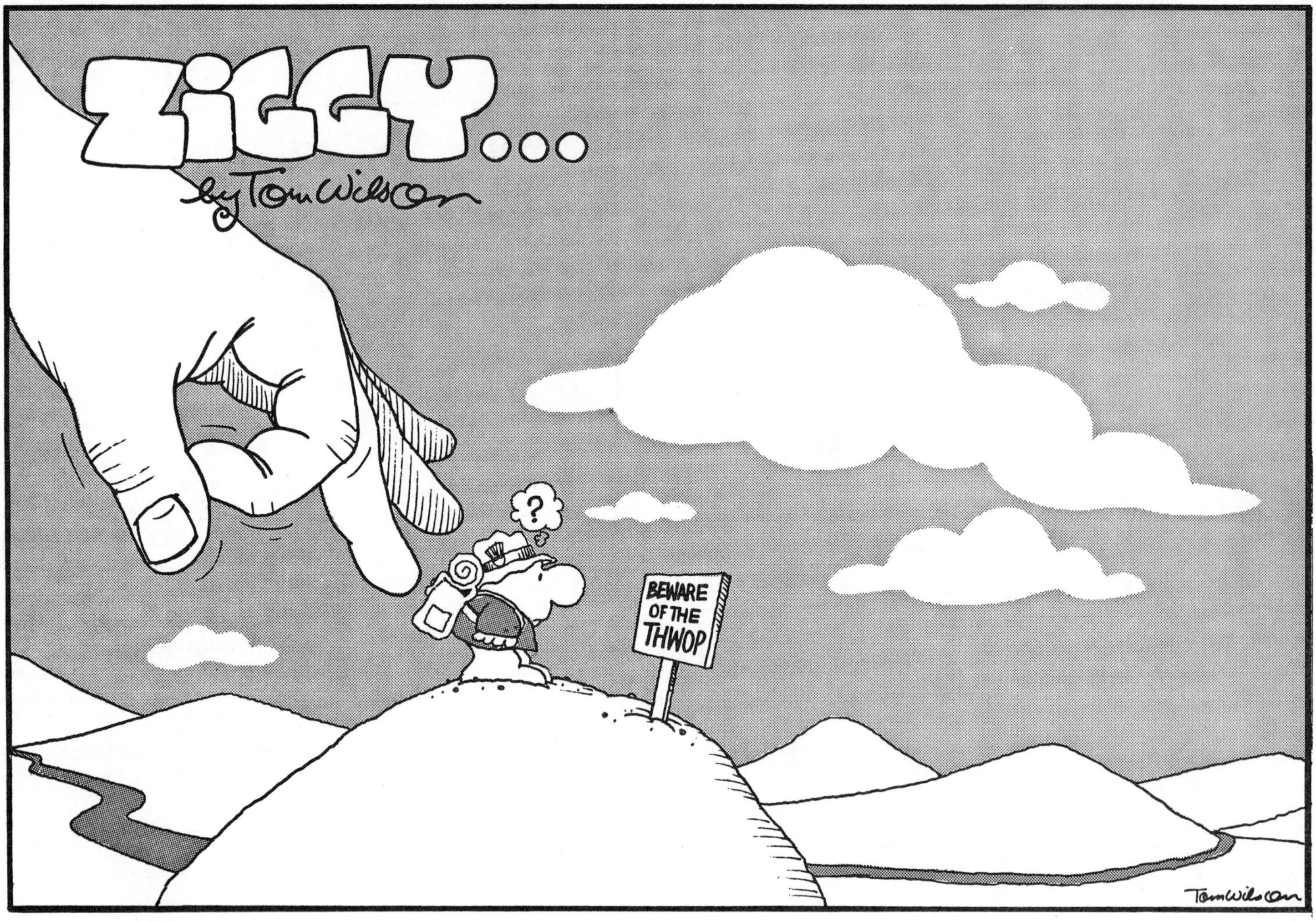
ZIGGY...
by Tom Wilson
BEWARE OF THE THWOP
?
Tom Wilson

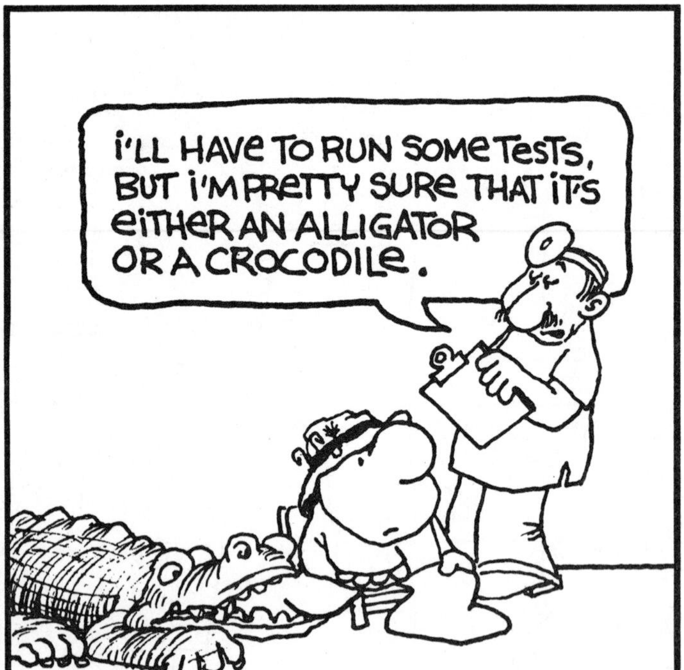
I'LL HAVE TO RUN SOME TESTS, BUT I'M PRETTY SURE THAT IT'S EITHER AN ALLIGATOR OR A CROCODILE.
Tom Wilson

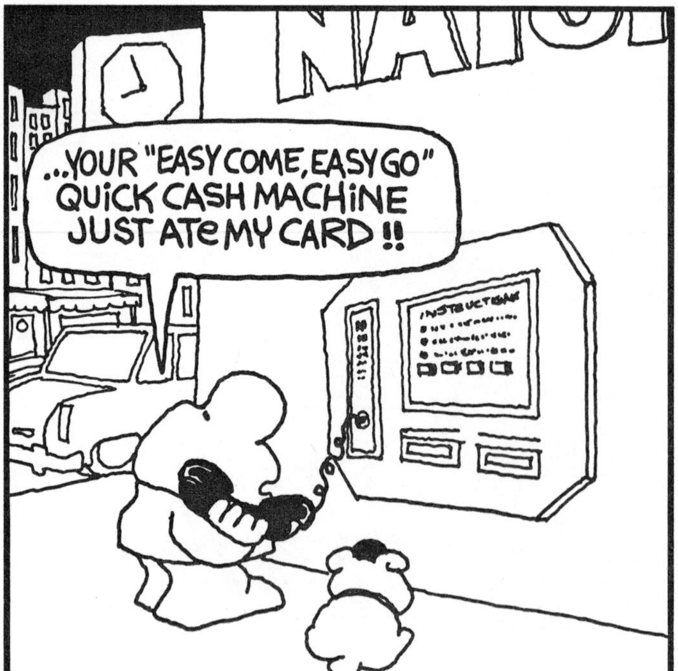
...YOUR "EASY COME, EASY GO" QUICK CASH MACHINE JUST ATE MY CARD!!
INSTRUCTIONS
Tom Wilson

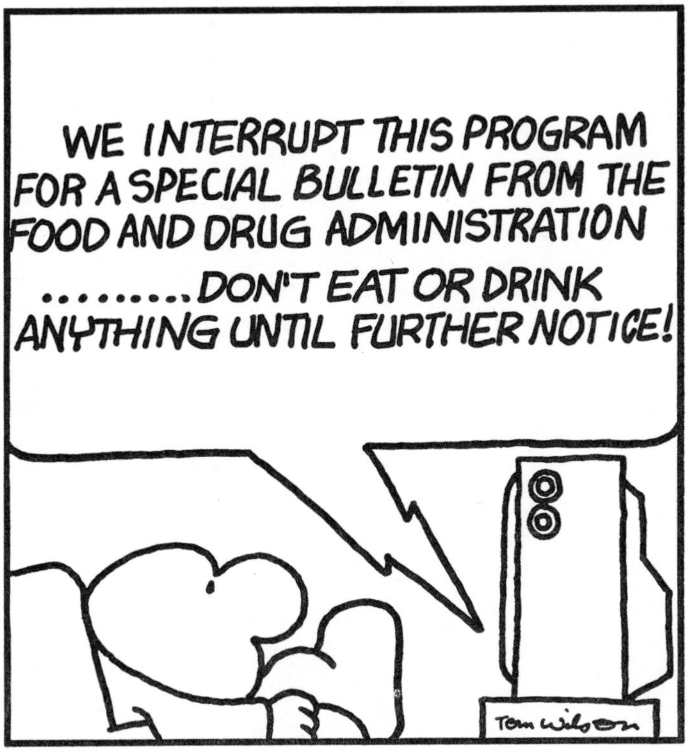
WE INTERRUPT THIS PROGRAM FOR A SPECIAL BULLETIN FROM THE FOOD AND DRUG ADMINISTRATION ....DON'T EAT OR DRINK ANYTHING UNTIL FURTHER NOTICE!
Tom Wilson

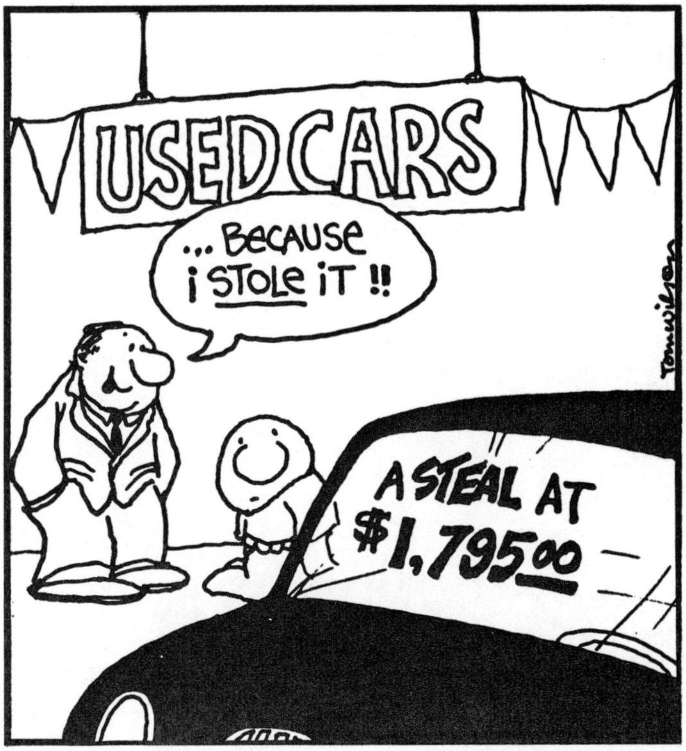
USED CARS
... Because i STOLe iT !!
A STEAL AT $1,795.00
Tom Wilson

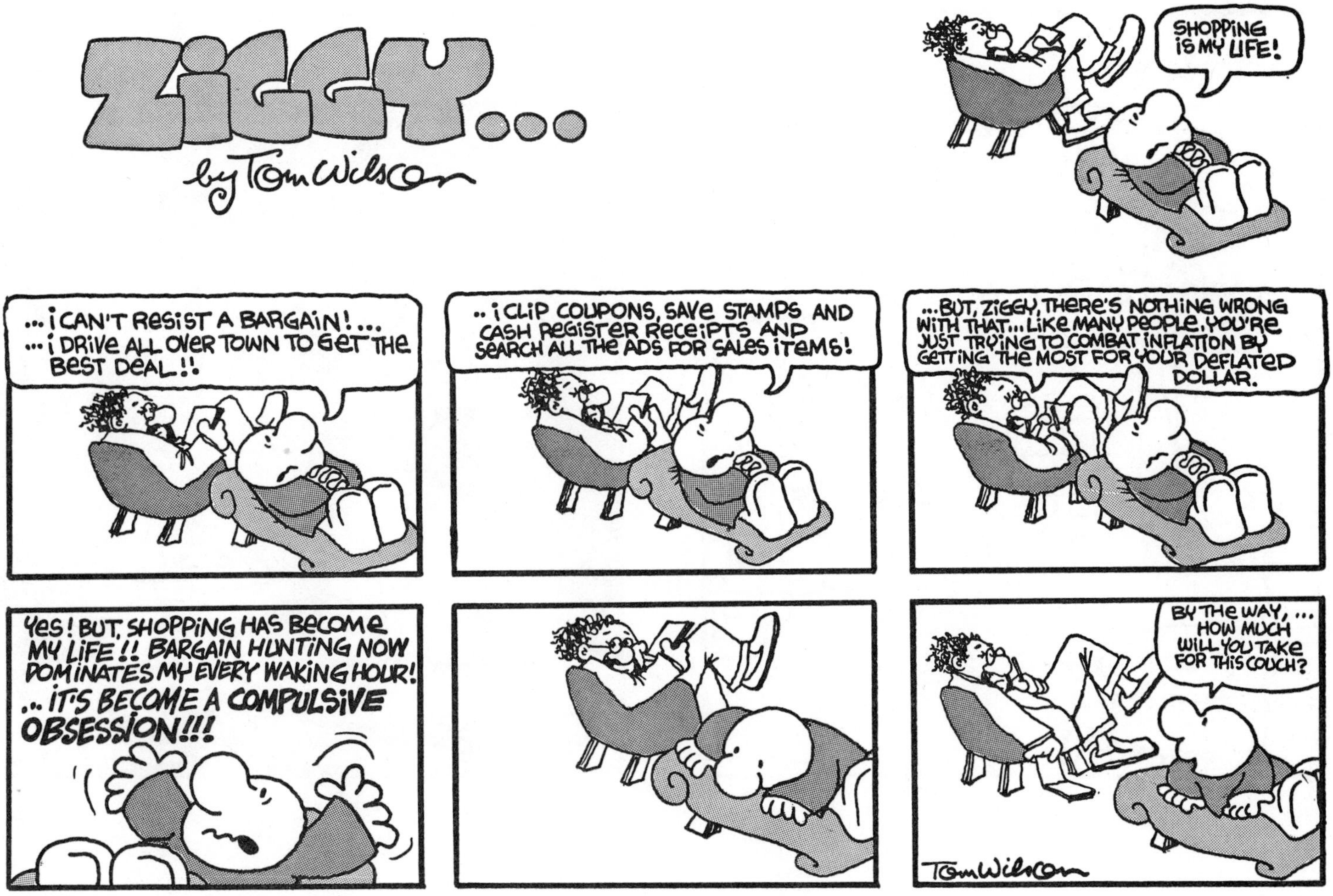
ZiGGY...
by Tom Wilson
SHOPPiNG iS MY LiFE!
... i CAN'T ReSiST A BARGAiN! ... ... i DRiVe ALL OVeR TOWN TO GeT THe BeST DeAL!!
.. i CLiP COUPONS, SAVe STAMPS AND CASH ReGiSTeR ReCeiPTS AND SeARCH ALL THe ADS FOR SALeS iTeMS!
...BUT, ZiGGY, THeRe'S NOTHiNG WRONG WiTH THAT... LiKe MANY PeOPLe, YOU'Re JUST TRYiNG TO COMBAT iNFLATiON BY GeTTiNG THe MOST FOR YOUR DeFLATeD DOLLAR.
YeS! BUT, SHOPPiNG HAS BeCOMe MY LiFe!! BARGAiN HUNTiNG NOW DOMiNATeS MY eVeRY WAKiNG HOUR! ... iT'S BeCOMe A COMPULSiVe OBSeSSiON!!!
BY THe WAY, ... HOW MUCH WiLL YOU TAKe FOR THiS COUCH?
Tom Wilson

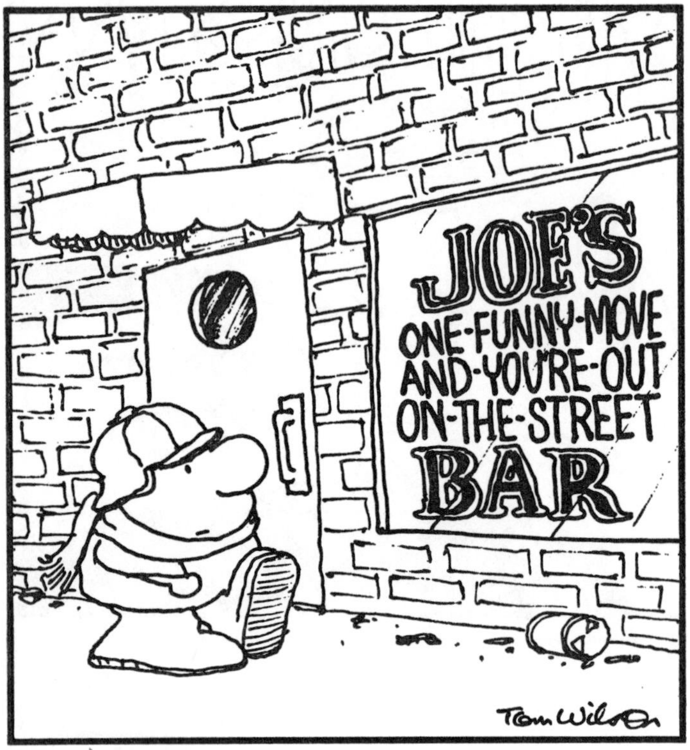
JOE'S
ONE-FUNNY-MOVE AND-YOU'RE-OUT ON-THE-STREET
BAR
Tom Wilson

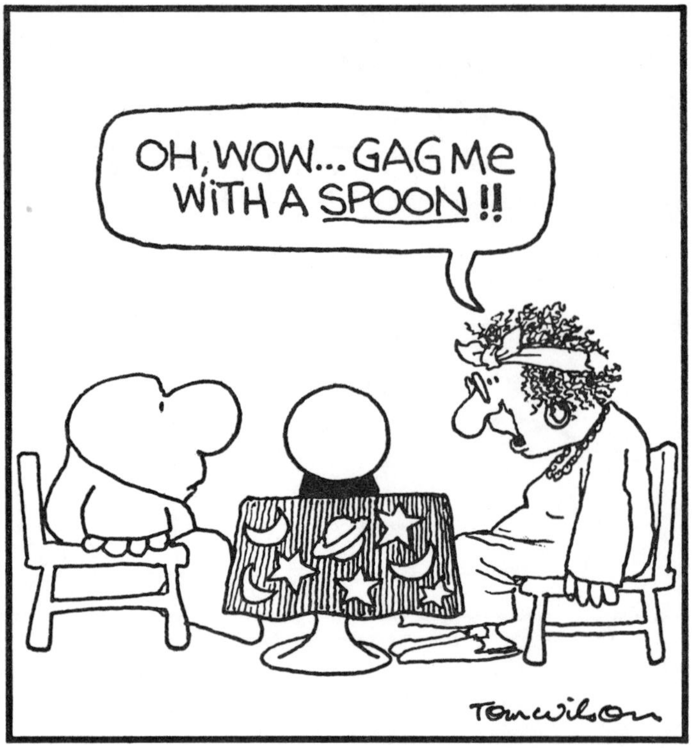
OH, WOW... GAG ME WITH A SPOON !!
Tom Wilson

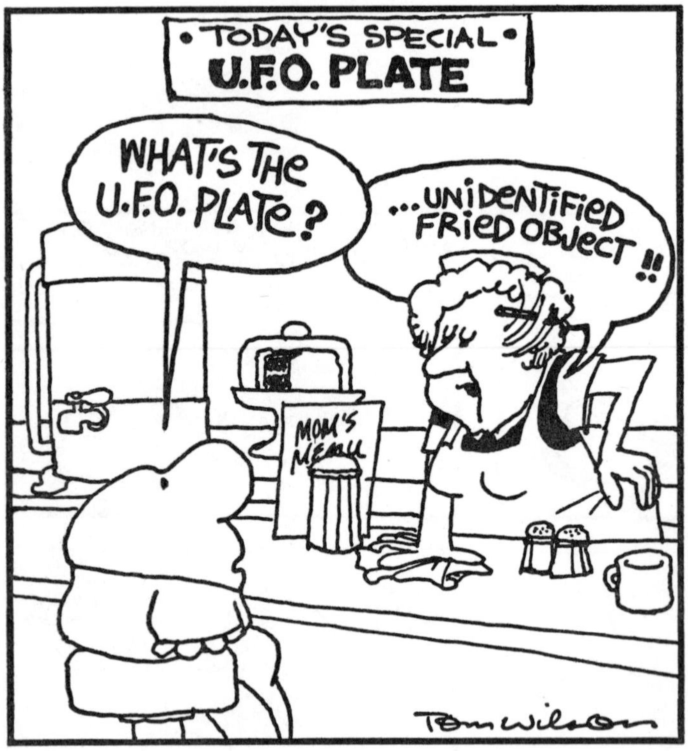
• TODAY'S SPECIAL •
U.F.O. PLATE
WHAT'S THE U.F.O. PLATE?
...UNIDENTIFIED FRIED OBJECT !!
MOM'S MENU
Tom Wilson

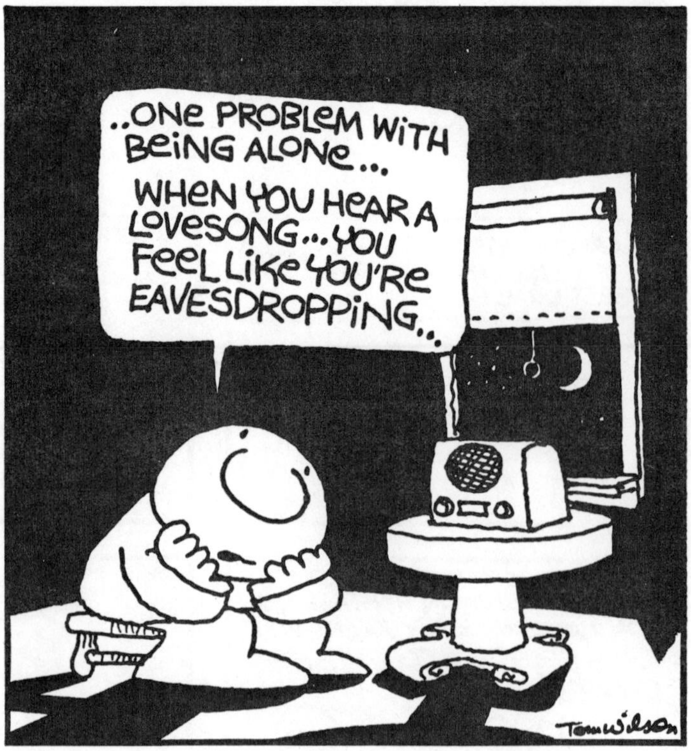
..ONE PROBLEM WITH BEING ALONE...
WHEN YOU HEAR A LOVESONG... YOU FEEL LIKE YOU'RE EAVESDROPPING...
Tom Wilson

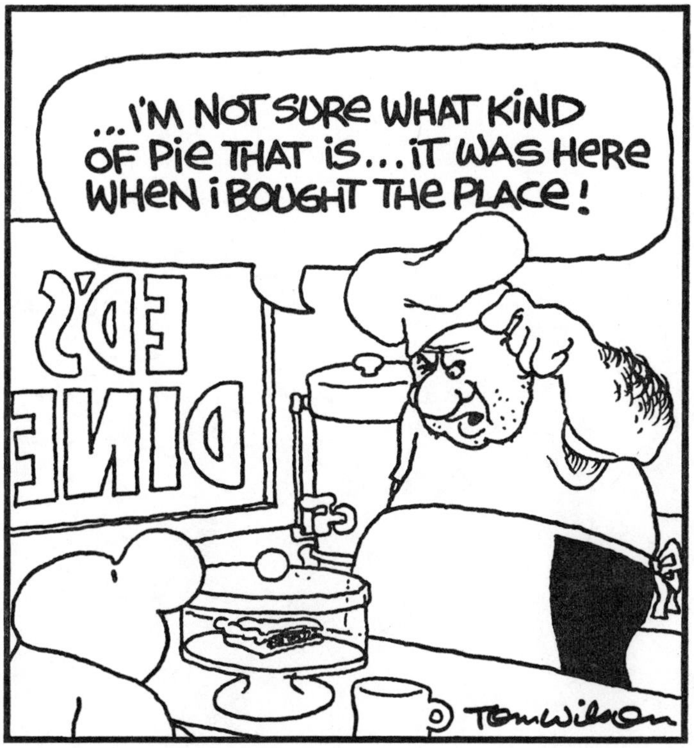
...I'M NOT SURE WHAT KIND OF PIE THAT IS... IT WAS HERE WHEN I BOUGHT THE PLACE!
ED'S DINE
© TOM WILSON

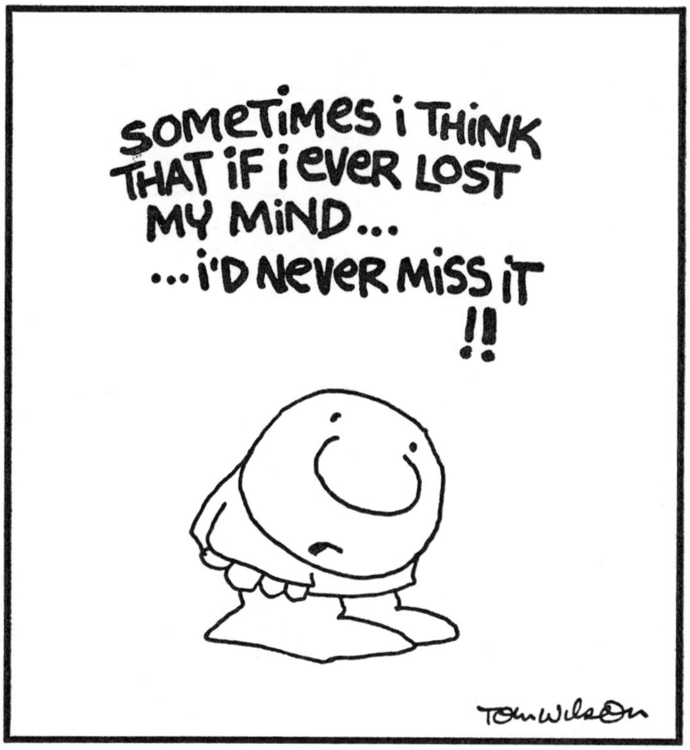
SOMETIMES I THINK THAT IF I EVER LOST MY MIND...
...I'D NEVER MISS IT !!
TOM WILSON

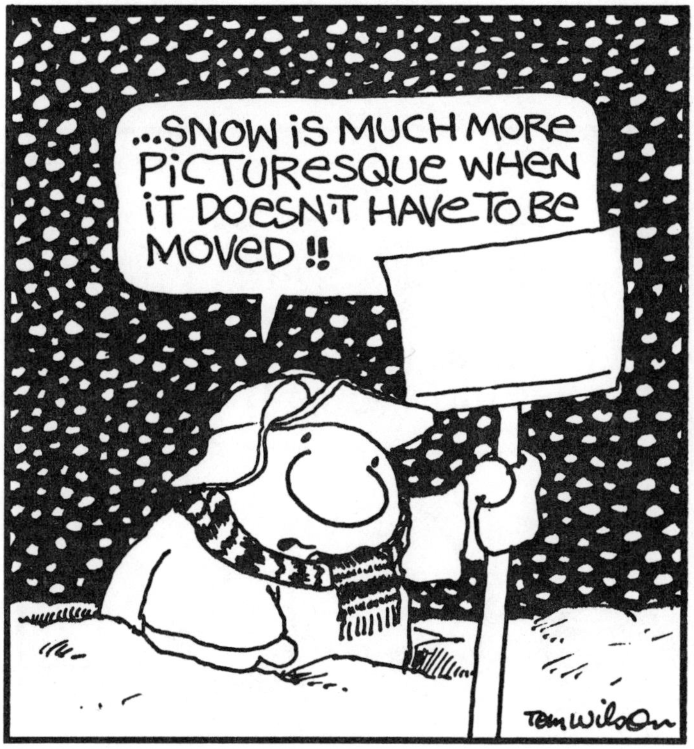
...SNOW IS MUCH MORE PICTURESQUE WHEN IT DOESN'T HAVE TO BE MOVED !!
TOM WILSON

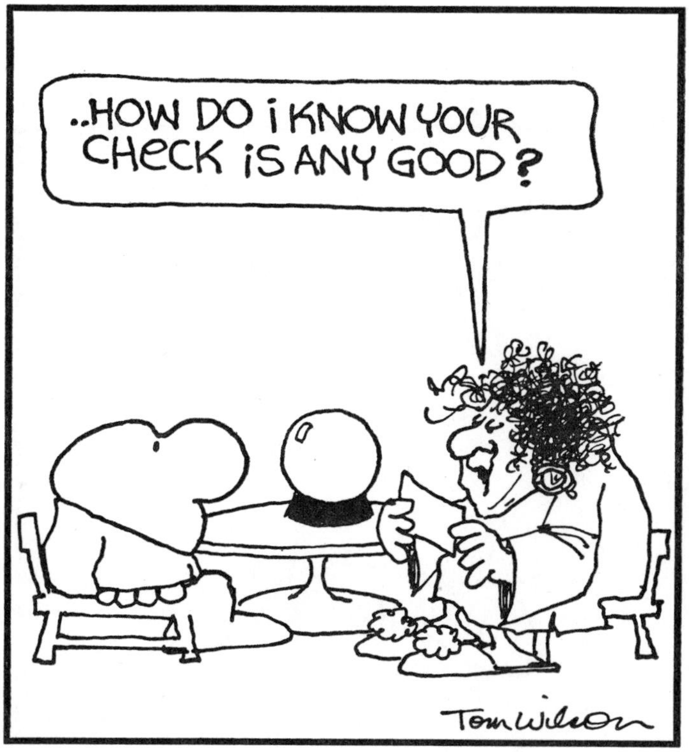
..HOW DO I KNOW YOUR CHECK IS ANY GOOD?
TOM WILSON

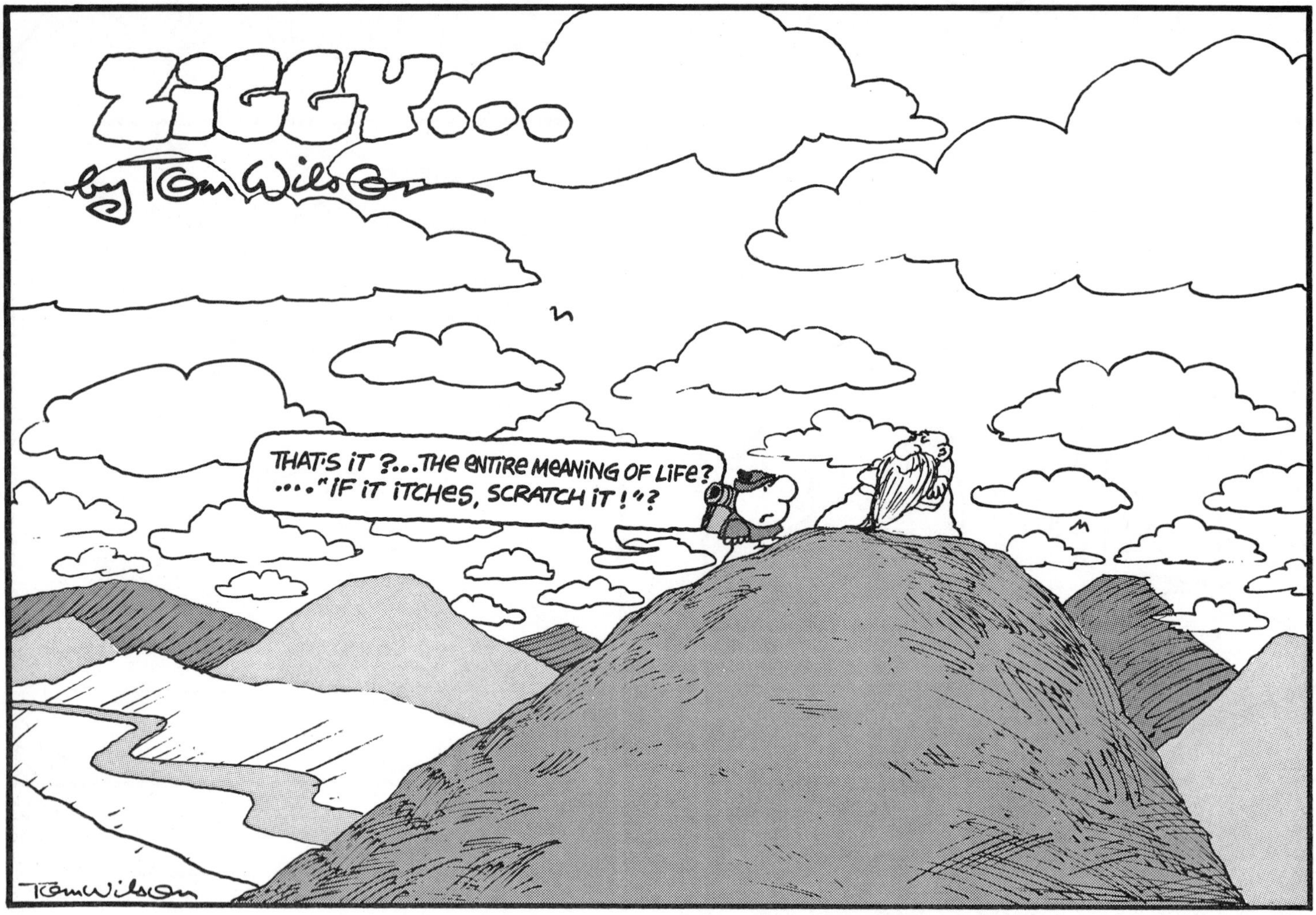
ZIGGY...
by Tom Wilson
THAT'S IT ?...THE ENTIRE MEANING OF LIFE? ...."IF IT ITCHES, SCRATCH IT !"?
TOM WILSON

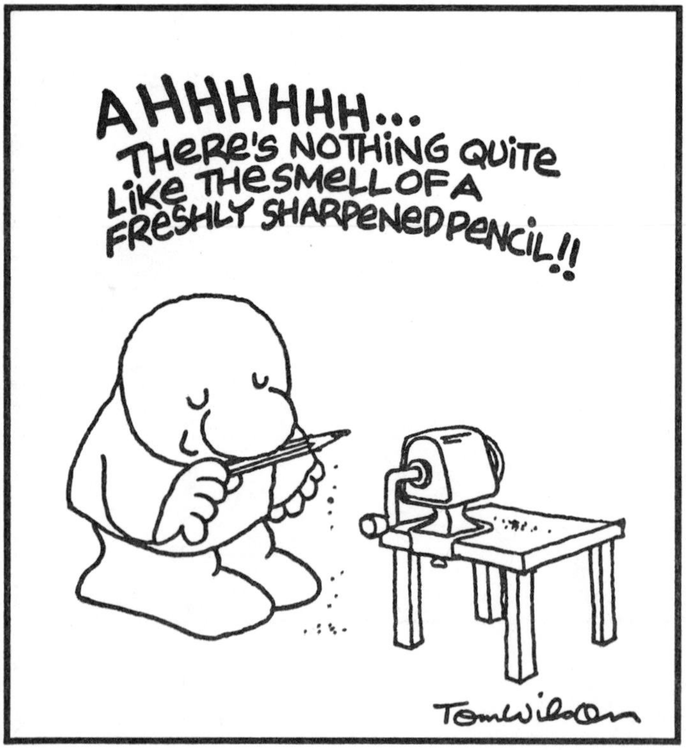
AHHHHHH... THERE'S NOTHING QUITE LIKE THE SMELL OF A FRESHLY SHARPENED PENCIL!!
TOM WILSON

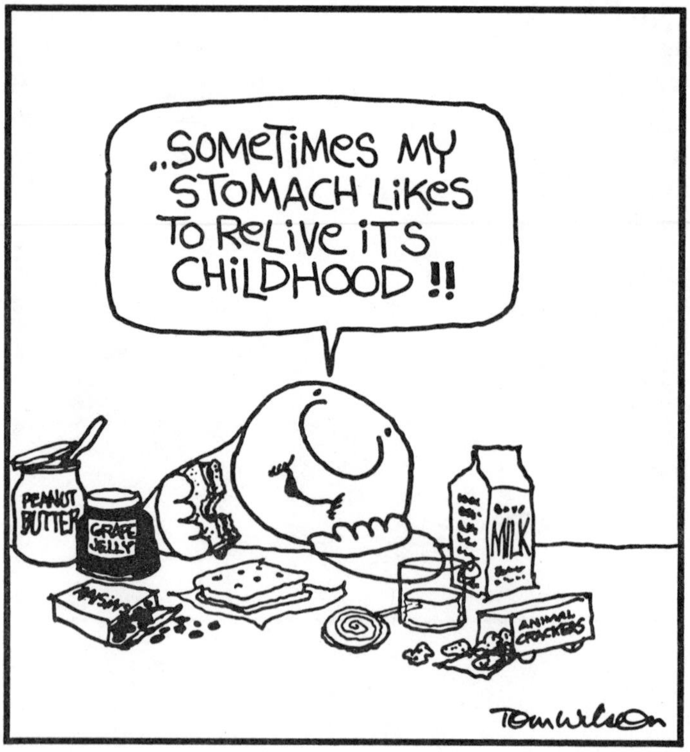
..SOMETIMES MY STOMACH LIKES TO RELIVE ITS CHILDHOOD !!
PEANUT BUTTER
GRAPE JELLY
MILK
ANIMAL CRACKERS
TOM WILSON

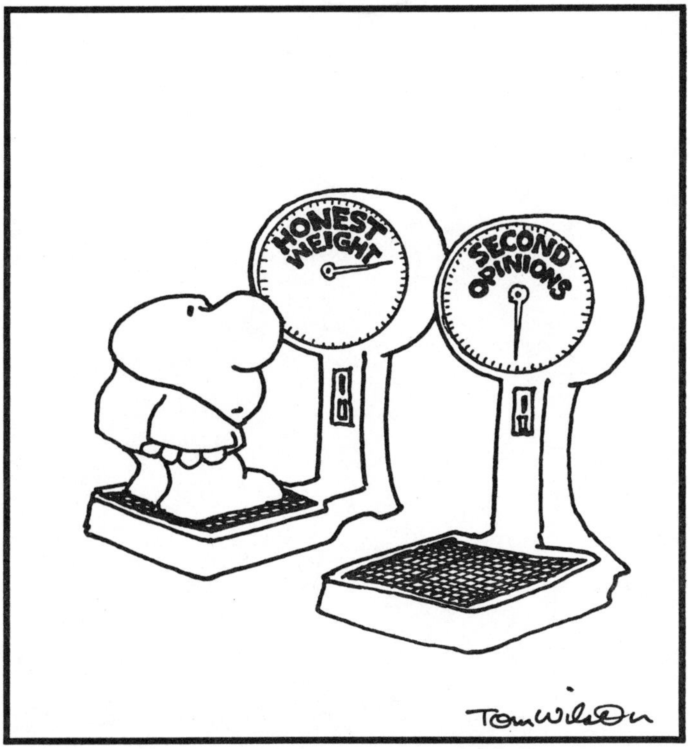
HONEST WEIGHT
SECOND OPINIONS
Tom Wilson

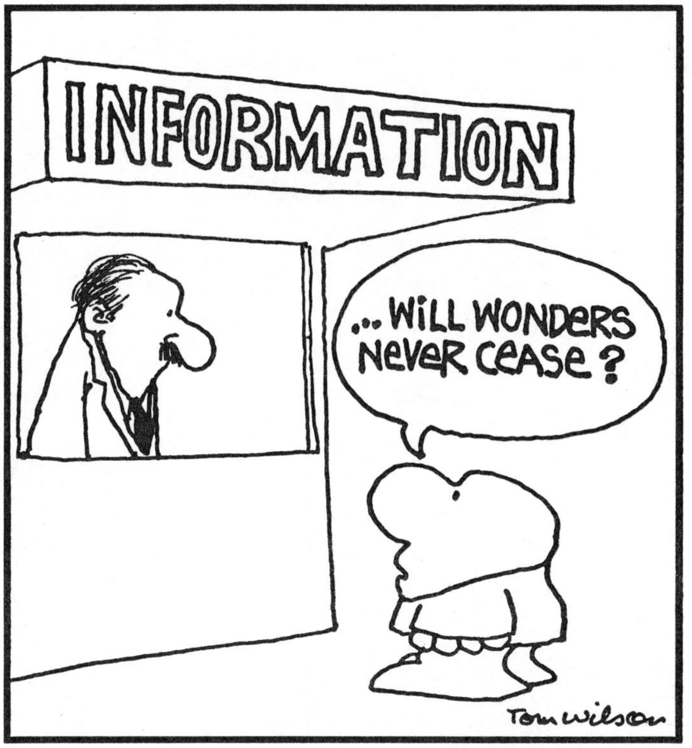
INFORMATION
...WiLL WONDERS NeVER CeASe?
Tom Wilson

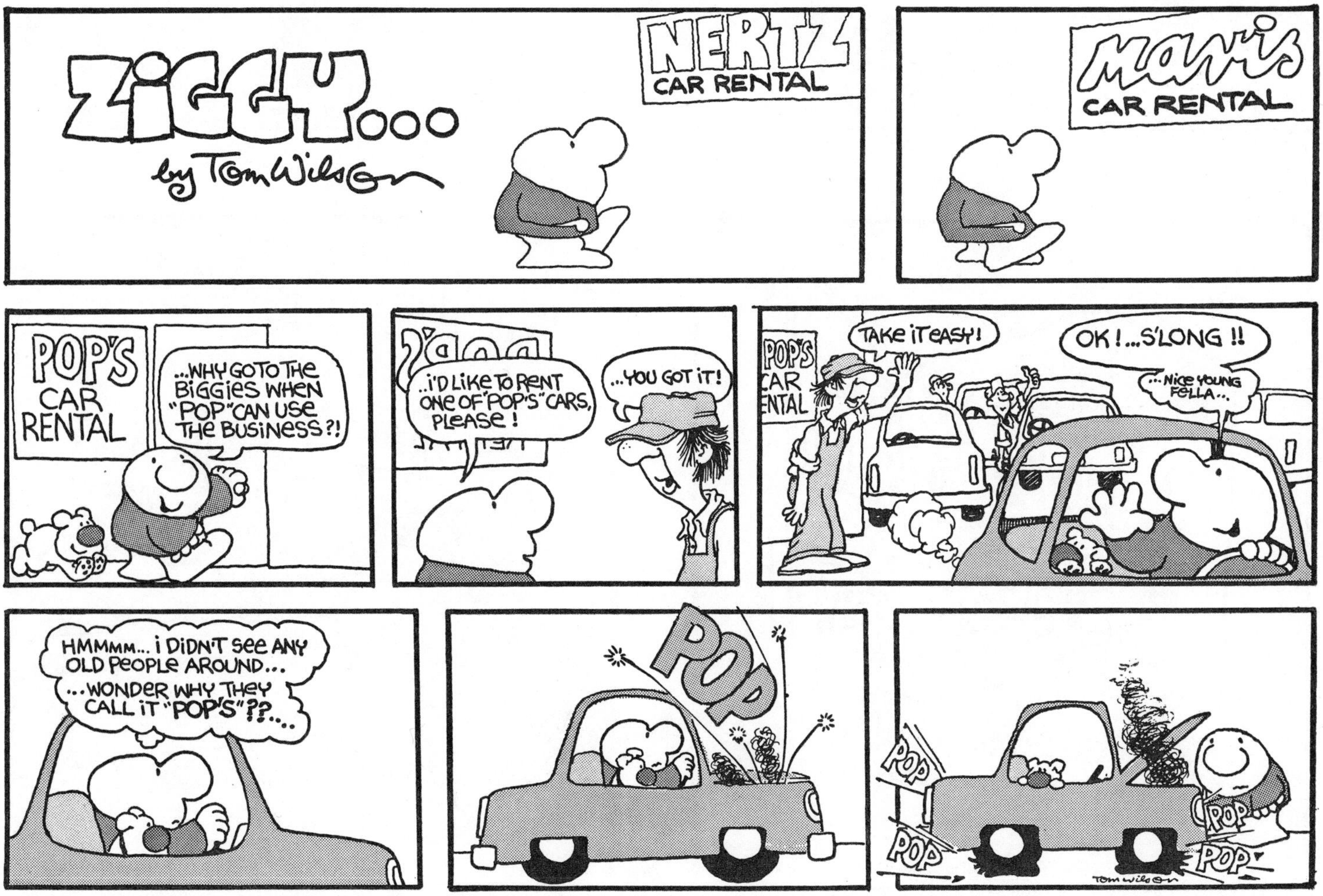
ZiGGY...
by Tom Wilson
NERTZ CAR RENTAL
Mavis CAR RENTAL
POP'S CAR RENTAL
...WHY GO TO THE BiGGiES WHEN "POP" CAN USE THE BUSiNESS?!
...i'D LiKE TO RENT ONE OF "POP'S" CARS, PLEASE!
...YOU GOT iT!
POP'S CAR RENTAL
TAKE iT EASY!
OK!...S'LONG!!
...NiCE YOUNG FELLA...
HMMMM... i DiDN'T SEE ANY OLD PEOPLE AROUND... ...WONDER WHY THEY CALL iT "POP'S"??...
POP
POP
POP
POP
POP
Tom Wilson

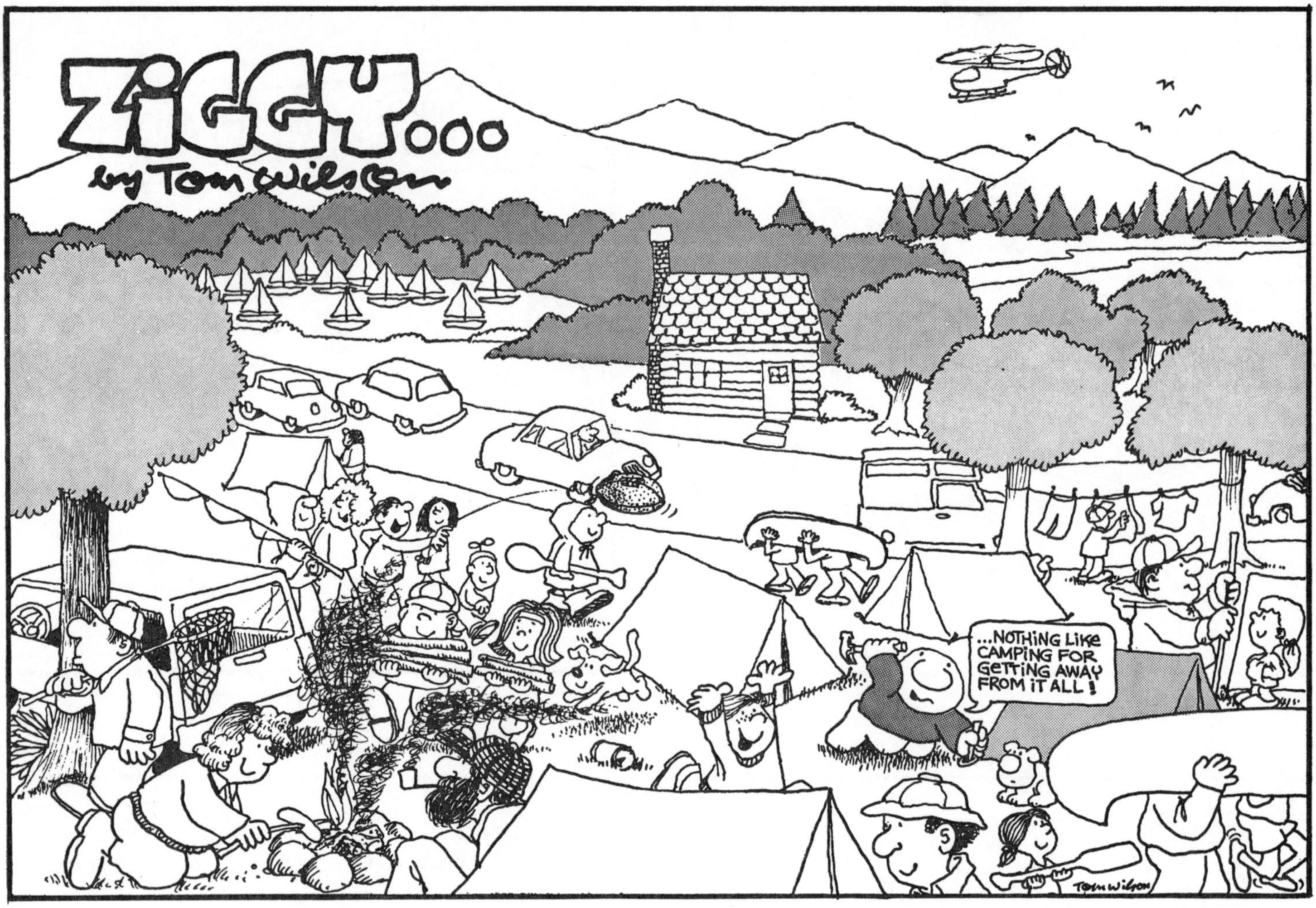
ZIGGY
by Tom Wilson
...NOTHING LIKE CAMPING FOR GETTING AWAY FROM IT ALL!
Tom Wilson

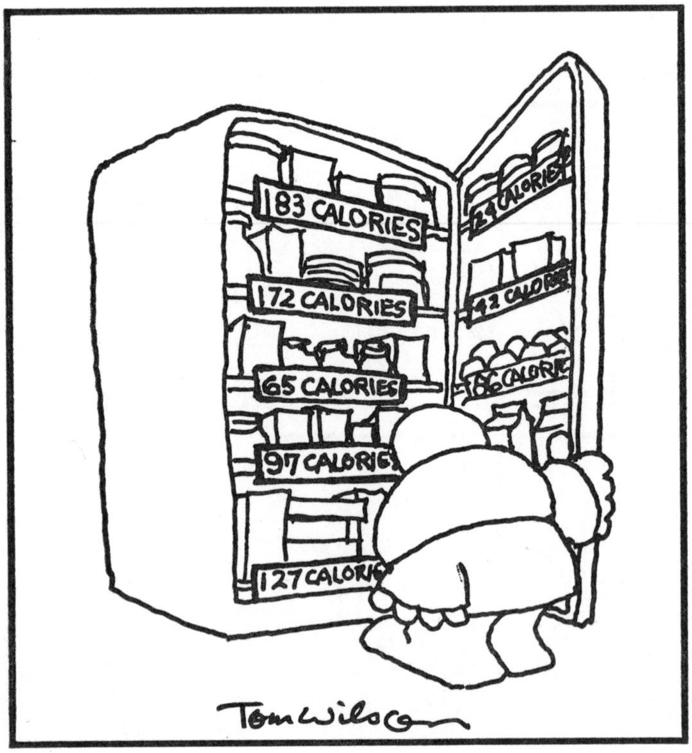
183 CALORIES
172 CALORIES
65 CALORIES
97 CALORIES
127 CALORIES
Tom Wilson

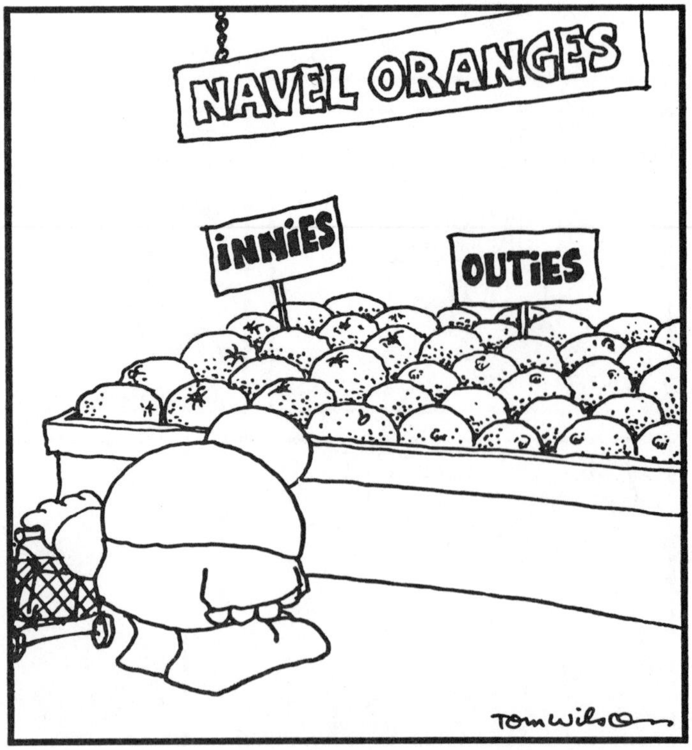
NAVEL ORANGES
INNIES
OUTIES
Tom Wilson

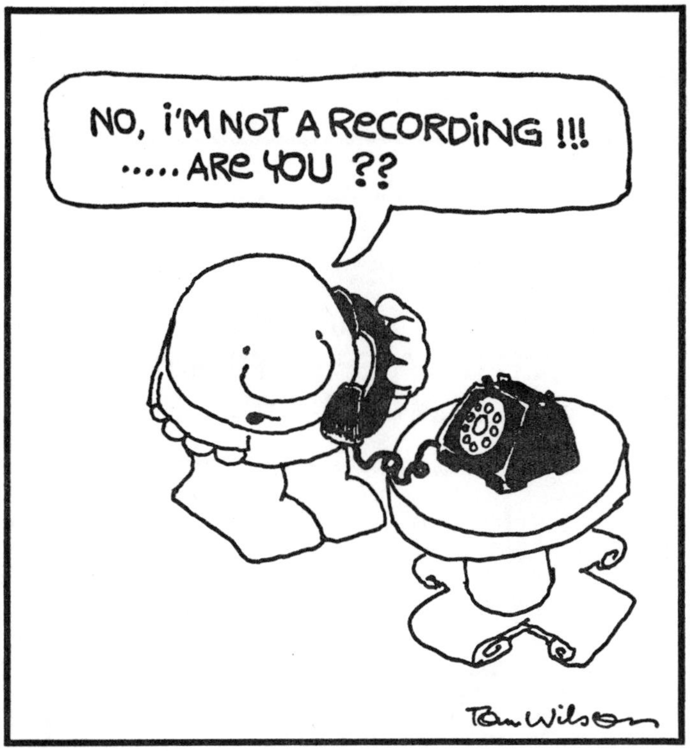
NO, I'M NOT A RECORDING !!! ..... ARE YOU ??
Tom Wilson

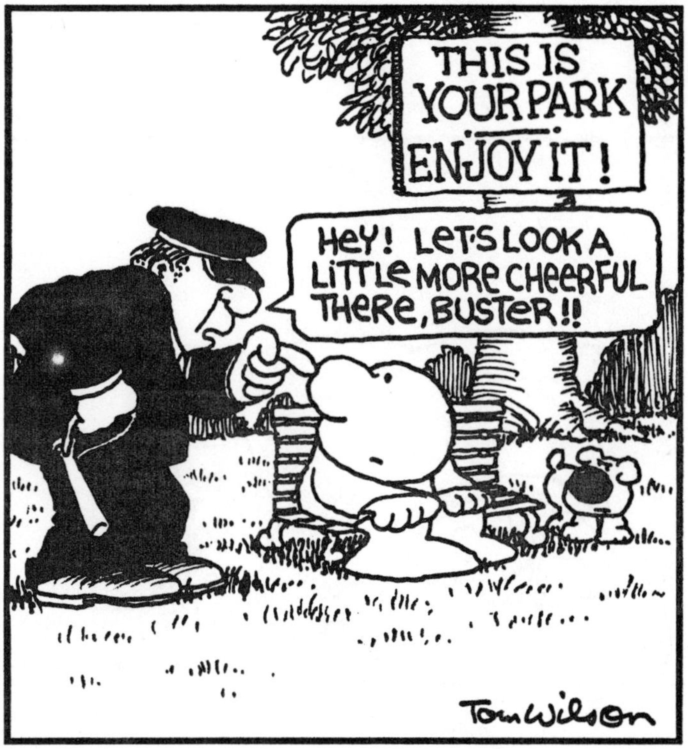
THIS IS YOUR PARK ENJOY IT !
HEY! LET'S LOOK A LITTLE MORE CHEERFUL THERE, BUSTER!!
Tom Wilson

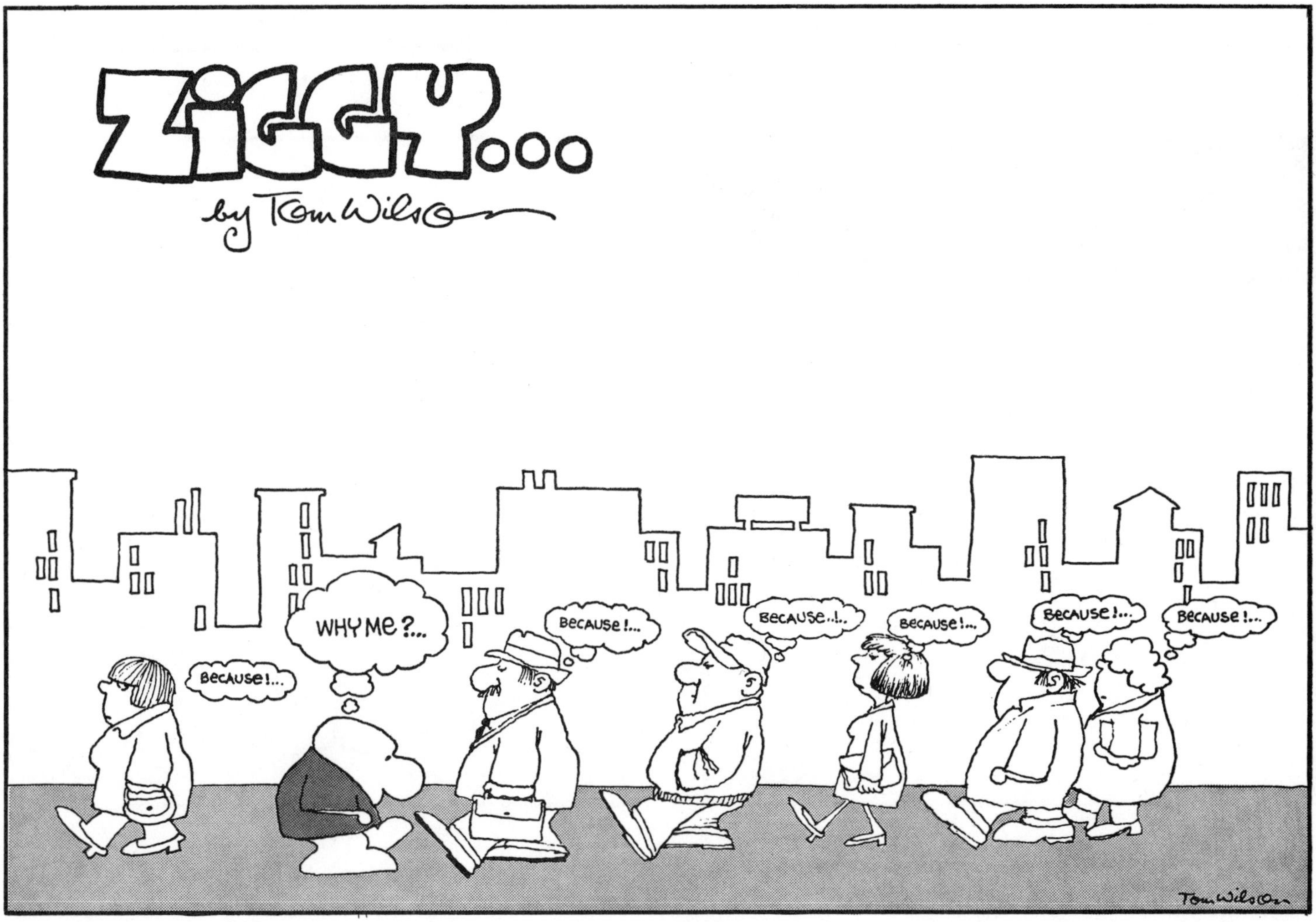
ZIGGY...
by Tom Wilson
BECAUSE!...
WHY ME?...
BECAUSE!...
BECAUSE..!..
BECAUSE!...
BECAUSE!...
BECAUSE!...
Tom Wilson

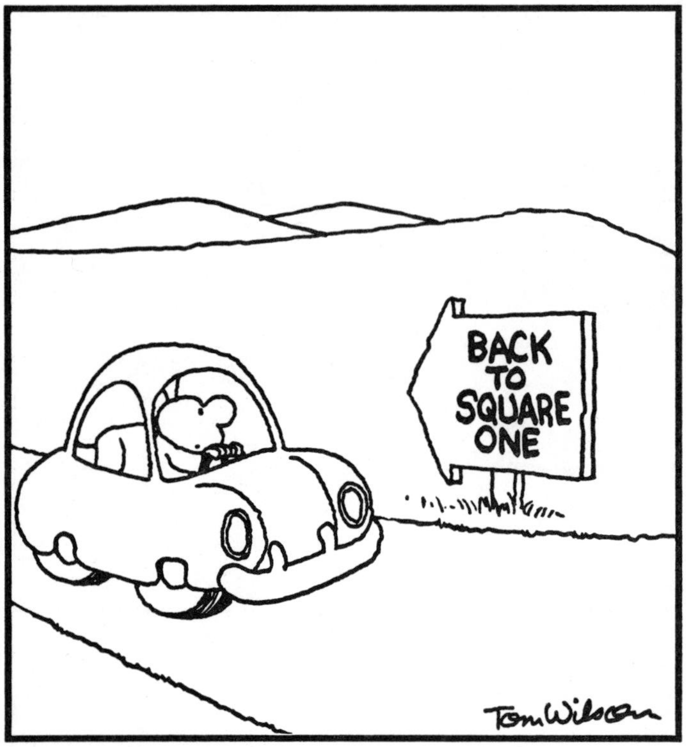
BACK TO SQUARE ONE
TomWilson

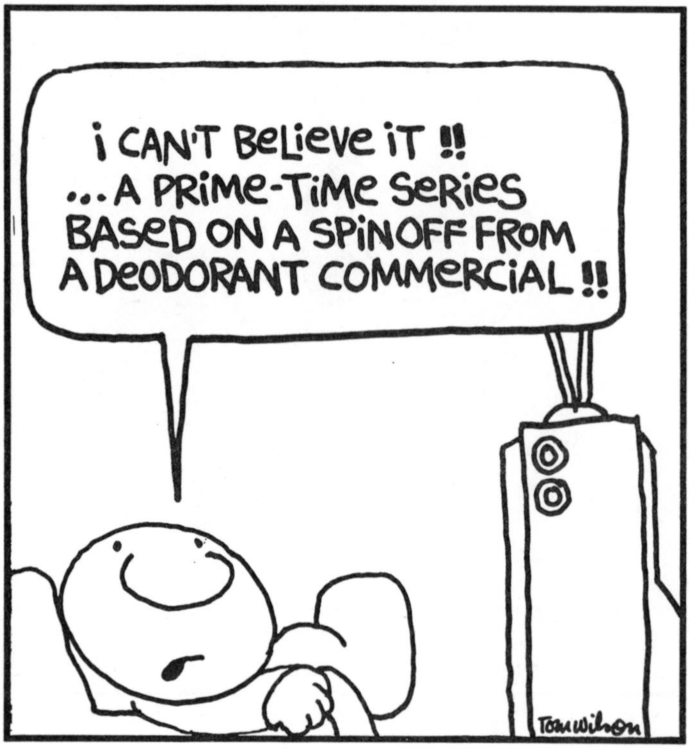
I CAN'T BELIEVE IT !! ...A PRIME-TIME SERIES BASED ON A SPINOFF FROM A DEODORANT COMMERCIAL !!
TomWilson

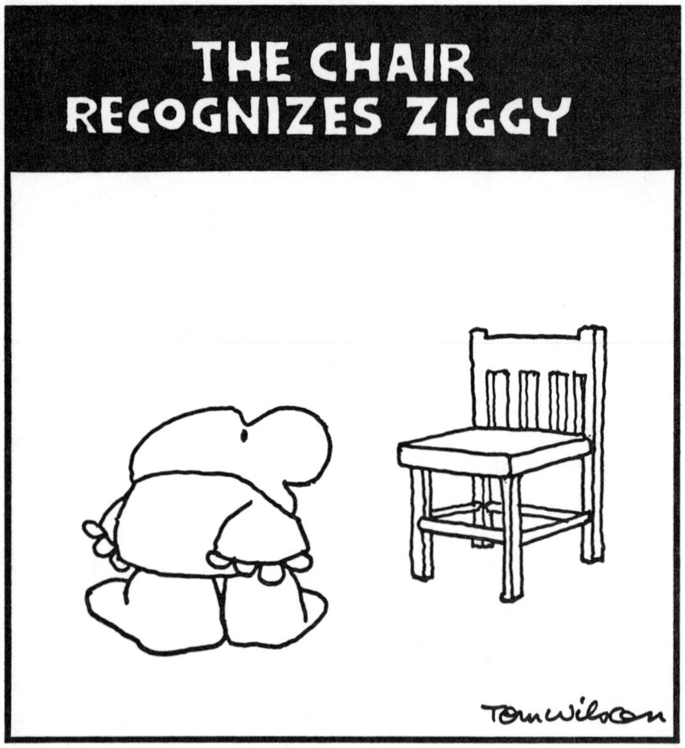
THE CHAIR RECOGNIZES ZIGGY
TomWilson

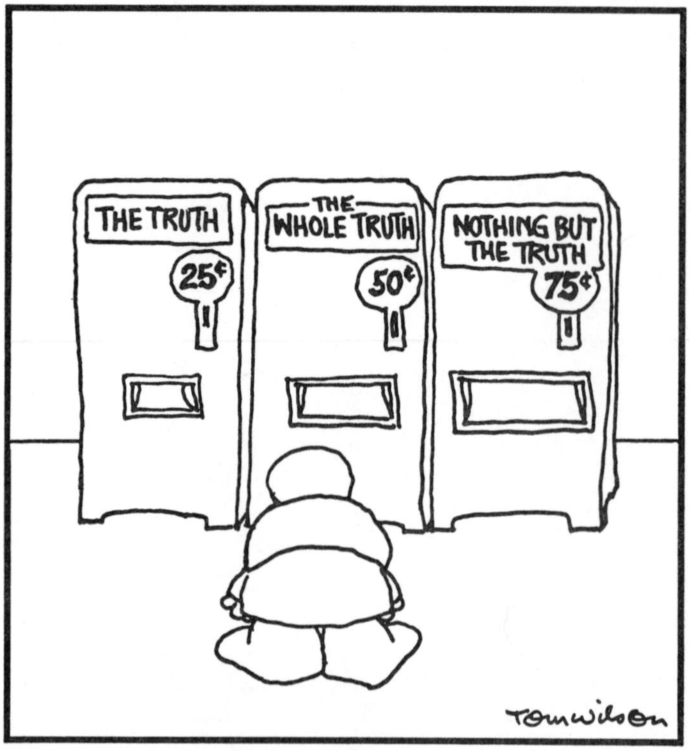
THE TRUTH
25¢
THE WHOLE TRUTH
50¢
NOTHING BUT THE TRUTH
75¢
TomWilson

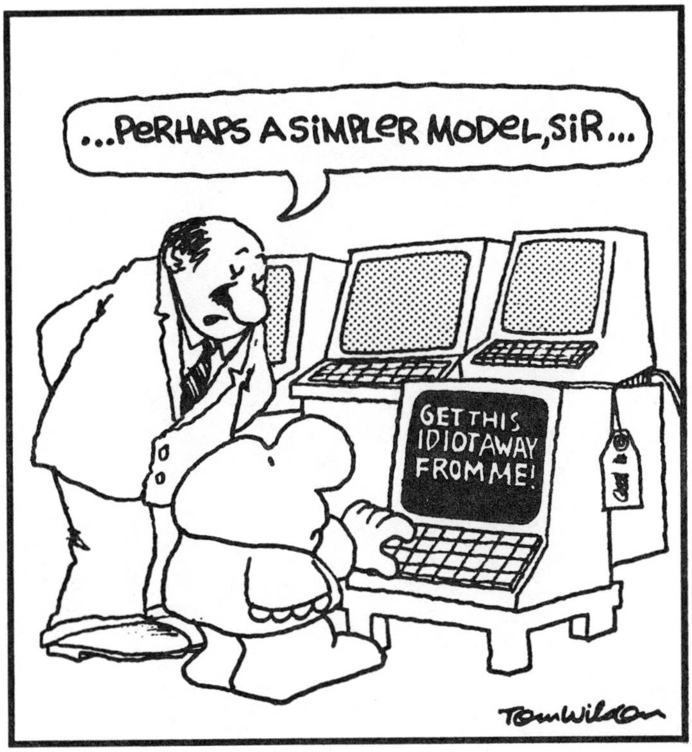
...PERHAPS A SIMPLER MODEL, SIR...
GET THIS IDIOT AWAY FROM ME!
TOM WILSON

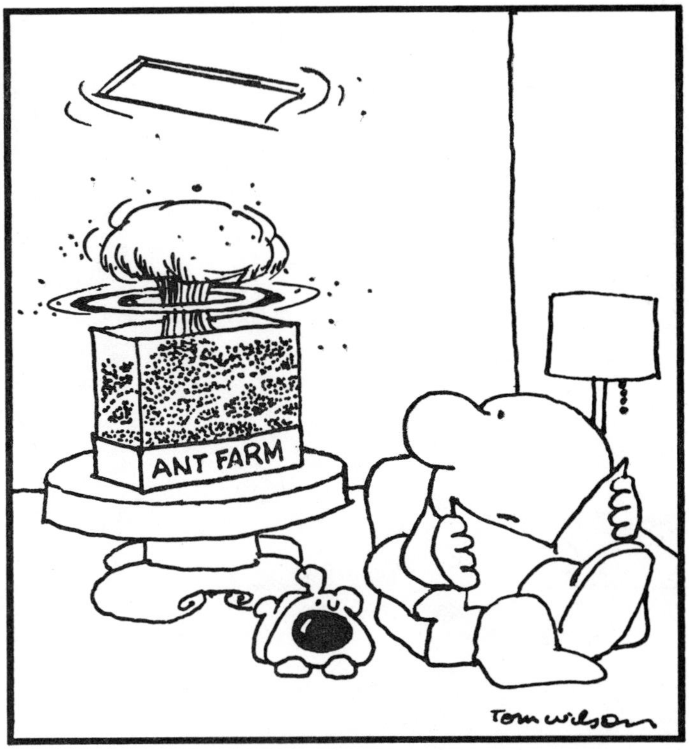
ANT FARM
TOM WILSON

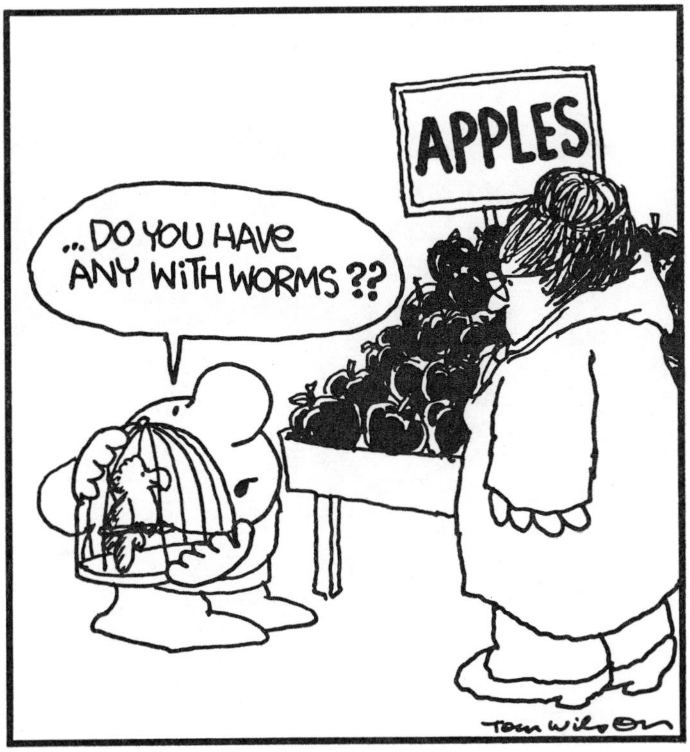
APPLES
...DO YOU HAVE ANY WITH WORMS ??
TOM WILSON

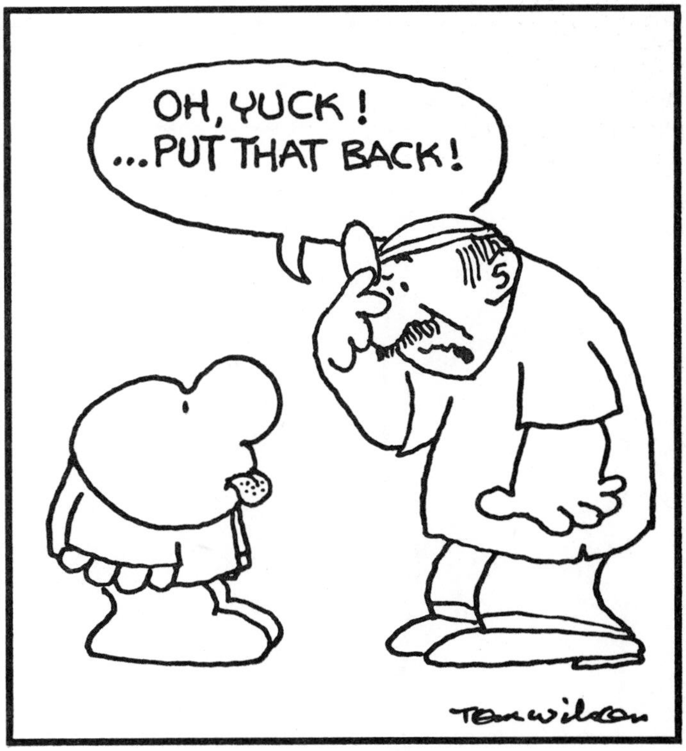
OH, YUCK! ...PUT THAT BACK!
TOM WILSON

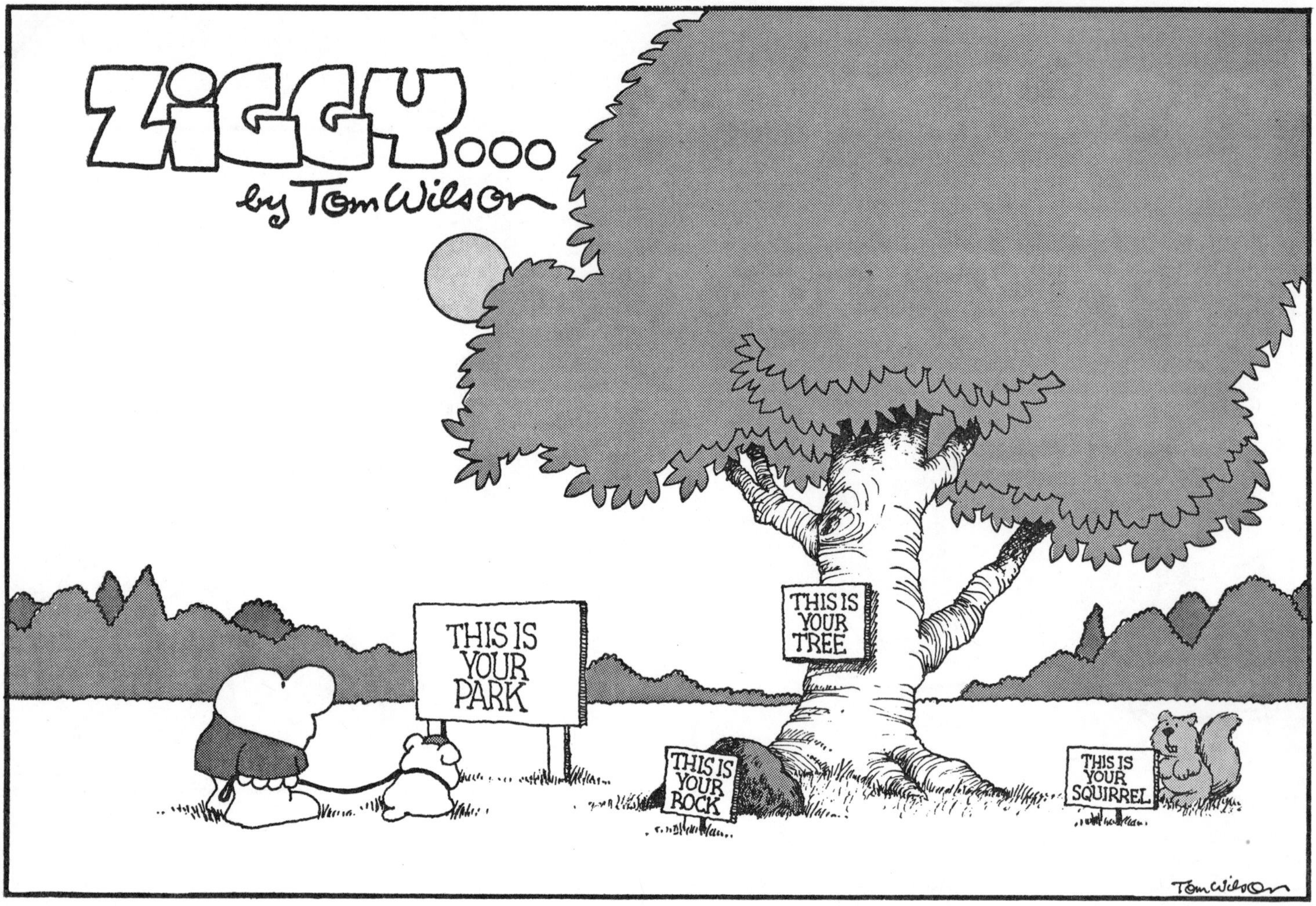
ZIGGY...
by Tom Wilson
THIS IS YOUR PARK
THIS IS YOUR TREE
THIS IS YOUR ROCK
THIS IS YOUR SQUIRREL
Tom Wilson

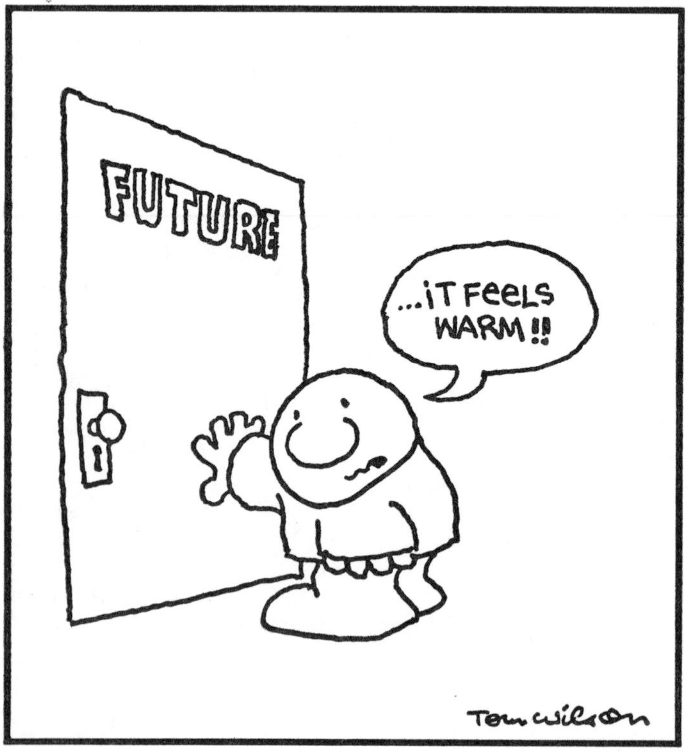
FUTURE
...iT FeeLS WARM!!
Tom Wilson

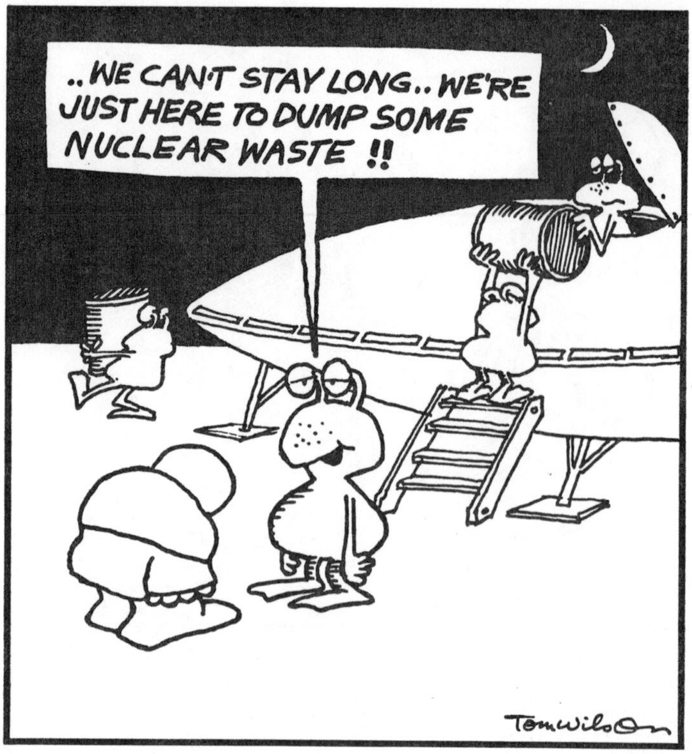
..WE CAN'T STAY LONG.. WE'RE JUST HERE TO DUMP SOME NUCLEAR WASTE !!
Tom Wilson

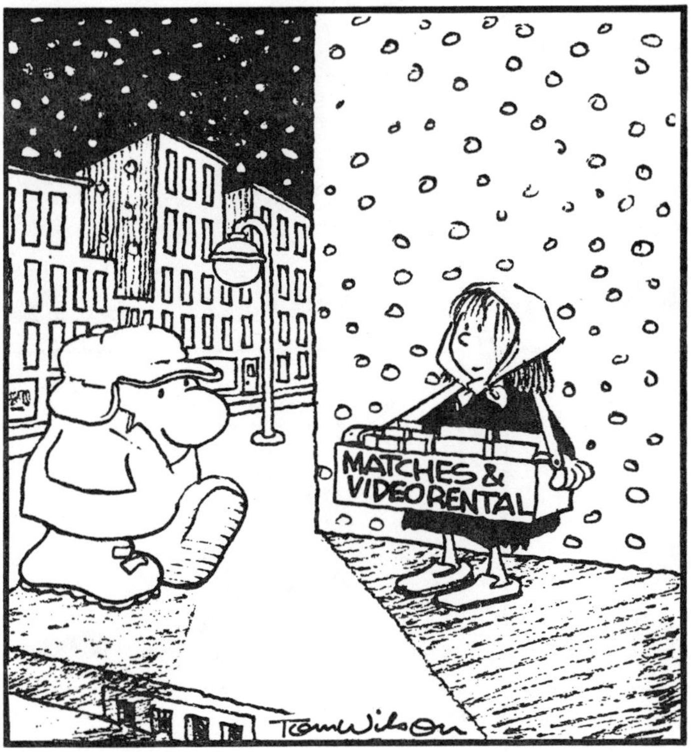
MATCHES & VIDEO RENTAL
TOM WILSON

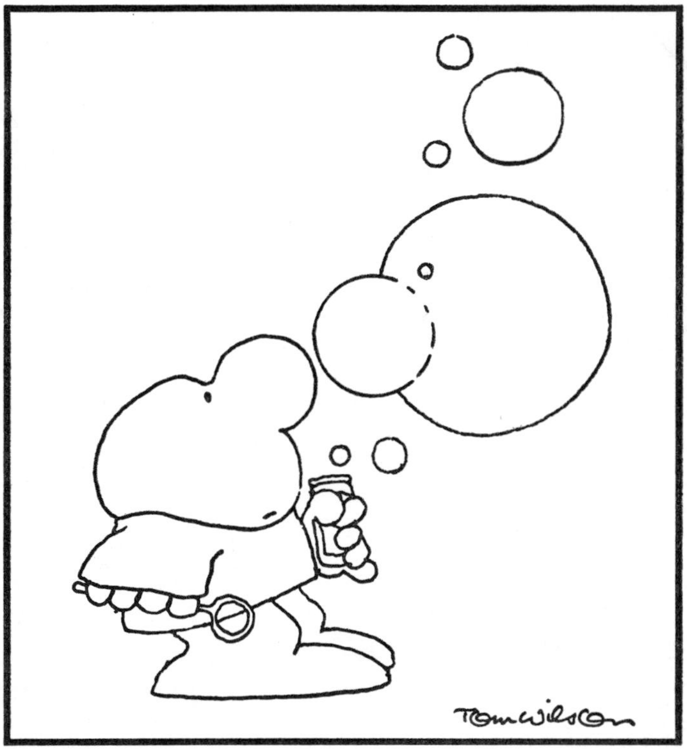
TOM WILSON

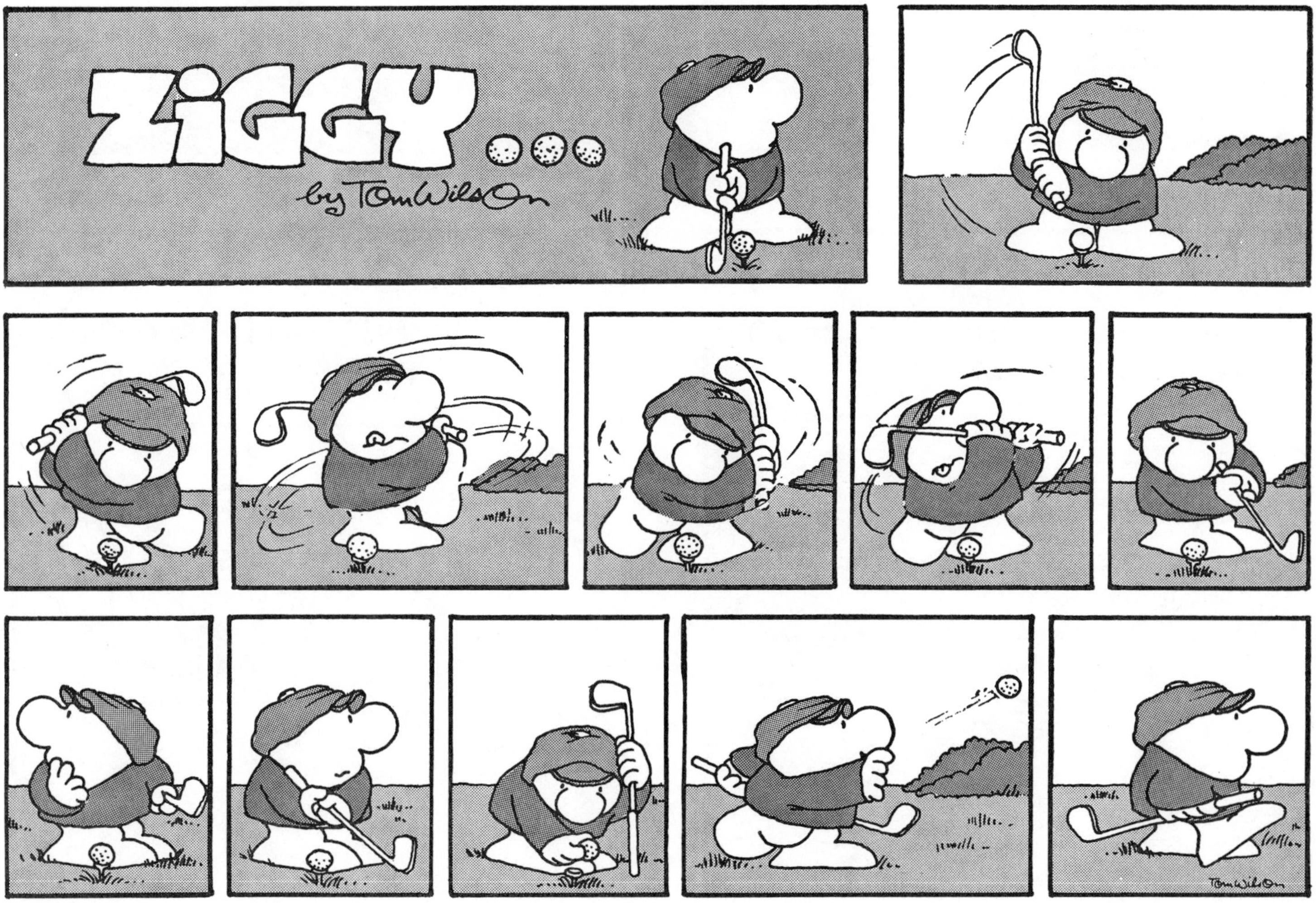
ZIGGY...
by TOM WILSON
TOM WILSON

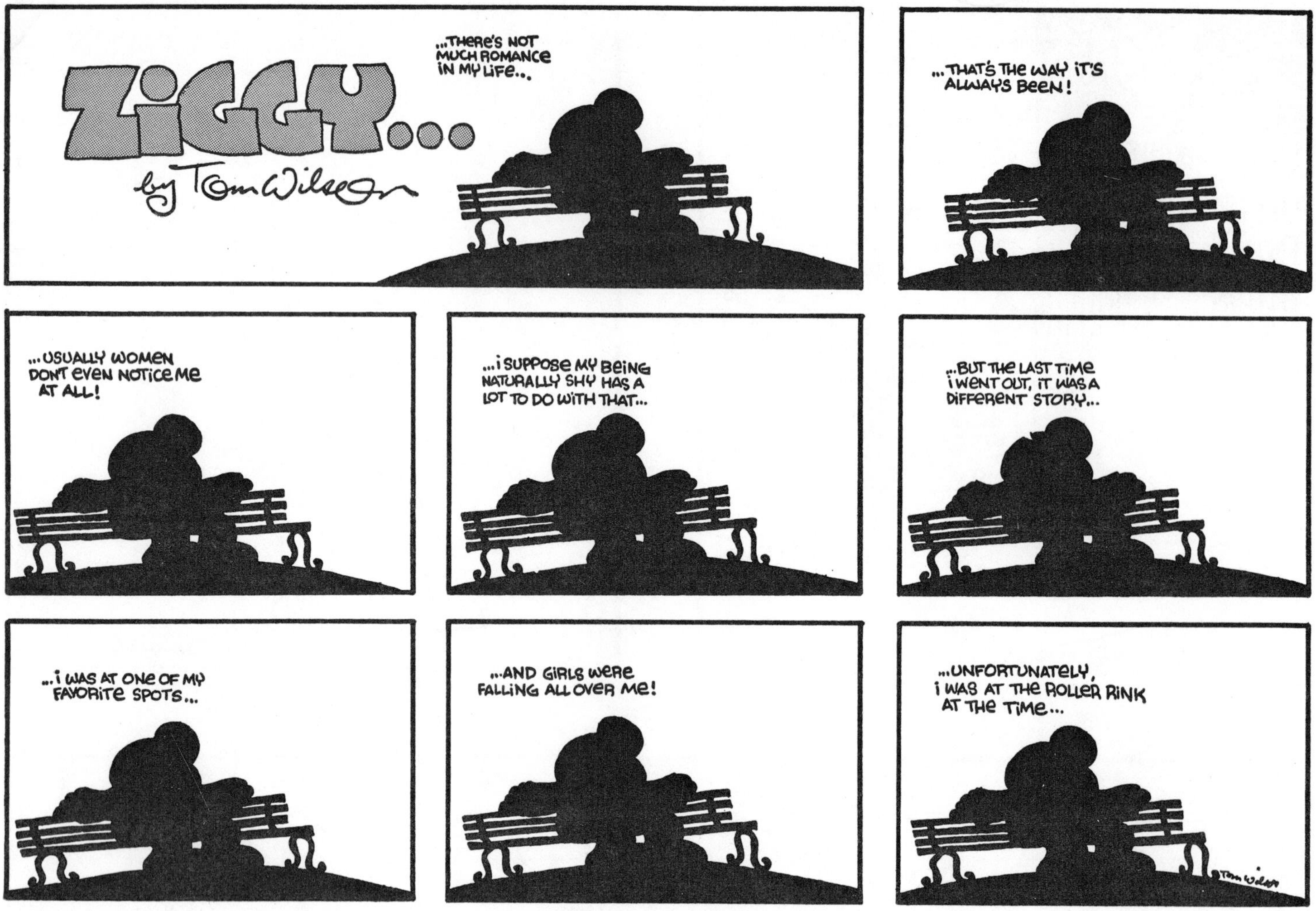
ZIGGY...
by Tom Wilson
...THERE'S NOT MUCH ROMANCE IN MY LIFE..
...THAT'S THE WAY IT'S ALWAYS BEEN!
...USUALLY WOMEN DON'T EVEN NOTICE ME AT ALL!
...I SUPPOSE MY BEING NATURALLY SHY HAS A LOT TO DO WITH THAT...
..BUT THE LAST TIME I WENT OUT, IT WAS A DIFFERENT STORY...
..I WAS AT ONE OF MY FAVORITE SPOTS...
..AND GIRLS WERE FALLING ALL OVER ME!
...UNFORTUNATELY, I WAS AT THE ROLLER RINK AT THE TIME...

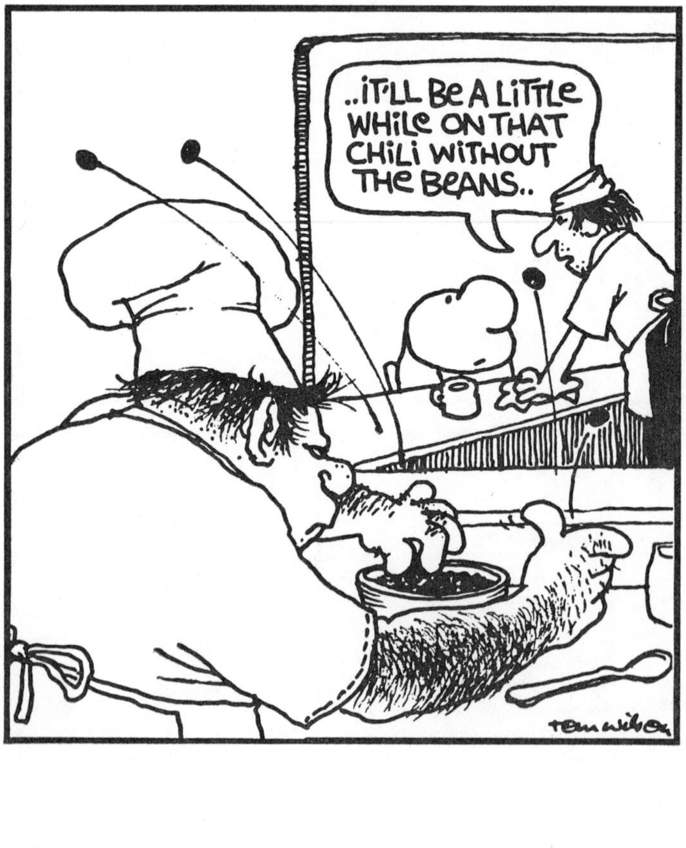
..IT'LL BE A LITTLE WHILE ON THAT CHILI WITHOUT THE BEANS..
Tom Wilson

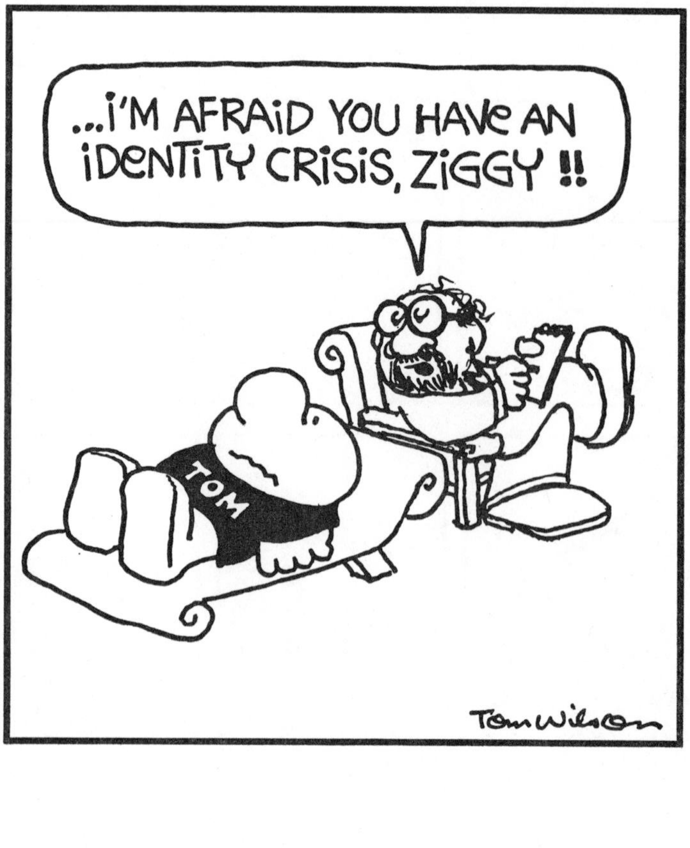
...I'M AFRAID YOU HAVE AN IDENTITY CRISIS, ZIGGY !!
TOM
Tom Wilson

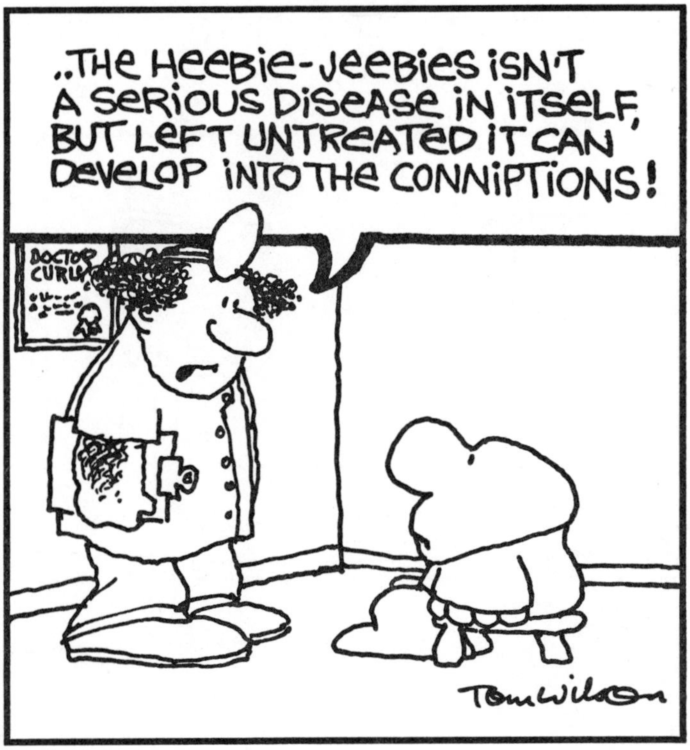
..THE HEEBIE-JEEBIES ISN'T A SERIOUS DISEASE IN ITSELF, BUT LEFT UNTREATED IT CAN DEVELOP INTO THE CONNIPTIONS!
DOCTOR CURLY
Tom Wilson

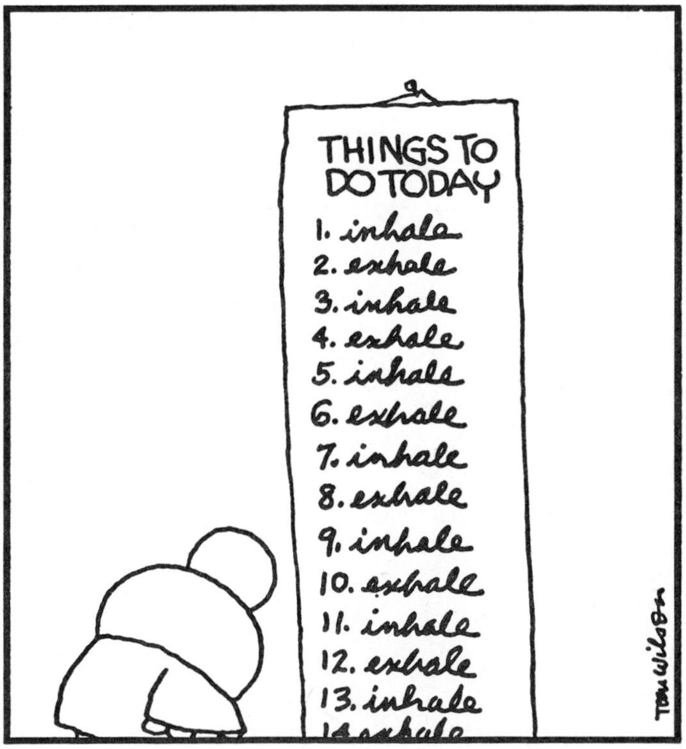
THINGS TO DO TODAY
1. inhale
2. exhale
3. inhale
4. exhale
5. inhale
6. exhale
7. inhale
8. exhale
9. inhale
10. exhale
11. inhale
12. exhale
13. inhale
Tom Wilson

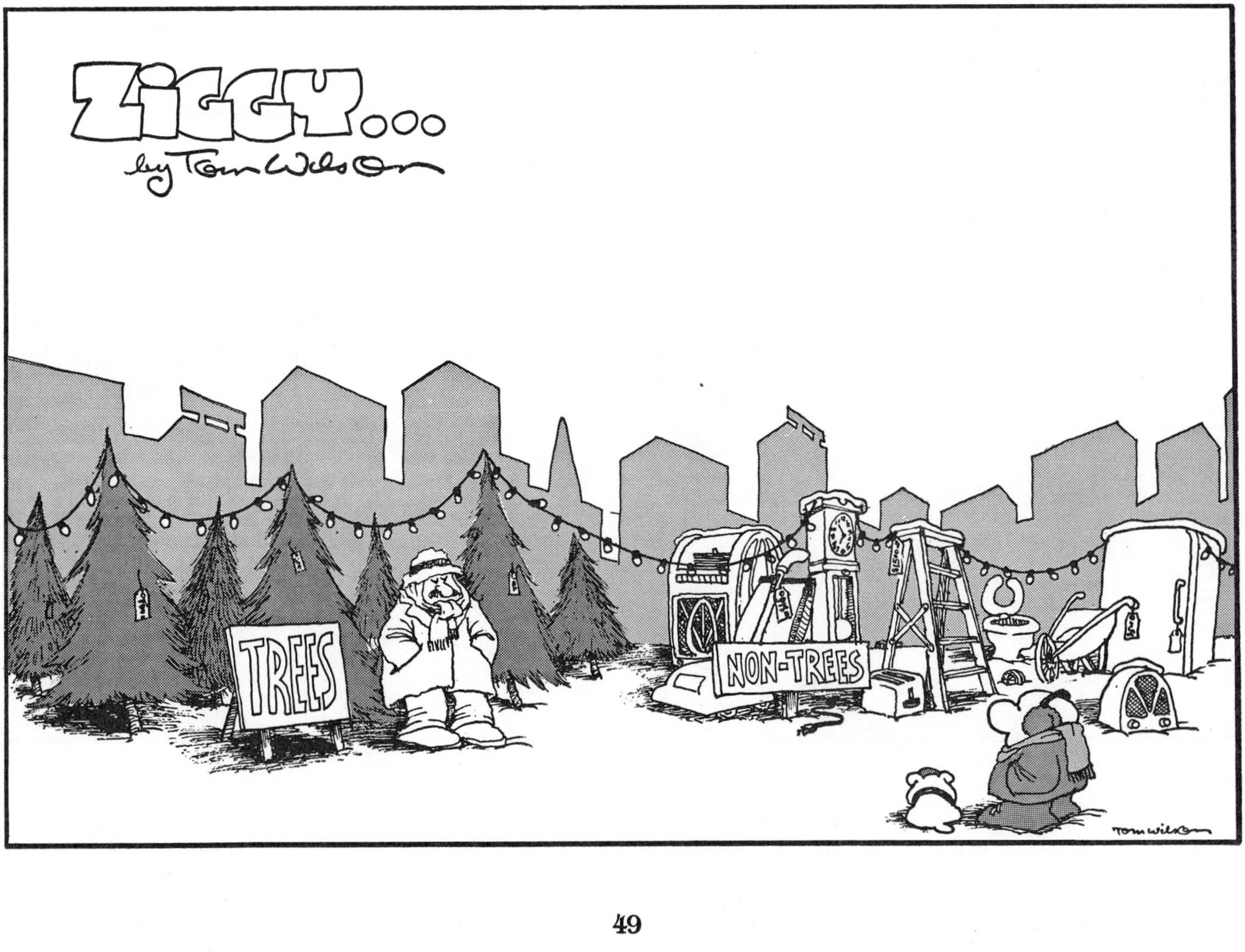
ZIGGY...
by Tom Wilson
TREES
NON-TREES
Tom Wilson

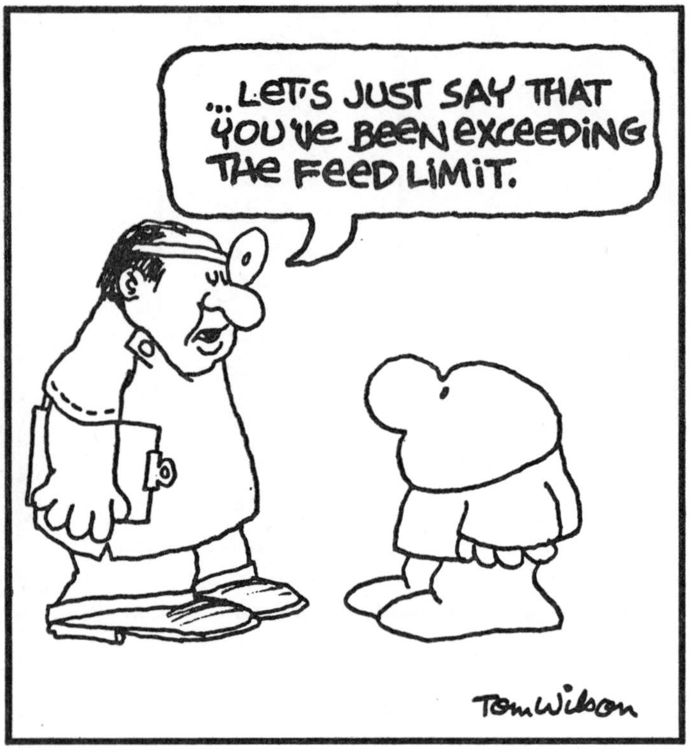
...LET'S JUST SAY THAT YOU'VE BEEN EXCEEDING THE FEED LIMIT.
Tom Wilson

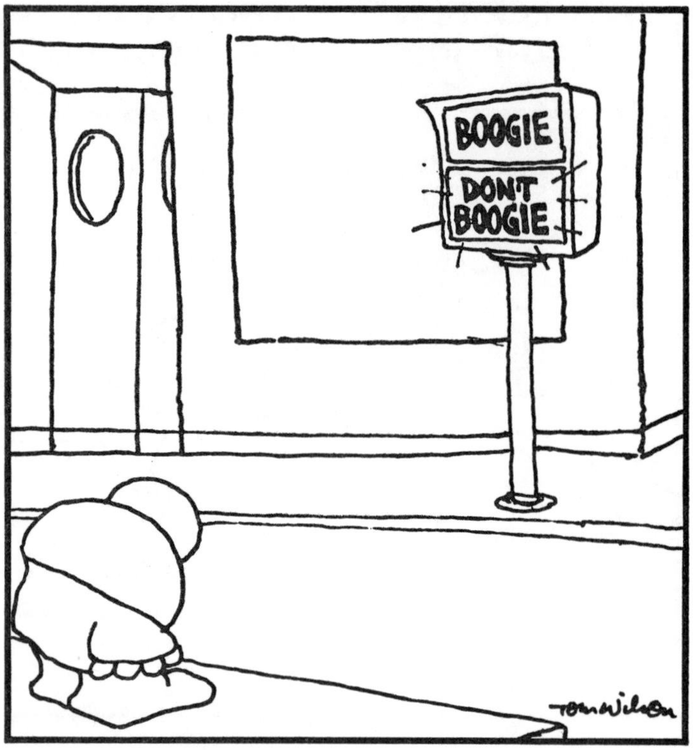
BOOGIE
DON'T BOOGIE
Tom Wilson

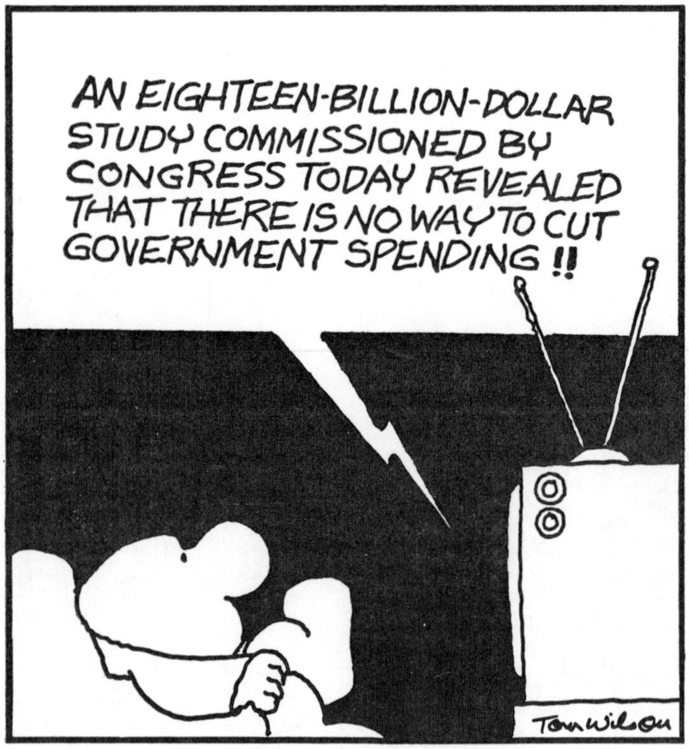
AN EIGHTEEN-BILLION-DOLLAR STUDY COMMISSIONED BY CONGRESS TODAY REVEALED THAT THERE IS NO WAY TO CUT GOVERNMENT SPENDING !!
Tom Wilson

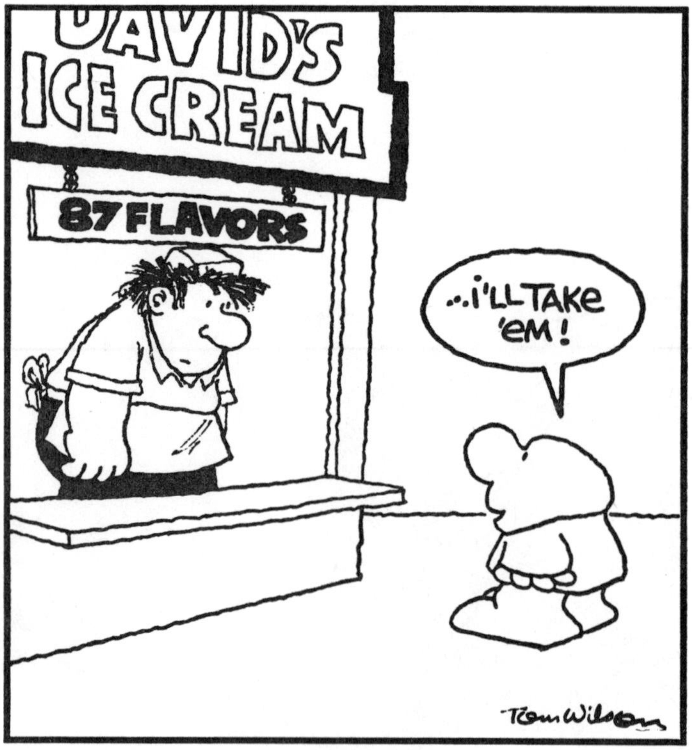
DAVID'S ICE CREAM
87 FLAVORS
..I'LL TAKE 'EM!
Tom Wilson

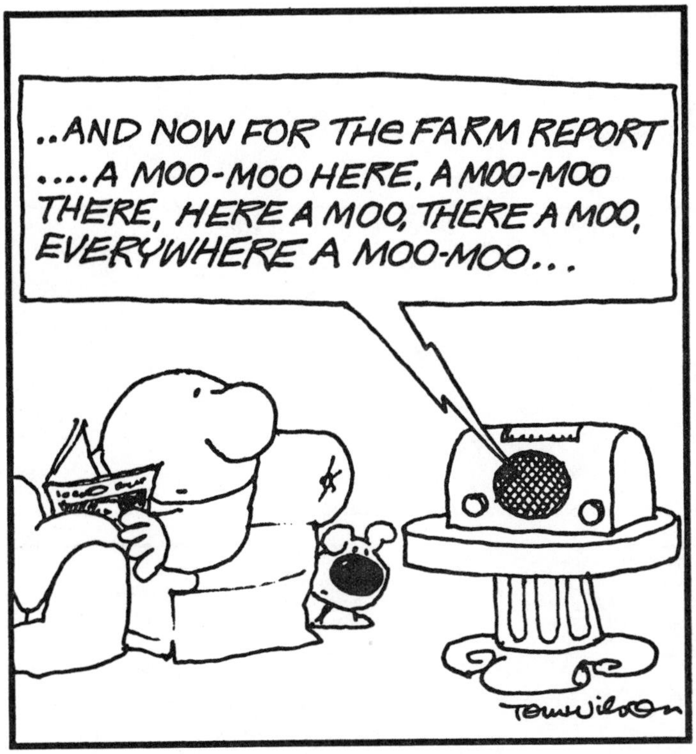
..AND NOW FOR THE FARM REPORT ....A MOO-MOO HERE, A MOO-MOO THERE, HERE A MOO, THERE A MOO, EVERYWHERE A MOO-MOO...

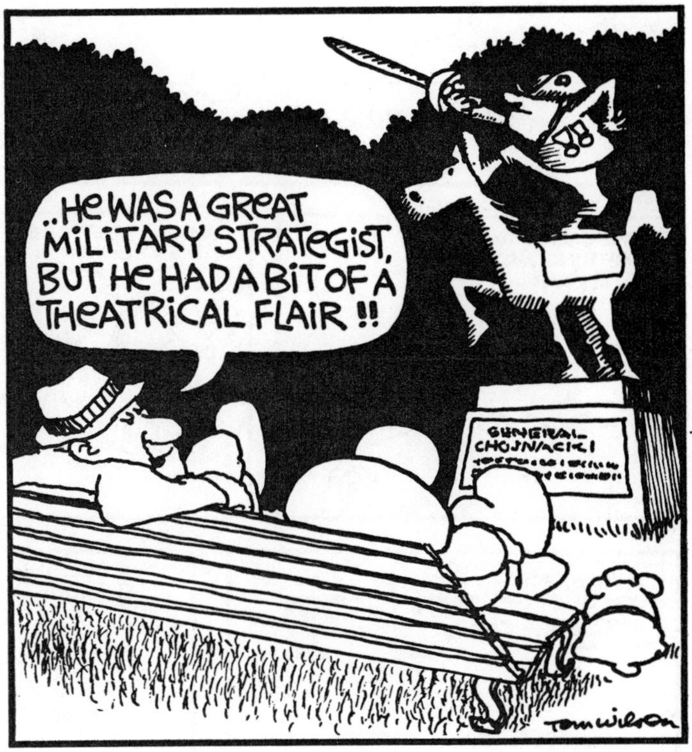
..HE WAS A GREAT MILITARY STRATEGIST, BUT HE HAD A BIT OF A THEATRICAL FLAIR !!
GENERAL CHOJNACKI

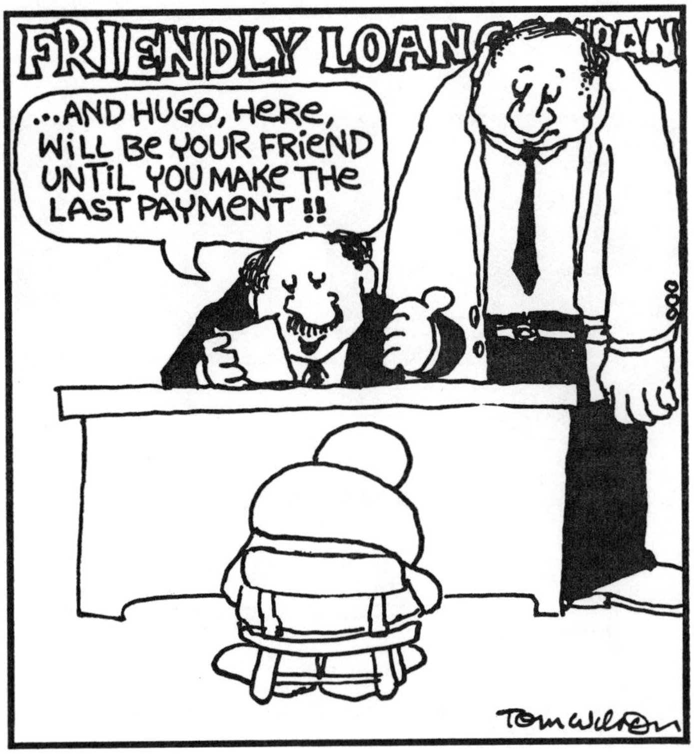
FRIENDLY LOAN
..AND HUGO, HERE, WILL BE YOUR FRIEND UNTIL YOU MAKE THE LAST PAYMENT !!

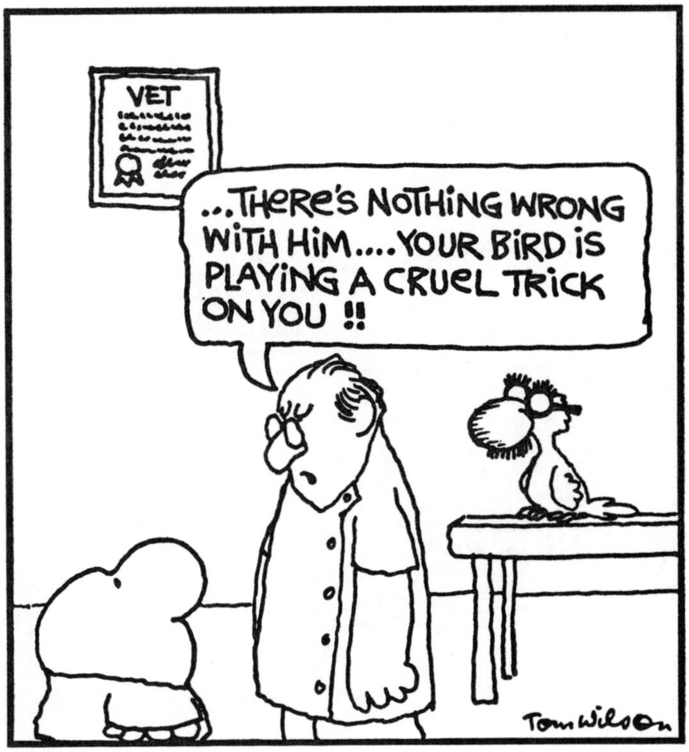
VET
...THERE'S NOTHING WRONG WITH HIM....YOUR BIRD IS PLAYING A CRUEL TRICK ON YOU !!

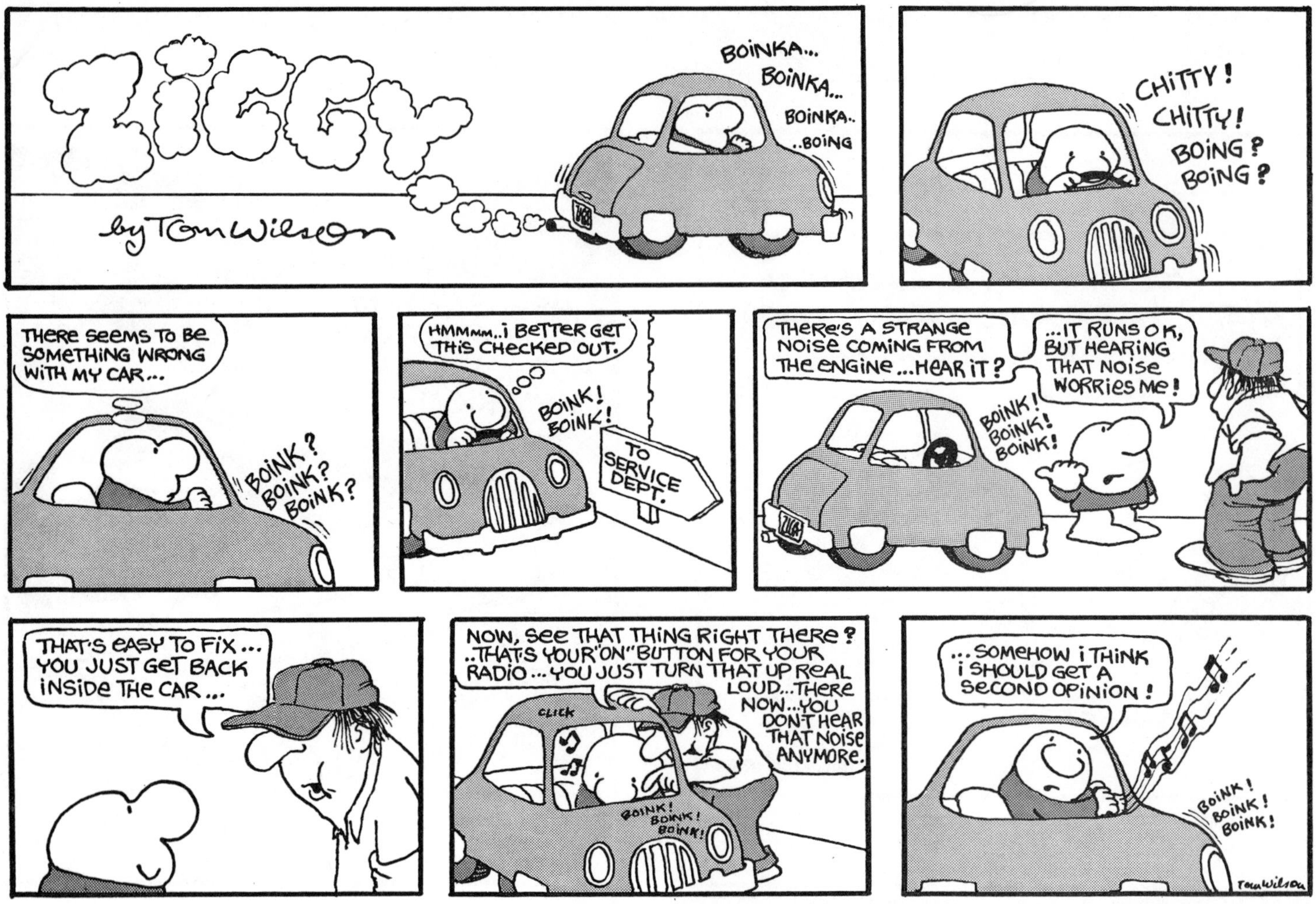
ZIGGY
by Tom Wilson
BOINKA... BOINKA... BOINKA.. ..BOING
CHITTY! CHITTY! BOING? BOING?
THERE SEEMS TO BE SOMETHING WRONG WITH MY CAR...
BOINK? BOINK? BOINK?
HMMMM..I BETTER GET THIS CHECKED OUT.
BOINK! BOINK!
TO SERVICE DEPT.
THERE'S A STRANGE NOISE COMING FROM THE ENGINE...HEAR IT?
...IT RUNS OK, BUT HEARING THAT NOISE WORRIES ME!
BOINK! BOINK! BOINK!
THAT'S EASY TO FIX... YOU JUST GET BACK INSIDE THE CAR...
NOW, SEE THAT THING RIGHT THERE? ..THAT'S YOUR "ON" BUTTON FOR YOUR RADIO...YOU JUST TURN THAT UP REAL LOUD...THERE NOW...YOU DON'T HEAR THAT NOISE ANYMORE.
CLICK
BOINK! BOINK! BOINK!
...SOMEHOW I THINK I SHOULD GET A SECOND OPINION!
BOINK! BOINK! BOINK!
Tom Wilson

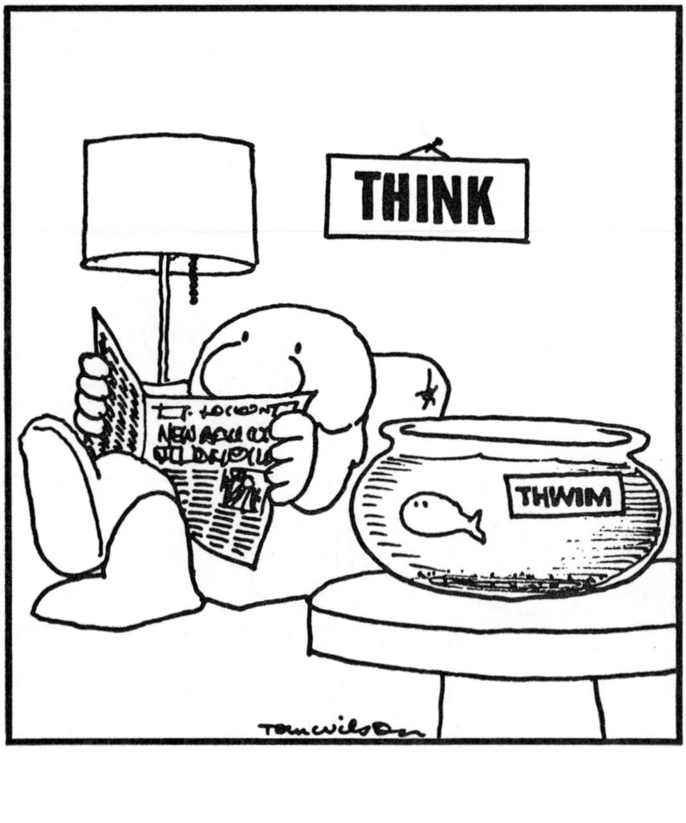
THINK
THWIM
Tom Wilson

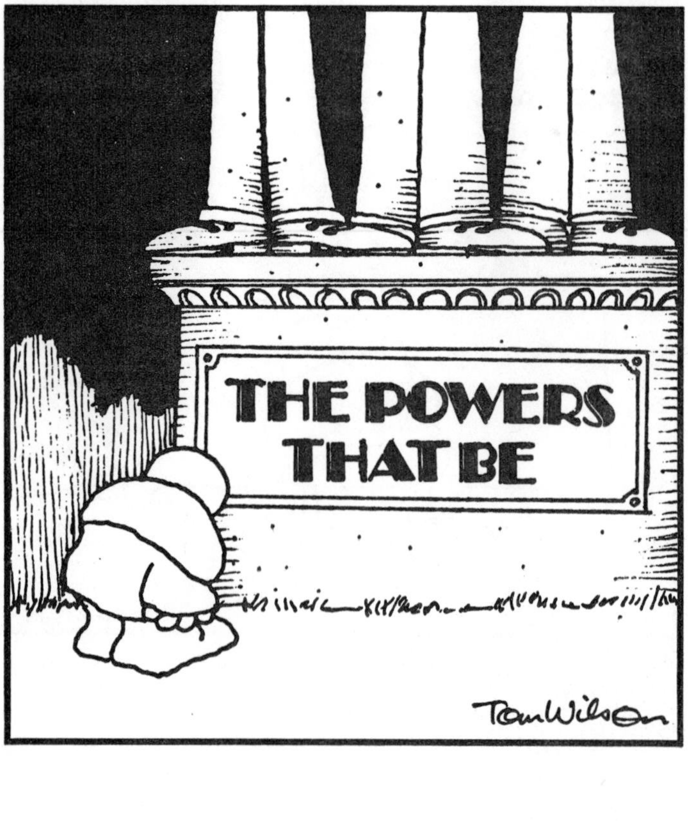
THE POWERS THAT BE
Tom Wilson

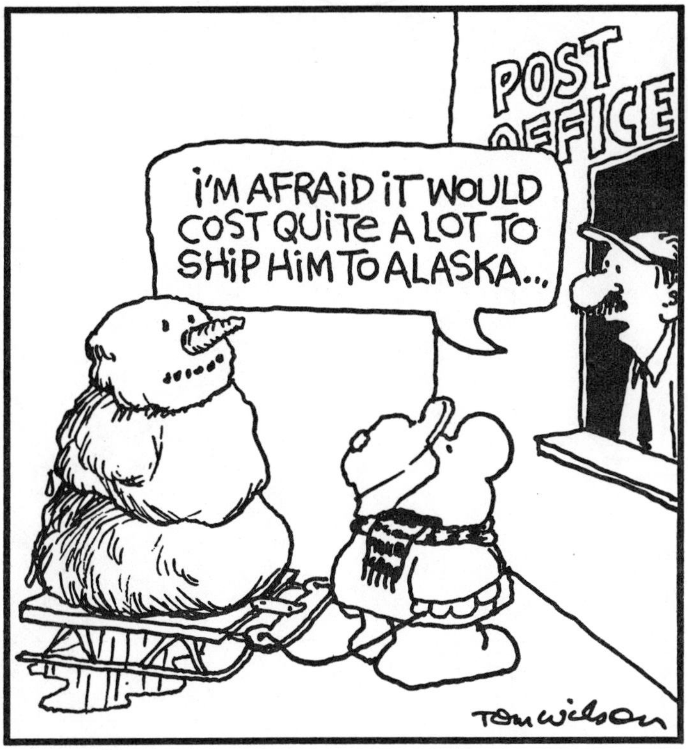
POST OFFICE
I'M AFRAID IT WOULD COST QUITE A LOT TO SHIP HIM TO ALASKA...
TOM WILSON

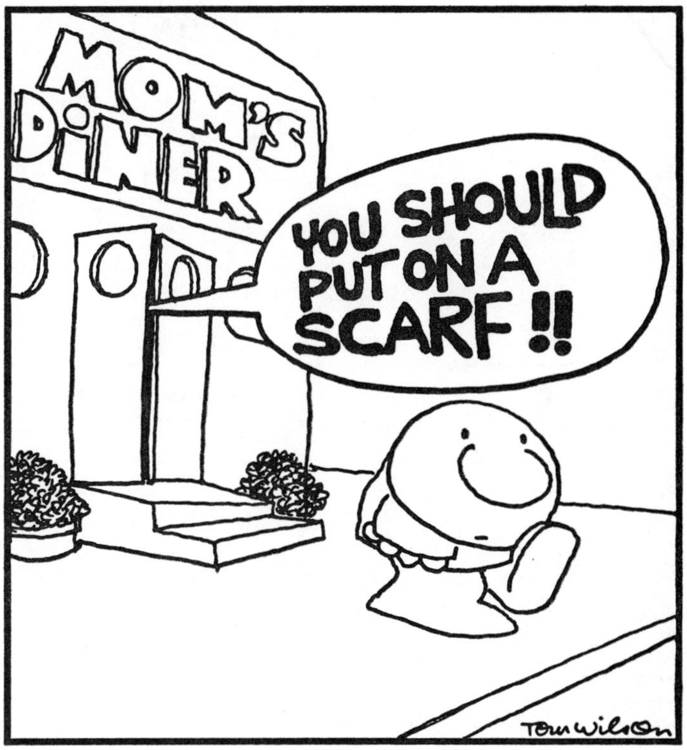
MOM'S DINER
YOU SHOULD PUT ON A SCARF !!
TOM WILSON

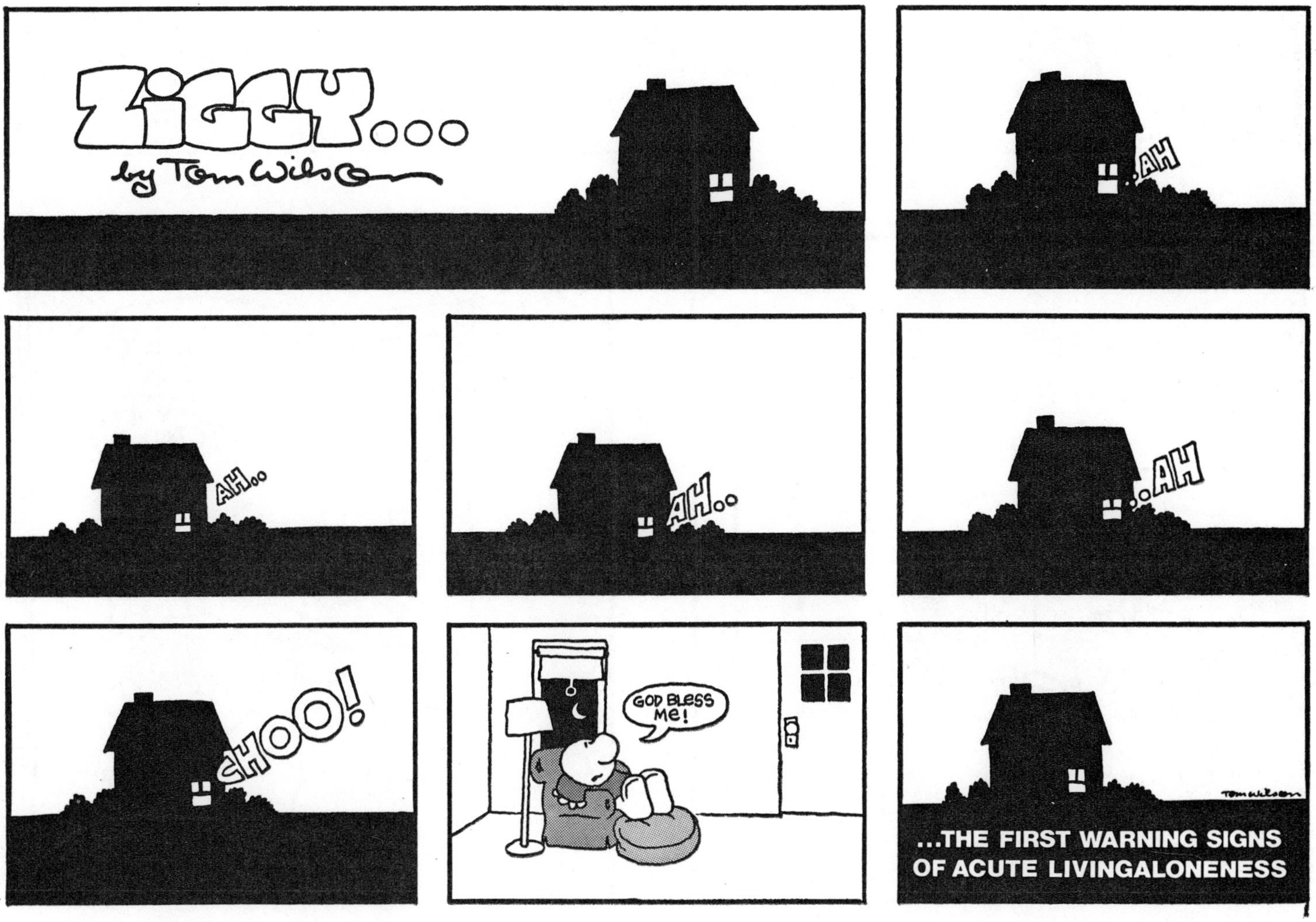
ZIGGY...
by Tom Wilson
AH
AH..
AH..
..AH
CHOO!
GOD BLESS ME!
TOM WILSON
...THE FIRST WARNING SIGNS OF ACUTE LIVINGALONENESS

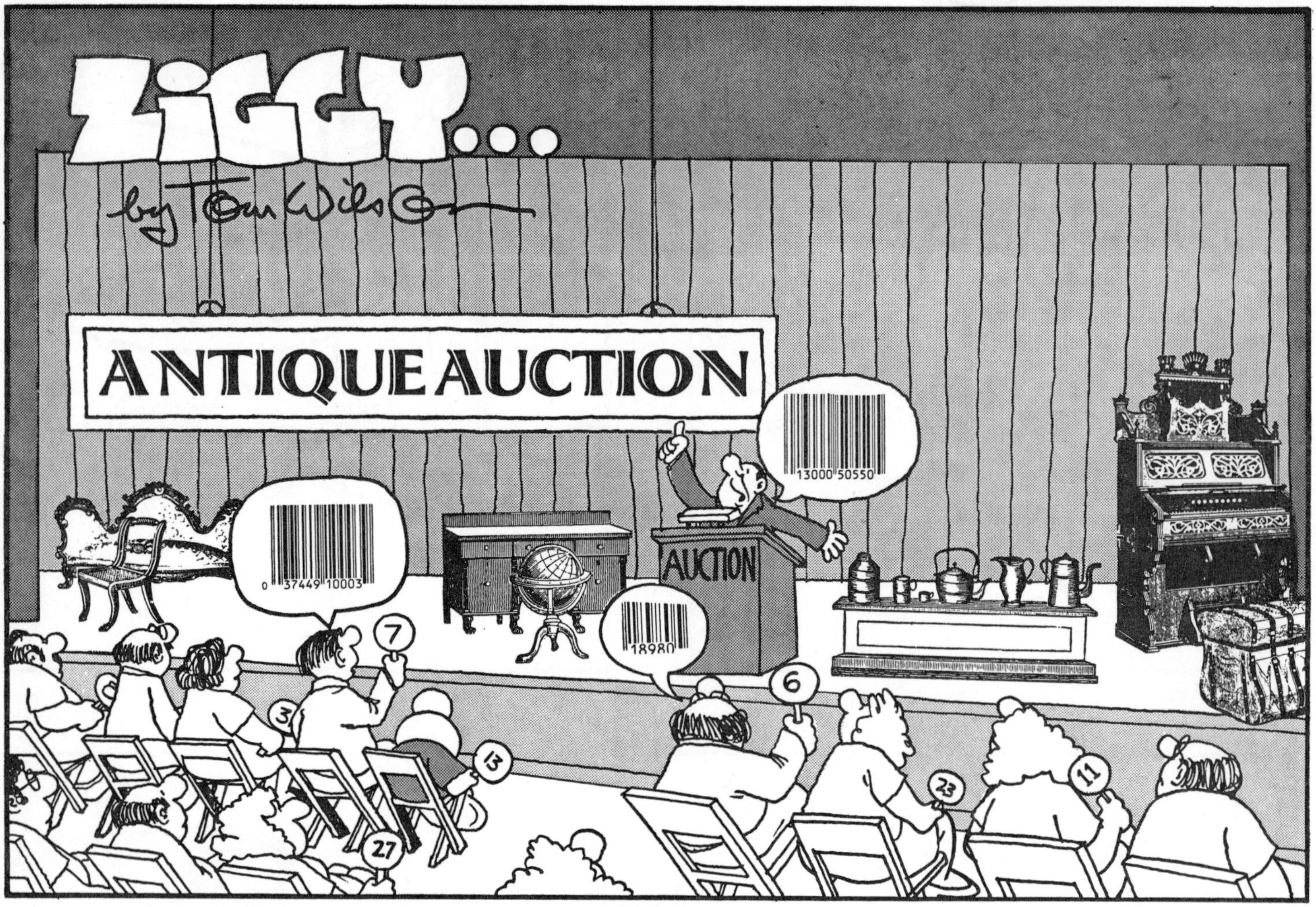
ZIGGY...
by Tom Wilson
ANTIQUE AUCTION
AUCTION
13000 50550
0 37449 10003
18980
7
3
13
27
6
23
11

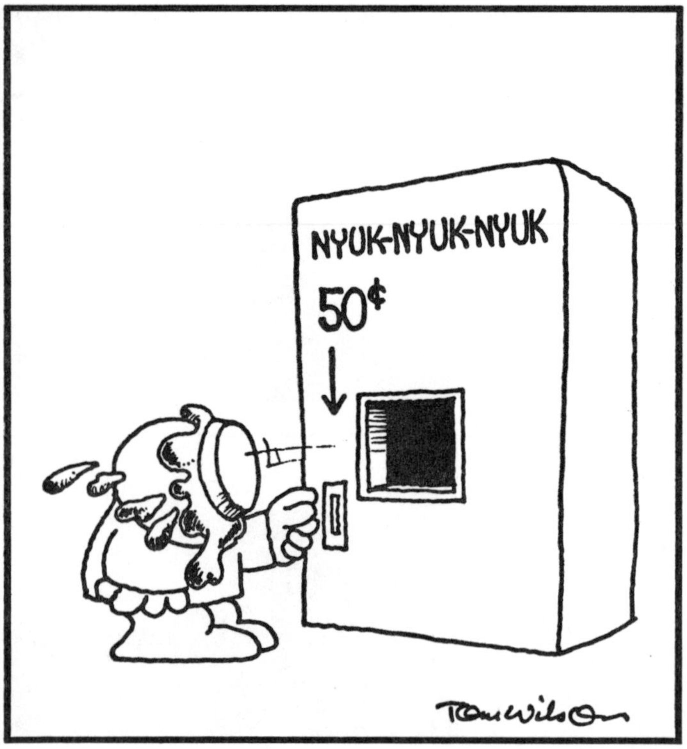
NYUK-NYUK-NYUK
50¢
Tom Wilson

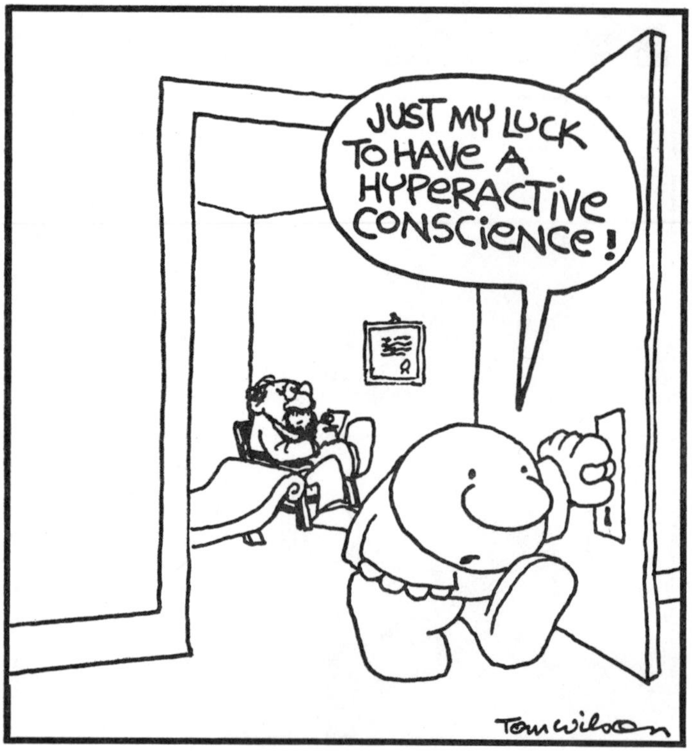
JUST MY LUCK TO HAVE A HYPERACTIVE CONSCIENCE!
Tom Wilson

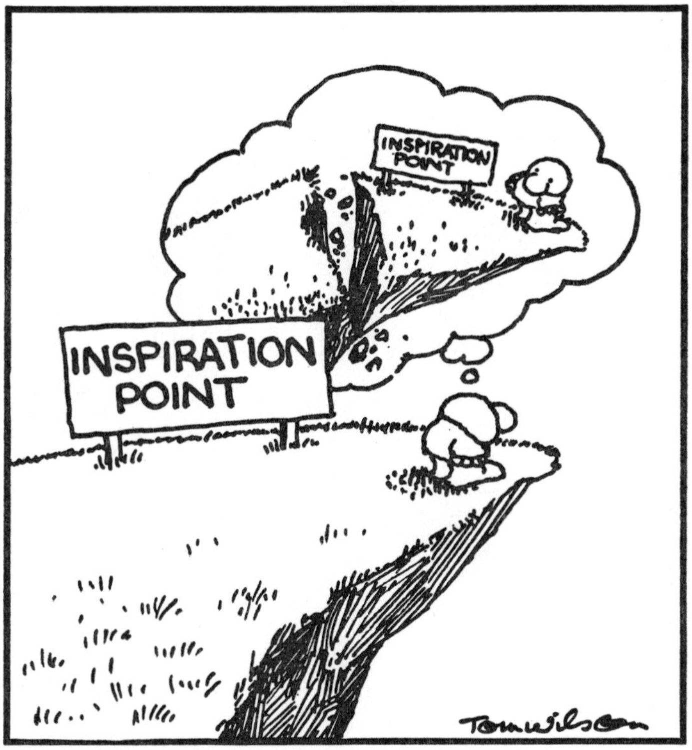
INSPIRATION POINT
INSPIRATION POINT
Tom Wilson

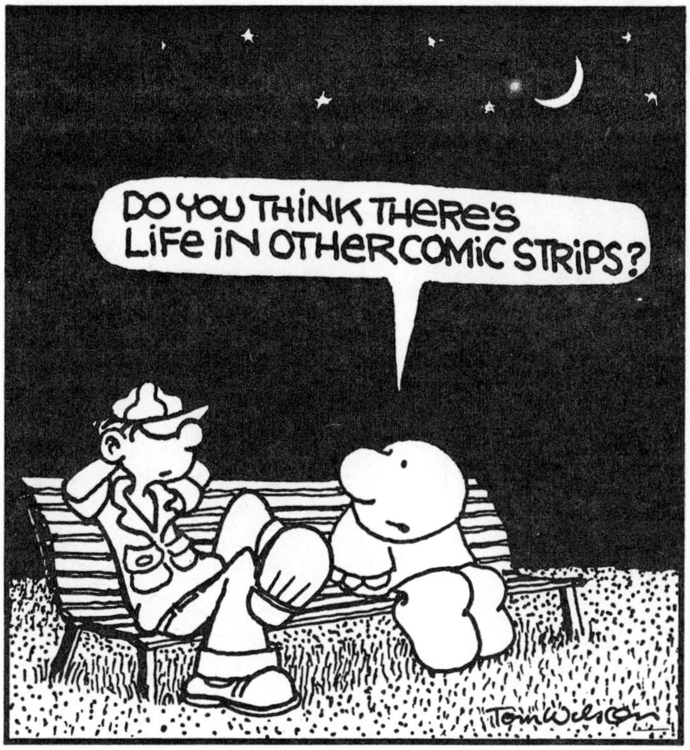
DO YOU THINK THERE'S LIFE IN OTHER COMIC STRIPS?
Tom Wilson

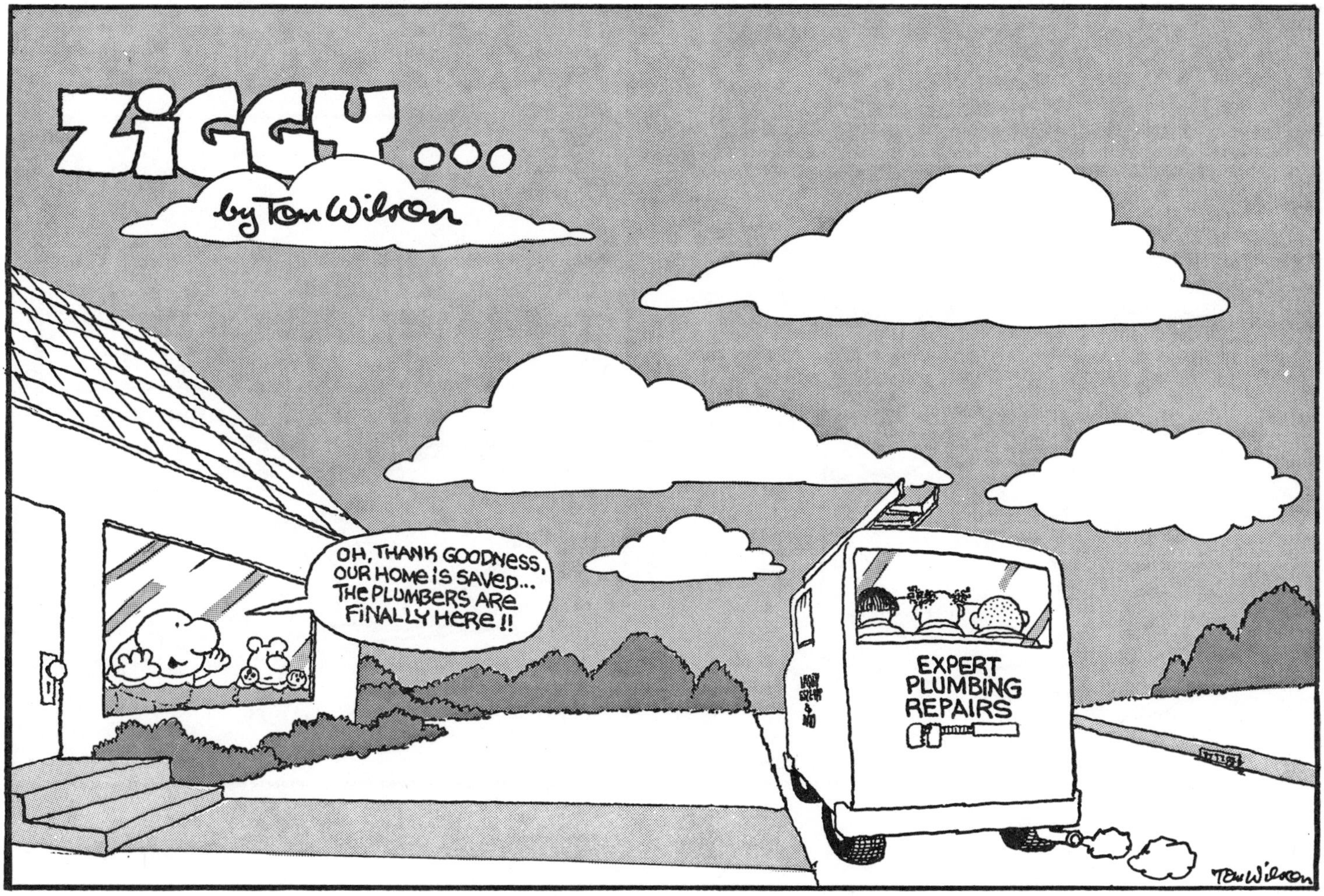
ZiGGY...
by Tom Wilson
OH, THANK GOODNESS, OUR HOME IS SAVED... THE PLUMBERS ARE FINALLY HERE!!
EXPERT PLUMBING REPAIRS
Tom Wilson

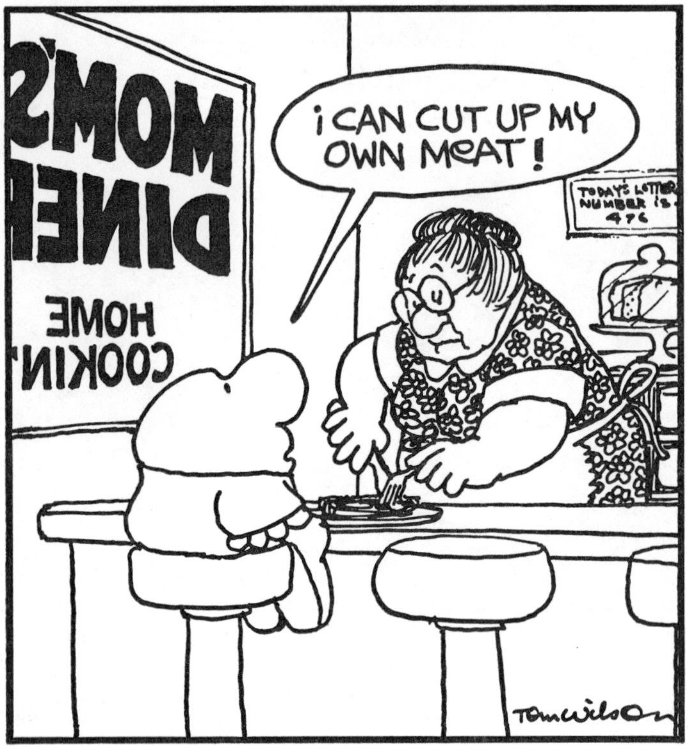
i CAN CUT UP MY OWN MEAT !
Tom Wilson

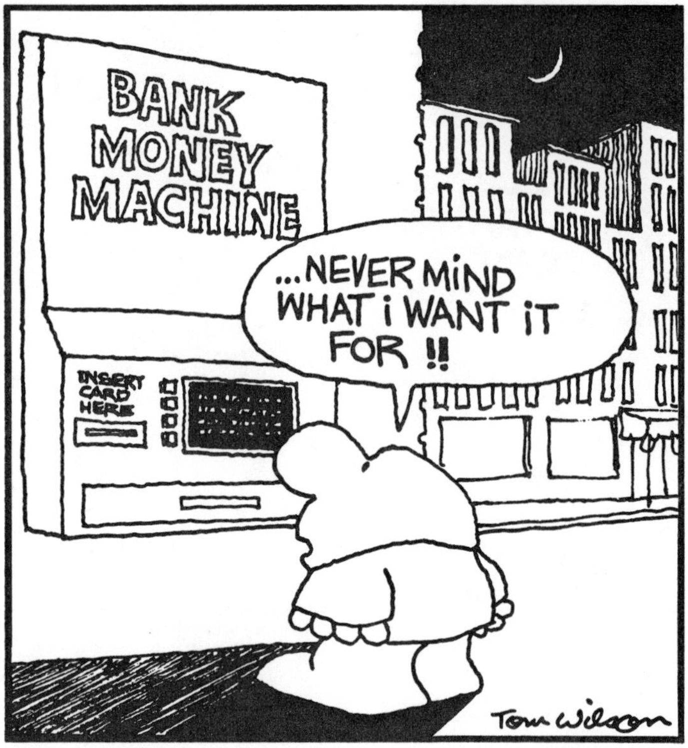
BANK MONEY MACHINE
INSERT CARD HERE
...NEVER MIND WHAT i WANT iT FOR !!
Tom Wilson

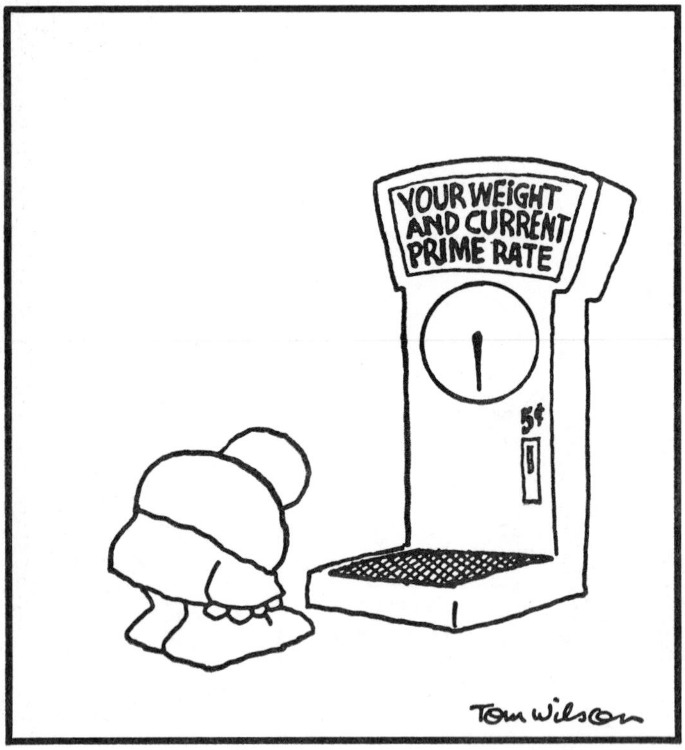
YOUR WEIGHT AND CURRENT PRIME RATE
5¢
Tom Wilson

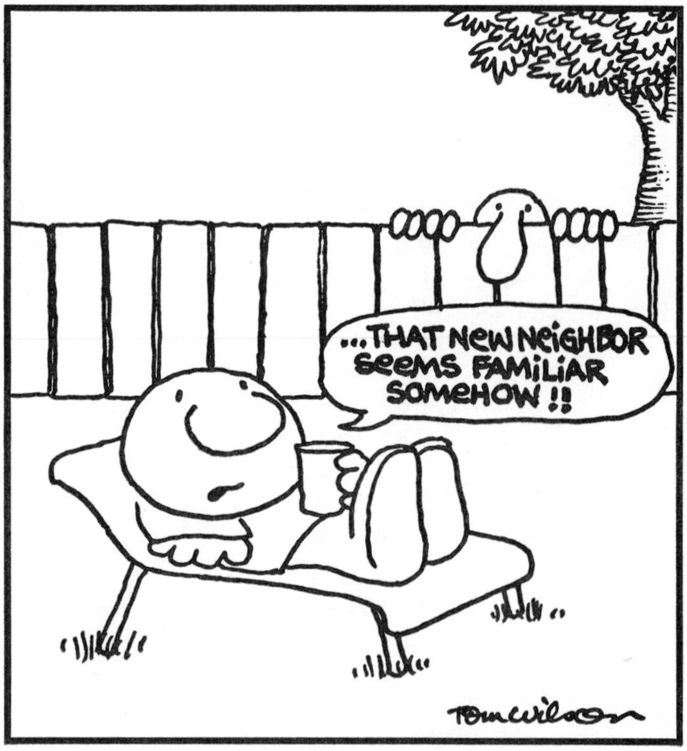
...THAT NEW NEIGHBOR SEEMS FAMILIAR SOMEHOW !!
Tom Wilson

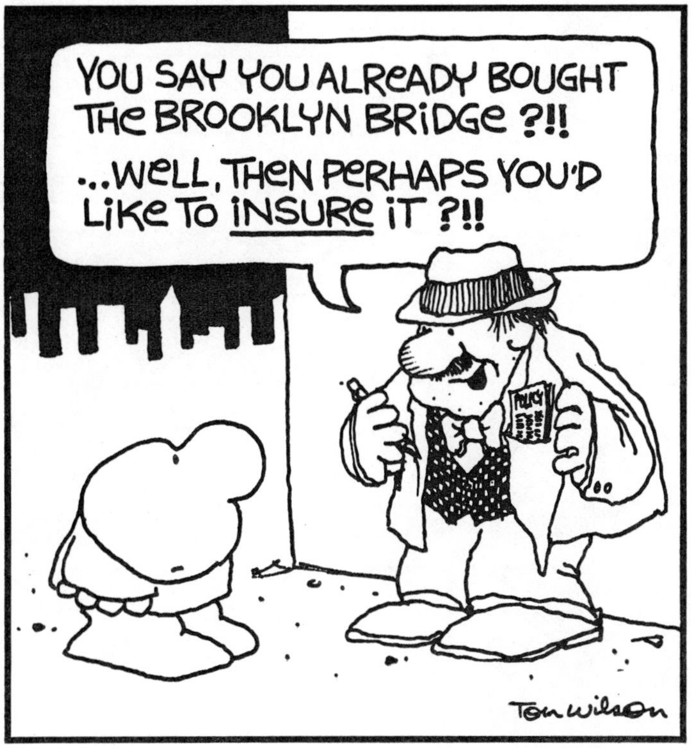
YOU SAY YOU ALREADY BOUGHT THE BROOKLYN BRIDGE ?!!
...WELL, THEN PERHAPS YOU'D LIKE TO INSURE IT ?!!
POLICY
TOM WILSON

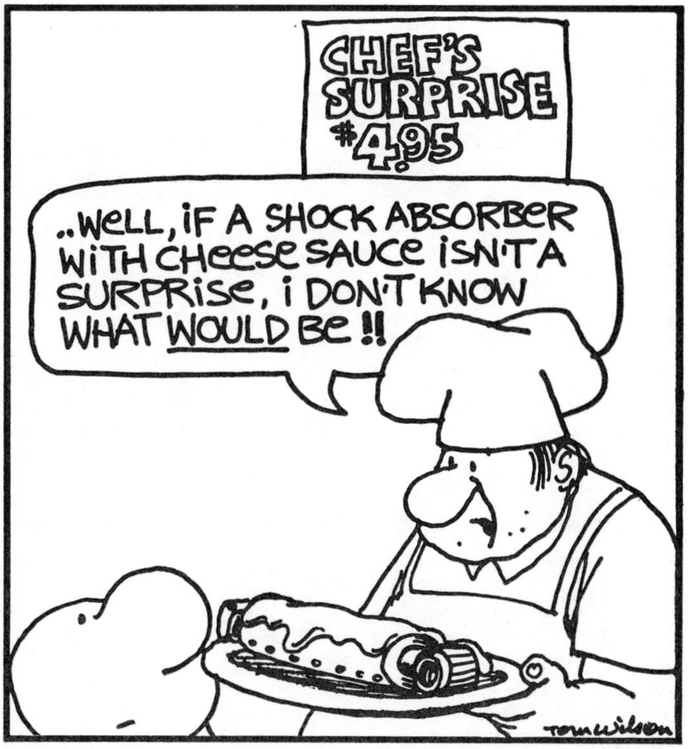
CHEF'S SURPRISE $4.95
..WELL, IF A SHOCK ABSORBER WITH CHEESE SAUCE ISN'T A SURPRISE, I DON'T KNOW WHAT WOULD BE !!
TOM WILSON

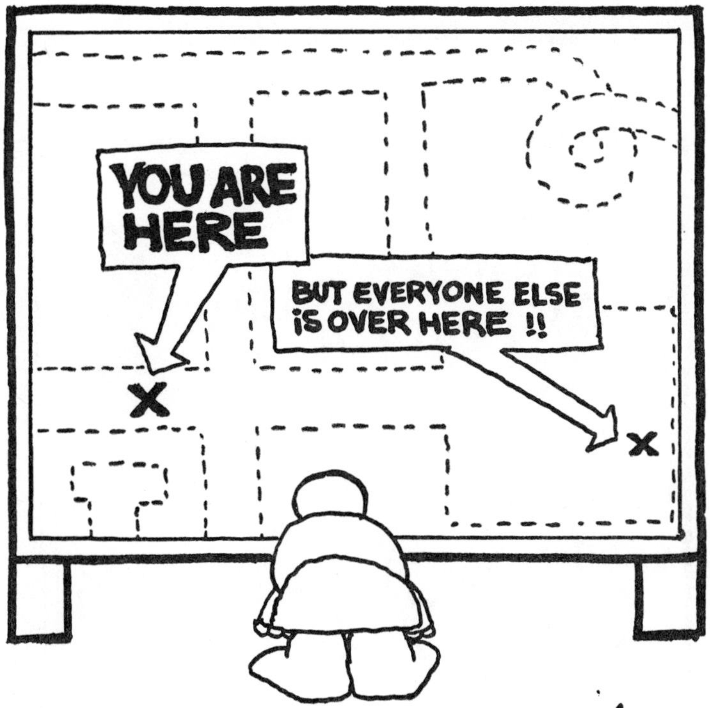
YOU ARE HERE
BUT EVERYONE ELSE IS OVER HERE !!
X
X
TOM WILSON

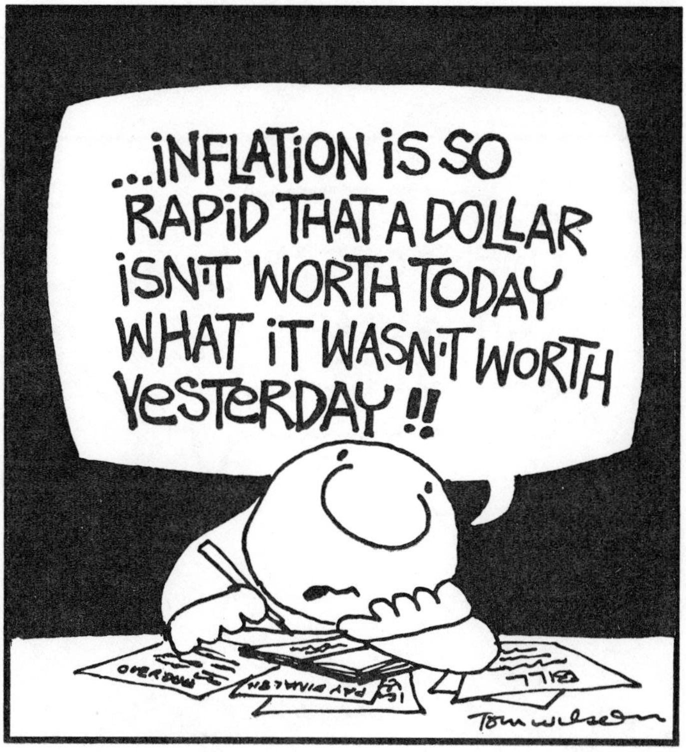
...INFLATION IS SO RAPID THAT A DOLLAR ISN'T WORTH TODAY WHAT IT WASN'T WORTH YESTERDAY !!
TOM WILSON

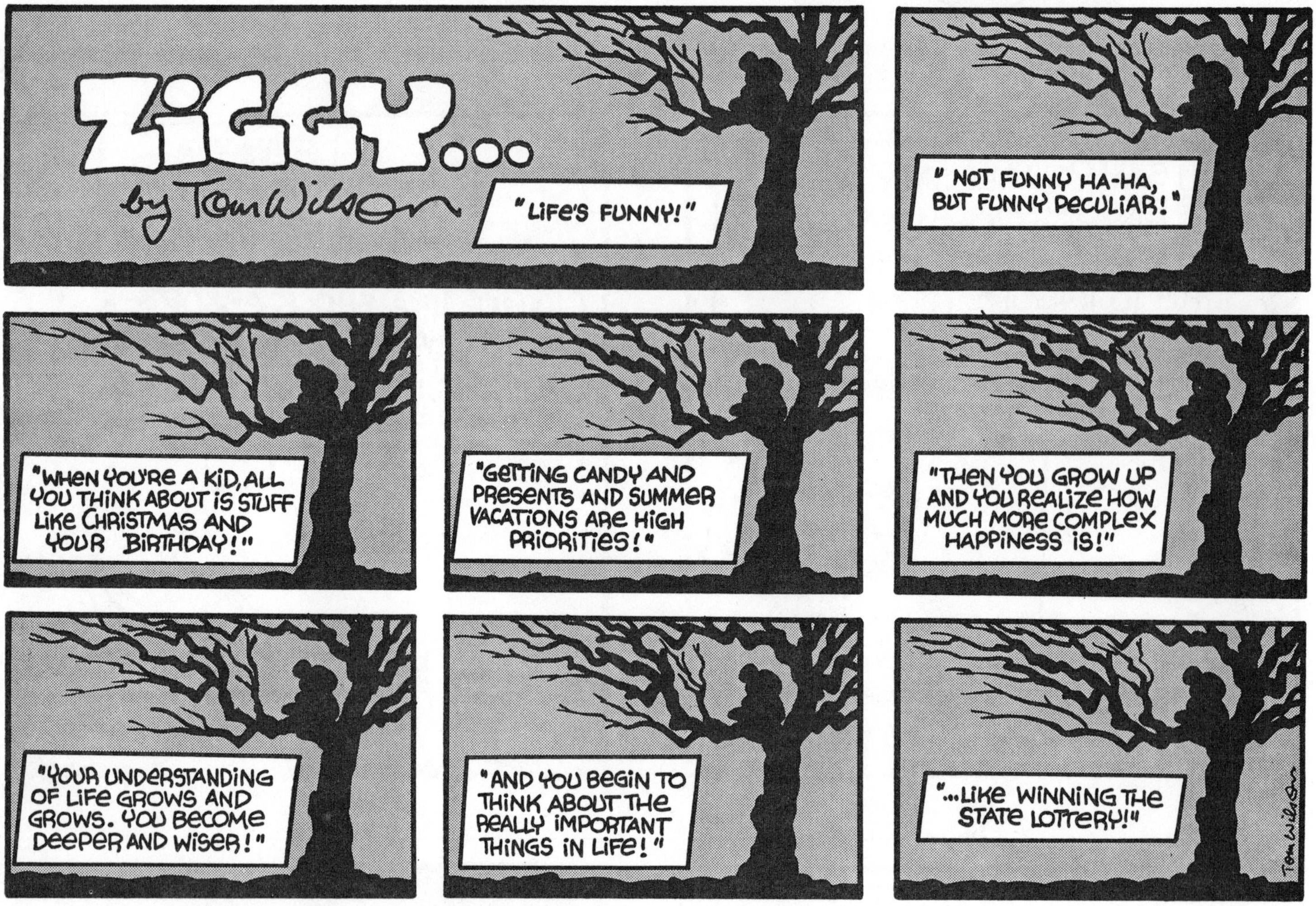
ZiGGY...
by Tom Wilson
"LIFE'S FUNNY!"
" NOT FUNNY HA-HA, BUT FUNNY PECULIAR!"
"WHEN YOU'RE A KID, ALL YOU THINK ABOUT IS STUFF LIKE CHRISTMAS AND YOUR BIRTHDAY!"
"GETTING CANDY AND PRESENTS AND SUMMER VACATIONS ARE HIGH PRIORITIES!"
"THEN YOU GROW UP AND YOU REALIZE HOW MUCH MORE COMPLEX HAPPINESS IS!"
"YOUR UNDERSTANDING OF LIFE GROWS AND GROWS. YOU BECOME DEEPER AND WISER!"
"AND YOU BEGIN TO THINK ABOUT THE REALLY IMPORTANT THINGS IN LIFE!"
"...LIKE WINNING THE STATE LOTTERY!"
Tom Wilson

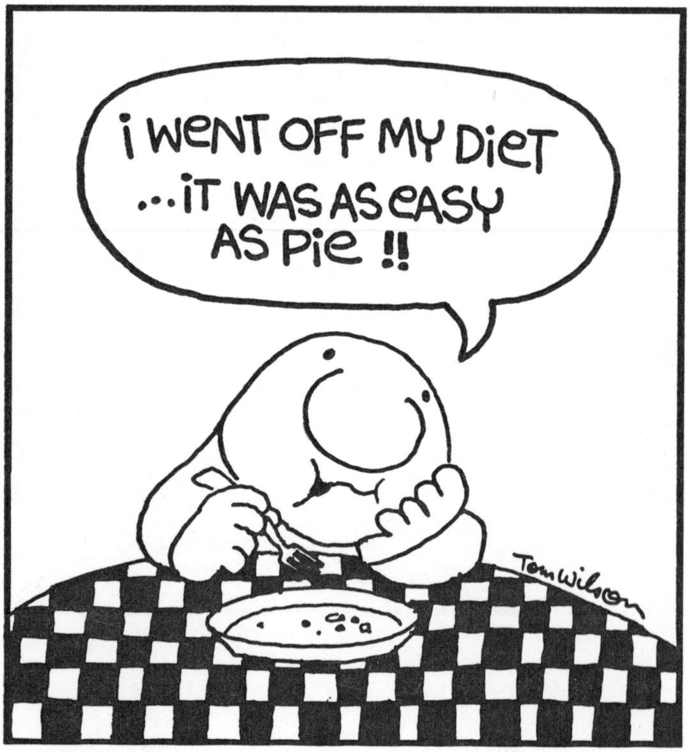
i WENT OFF MY DIET ...iT WAS AS EASY AS PIE !!
Tom Wilson

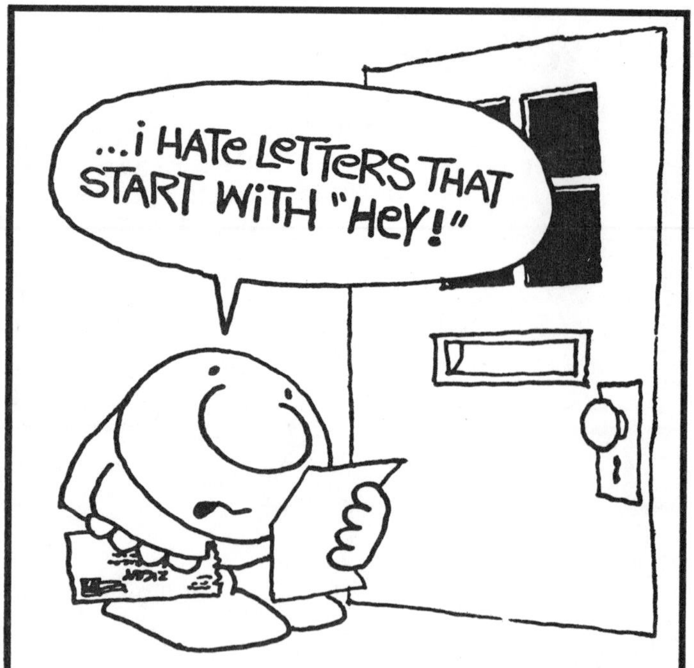
...i HATE LETTERS THAT START WITH "HEY!"
Tom Wilson

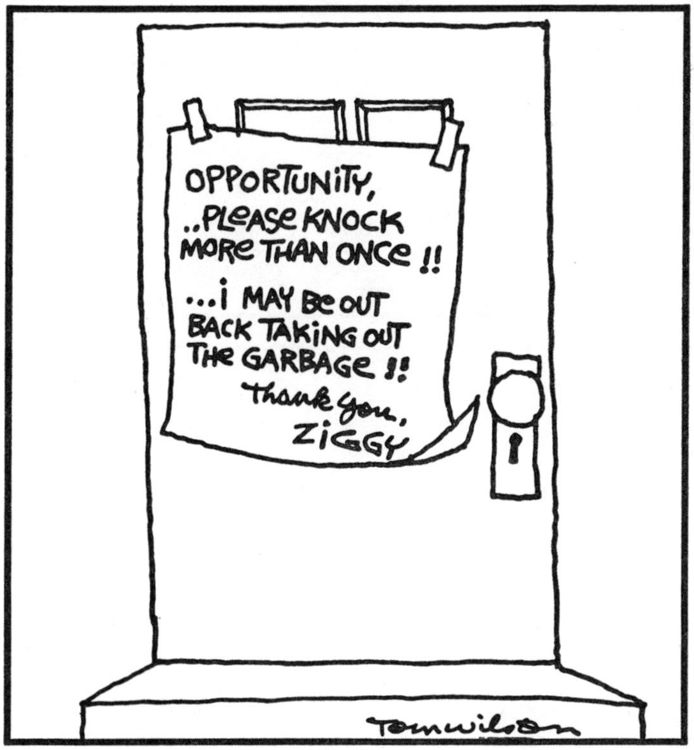
OPPORTUNITY,
..PLEASE KNOCK MORE THAN ONCE !!
...I MAY BE OUT BACK TAKING OUT THE GARBAGE !!
Thank you,
ZIGGY
Tom Wilson

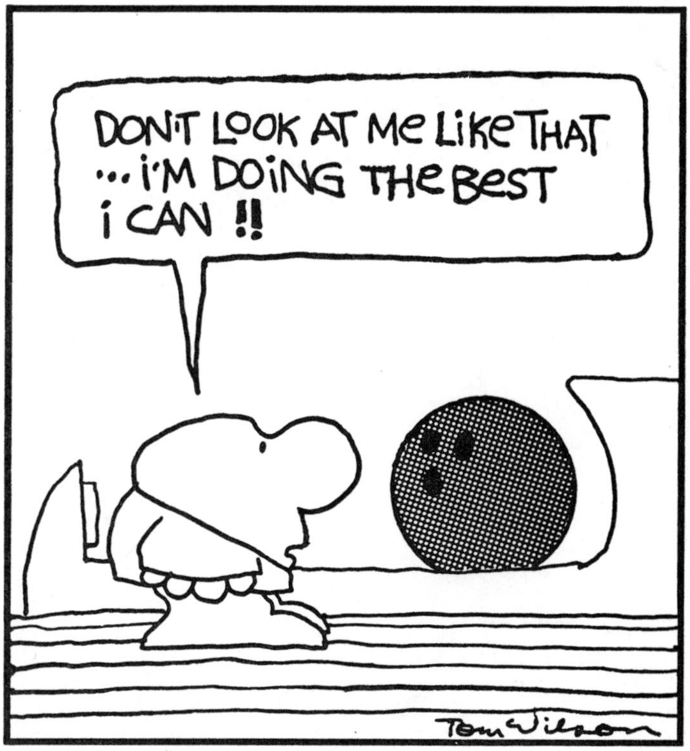
DON'T LOOK AT ME LIKE THAT ... I'M DOING THE BEST I CAN !!
Tom Wilson

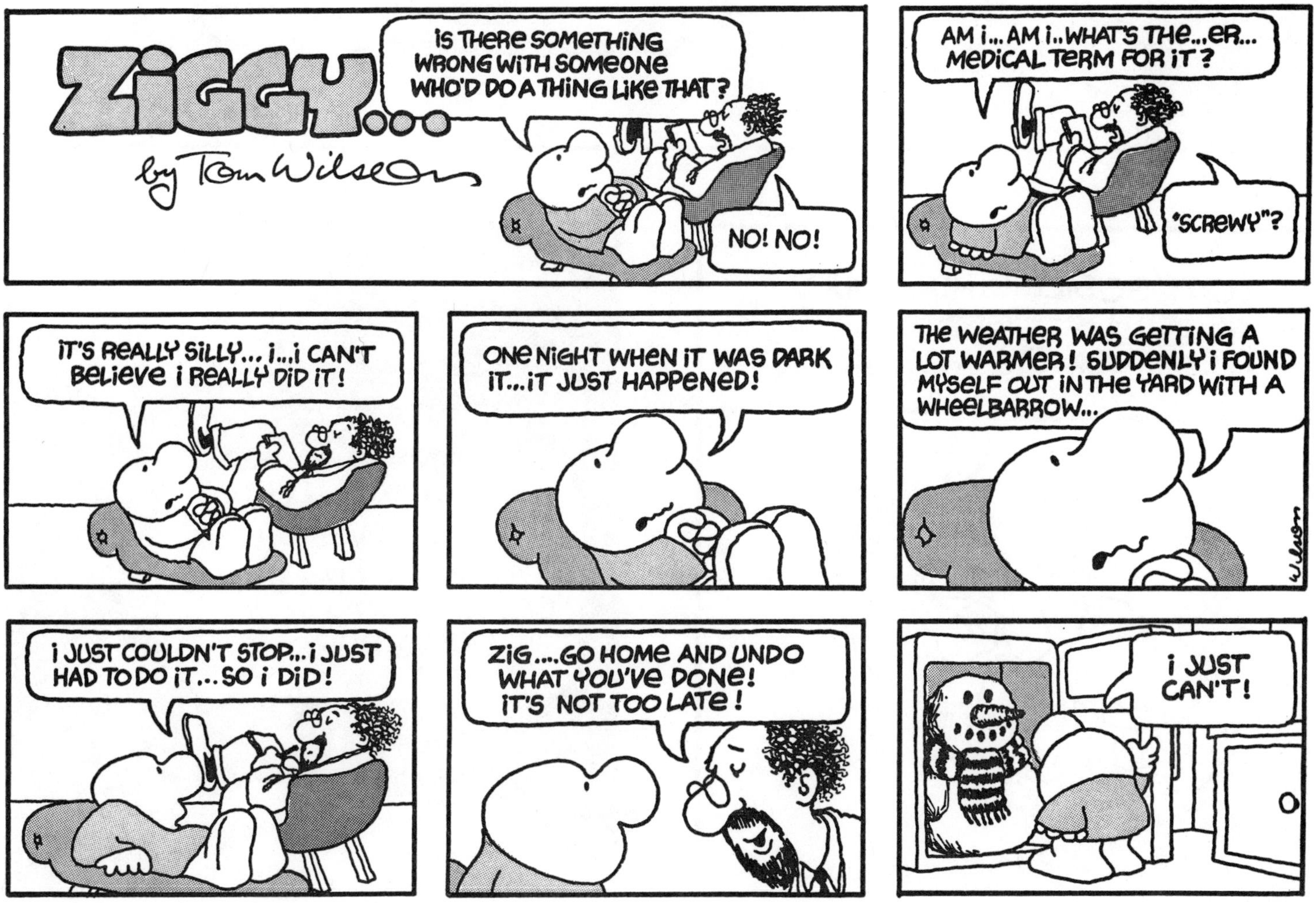
ZIGGY...
by Tom Wilson
IS THERE SOMETHING WRONG WITH SOMEONE WHO'D DO A THING LIKE THAT?
NO! NO!
AM I... AM I.. WHAT'S THE...ER... MEDICAL TERM FOR IT ?
"SCREWY"?
IT'S REALLY SILLY... I...I CAN'T BELIEVE I REALLY DID IT!
ONE NIGHT WHEN IT WAS DARK IT...IT JUST HAPPENED!
THE WEATHER WAS GETTING A LOT WARMER! SUDDENLY I FOUND MYSELF OUT IN THE YARD WITH A WHEELBARROW...
Wilson
I JUST COULDN'T STOP...I JUST HAD TO DO IT... SO I DID!
ZIG....GO HOME AND UNDO WHAT YOU'VE DONE! IT'S NOT TOO LATE!
I JUST CAN'T!

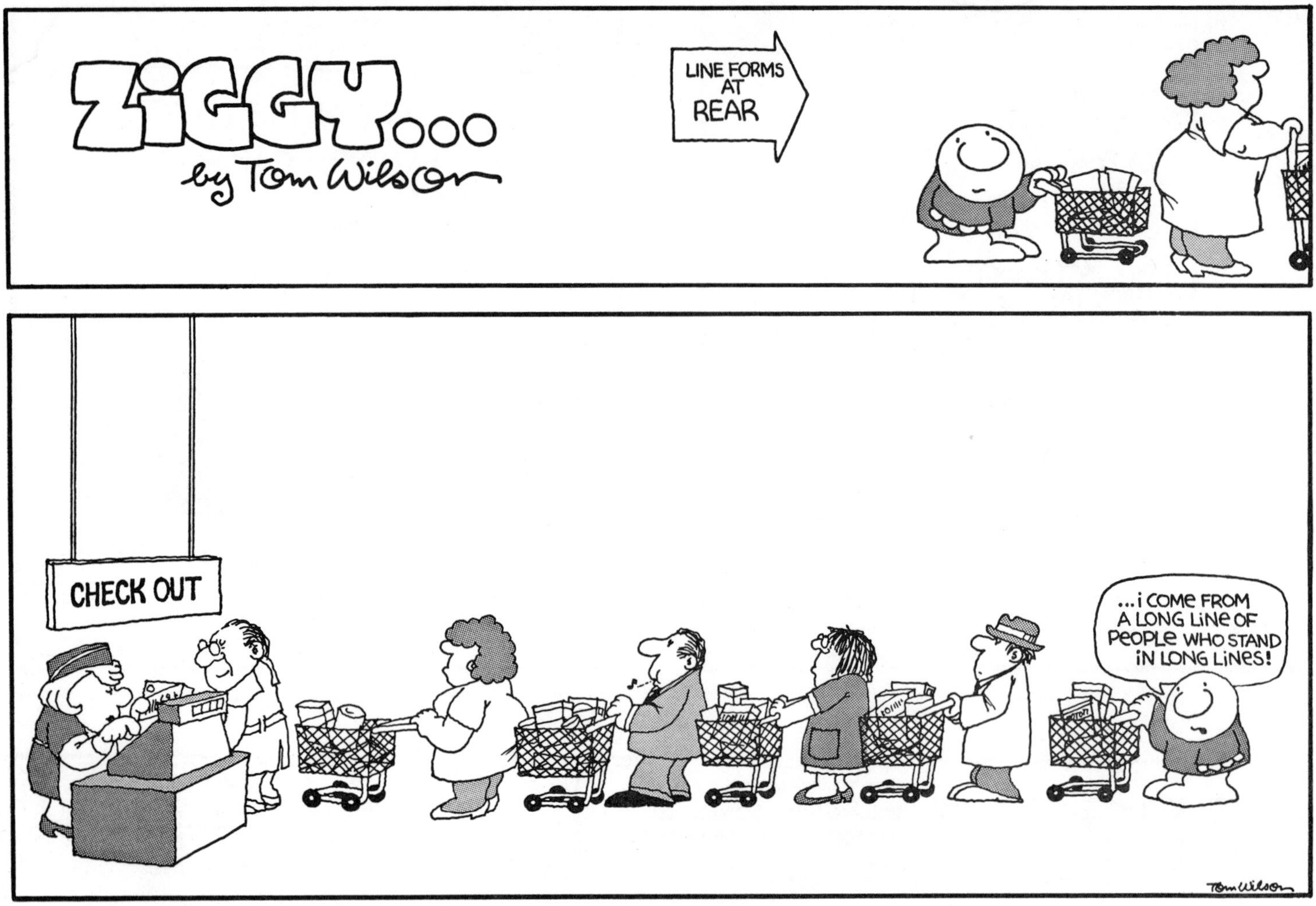
ZIGGY...
by Tom Wilson
LINE FORMS AT REAR
CHECK OUT
...i COME FROM A LONG LiNe OF PeOPLe WHO STAND iN LONG LiNeS!
Tom Wilson

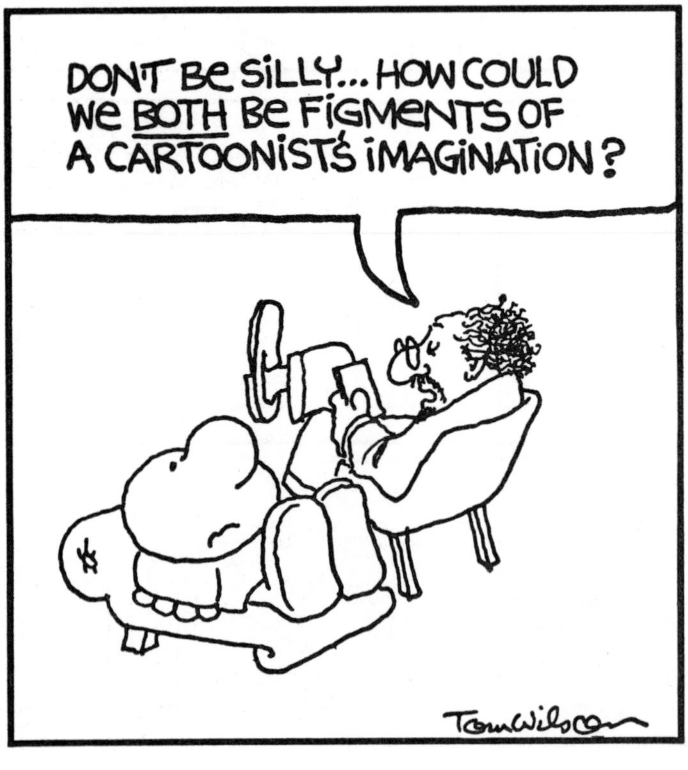
DON'T Be SiLLY... HOW COULD We BOTH Be FiGMENTS OF A CARTOONIST'S iMAGiNATiON?
Tom Wilson

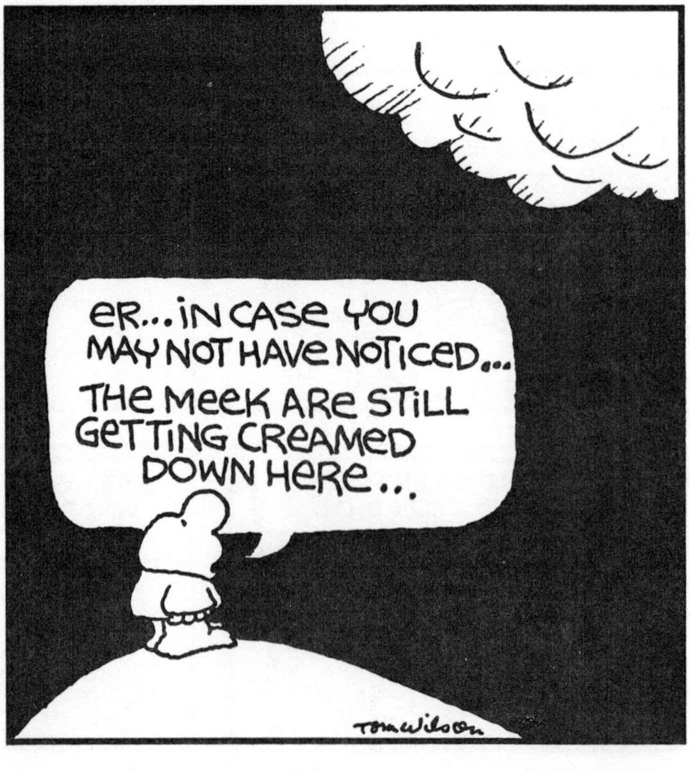
eR...iN CASe YOU MAY NOT HAVe NOTiCeD... THe MeeK ARe STiLL GeTTiNG CReAMeD DOWN HeRe...
Tom Wilson

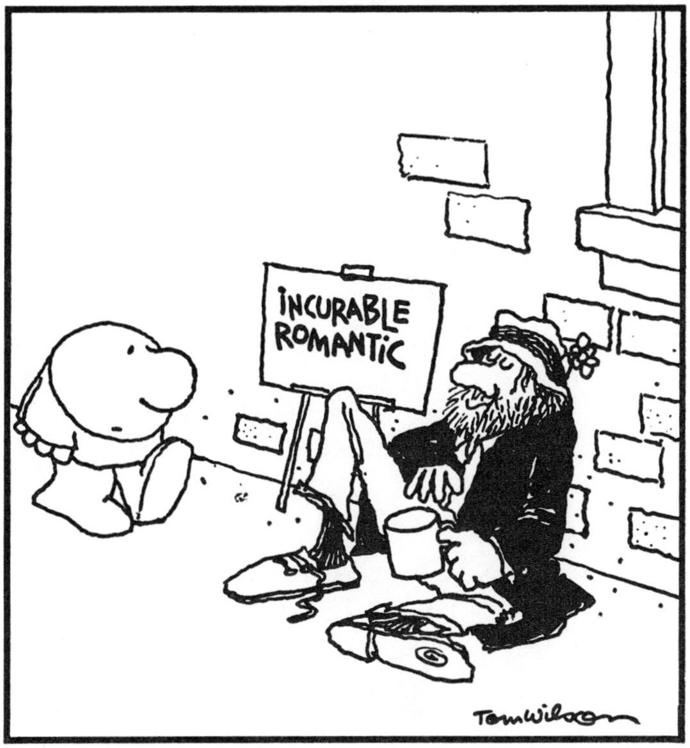

INCURABLE ROMANTIC
Tom Wilson

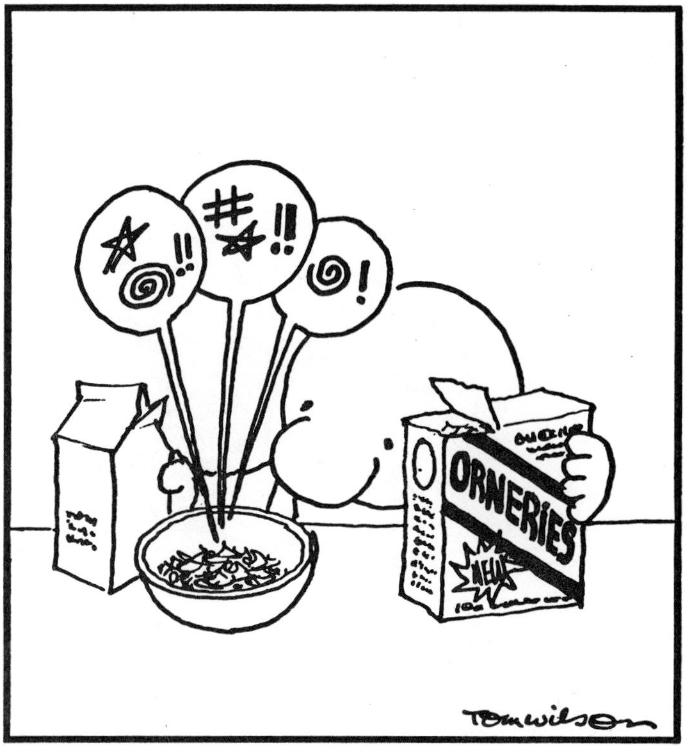

ORNERIES
Tom Wilson

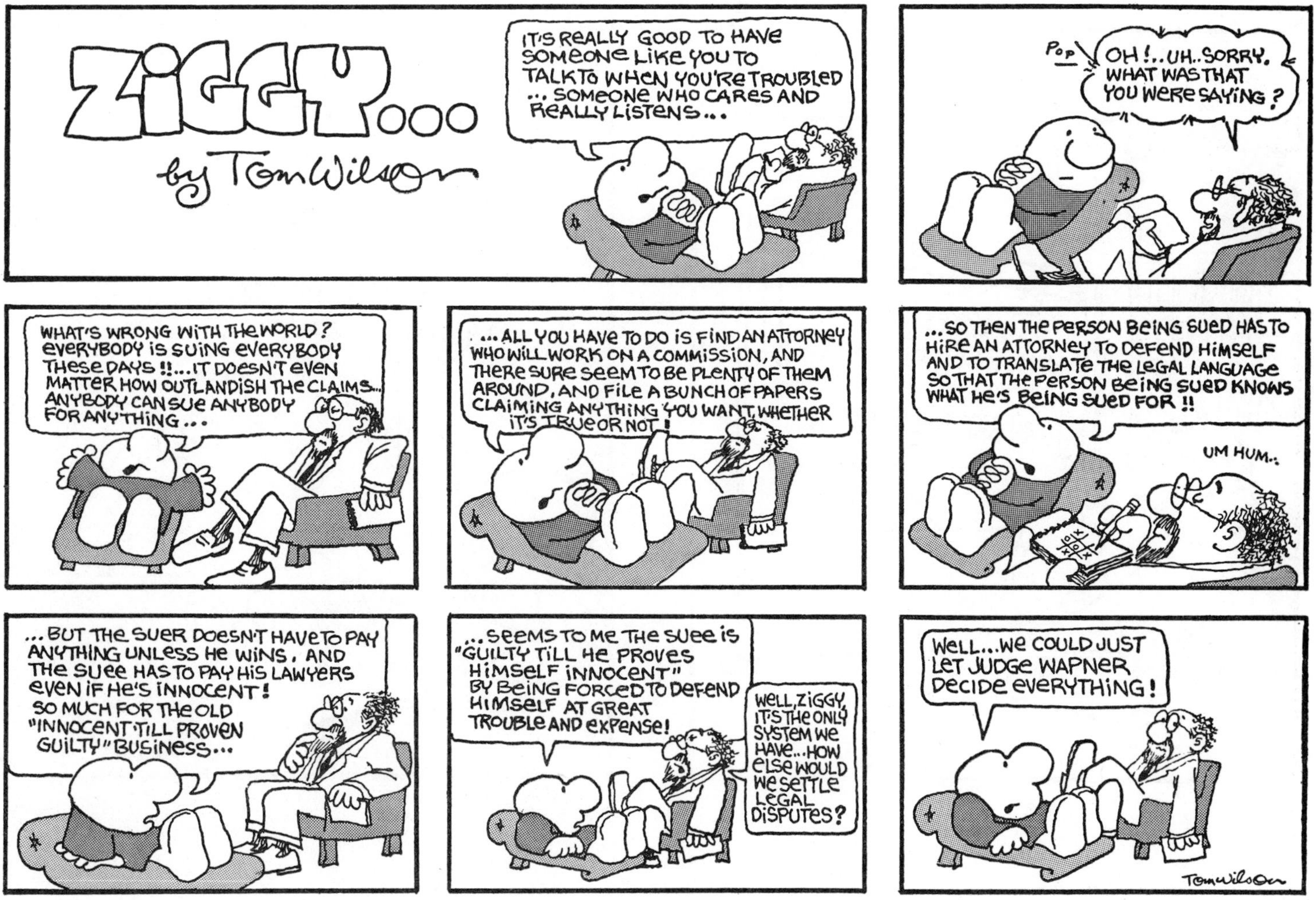

ZIGGY...
by Tom Wilson
IT'S REALLY GOOD TO HAVE SOMEONE LIKE YOU TO TALK TO WHEN YOU'RE TROUBLED ... SOMEONE WHO CARES AND REALLY LISTENS...
POP
OH!..UH..SORRY. WHAT WAS THAT YOU WERE SAYING?
WHAT'S WRONG WITH THE WORLD? EVERYBODY IS SUING EVERYBODY THESE DAYS !!...IT DOESN'T EVEN MATTER HOW OUTLANDISH THE CLAIMS... ANYBODY CAN SUE ANYBODY FOR ANYTHING...
...ALL YOU HAVE TO DO IS FIND AN ATTORNEY WHO WILL WORK ON A COMMISSION, AND THERE SURE SEEM TO BE PLENTY OF THEM AROUND, AND FILE A BUNCH OF PAPERS CLAIMING ANYTHING YOU WANT, WHETHER IT'S TRUE OR NOT!
...SO THEN THE PERSON BEING SUED HAS TO HIRE AN ATTORNEY TO DEFEND HIMSELF AND TO TRANSLATE THE LEGAL LANGUAGE SO THAT THE PERSON BEING SUED KNOWS WHAT HE'S BEING SUED FOR !!
UM HUM..
...BUT THE SUER DOESN'T HAVE TO PAY ANYTHING UNLESS HE WINS, AND THE SUEE HAS TO PAY HIS LAWYERS EVEN IF HE'S INNOCENT! SO MUCH FOR THE OLD "INNOCENT TILL PROVEN GUILTY" BUSINESS...
...SEEMS TO ME THE SUEE IS "GUILTY TILL HE PROVES HIMSELF INNOCENT" BY BEING FORCED TO DEFEND HIMSELF AT GREAT TROUBLE AND EXPENSE!
WELL, ZIGGY, IT'S THE ONLY SYSTEM WE HAVE...HOW ELSE WOULD WE SETTLE LEGAL DISPUTES?
WELL...WE COULD JUST LET JUDGE WAPNER DECIDE EVERYTHING!
Tom Wilson

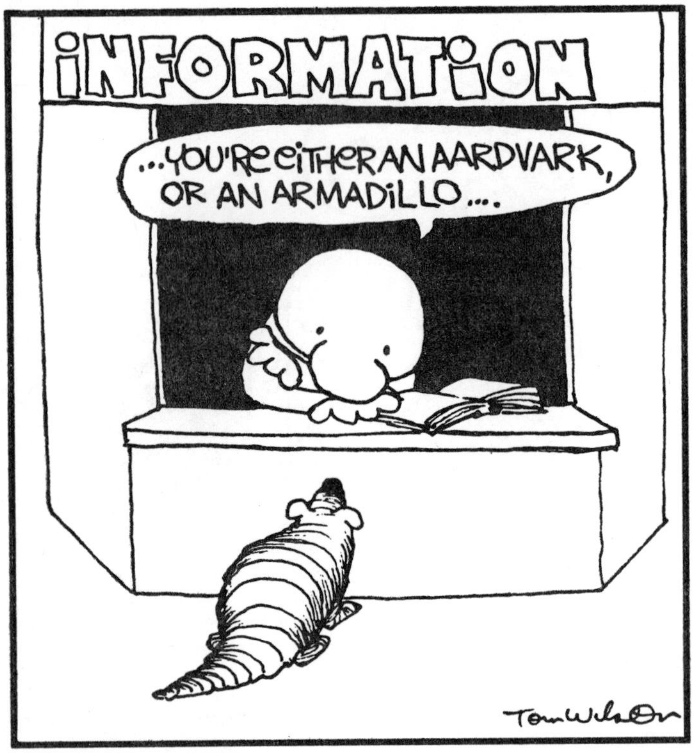
INFORMATION
...YOU'RE EITHER AN AARDVARK, OR AN ARMADILLO....
TOM WILSON

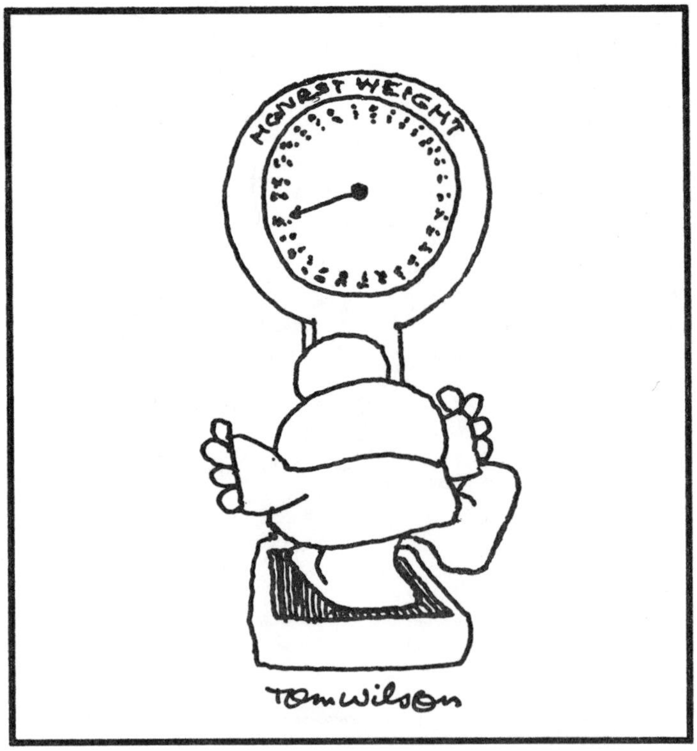
HONEST WEIGHT
TOM WILSON

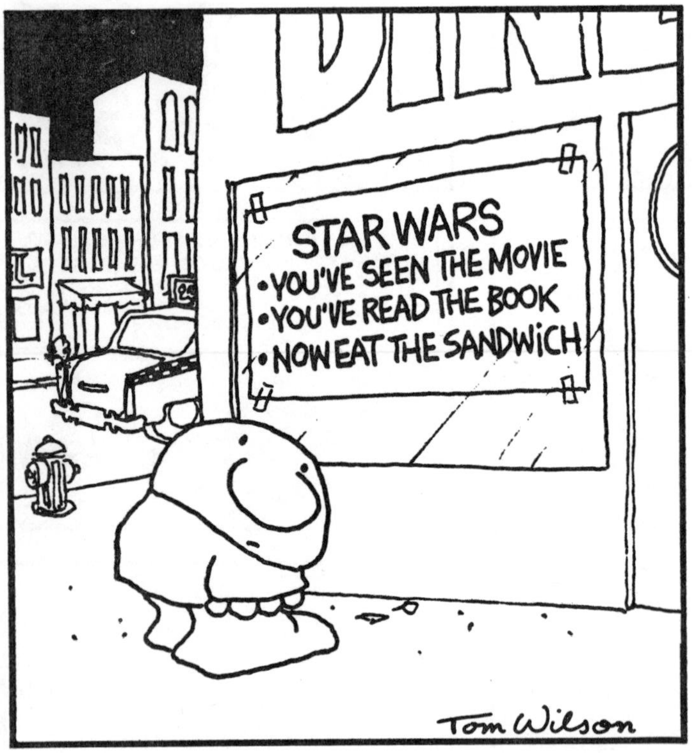
STAR WARS
•YOU'VE SEEN THE MOVIE
•YOU'VE READ THE BOOK
•NOW EAT THE SANDWICH
Tom Wilson

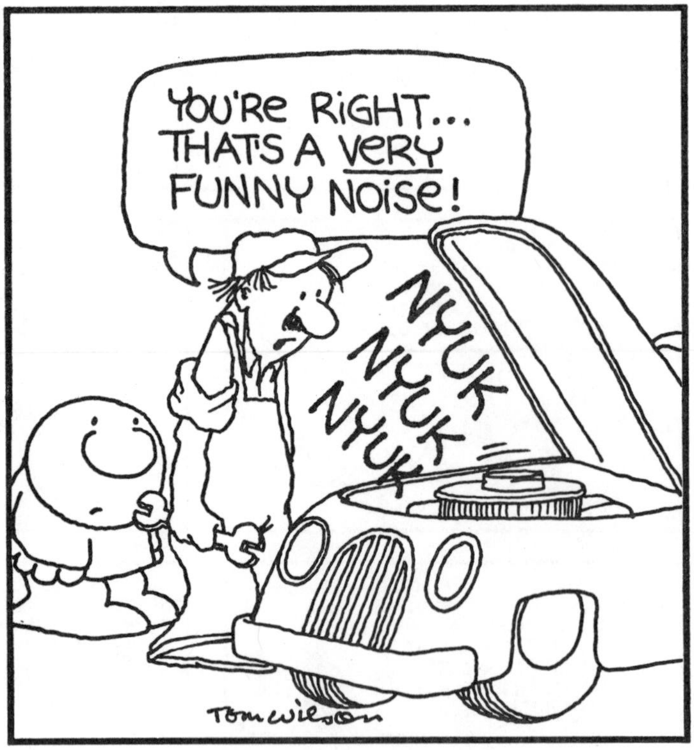
YOU'RE RIGHT... THAT'S A VERY FUNNY NOISE!
NYUK NYUK NYUK
TOM WILSON

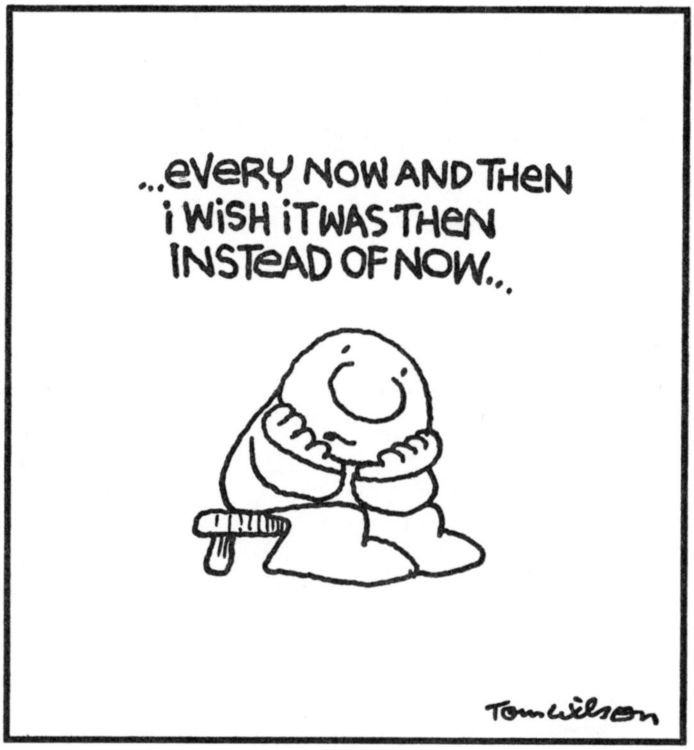
...every NOW AND THEN i WiSH iTWAS THEN INSTEAD OF NOW...
TomWilson

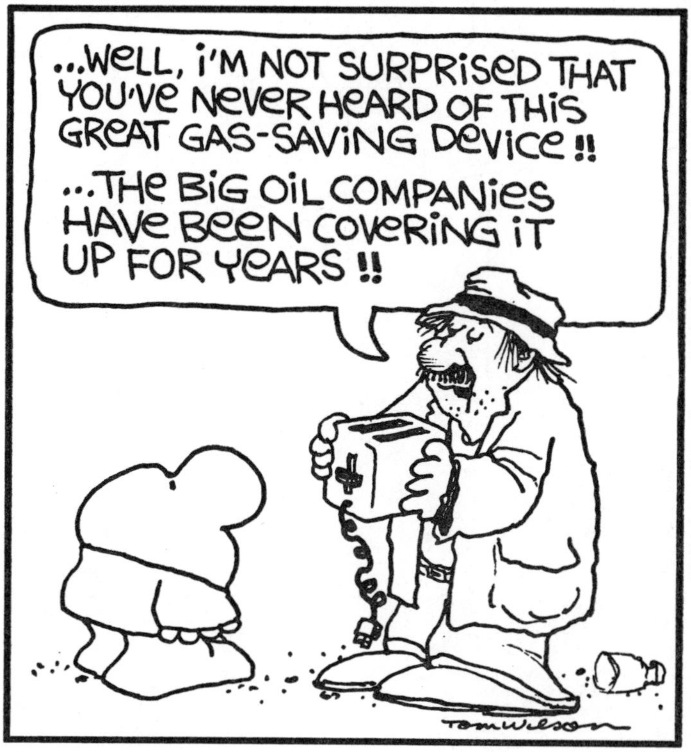
...WELL, i'M NOT SURPRISED THAT YOU'VE NEVER HEARD OF THIS GREAT GAS-SAVING DEVICE!!
...THE BIG OIL COMPANIES HAVE BEEN COVERING IT UP FOR YEARS!!
TomWilson

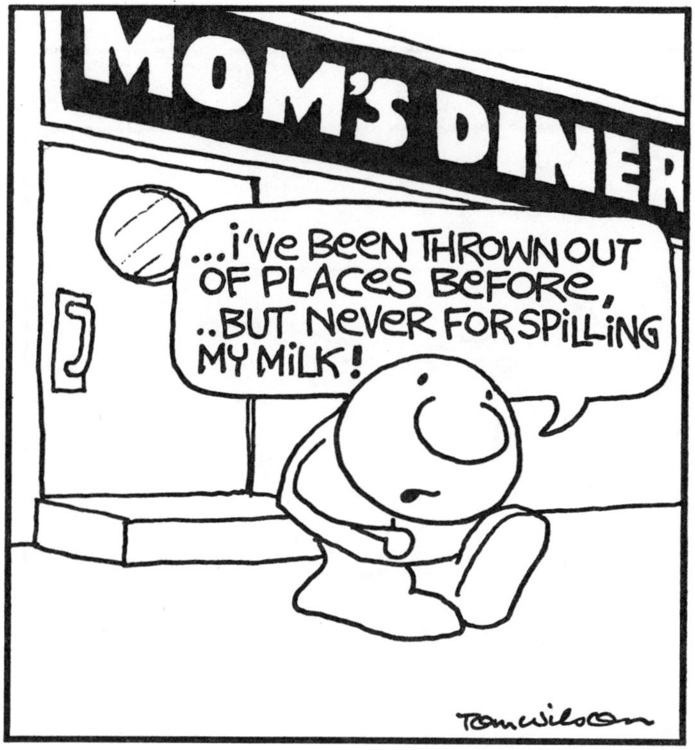
MOM'S DINER
...i've BEEN THROWN OUT OF PLACES BEFORE, ..BUT NEVER FOR SPILLING MY MILK!
TomWilson

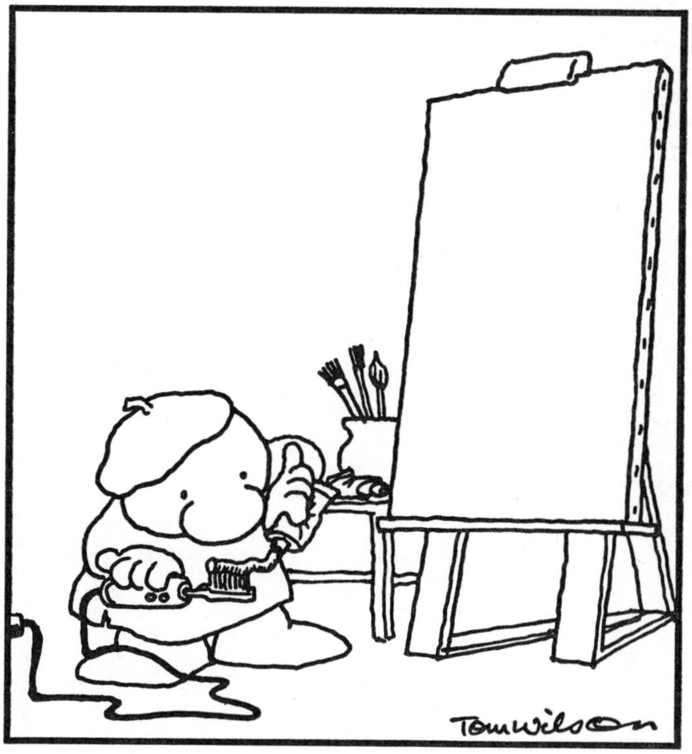
TomWilson

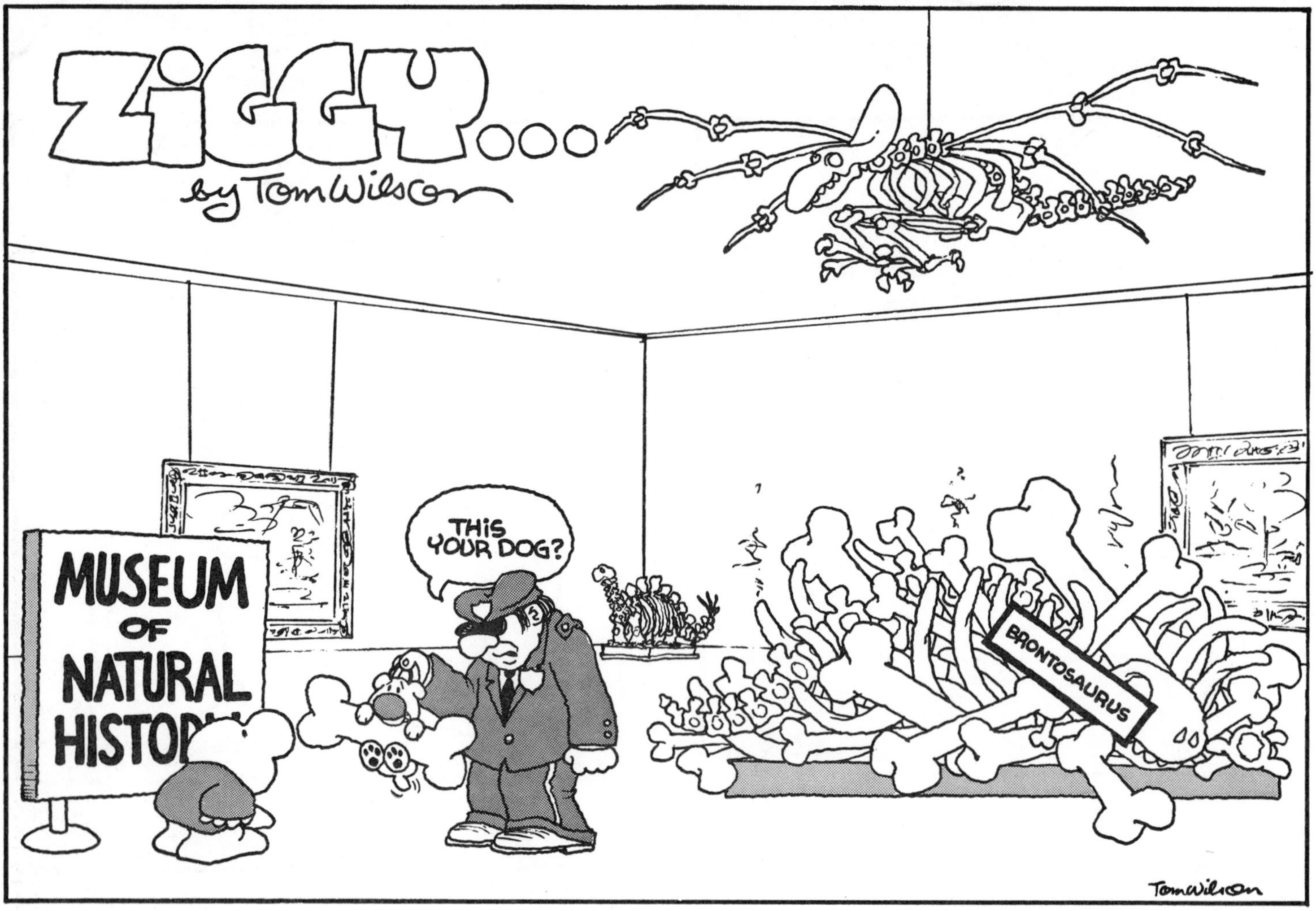
ZIGGY...
by Tom Wilson
MUSEUM OF NATURAL HISTOR
THIS YOUR DOG?
BRONTOSAURUS
Tom Wilson

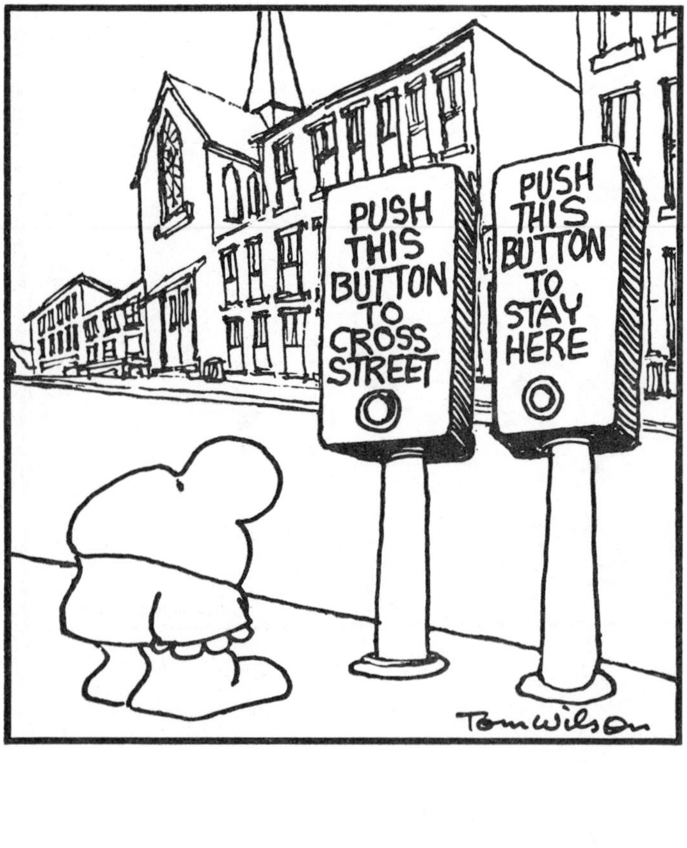
PUSH THIS BUTTON TO CROSS STREET
PUSH THIS BUTTON TO STAY HERE
Tom Wilson

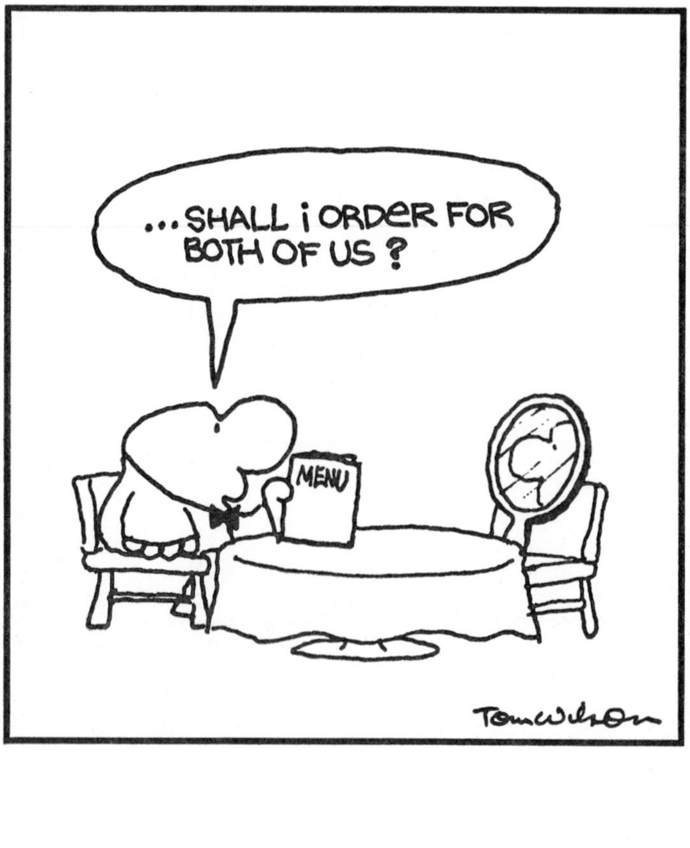
...SHALL i ORDER FOR BOTH OF US ?
MENU
Tom Wilson

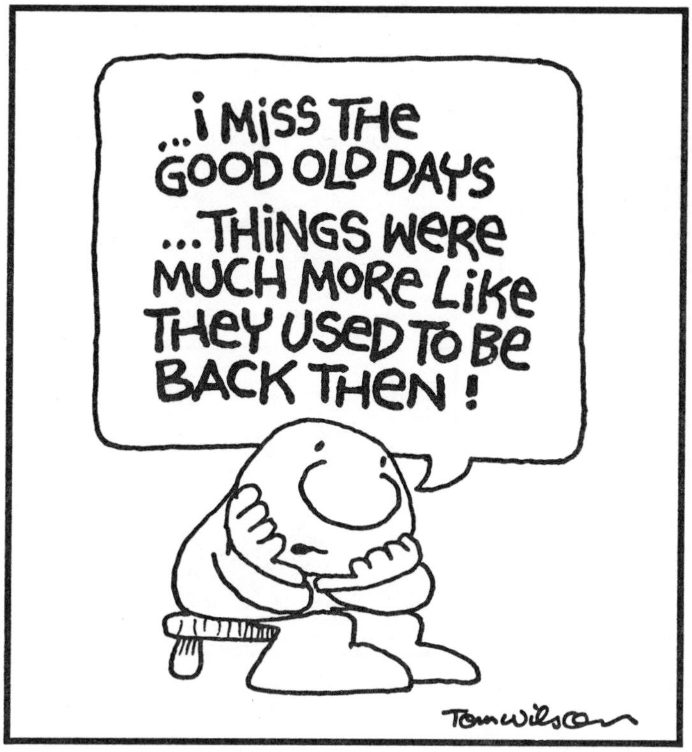
...i MISS THE GOOD OLD DAYS ...THINGS WERE MUCH MORE LIKE THEY USED TO BE BACK THEN !
Tom Wilson

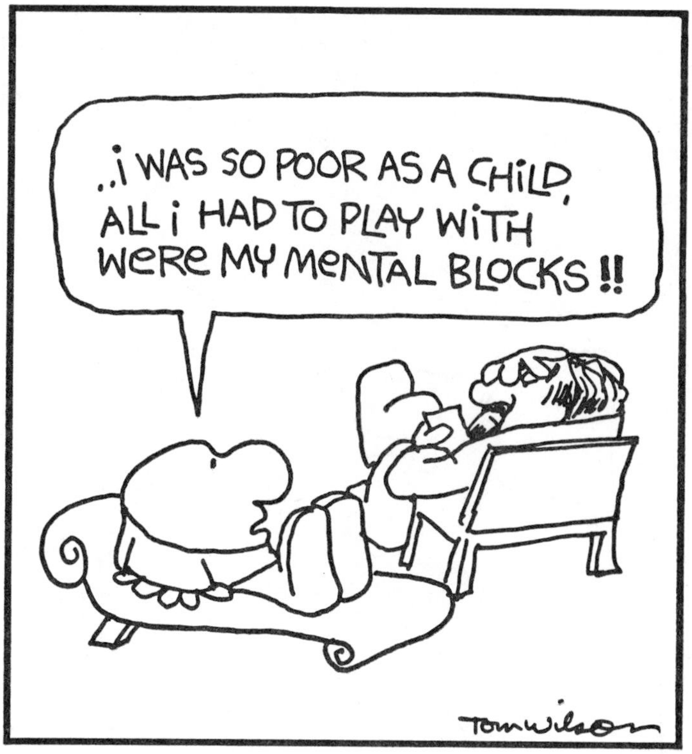
..i WAS SO POOR AS A CHILD, ALL i HAD TO PLAY WITH WERE MY MENTAL BLOCKS !!
Tom Wilson

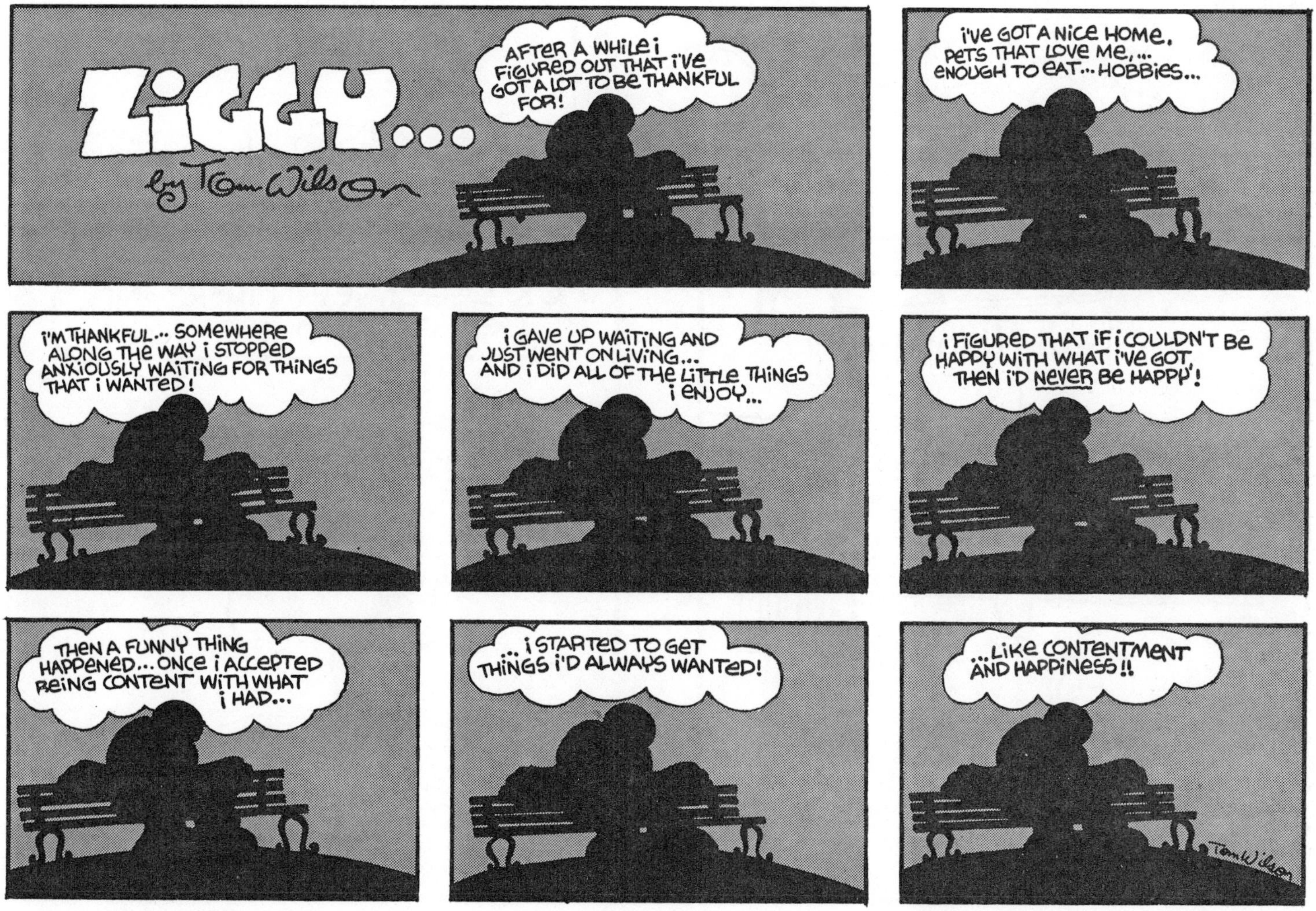
ZIGGY...
by Tom Wilson
AFTER A WHILE i FIGURED OUT THAT i'VE GOT A LOT TO BE THANKFUL FOR!
i'VE GOT A NICE HOME, PETS THAT LOVE ME, ... ENOUGH TO EAT... HOBBIES...
i'M THANKFUL... SOMEWHERE ALONG THE WAY i STOPPED ANXIOUSLY WAITING FOR THINGS THAT i WANTED!
i GAVE UP WAITING AND JUST WENT ON LIVING... AND i DID ALL OF THE LITTLE THINGS i ENJOY...
i FIGURED THAT IF i COULDN'T BE HAPPY WITH WHAT i'VE GOT, THEN i'D NEVER BE HAPPY!
THEN A FUNNY THING HAPPENED... ONCE i ACCEPTED BEING CONTENT WITH WHAT i HAD...
... i STARTED TO GET THINGS i'D ALWAYS WANTED!
...LIKE CONTENTMENT AND HAPPINESS !!
Tom Wilson

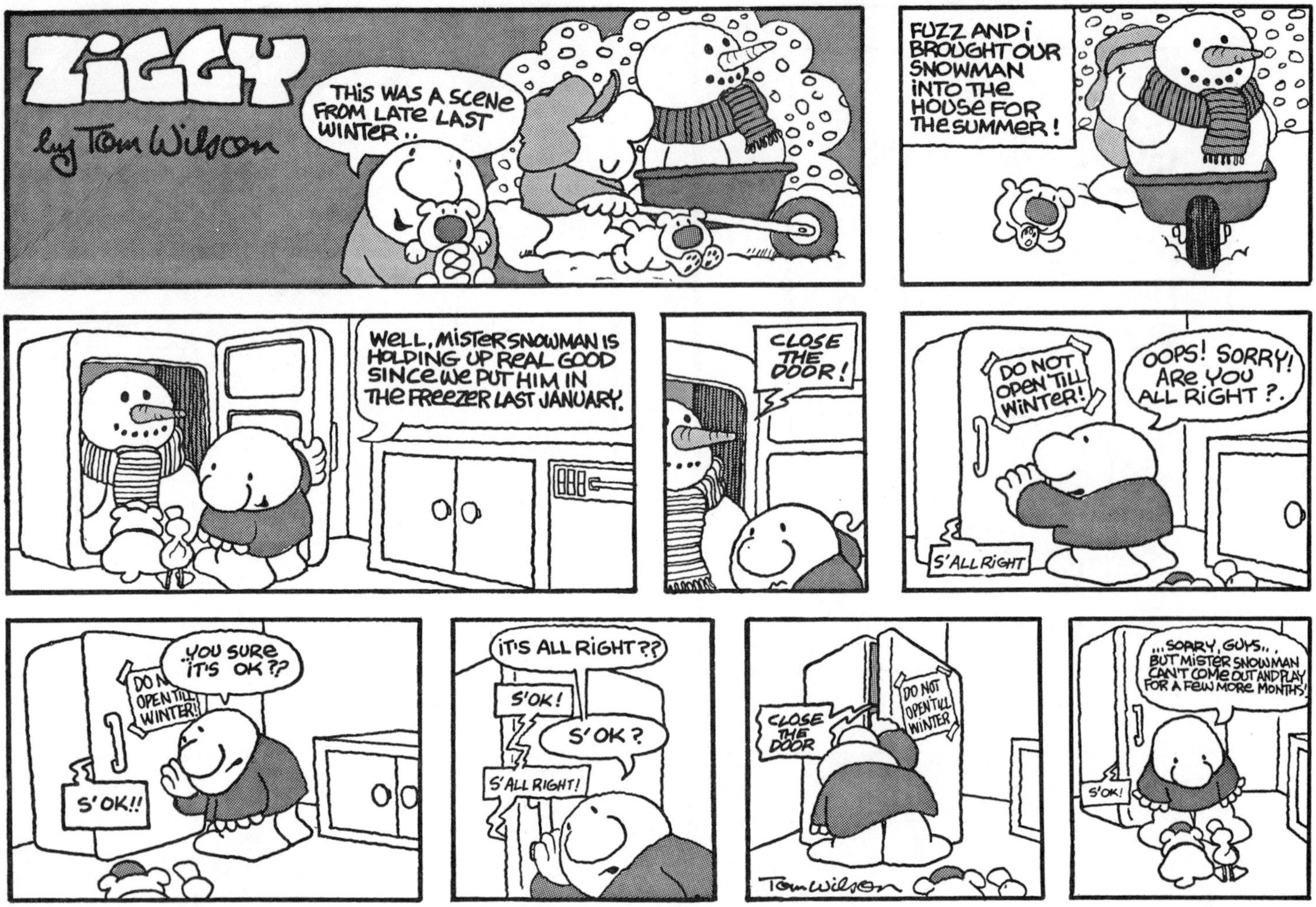
ZiGGY
by Tom Wilson
THIS WAS A SCENE FROM LATE LAST WINTER..
FUZZ AND i BROUGHT OUR SNOWMAN iNTO THE HOUSE FOR THE SUMMER!
WELL, MISTER SNOWMAN IS HOLDING UP REAL GOOD SINCE WE PUT HIM IN THE FREEZER LAST JANUARY.
CLOSE THE DOOR!
DO NOT OPEN TILL WINTER!
OOPS! SORRY! ARE YOU ALL RIGHT?.
S'ALL RIGHT
YOU SURE IT'S OK??
S'OK!!
IT'S ALL RIGHT??
S'OK!
S'OK?
S'ALL RIGHT!
CLOSE THE DOOR
DO NOT OPEN TILL WINTER
...SORRY, GUYS...
BUT MISTER SNOWMAN CAN'T COME OUT AND PLAY FOR A FEW MORE MONTHS!
S'OK!
Tom Wilson

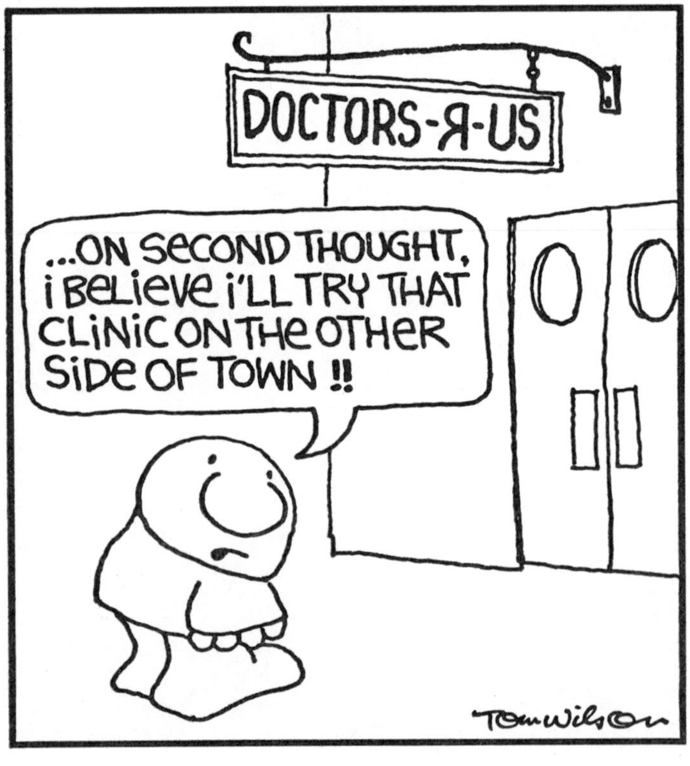
DOCTORS-Я-US
...ON SECOND THOUGHT, I BELIEVE I'LL TRY THAT CLINIC ON THE OTHER SIDE OF TOWN!!
Tom Wilson

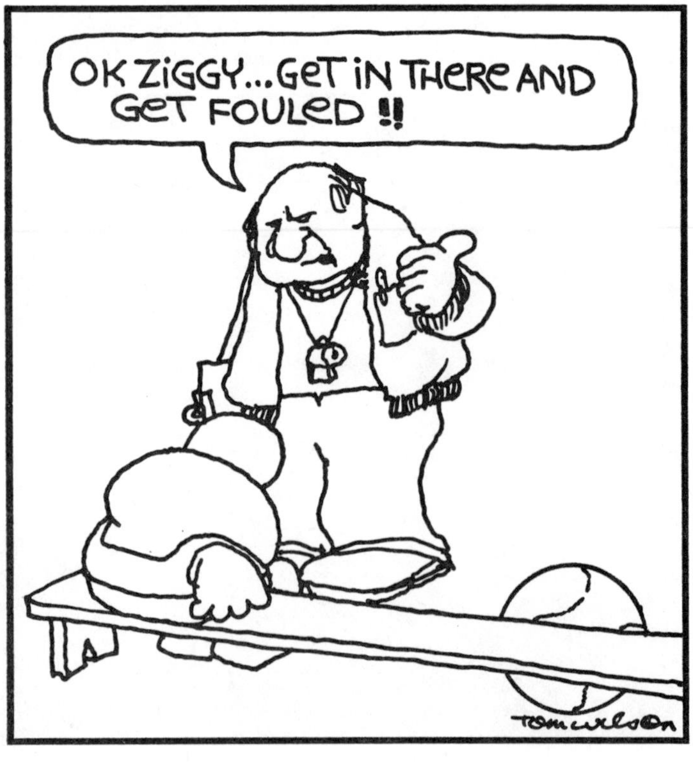
OK ZIGGY...GET IN THERE AND GET FOULED!!
Tom Wilson

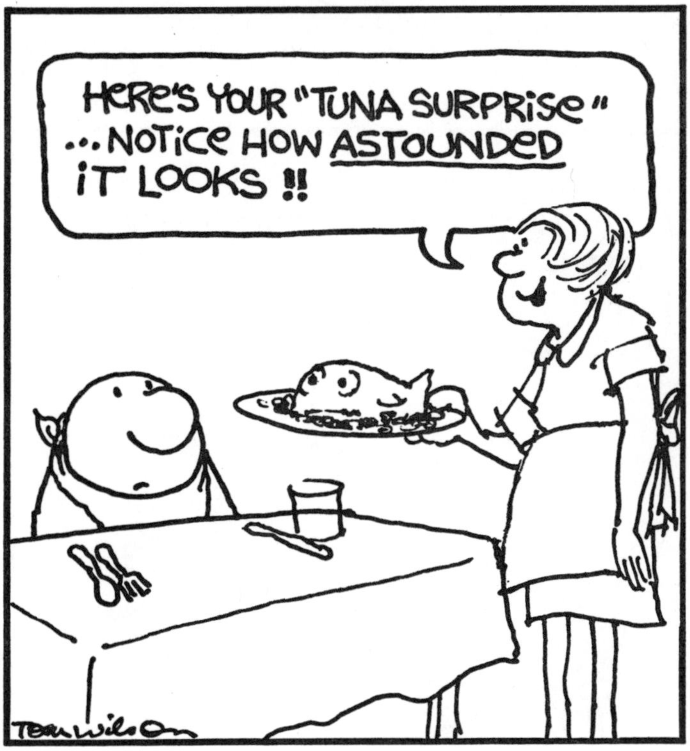

HERE'S YOUR "TUNA SURPRISE" ...NOTICE HOW ASTOUNDED IT LOOKS !!
Tom Wilson

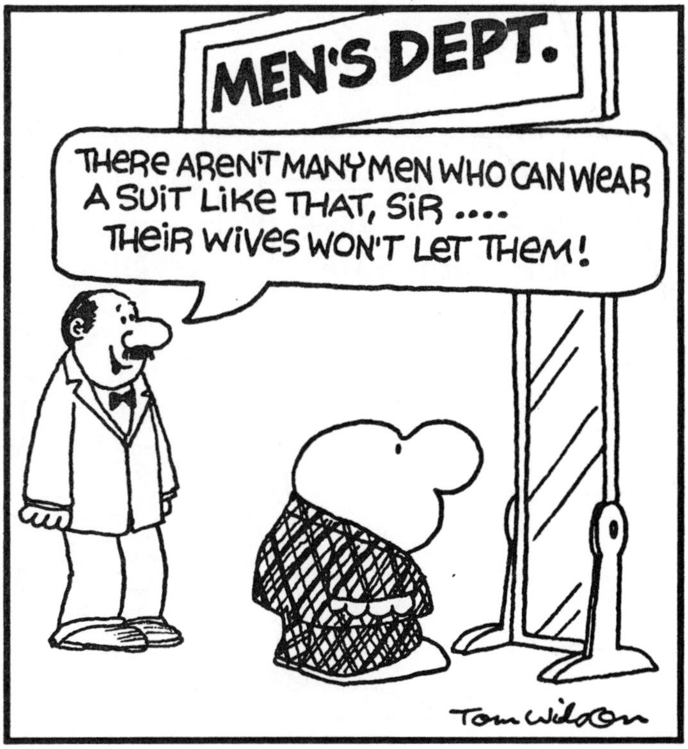

MEN'S DEPT.
THERE AREN'T MANY MEN WHO CAN WEAR A SUIT LIKE THAT, SIR .... THEIR WIVES WON'T LET THEM!
Tom Wilson

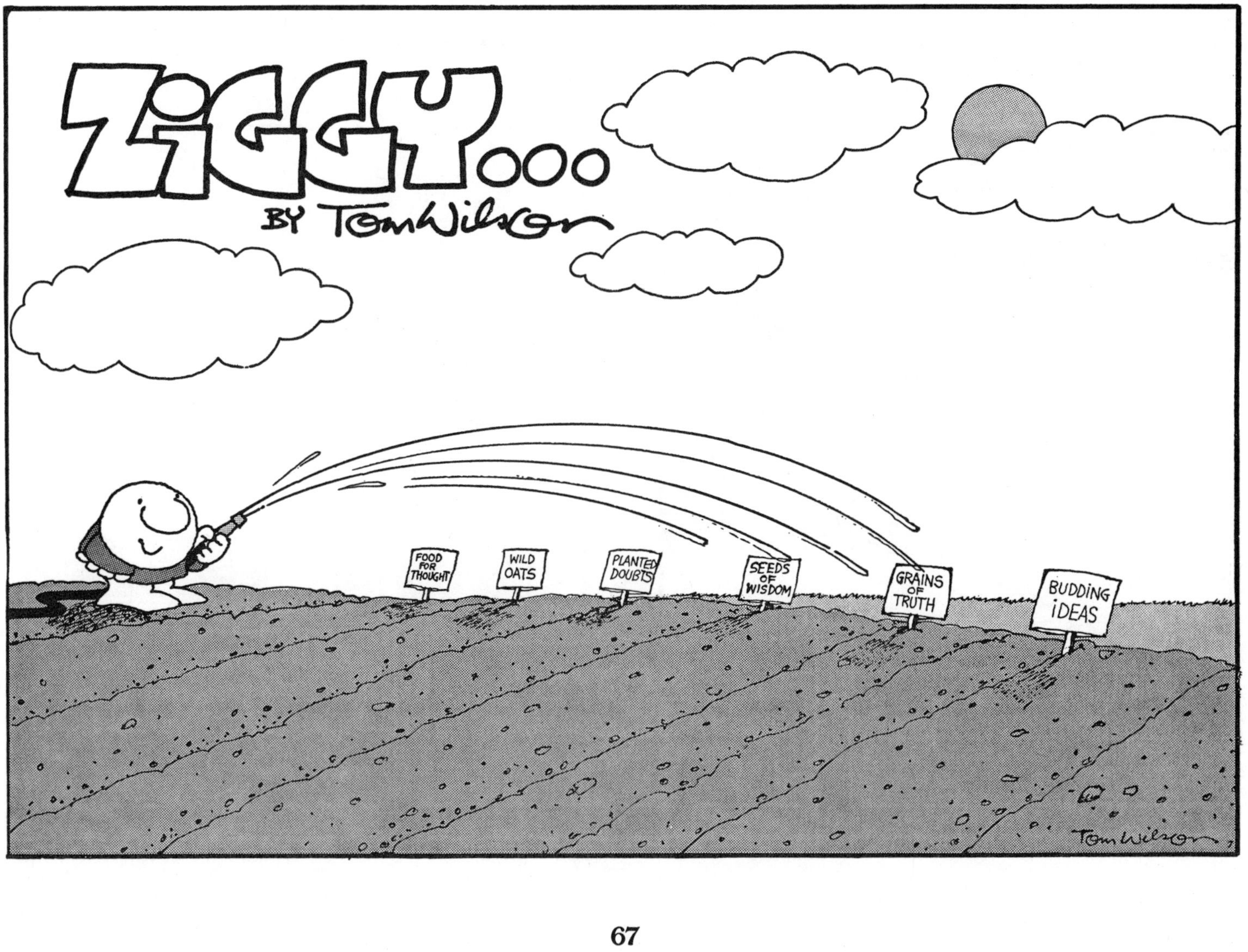

ZIGGY ooo
BY Tom Wilson
FOOD FOR THOUGHT
WILD OATS
PLANTED DOUBTS
SEEDS OF WISDOM
GRAINS OF TRUTH
BUDDING IDEAS
Tom Wilson

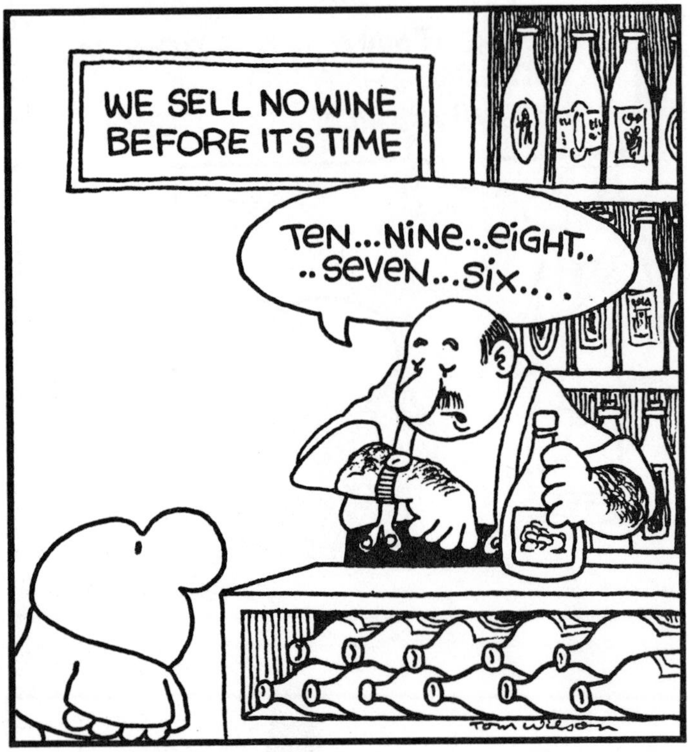
WE SELL NO WINE BEFORE ITS TIME
TEN...NINE...EIGHT.. ..SEVEN...SIX....
Tom Wilson

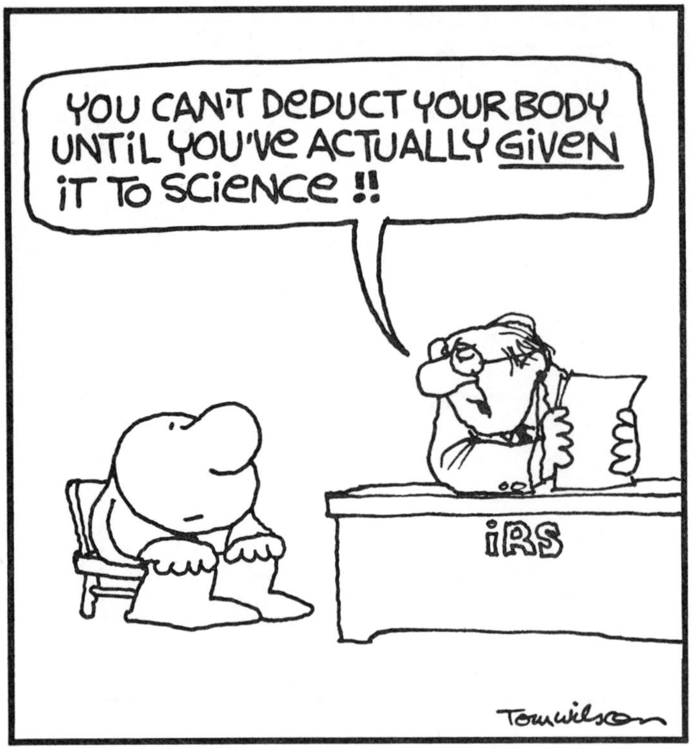
YOU CAN'T DEDUCT YOUR BODY UNTIL YOU'VE ACTUALLY GIVEN IT TO SCIENCE !!
IRS
Tom Wilson

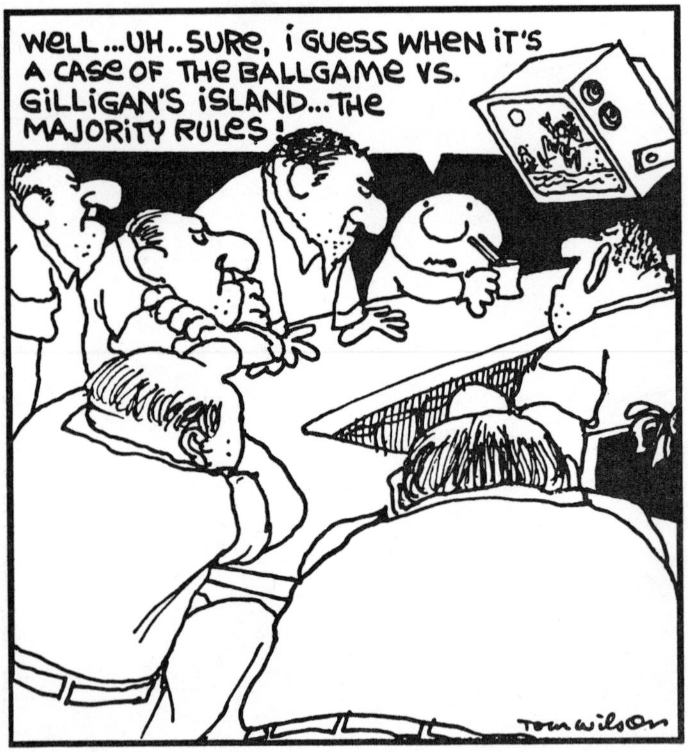
WELL...UH..SURE, I GUESS WHEN IT'S A CASE OF THE BALLGAME VS. GILLIGAN'S ISLAND...THE MAJORITY RULES!
Tom Wilson

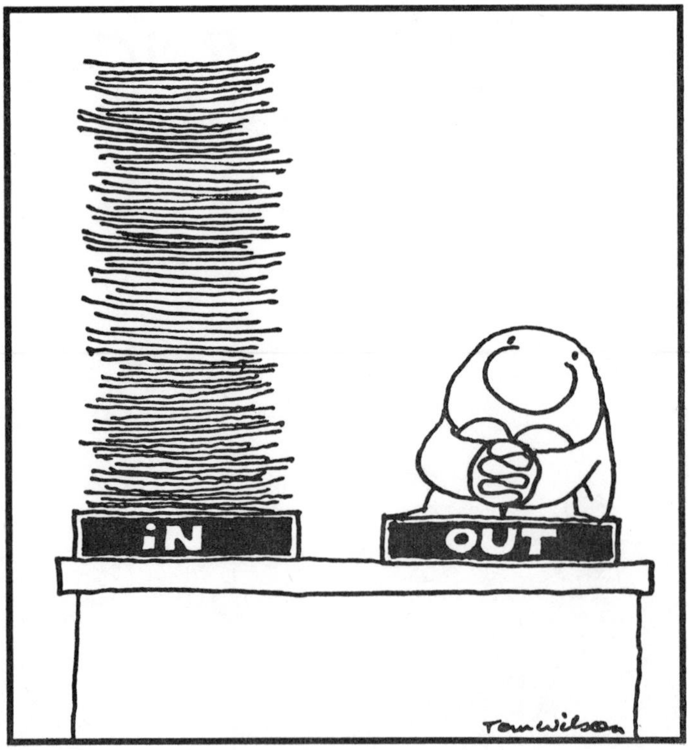
IN
OUT
Tom Wilson

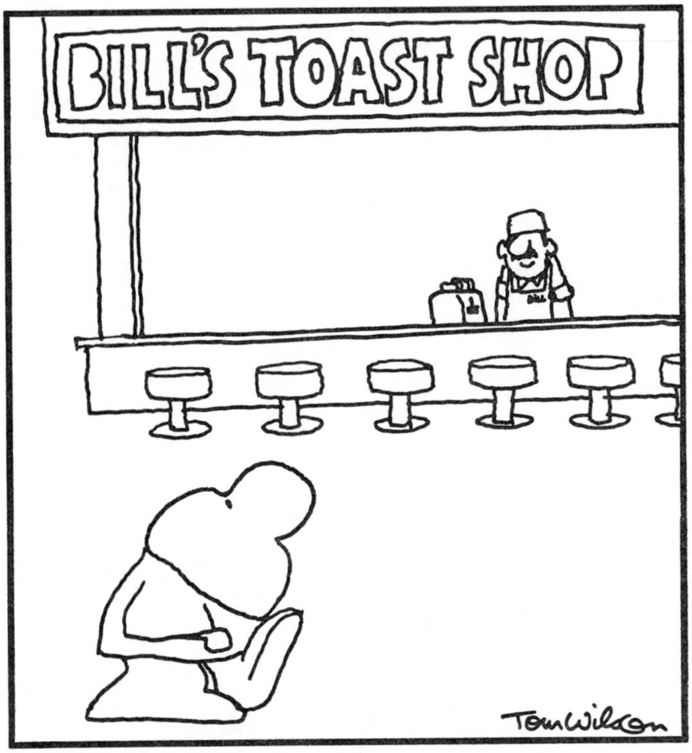
BILL'S TOAST SHOP
TOM WILSON

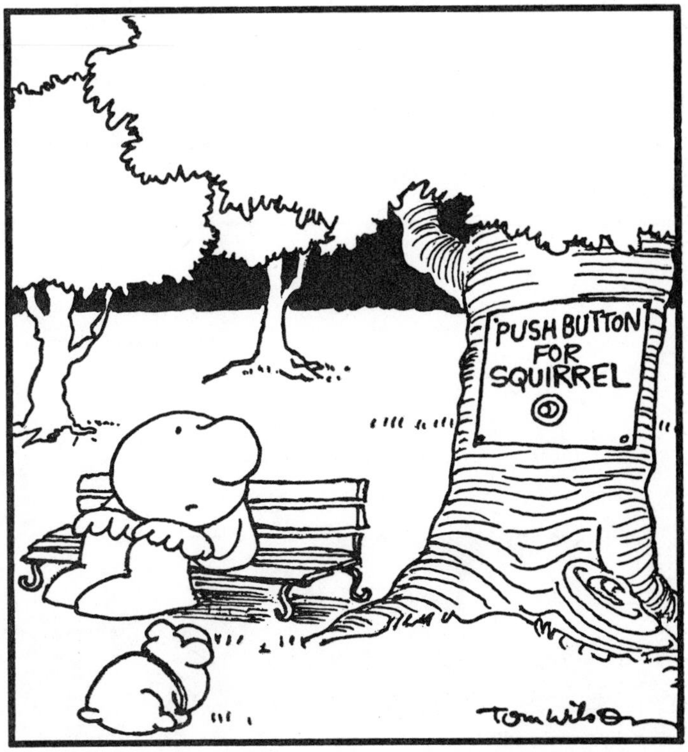
PUSH BUTTON FOR SQUIRREL
TOM WILSON

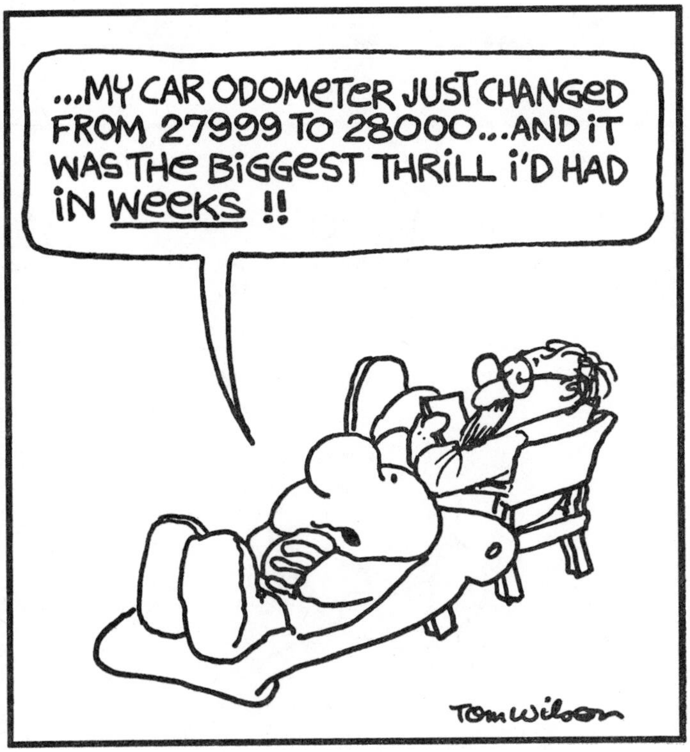
...MY CAR ODOMETER JUST CHANGED FROM 27999 TO 28000...AND IT WAS THE BIGGEST THRILL I'D HAD IN WEEKS !!
TOM WILSON

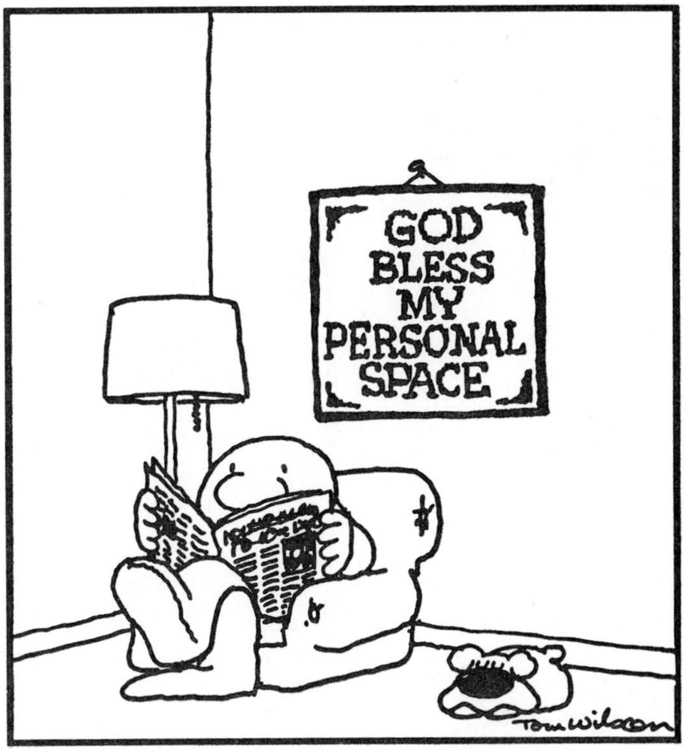
GOD BLESS MY PERSONAL SPACE
TOM WILSON

ZIGGY...

BY TOM WILSON

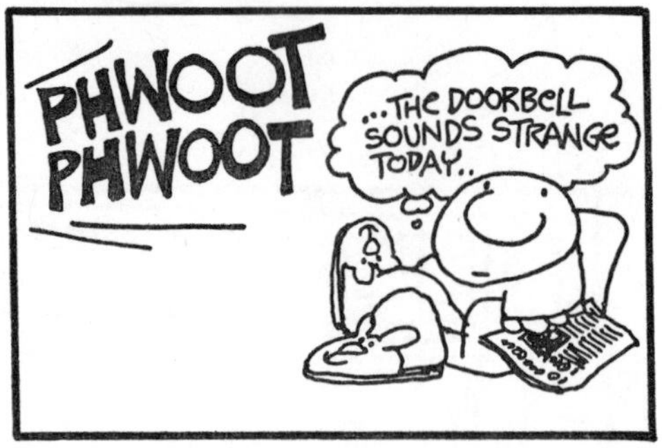
PHWOOT PHWOOT
...THE DOORBELL SOUNDS STRANGE TODAY..

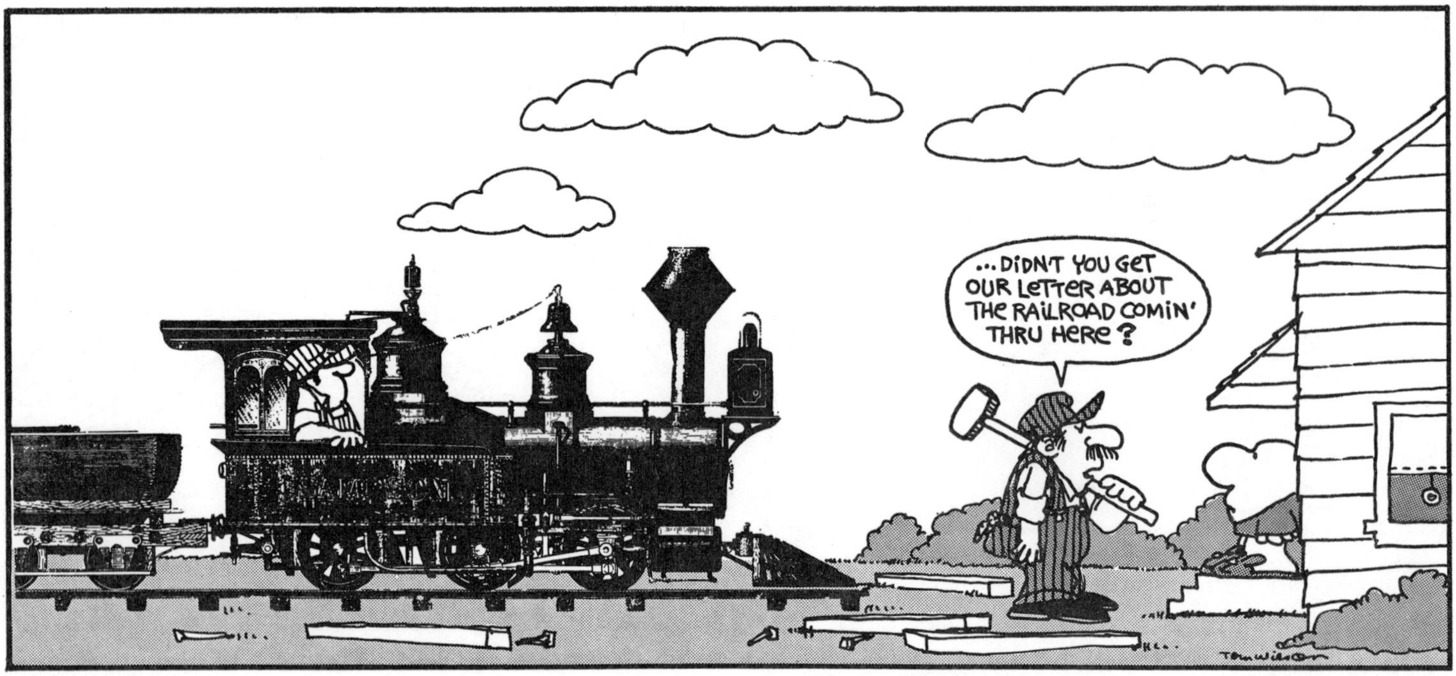
...DIDN'T YOU GET OUR LETTER ABOUT THE RAILROAD COMIN' THRU HERE?
TOM WILSON

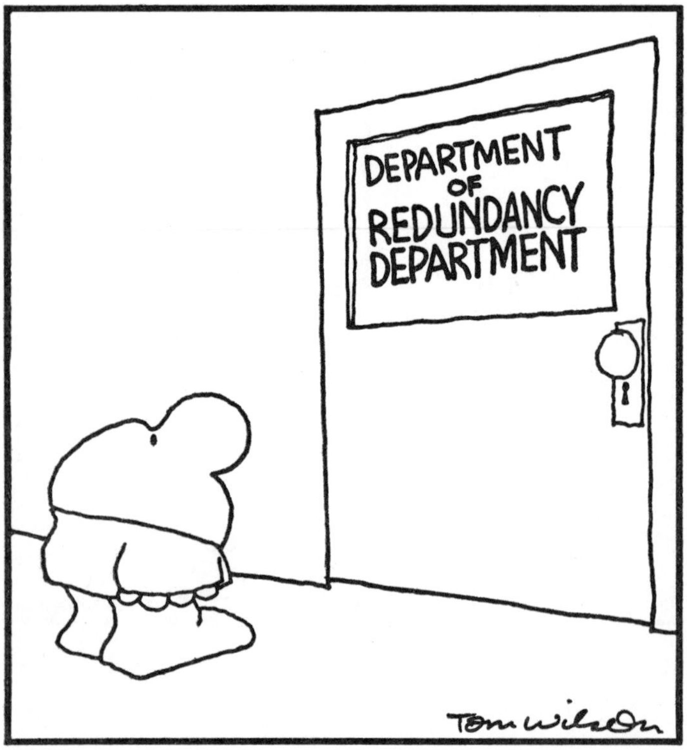
DEPARTMENT OF REDUNDANCY DEPARTMENT
TOM WILSON

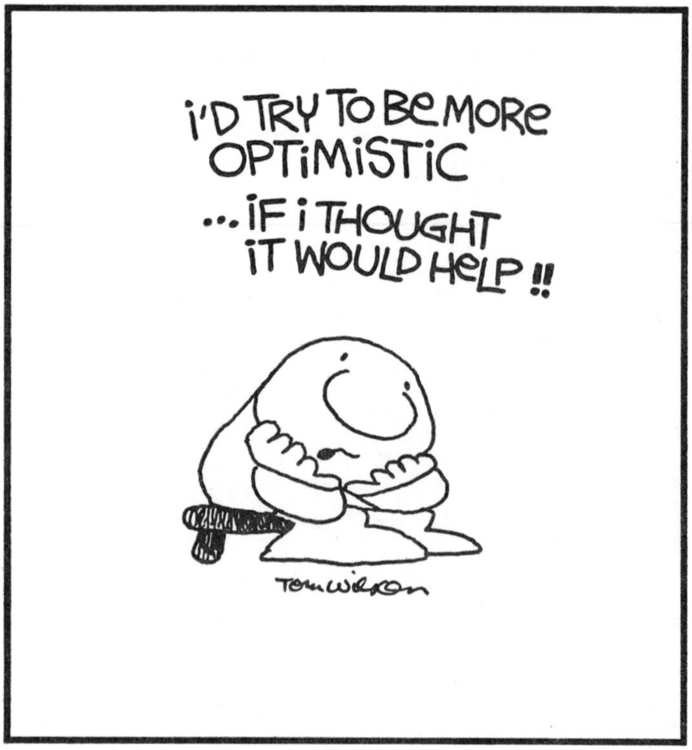
I'D TRY TO BE MORE OPTIMISTIC
...IF I THOUGHT IT WOULD HELP!!
TOM WILSON

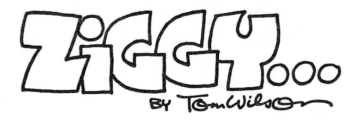

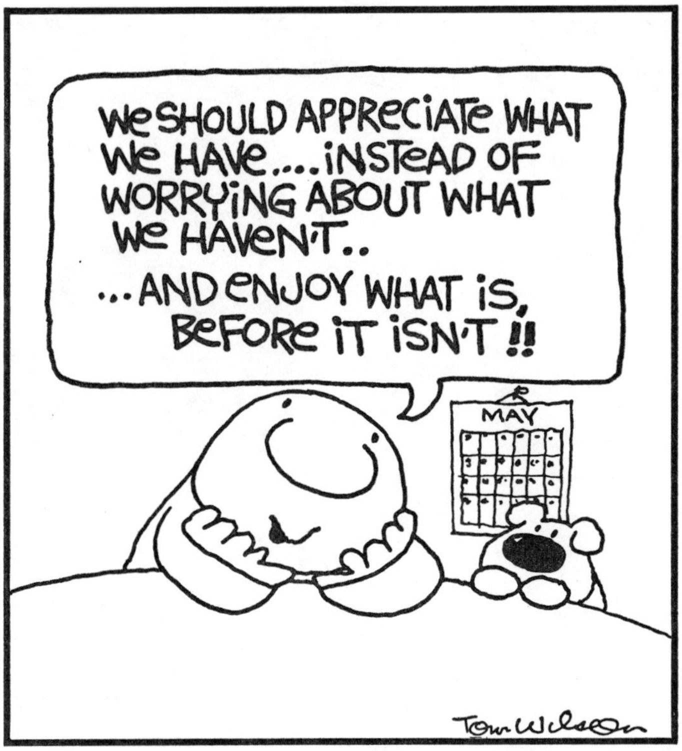
WE SHOULD APPRECIATE WHAT WE HAVE....INSTEAD OF WORRYING ABOUT WHAT WE HAVEN'T..
...AND ENJOY WHAT IS, BEFORE IT ISN'T !!
MAY
Tom Wilson

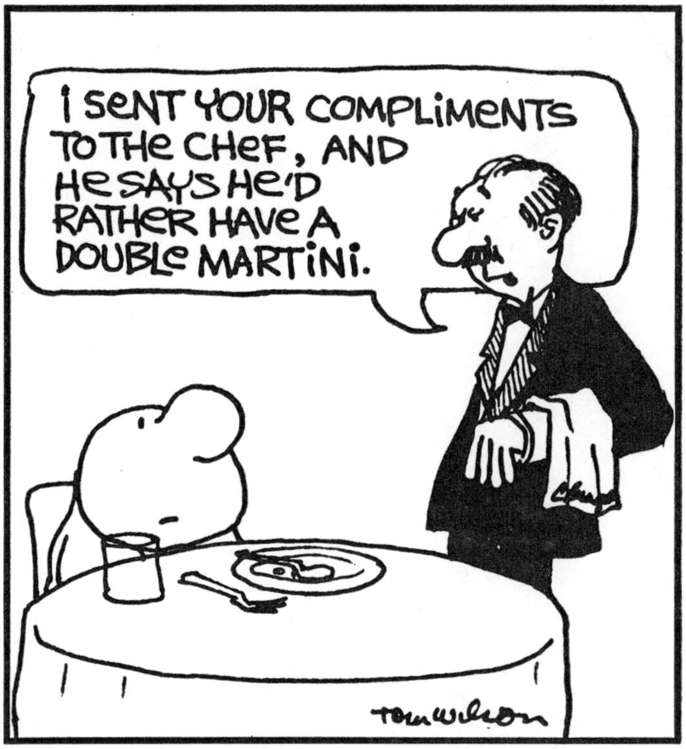
I SENT YOUR COMPLIMENTS TO THE CHEF, AND HE SAYS HE'D RATHER HAVE A DOUBLE MARTINI.
Tom Wilson

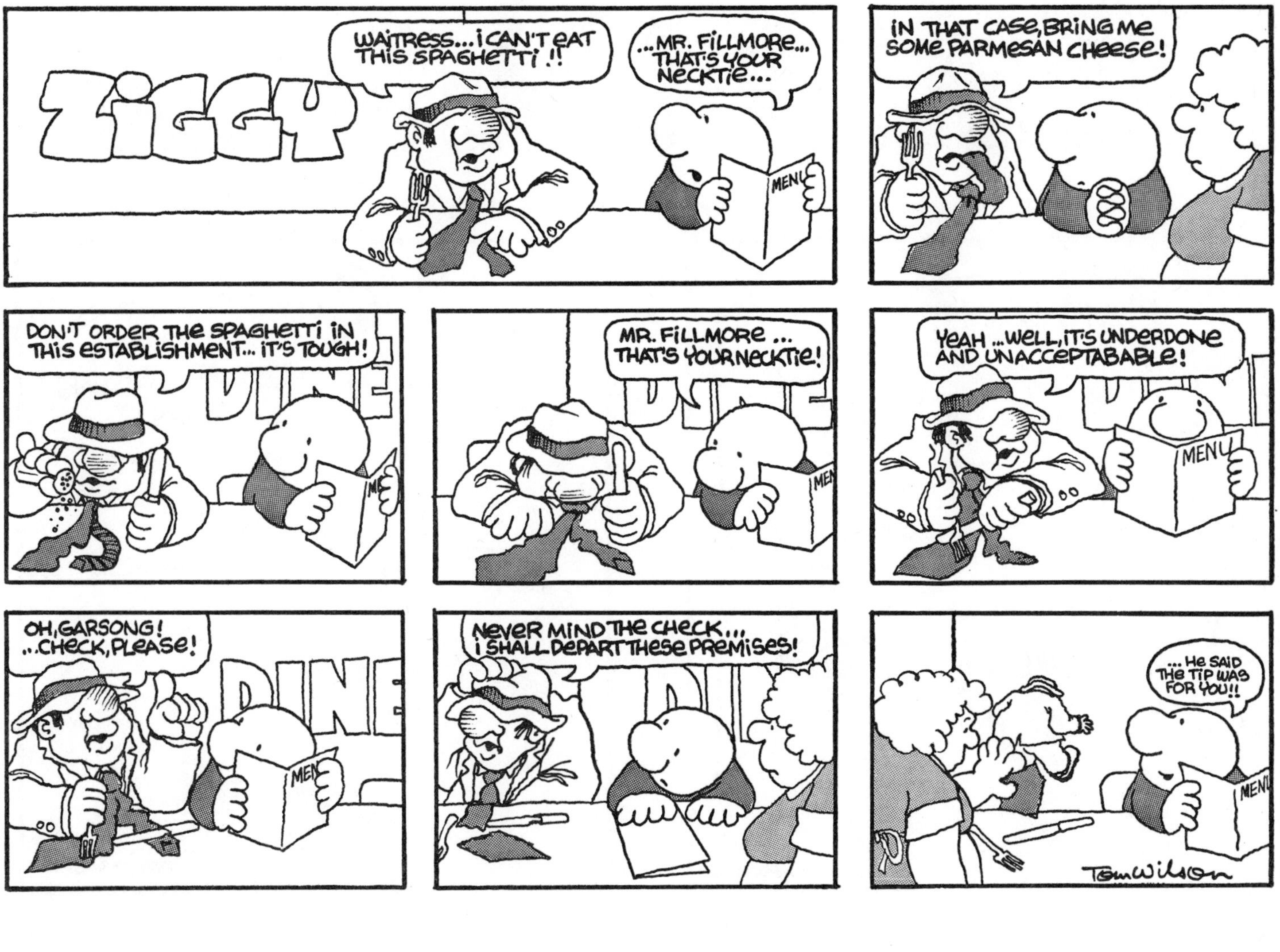
ZIGGY
WAITRESS...I CAN'T EAT THIS SPAGHETTI !!
...MR. FILLMORE... THAT'S YOUR NECKTIE...
MENU
IN THAT CASE, BRING ME SOME PARMESAN CHEESE!
DON'T ORDER THE SPAGHETTI IN THIS ESTABLISHMENT... IT'S TOUGH!
DINE
MR. FILLMORE ... THAT'S YOUR NECKTIE!
YEAH ...WELL, IT'S UNDERDONE AND UNACCEPTABABLE!
MENU
OH, GARSONG! ..CHECK, PLEASE!
DINE
NEVER MIND THE CHECK... I SHALL DEPART THESE PREMISES!
... HE SAID THE TIP WAS FOR YOU!!
MENU
Tom Wilson

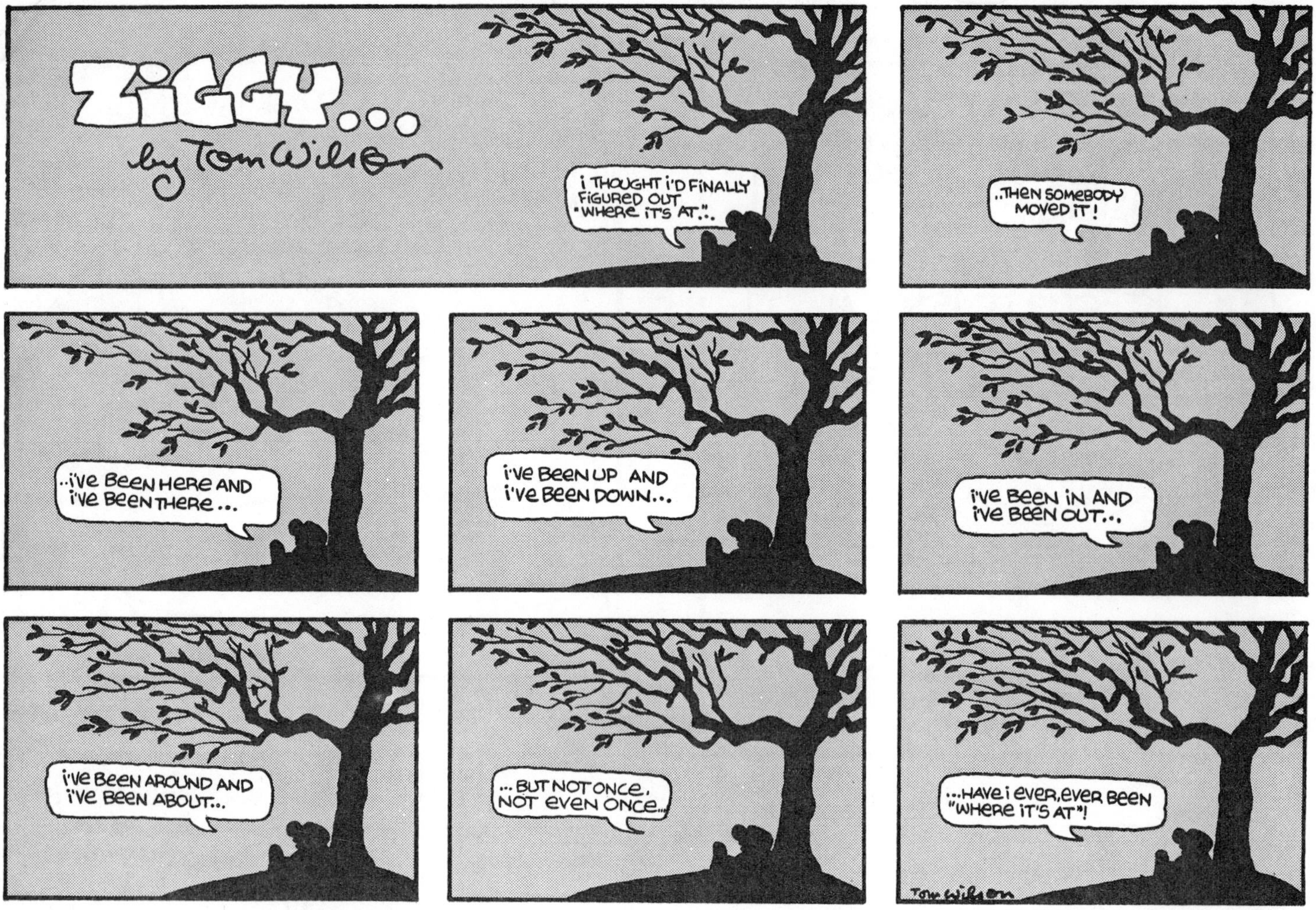
ZIGGY...
by Tom Wilson
i THOUGHT i'D FINALLY FIGURED OUT "WHERE iT'S AT."..
..THEN SOMEBODY MOVED iT!
..i've BEEN HERE AND i've BEEN THERE...
i've BEEN UP AND i've BEEN DOWN...
i've BEEN iN AND i've BEEN OUT...
i've BEEN AROUND AND i've BEEN ABOUT...
...BUT NOT ONCE, NOT EVEN ONCE...
...HAVE i EVER, EVER BEEN "WHERE iT'S AT"!
Tom Wilson

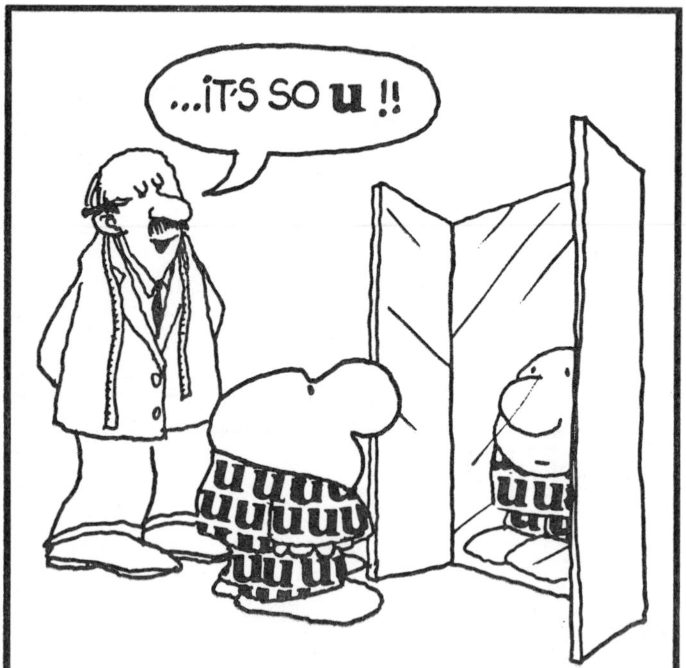
...iT'S SO u !!
Tom Wilson

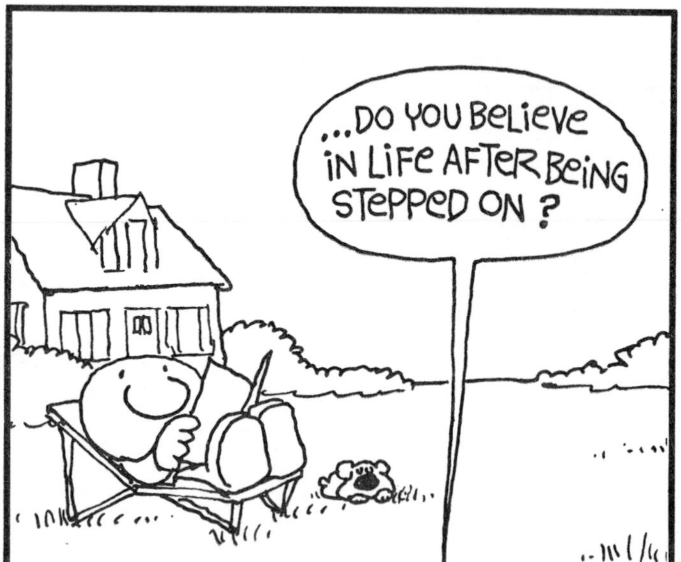
...DO YOU BELIEVE iN LIFE AFTER BEiNG STEPPED ON ?
Tom Wilson

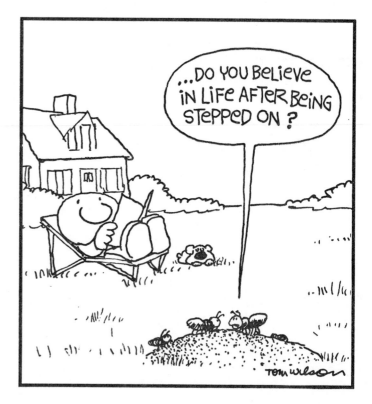

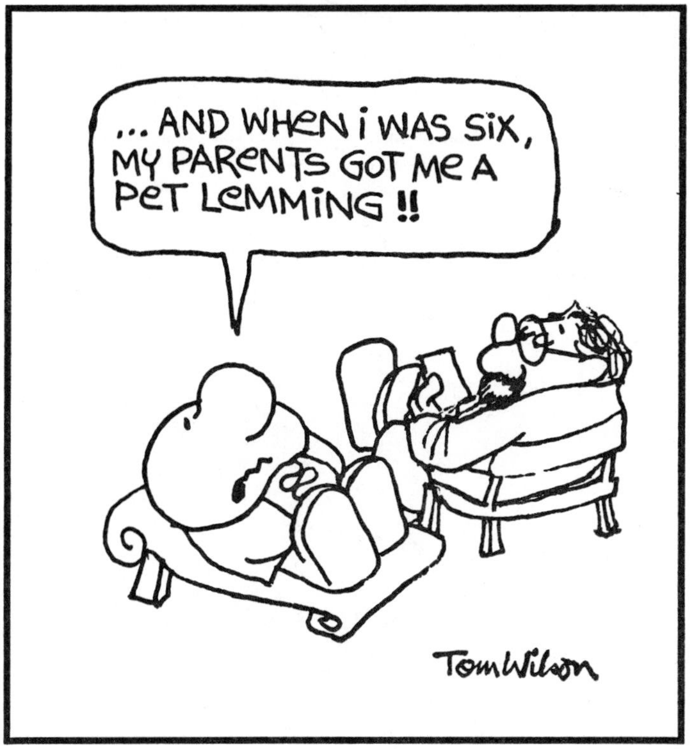

...AND WHEN i WAS SIX, MY PARENTS GOT ME A PET LEMMING !!
Tom Wilson

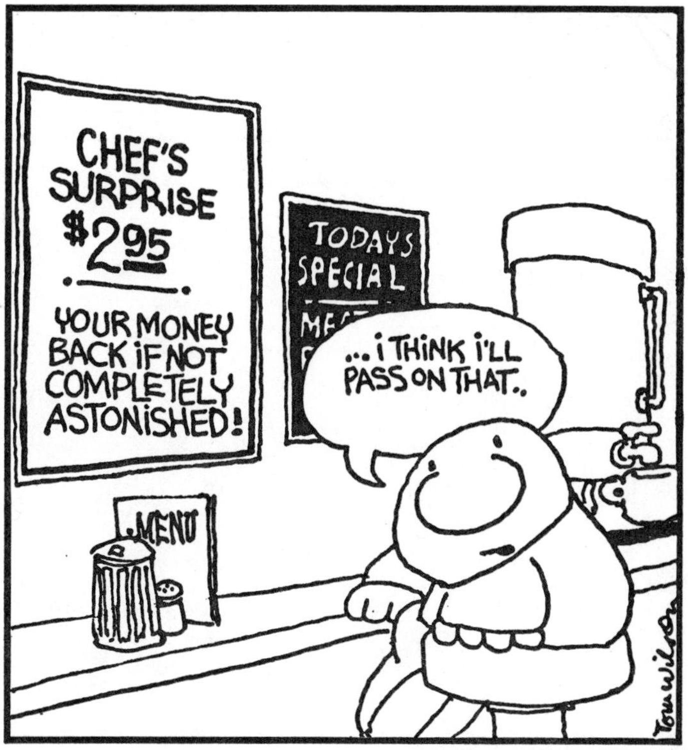

CHEF'S SURPRISE $2.95
YOUR MONEY BACK IF NOT COMPLETELY ASTONISHED!
TODAYS SPECIAL
MENU
...i THINK i'LL PASS ON THAT..
Tom Wilson

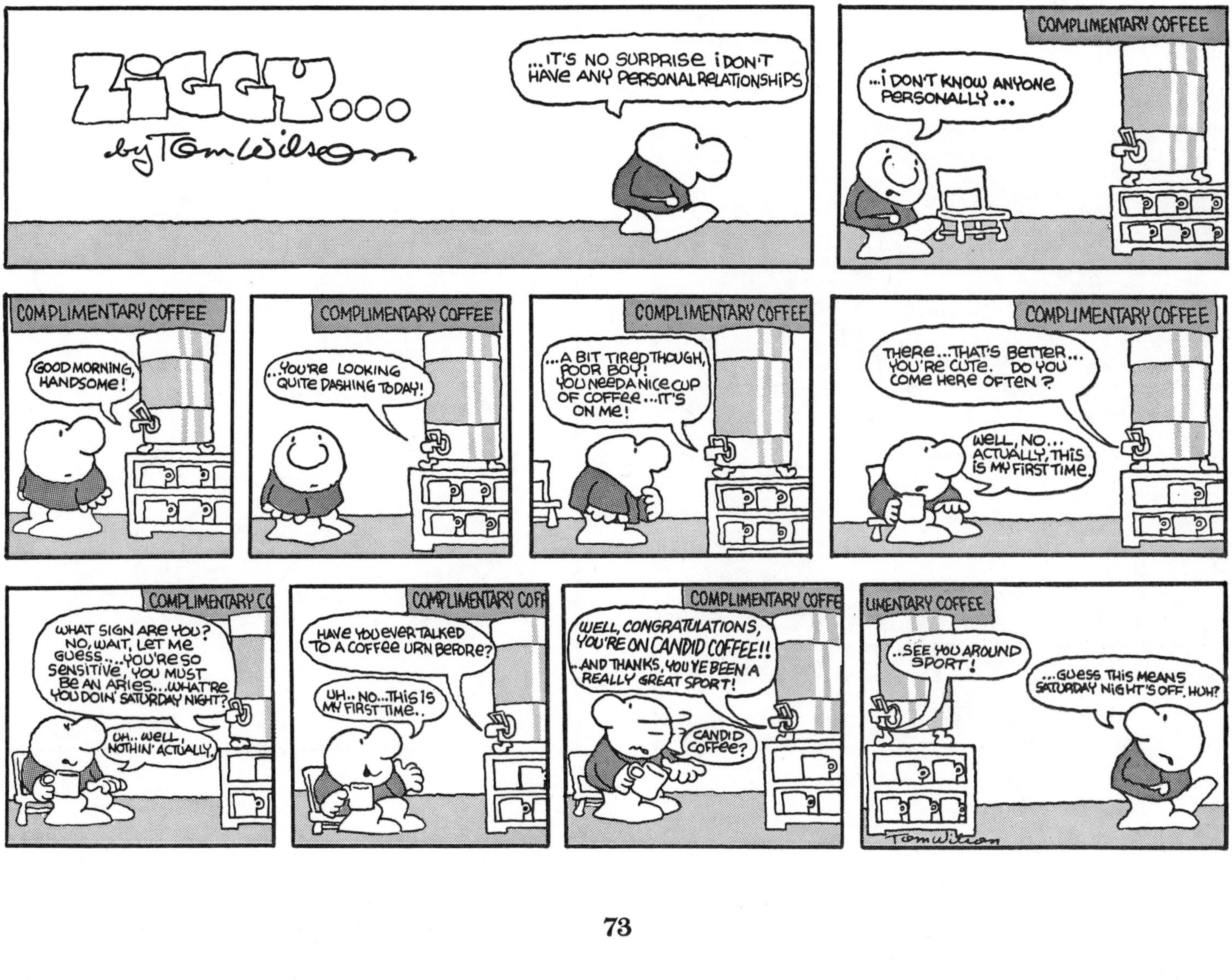

ZIGGY...
by Tom Wilson
...IT'S NO SURPRISE i DON'T HAVE ANY PERSONAL RELATIONSHIPS
COMPLIMENTARY COFFEE
...i DON'T KNOW ANYONE PERSONALLY...
GOOD MORNING, HANDSOME!
...YOU'RE LOOKING QUITE DASHING TODAY!
...A BIT TIRED THOUGH, POOR BOY! YOU NEED A NICE CUP OF COFFEE...IT'S ON ME!
THERE...THAT'S BETTER... YOU'RE CUTE. DO YOU COME HERE OFTEN ?
WELL, NO... ACTUALLY, THIS IS MY FIRST TIME.
WHAT SIGN ARE YOU? NO, WAIT, LET ME GUESS...YOU'RE SO SENSITIVE, YOU MUST BE AN ARIES...WHAT'RE YOU DOIN' SATURDAY NIGHT?
UH.. WELL, NOTHIN' ACTUALLY.
HAVE YOU EVER TALKED TO A COFFEE URN BEFORE?
UH.. NO...THIS IS MY FIRST TIME..
WELL, CONGRATULATIONS, YOU'RE ON CANDID COFFEE!! ...AND THANKS, YOU'VE BEEN A REALLY GREAT SPORT!
CANDID COFFEE?
...SEE YOU AROUND SPORT!
...GUESS THIS MEANS SATURDAY NIGHT'S OFF, HUH?
Tom Wilson

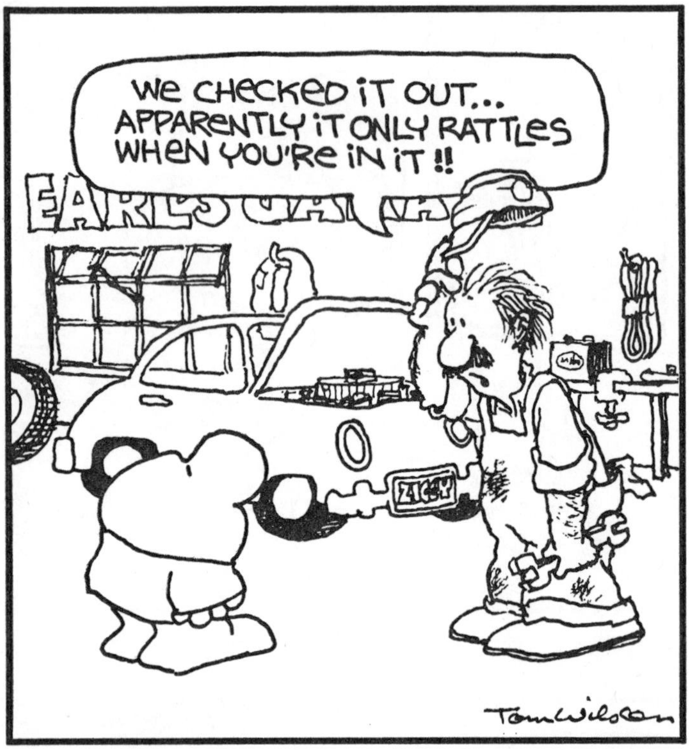
WE CHECKED IT OUT... APPARENTLY IT ONLY RATTLES WHEN YOU'RE IN IT !!
Tom Wilson

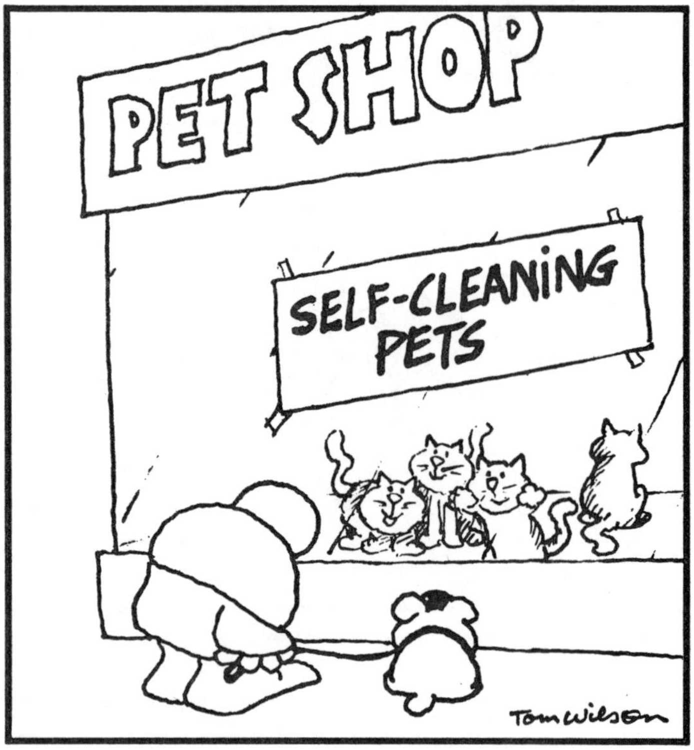
PET SHOP
SELF-CLEANING PETS
Tom Wilson

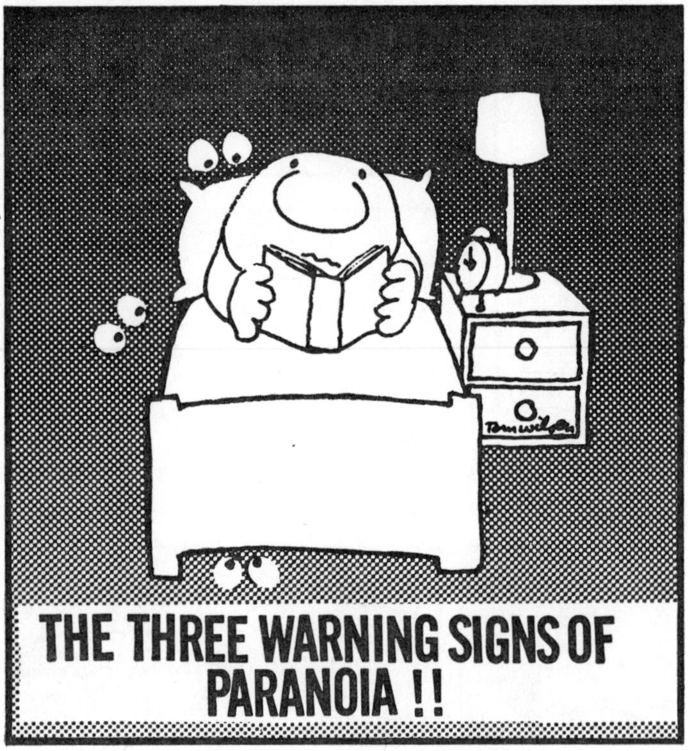
Tom Wilson
THE THREE WARNING SIGNS OF PARANOIA !!

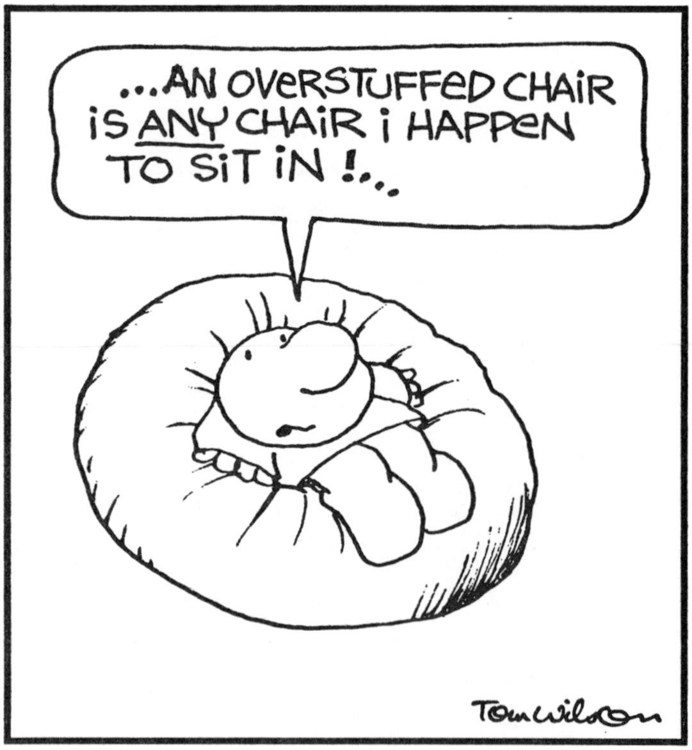
...AN OVERSTUFFED CHAIR IS ANY CHAIR I HAPPEN TO SIT IN !...
Tom Wilson

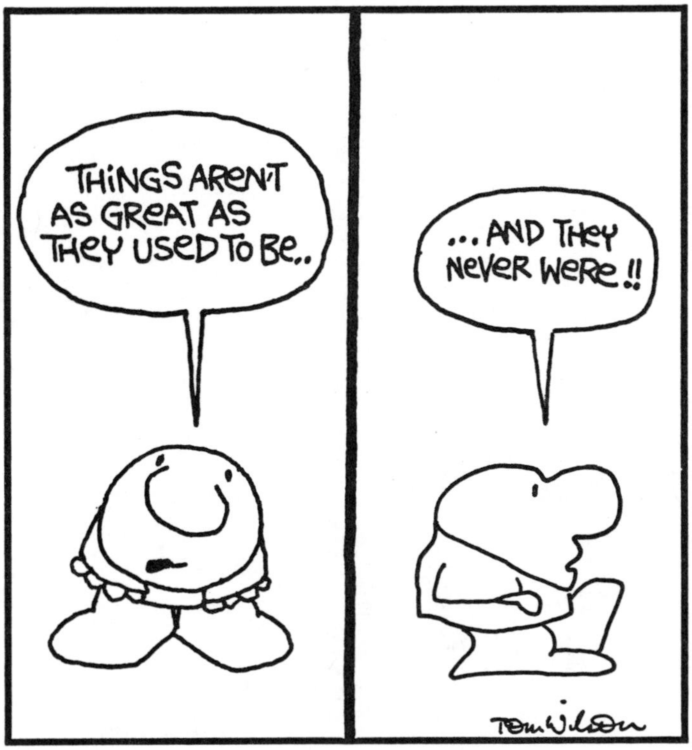
THINGS AREN'T AS GREAT AS THEY USED TO BE..
...AND THEY NEVER WERE!!
Tom Wilson

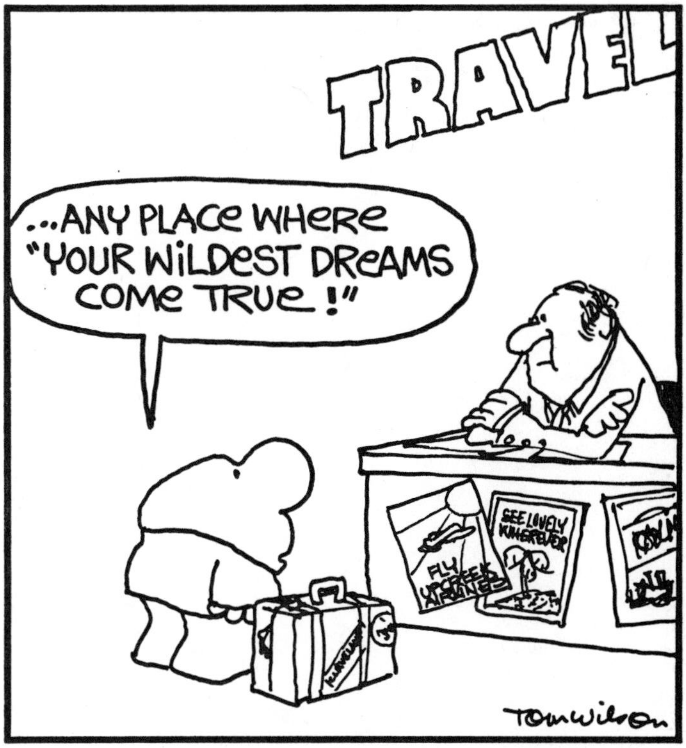
TRAVEL
...ANY PLACE WHERE "YOUR WILDEST DREAMS COME TRUE!"
Tom Wilson

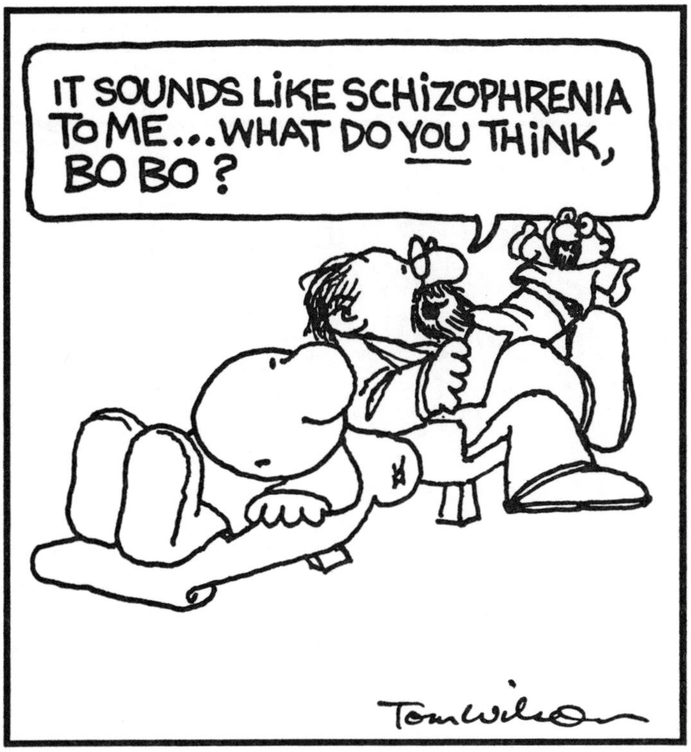
IT SOUNDS LIKE SCHIZOPHRENIA TO ME...WHAT DO YOU THINK, BO BO?
Tom Wilson

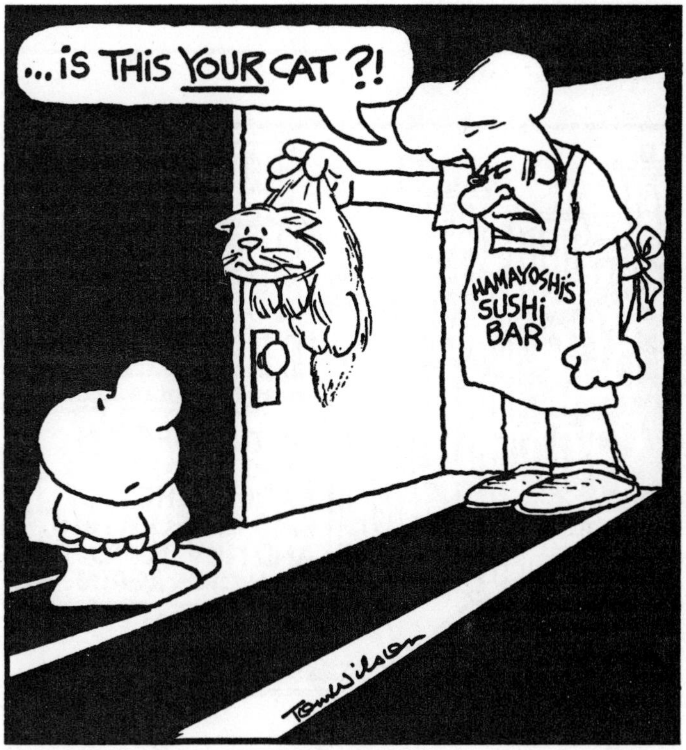
...IS THIS YOUR CAT?!
HAMAYOSHI'S SUSHI BAR
Tom Wilson

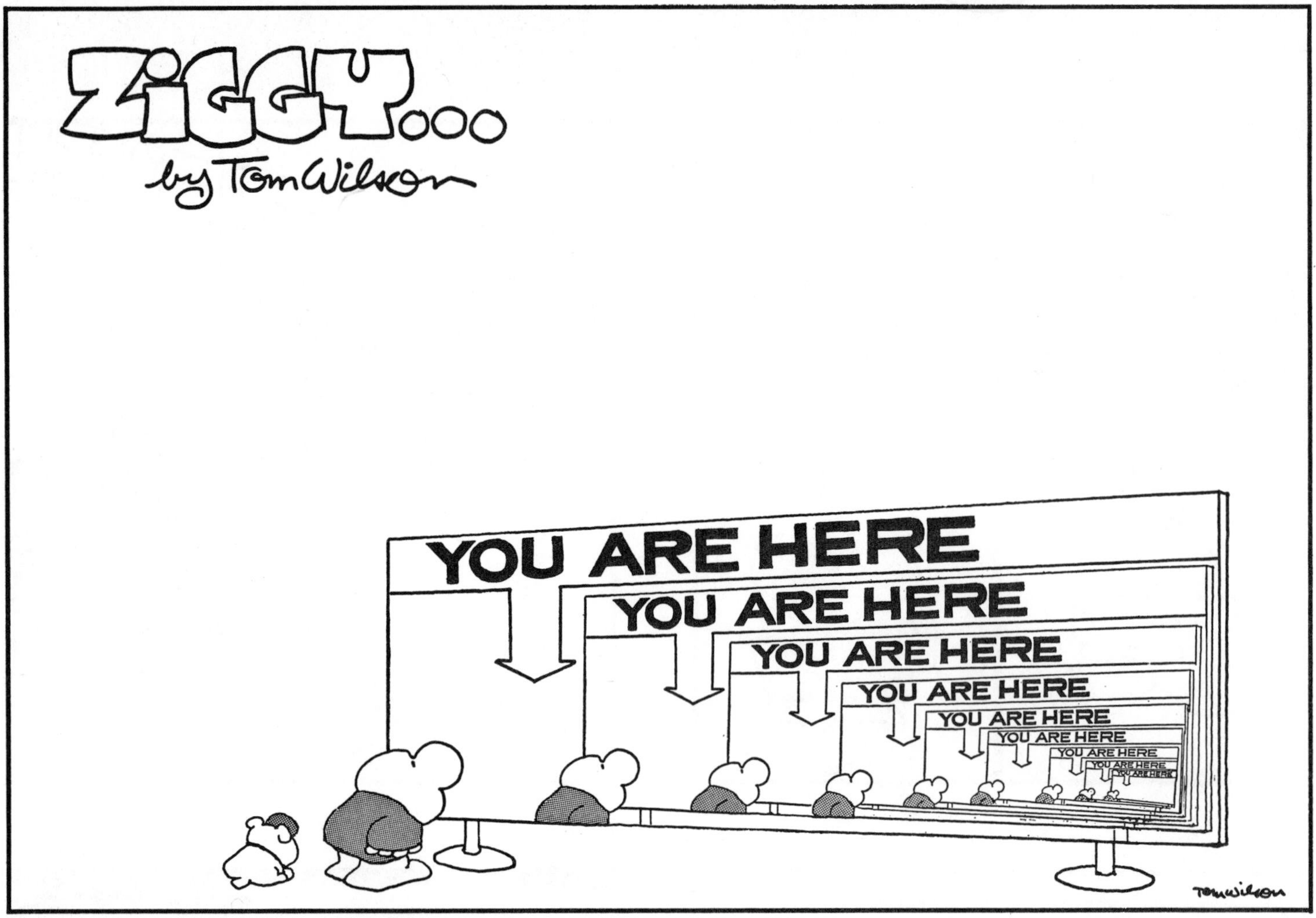
ZIGGY
by Tom Wilson
YOU ARE HERE
YOU ARE HERE
YOU ARE HERE
YOU ARE HERE
YOU ARE HERE
YOU ARE HERE
TOM WILSON

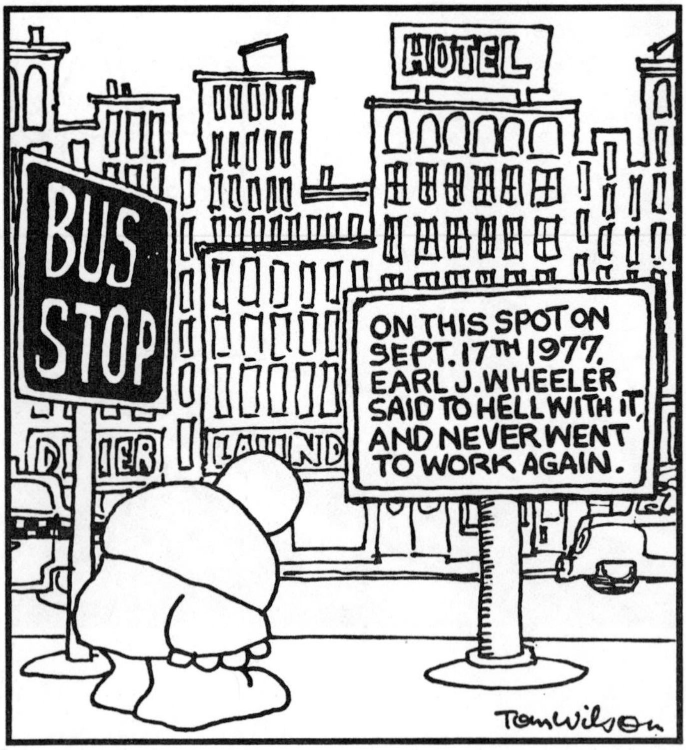
HOTEL
BUS STOP
ON THIS SPOT ON SEPT. 17TH 1977, EARL J. WHEELER SAID TO HELL WITH IT, AND NEVER WENT TO WORK AGAIN.
TOM WILSON

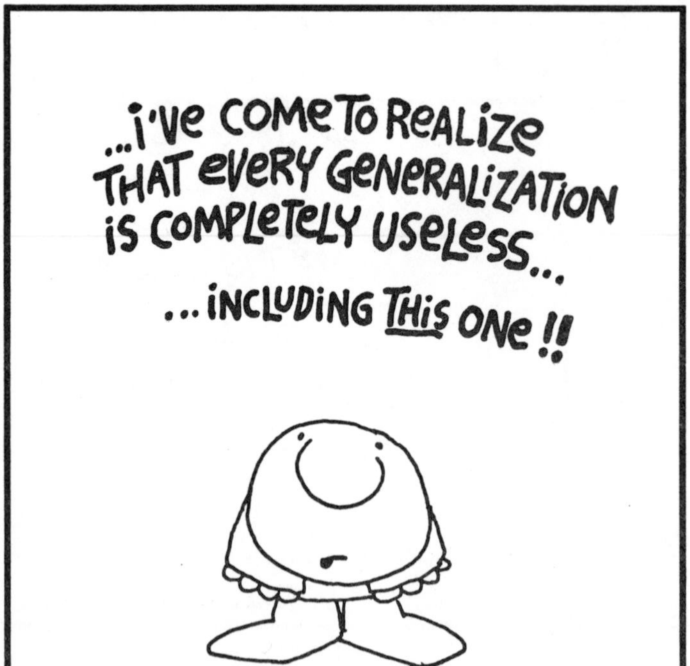
...i've come to realize that every generalization is completely useless...
...including this one!!
Tom Wilson

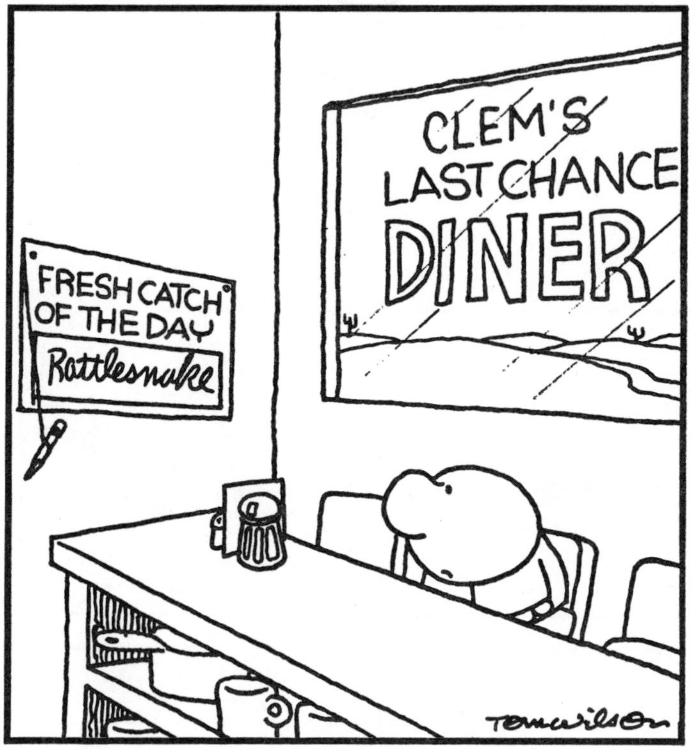
CLEM'S
LAST CHANCE
DINER
FRESH CATCH
OF THE DAY
Rattlesnake
TOM WILSON

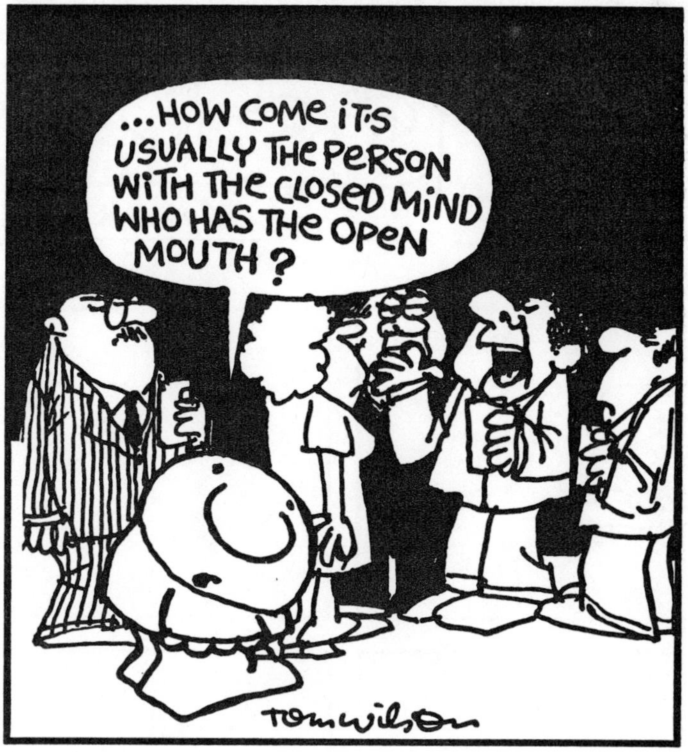
...HOW COME IT'S USUALLY THE PERSON WITH THE CLOSED MIND WHO HAS THE OPEN MOUTH ?
TOM WILSON

ZIGGY...

BY Tom Wilson

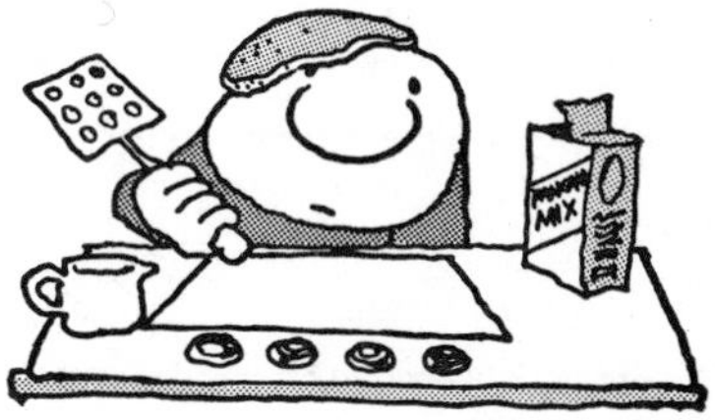

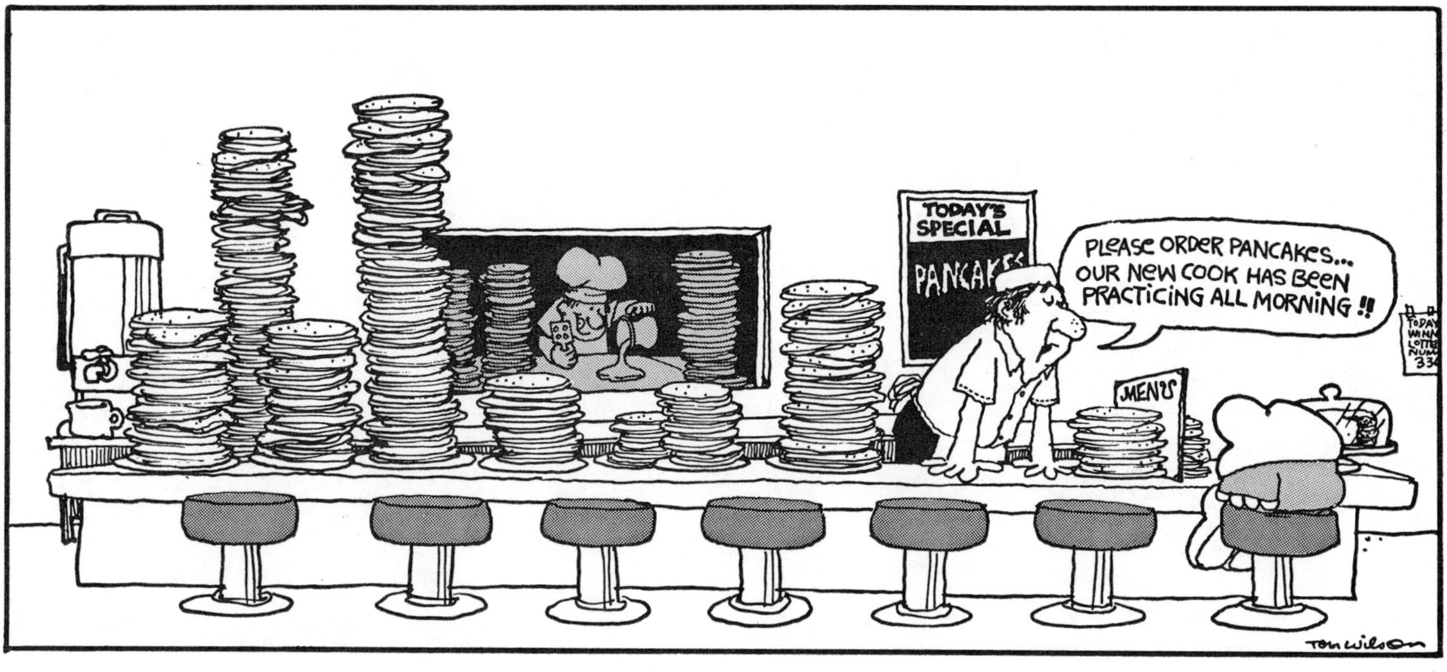
TODAY'S
SPECIAL
PLEASE ORDER PANCAKES... OUR NEW COOK HAS BEEN PRACTICING ALL MORNING !!
TOM WILSON

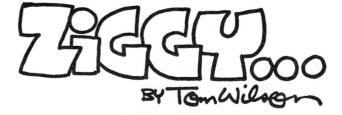

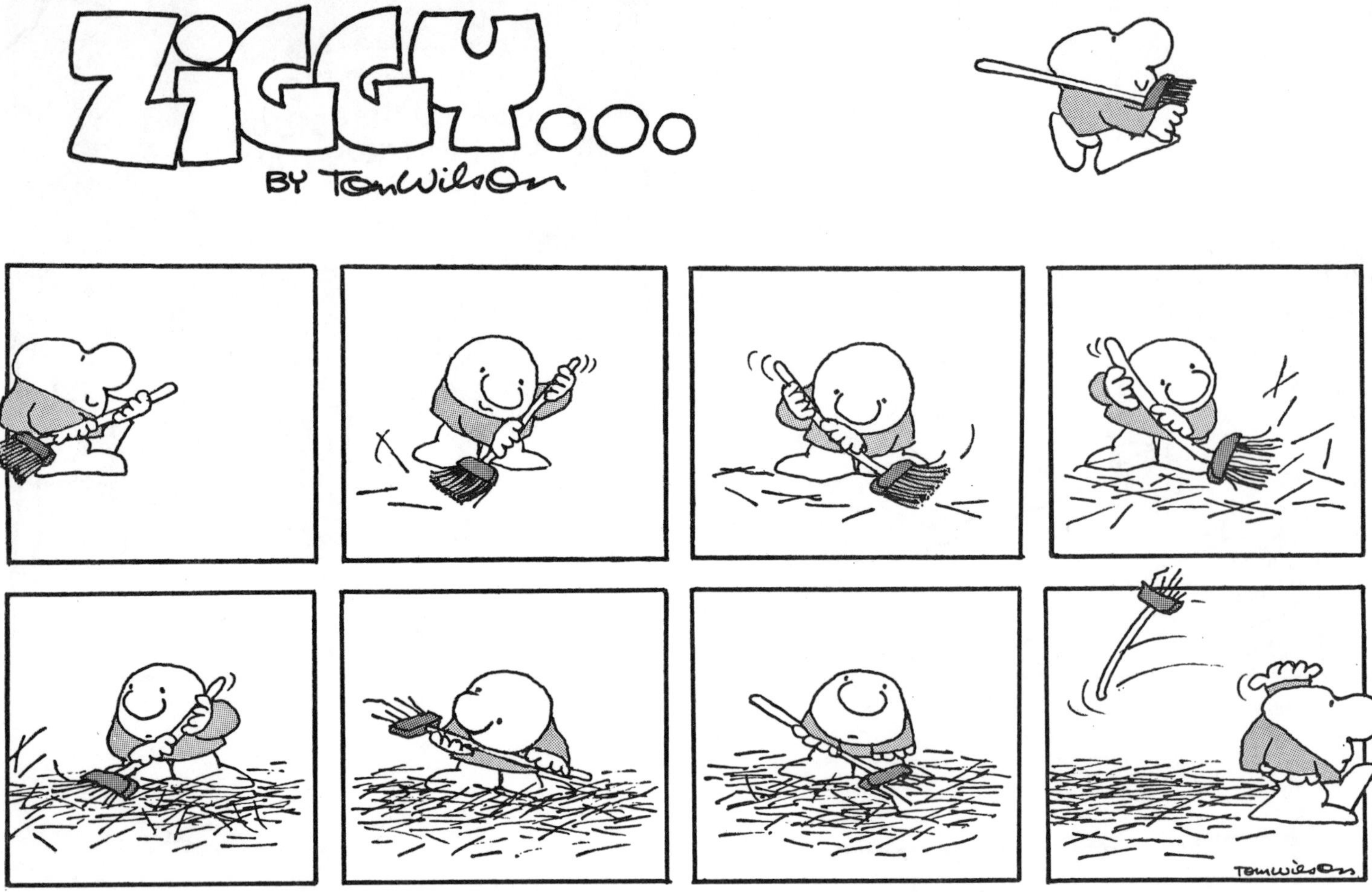
ZIGGY...
BY Tom Wilson
Tom Wilson

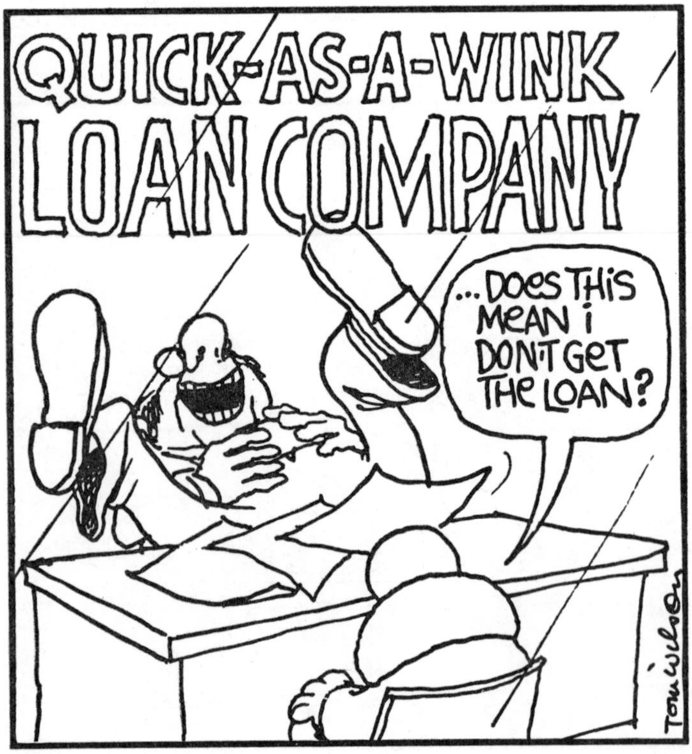
QUICK-AS-A-WINK
LOAN COMPANY
...DOES THIS MEAN i DON'T GET THE LOAN?
Tom Wilson

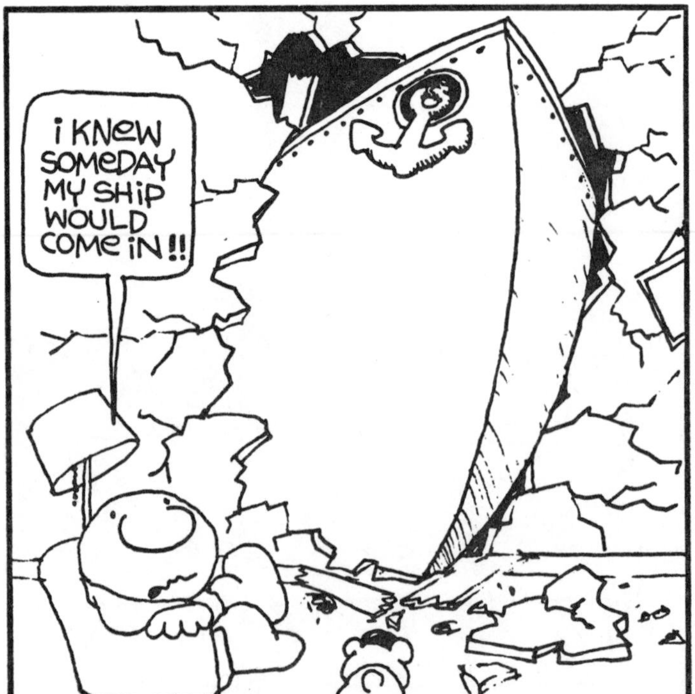
i KNEW SOMEDAY MY SHiP WOULD COME iN!!
Tom Wilson

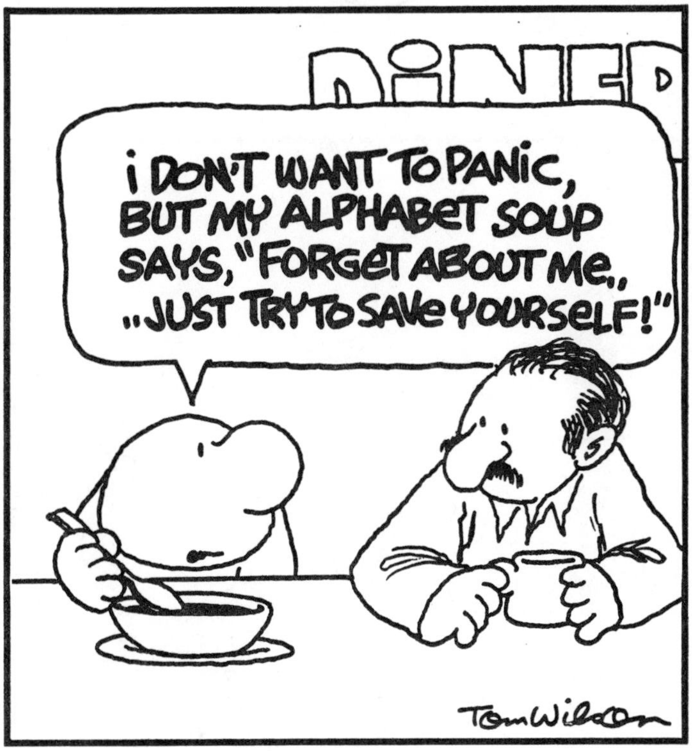
DiNER
i DON'T WANT TO PANIC, BUT MY ALPHABET SOUP SAYS, "FORGET ABOUT ME.. ..JUST TRY TO SAVE YOURSELF!"
TOM WILSON

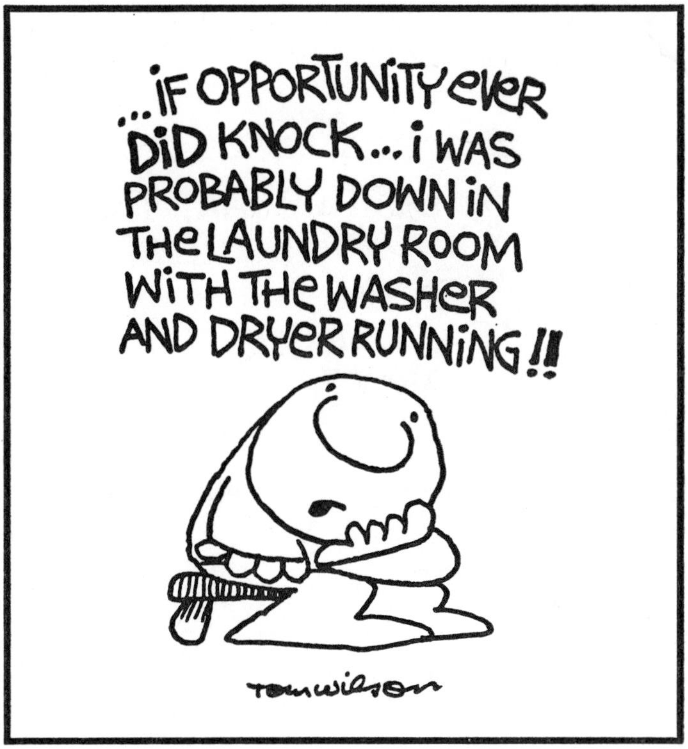
...iF OPPORTUNITY EVER DiD KNOCK... i WAS PROBABLY DOWN iN THE LAUNDRY ROOM WiTH THE WASHER AND DRYER RUNNiNG !!
TOM WILSON

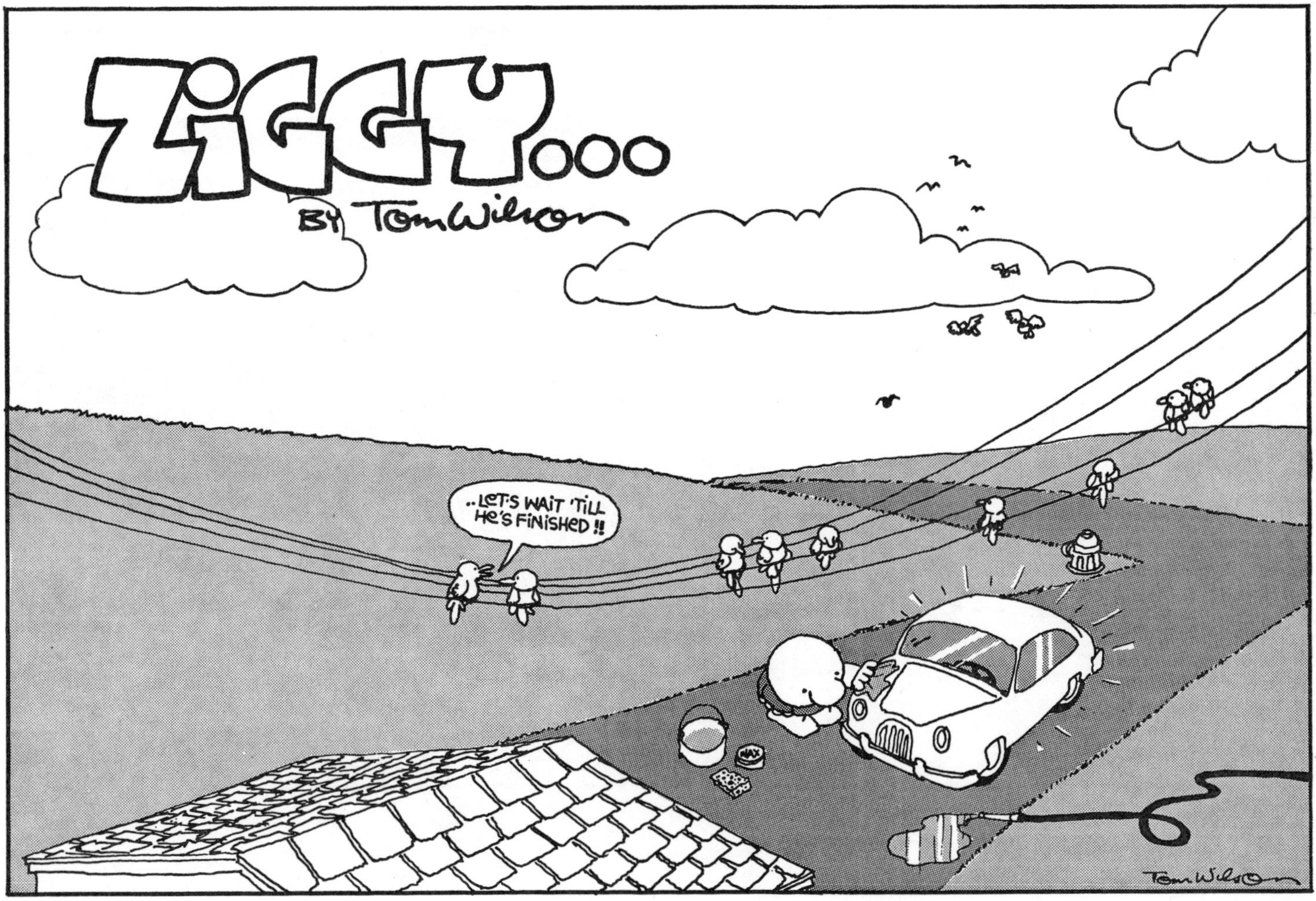
ZiGGY...
BY TOM WILSON
..LET'S WAIT 'TILL HE'S FINISHED !!
WAX
TOM WILSON

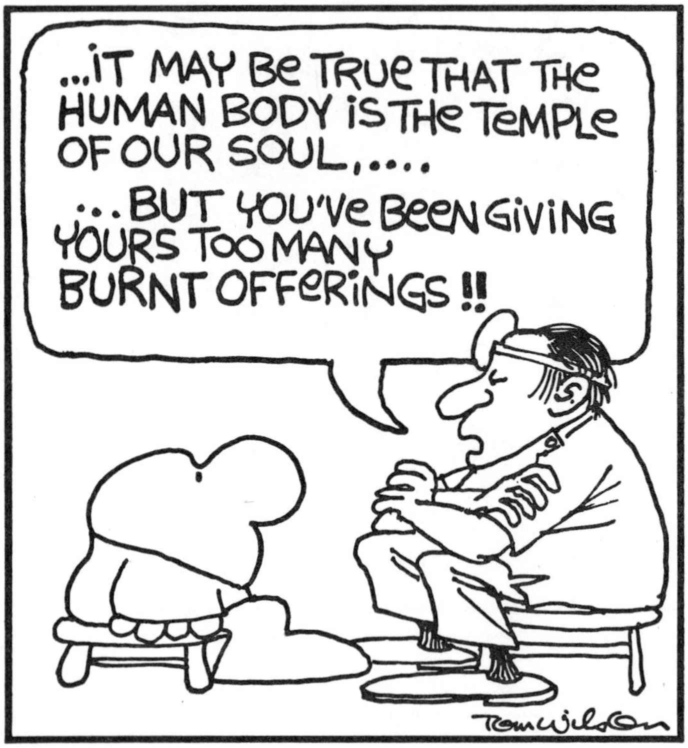
...IT MAY BE TRUE THAT THE HUMAN BODY IS THE TEMPLE OF OUR SOUL,....
...BUT YOU'VE BEEN GIVING YOURS TOO MANY BURNT OFFERINGS !!

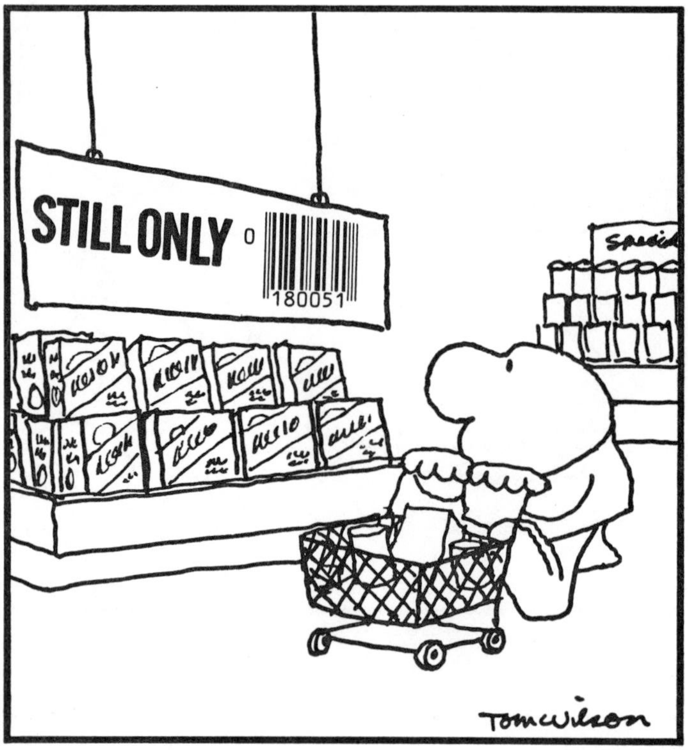
STILL ONLY
180051

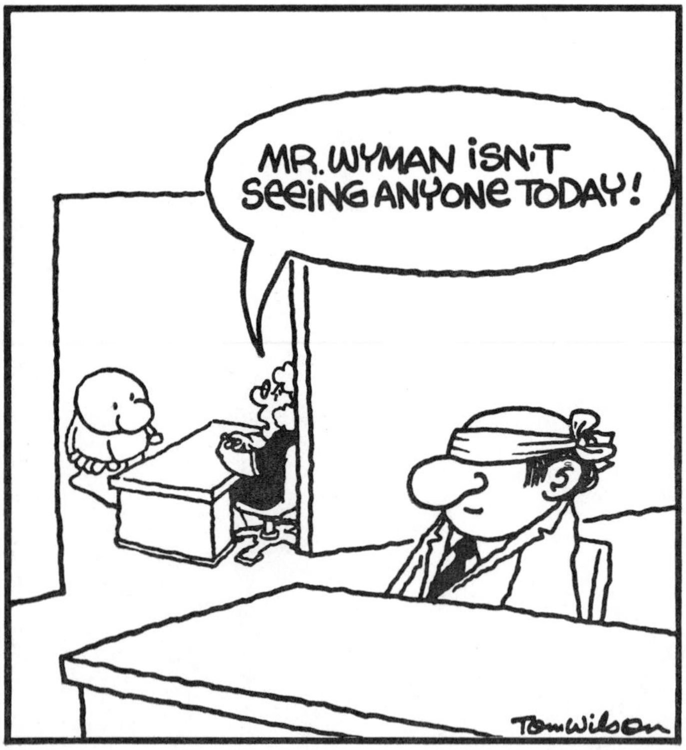
MR. WYMAN ISN'T SEEING ANYONE TODAY!

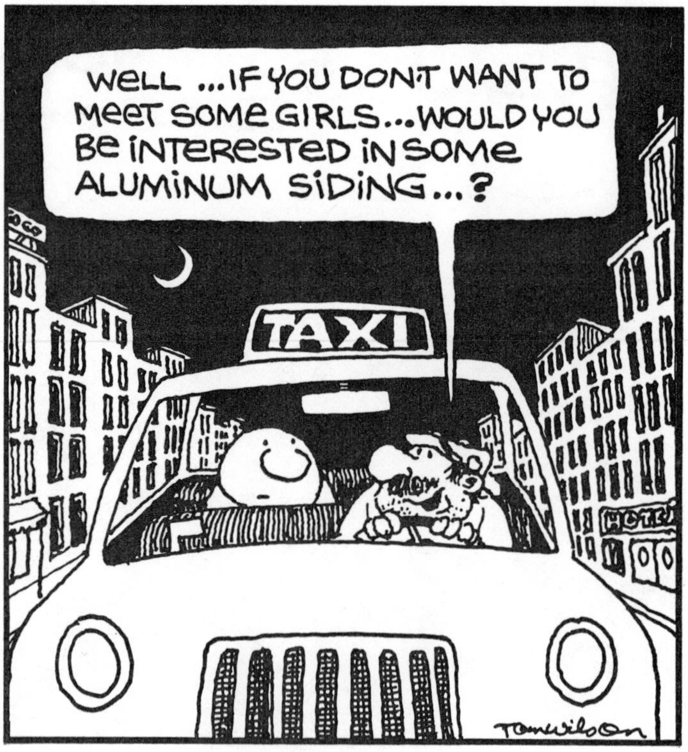
WELL ...IF YOU DON'T WANT TO MEET SOME GIRLS...WOULD YOU BE INTERESTED IN SOME ALUMINUM SIDING...?
TAXI

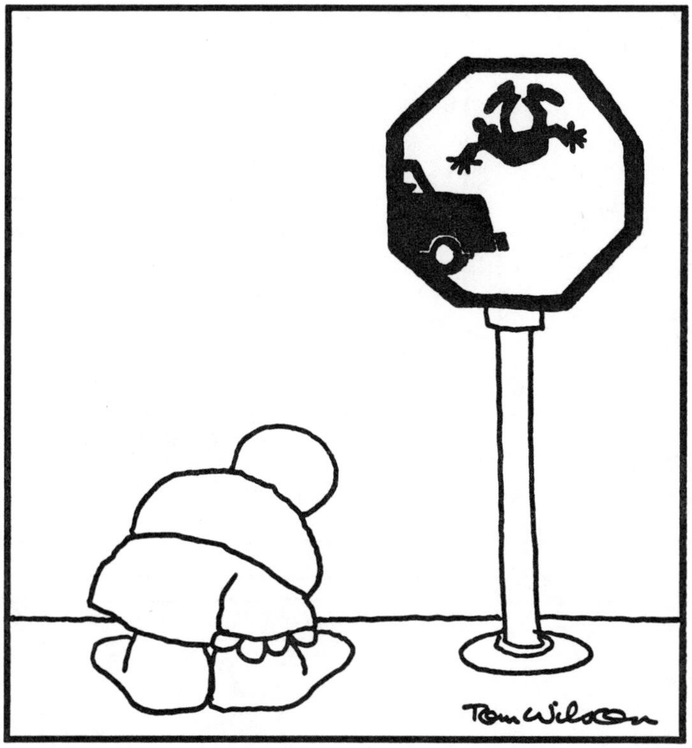
Tom Wilson

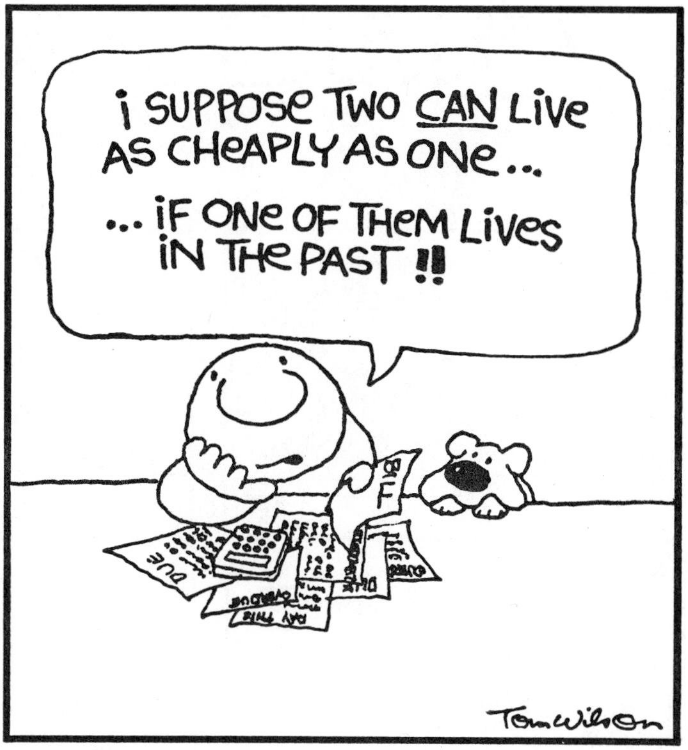
i SUPPOSE TWO CAN LiVe AS CHeAPLY AS ONe...
... iF ONe OF THeM LiVeS iN THe PAST !!
BILL
Tom Wilson

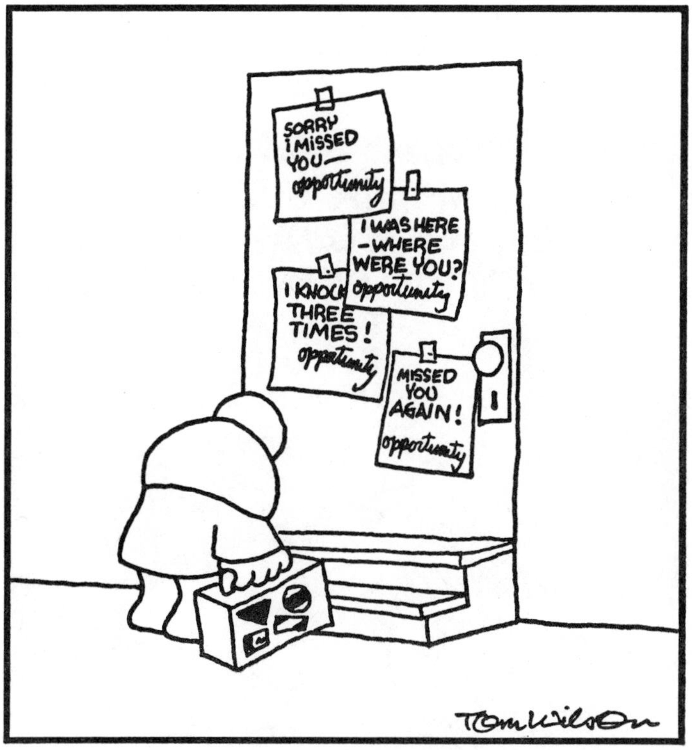
SORRY I MISSED YOU— opportunity
I WAS HERE —WHERE WERE YOU? opportunity
I KNOCK THREE TIMES! opportunity
MISSED YOU AGAIN! opportunity
Tom Wilson

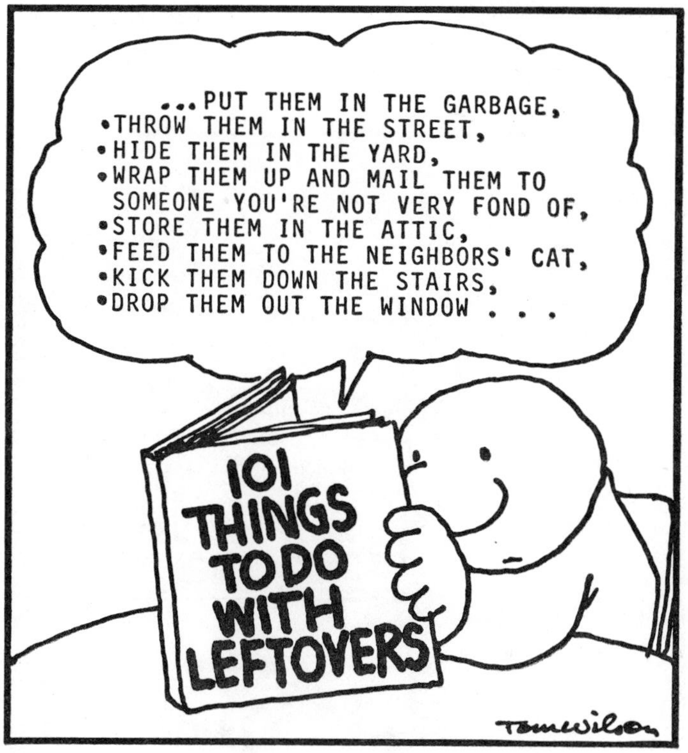
...PUT THEM IN THE GARBAGE,
•THROW THEM IN THE STREET,
•HIDE THEM IN THE YARD,
•WRAP THEM UP AND MAIL THEM TO SOMEONE YOU'RE NOT VERY FOND OF,
•STORE THEM IN THE ATTIC,
•FEED THEM TO THE NEIGHBORS' CAT,
•KICK THEM DOWN THE STAIRS,
•DROP THEM OUT THE WINDOW . . .
101 THINGS TO DO WITH LEFTOVERS
Tom Wilson

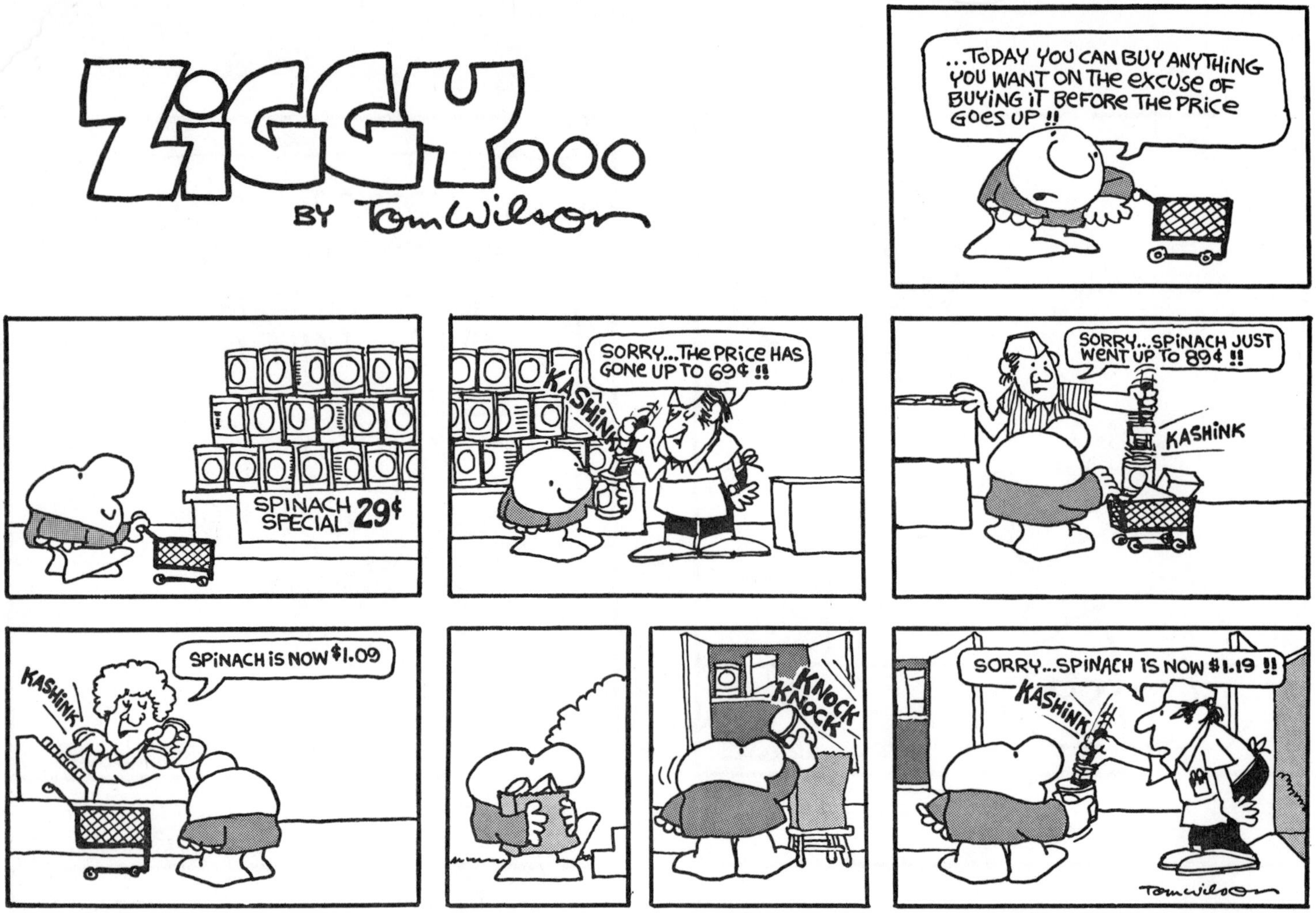

ZIGGY
BY Tom Wilson
...TODAY YOU CAN BUY ANYTHING YOU WANT ON THE EXCUSE OF BUYING IT BEFORE THE PRICE GOES UP !!
SPINACH SPECIAL 29¢
SORRY...THE PRICE HAS GONE UP TO 69¢ !!
KASHINK
SORRY...SPINACH JUST WENT UP TO 89¢ !!
KASHINK
SPINACH IS NOW $1.09
KASHINK
KNOCK KNOCK
SORRY...SPINACH IS NOW $1.19 !!
KASHINK
Tom Wilson

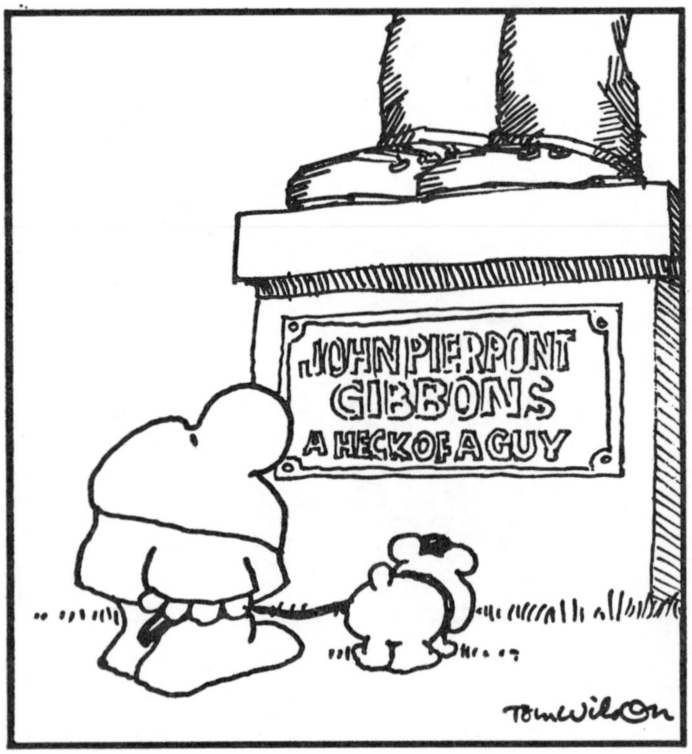

JOHN PIERPONT GIBBONS A HECK OF A GUY
Tom Wilson

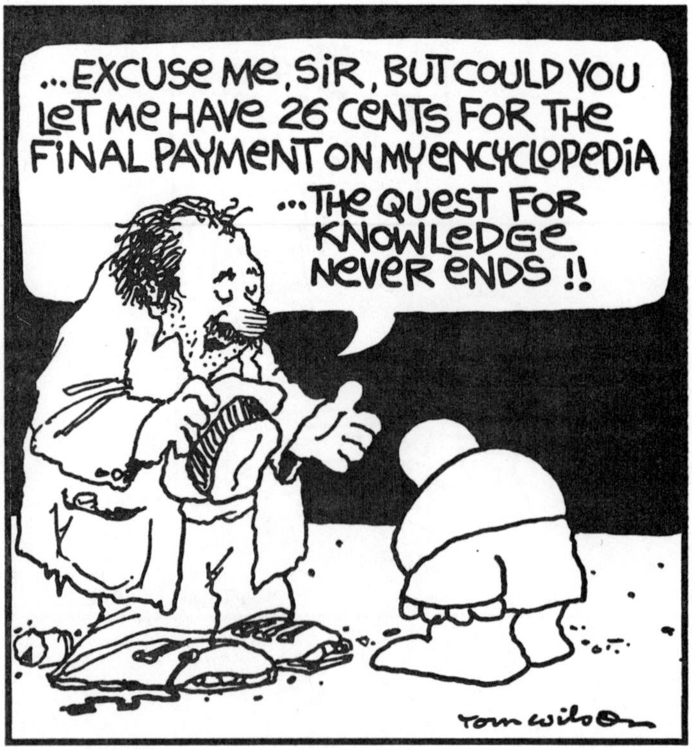

...EXCUSE ME, SIR, BUT COULD YOU LET ME HAVE 26 CENTS FOR THE FINAL PAYMENT ON MY ENCYCLOPEDIA ...THE QUEST FOR KNOWLEDGE NEVER ENDS !!
Tom Wilson

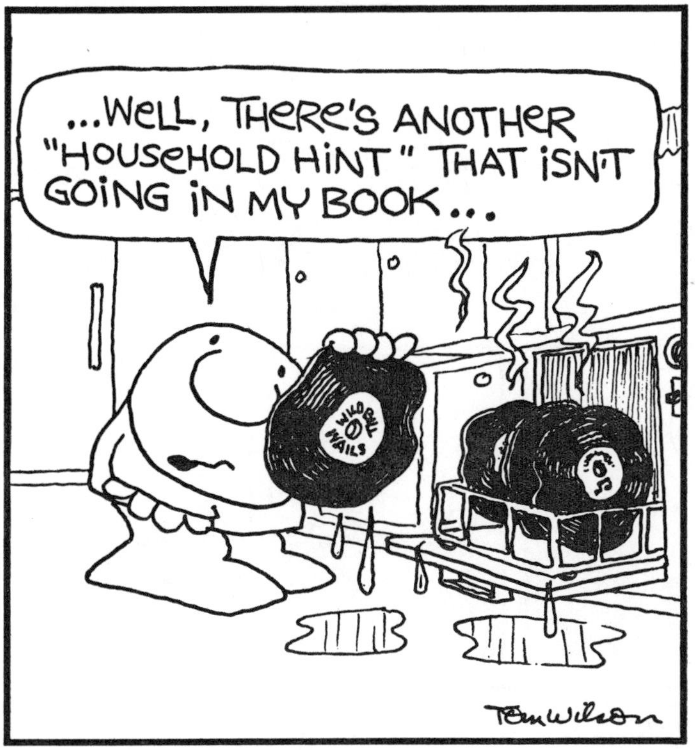
...WELL, THERE'S ANOTHER "HOUSEHOLD HINT" THAT ISN'T GOING IN MY BOOK...
WILD BILL WAILS
TOM WILSON

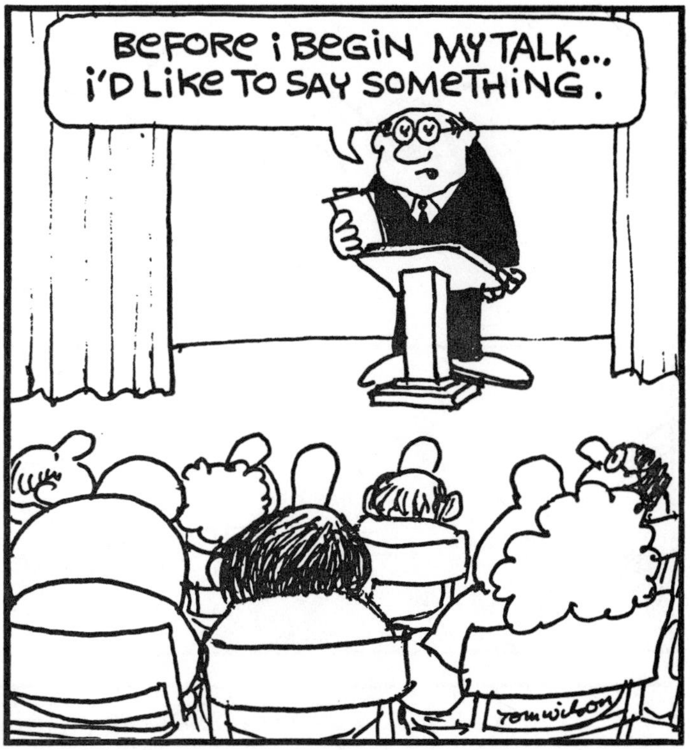
BEFORE I BEGIN MY TALK... I'D LIKE TO SAY SOMETHING.
TOM WILSON

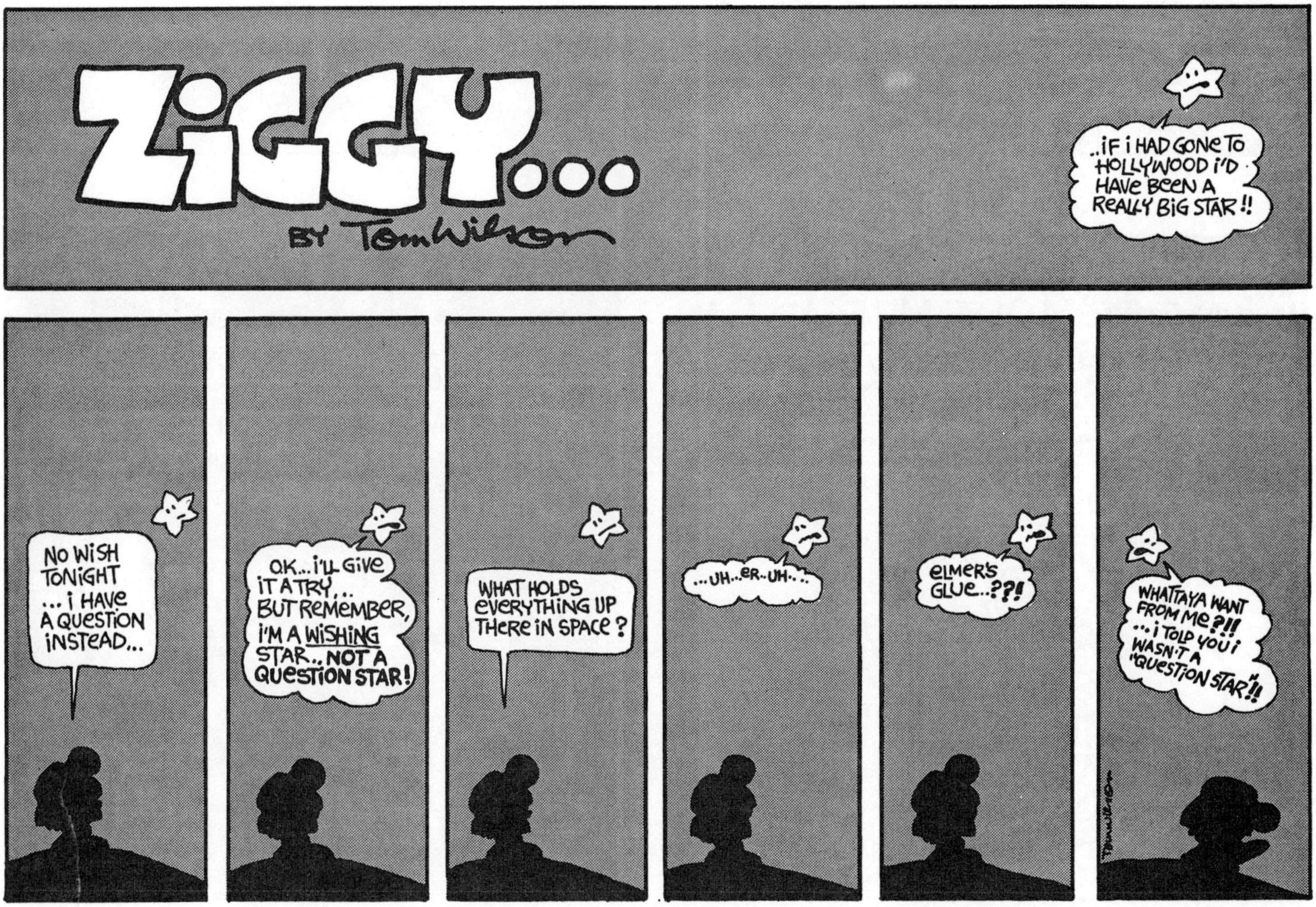
ZIGGY...
BY TOM WILSON
..IF I HAD GONE TO HOLLYWOOD I'D HAVE BEEN A REALLY BIG STAR!!
NO WISH TONIGHT ...I HAVE A QUESTION INSTEAD...
O.K... I'LL GIVE IT A TRY... BUT REMEMBER, I'M A WISHING STAR.. NOT A QUESTION STAR!
WHAT HOLDS EVERYTHING UP THERE IN SPACE?
...UH..ER..UH...
ELMER'S GLUE..??!
WHATTAYA WANT FROM ME?!! ...I TOLD YOU I WASN'T A "QUESTION STAR"!!
TOM WILSON

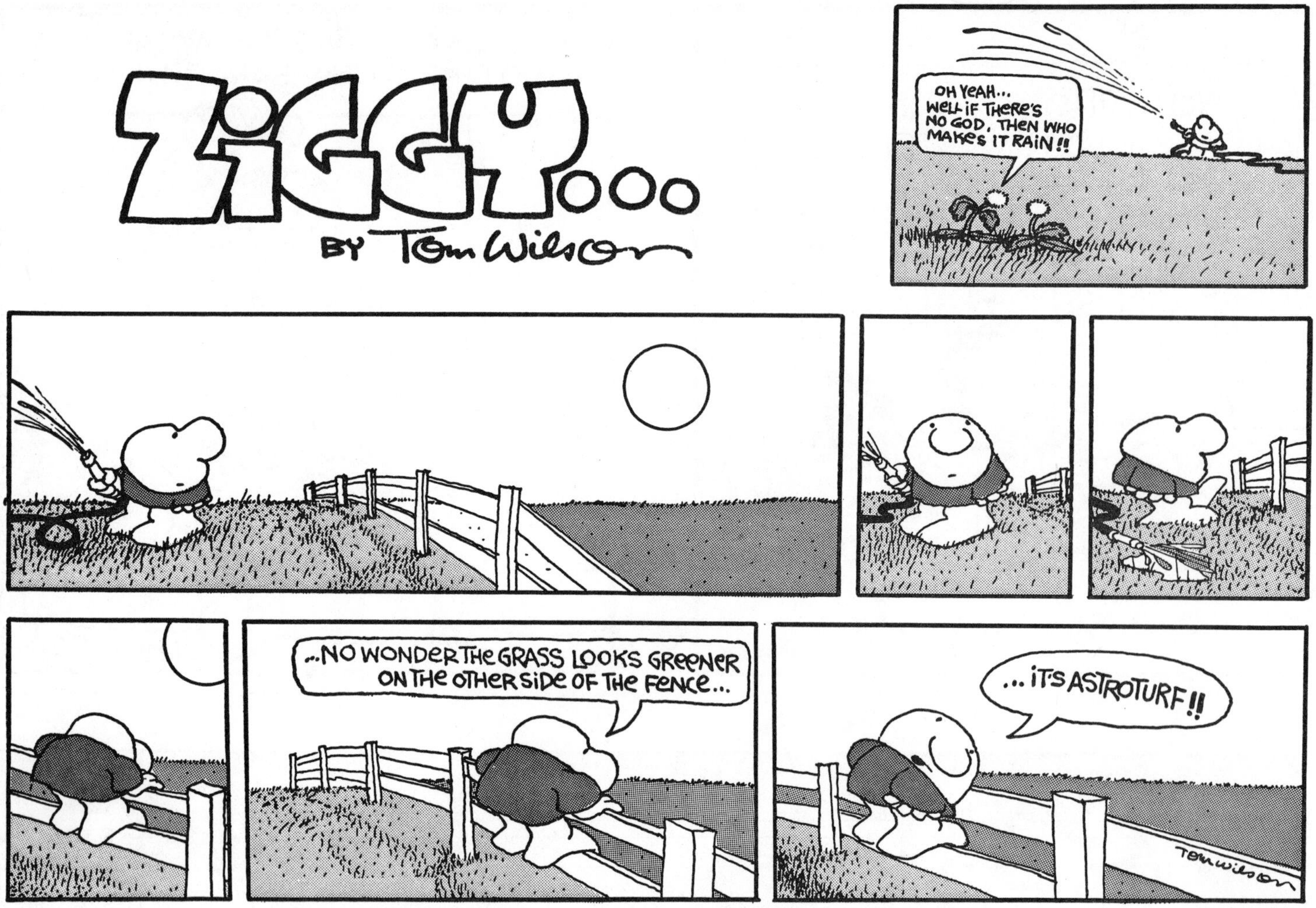
ZiGGY
BY Tom Wilson
OH YEAH... WELL IF THERE'S NO GOD, THEN WHO MAKES IT RAIN!!
...NO WONDER THE GRASS LOOKS GREENER ON THE OTHER SIDE OF THE FENCE...
...iT'S ASTROTURF!!
Tom Wilson

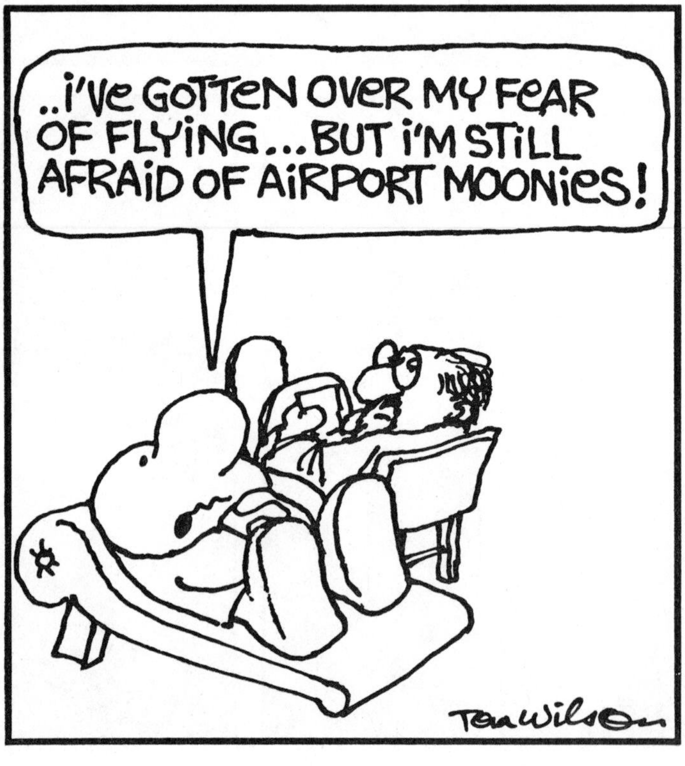
..i've GOTTEN OVER MY FEAR OF FLYiNG...BUT i'M STiLL AFRAiD OF AiRPORT MOONieS!
Tom Wilson

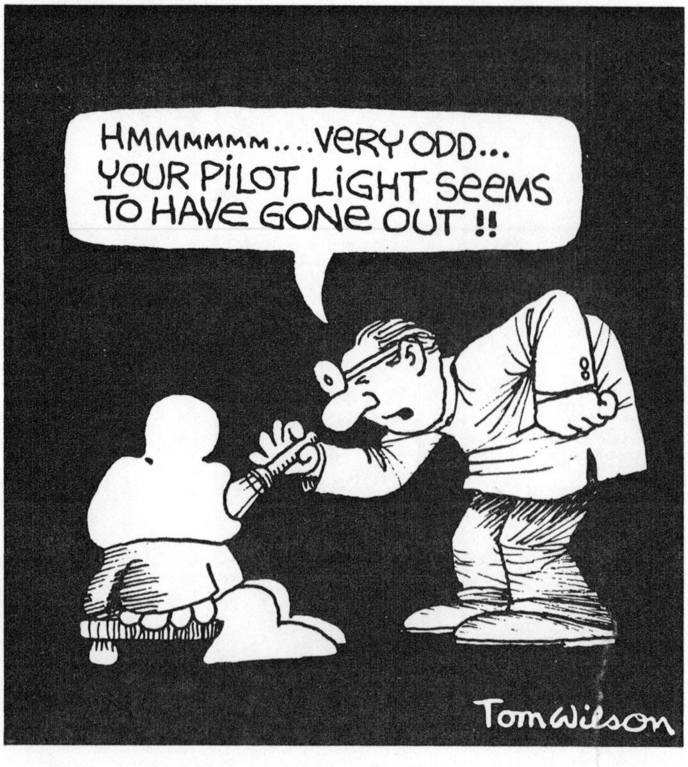
HMMMMMM....VERY ODD... YOUR PiLOT LiGHT SEEMS TO HAVE GONE OUT!!
Tom Wilson

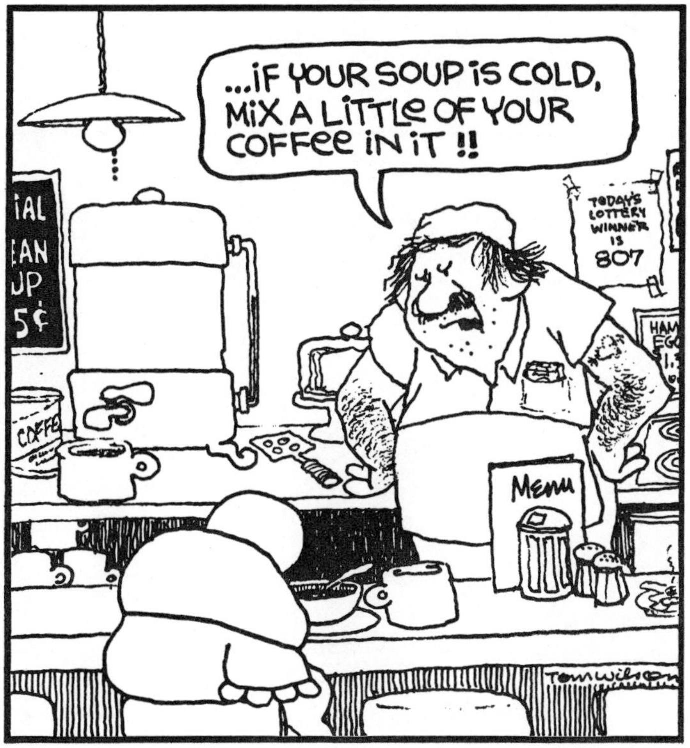
...iF YOUR SOUP iS COLD, MiX A LiTTLe OF YOUR COFFee iN iT !!
TODAY'S LOTTERY WINNER IS 807
MENU
TOM WILSON

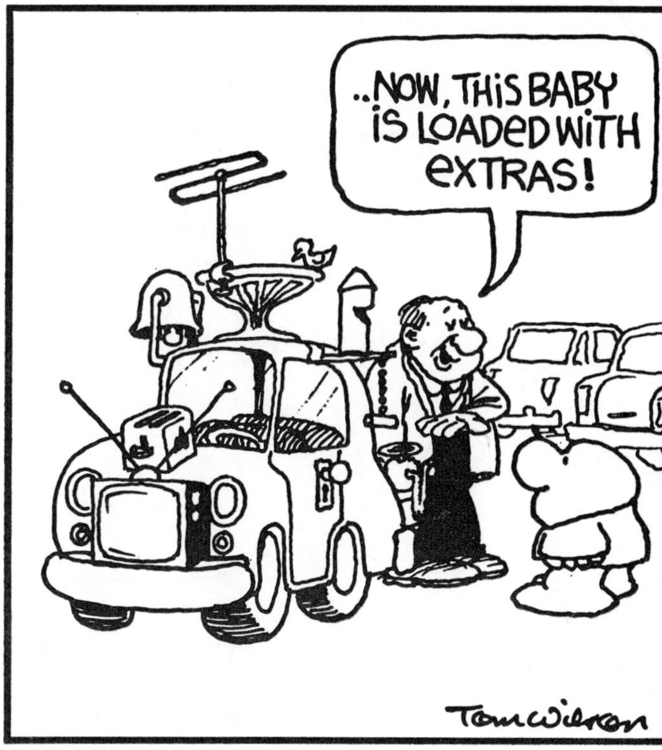
..NOW, THiS BABY iS LOADeD WiTH eXTRAS!
TOM WILSON

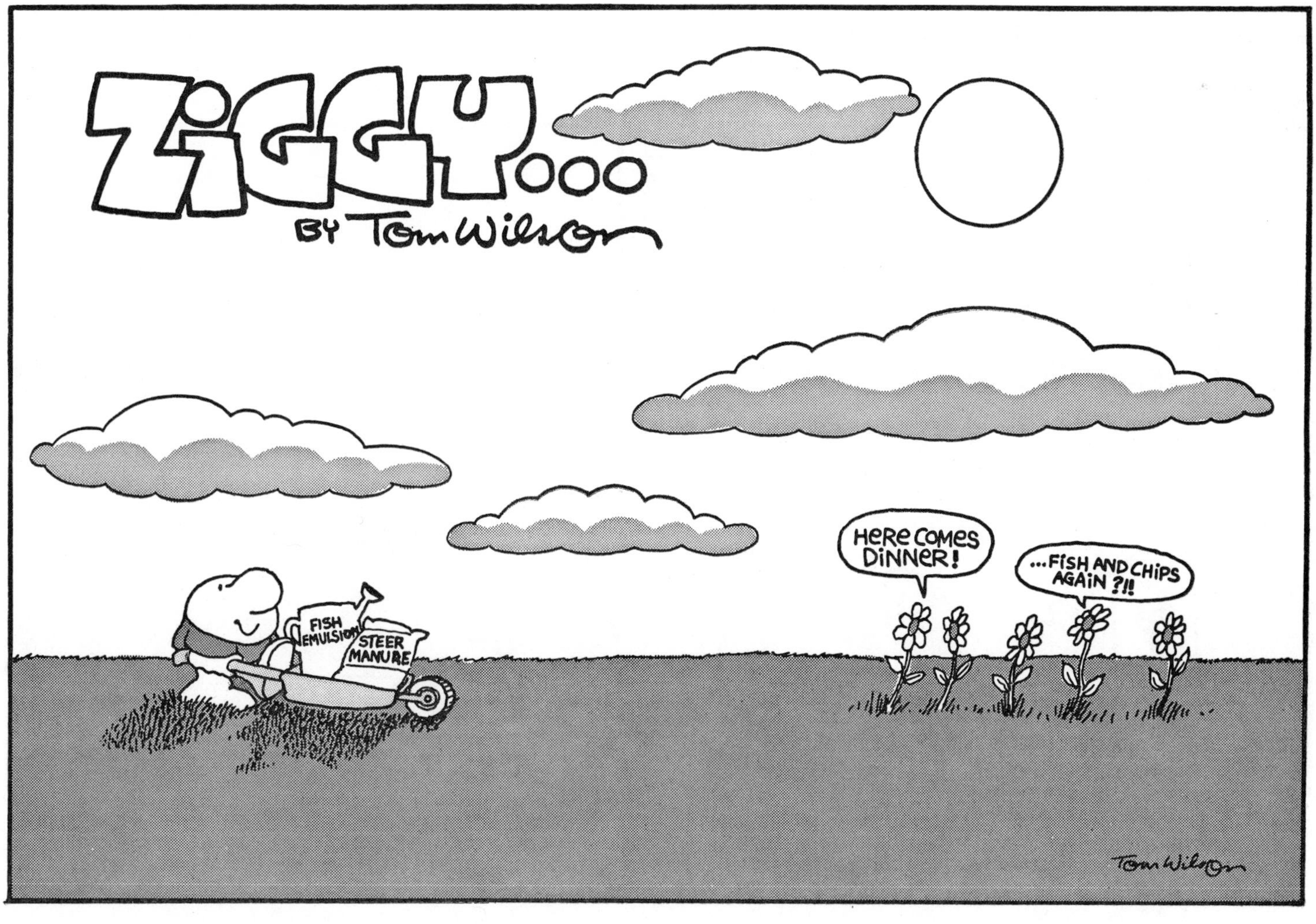
ZiGGY
BY TOM WILSON
FISH EMULSION
STEER MANURE
HeRe COMeS DiNNeR!
...FiSH AND CHiPS AGAiN ?!!
TOM WILSON

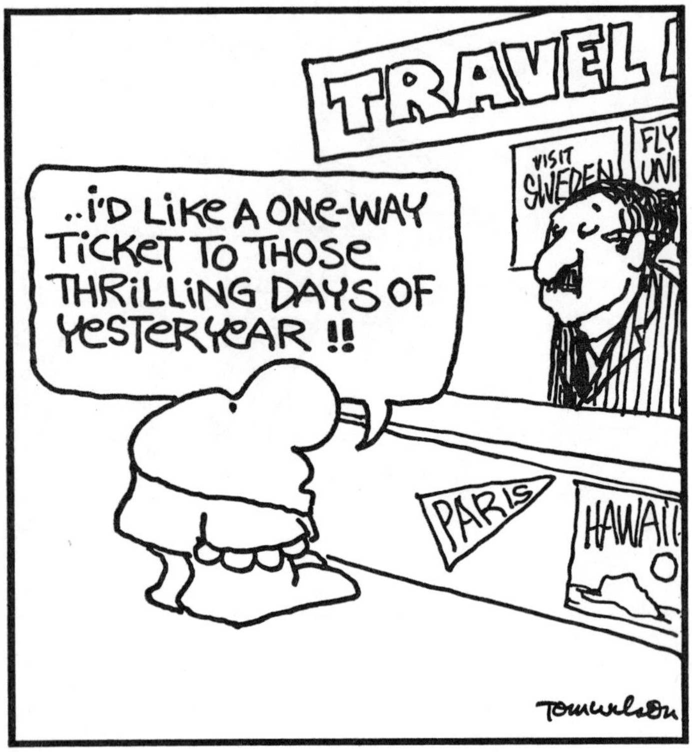
TRAVEL
VISIT SWEDEN
FLY UNI
..I'D LIKE A ONE-WAY TICKET TO THOSE THRILLING DAYS OF YESTERYEAR !!
PARIS
HAWAII
TomWilson

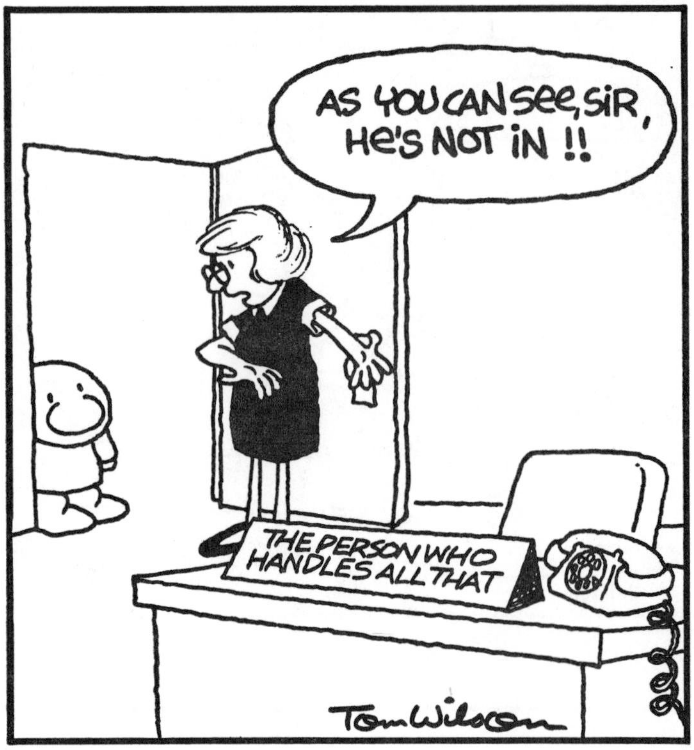
AS YOU CAN SEE, SIR, HE'S NOT IN !!
THE PERSON WHO HANDLES ALL THAT
TomWilson

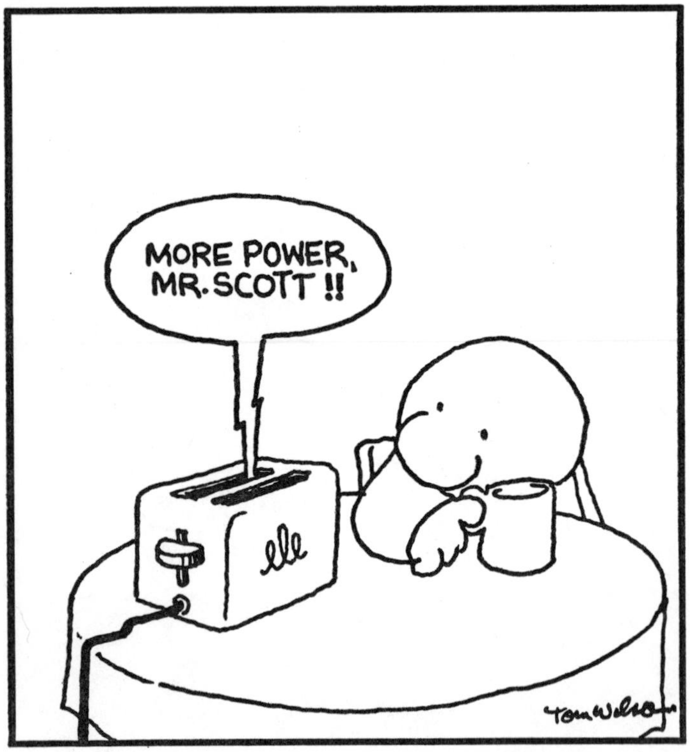
MORE POWER, MR. SCOTT !!
TomWilson

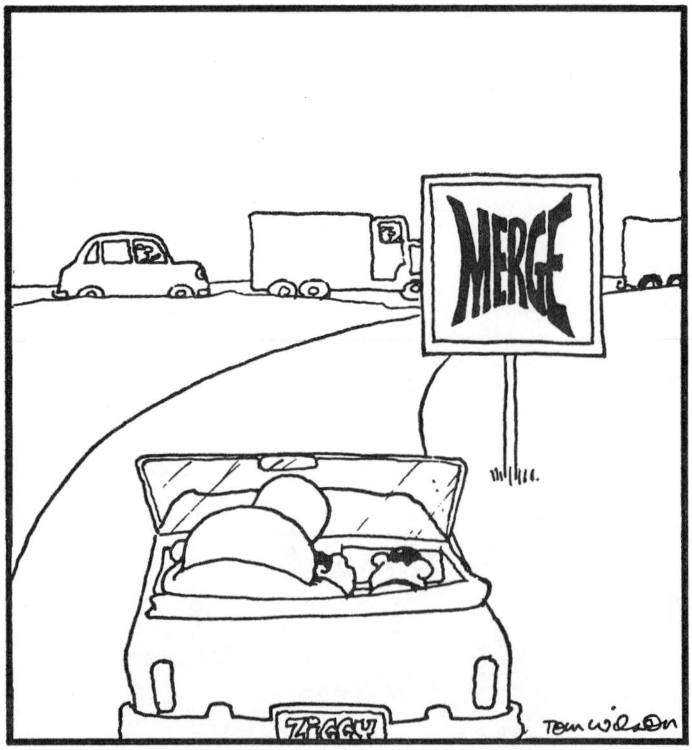
MERGE
ZIGGY
TomWilson

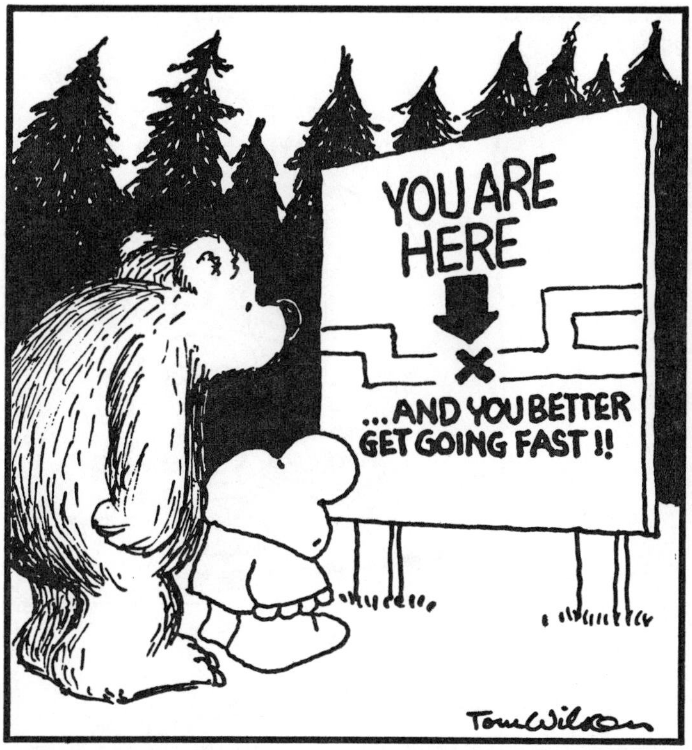
YOU ARE HERE
...AND YOU BETTER GET GOING FAST !!
Tom Wilson

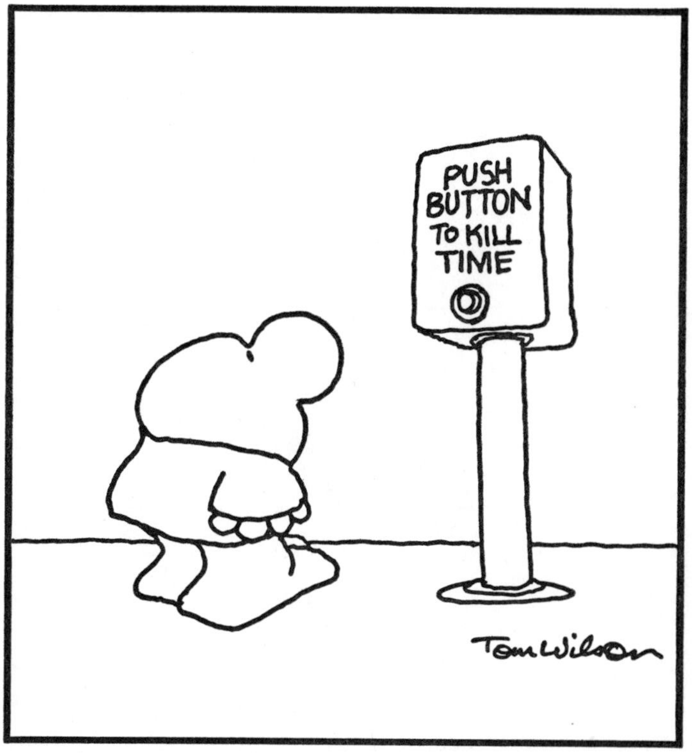
PUSH BUTTON TO KILL TIME
Tom Wilson

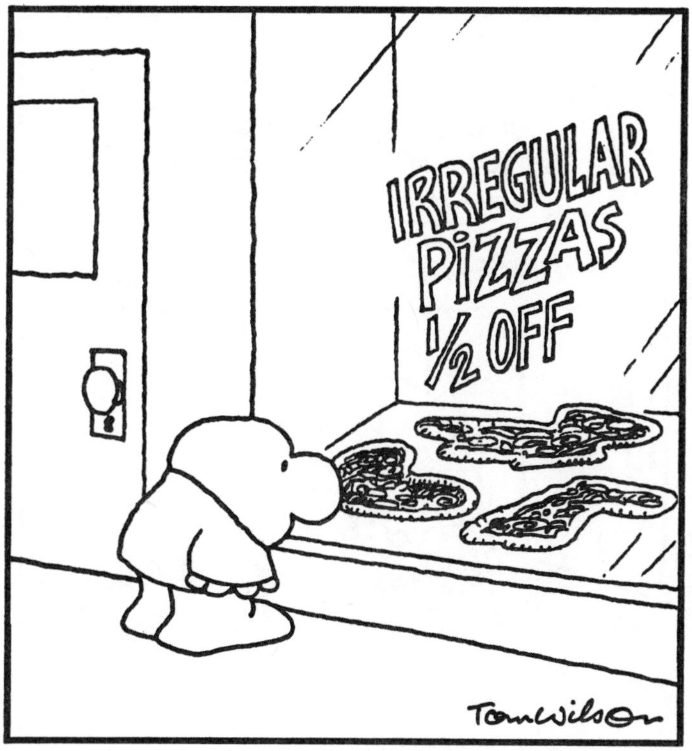
IRREGULAR PIZZAS 1/2 OFF
Tom Wilson

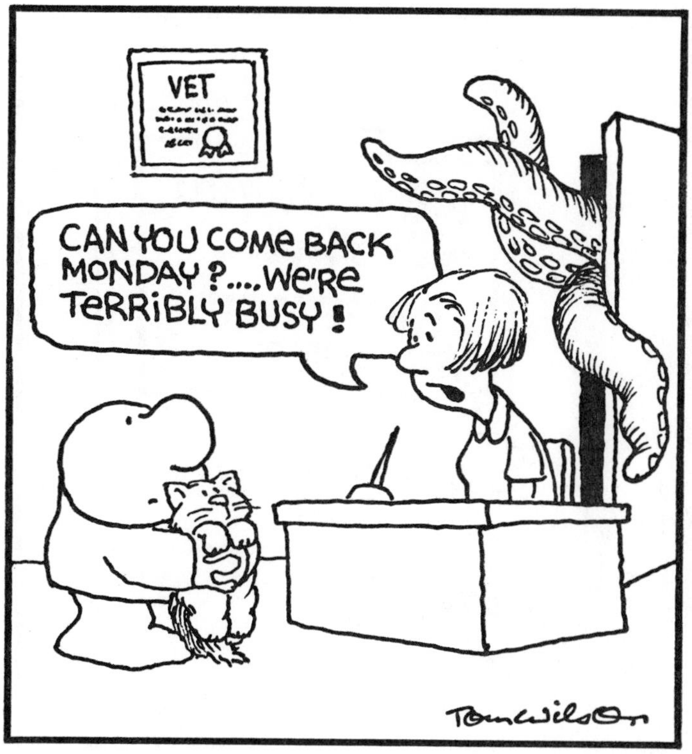
VET
CAN YOU COME BACK MONDAY ?....WE'RE TERRIBLY BUSY !
Tom Wilson

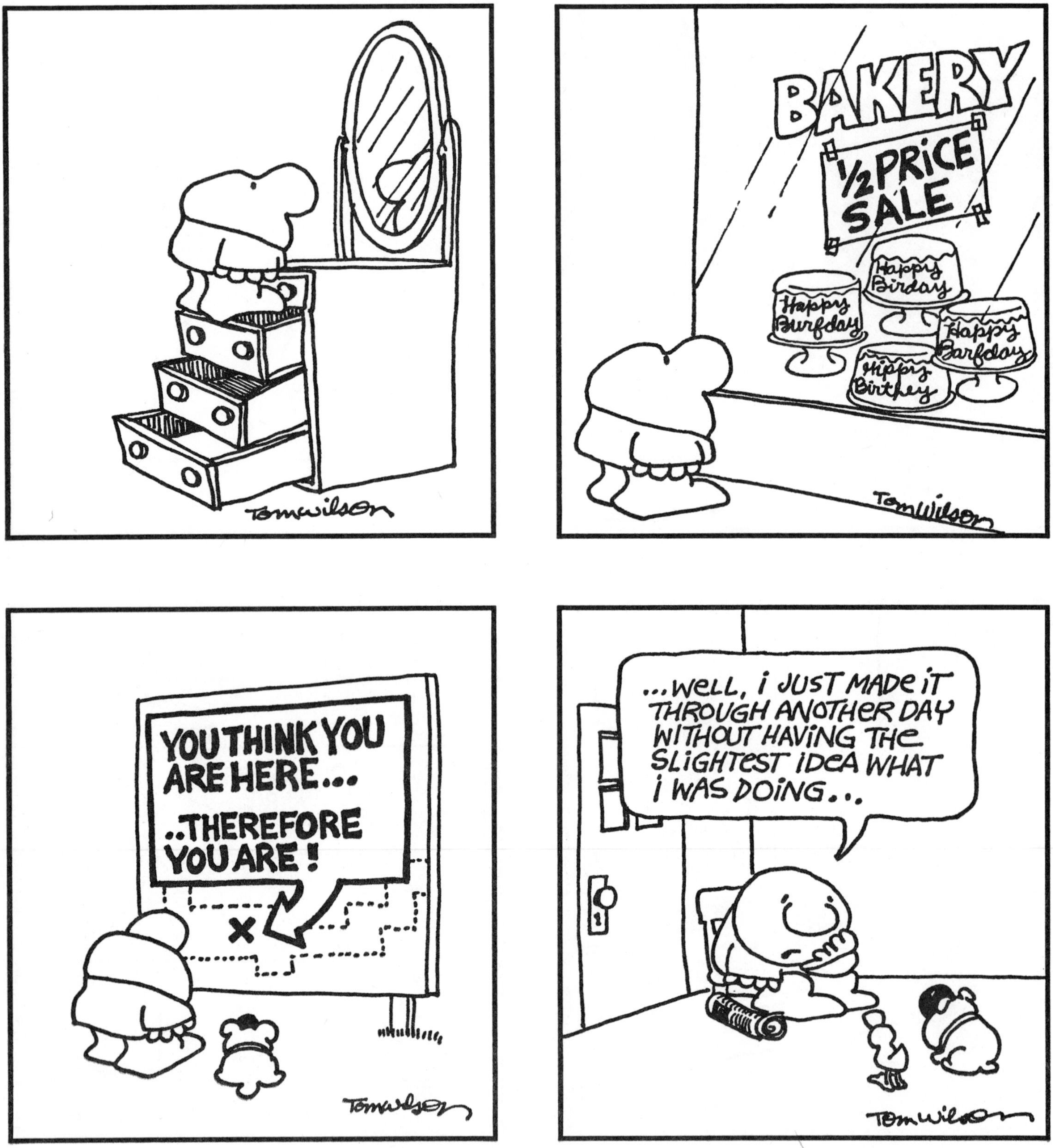
TomWilson
BAKERY
1/2 PRICE SALE
Happy Birday
Happy Burfday
Happy Barfday
Hippy Birthey
TomWilson
YOU THINK YOU ARE HERE...
..THEREFORE YOU ARE!
X
TomWilson
...WELL, I JUST MADE IT THROUGH ANOTHER DAY WITHOUT HAVING THE SLIGHTEST IDEA WHAT I WAS DOING...
TomWilson

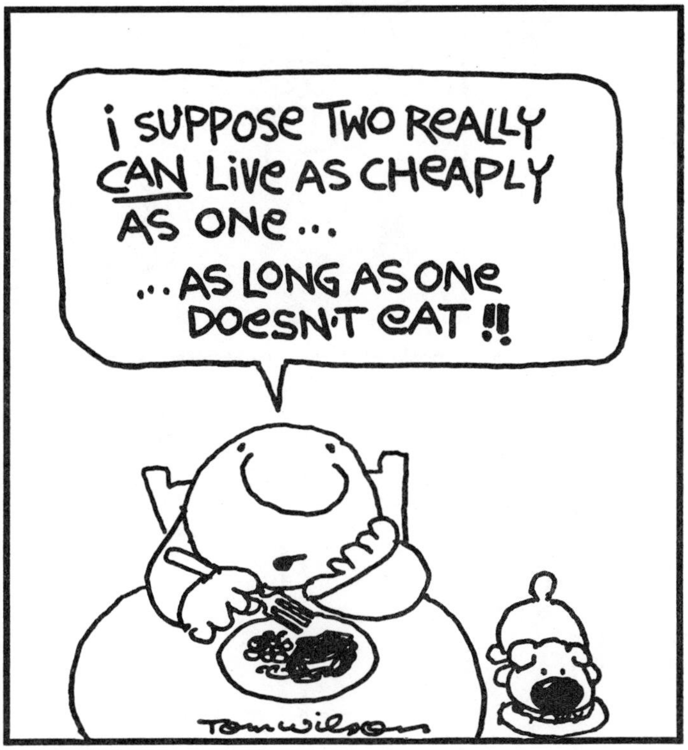
i SUPPOSE TWO REALLY CAN LIVE AS CHEAPLY AS ONE...
...AS LONG AS ONE DOESN'T EAT !!
Tom Wilson

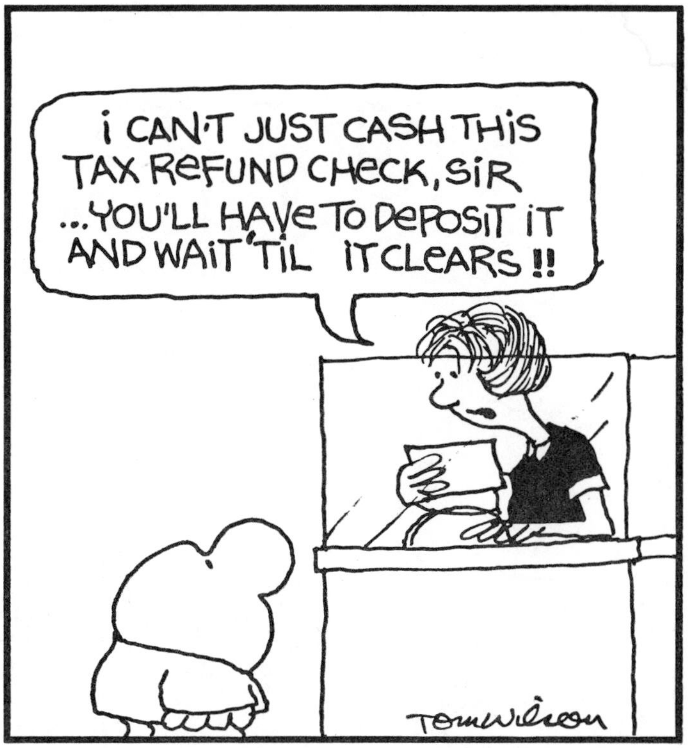
i CAN'T JUST CASH THIS TAX REFUND CHECK, SIR ...YOU'LL HAVE TO DEPOSIT IT AND WAIT 'TIL IT CLEARS !!
Tom Wilson

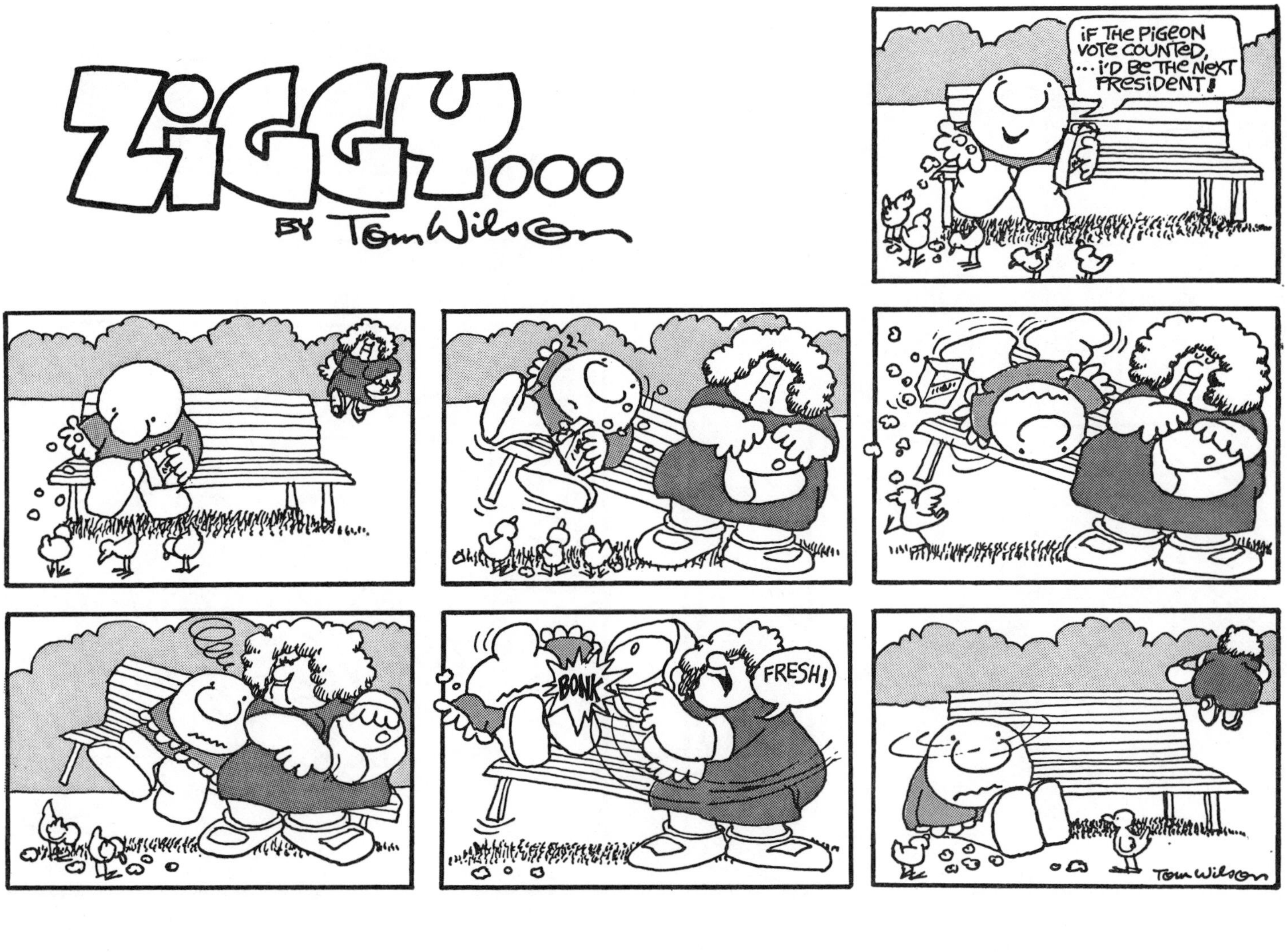
ZiGGY ooo
BY Tom Wilson
iF THE PIGEON VOTE COUNTED, ...i'D BE THE NEXT PRESIDENT!
BONK
FRESH!
Tom Wilson

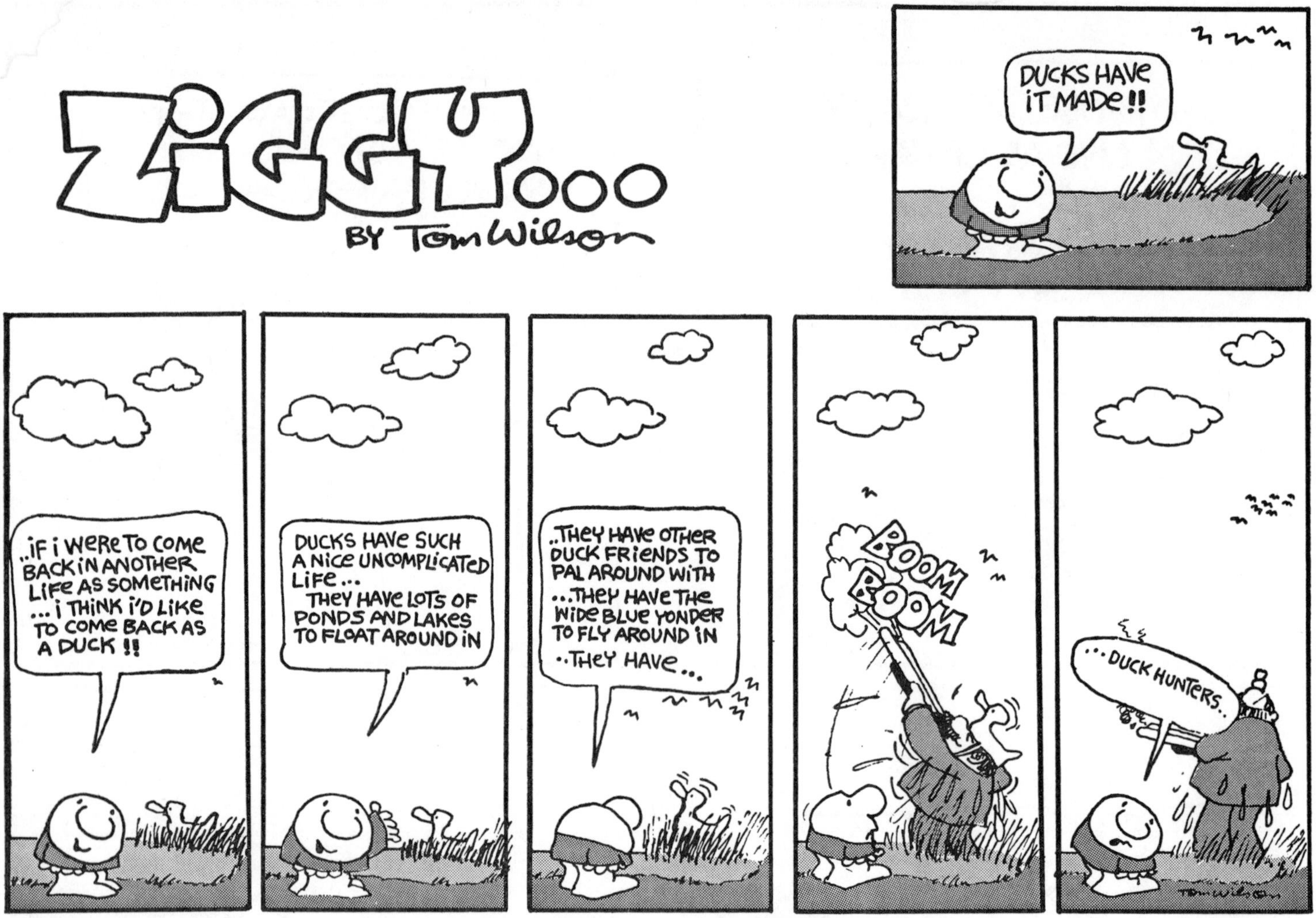
ZIGGY
BY Tom Wilson
DUCKS HAVE IT MADE !!
..IF I WERE TO COME BACK IN ANOTHER LIFE AS SOMETHING ...I THINK I'D LIKE TO COME BACK AS A DUCK !!
DUCKS HAVE SUCH A NICE UNCOMPLICATED LIFE... THEY HAVE LOTS OF PONDS AND LAKES TO FLOAT AROUND IN
..THEY HAVE OTHER DUCK FRIENDS TO PAL AROUND WITH ...THEY HAVE THE WIDE BLUE YONDER TO FLY AROUND IN ..THEY HAVE...
BOOM
BOOM
...DUCK HUNTERS..
Tom Wilson

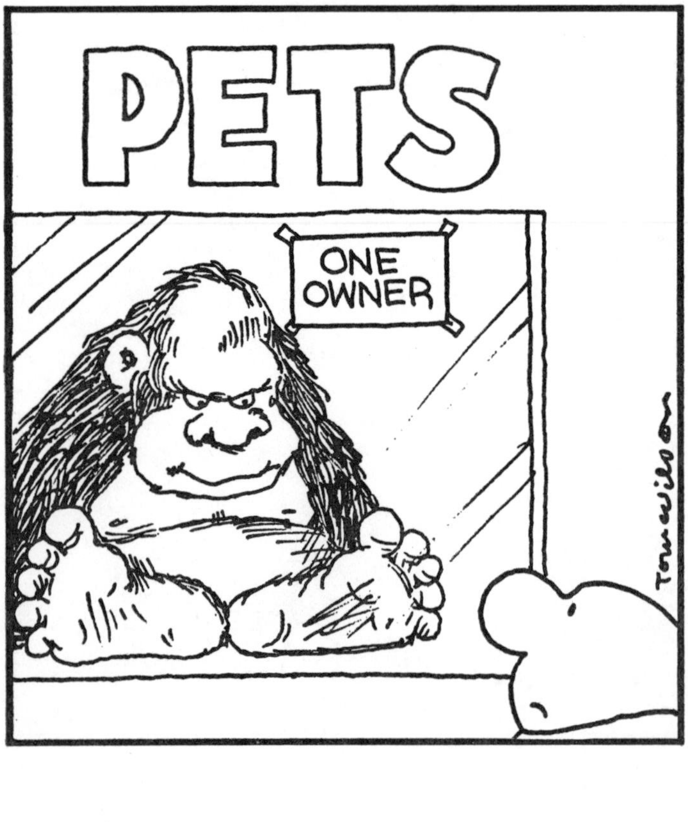
PETS
ONE OWNER
Tom Wilson

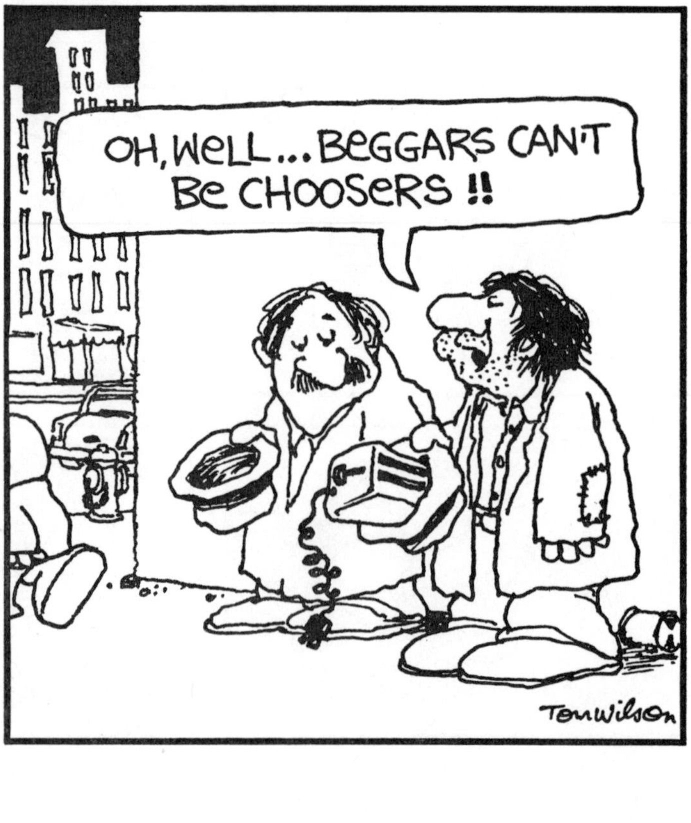
OH, WELL... BEGGARS CAN'T BE CHOOSERS !!
Tom Wilson

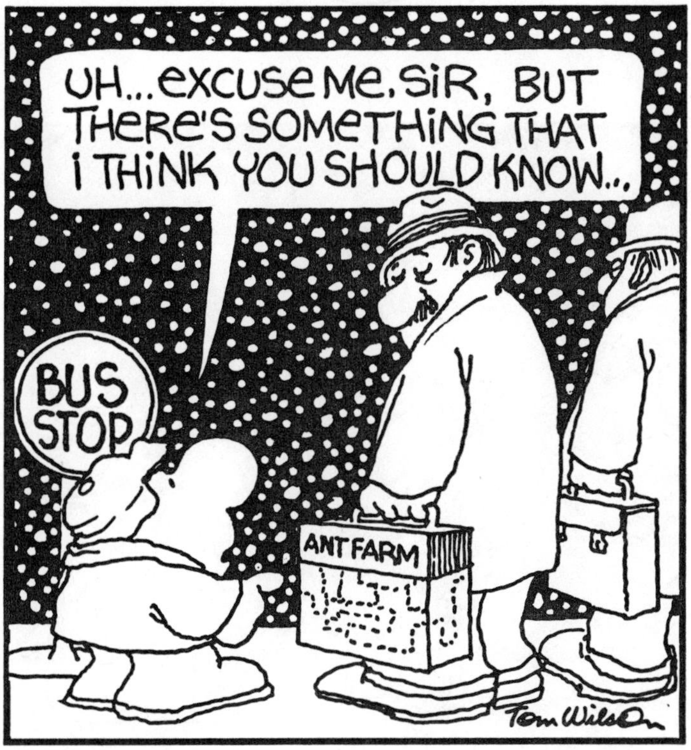
UH...EXCUSE ME, SIR, BUT THERE'S SOMETHING THAT I THINK YOU SHOULD KNOW...
BUS STOP
ANT FARM
Tom Wilson

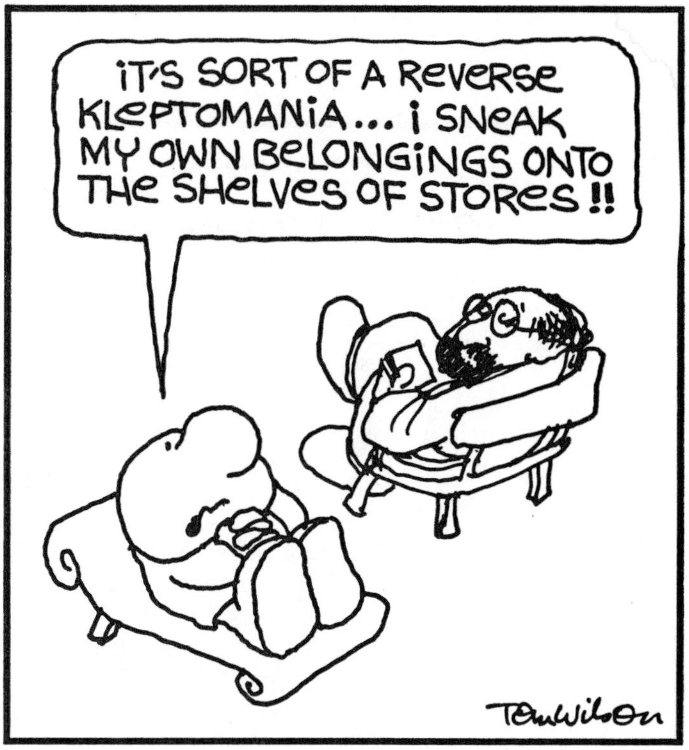
IT'S SORT OF A REVERSE KLEPTOMANIA... I SNEAK MY OWN BELONGINGS ONTO THE SHELVES OF STORES !!
Tom Wilson

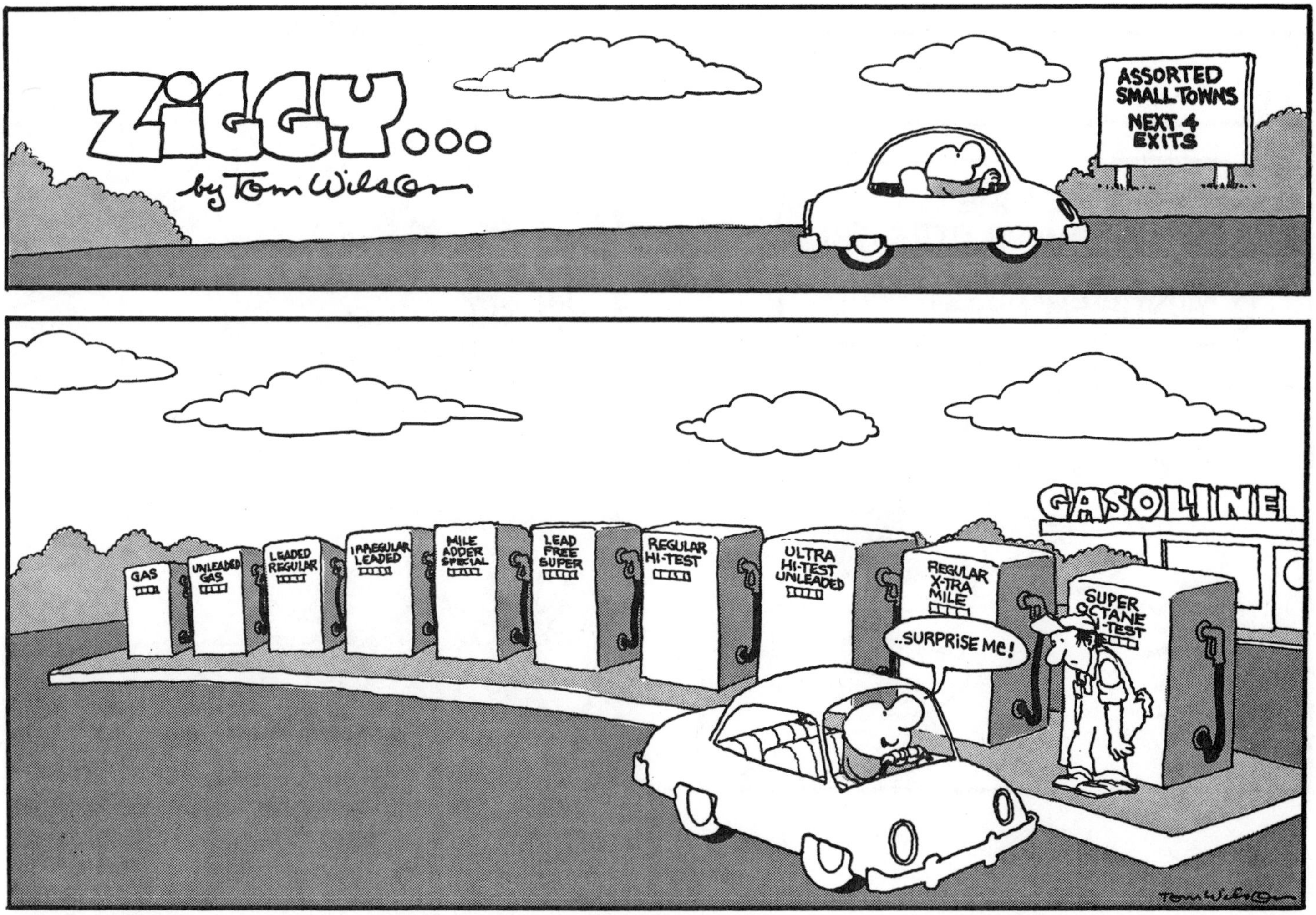
ZIGGY...
by Tom Wilson
ASSORTED SMALL TOWNS NEXT 4 EXITS
GASOLINE
GAS
UNLEADED GAS
LEADED REGULAR
IRREGULAR LEADED
MILE ADDER SPECIAL
LEAD FREE SUPER
REGULAR HI-TEST
ULTRA HI-TEST UNLEADED
REGULAR X-TRA MILE
..SURPRISE ME!
Tom Wilson

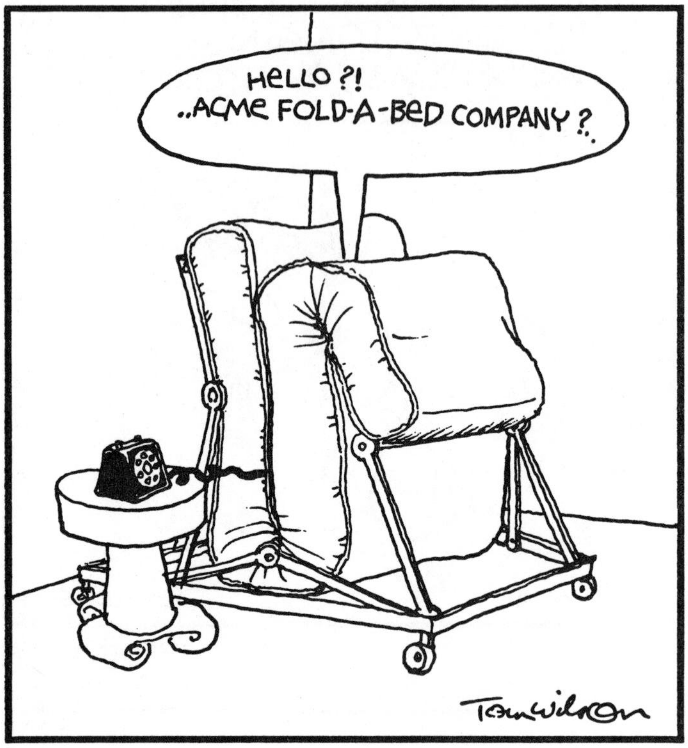
HELLO ?!
..ACME FOLD-A-BED COMPANY ?..
TOM WILSON

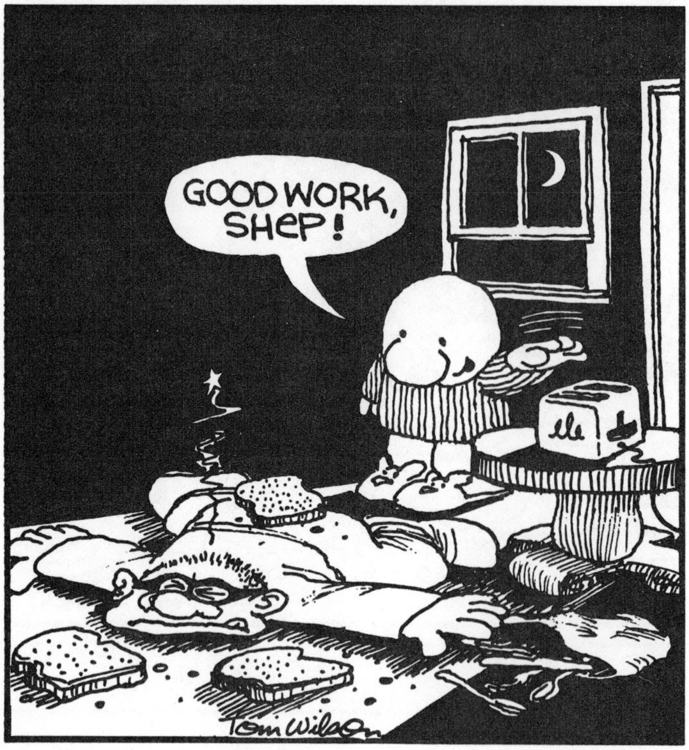
GOOD WORK,
SHEP !
TOM WILSON

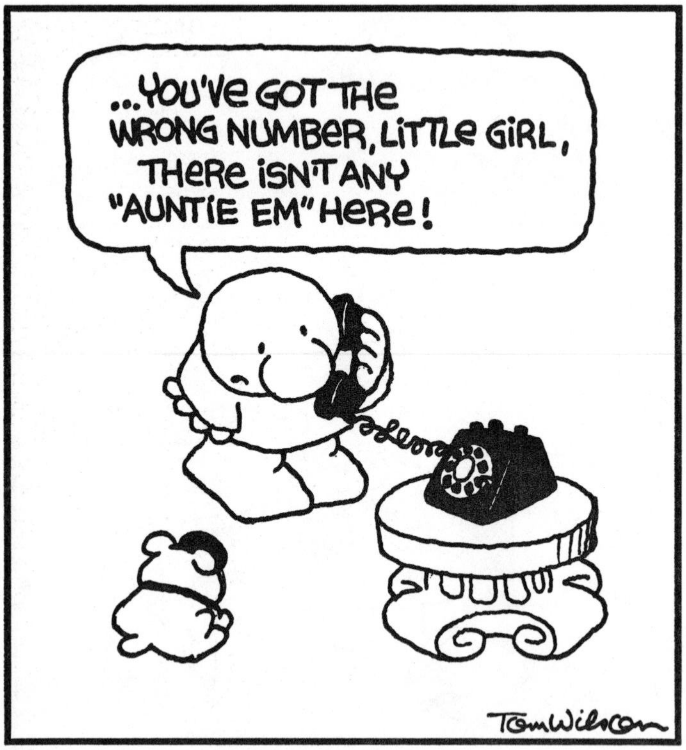
...YOU'VE GOT THE
WRONG NUMBER, LITTLE GIRL,
THERE ISN'T ANY
"AUNTIE EM" HERE !
TOM WILSON

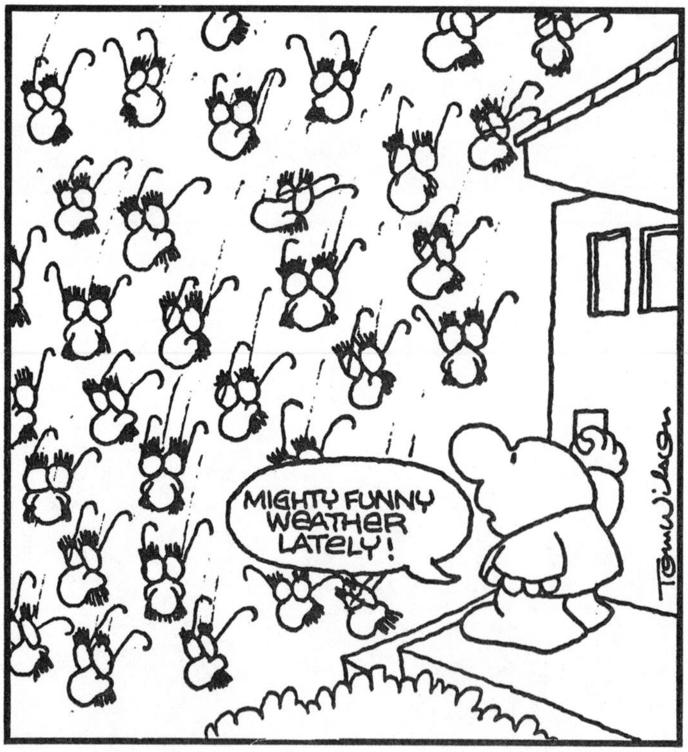
MIGHTY FUNNY
WEATHER
LATELY !
TOM WILSON

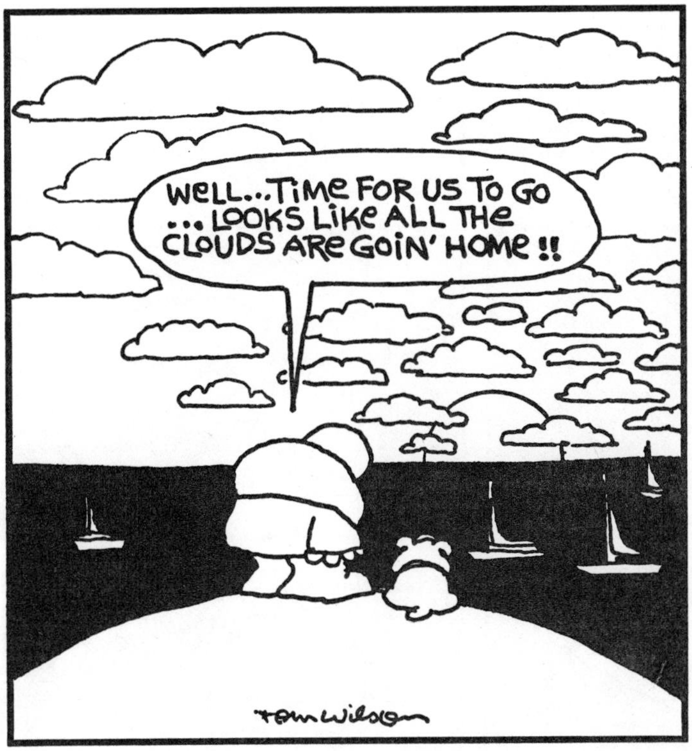
WELL...TIME FOR US TO GO ...LOOKS LIKE ALL THE CLOUDS ARE GOIN' HOME !!
TOM WILSON

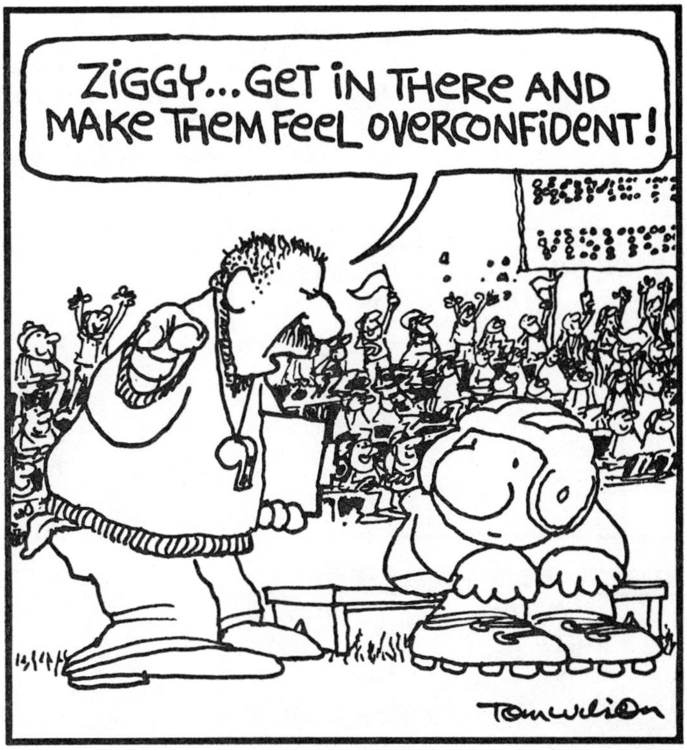
ZIGGY...GET IN THERE AND MAKE THEM FEEL OVERCONFIDENT!
TOM WILSON

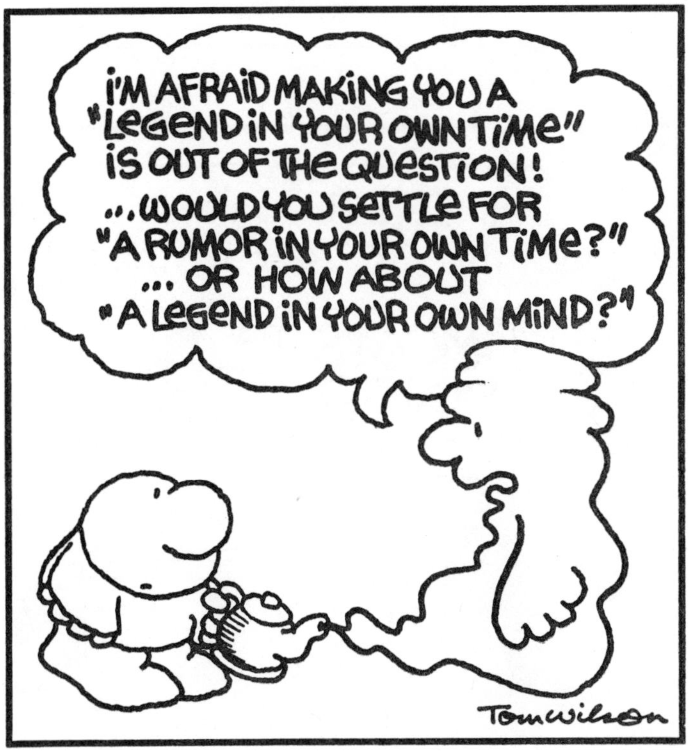
I'M AFRAID MAKING YOU A "LEGEND IN YOUR OWN TIME" IS OUT OF THE QUESTION! ...WOULD YOU SETTLE FOR "A RUMOR IN YOUR OWN TIME?" ...OR HOW ABOUT "A LEGEND IN YOUR OWN MIND?"
TOM WILSON

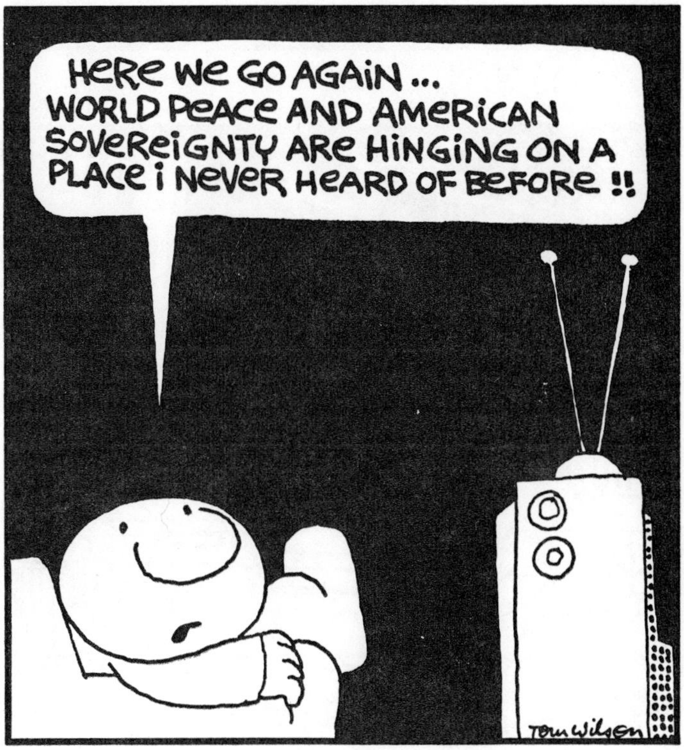
HERE WE GO AGAIN... WORLD PEACE AND AMERICAN SOVEREIGNTY ARE HINGING ON A PLACE I NEVER HEARD OF BEFORE !!
TOM WILSON

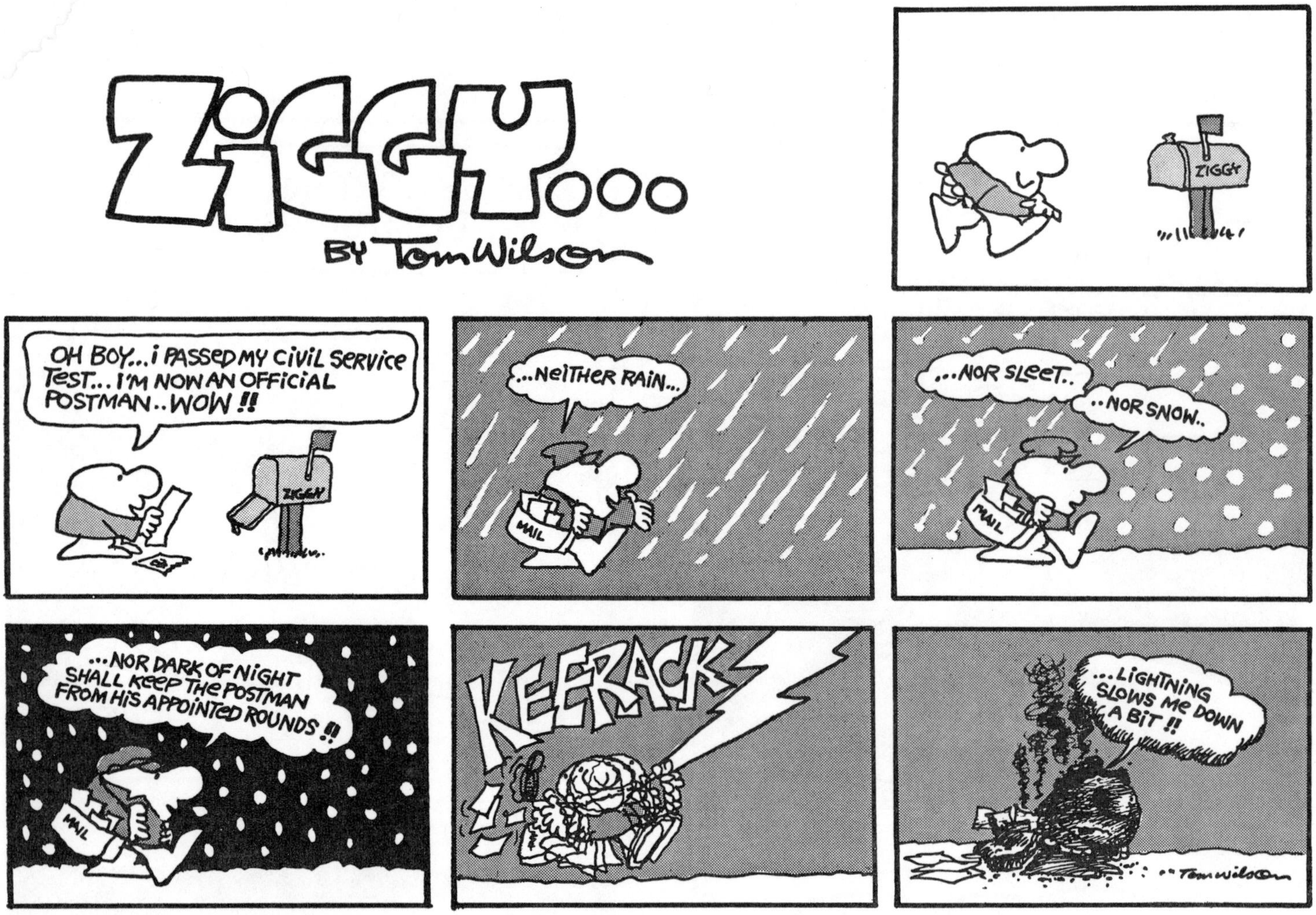
ZIGGY...
BY Tom Wilson
ZIGGY
OH BOY...i PASSED MY CIVIL SERVICE TEST... I'M NOW AN OFFICIAL POSTMAN..WOW !!
ZIGGY
MAIL
...NEITHER RAIN...
...NOR SLEET..
..NOR SNOW..
MAIL
...NOR DARK OF NIGHT SHALL KEEP THE POSTMAN FROM HIS APPOINTED ROUNDS !!
MAIL
KEERACK
...LIGHTNING SLOWS ME DOWN A BIT !!
Tom Wilson

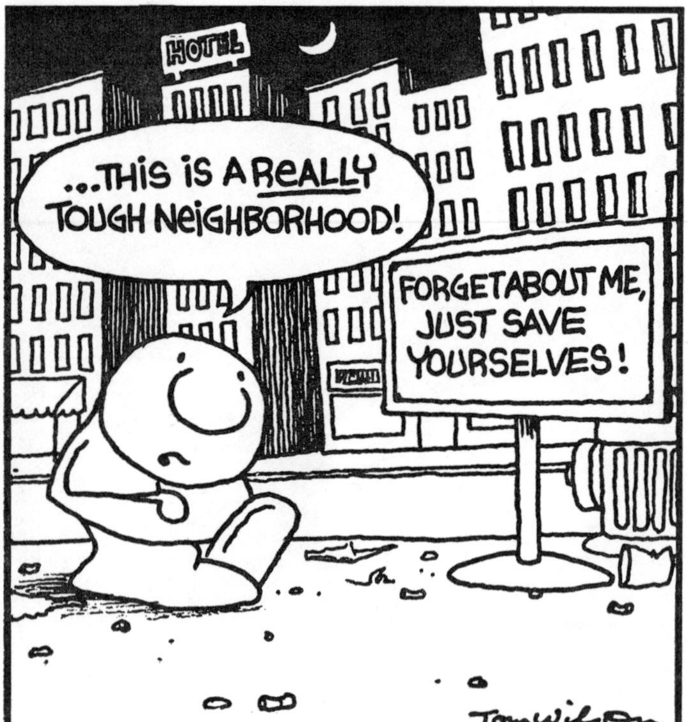
HOTEL
...THIS IS A REALLY TOUGH NEIGHBORHOOD!
FORGET ABOUT ME, JUST SAVE YOURSELVES!
Tom Wilson

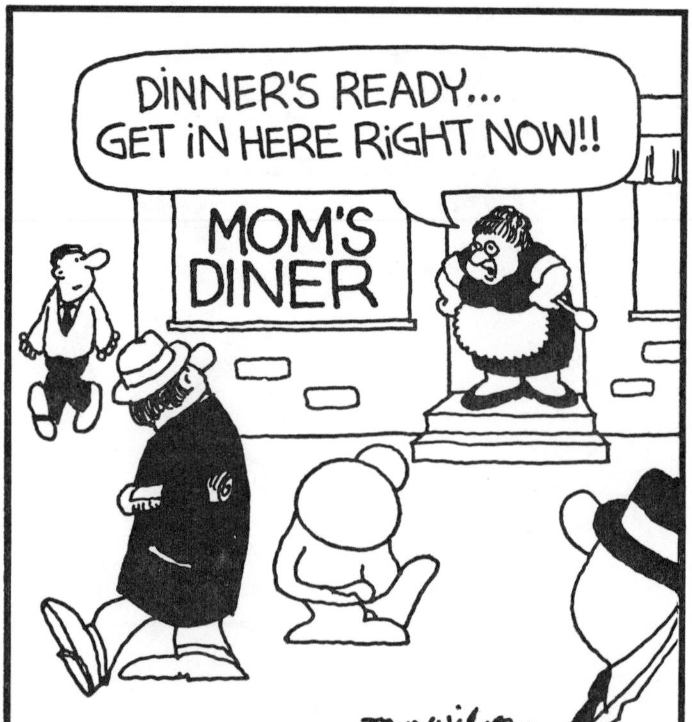
DINNER'S READY... GET IN HERE RIGHT NOW!!
MOM'S DINER
Tom Wilson

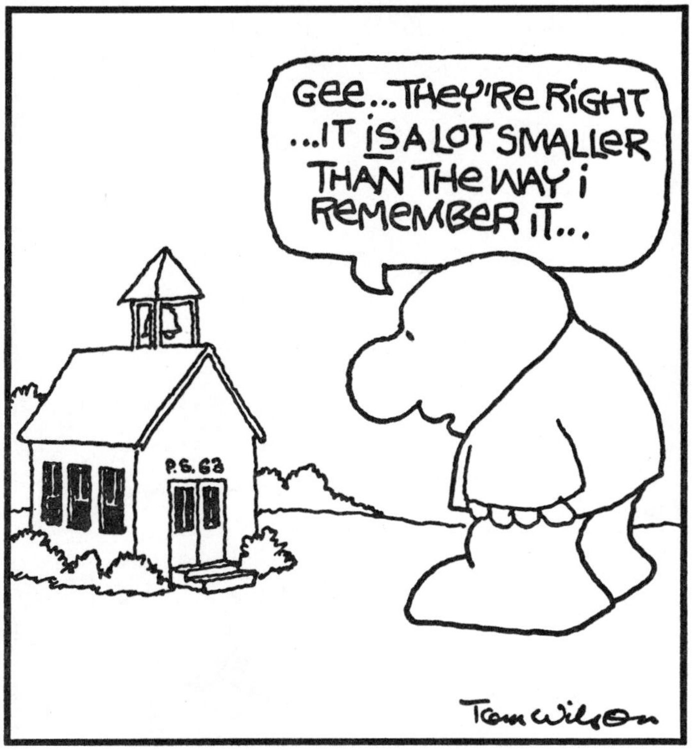
GEE...THEY'RE RIGHT ...IT IS A LOT SMALLER THAN THE WAY I REMEMBER IT...
P.S. 63
Tom Wilson

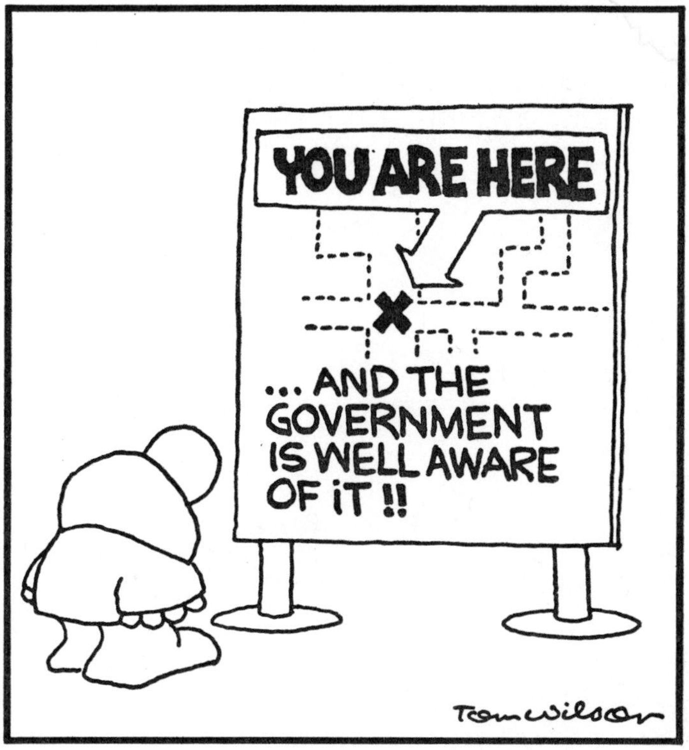
YOU ARE HERE
... AND THE GOVERNMENT IS WELL AWARE OF IT !!
Tom Wilson

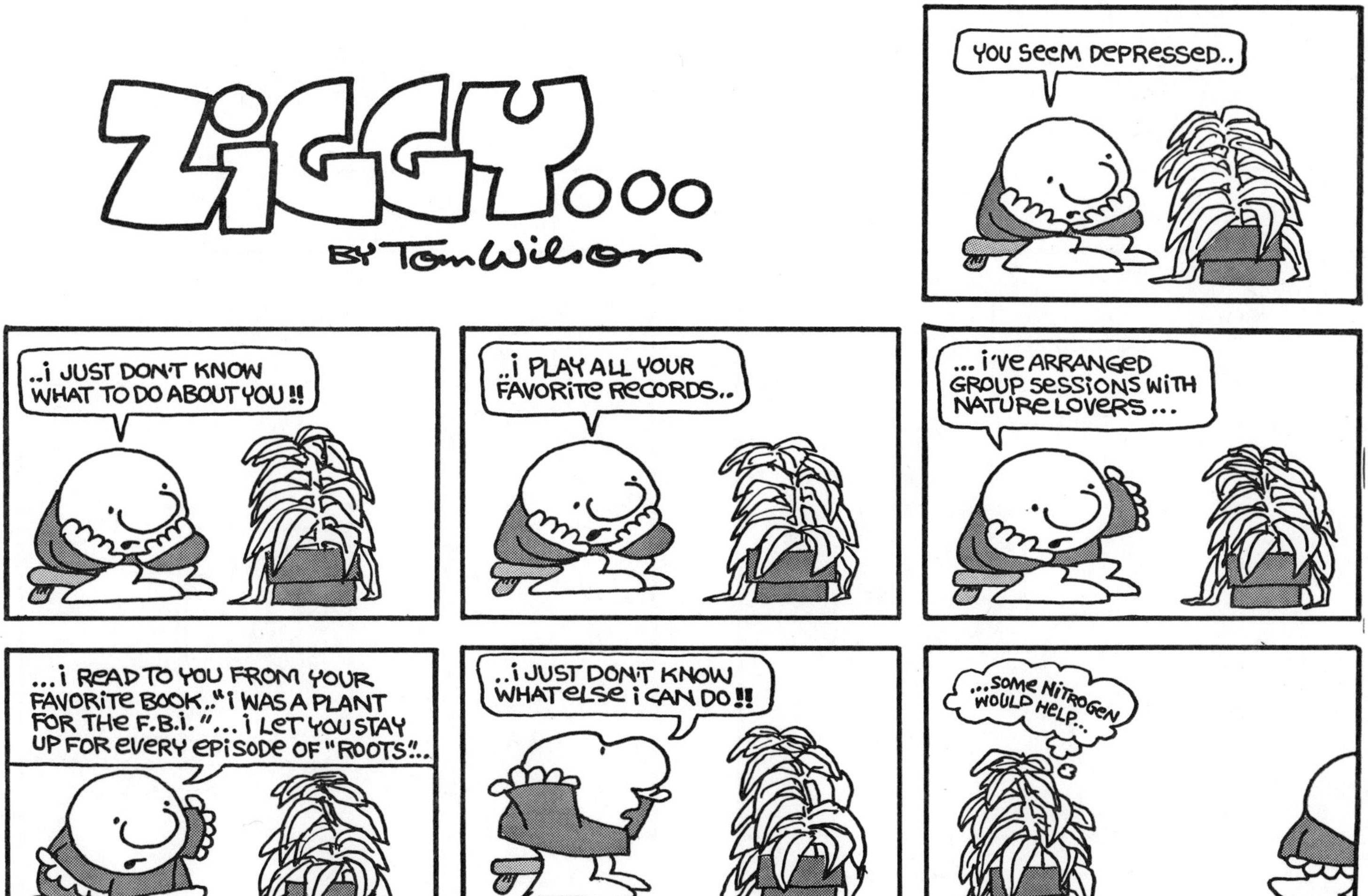
ZIGGY...
BY Tom Wilson
YOU SEEM DEPRESSED..
..I JUST DON'T KNOW WHAT TO DO ABOUT YOU !!
..I PLAY ALL YOUR FAVORITE RECORDS..
... I'VE ARRANGED GROUP SESSIONS WITH NATURE LOVERS ...
...I READ TO YOU FROM YOUR FAVORITE BOOK.."I WAS A PLANT FOR THE F.B.I."... I LET YOU STAY UP FOR EVERY EPISODE OF "ROOTS"...
..I JUST DON'T KNOW WHAT ELSE I CAN DO !!
...SOME NITROGEN WOULD HELP...
Tom Wilson

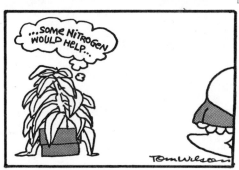

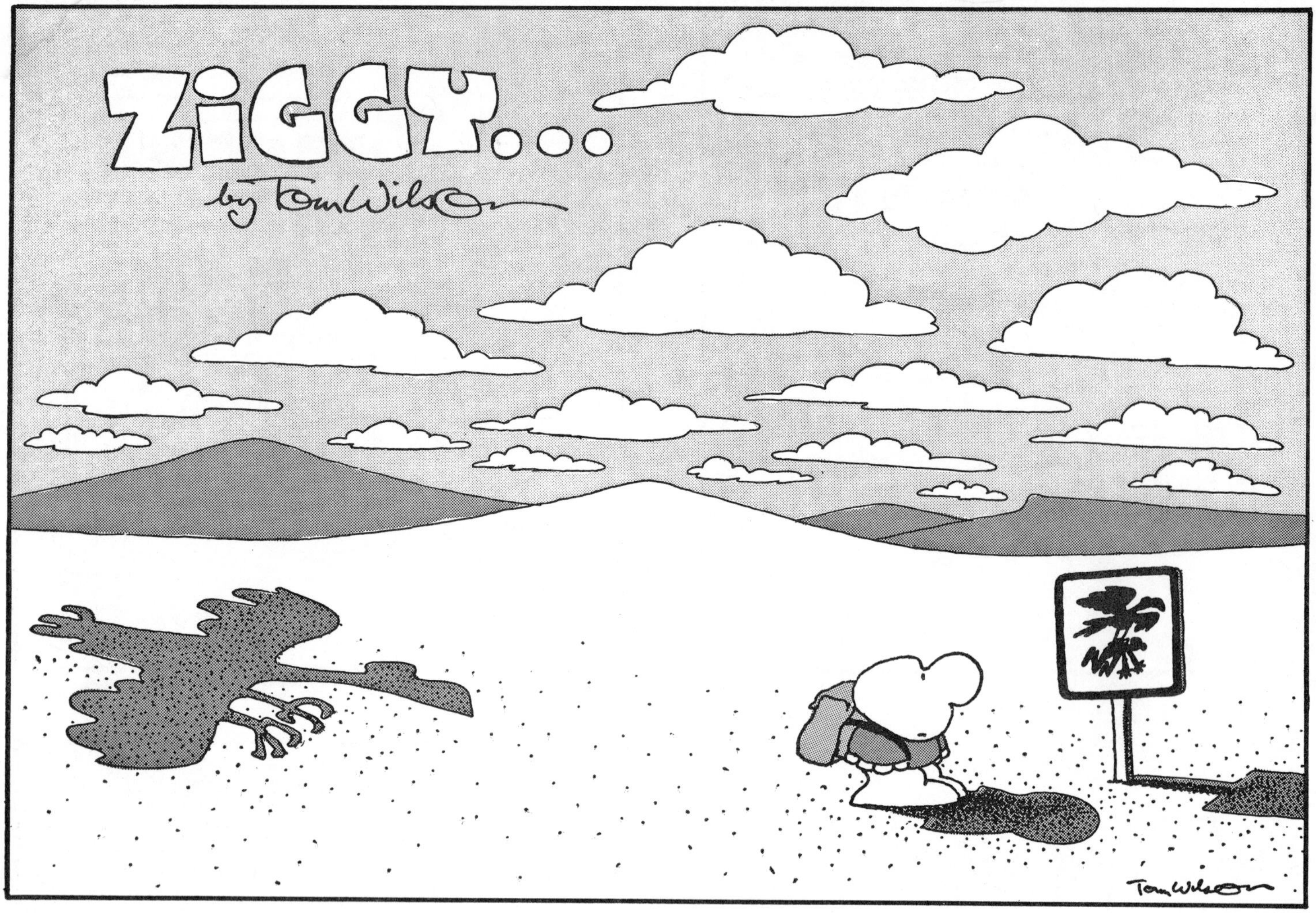
ZiGGY...
by Tom Wilson
Tom Wilson

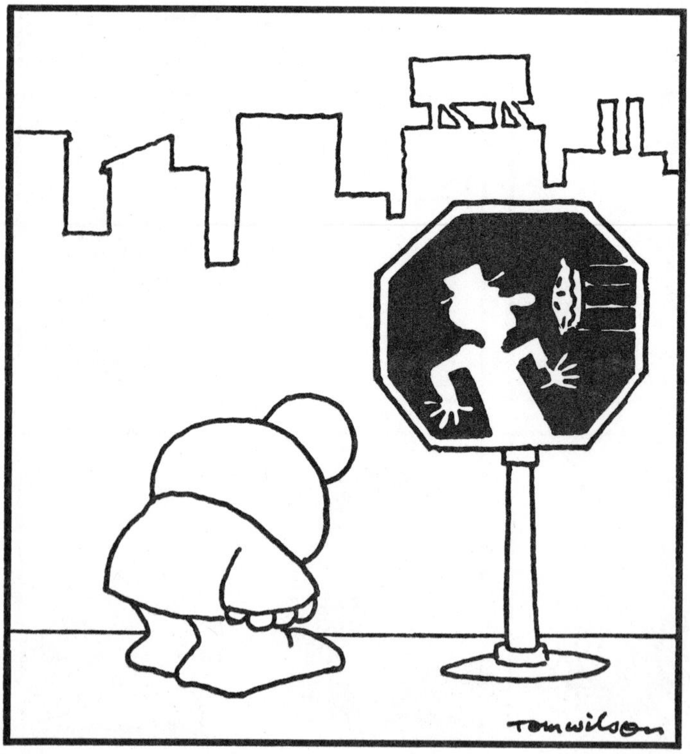
Tom Wilson

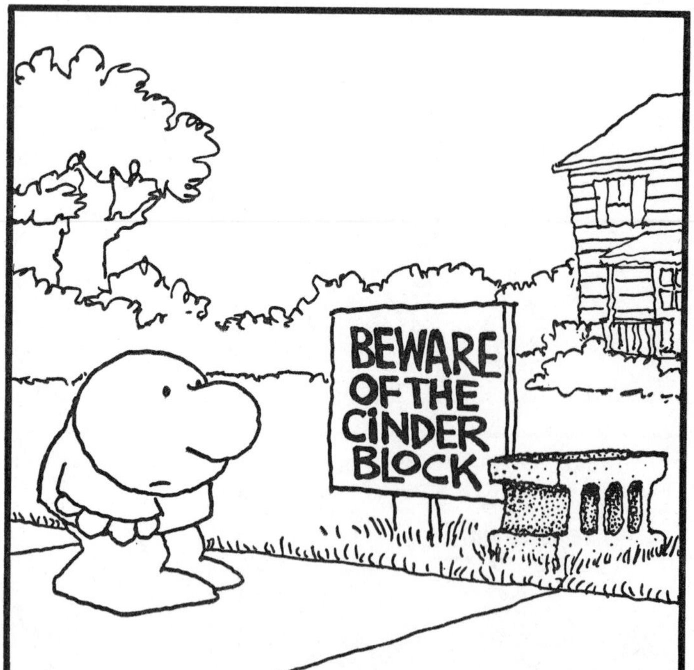
BEWARE OF THE CINDER BLOCK
Tom Wilson

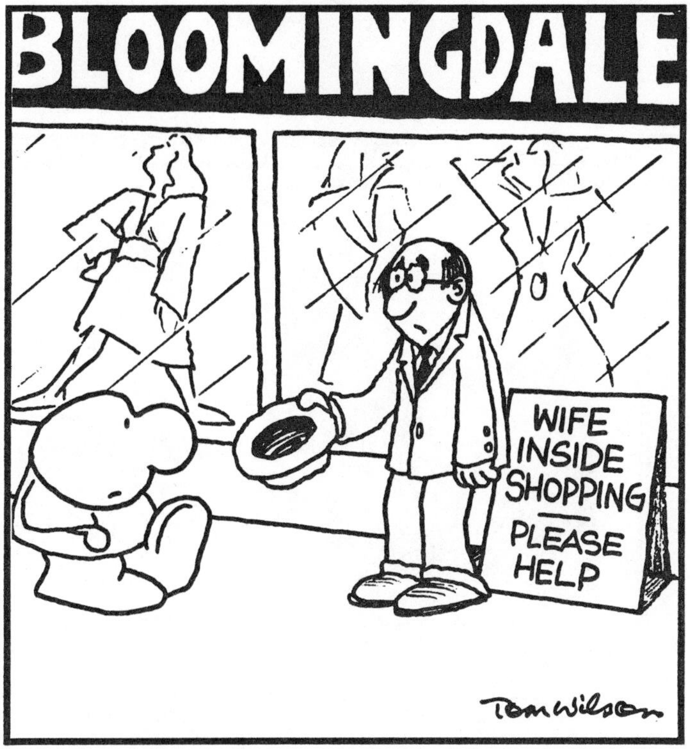
BLOOMINGDALE
WIFE INSIDE SHOPPING
PLEASE HELP
Tom Wilson

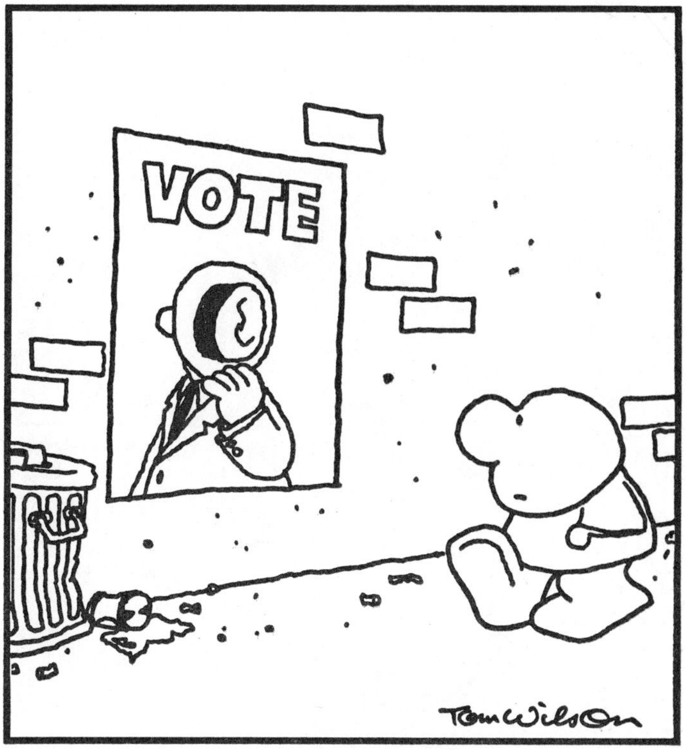
VOTE
Tom Wilson

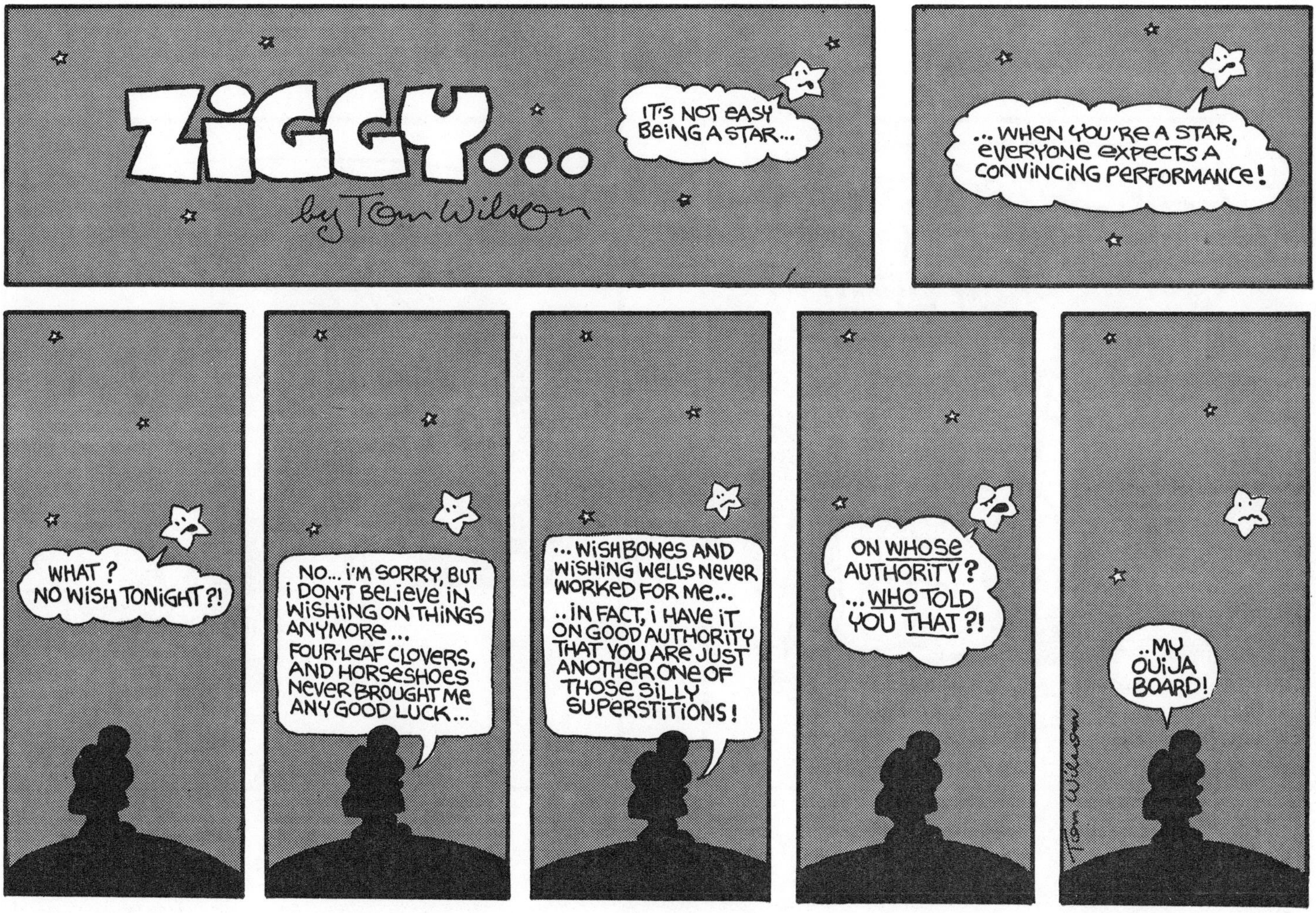
ZiGGY...
by Tom Wilson
IT'S NOT easy BeiNG A STAR...
... WHEN YOU'Re A STAR, eVERYONE eXPECTS A CONVINCING PERFORMANCE!
WHAT ? NO WiSH TONiGHT ?!
NO... i'M SORRY, BUT i DON'T BeLieve iN WiSHiNG ON THiNGS ANYMORE... FOUR-LeAF CLOVERS, AND HORSeSHOeS NeVeR BROUGHT Me ANY GOOD LUCK...
... WiSHBONeS AND WiSHiNG WeLLS NeVeR WORKeD FOR Me... .. iN FACT, i HAVe iT ON GOOD AUTHORiTY THAT YOU ARe JUST ANOTHeR ONe OF THOSe SiLLY SUPeRSTiTiONS!
ON WHOSe AUTHORiTY ? ... WHO TOLD YOU THAT ?!
.. MY OUiJA BOARD!
Tom Wilson

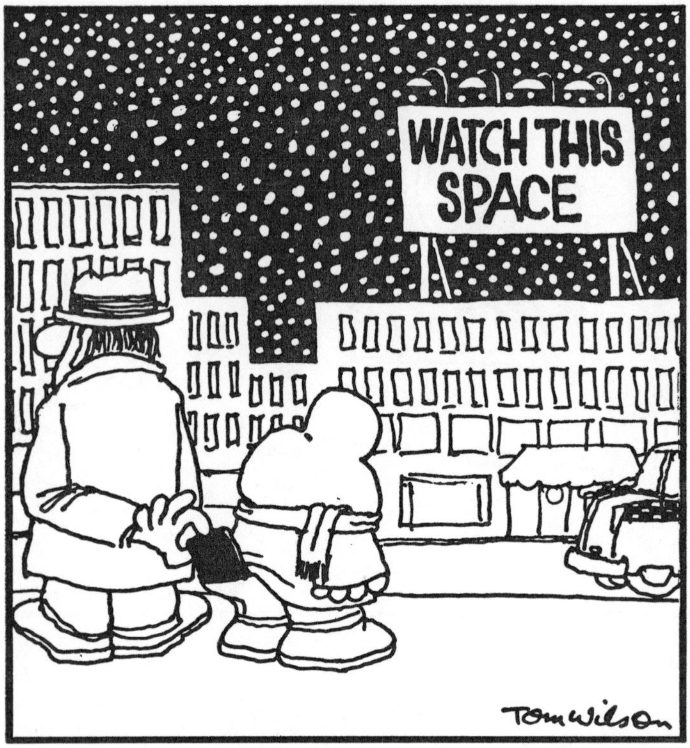
WATCH THIS SPACE

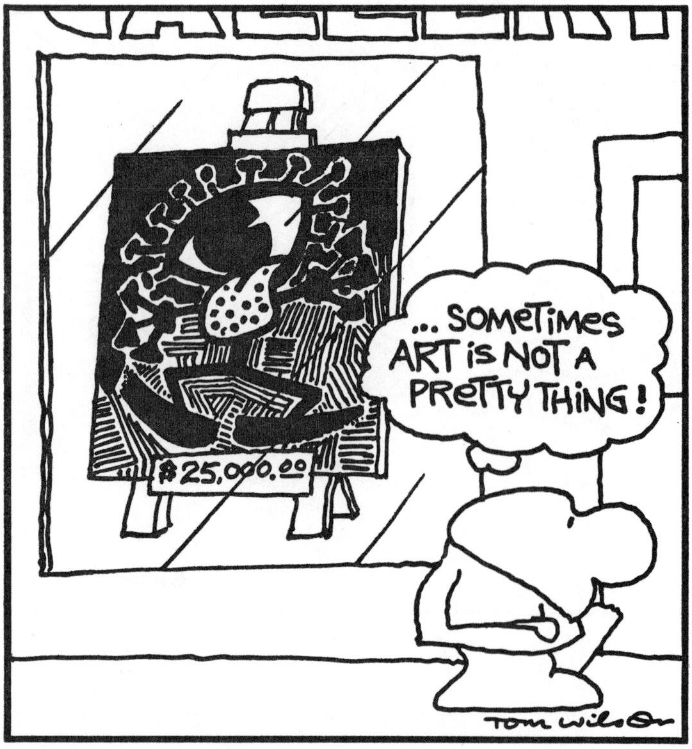
$25,000.00
... SOMETIMES ART IS NOT A PRETTY THING!

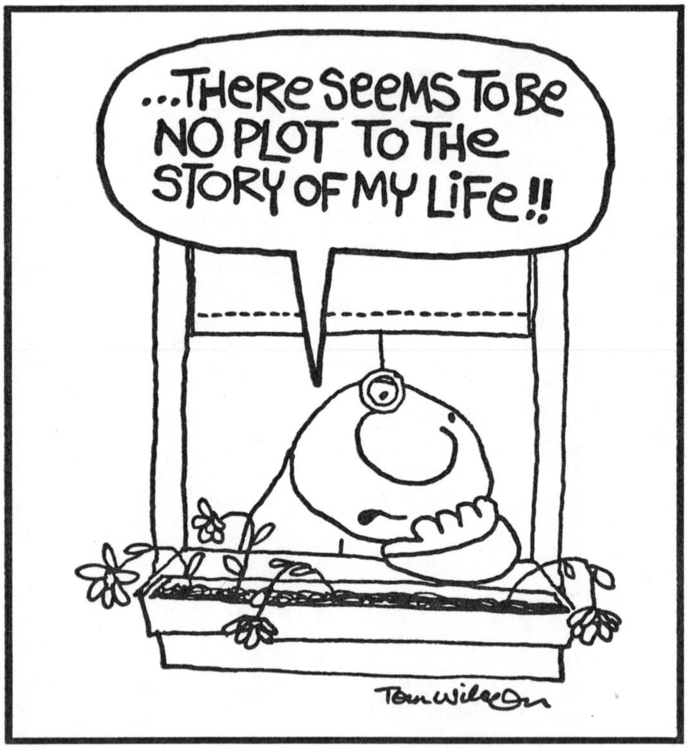
...THERE SEEMS TO BE NO PLOT TO THE STORY OF MY LIFE!!

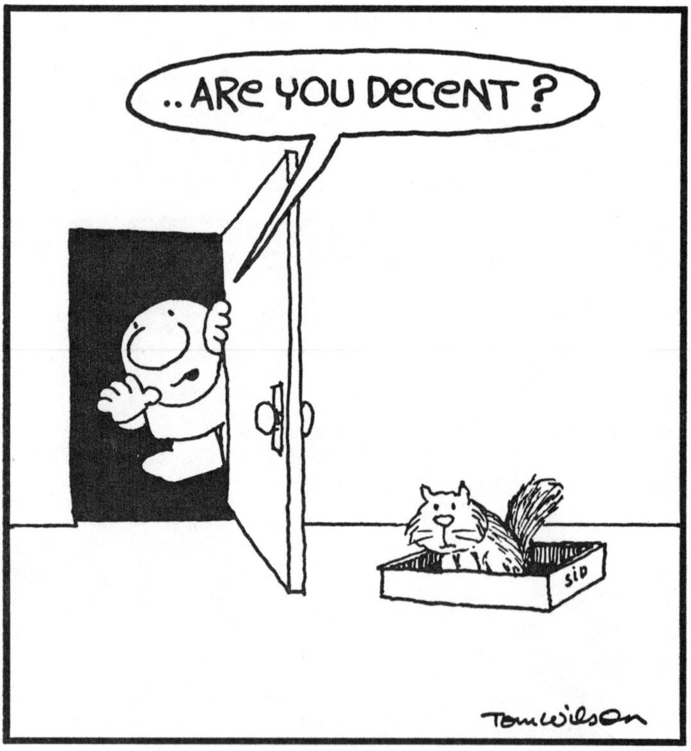
..ARE YOU DECENT?
SID

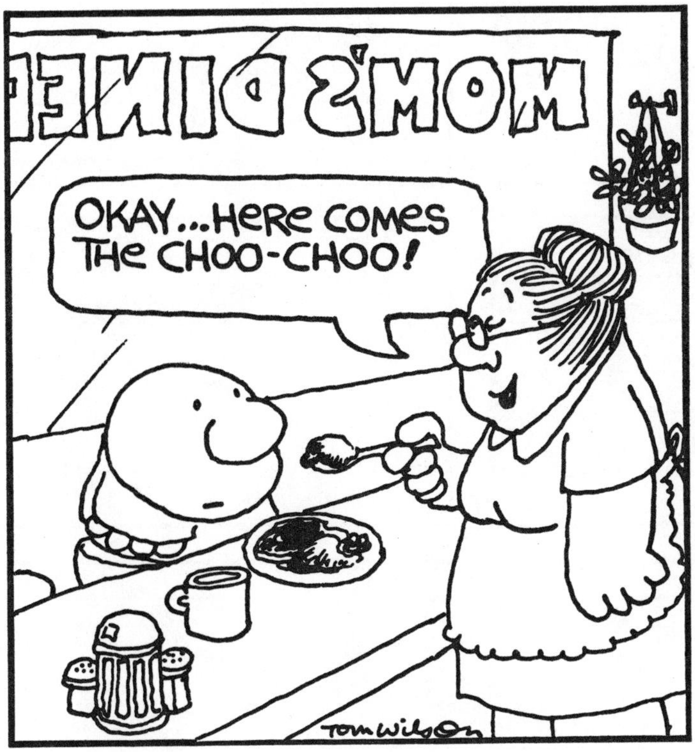
OKAY...HERE COMES THE CHOO-CHOO!
Tom Wilson

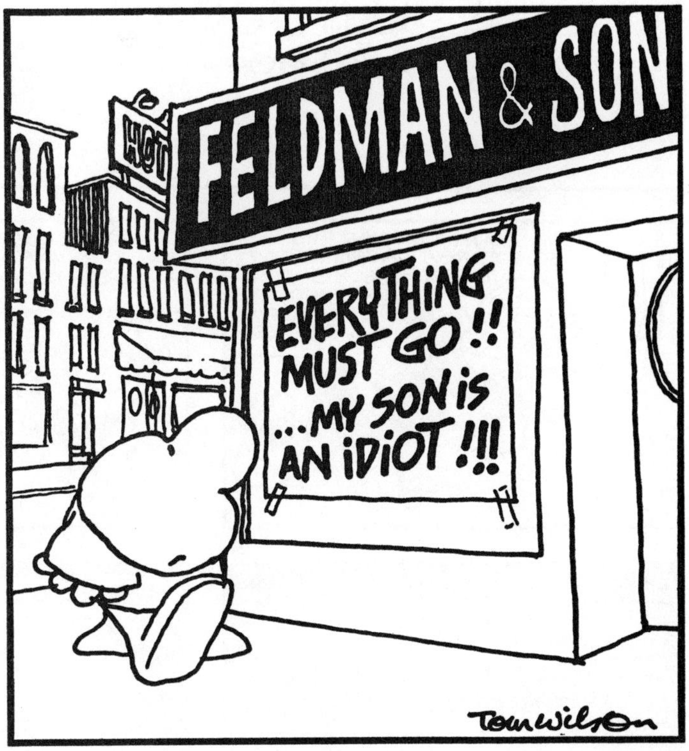
FELDMAN & SON
EVERYTHING MUST GO!! ...MY SON IS AN IDIOT!!!
Tom Wilson

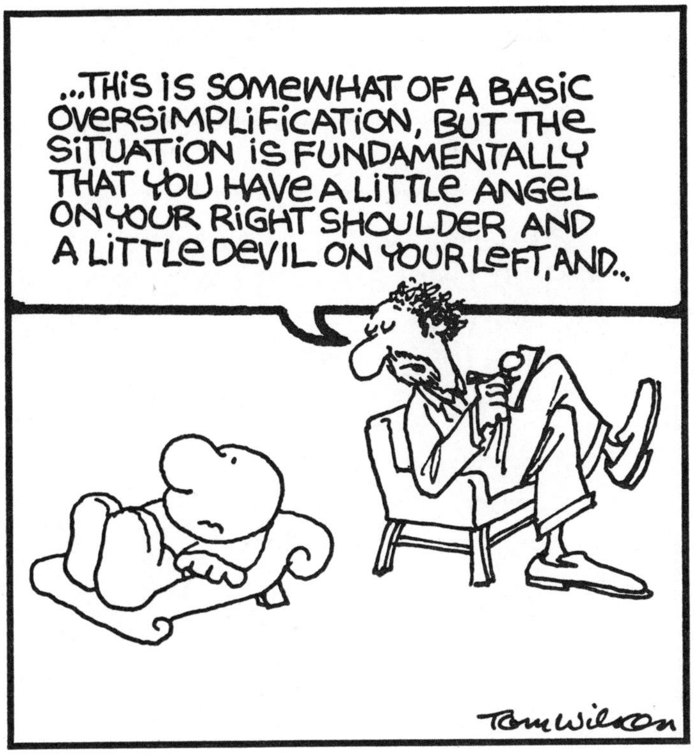
...THIS IS SOMEWHAT OF A BASIC OVERSIMPLIFICATION, BUT THE SITUATION IS FUNDAMENTALLY THAT YOU HAVE A LITTLE ANGEL ON YOUR RIGHT SHOULDER AND A LITTLE DEVIL ON YOUR LEFT, AND...
Tom Wilson

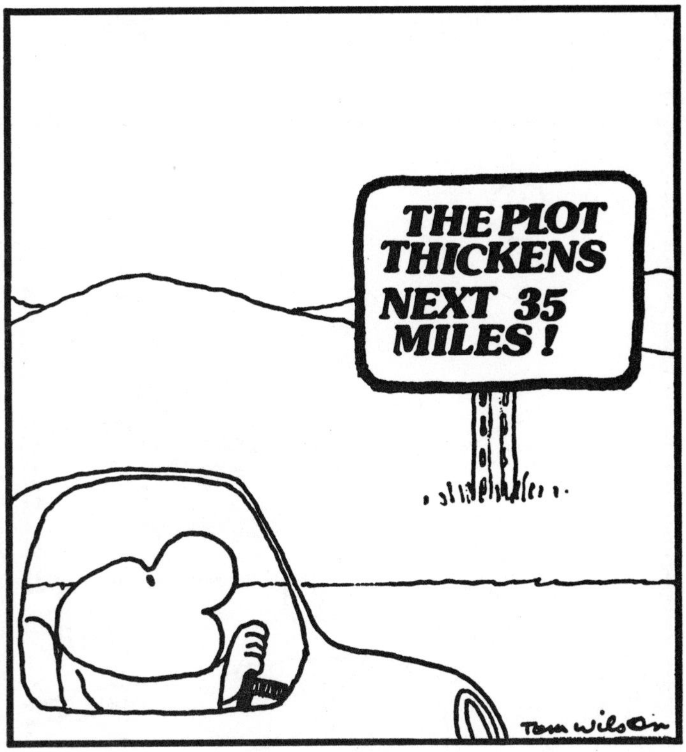
THE PLOT THICKENS NEXT 35 MILES!
Tom Wilson

ZIGGY...
by Tom Wilson
PROTECTO
BUILD A REPLICA OF YOURSELF
FOOL BURGLARS
EVERYTHING YOU NEED
PROTECTO
BUILD A REPLICA OF YOURSELF
FOOL BURGLARS
I'M SEWING TOGETHER THIS STUFFED REPLICA OF MYSELF, FUZZ, TO FOOL BURGLARS WHEN YOU AND I ARE AWAY FROM THE HOUSE...
THERE! I'LL LEAVE HIM IN MY FAVORITE CHAIR, WITH THE LAMP ON AND WE CAN LEAVE FEELING SECURE.
...A PERSON CAN'T BE TOO CAREFUL THESE DAYS, FUZZ ...BETTER SAFE THAN SORRY."
LATER
...AHHH HERE WE ARE. HOME AGAIN.. THERE'S OUR HOUSE...
YAP!
...SAFE AND SOUND!
HOME SWEET HOME
Tom Wilson

FIVE WILL GET YOU TEN THAT YOU ARE NOW ENTERING THE STATE OF NEVADA
Tom Wilson

ZIGGY, I'M AFRAID YOUR GREAT UNCLE AMOS WATCHED TOO MUCH T.V. HIS WILL JUST SAYS, "LEAVE IT TO BEAVER."
Tom Wilson

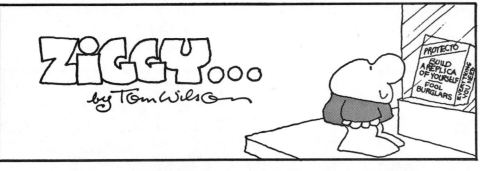

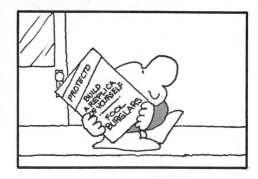

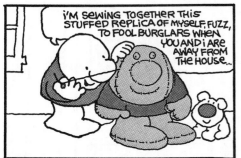

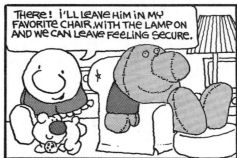

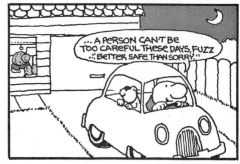

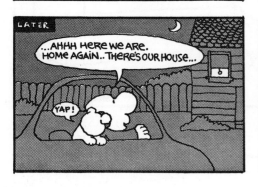

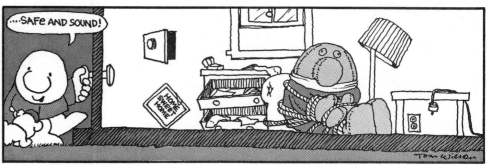

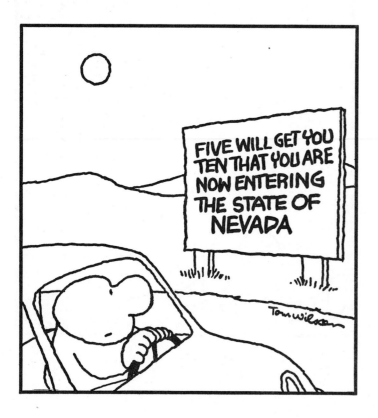

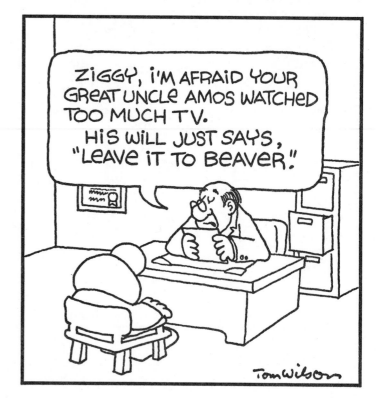

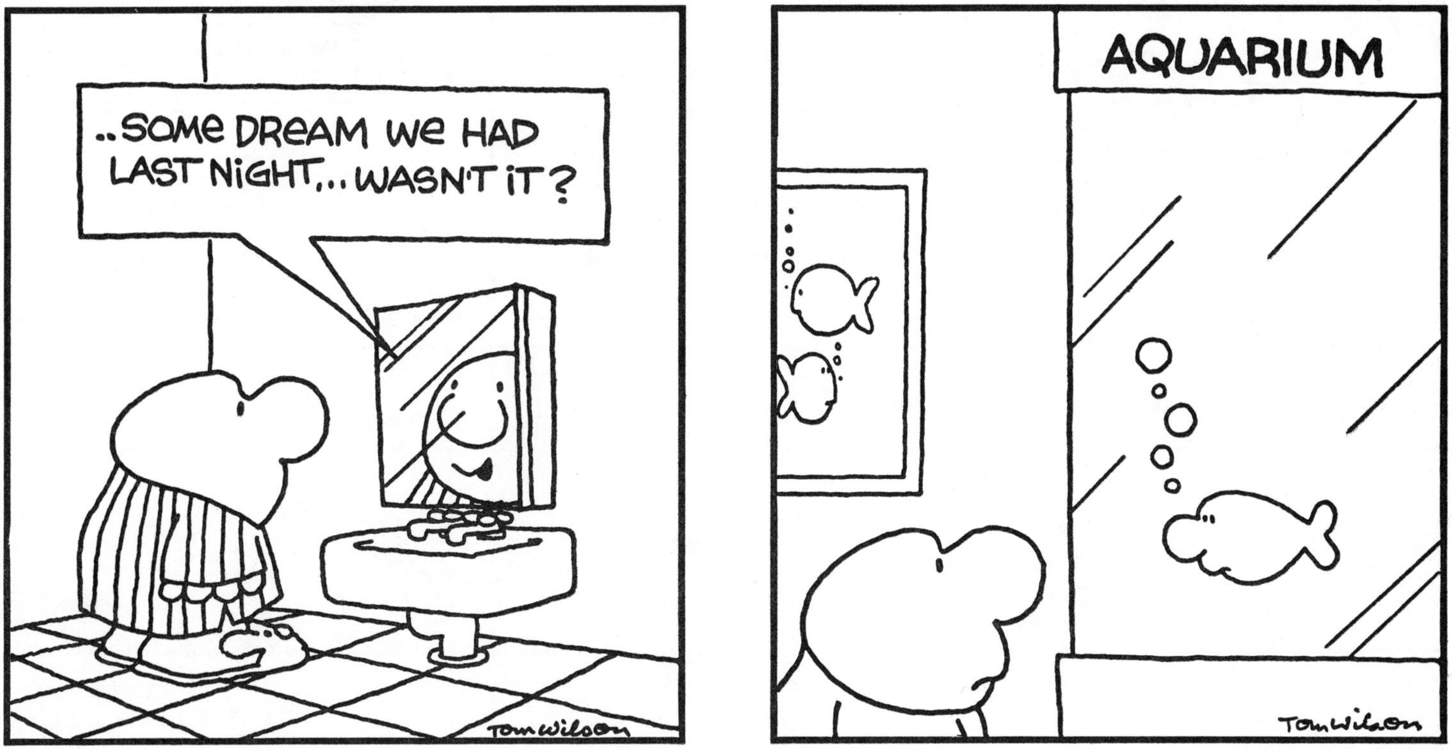
..SOME DREAM WE HAD LAST NIGHT... WASN'T IT?
AQUARIUM
Tom Wilson
Tom Wilson

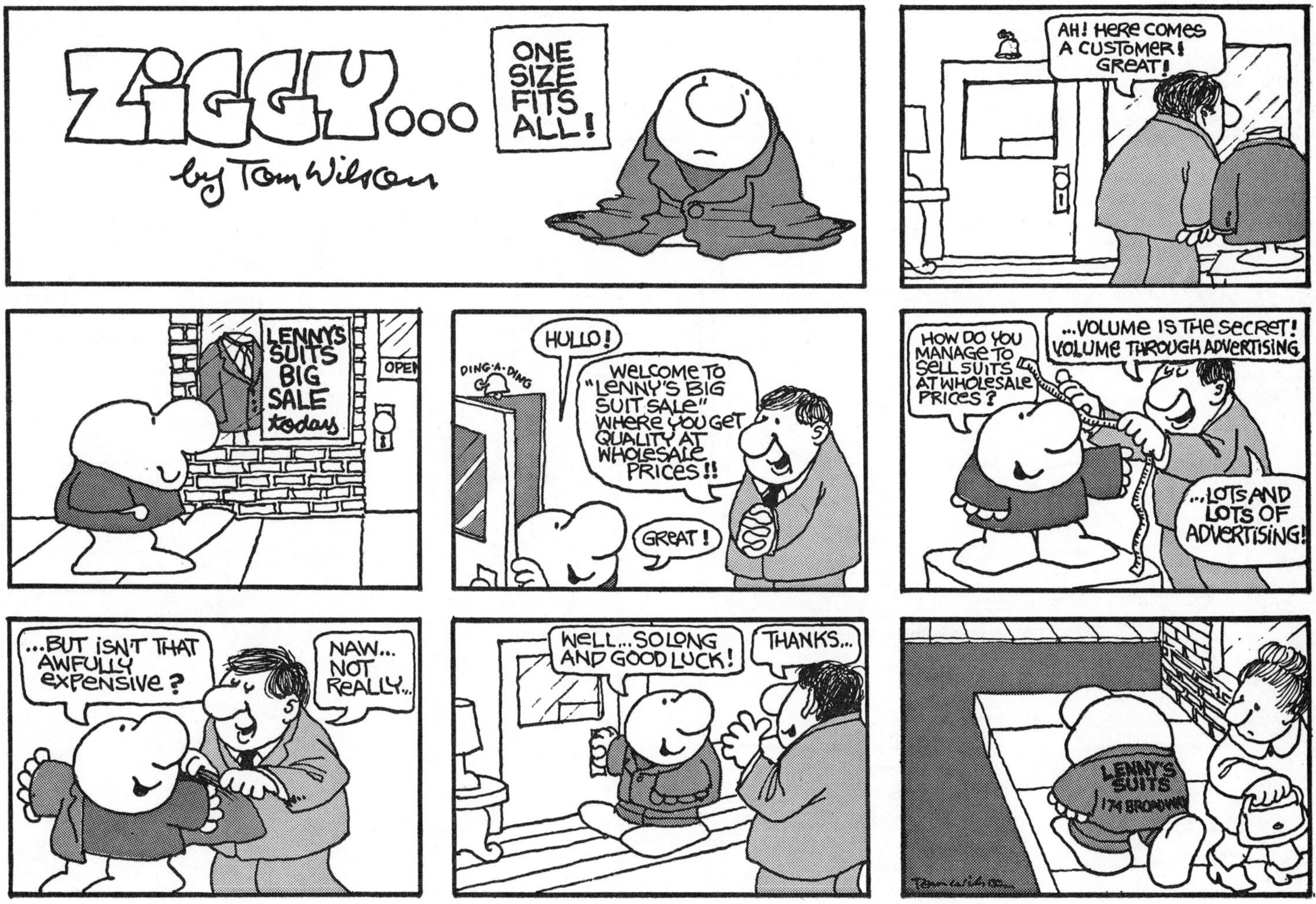
ZIGGY...
ONE SIZE FITS ALL!
by Tom Wilson
AH! HERE COMES A CUSTOMER! GREAT!
LENNY'S SUITS BIG SALE today
OPEN
HULLO!
DING-A-DING
WELCOME TO "LENNY'S BIG SUIT SALE" WHERE YOU GET QUALITY AT WHOLESALE PRICES!!
GREAT!
HOW DO YOU MANAGE TO SELL SUITS AT WHOLESALE PRICES?
...VOLUME IS THE SECRET! VOLUME THROUGH ADVERTISING
...LOTS AND LOTS OF ADVERTISING!
...BUT ISN'T THAT AWFULLY EXPENSIVE?
NAW... NOT REALLY...
WELL... SO LONG AND GOOD LUCK!
THANKS...
LENNY'S SUITS 174 BROADWAY
Tom Wilson

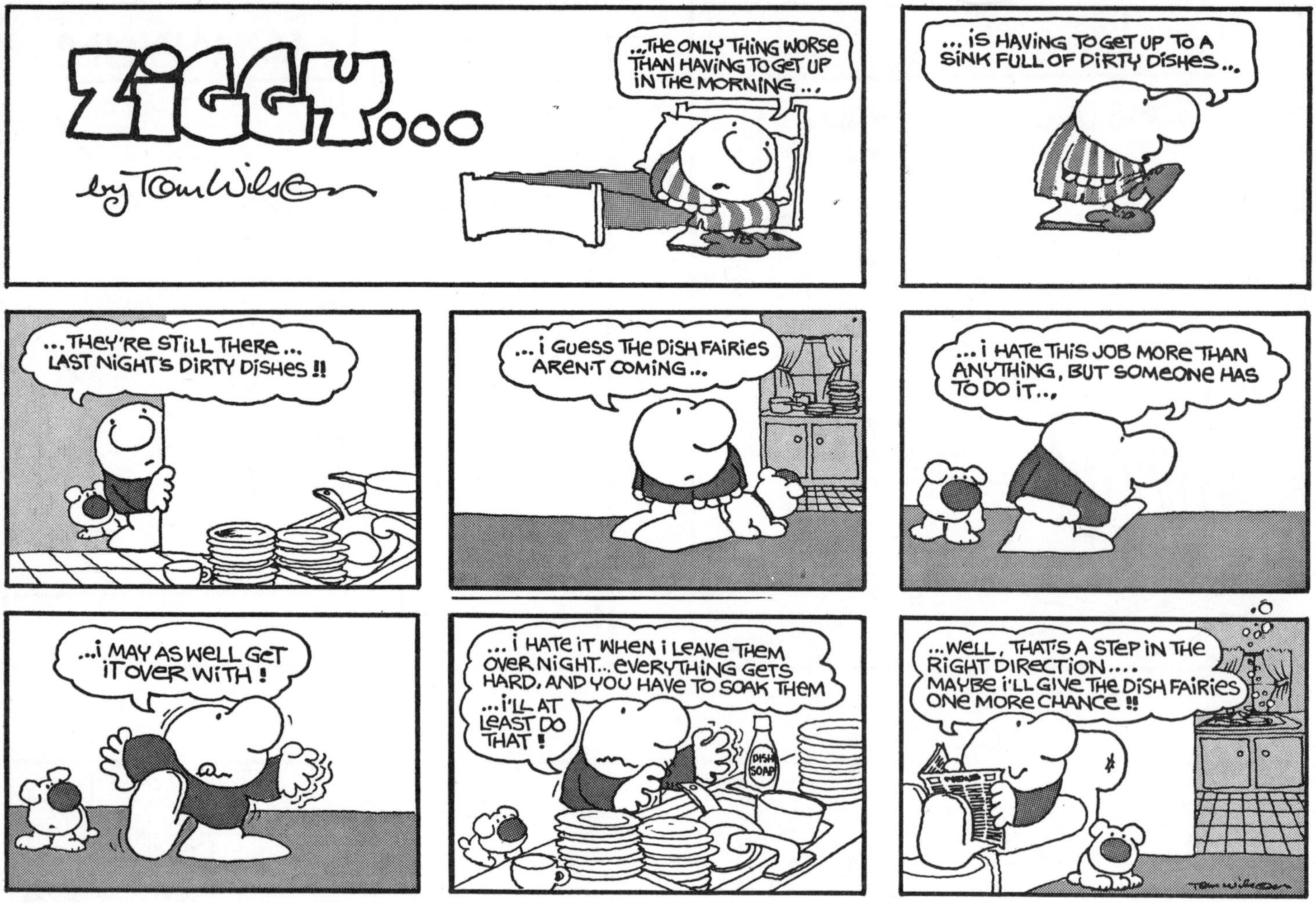
ZIGGY
by Tom Wilson
...THE ONLY THING WORSE THAN HAVING TO GET UP IN THE MORNING...
...IS HAVING TO GET UP TO A SINK FULL OF DIRTY DISHES...
...THEY'RE STILL THERE... LAST NIGHT'S DIRTY DISHES !!
...I GUESS THE DISH FAIRIES AREN'T COMING...
...I HATE THIS JOB MORE THAN ANYTHING, BUT SOMEONE HAS TO DO IT...
...I MAY AS WELL GET IT OVER WITH !
...I HATE IT WHEN I LEAVE THEM OVERNIGHT... EVERYTHING GETS HARD, AND YOU HAVE TO SOAK THEM
...I'LL AT LEAST DO THAT !
DISH SOAP
...WELL, THAT'S A STEP IN THE RIGHT DIRECTION.... MAYBE I'LL GIVE THE DISH FAIRIES ONE MORE CHANCE !!

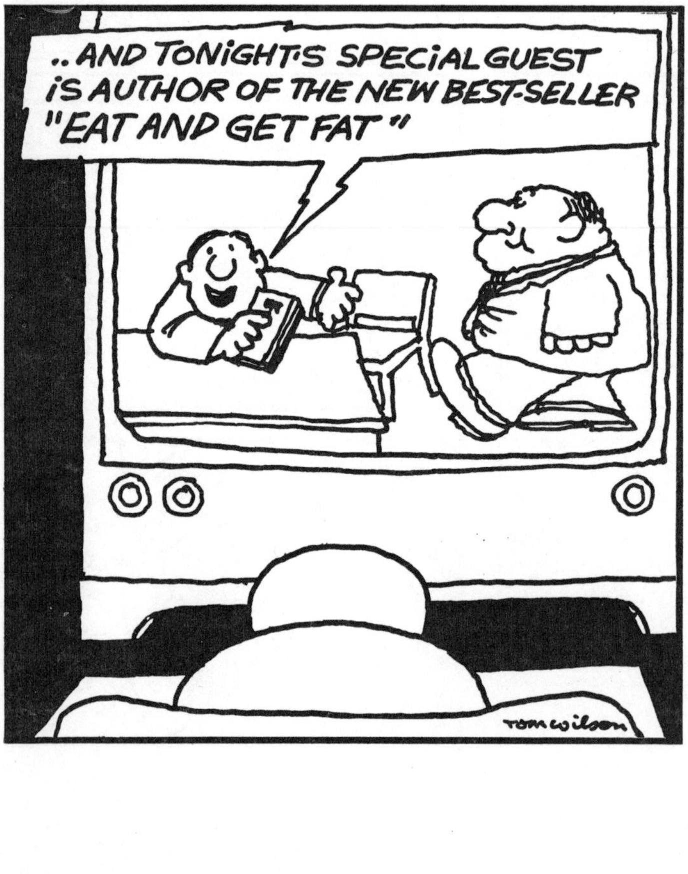
..AND TONIGHT'S SPECIAL GUEST IS AUTHOR OF THE NEW BEST-SELLER "EAT AND GET FAT"

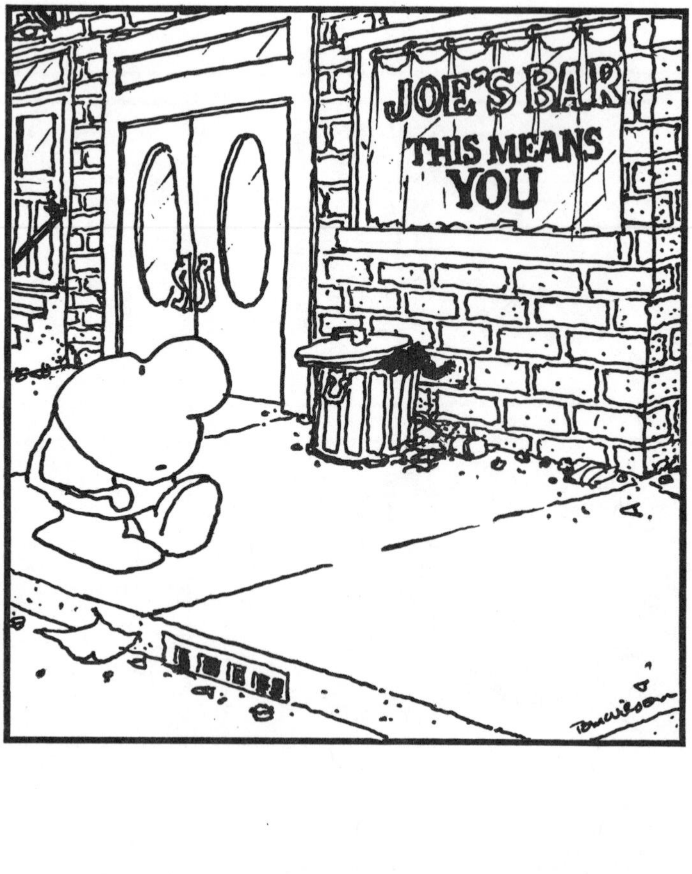
JOE'S BAR
THIS MEANS YOU

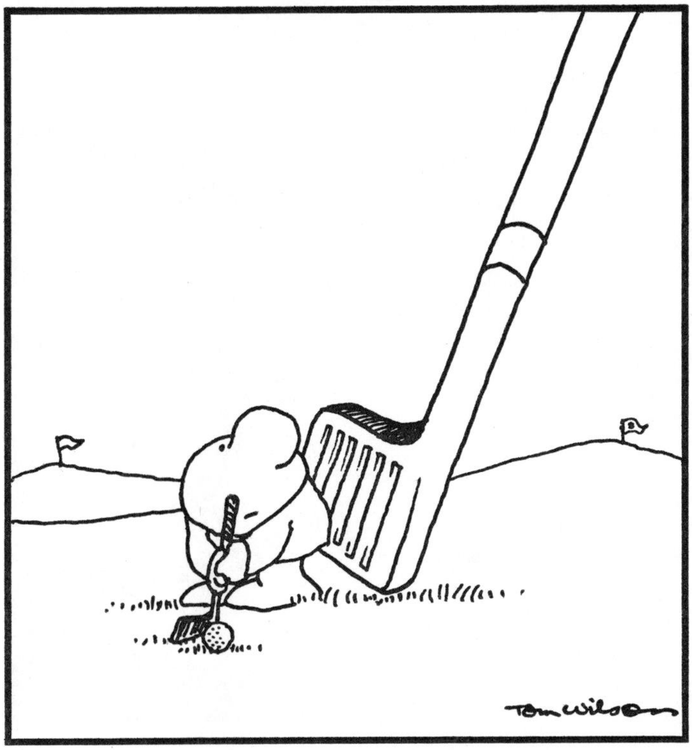
Tom Wilson

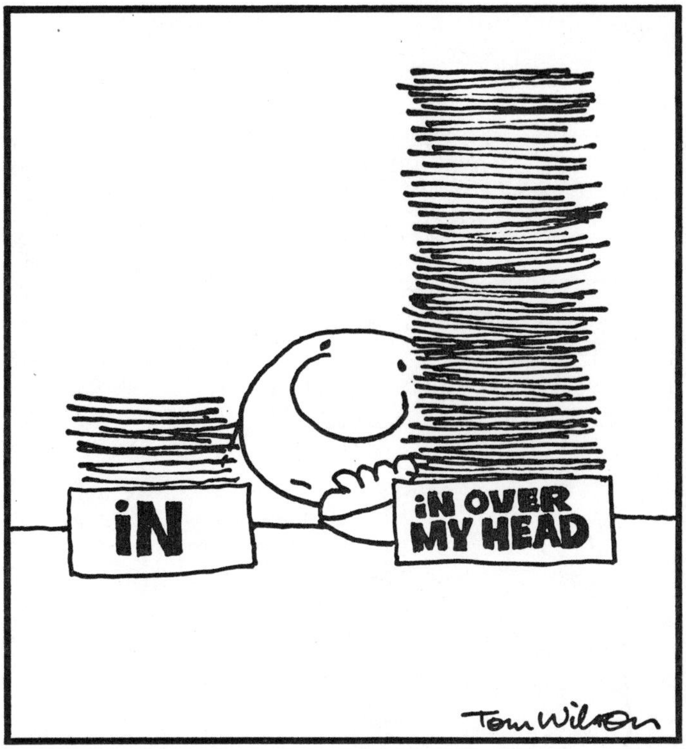
iN
iN OVER MY HEAD
Tom Wilson

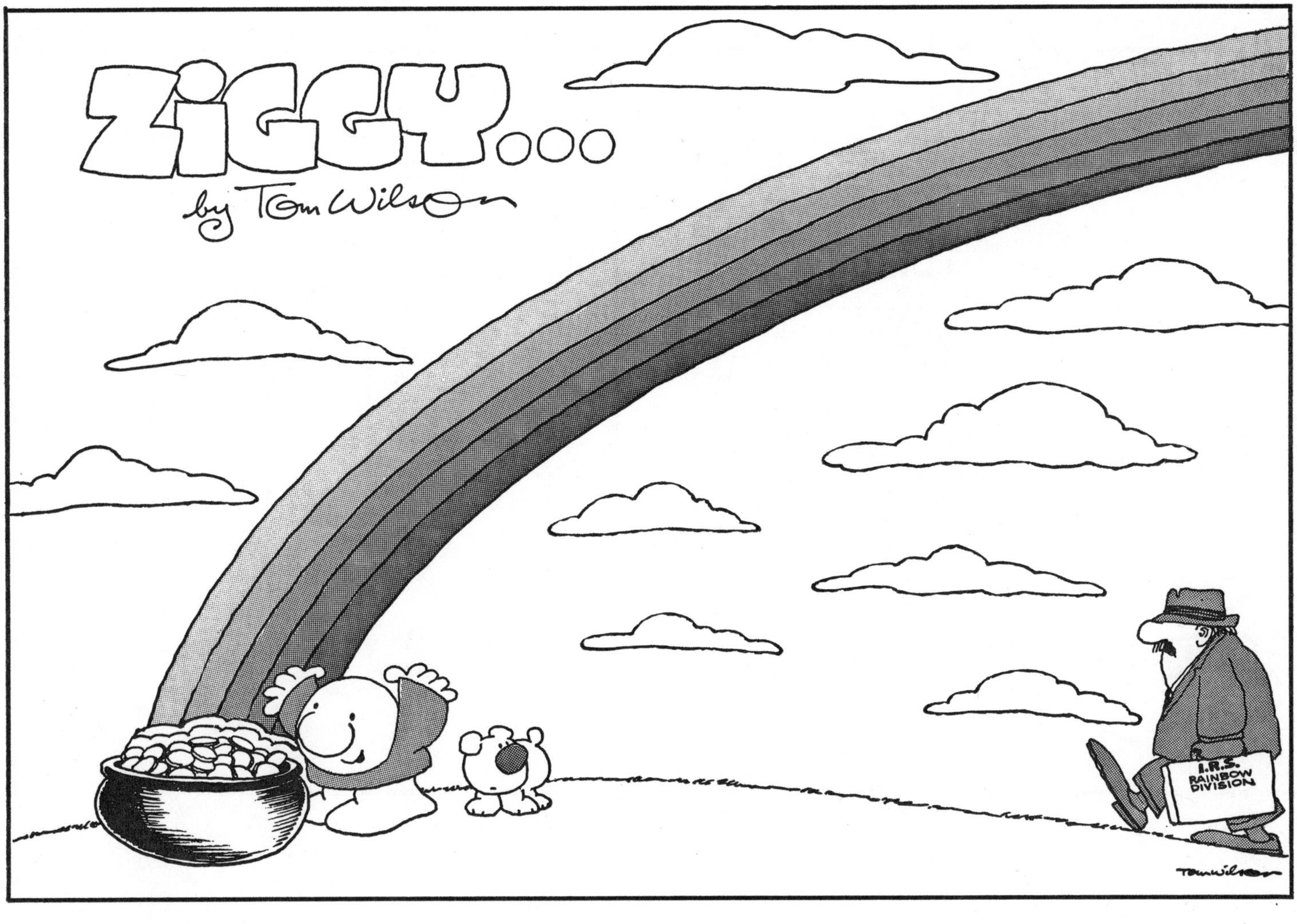
ZiGGY...
by Tom Wilson
I.R.S. RAINBOW DIVISION
Tom Wilson

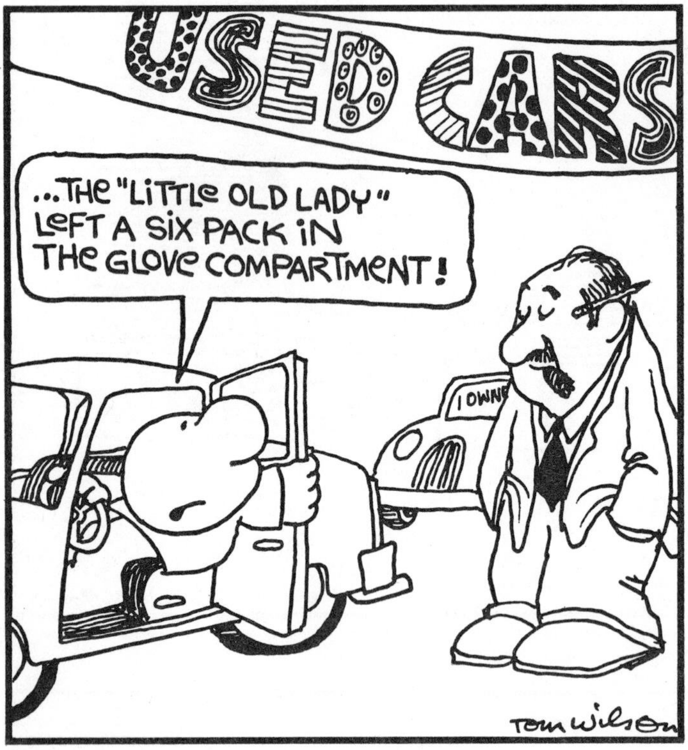
USED CARS
...THE "LITTLE OLD LADY" LEFT A SIX PACK IN THE GLOVE COMPARTMENT!
Tom Wilson

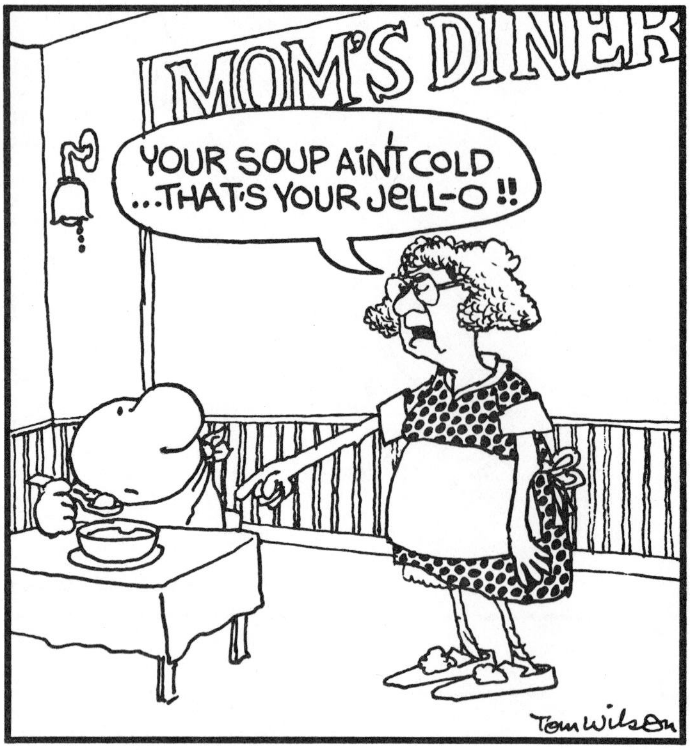
MOM'S DINER
YOUR SOUP AIN'T COLD ...THAT'S YOUR JELL-O !!
Tom Wilson

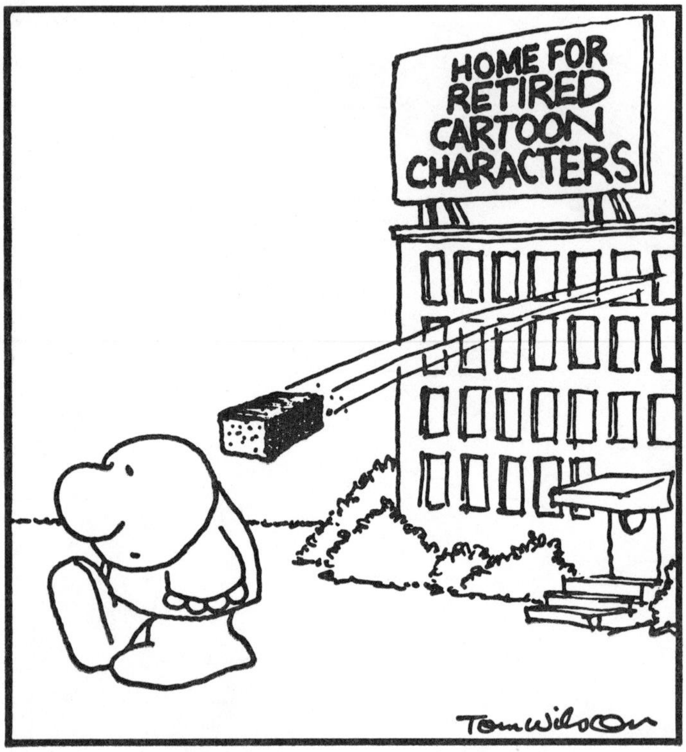
HOME FOR RETIRED CARTOON CHARACTERS
Tom Wilson

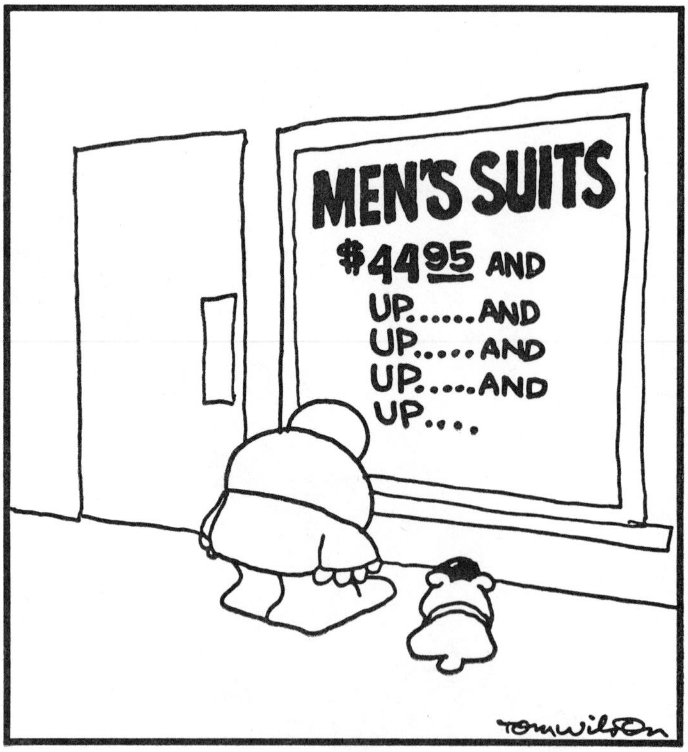
MEN'S SUITS
$44 95 AND
UP......AND
UP.....AND
UP.....AND
UP....
Tom Wilson

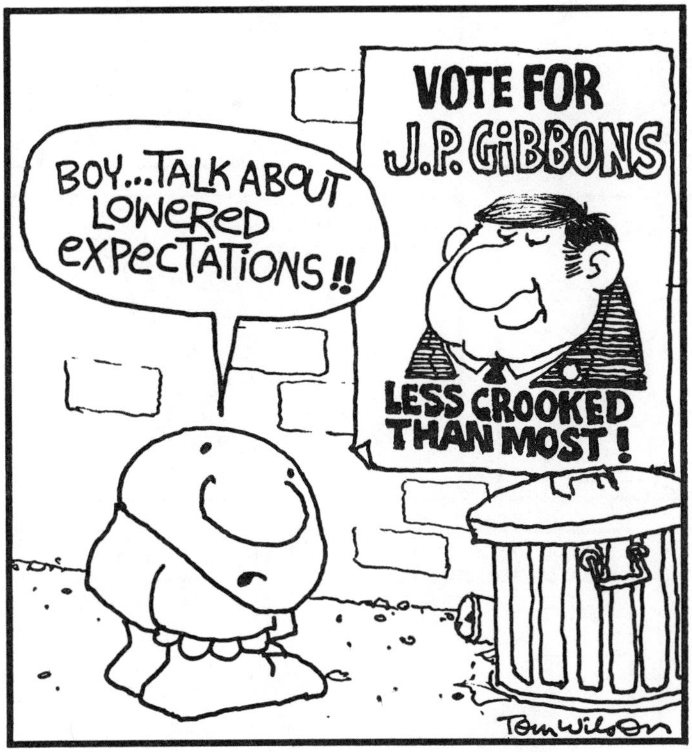
VOTE FOR
J.P. GIBBONS
LESS CROOKED THAN MOST!
BOY...TALK ABOUT LOWERED EXPECTATIONS!!
Tom Wilson

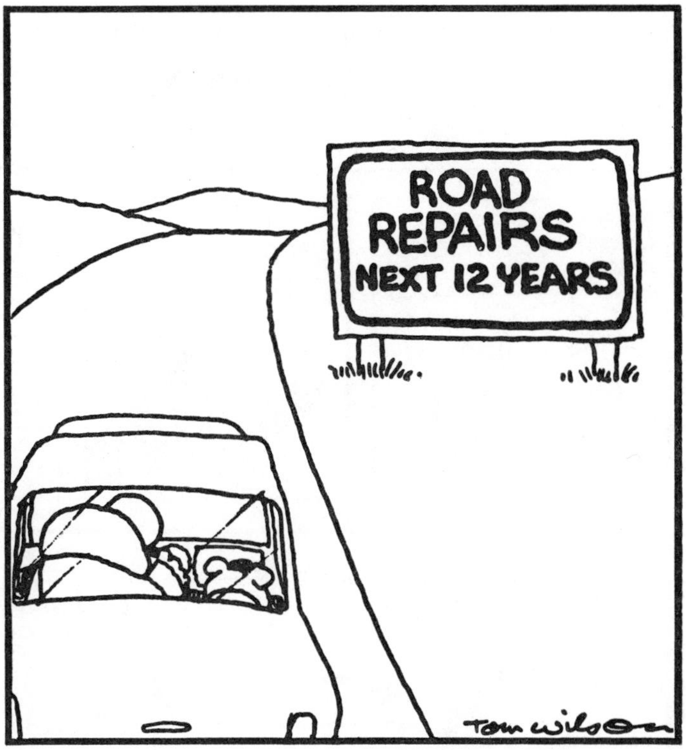
ROAD REPAIRS
NEXT 12 YEARS
Tom Wilson

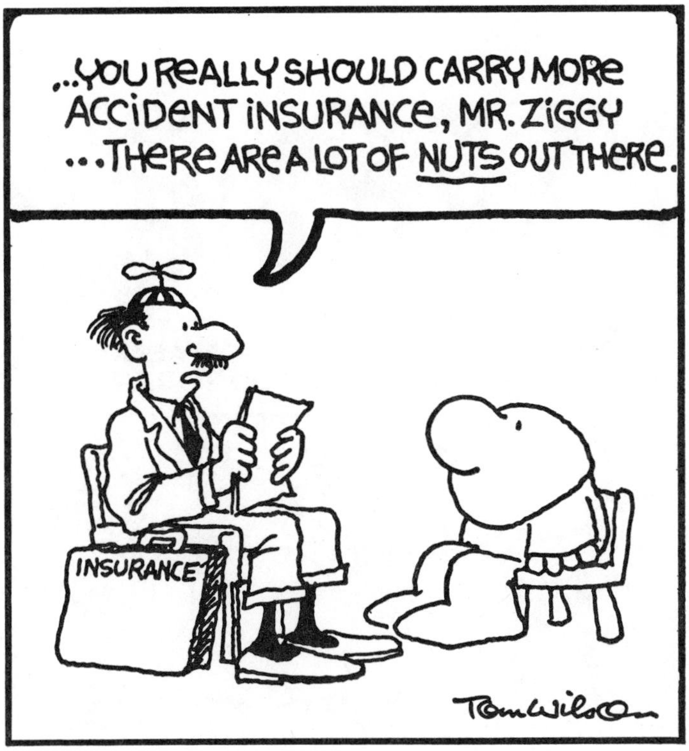
...YOU REALLY SHOULD CARRY MORE ACCIDENT INSURANCE, MR. ZIGGY ...THERE ARE A LOT OF NUTS OUT THERE.
INSURANCE
Tom Wilson

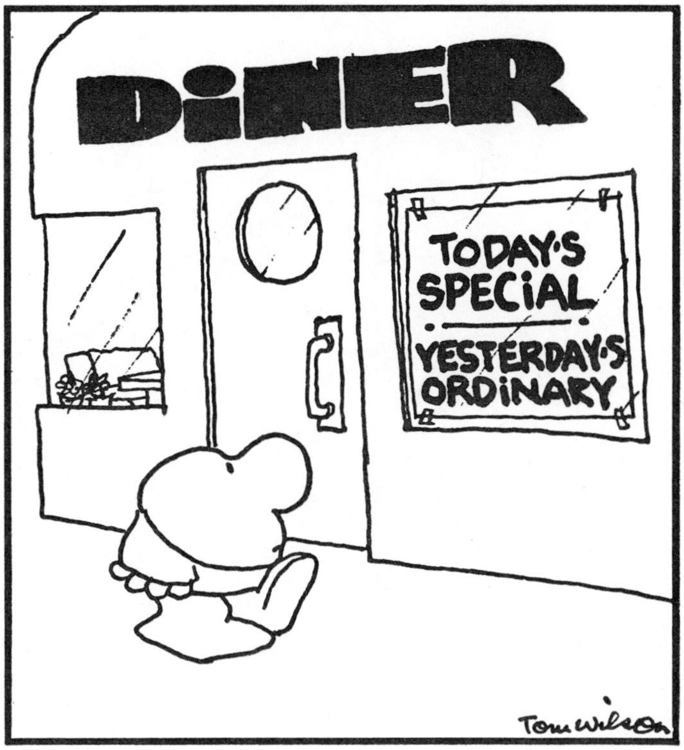
DINER
TODAY'S SPECIAL
YESTERDAY'S ORDINARY
Tom Wilson

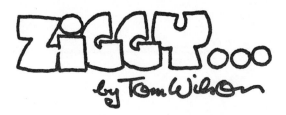

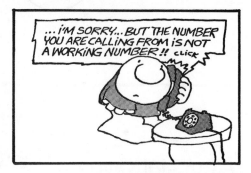

ZIGGY
by Tom Wilson
DIAL DIAL DIAL
... I'M SORRY... BUT THE NUMBER YOU ARE CALLING FROM IS NOT A WORKING NUMBER!! CLICK
THERE'S A NEW SERVICE CALLED "DIAL-A-FRIEND" ...SO I'M GIVING IT A TRY...
"DIAL-A-FRIEND." PLEASE HOLD!!
THIS IS GREAT!! ....EVERYBODY NEEDS A FRIEND...
HELLO?
HELLO? "DIAL-A-FRIEND"? HI! WHAT'S UP?
PLEASE HOLD.
..THIS SERVICE IS DESIGNED FOR PEOPLE LIKE ME, WHO NEED SOMEONE TO TALK TO...
HELLO? ARE YOU STILL THERE?!
YES!
PLEASE HOLD THE LINE.... ..OK SIR, GO AHEAD.
HI! MY NAME IS ZIGGY, AND I UNDERSTAND YOU'LL BE MY FRIEND, AND WE CAN CALL EACH OTHER UP AND EVERYTHING!!
HEY! YOU BET... GEE, THIS IS GREAT.
... SAY, LISTEN ZIG, OLD BUDDY... COULD YOU LET ME HAVE TEN BUCKS TILL THURSDAY?
Tom Wilson

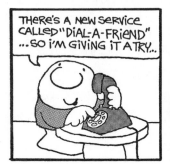

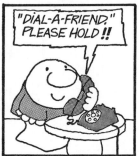

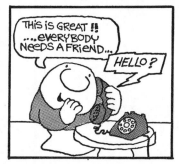

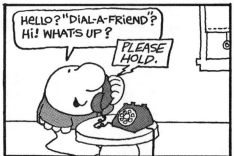

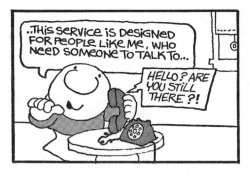

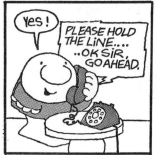

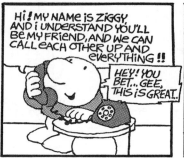

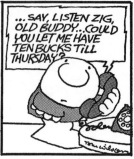

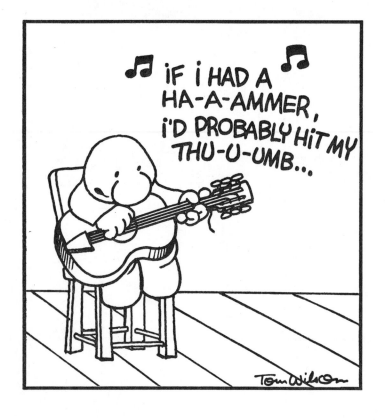

IF I HAD A HA-A-AMMER, I'D PROBABLY HIT MY THU-U-UMB...
Tom Wilson

...TELEPHONY ENOUGH FOR YOU TODAY?
BUS STOP
Tom Wilson

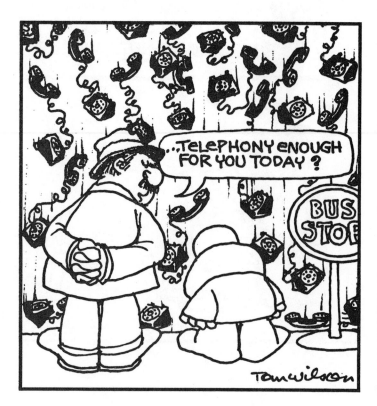

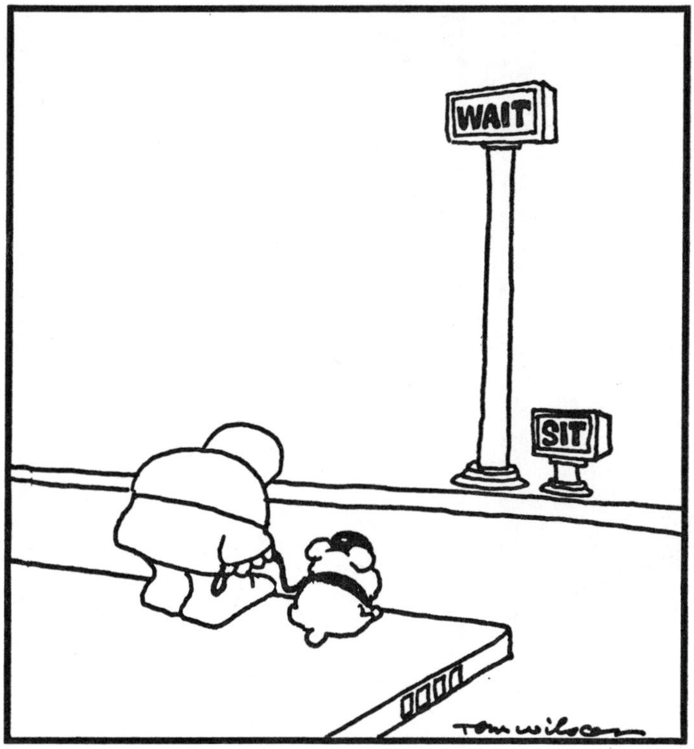
WAIT
SIT
Tom Wilson

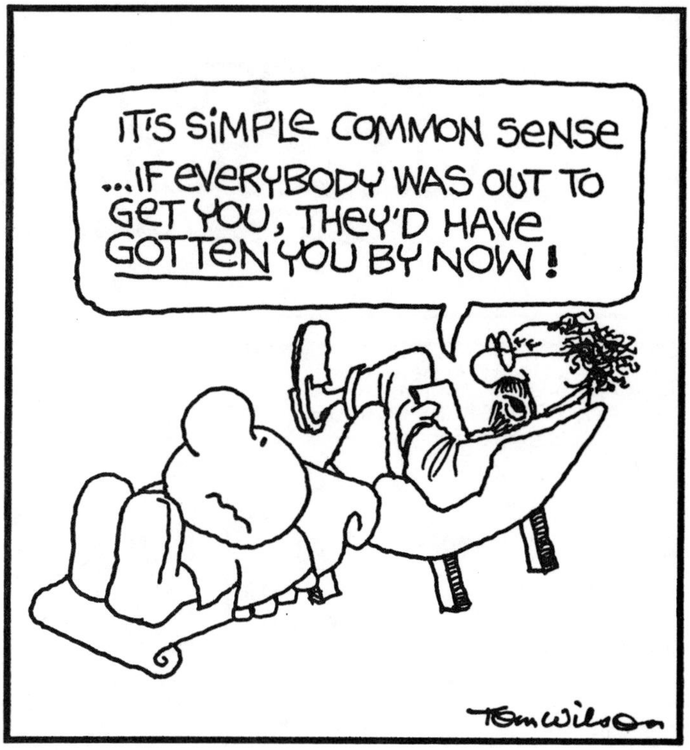
IT'S SIMPLE COMMON SENSE ...IF EVERYBODY WAS OUT TO GET YOU, THEY'D HAVE GOTTEN YOU BY NOW!
Tom Wilson

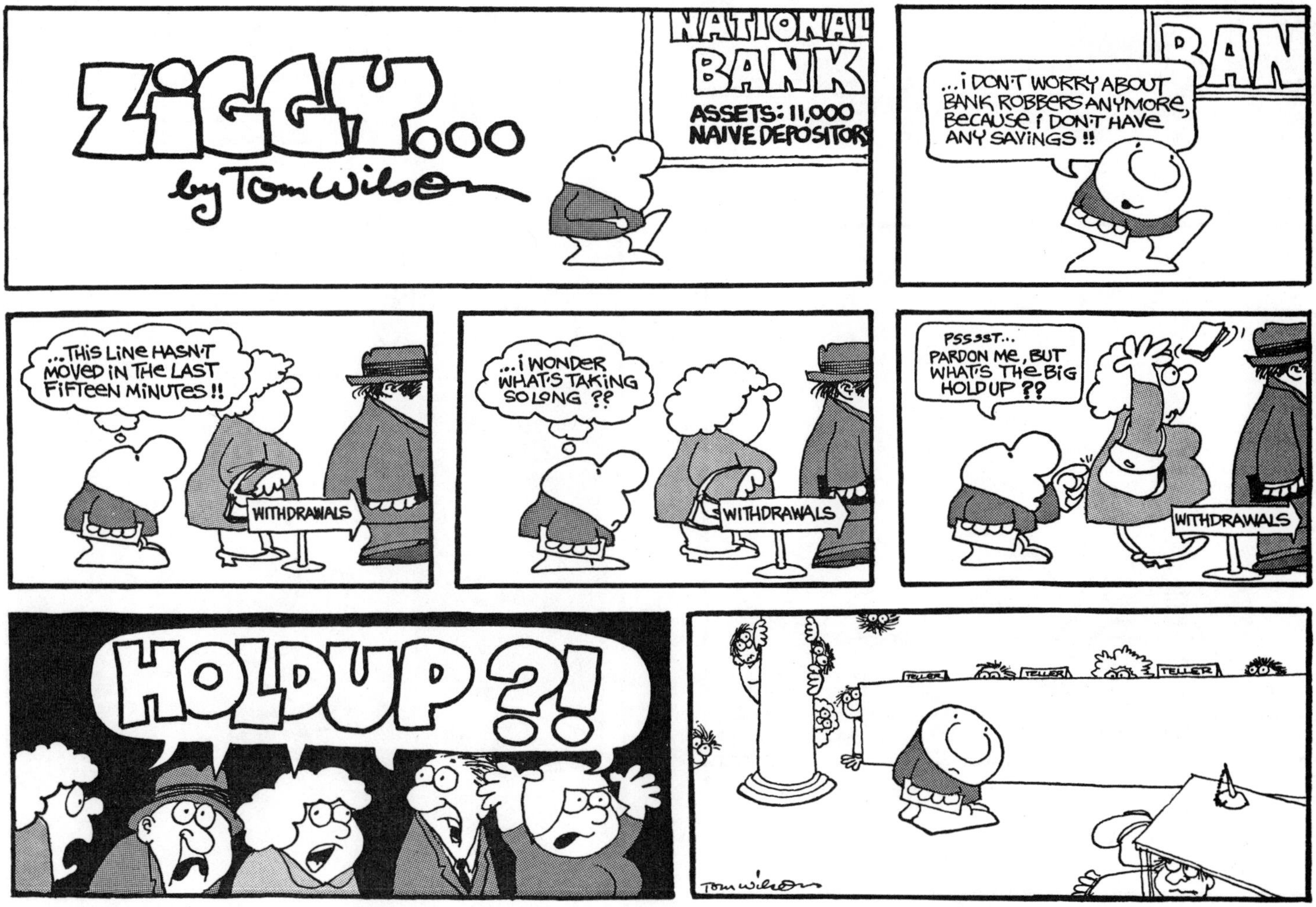
ZIGGY.000
by Tom Wilson
NATIONAL BANK
ASSETS: 11,000 NAIVE DEPOSITORS
...I DON'T WORRY ABOUT BANK ROBBERS ANYMORE, BECAUSE I DON'T HAVE ANY SAVINGS!!
...THIS LINE HASN'T MOVED IN THE LAST FIFTEEN MINUTES!!
WITHDRAWALS
...I WONDER WHAT'S TAKING SO LONG ??
WITHDRAWALS
PSSSST... PARDON ME, BUT WHAT'S THE BIG HOLDUP ??
WITHDRAWALS
HOLDUP ?!
TELLER
TELLER
TELLER
Tom Wilson

ZIGGY
by Tom Wilson
...GUESS THIS is iT ...i'M ON !!
...DiD YOU eVeR HAVE THE FeeLiNG THAT THE WHOLE WORLD iS WATCHiNG YOU?
...LiKe YOU'Re iN THE SPOTLiGHT, AND THE AUDieNCe iS WAiTiNG OUT THeRe FOR YOU TO DO SOMeTHiNG...
BUT WHAT...??
YOU CAN'T DANCe... ..YOU CAN'T SiNG...CAN'T DO iMPReSSiONS...YOU'Re ReALLY iN TROUBLe...
...AND THeN SUDDeNLY YOU ReALiZe... ALL YOU GOTTA DO iS Be YOURSeLF !! THAT'S THe SeCReT, THAT'S ALL THe WORLD eXPeCTS OF YOU...
SNAP
Tom Wilson

EENIE
MEENIE
MINEY
MOE
Tom Wilson

...i DON'T THiNK SHe WANTS TO TALK ABOUT iT...
Tom Wilson

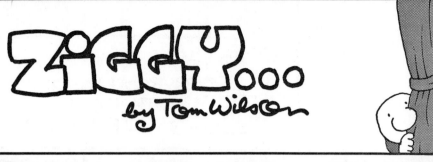

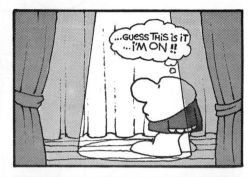

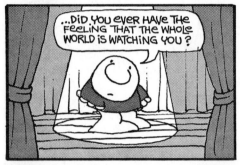

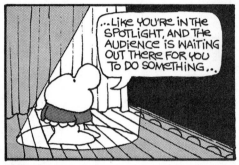

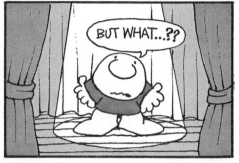

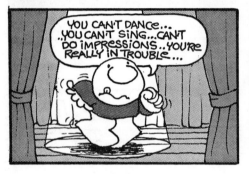

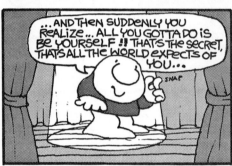

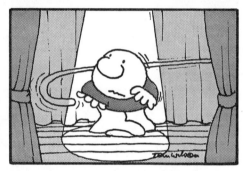

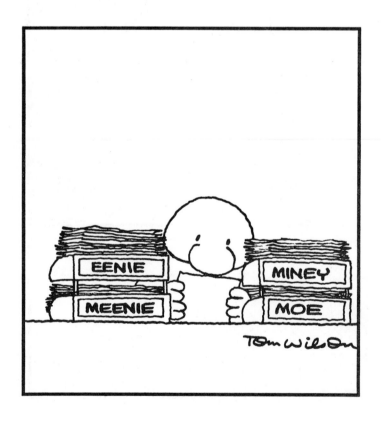

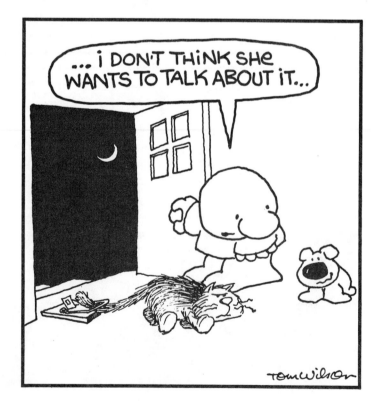

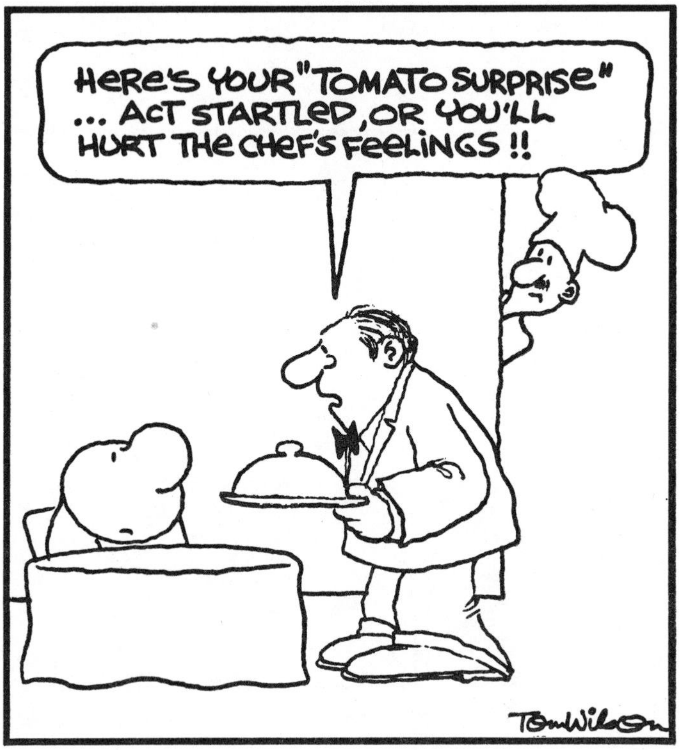
HERE'S YOUR "TOMATO SURPRISE" ... ACT STARTLED, OR YOU'LL HURT THE CHEF'S FEELINGS !!
Tom Wilson

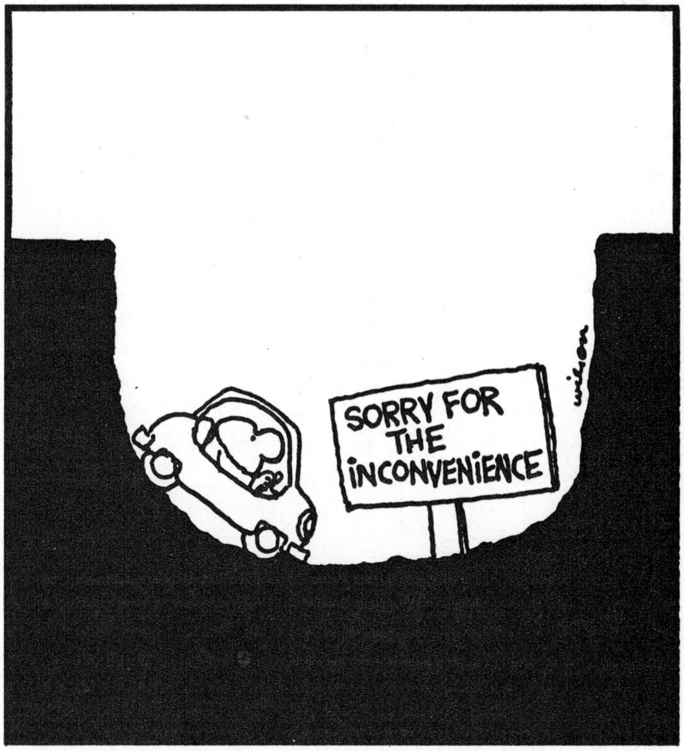
SORRY FOR THE INCONVENIENCE
wilson

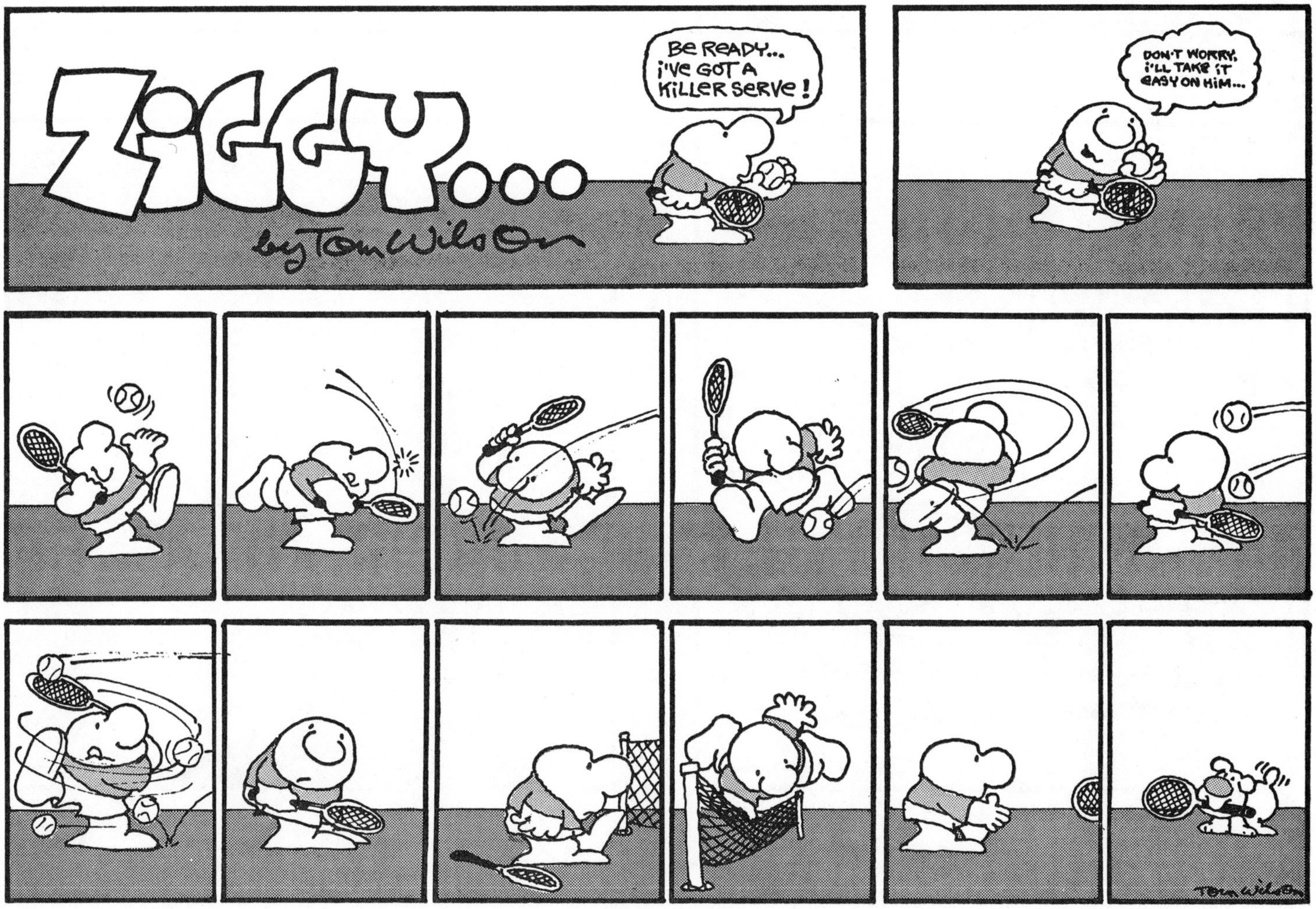
ZIGGY...
by Tom Wilson
BE READY... I'VE GOT A KILLER SERVE!
DON'T WORRY, I'LL TAKE IT EASY ON HIM...
Tom Wilson

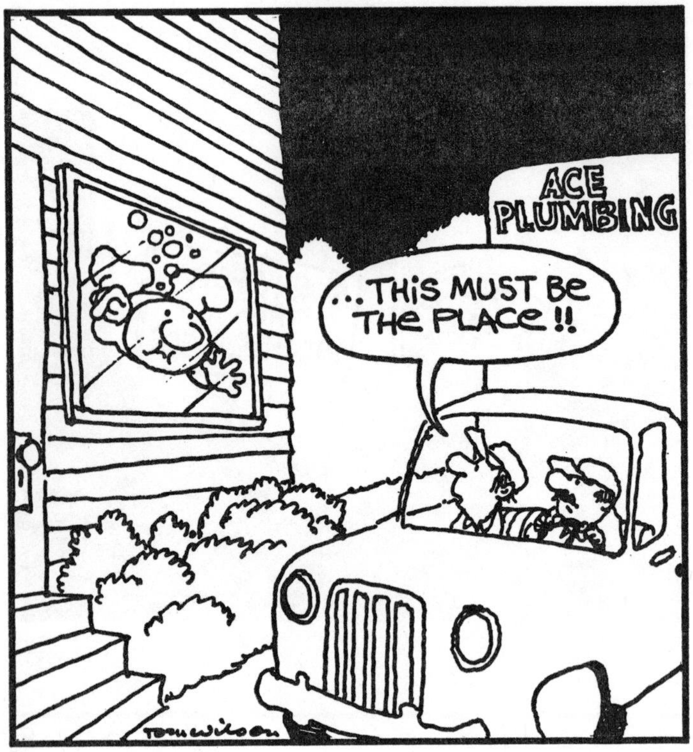
ACE PLUMBING
...THIS MUST BE THE PLACE!!
TOM WILSON

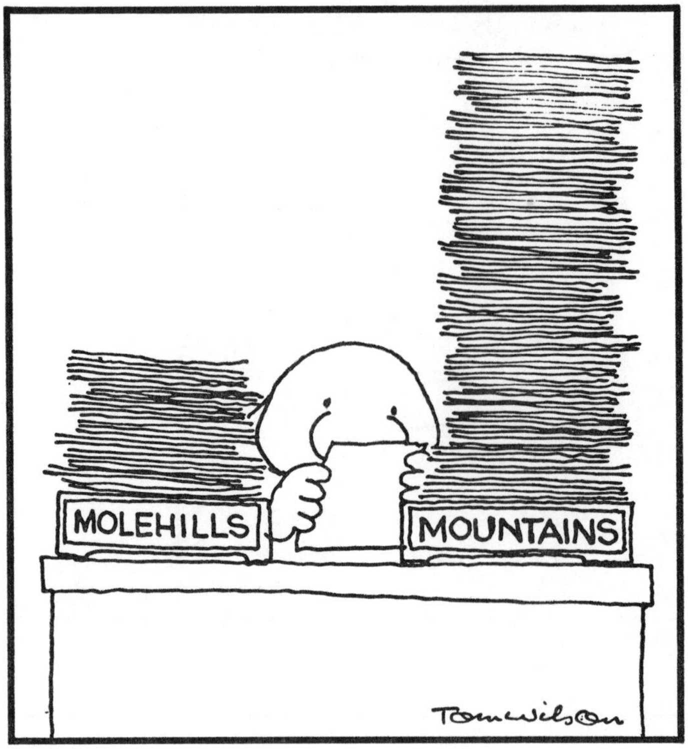
MOLEHILLS
MOUNTAINS
TOM WILSON

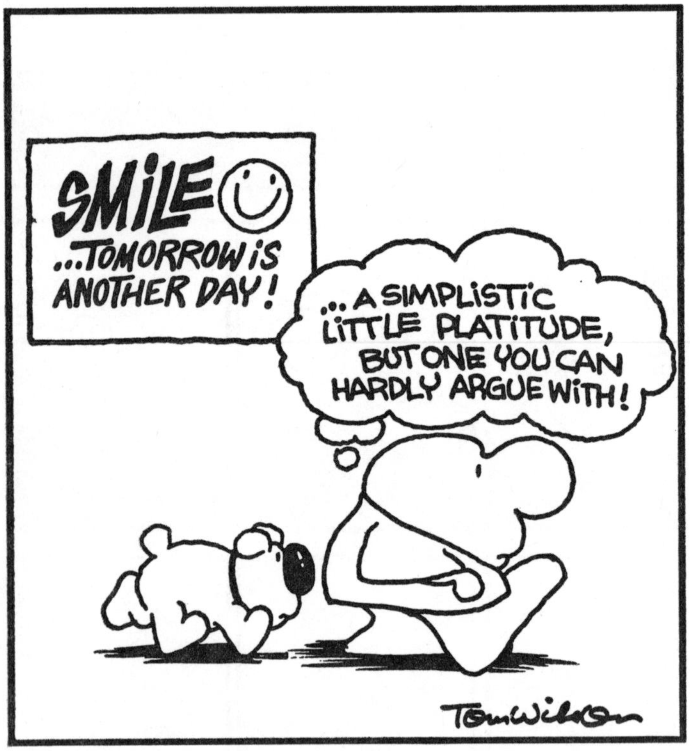
SMILE ...TOMORROW IS ANOTHER DAY!
...A SIMPLISTIC LITTLE PLATITUDE, BUT ONE YOU CAN HARDLY ARGUE WITH!
TOM WILSON

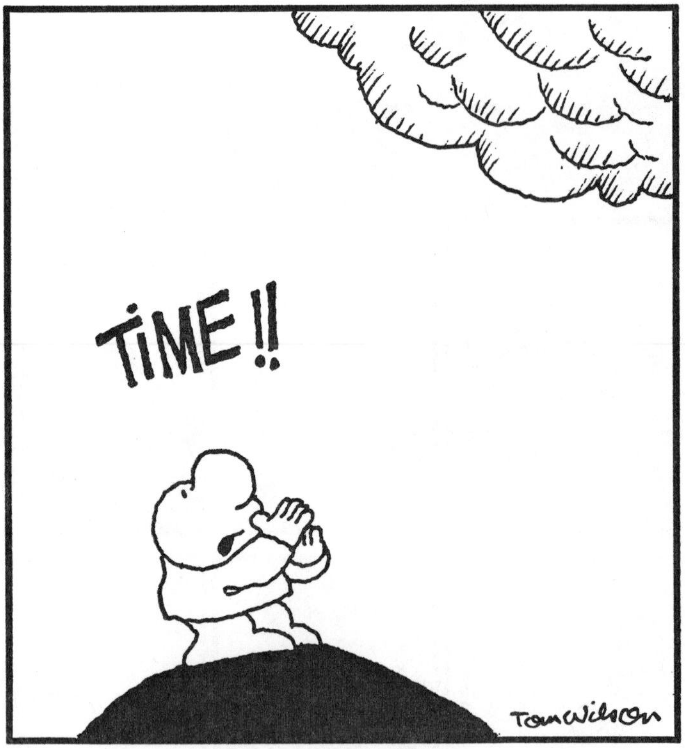
TIME!!
TOM WILSON

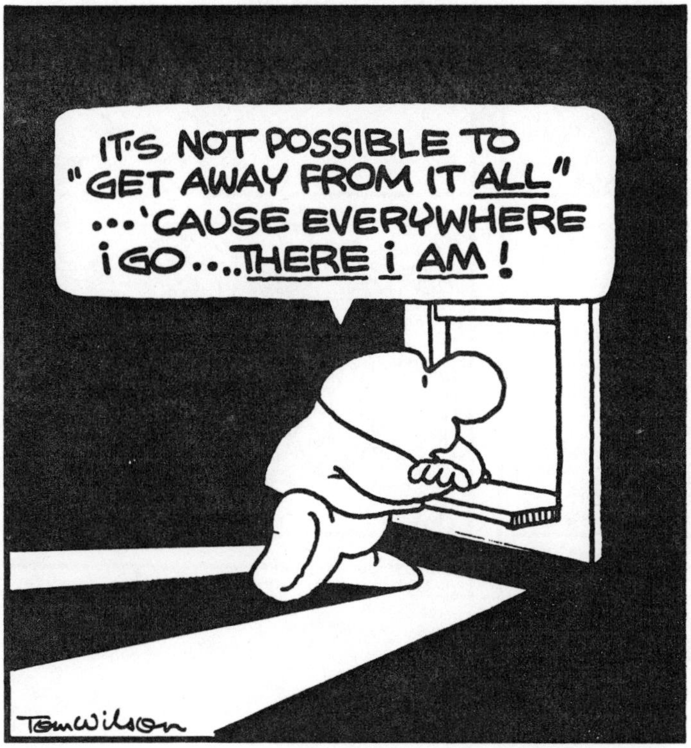
IT'S NOT POSSIBLE TO "GET AWAY FROM IT ALL" ...'CAUSE EVERYWHERE I GO... THERE I AM!
TOM WILSON

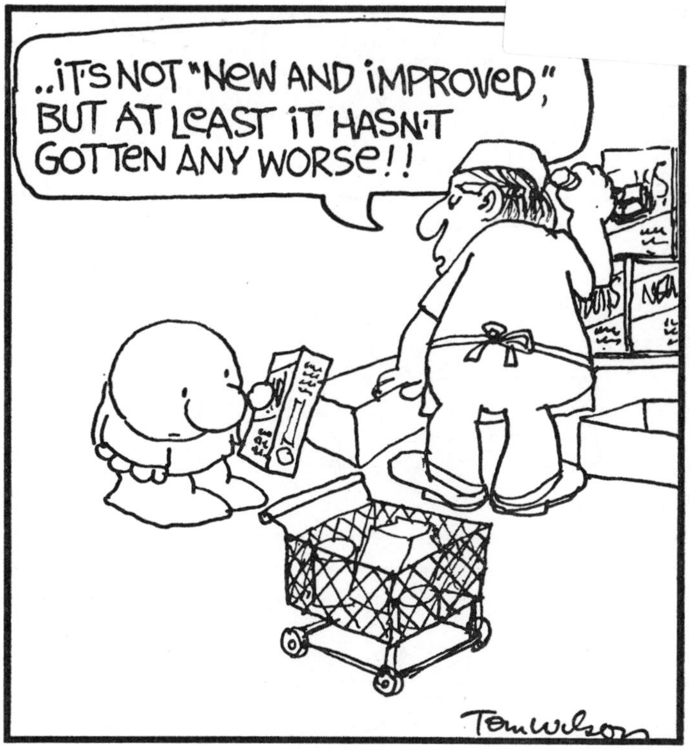
..IT'S NOT "NEW AND IMPROVED," BUT AT LEAST IT HASN'T GOTTEN ANY WORSE!!
TOM WILSON

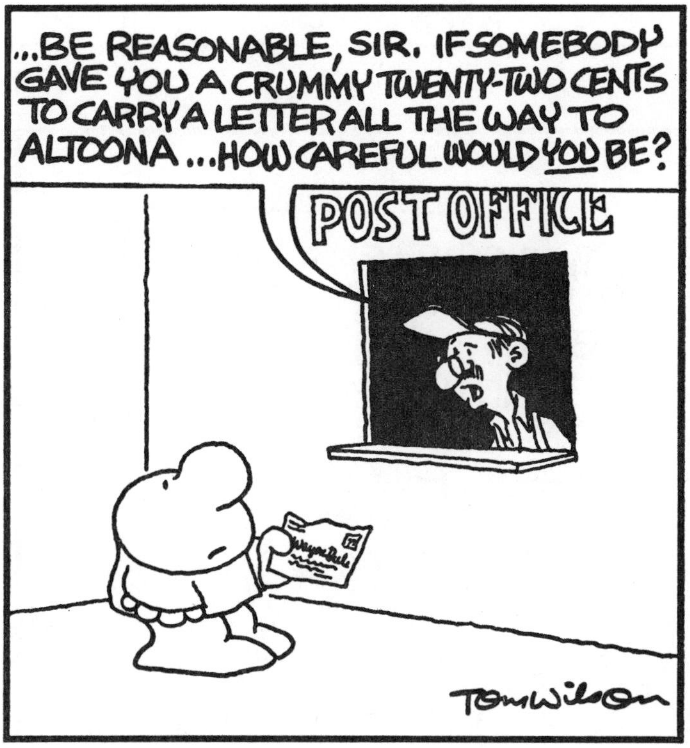
...BE REASONABLE, SIR. IF SOMEBODY GAVE YOU A CRUMMY TWENTY-TWO CENTS TO CARRY A LETTER ALL THE WAY TO ALTOONA ...HOW CAREFUL WOULD YOU BE?
POST OFFICE
TOM WILSON

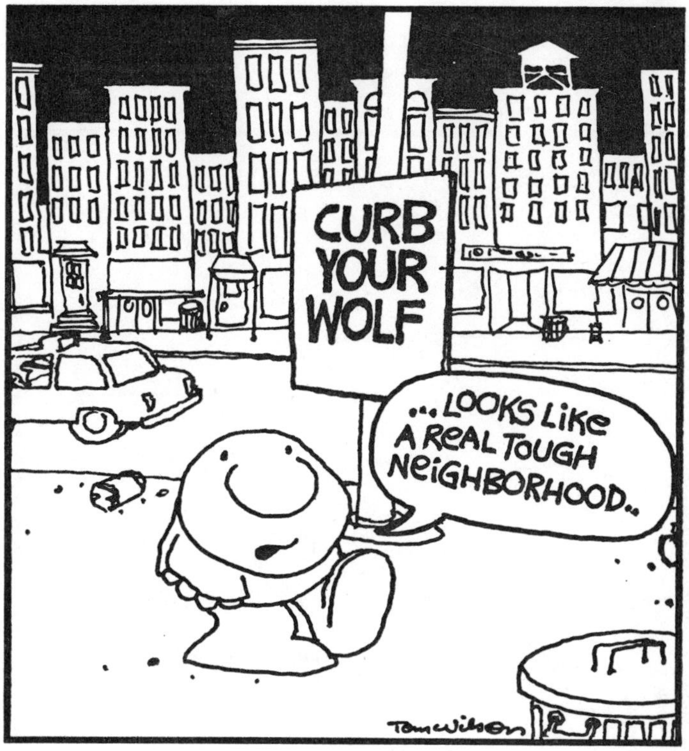
CURB YOUR WOLF
...LOOKS LIKE A REAL TOUGH NEIGHBORHOOD..
TOM WILSON

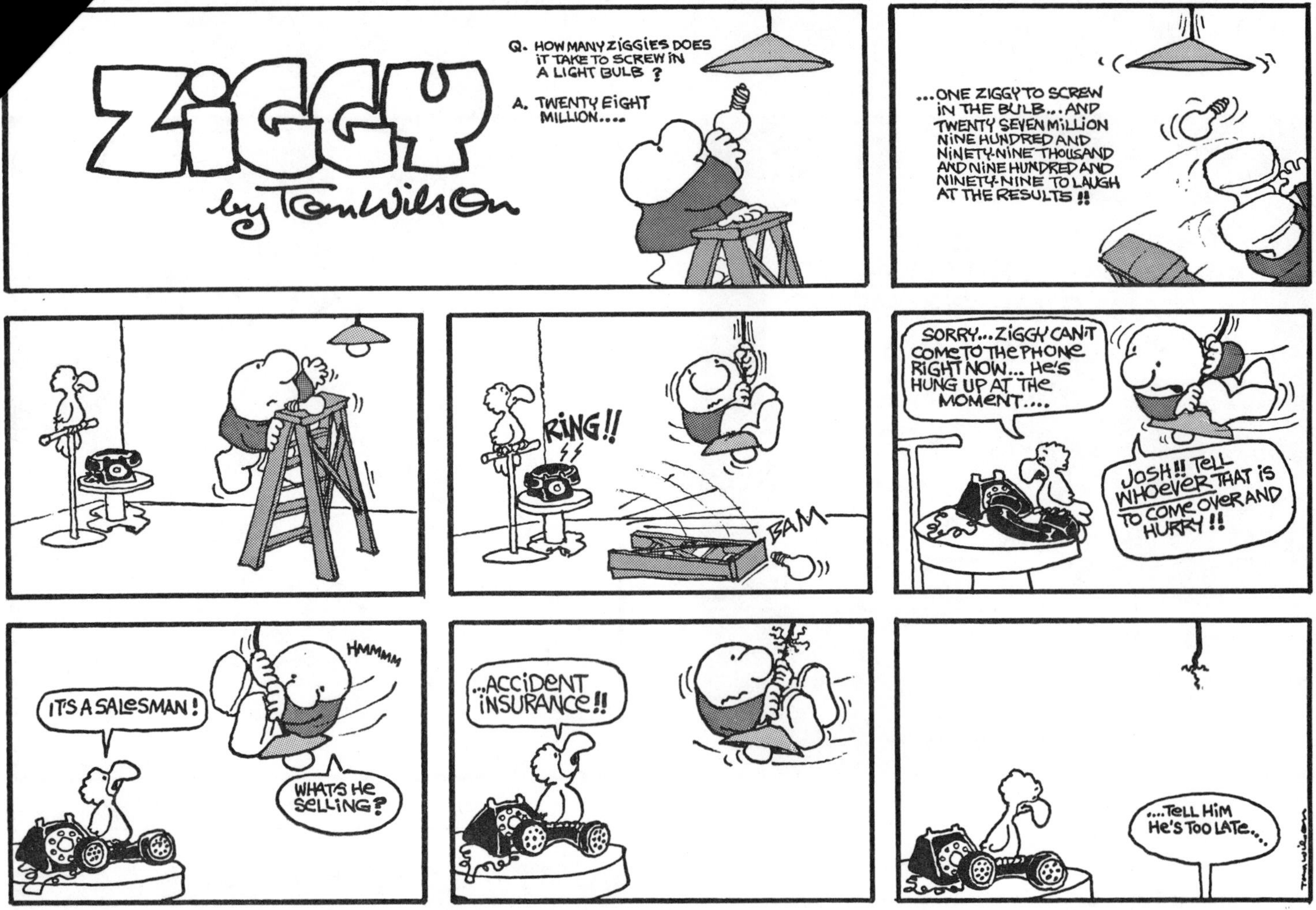
ZIGGY
by Tom Wilson
Q. HOW MANY ZIGGIES DOES IT TAKE TO SCREW IN A LIGHT BULB ?
A. TWENTY EIGHT MILLION....
...ONE ZIGGY TO SCREW IN THE BULB...AND TWENTY SEVEN MILLION NINE HUNDRED AND NINETY-NINE THOUSAND AND NINE HUNDRED AND NINETY-NINE TO LAUGH AT THE RESULTS !!
RING !!
BAM
SORRY...ZIGGY CAN'T COME TO THE PHONE RIGHT NOW... HE'S HUNG UP AT THE MOMENT....
JOSH !! TELL WHOEVER THAT IS TO COME OVER AND HURRY !!
IT'S A SALESMAN !
HMMMM
WHAT'S HE SELLING ?
...ACCIDENT INSURANCE !!
...TELL HIM HE'S TOO LATE....

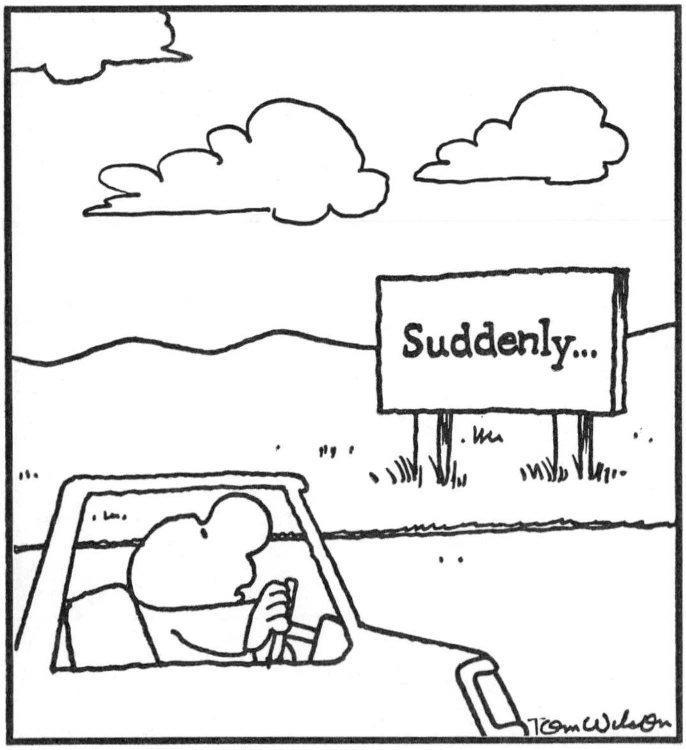
Suddenly...
Tom Wilson

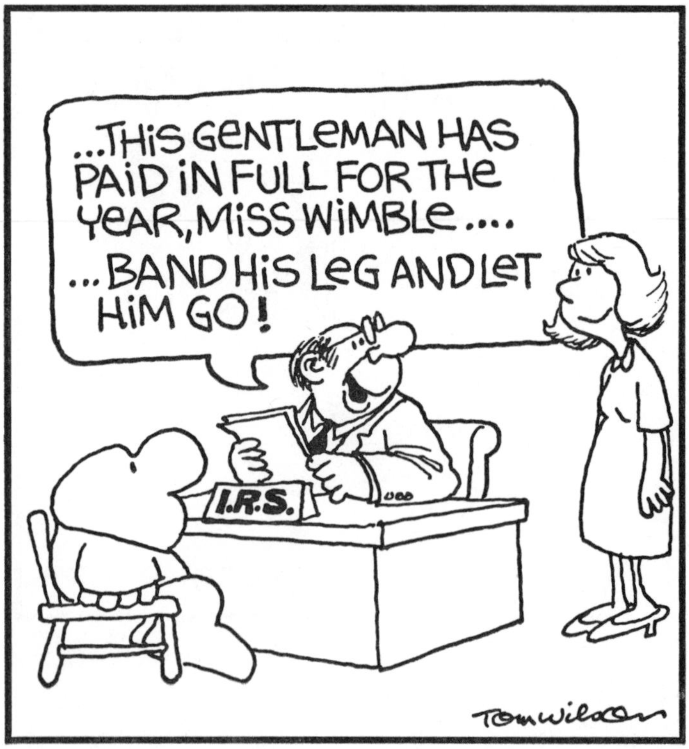
...THIS GENTLEMAN HAS PAID IN FULL FOR THE YEAR, MISS WIMBLE ....
...BAND HIS LEG AND LET HIM GO !
I.R.S.
Tom Wilson

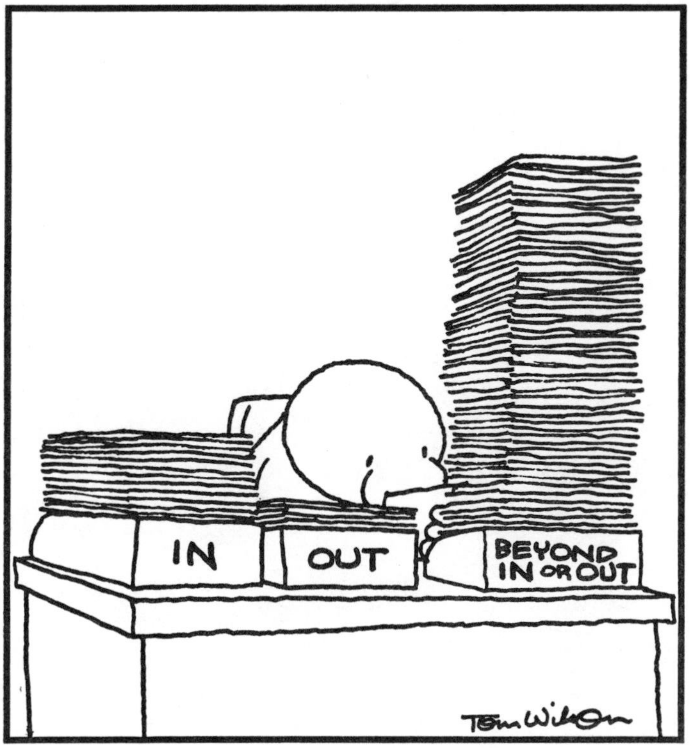
IN
OUT
BEYOND IN OR OUT
Tom Wilson

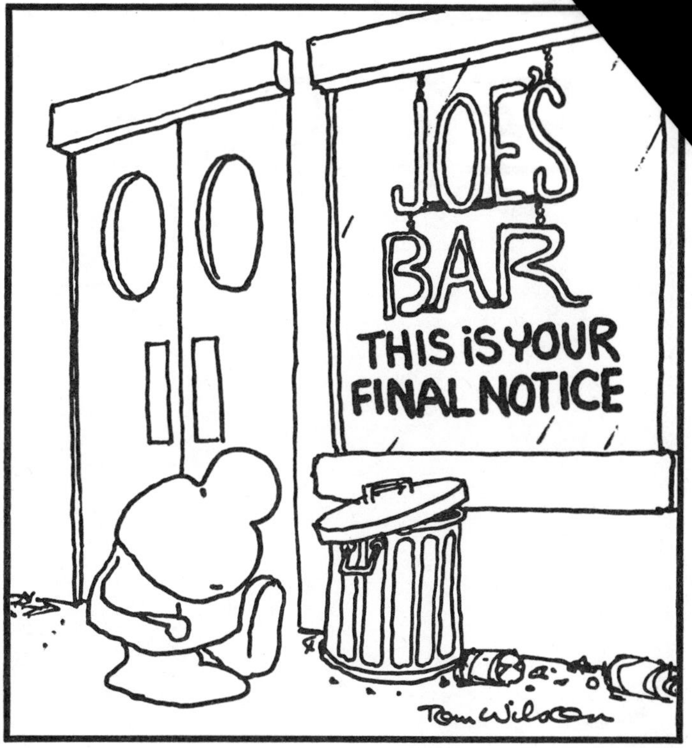
JOE'S
BAR
THIS iS YOUR FINAL NOTICE
Tom Wilson

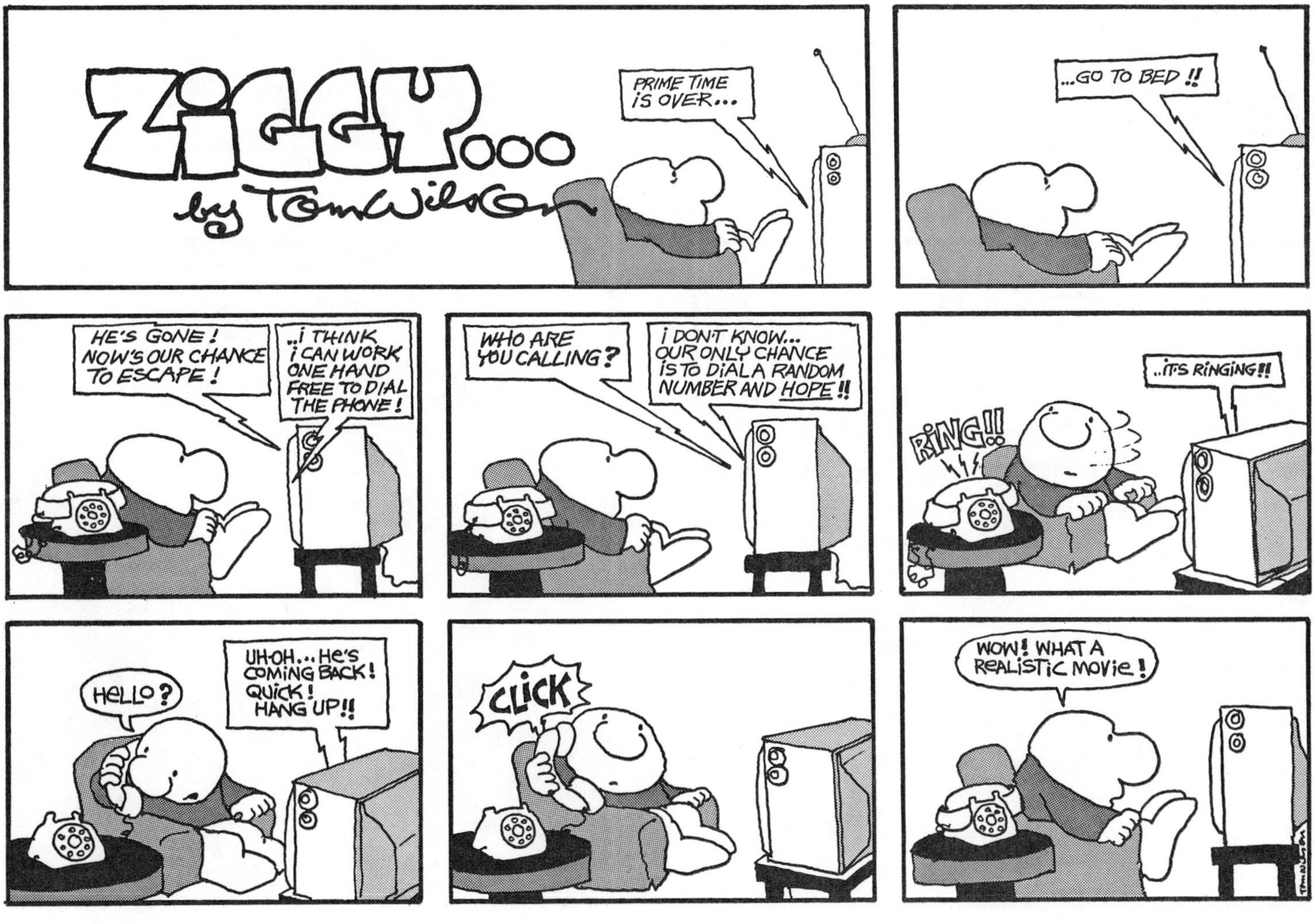
ZiGGY...
by Tom Wilson
PRIME TIME IS OVER...
...GO TO BED !!
HE'S GONE ! NOW'S OUR CHANCE TO ESCAPE !
..i THINK i CAN WORK ONE HAND FREE TO DIAL THE PHONE !
WHO ARE YOU CALLING ?
i DON'T KNOW... OUR ONLY CHANCE iS TO DIAL A RANDOM NUMBER AND HOPE !!
RING!!
..IT'S RiNGING!!
HELLO ?
UH-OH... He's COMING BACK ! QUICK ! HANG UP !!
CLICK
WOW! WHAT A REALISTIC MOVIE !

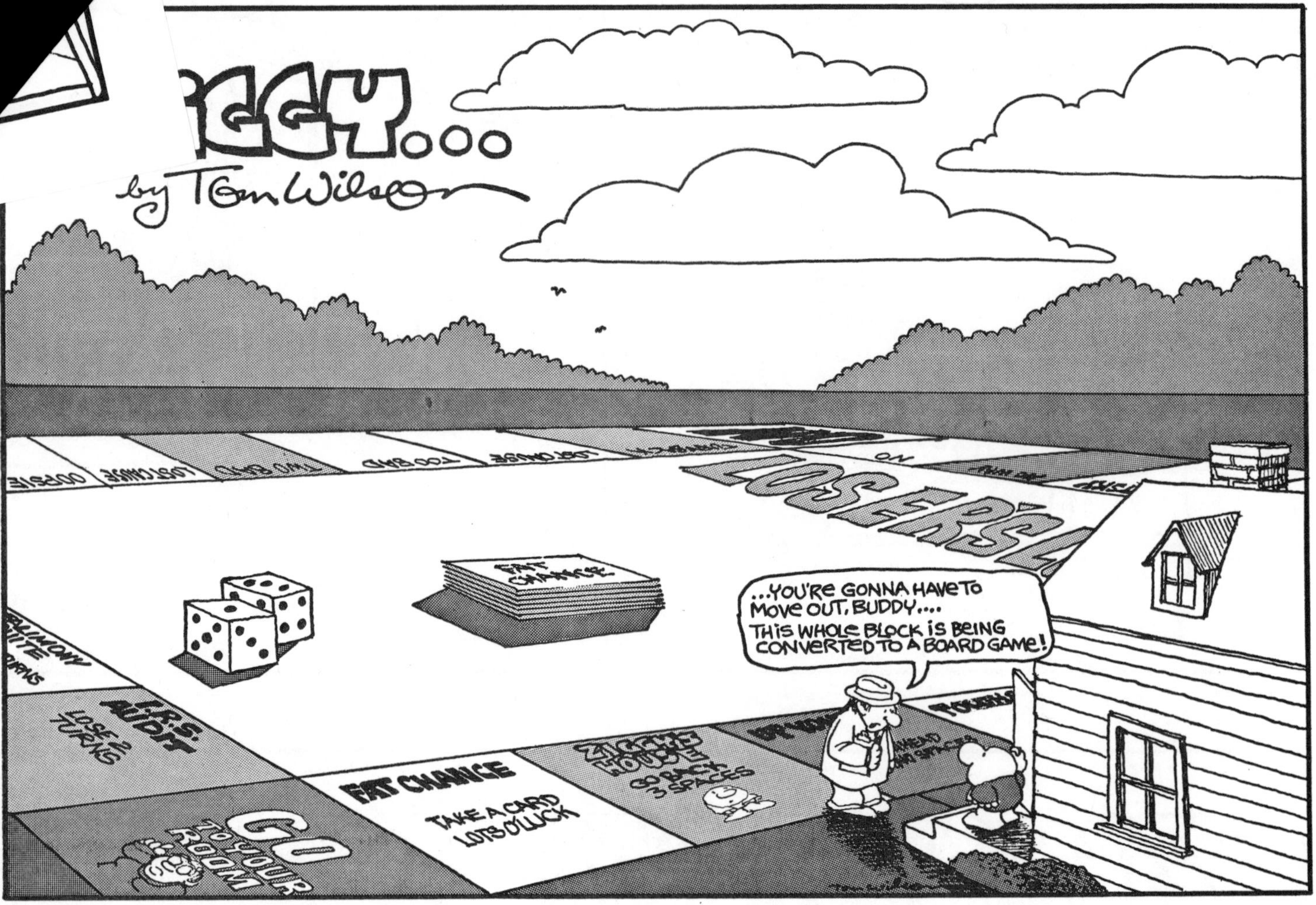
by Tom Wilson
...YOU'RE GONNA HAVE TO MOVE OUT, BUDDY.... THIS WHOLE BLOCK IS BEING CONVERTED TO A BOARD GAME!
LOSERS
FAT CHANCE
FAT CHANCE TAKE A CARD LOTS O'LUCK
I.R.S. AUDIT LOSE 2 TURNS
GO TO YOUR ROOM
GO BACK 3 SPACES

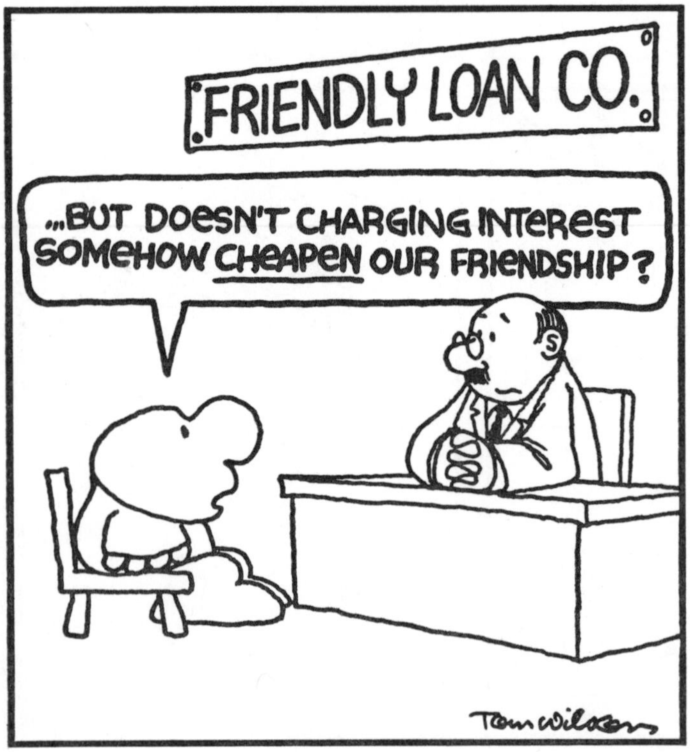
FRIENDLY LOAN CO.
...BUT DOESN'T CHARGING INTEREST SOMEHOW CHEAPEN OUR FRIENDSHIP?
Tom Wilson

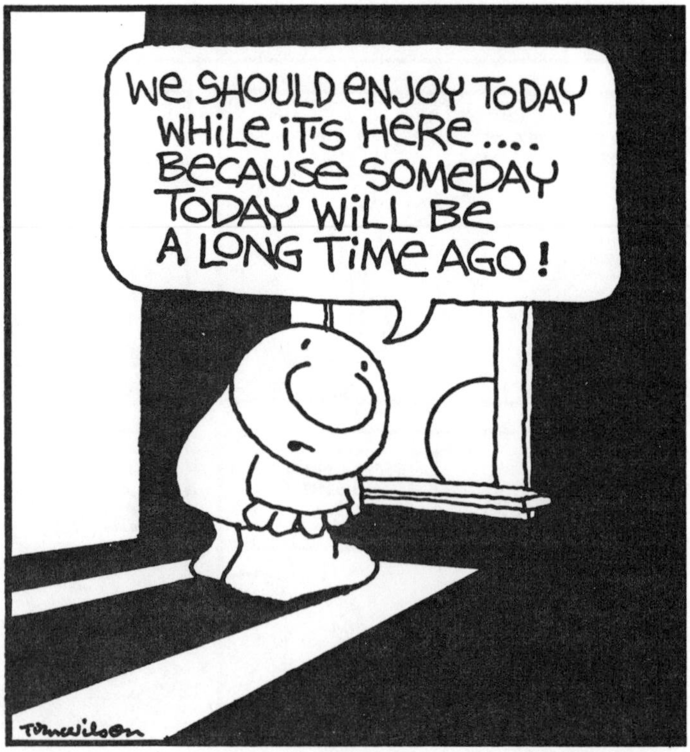
WE SHOULD ENJOY TODAY WHILE IT'S HERE.... BECAUSE SOMEDAY TODAY WILL BE A LONG TIME AGO!
Tom Wilson

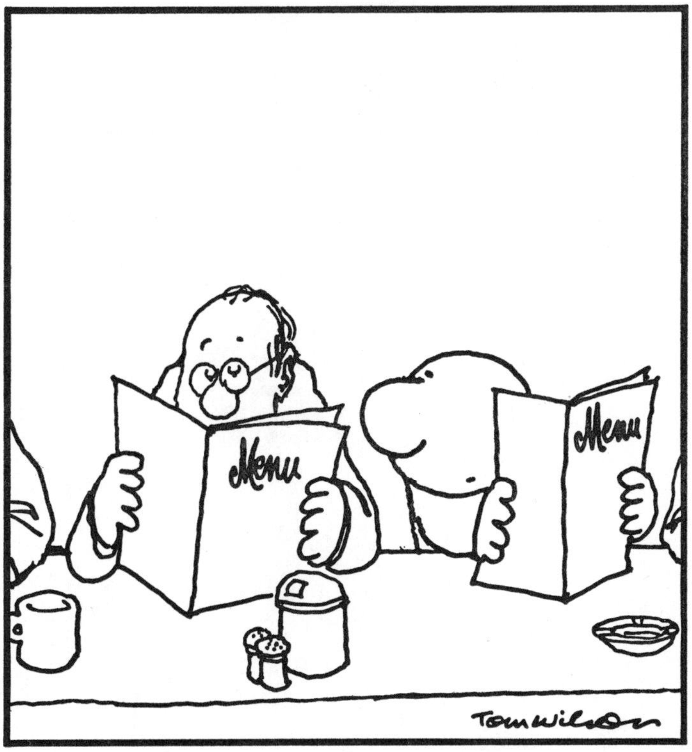
Menu
Menu
Tom Wilson

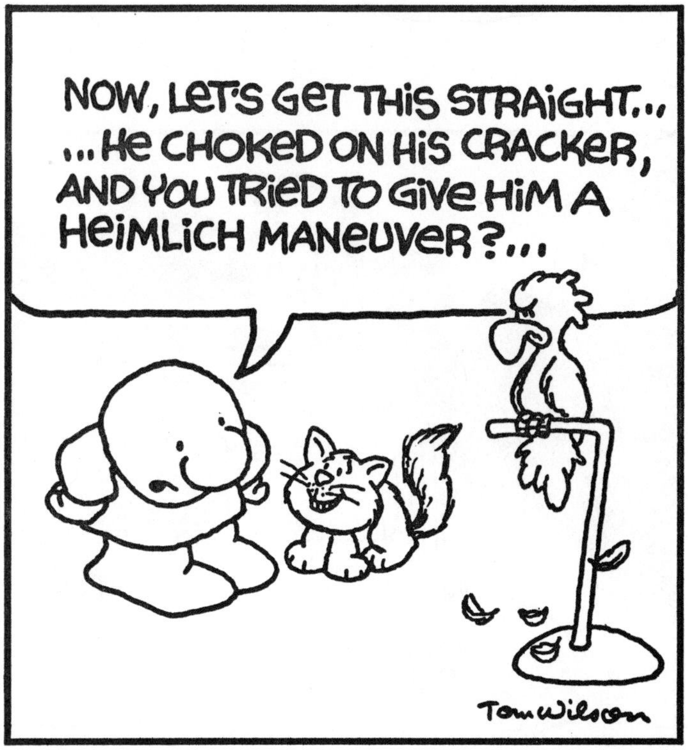
NOW, LET'S GET THIS STRAIGHT... ...HE CHOKED ON HIS CRACKER, AND YOU TRIED TO GIVE HIM A HEIMLICH MANEUVER?...
Tom Wilson

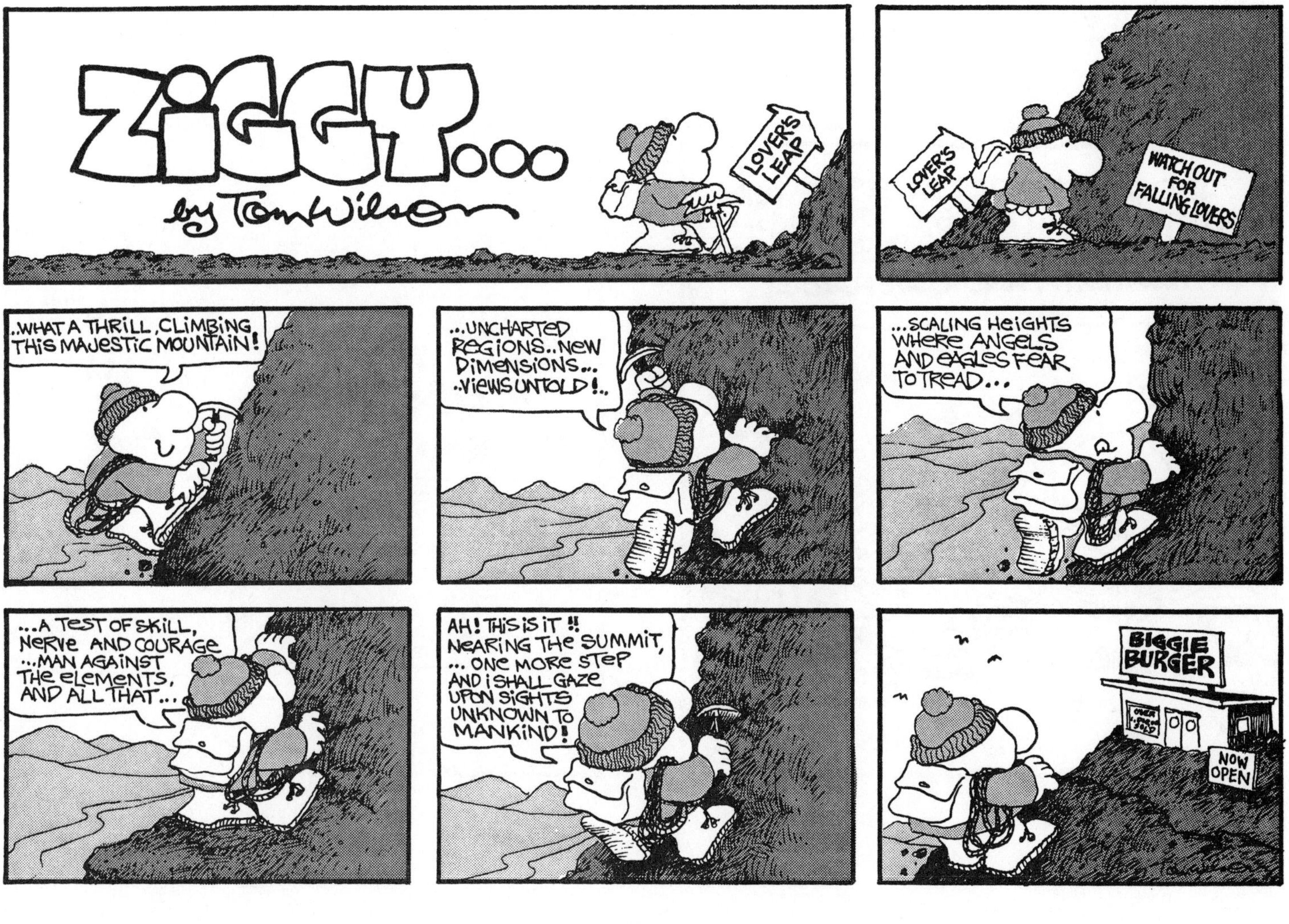
ZIGGY...
by Tom Wilson
LOVER'S LEAP
LOVER'S LEAP
WATCH OUT FOR FALLING LOVERS
..WHAT A THRILL, CLIMBING THIS MAJESTIC MOUNTAIN!
..UNCHARTED REGIONS..NEW DIMENSIONS... ..VIEWS UNTOLD!..
...SCALING HEIGHTS WHERE ANGELS AND EAGLES FEAR TO TREAD...
...A TEST OF SKILL, NERVE AND COURAGE ...MAN AGAINST THE ELEMENTS, AND ALL THAT...
AH! THIS IS IT !! NEARING THE SUMMIT, ... ONE MORE STEP AND I SHALL GAZE UPON SIGHTS UNKNOWN TO MANKIND!
BIGGIE BURGER
NOW OPEN

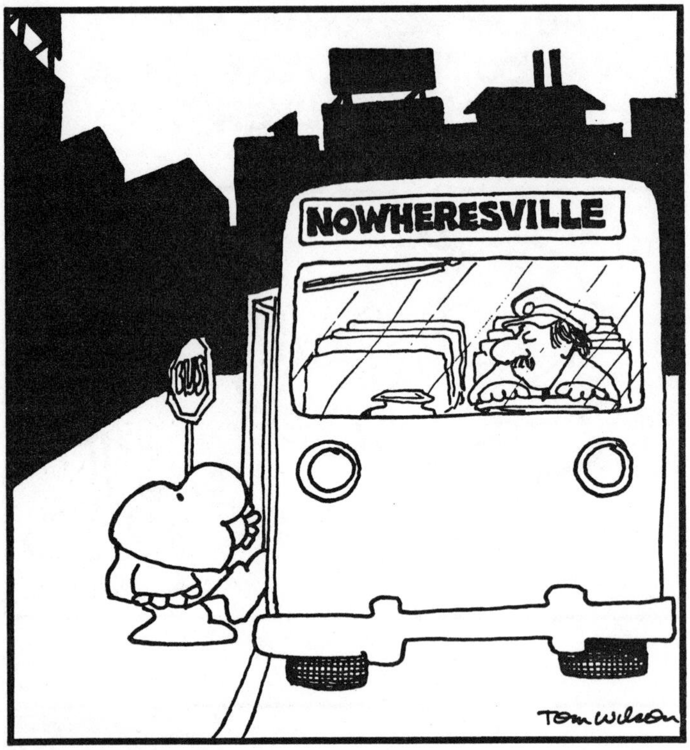
NOWHERESVILLE
BUS
TOM WILSON

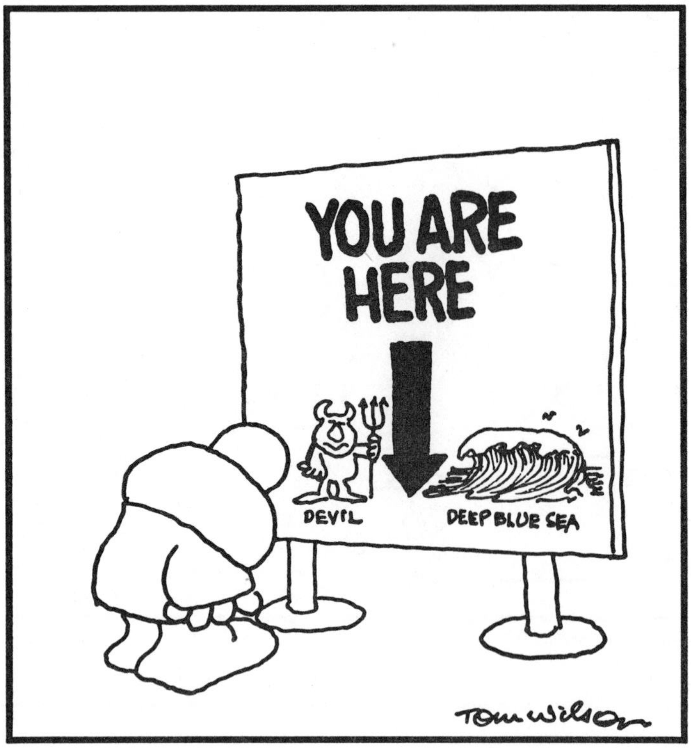
YOU ARE HERE
DEVIL
DEEP BLUE SEA
TOM WILSON

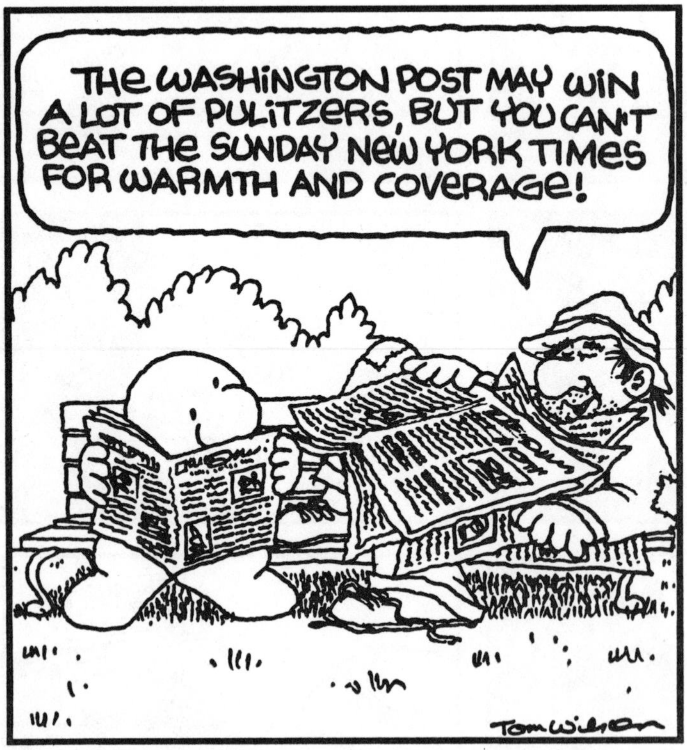
THE WASHINGTON POST MAY WIN A LOT OF PULITZERS, BUT YOU CAN'T BEAT THE SUNDAY NEW YORK TIMES FOR WARMTH AND COVERAGE!
TOM WILSON

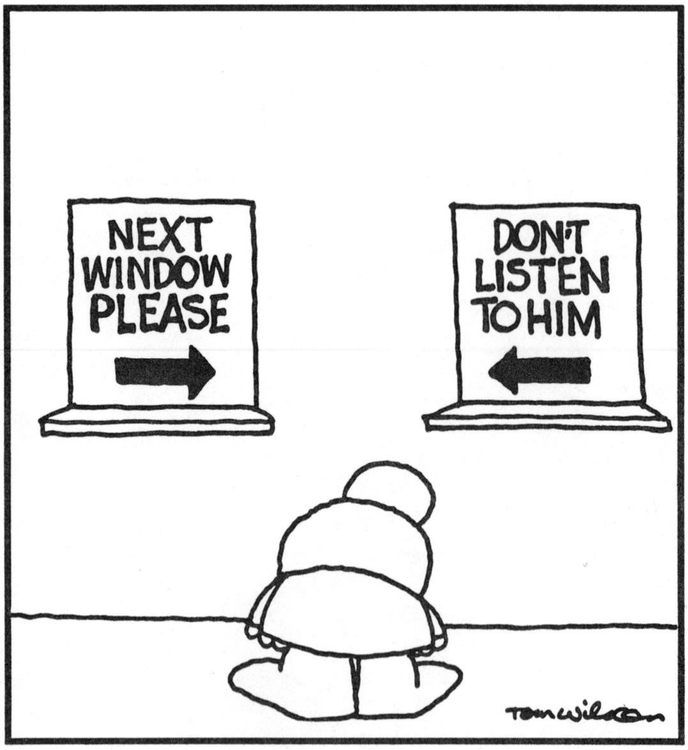
NEXT WINDOW PLEASE
DON'T LISTEN TO HIM
TOM WILSON

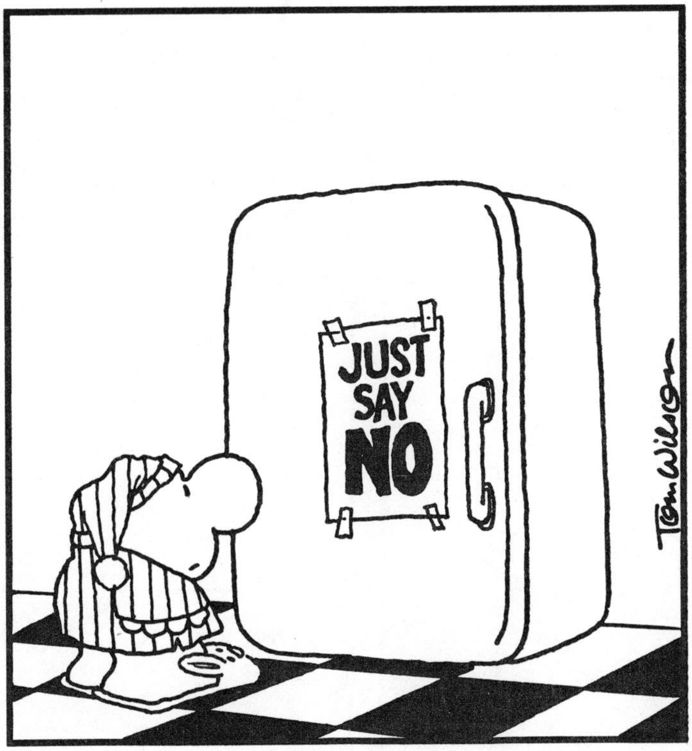
JUST SAY NO
Tom Wilson

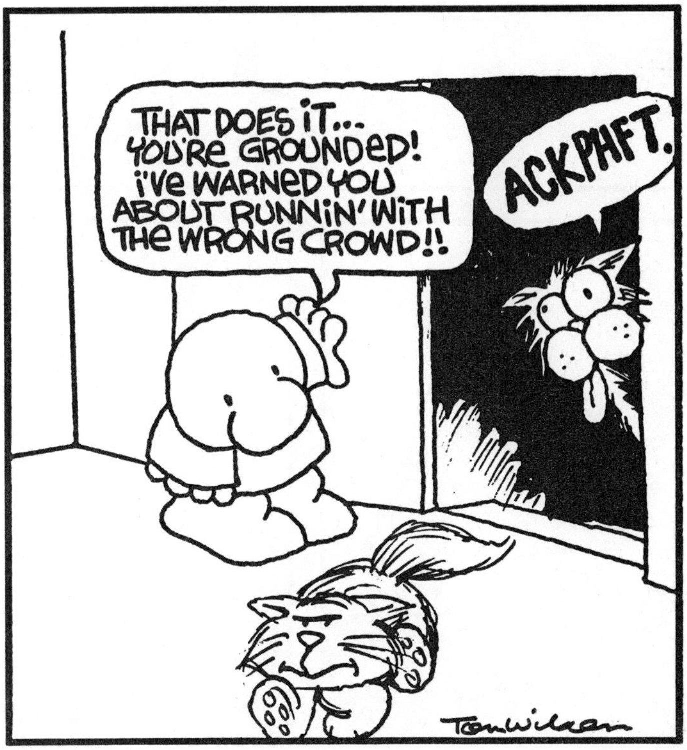
THAT DOES IT... YOU'RE GROUNDED! I'VE WARNED YOU ABOUT RUNNIN' WITH THE WRONG CROWD!!
ACKPHFT.
Tom Wilson

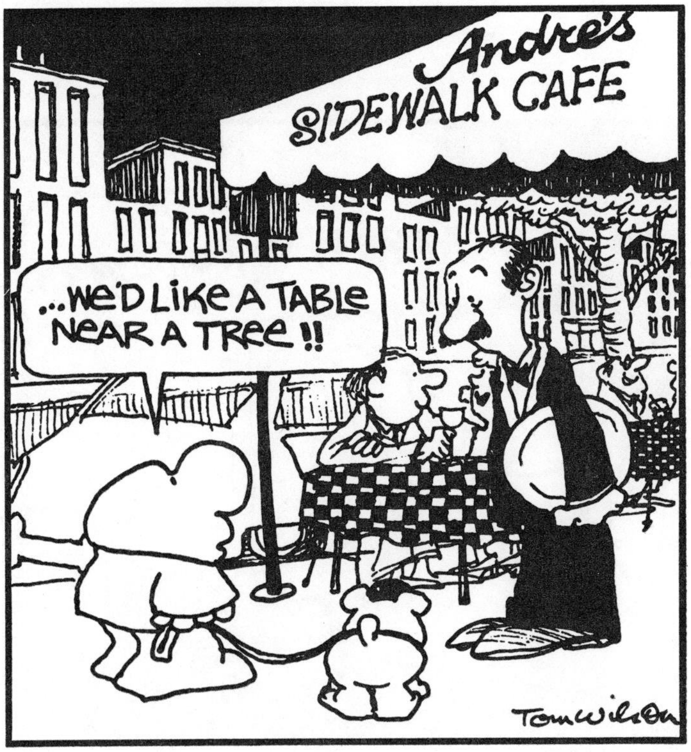
Andre's SIDEWALK CAFE
...WE'D LIKE A TABLE NEAR A TREE !!
Tom Wilson

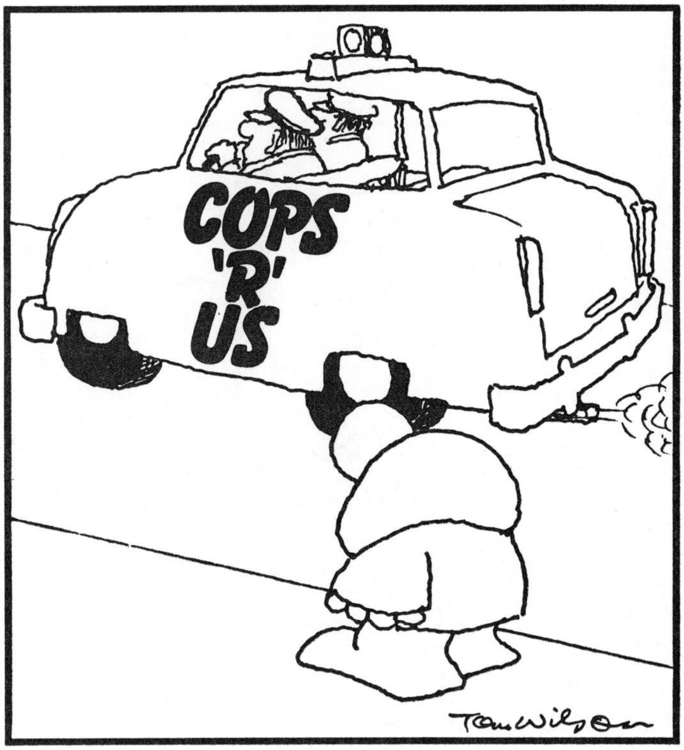
COPS 'R' US
Tom Wilson

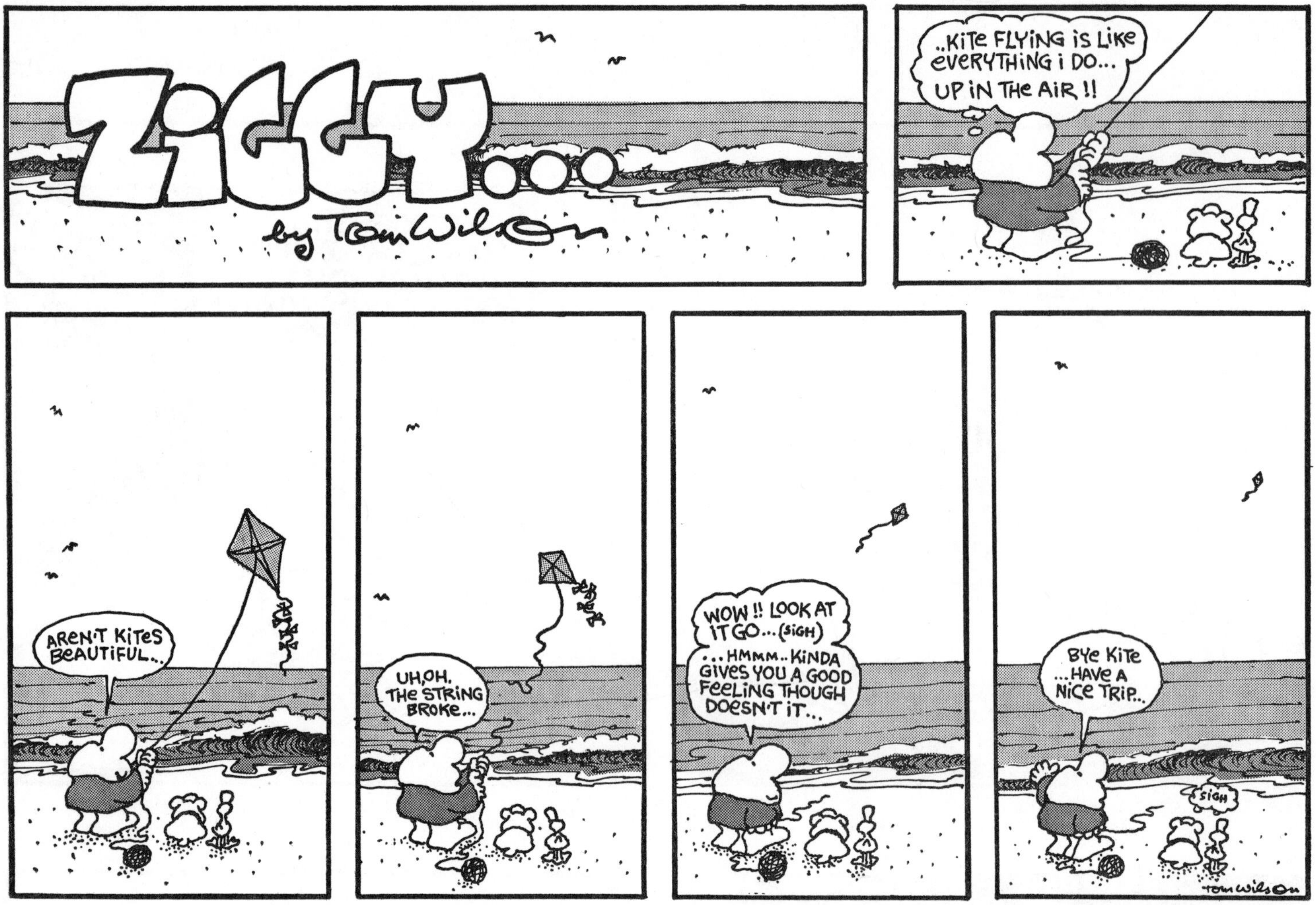
ZiGGY...
by Tom Wilson
..KiTe FLYiNG iS LiKe EVERYTHiNG i DO... UP iN THe AiR !!
AREN'T KiTeS BeAUTiFUL..
UH,OH, THe STRiNG BROKe...
WOW !! LOOK AT IT GO...(SiGH) ..HMMM..KiNDA GIVES YOU A GOOD FeeLiNG THOUGH DOESN'T iT...
BYe KiTe ...HAVe A NiCe TRiP..
SiGH
Tom Wilson

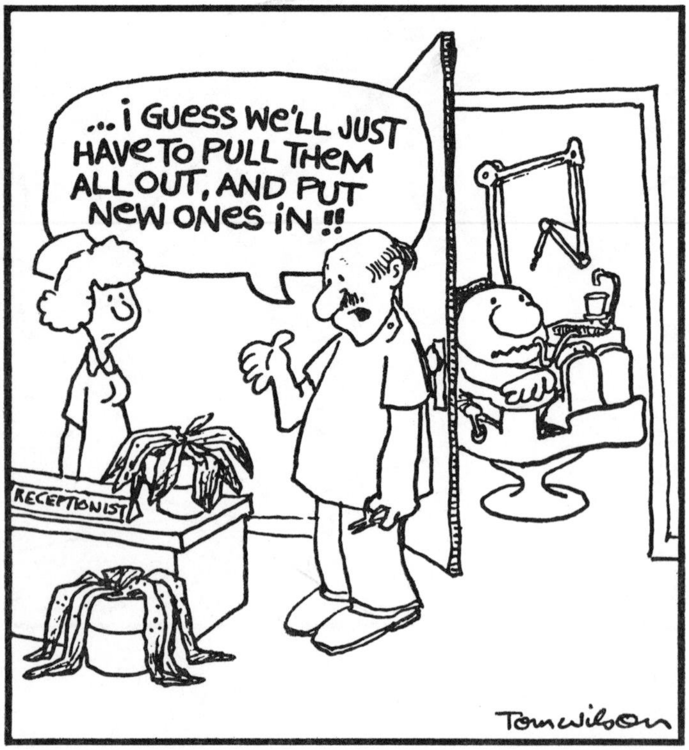
...i GUeSS We'LL JUST HAVe TO PULL THeM ALL OUT, AND PUT NeW ONeS iN !!
RECEPTIONIST
Tom Wilson

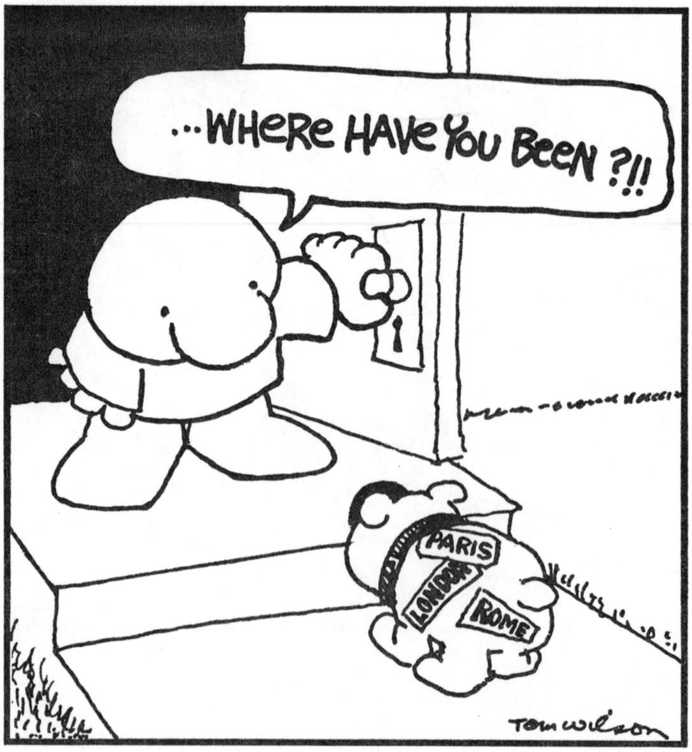
...WHeRe HAVe YOU BeeN ?!!
PARIS
LONDON
ROME
Tom Wilson

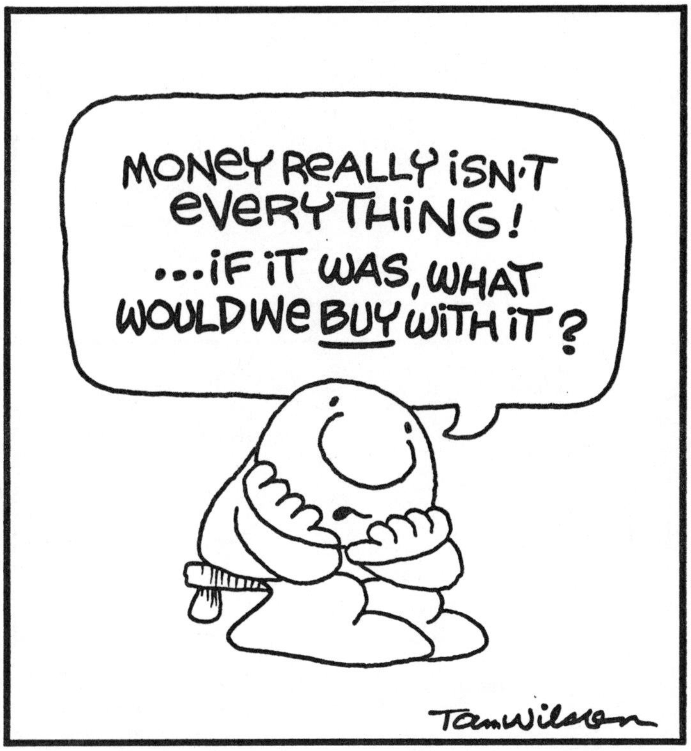
MONEY REALLY ISN'T EVERYTHING! ...IF IT WAS, WHAT WOULD WE BUY WITH IT?

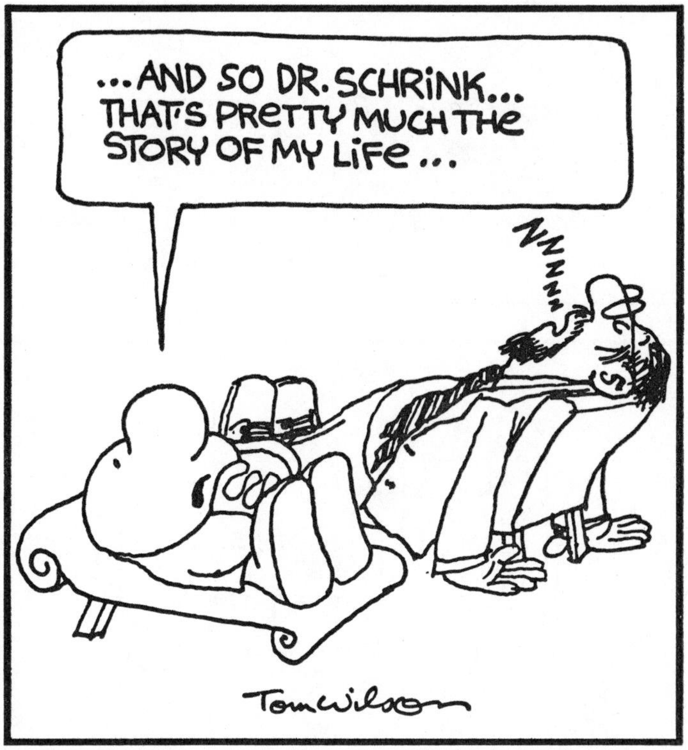
...AND SO DR. SCHRINK... THAT'S PRETTY MUCH THE STORY OF MY LIFE...
ZZZZZ

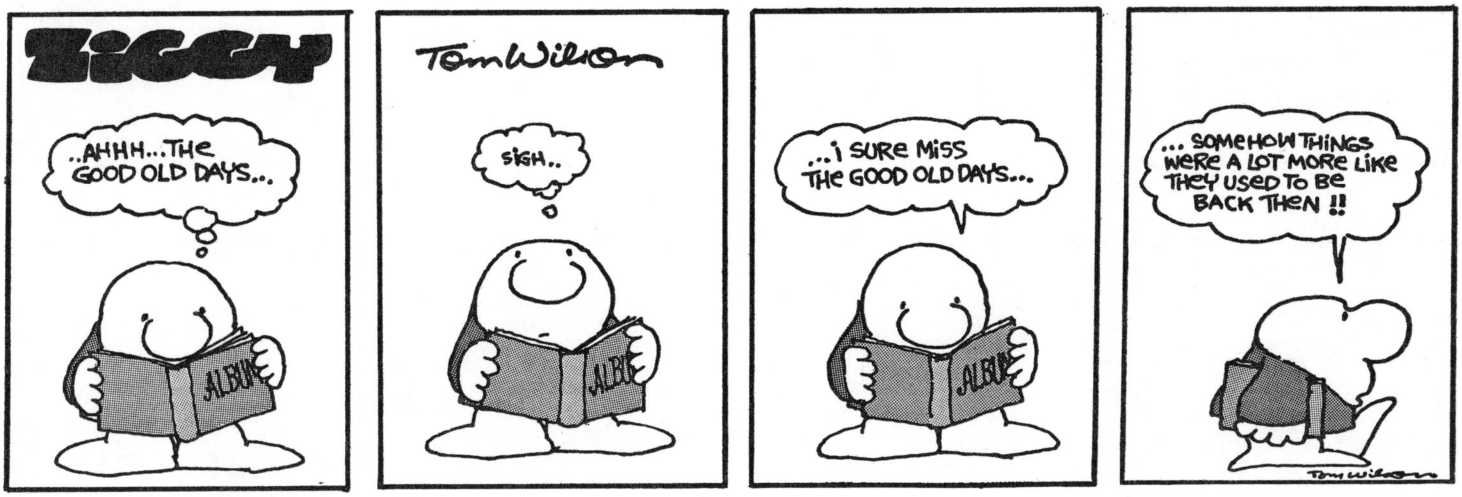
ZIGGY
..AHHH...THE GOOD OLD DAYS...
SIGH..
...I SURE MISS THE GOOD OLD DAYS...
... SOMEHOW THINGS WERE A LOT MORE LIKE THEY USED TO BE BACK THEN !!

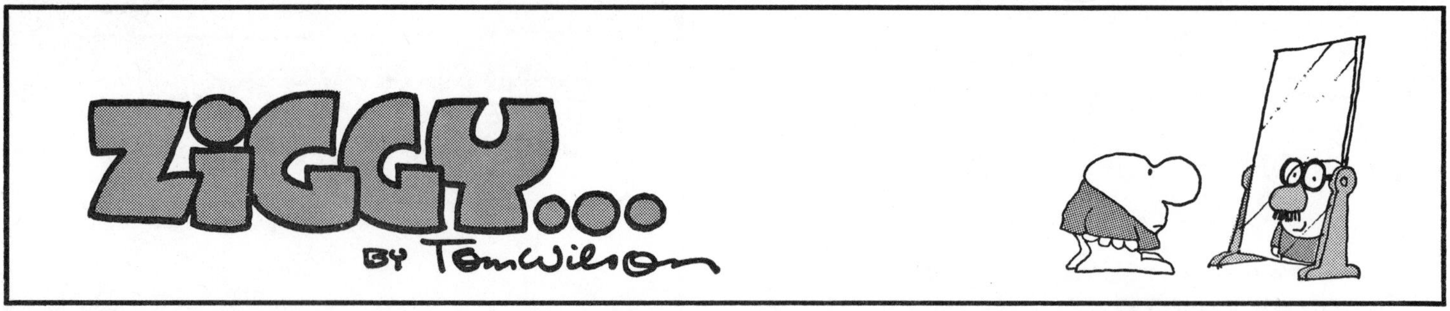
ZiGGY...
BY Tom Wilson

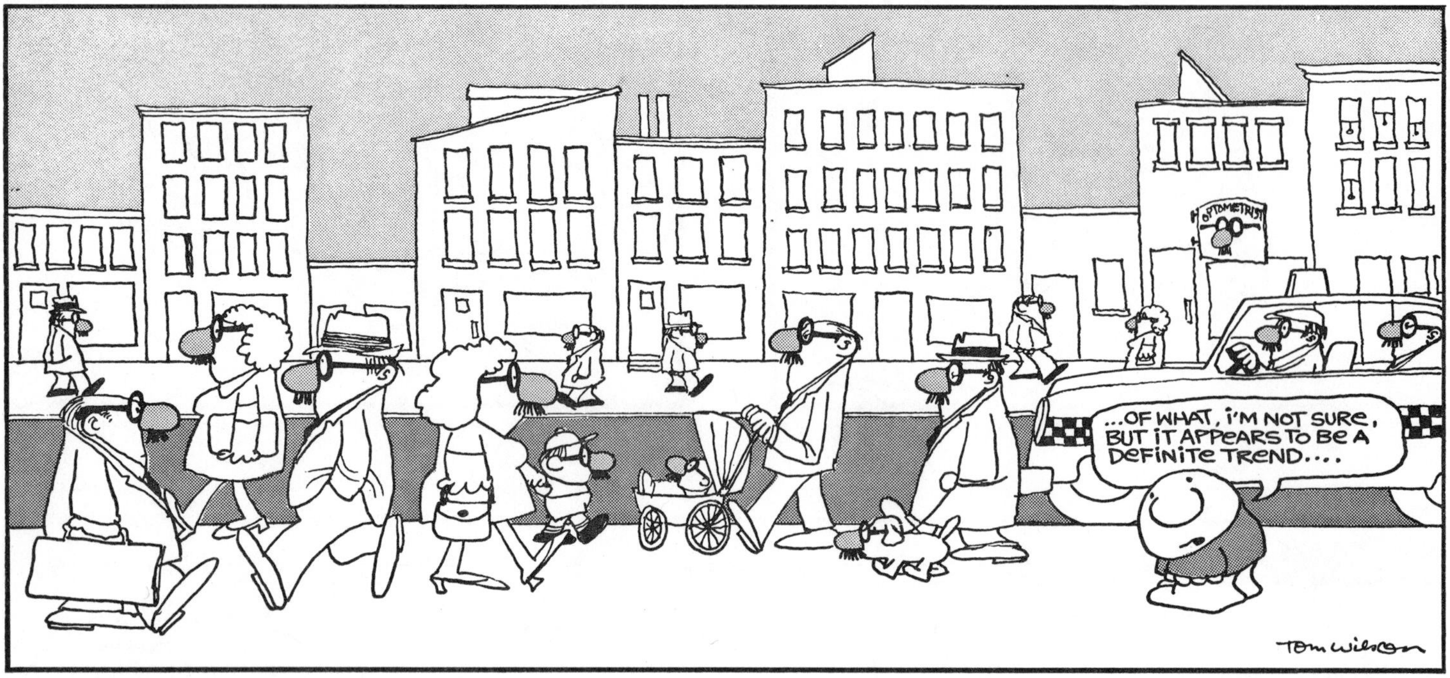
OPTOMETRIST
...OF WHAT, i'M NOT SURE, BUT iT APPEARS TO BE A DEFINITE TREND....
Tom Wilson

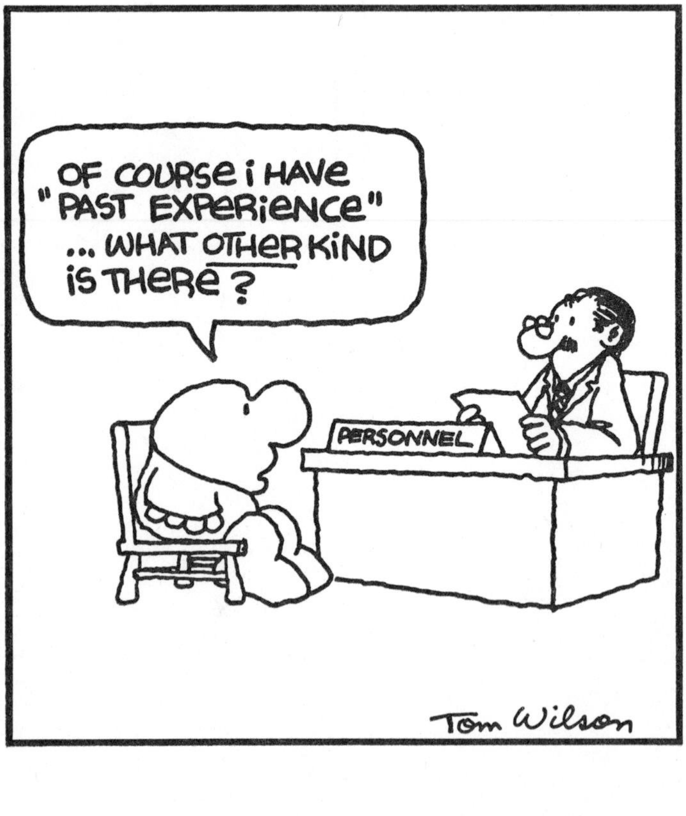
OF COURSE i HAVE "PAST EXPERiENCE" ... WHAT OTHER KiND iS THERE?
PERSONNEL
Tom Wilson

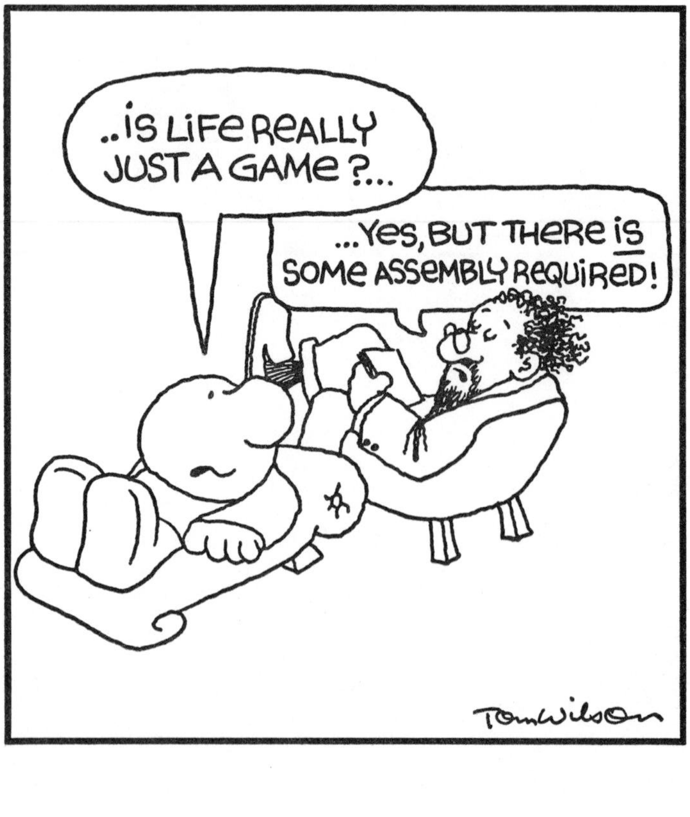
..iS LiFE REALLY JUST A GAME?...
...YES, BUT THERE iS SOME ASSEMBLY REQUiRED!
Tom Wilson

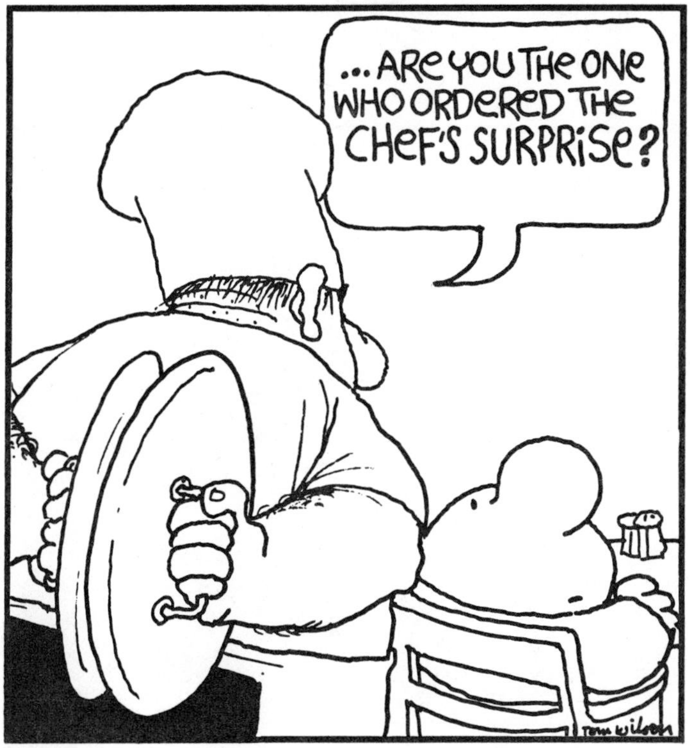
...ARE YOU THE ONE WHO ORDERED THE CHEF'S SURPRISE?
Tom Wilson

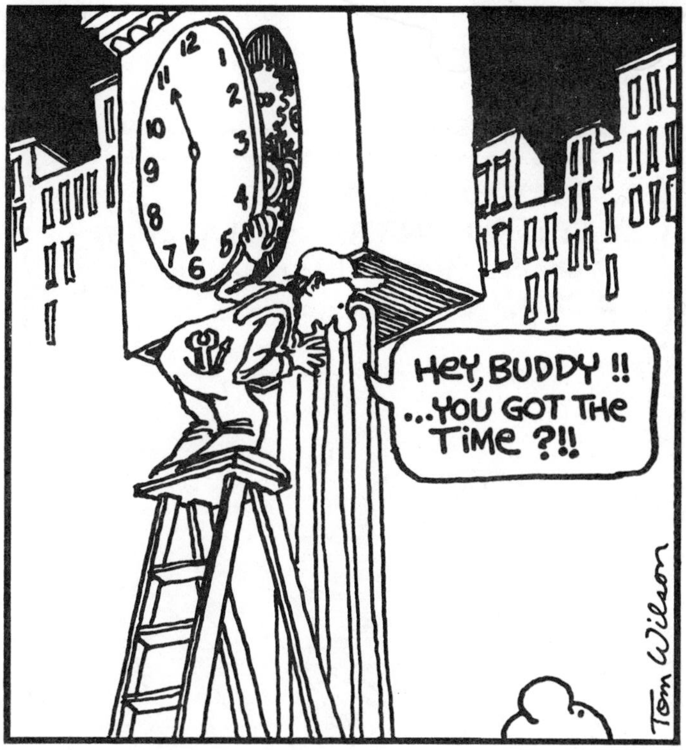
HEY, BUDDY !! ...YOU GOT THE TIME ?!!
Tom Wilson

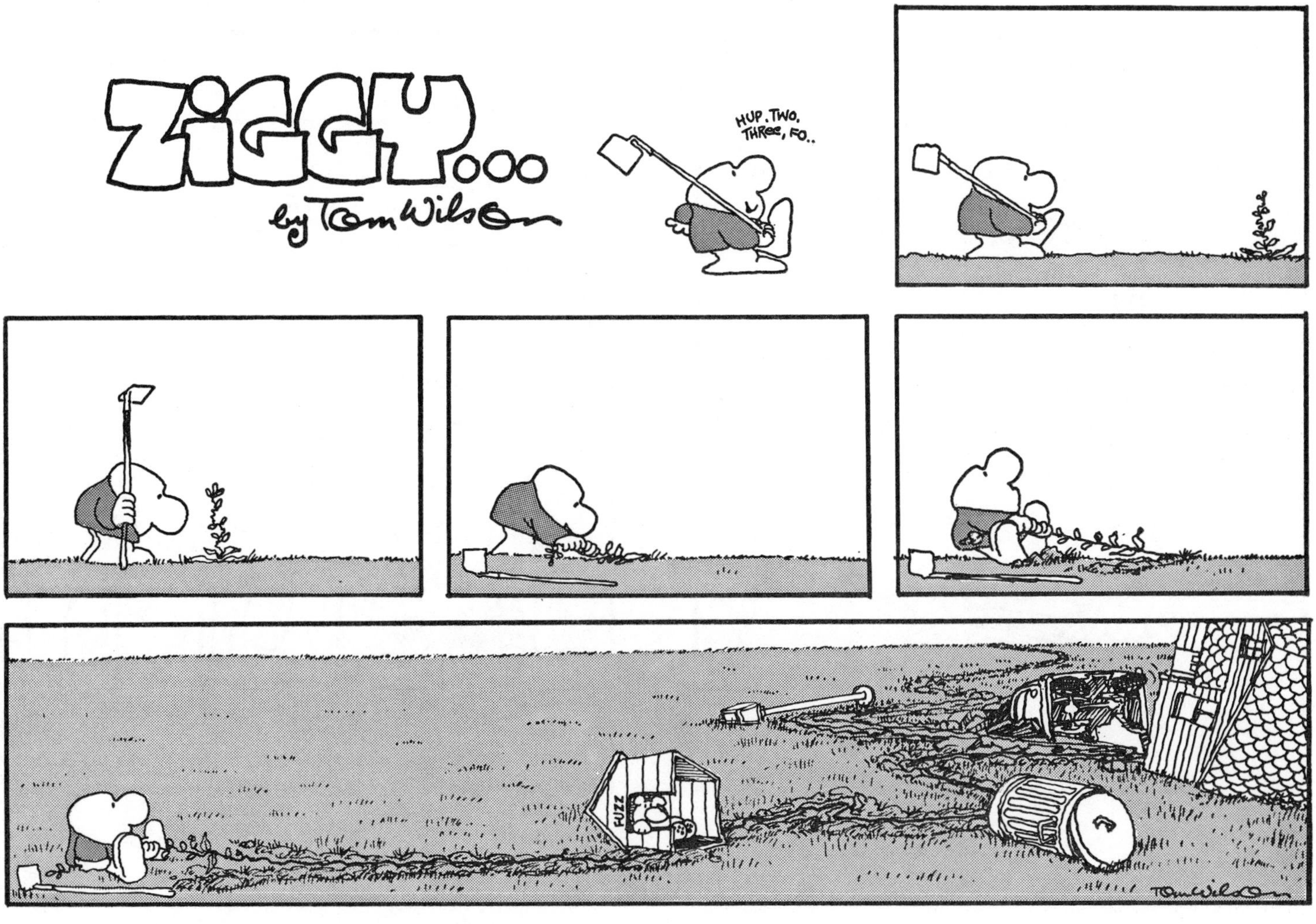
ZIGGY
by Tom Wilson
HUP, TWO. THREE, FO..
FUZZ
Tom Wilson

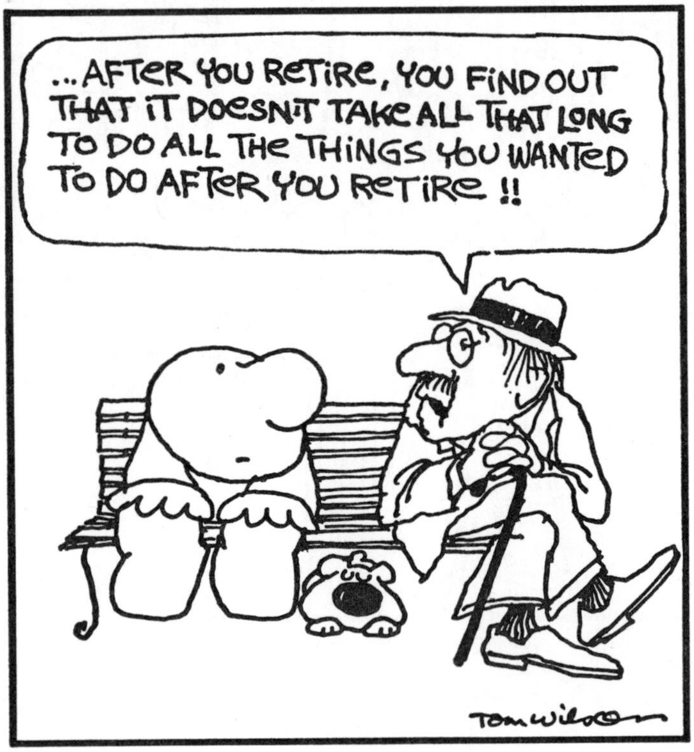
...AFTER YOU RETIRE, YOU FIND OUT THAT IT DOESN'T TAKE ALL THAT LONG TO DO ALL THE THINGS YOU WANTED TO DO AFTER YOU RETIRE !!
Tom Wilson

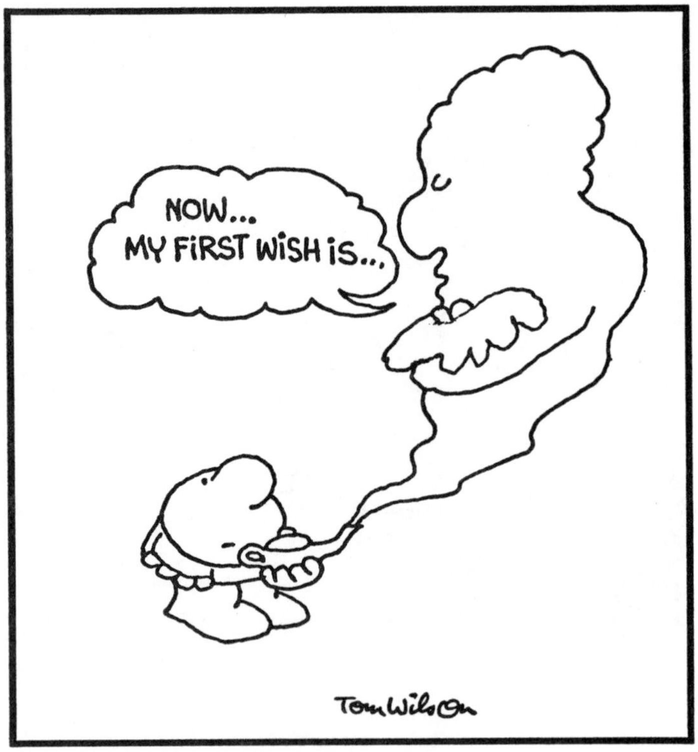
NOW... MY FIRST WISH IS...
Tom Wilson

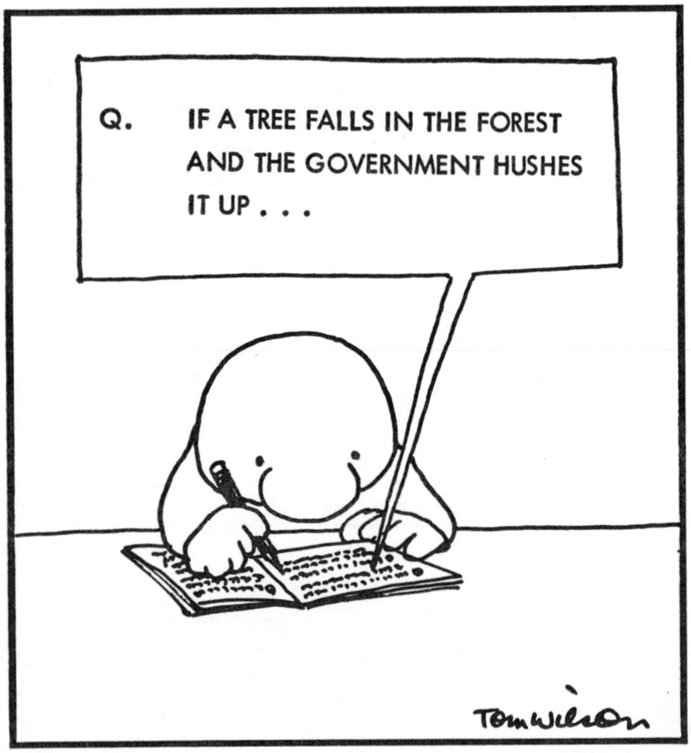
Q. IF A TREE FALLS IN THE FOREST AND THE GOVERNMENT HUSHES IT UP . . .
Tom Wilson

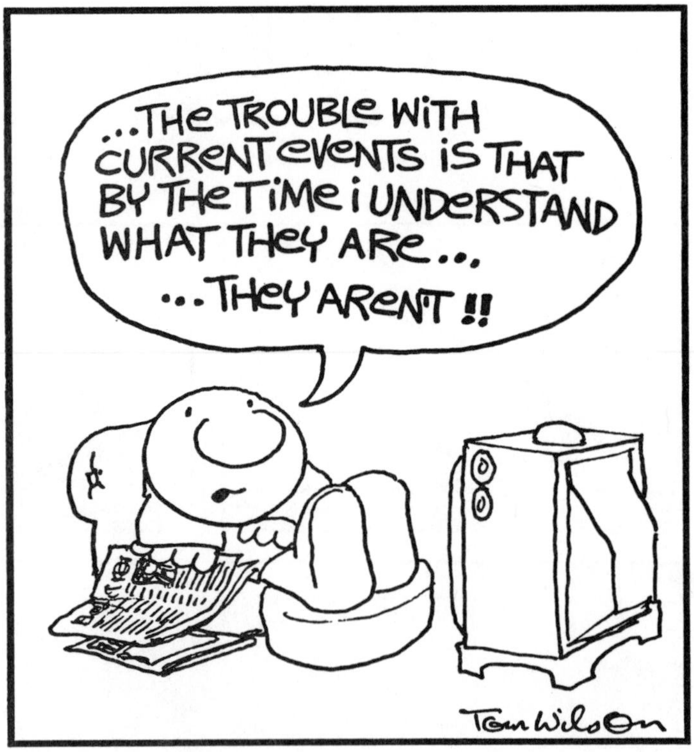
...THE TROUBLE WITH CURRENT EVENTS IS THAT BY THE TIME I UNDERSTAND WHAT THEY ARE...
...THEY AREN'T !!
Tom Wilson

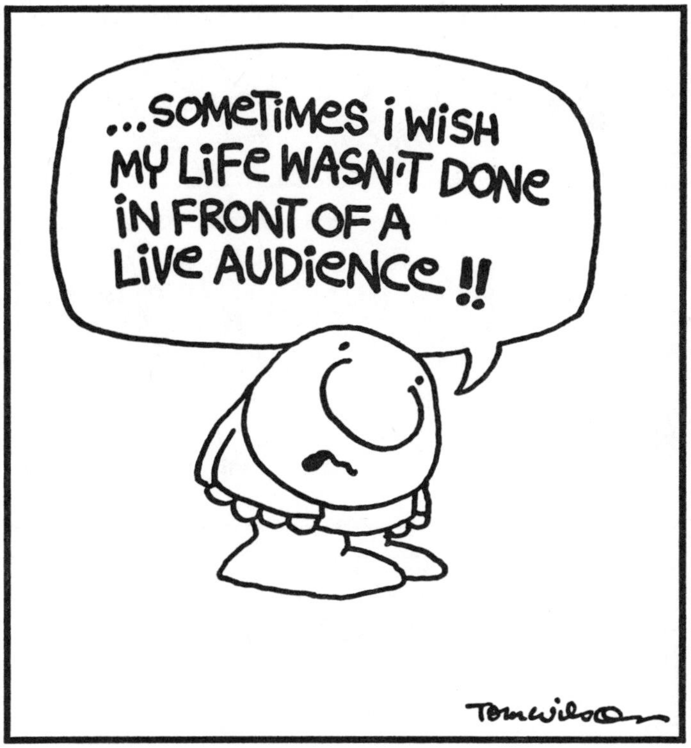
...SOMETIMES I WISH MY LIFE WASN'T DONE IN FRONT OF A LIVE AUDIENCE !!
Tom Wilson

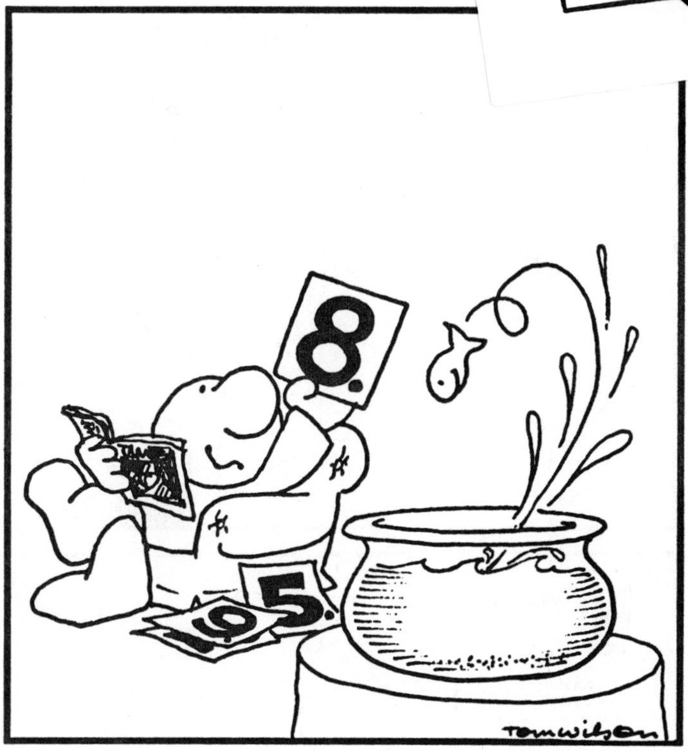
8.
5.
Tom Wilson

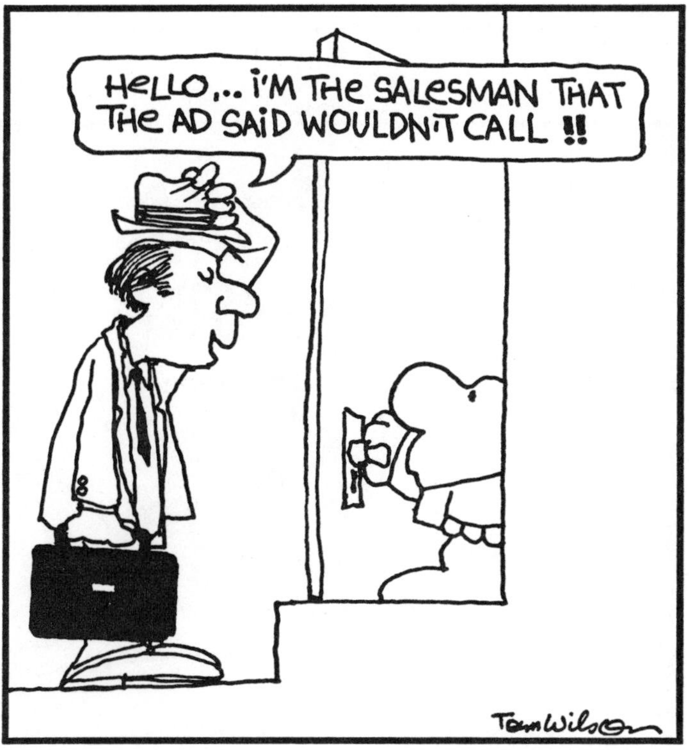
HELLO,... I'M THE SALESMAN THAT THE AD SAID WOULDN'T CALL !!
Tom Wilson

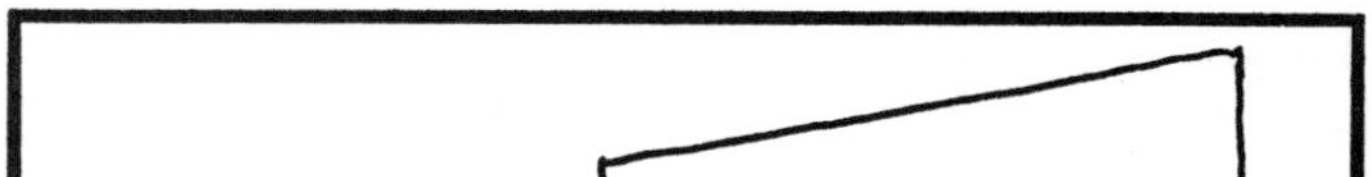
KNOCKED WHILE YOU WERE OUT. —OPPORTUNITY
Tom Wilson

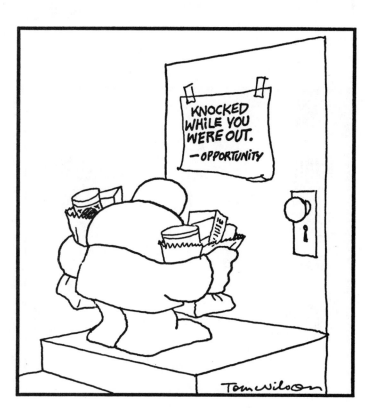

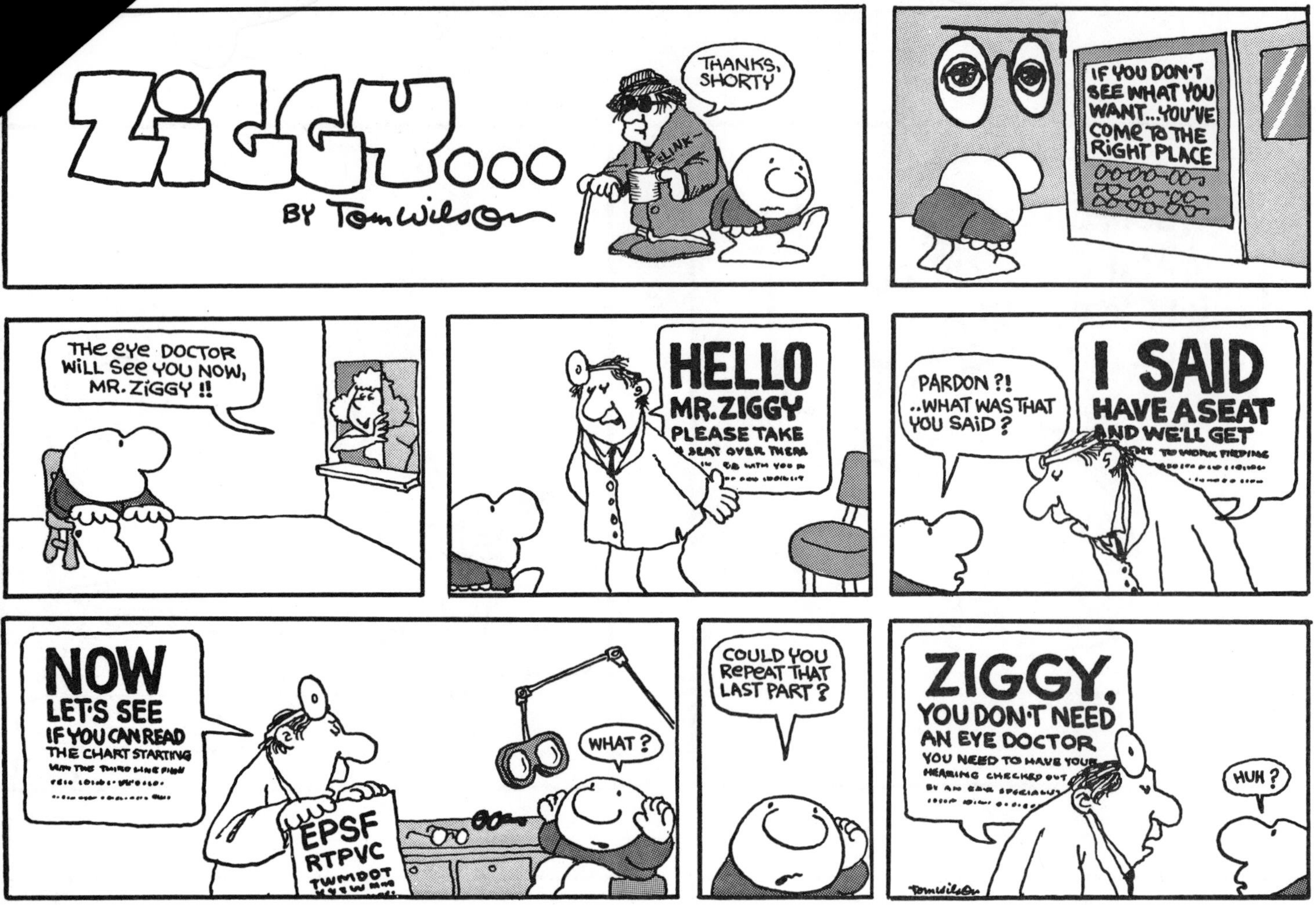
ZIGGY
BY Tom Wilson
THANKS, SHORTY
CLINK
IF YOU DON'T SEE WHAT YOU WANT...YOU'VE COME TO THE RIGHT PLACE
THE EYE DOCTOR WILL SEE YOU NOW, MR. ZIGGY !!
HELLO MR. ZIGGY PLEASE TAKE
PARDON ?! ..WHAT WAS THAT YOU SAID ?
I SAID HAVE A SEAT AND WE'LL GET
NOW LET'S SEE IF YOU CAN READ THE CHART STARTING
EPSF
RTPVC
TWMDOT
WHAT ?
COULD YOU REPEAT THAT LAST PART ?
ZIGGY, YOU DON'T NEED AN EYE DOCTOR YOU NEED TO HAVE YOUR HEARING CHECKED OUT
HUH ?
Tom Wilson

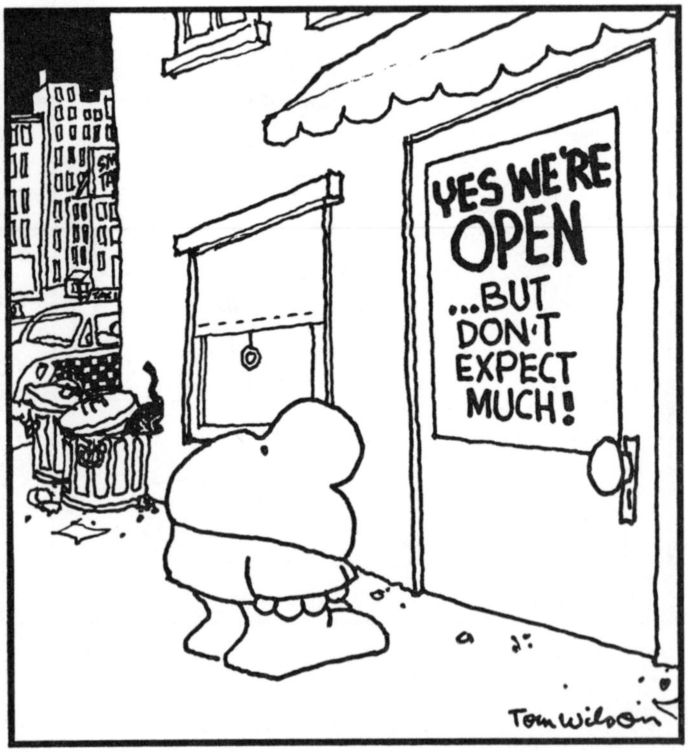
YES WE'RE OPEN ...BUT DON'T EXPECT MUCH!
Tom Wilson

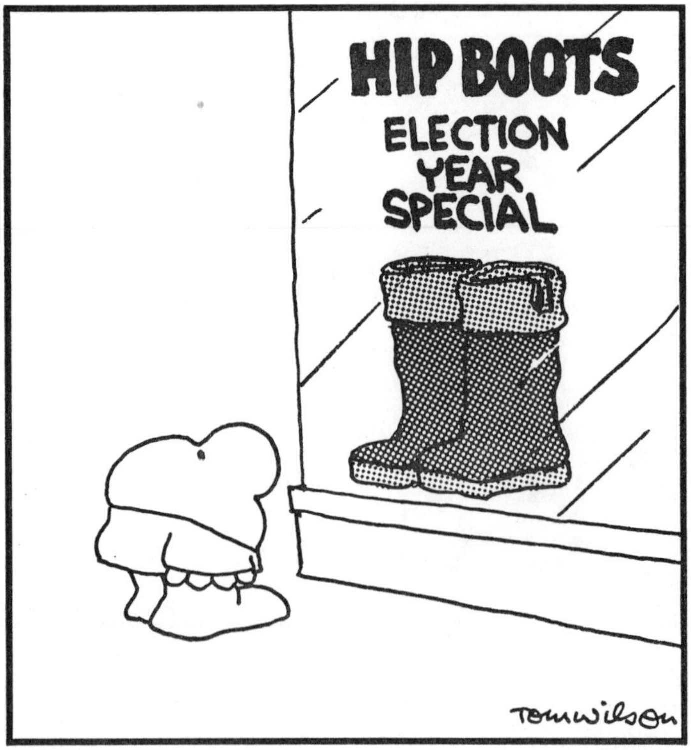
HIP BOOTS
ELECTION YEAR SPECIAL
Tom Wilson

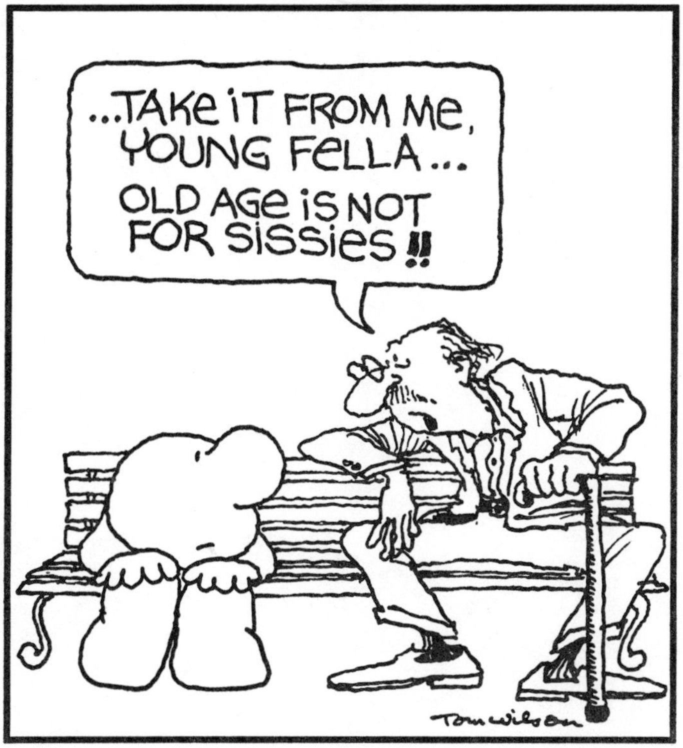
...TAKE IT FROM ME, YOUNG FELLA... OLD AGE IS NOT FOR SISSIES !!
Tom Wilson

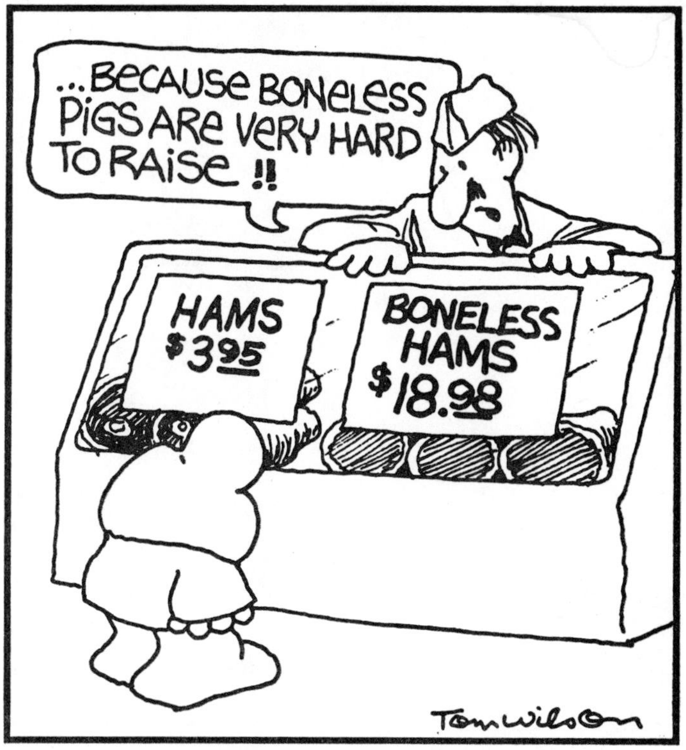
...BECAUSE BONELESS PIGS ARE VERY HARD TO RAISE !!
HAMS $3.95
BONELESS HAMS $18.98
Tom Wilson

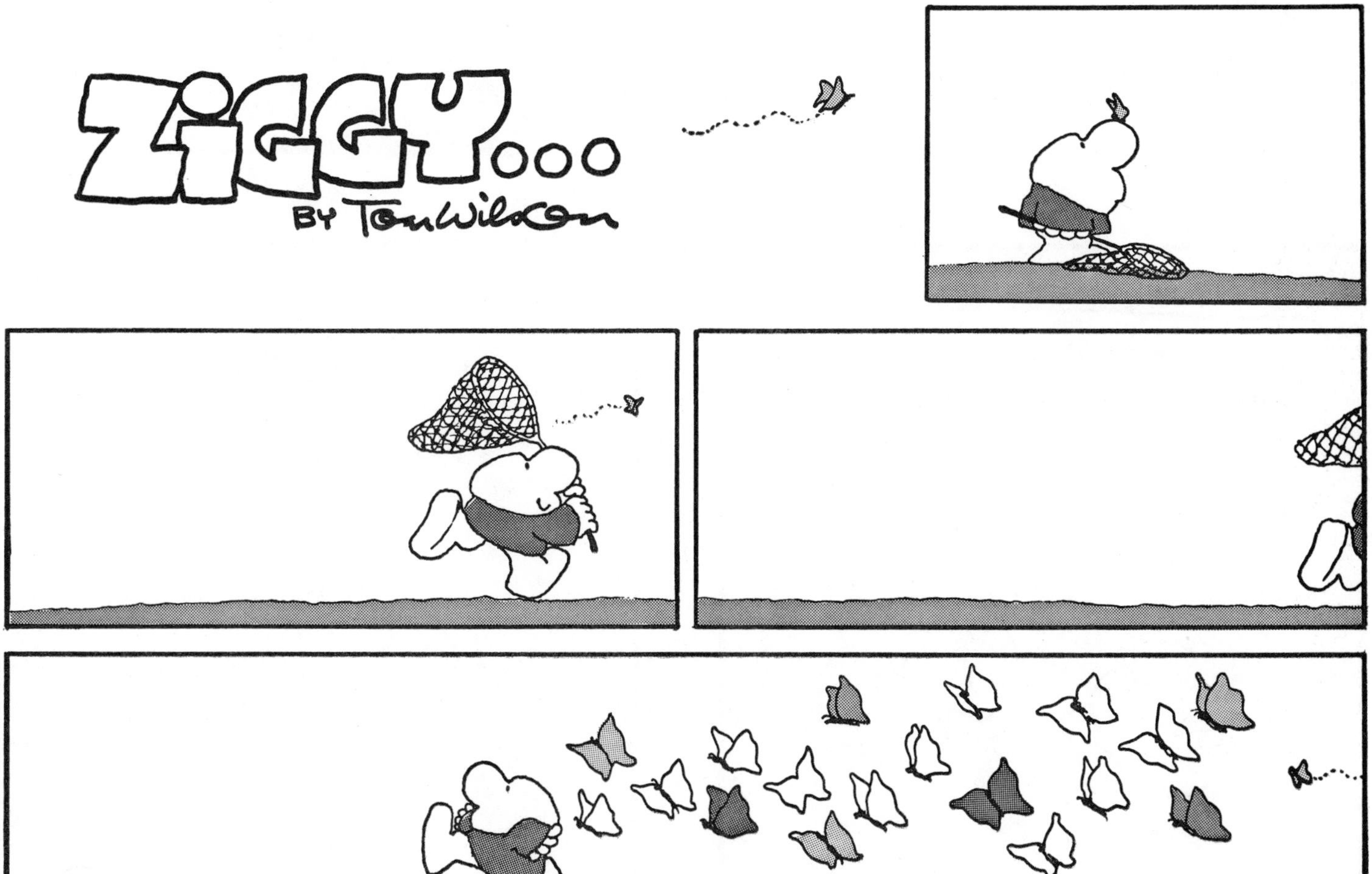
ZIGGY...
BY Tom Wilson
Tom Wilson

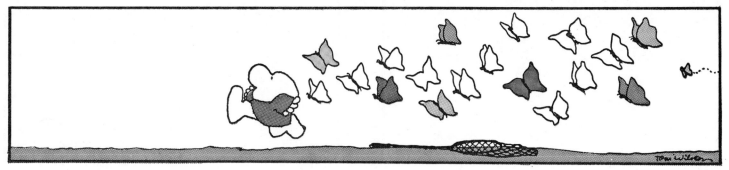

ZiGGY...
by Tom Wilson
...SO THIS iS WHERE THE CLOUDS ARE MADE!!
Tom Wilson

...iT'S NOTHiNG TO BE ASHAMED OF...A LOT OF CARTOON CHARACTERS AREN'T DRAWN VERY WELL!
Tom Wilson

WHEN THE GOiNG GETS TOUGH... ...i EAT DONUTS!!
Tom Wilson

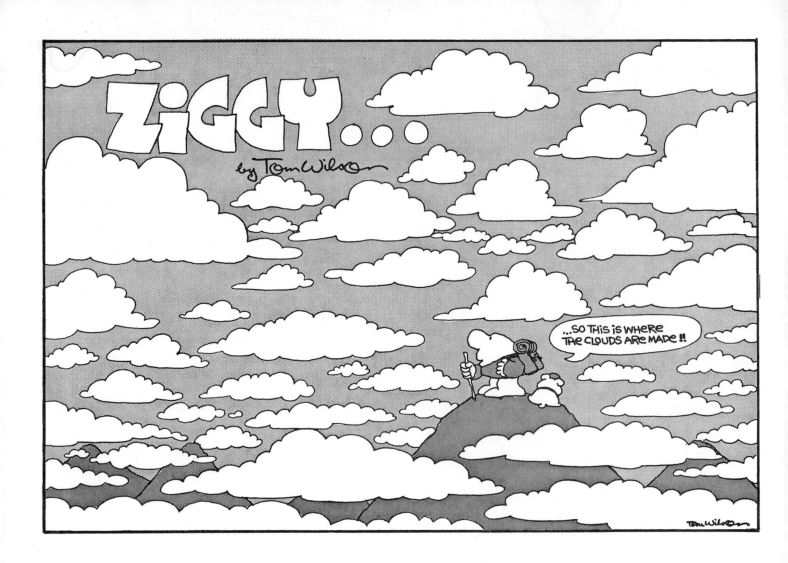

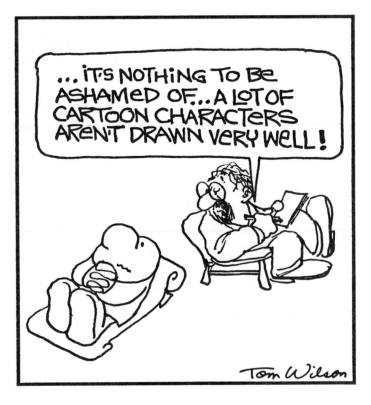

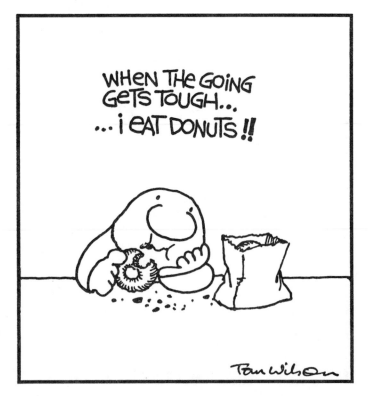

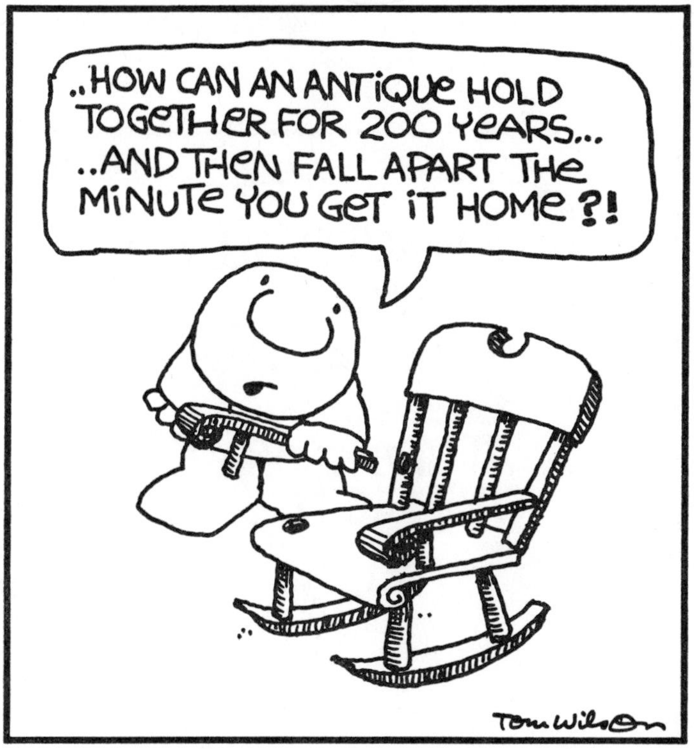
..HOW CAN AN ANTIQUE HOLD TOGETHER FOR 200 YEARS... ..AND THEN FALL APART THE MINUTE YOU GET IT HOME ?!
Tom Wilson

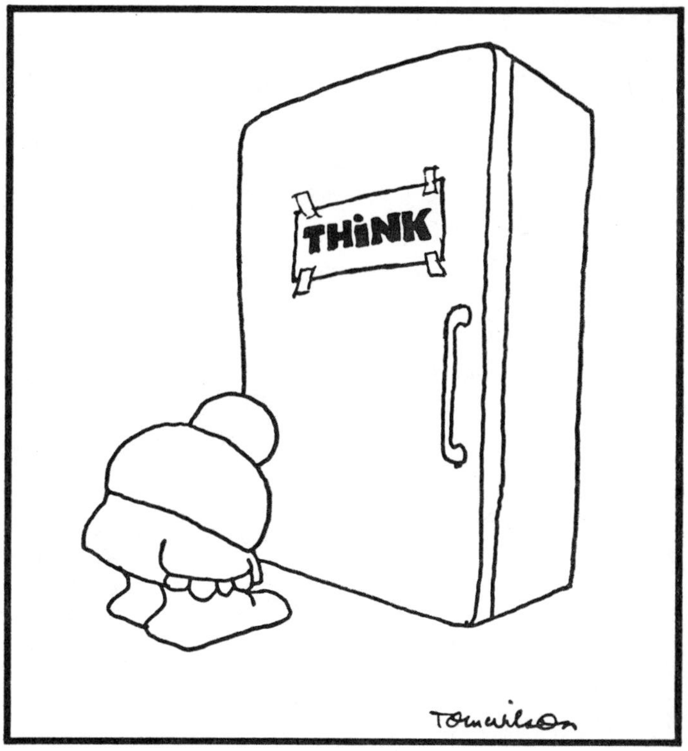
THINK
Tom Wilson

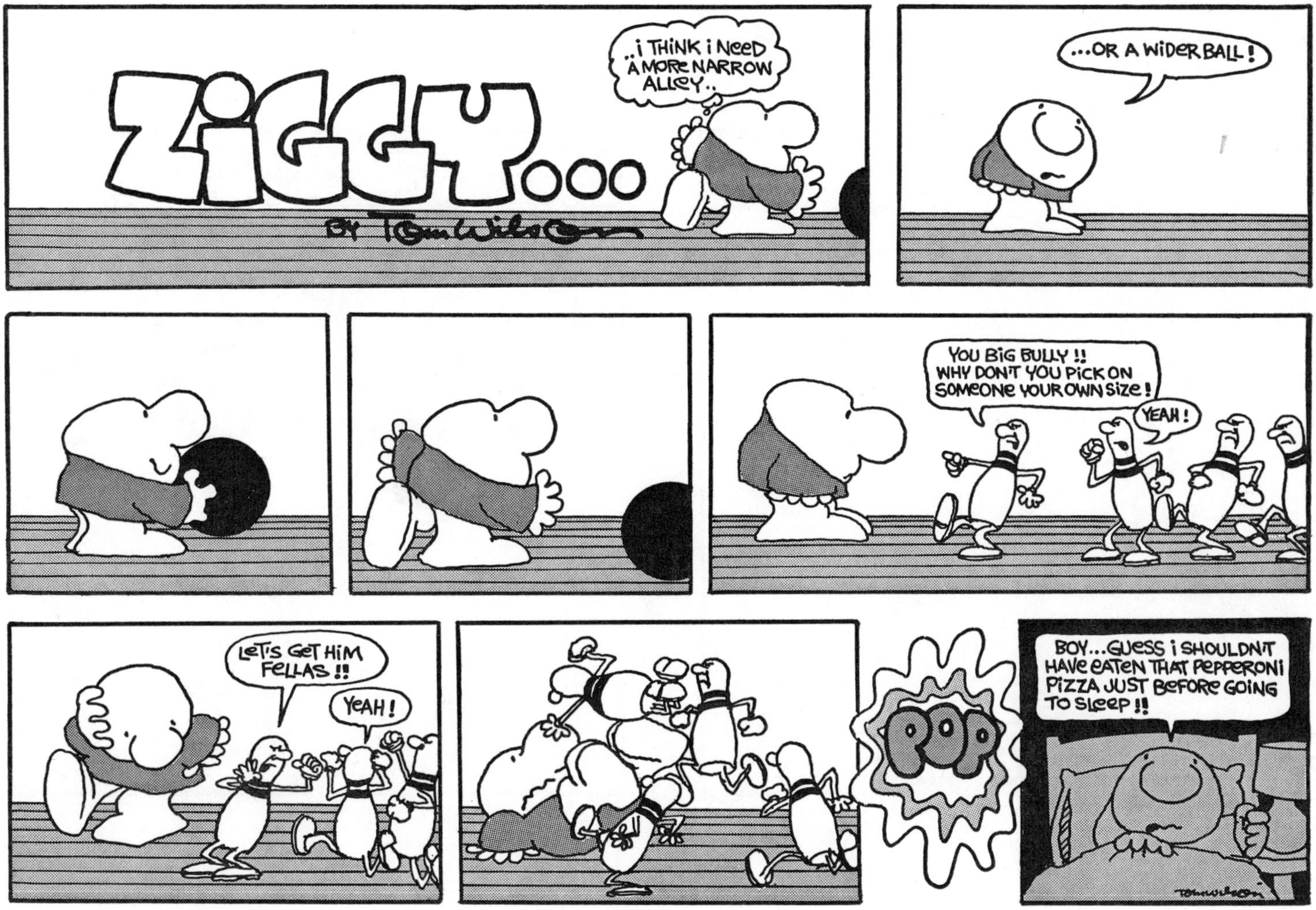
ZIGGY...
BY Tom Wilson
..I THINK I NEED A MORE NARROW ALLEY..
...OR A WIDER BALL!
YOU BIG BULLY!! WHY DON'T YOU PICK ON SOMEONE YOUR OWN SIZE!
YEAH!
LET'S GET HIM FELLAS!!
YEAH!
POP
BOY...GUESS I SHOULDN'T HAVE EATEN THAT PEPPERONI PIZZA JUST BEFORE GOING TO SLEEP!!
Tom Wilson

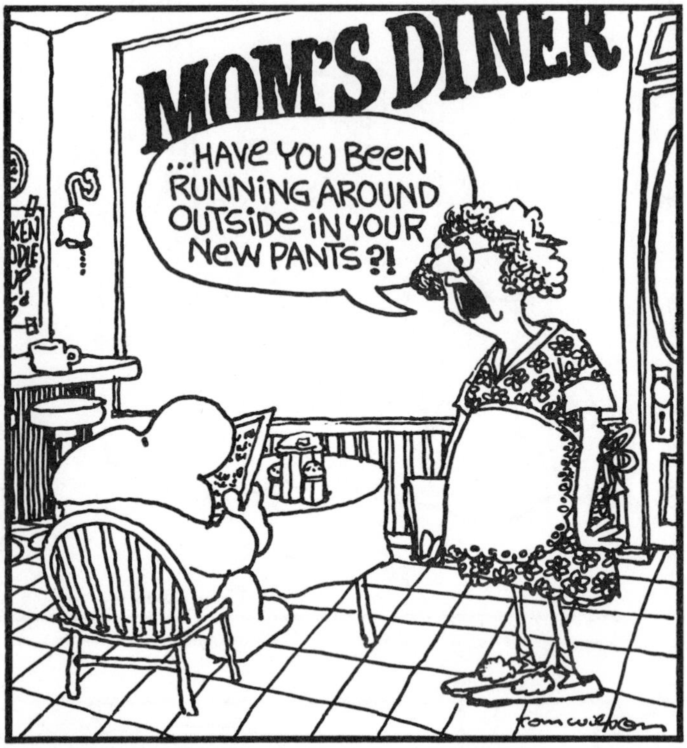
MOM'S DINER
...HAVE YOU BEEN RUNNING AROUND OUTSIDE IN YOUR NEW PANTS ?!
Tom Wilson

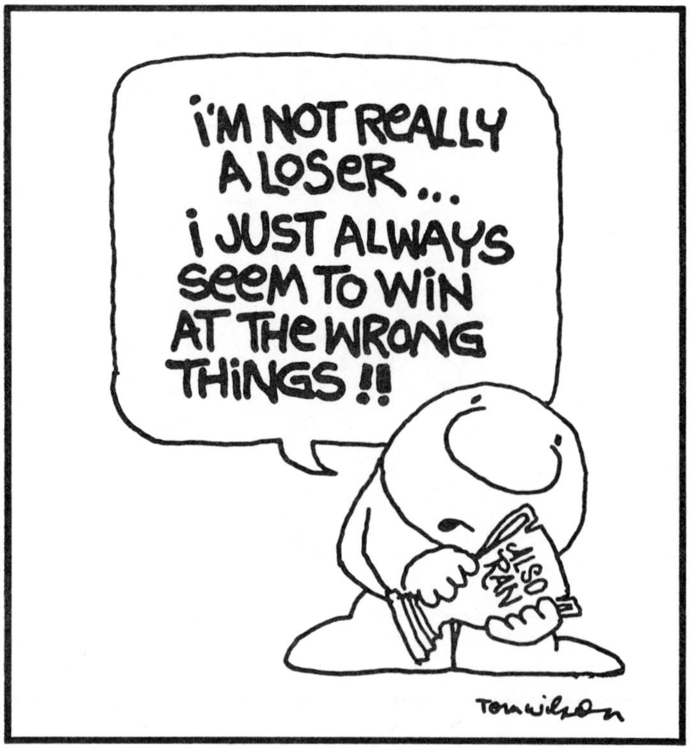
I'M NOT REALLY A LOSER... I JUST ALWAYS SEEM TO WIN AT THE WRONG THINGS !!
ALSO RAN
Tom Wilson

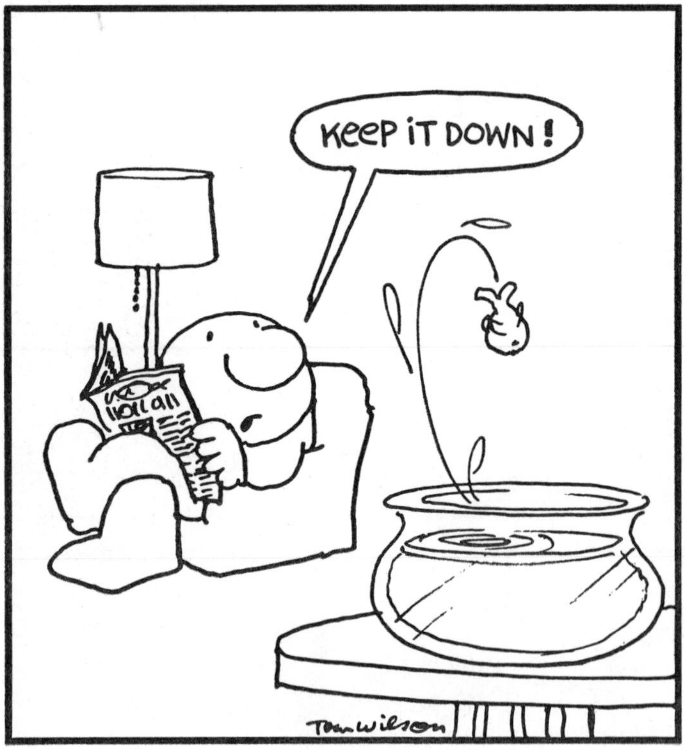
KEEP IT DOWN!
Tom Wilson

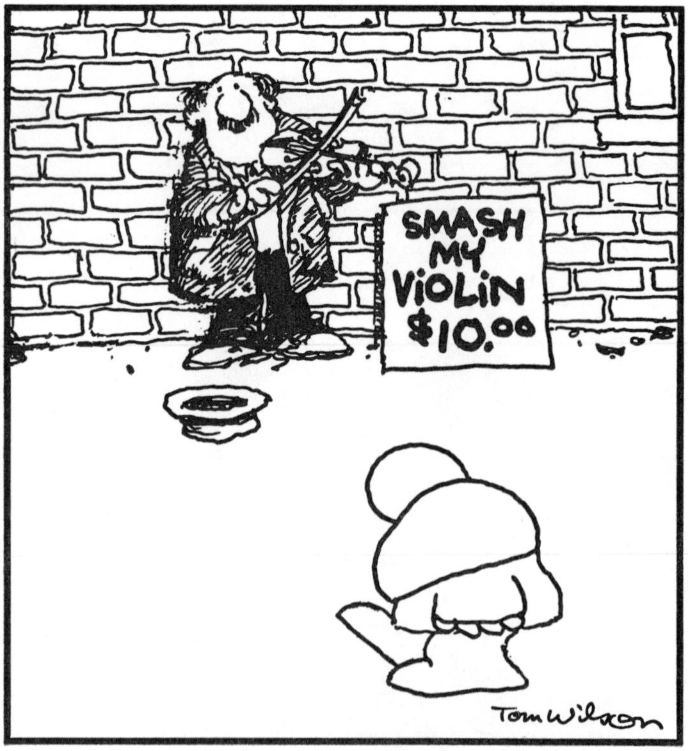
SMASH MY VIOLIN $10.00
Tom Wilson

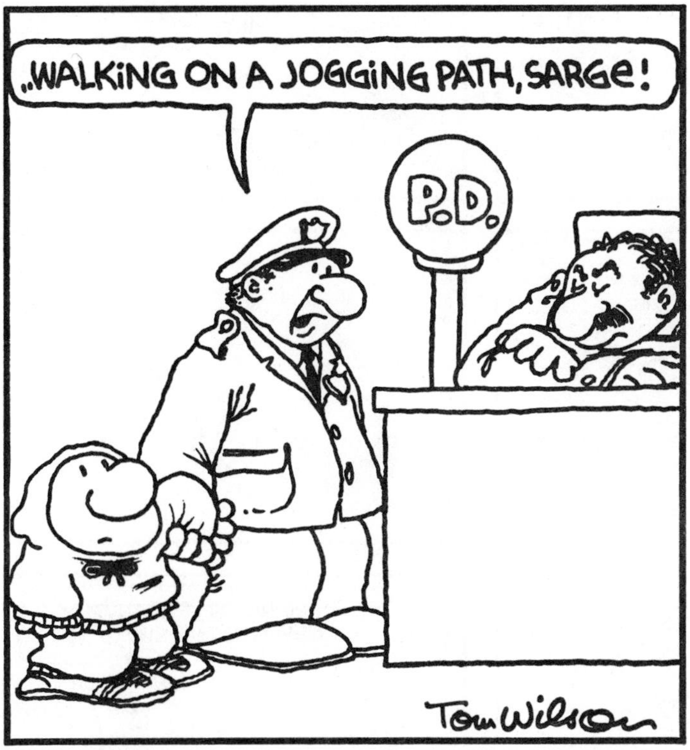
..WALKING ON A JOGGING PATH, SARGE!
P.D.
Tom Wilson

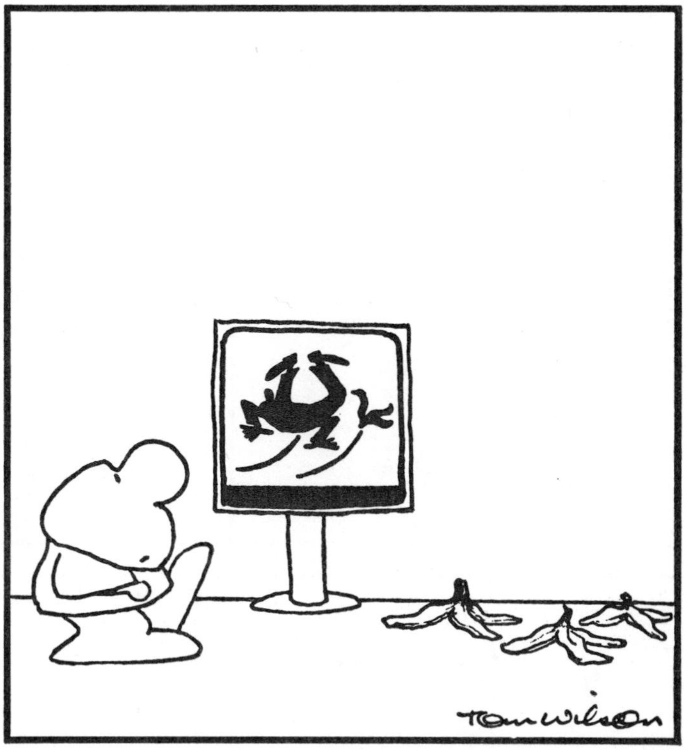
Tom Wilson

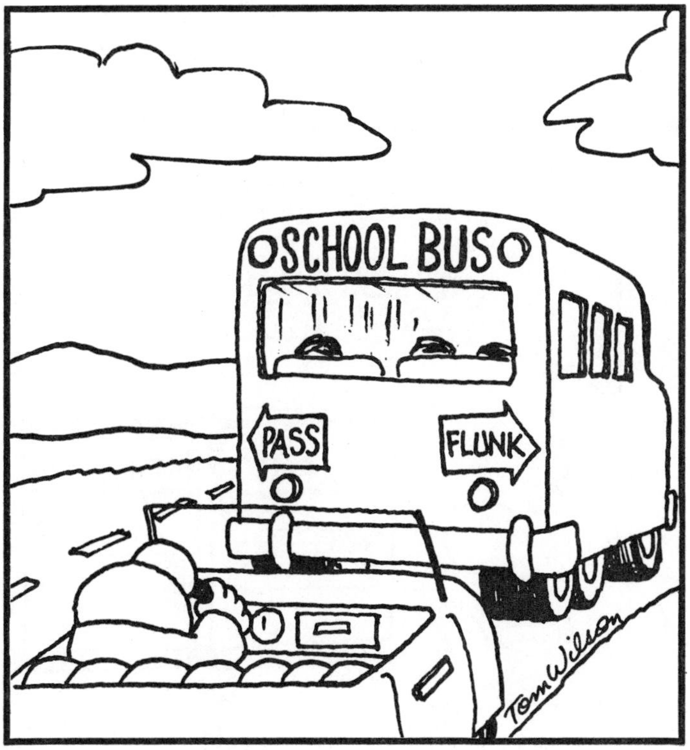
SCHOOL BUS
PASS
FLUNK
Tom Wilson

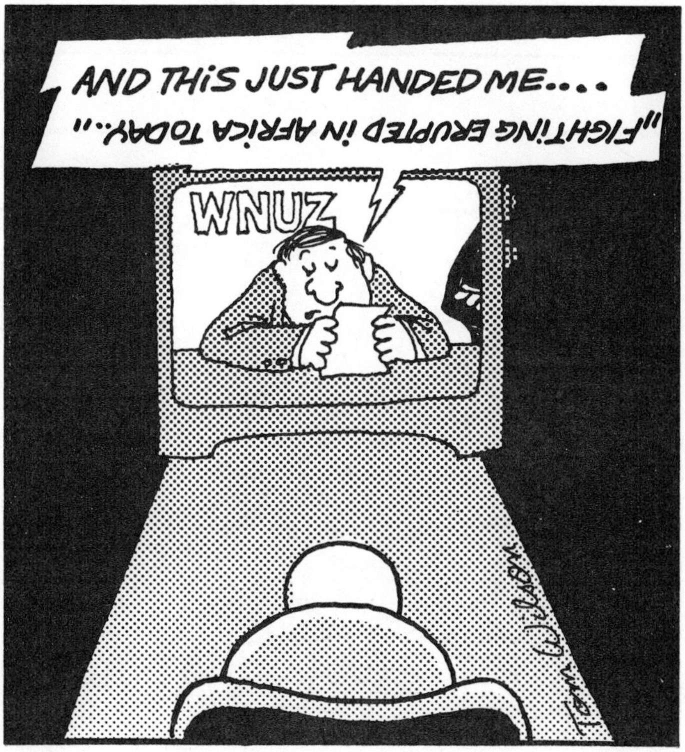
AND THIS JUST HANDED ME....
"FIGHTING ERUPTED IN AFRICA TODAY..."
WNUZ
Tom Wilson

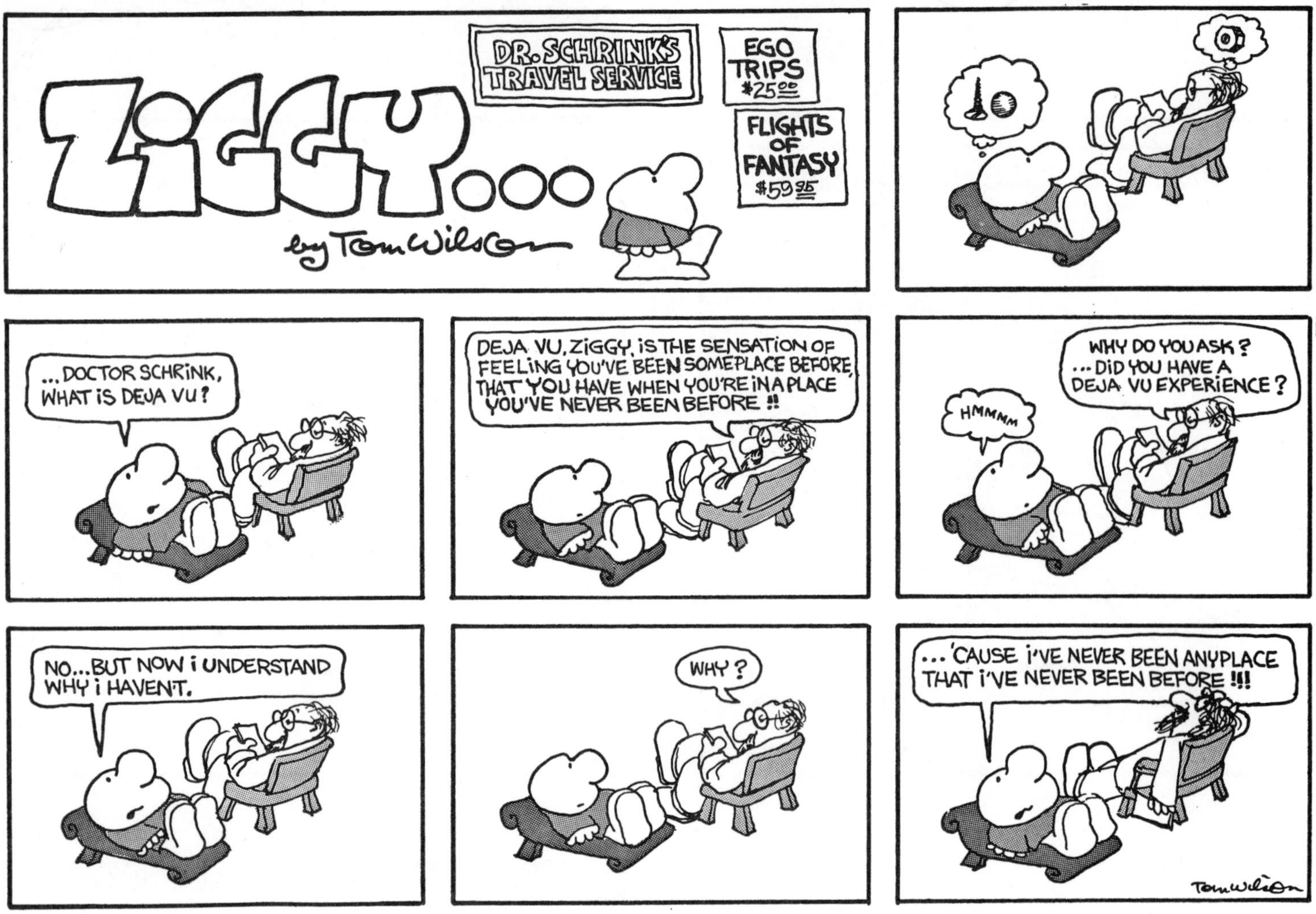
ZIGGY...
by Tom Wilson
DR. SCHRINK'S TRAVEL SERVICE
EGO TRIPS $25.00
FLIGHTS OF FANTASY $59.95
... DOCTOR SCHRINK, WHAT IS DEJA VU?
DEJA VU, ZIGGY, IS THE SENSATION OF FEELING YOU'VE BEEN SOMEPLACE BEFORE, THAT YOU HAVE WHEN YOU'RE IN A PLACE YOU'VE NEVER BEEN BEFORE !!
HMMMM
WHY DO YOU ASK? ... DID YOU HAVE A DEJA VU EXPERIENCE?
NO... BUT NOW I UNDERSTAND WHY I HAVEN'T.
WHY?
... 'CAUSE I'VE NEVER BEEN ANYPLACE THAT I'VE NEVER BEEN BEFORE !!!
Tom Wilson

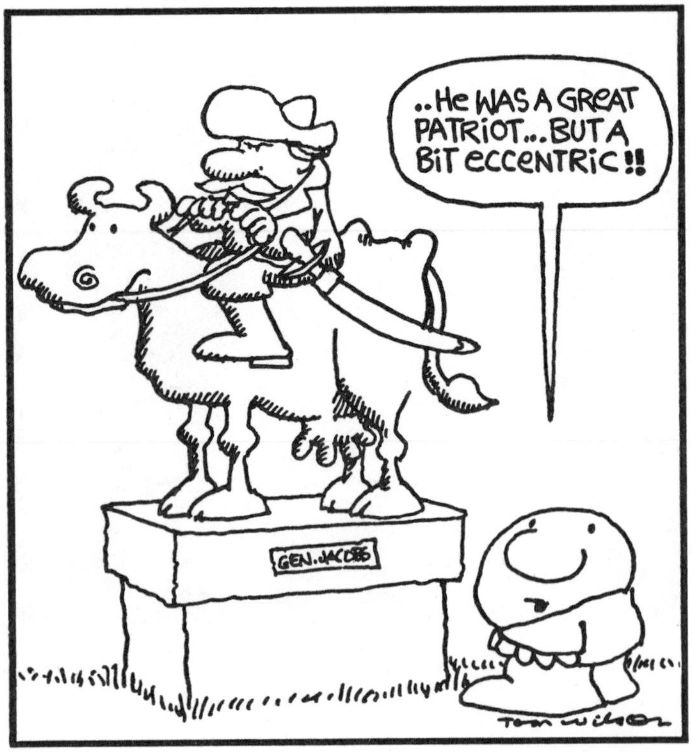
..He WAS A GREAT PATRIOT... BUT A BIT ECCENTRIC !!
GEN. JACOBS
Tom Wilson

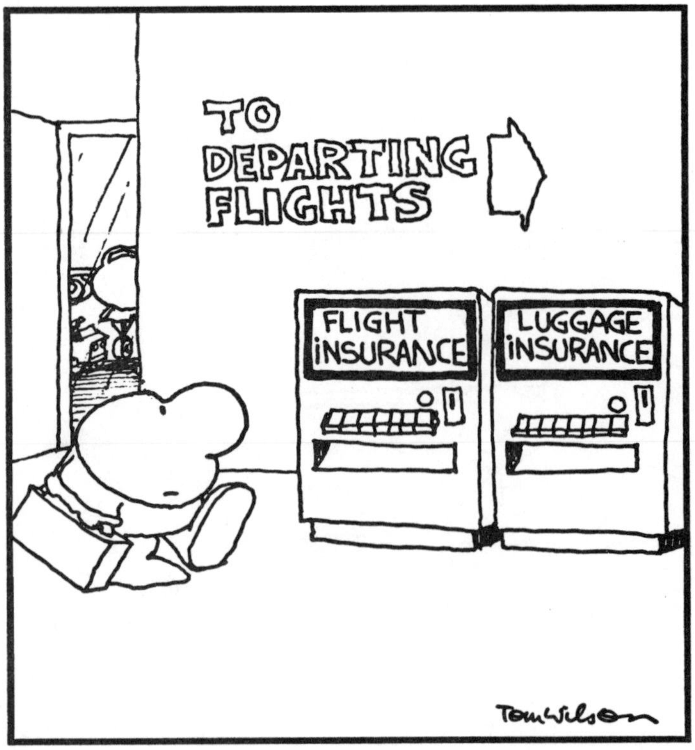
TO DEPARTING FLIGHTS
FLIGHT INSURANCE
LUGGAGE INSURANCE
Tom Wilson

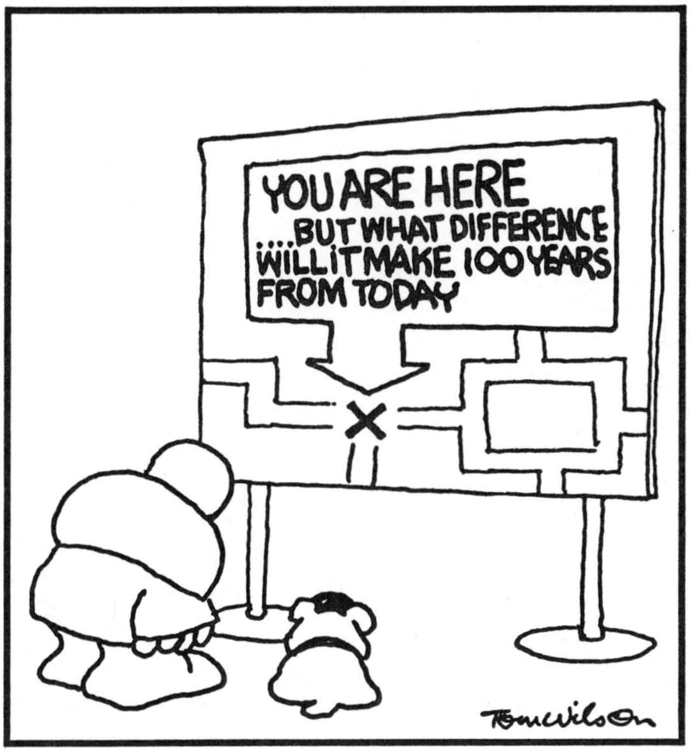
YOU ARE HERE
....BUT WHAT DIFFERENCE WILL IT MAKE 100 YEARS FROM TODAY
Tom Wilson

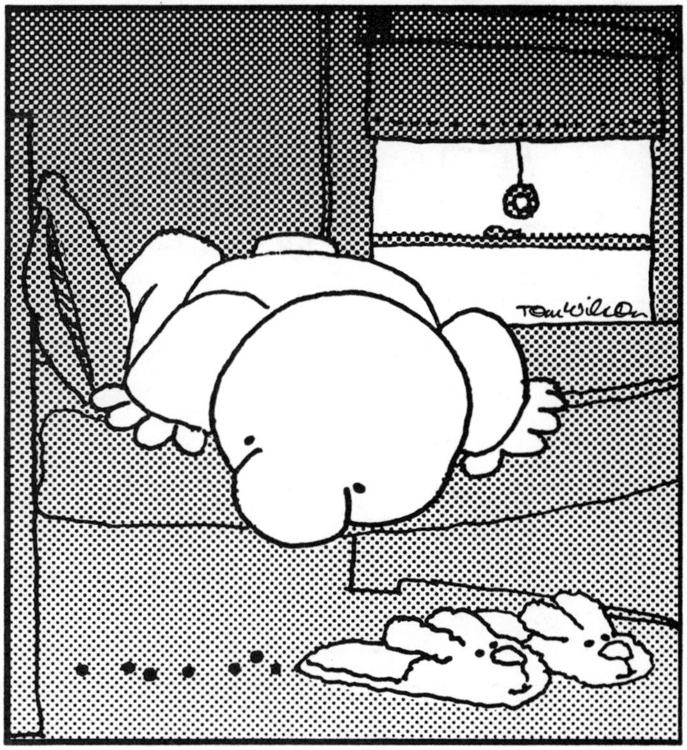
Tom Wilson

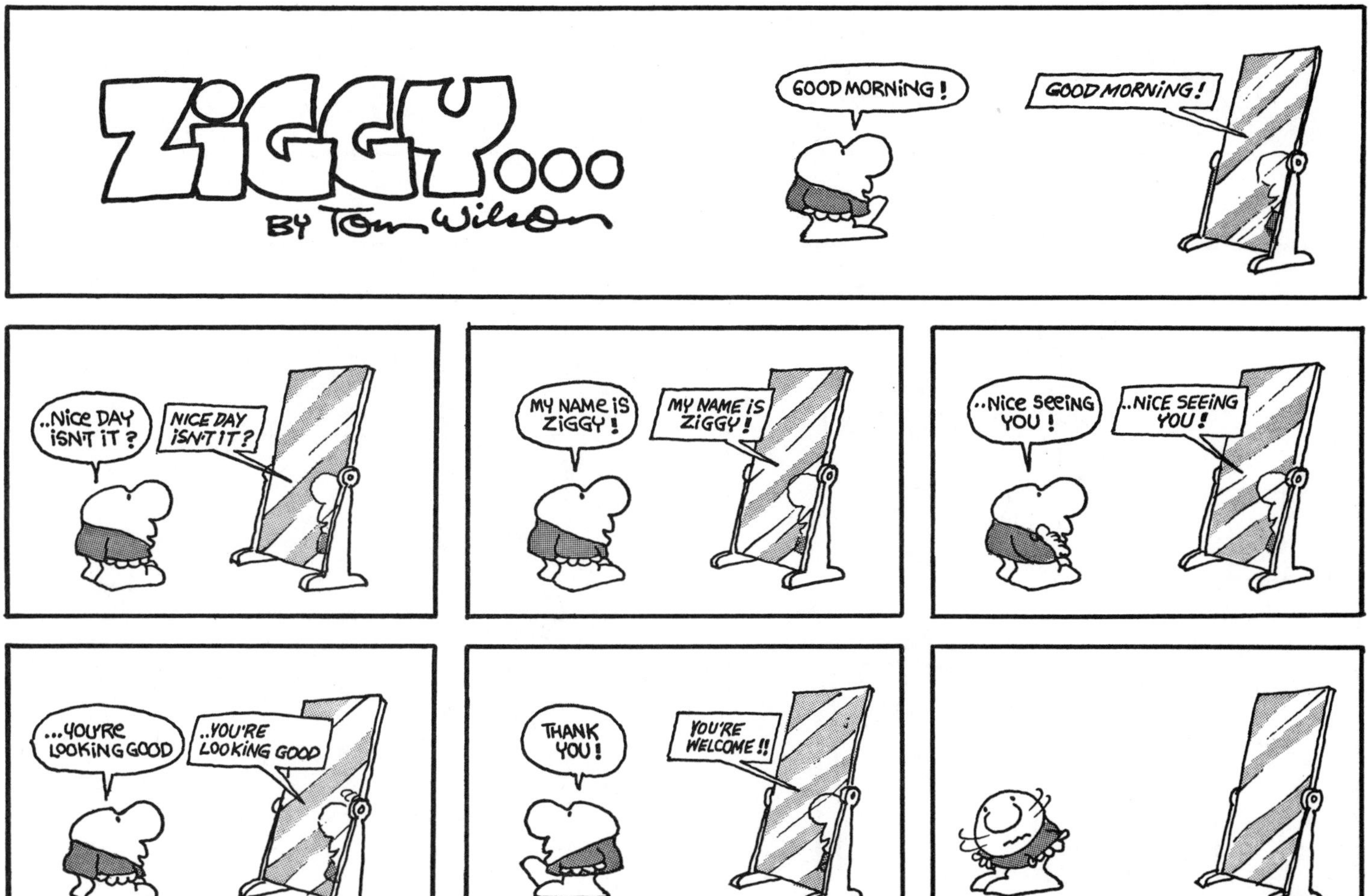
ZIGGY ooo
BY Tom Wilson
GOOD MORNING!
GOOD MORNING!
..Nice DAY isn't it?
NICE DAY isn't it?
MY NAME is ZIGGY!
MY NAME is ZIGGY!
..Nice SEEING YOU!
..NICE SEEING YOU!
...YOU'RE LOOKING GOOD
..YOU'RE LOOKING GOOD
THANK YOU!
YOU'RE WELCOME!!
Tom Wilson

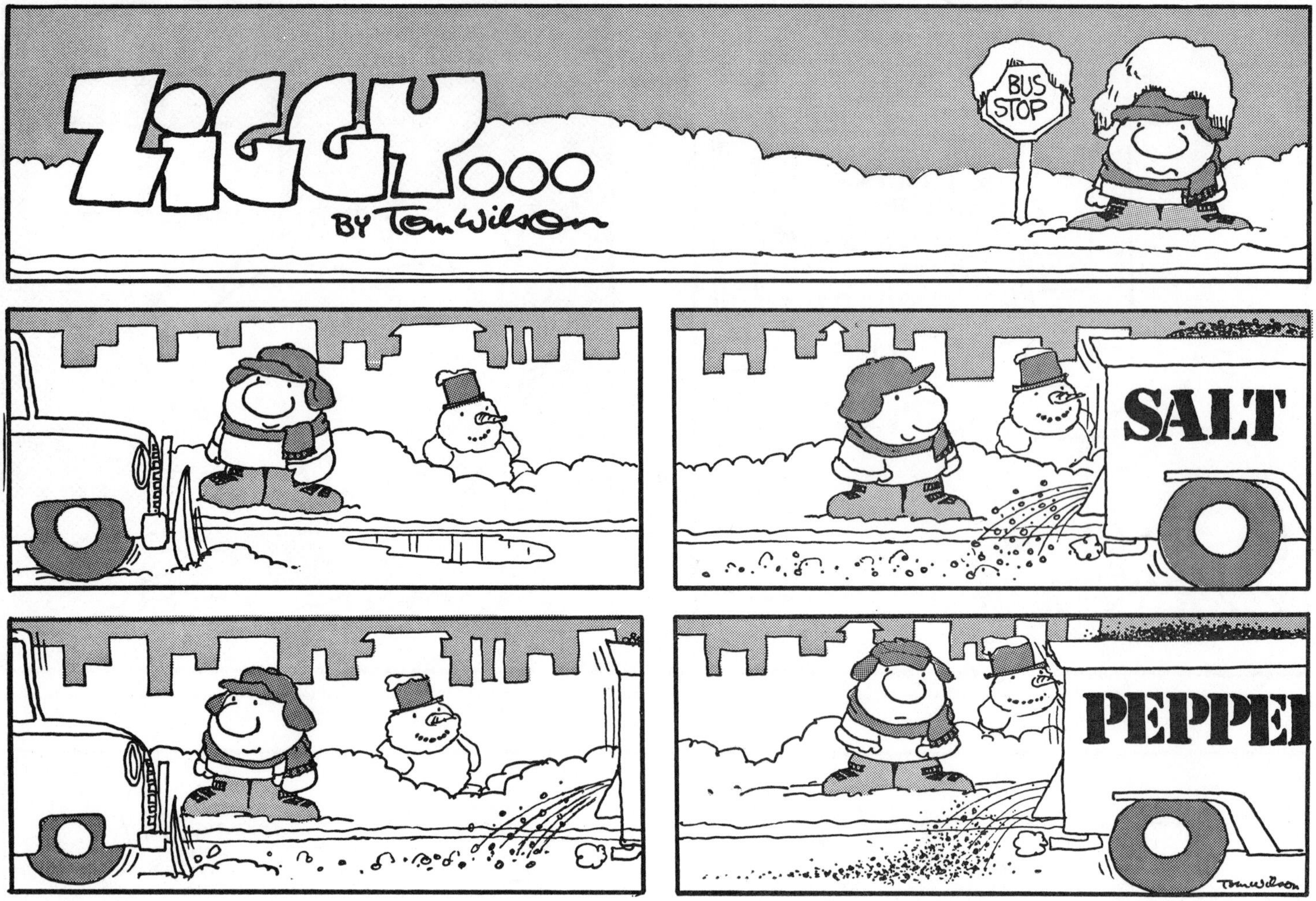
ZIGGY
BY Tom Wilson
BUS STOP
SALT
PEPPE
Tom Wilson

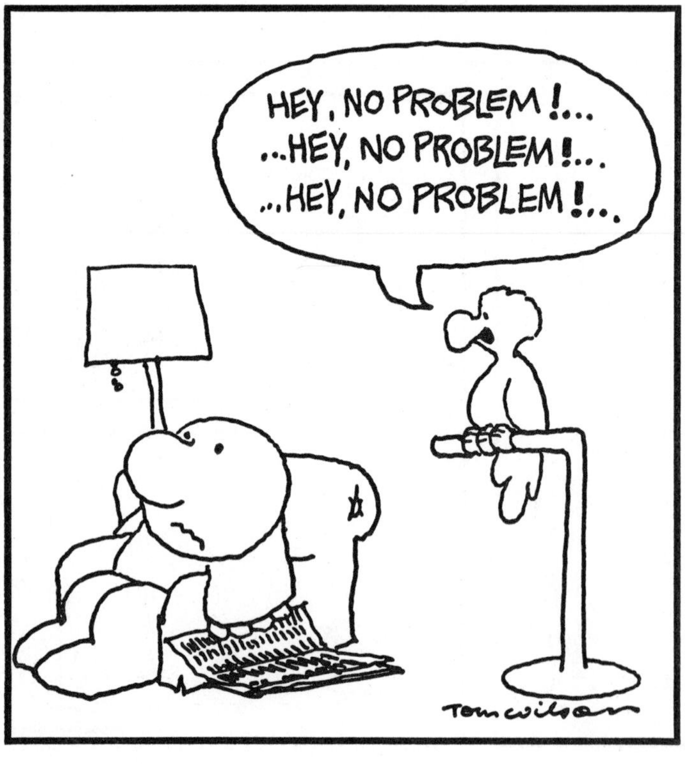
HEY, NO PROBLEM!... ...HEY, NO PROBLEM!... ...HEY, NO PROBLEM!...
Tom Wilson

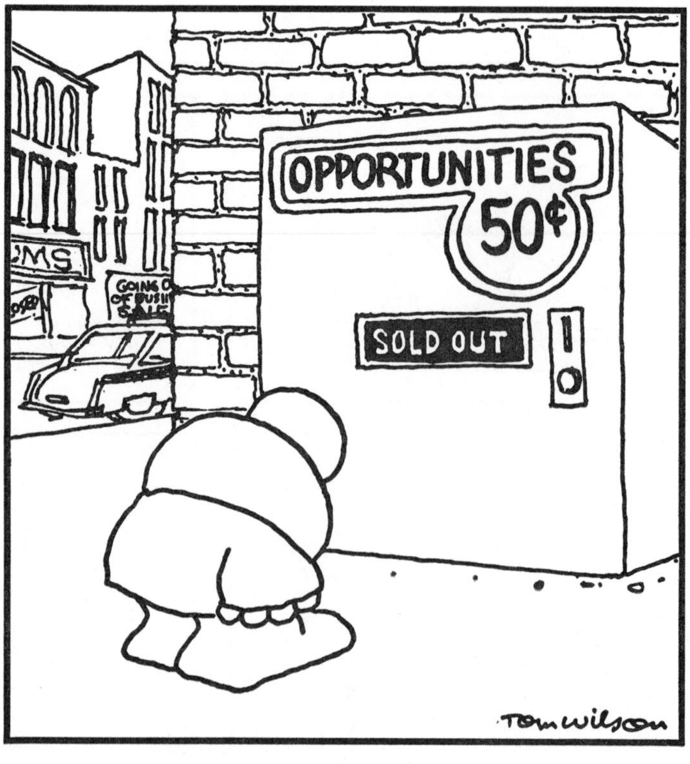
OPPORTUNITIES 50¢
SOLD OUT
Tom Wilson

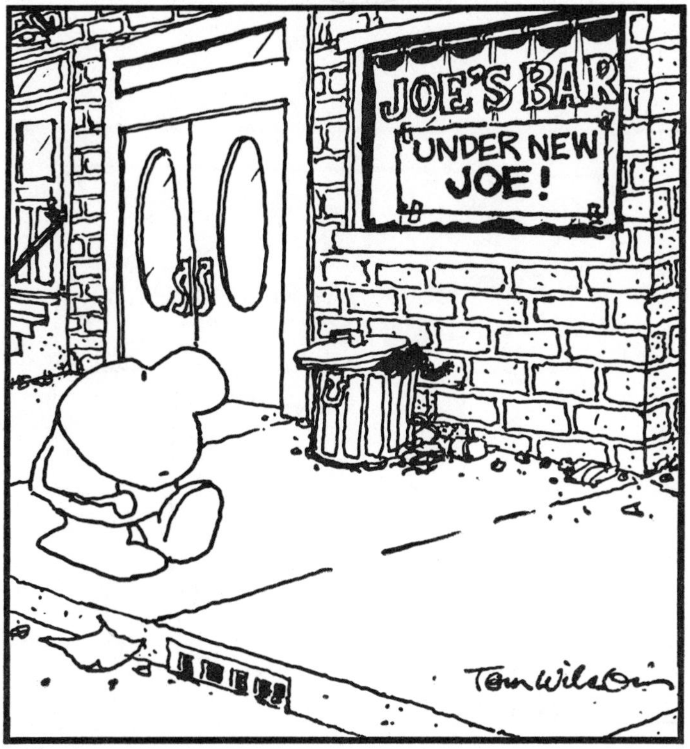
JOE'S BAR
UNDER NEW JOE!
Tom Wilson

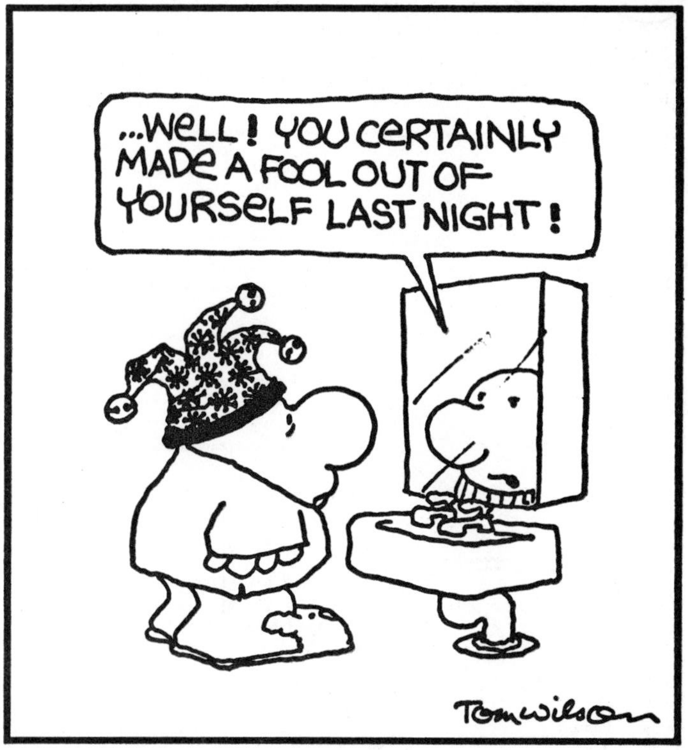
...WELL! YOU CERTAINLY MADE A FOOL OUT OF YOURSELF LAST NIGHT!
Tom Wilson

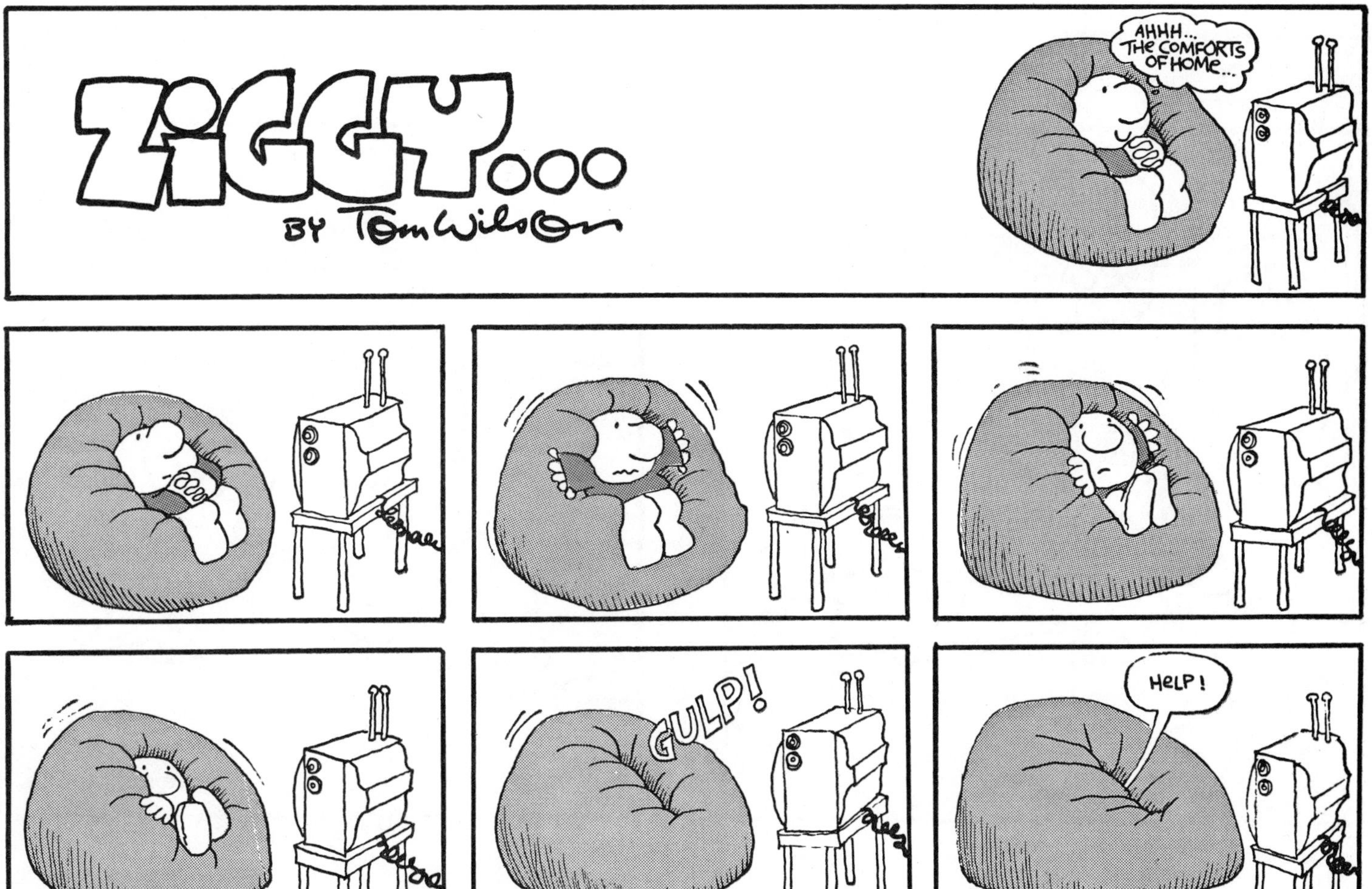
ZIGGY...
BY Tom Wilson
AHHH... THE COMFORTS OF HOME...
GULP!
HELP!

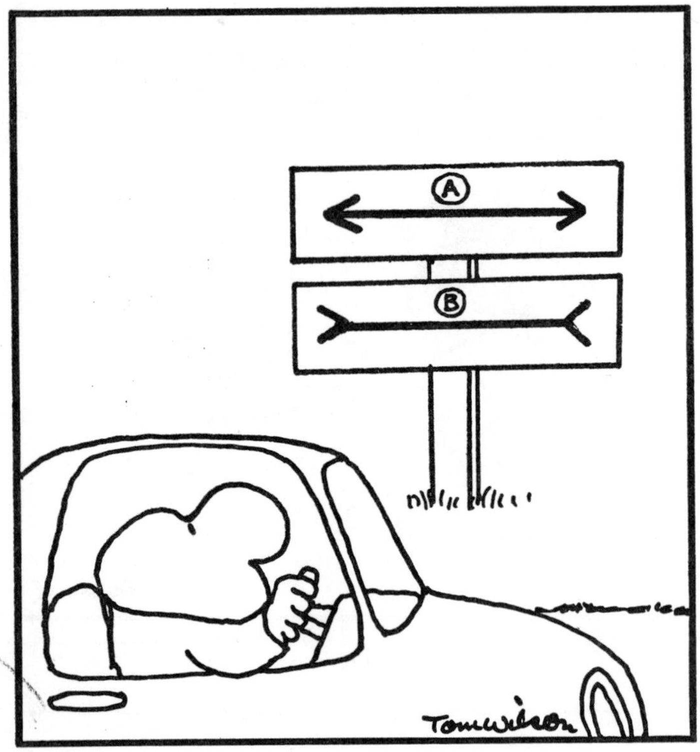

A
B
TomWilson

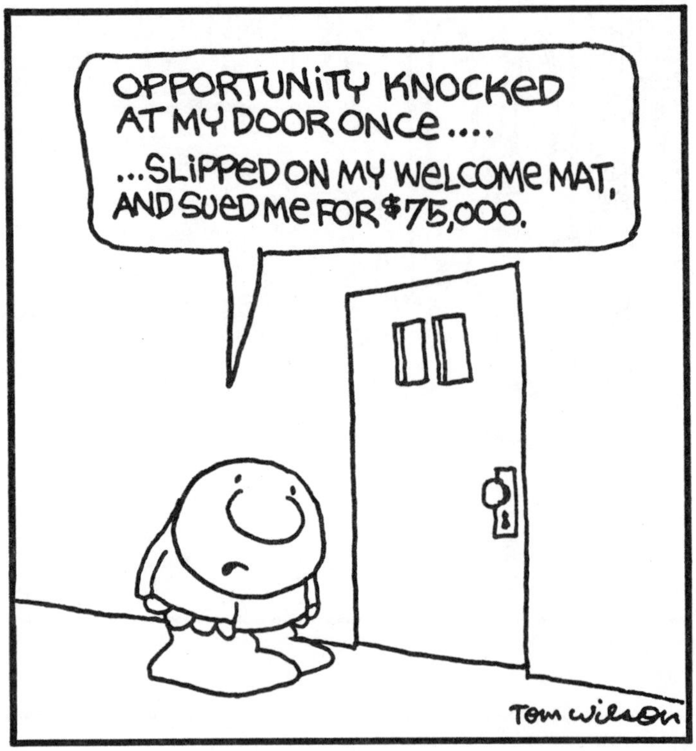

OPPORTUNITY KNOCKED AT MY DOOR ONCE.... ...SLIPPED ON MY WELCOME MAT, AND SUED ME FOR $75,000.
TOM WILSON

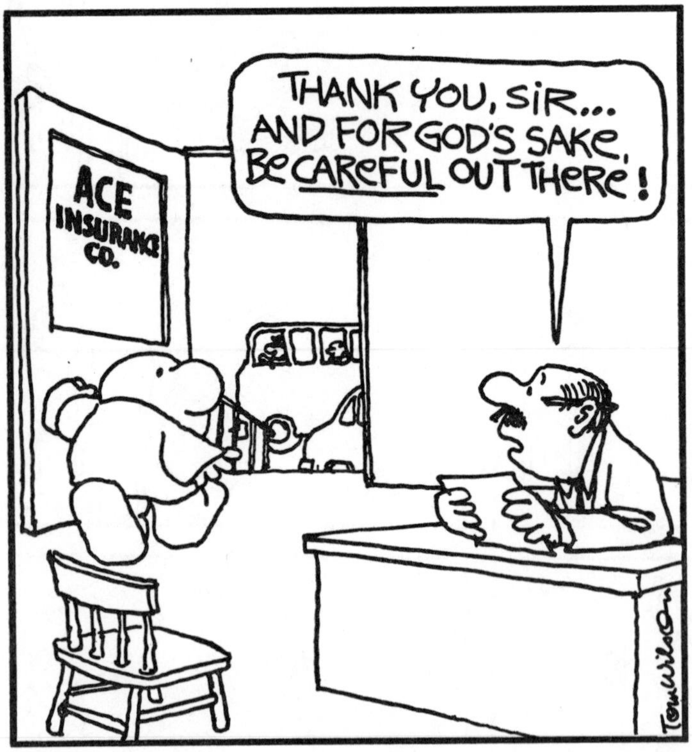

THANK YOU, SIR... AND FOR GOD'S SAKE, BE CAREFUL OUT THERE!
ACE INSURANCE CO.
TomWilson

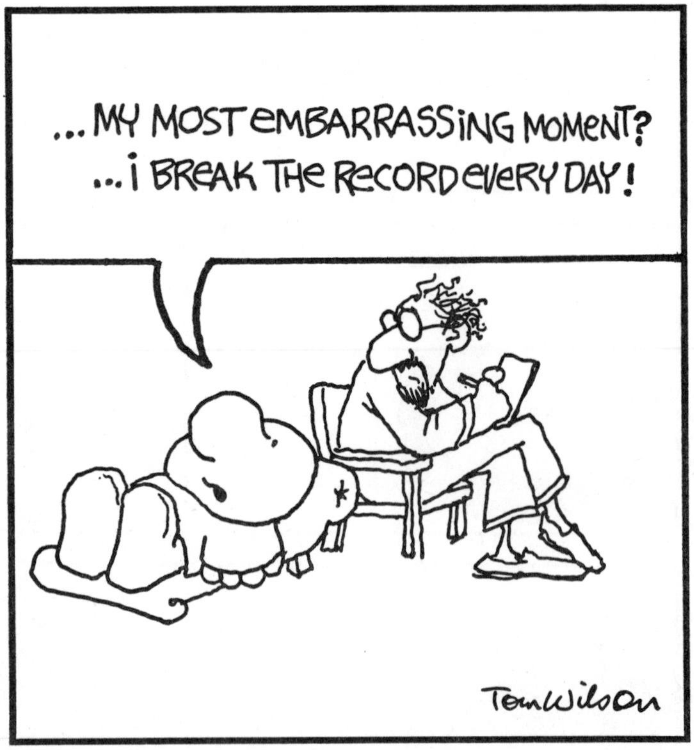

...MY MOST EMBARRASSING MOMENT? ...I BREAK THE RECORD EVERY DAY!
TomWilson

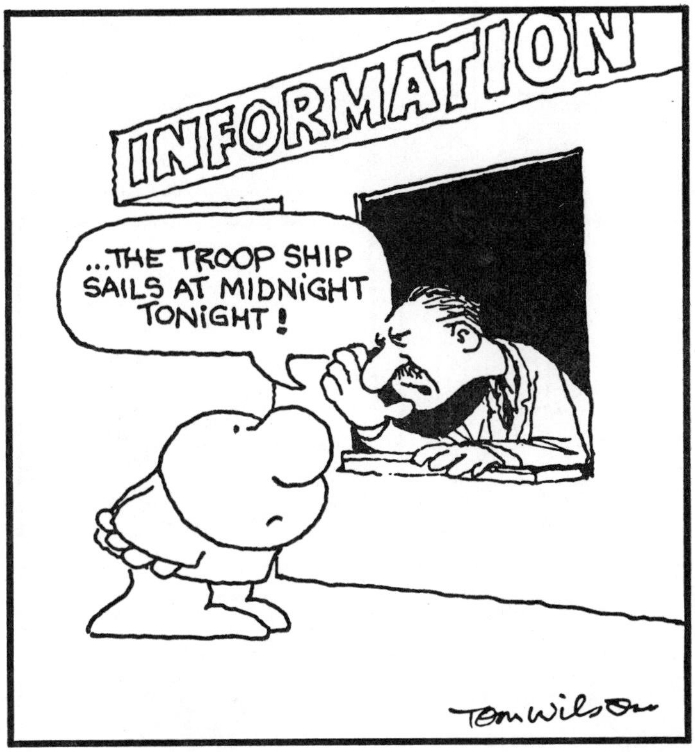
INFORMATION
...THE TROOP SHIP SAILS AT MIDNIGHT TONIGHT!
Tom Wilson

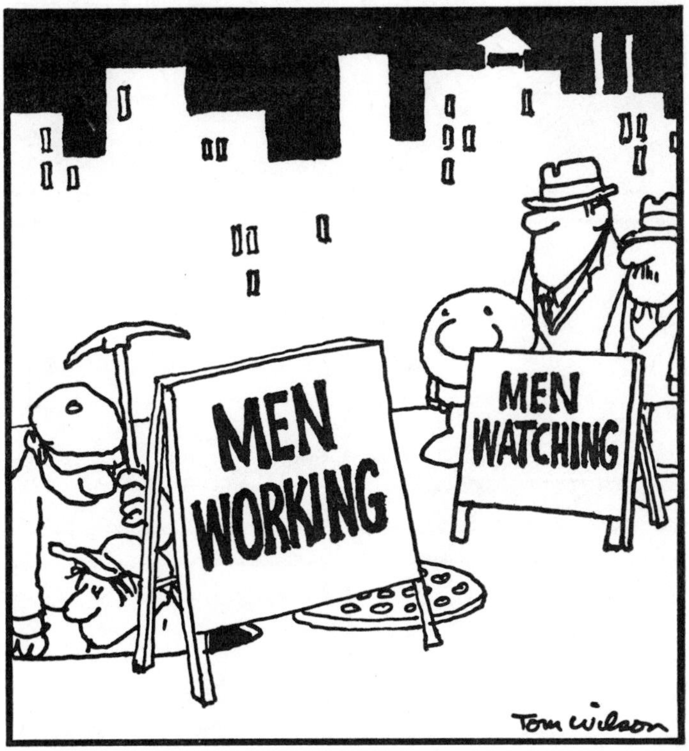
MEN WORKING
MEN WATCHING
Tom Wilson

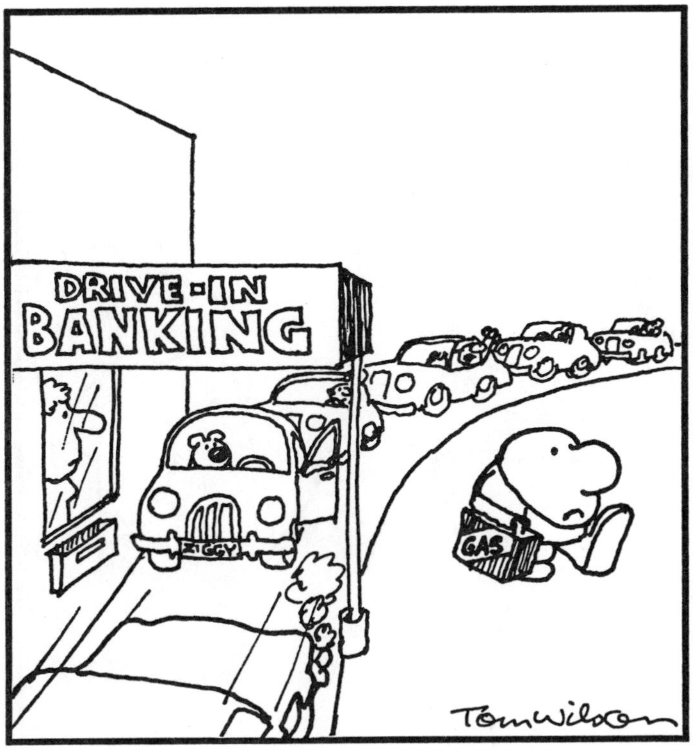
DRIVE-IN BANKING
ZIGGY
GAS
Tom Wilson

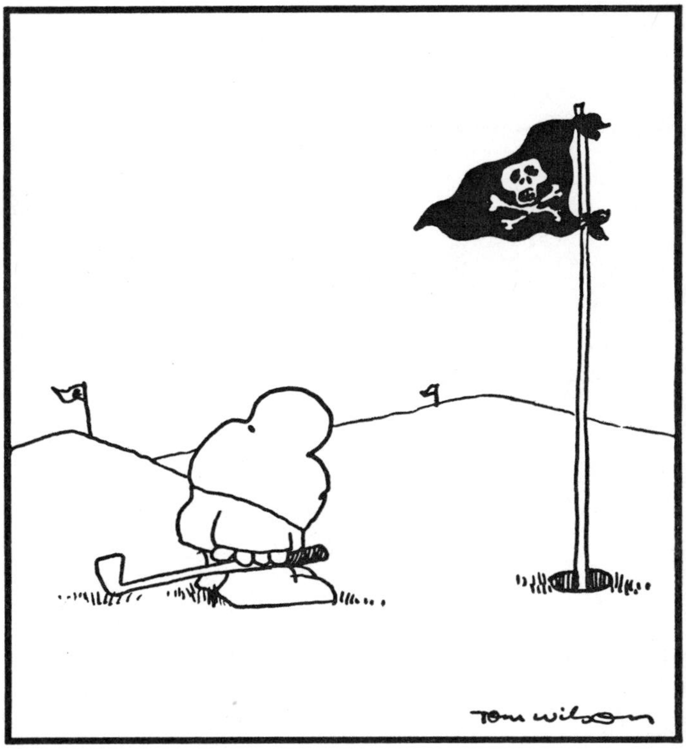
Tom Wilson

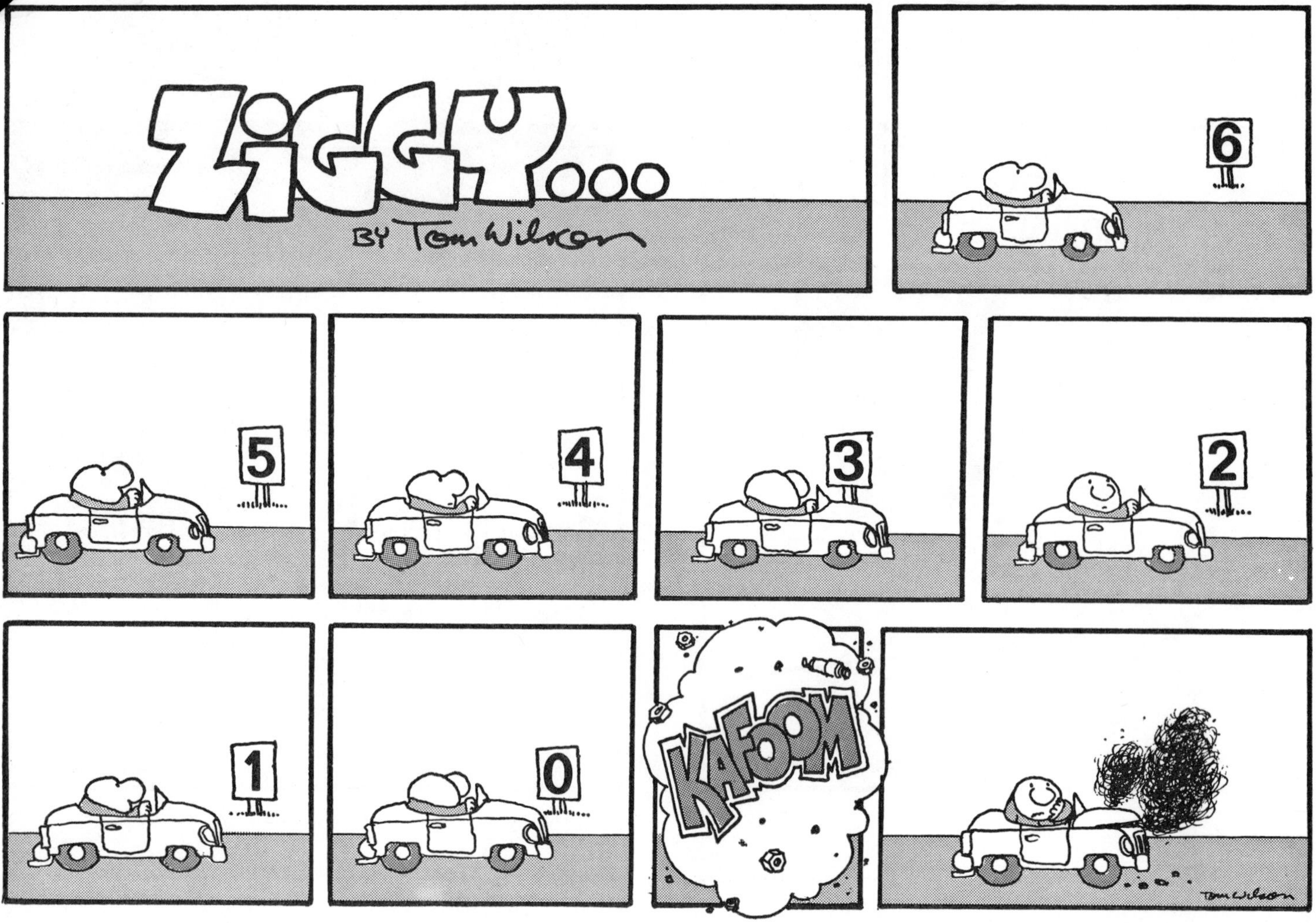
ZIGGY...
BY Tom Wilson
6
5
4
3
2
1
0
KAFOOM
Tom Wilson

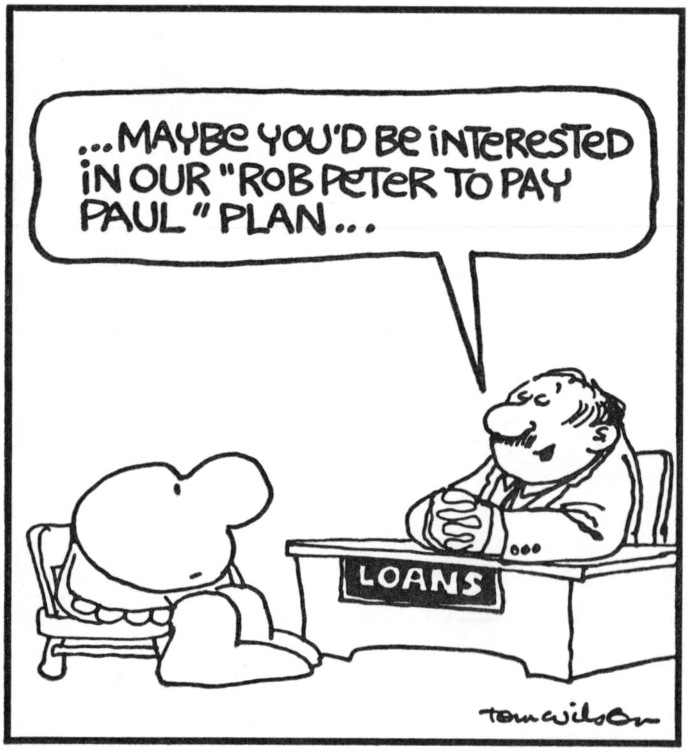
...MAYBE YOU'D BE INTERESTED IN OUR "ROB PETER TO PAY PAUL" PLAN...
LOANS
Tom Wilson

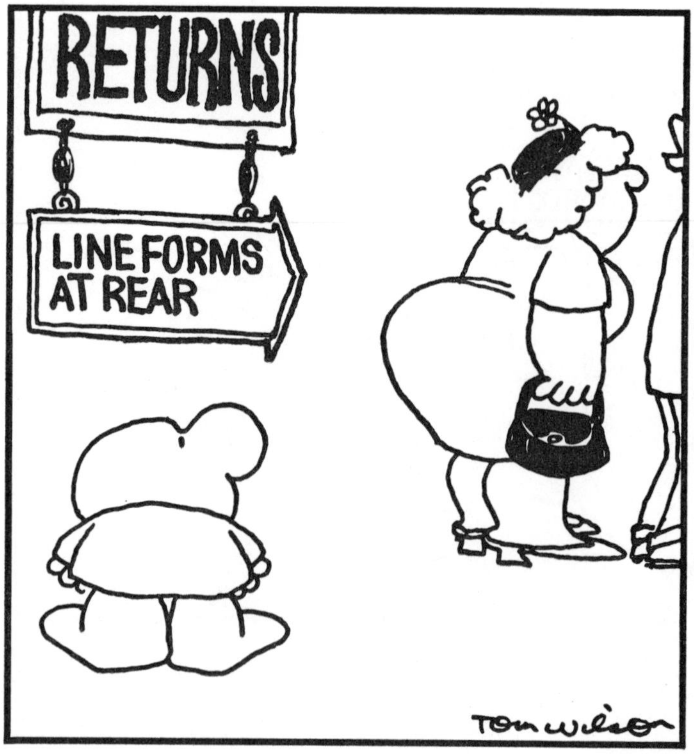
RETURNS
LINE FORMS AT REAR
Tom Wilson

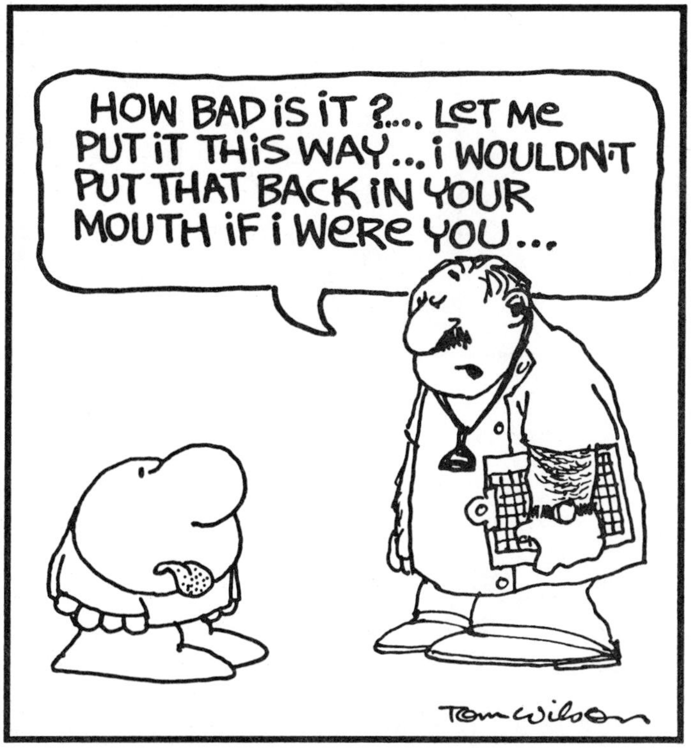
HOW BAD IS IT ?... LET ME PUT IT THIS WAY... I WOULDN'T PUT THAT BACK IN YOUR MOUTH IF I WERE YOU...
Tom Wilson

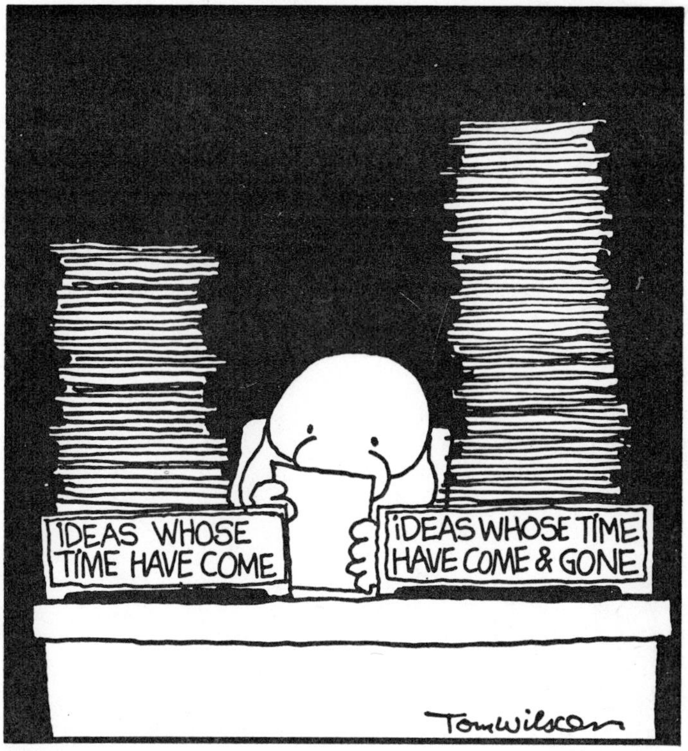
IDEAS WHOSE TIME HAVE COME
IDEAS WHOSE TIME HAVE COME & GONE
Tom Wilson

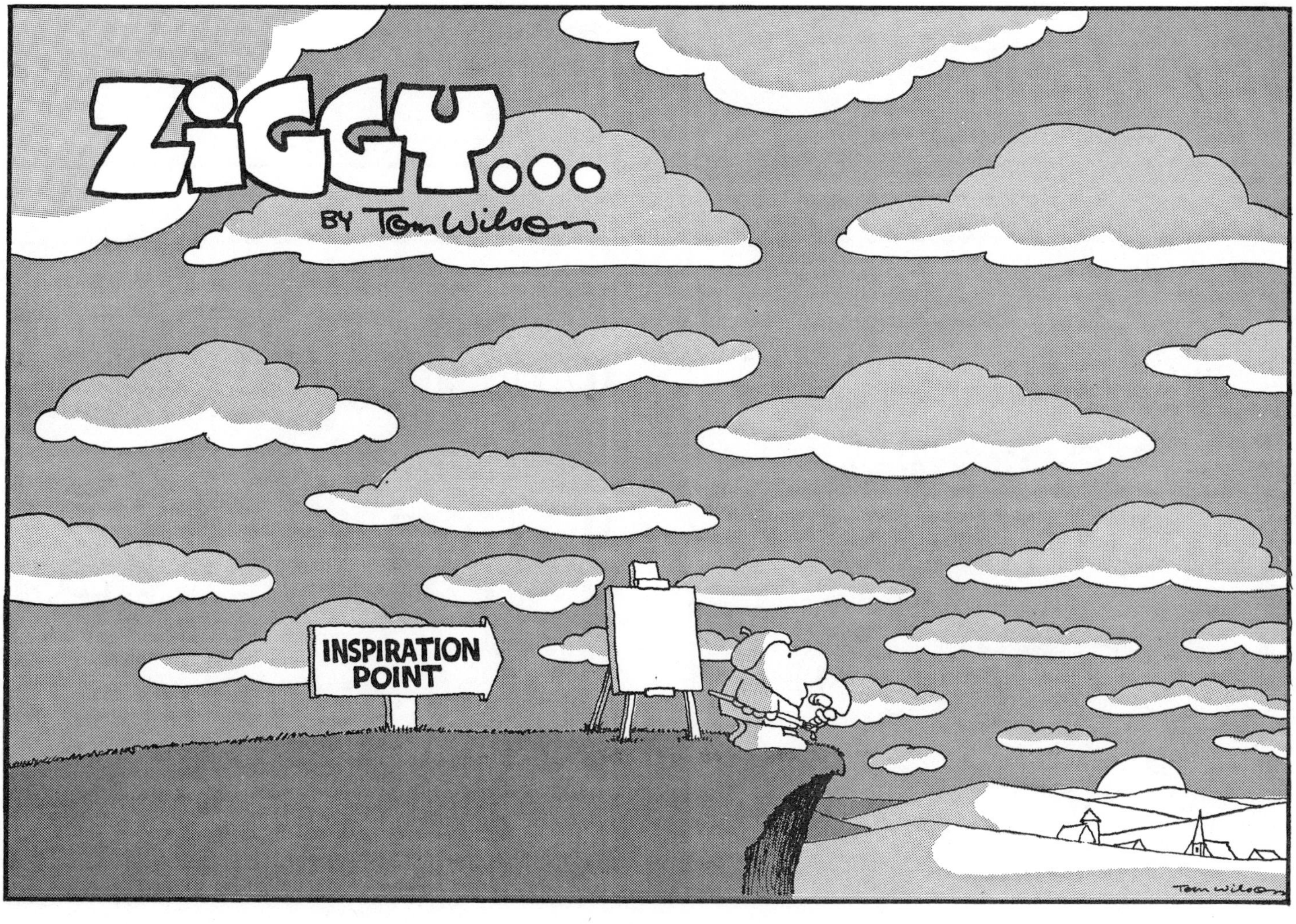
ZIGGY...
BY Tom Wilson
INSPIRATION POINT
Tom Wilson

ZIGGY...

BY Tom Wilson

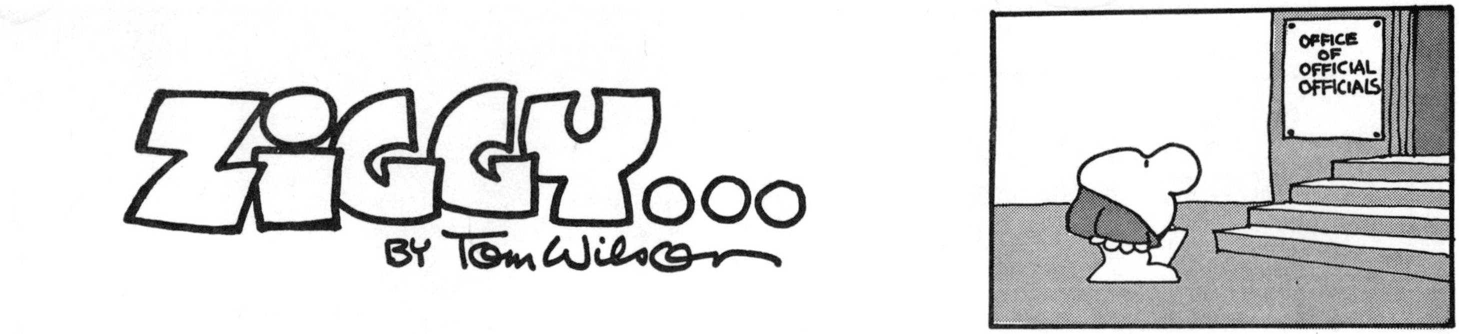
OFFICE OF OFFICIAL OFFICIALS

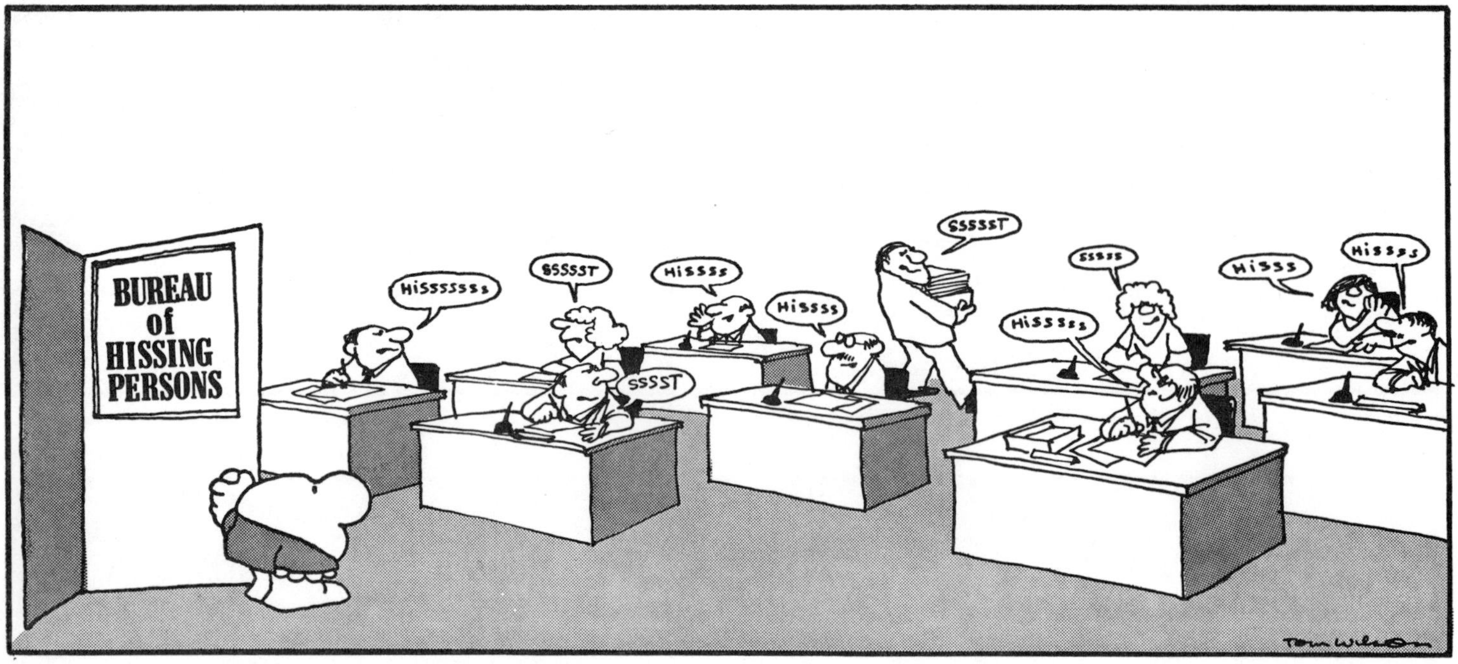
BUREAU of HISSING PERSONS
HiSSSSSSSs
SSSSST
HiSSSSs
SSSST
HiSSSS
SSSSST
HiSSSSSs
SSSSS
HiSSS
HiSSSSs
Tom Wilson

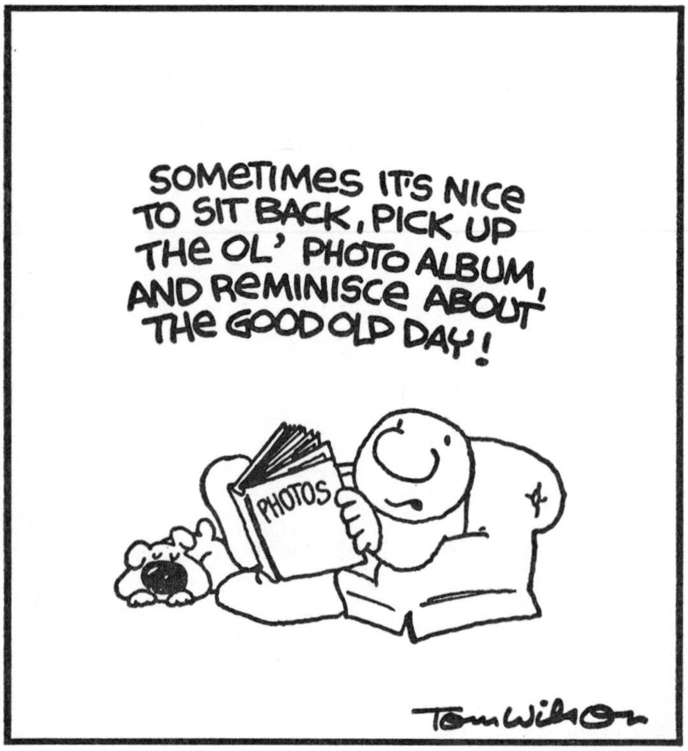
SOMETIMES IT'S NICE TO SIT BACK, PICK UP THE OL' PHOTO ALBUM AND REMINISCE ABOUT THE GOOD OLD DAY!
PHOTOS
Tom Wilson

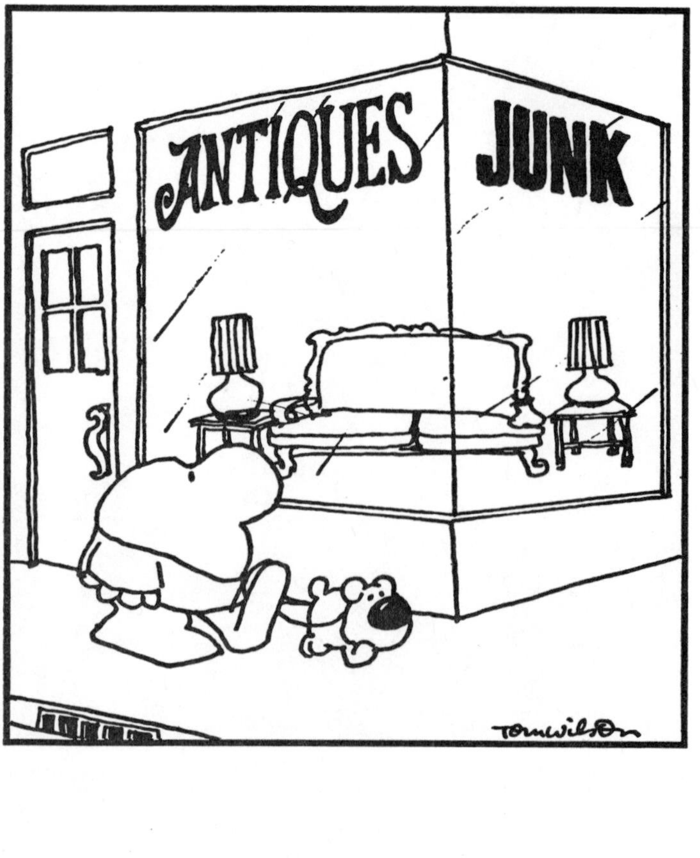
ANTIQUES
JUNK
Tom Wilson

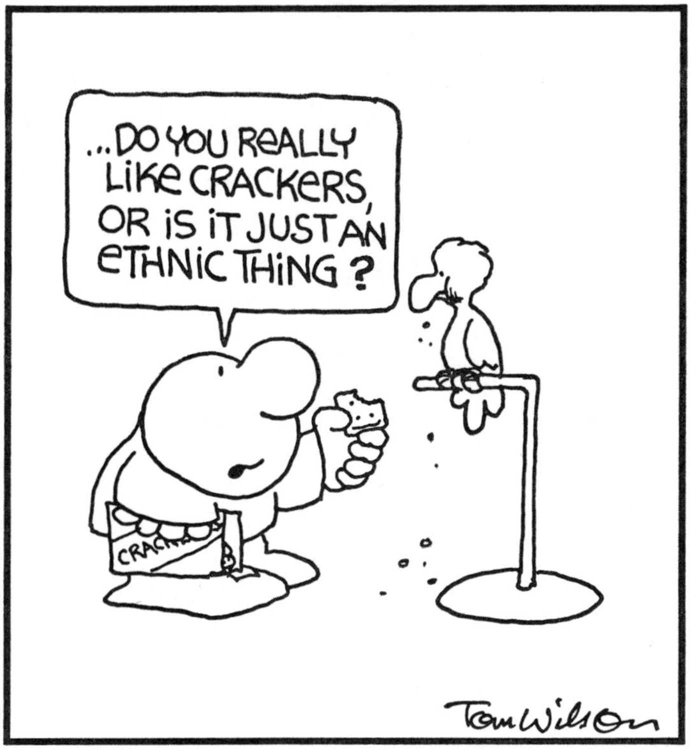
...DO YOU REALLY LIKE CRACKERS, OR IS IT JUST AN ETHNIC THING?
Tom Wilson

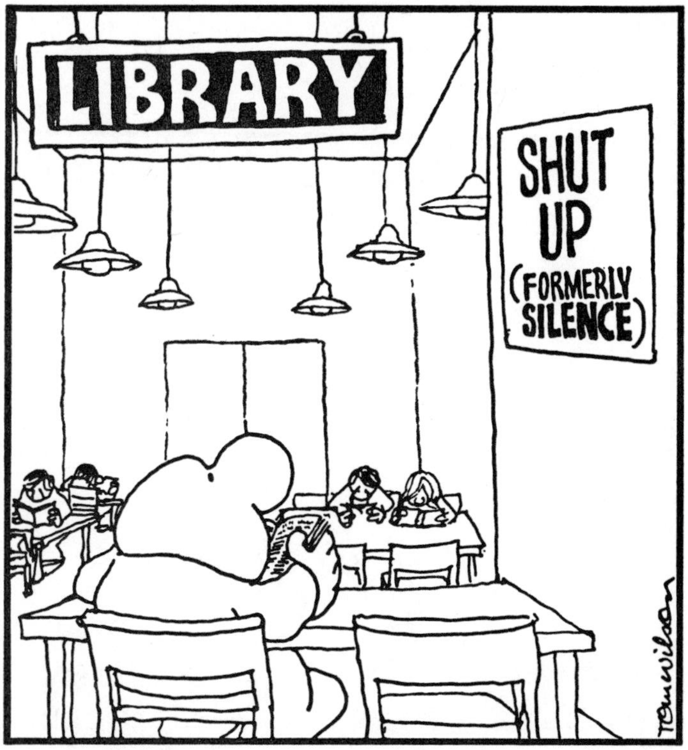
LIBRARY
SHUT UP (FORMERLY SILENCE)
Tom Wilson

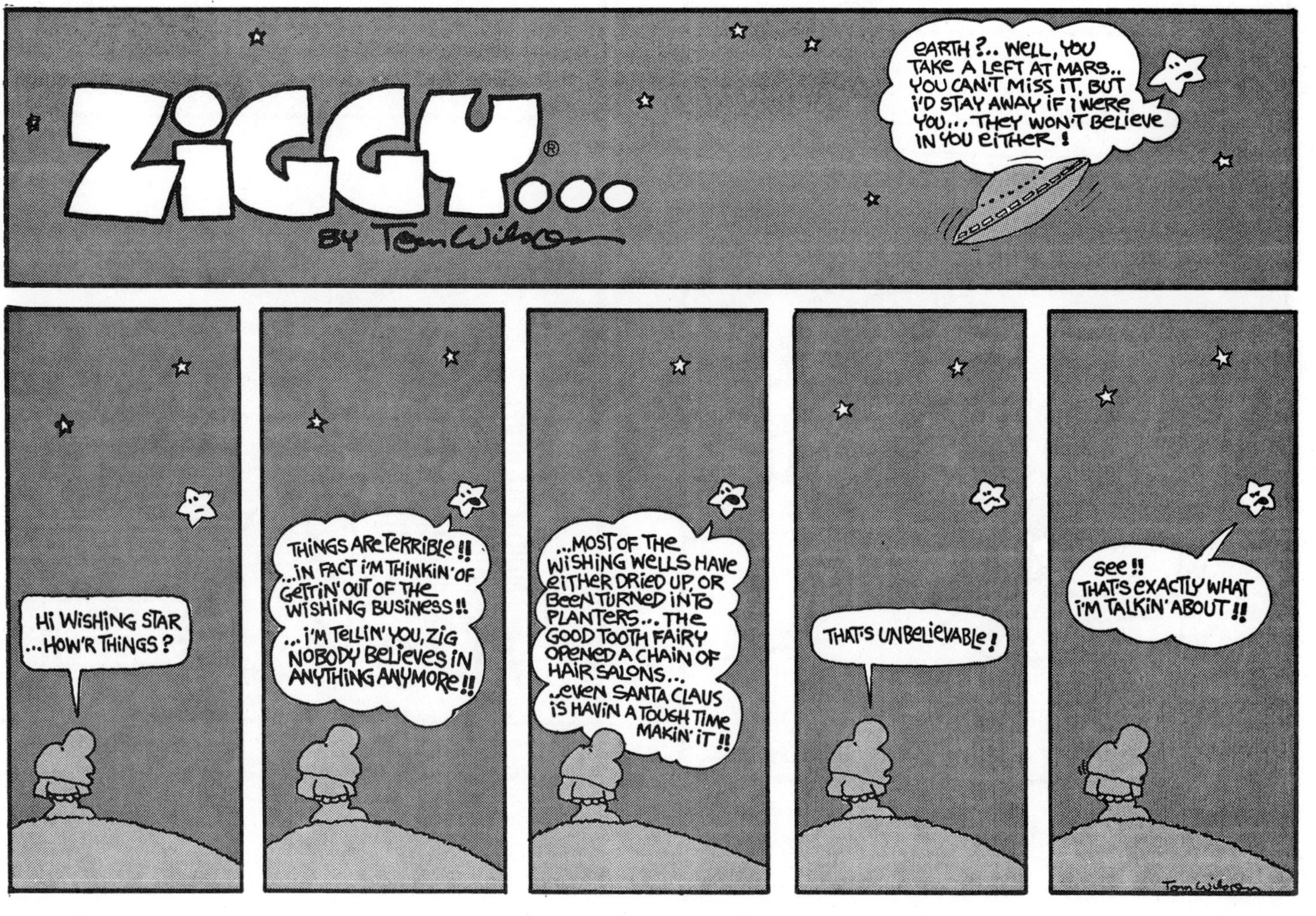
ZIGGY...
BY Tom Wilson
EARTH?.. WELL, YOU TAKE A LEFT AT MARS.. YOU CAN'T MISS IT, BUT I'D STAY AWAY IF I WERE YOU... THEY WON'T BELIEVE IN YOU EITHER!
HI WISHING STAR ...HOW'R THINGS?
THINGS ARE TERRIBLE!! ..IN FACT I'M THINKIN' OF GETTIN' OUT OF THE WISHING BUSINESS!! ...I'M TELLIN' YOU, ZIG NOBODY BELIEVES IN ANYTHING ANYMORE!!
...MOST OF THE WISHING WELLS HAVE EITHER DRIED UP OR BEEN TURNED INTO PLANTERS... THE GOOD TOOTH FAIRY OPENED A CHAIN OF HAIR SALONS... ..EVEN SANTA CLAUS IS HAVIN A TOUGH TIME MAKIN' IT!!
THAT'S UNBELIEVABLE!
SEE!! THAT'S EXACTLY WHAT I'M TALKIN' ABOUT!!

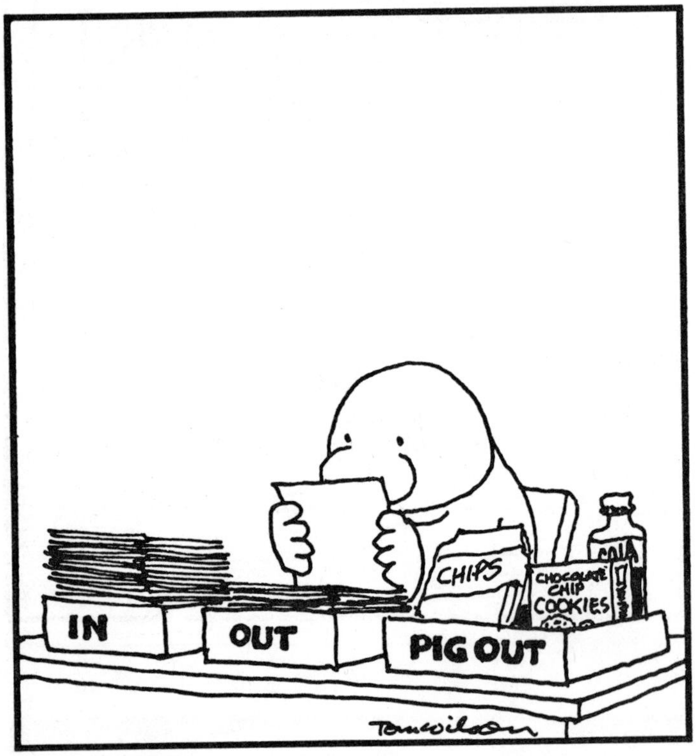
IN
OUT
PIG OUT
CHIPS
CHOCOLATE CHIP COOKIES
COLA

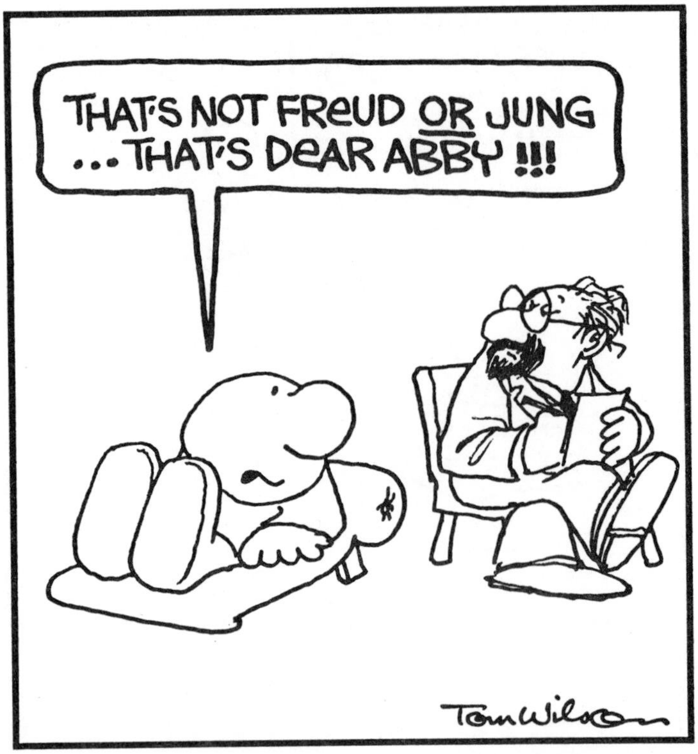
THAT'S NOT FREUD OR JUNG ...THAT'S DEAR ABBY !!!

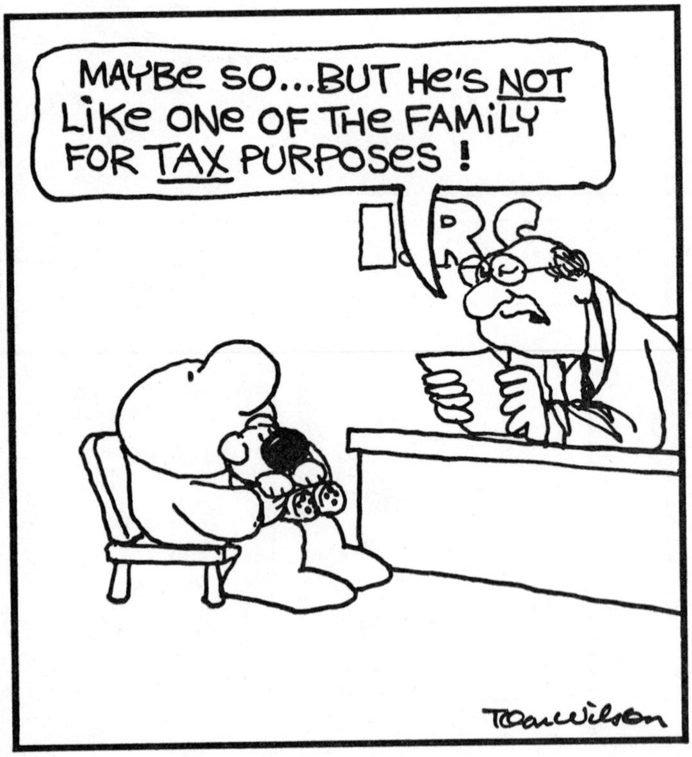
MAYBE SO...BUT HE'S NOT LIKE ONE OF THE FAMILY FOR TAX PURPOSES !

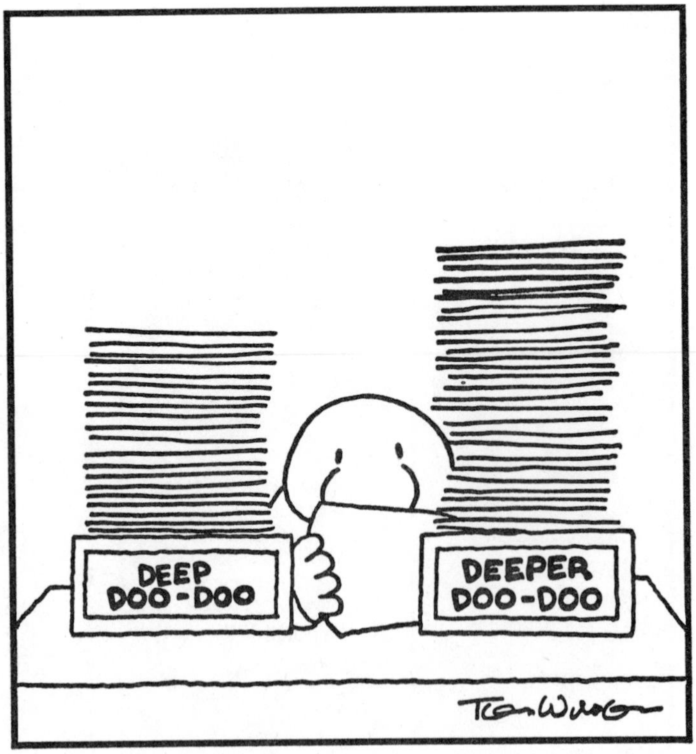
DEEP DOO-DOO
DEEPER DOO-DOO

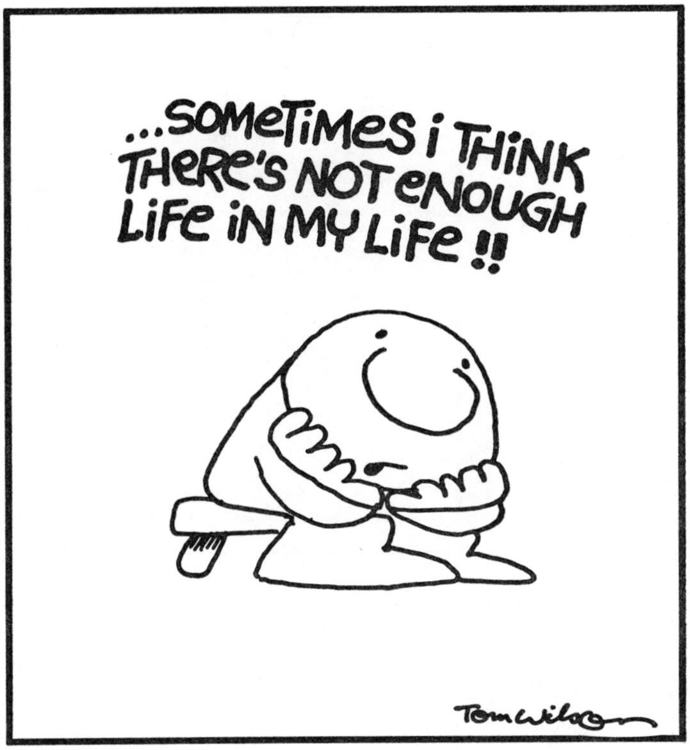
...SOMETIMES I THINK THERE'S NOT ENOUGH LIFE IN MY LIFE !!
Tom Wilson

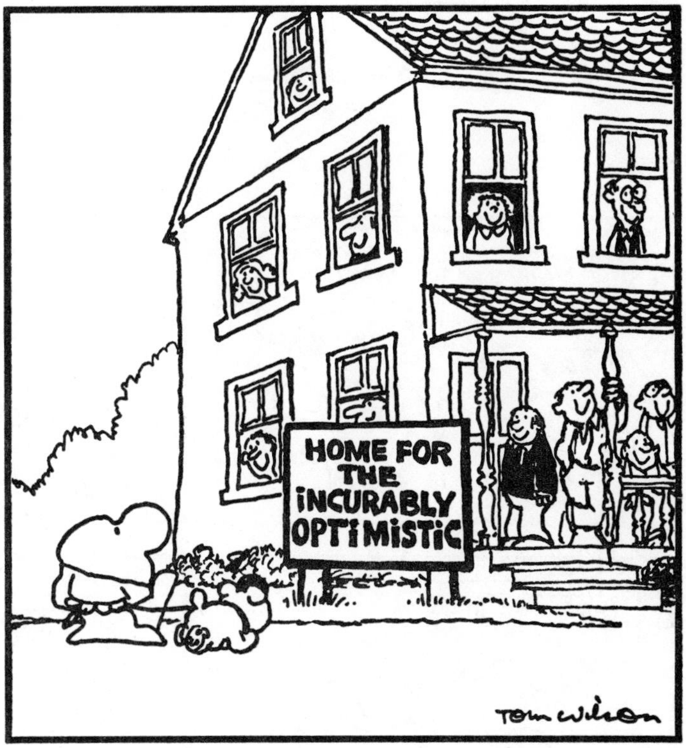
HOME FOR THE INCURABLY OPTIMISTIC
Tom Wilson

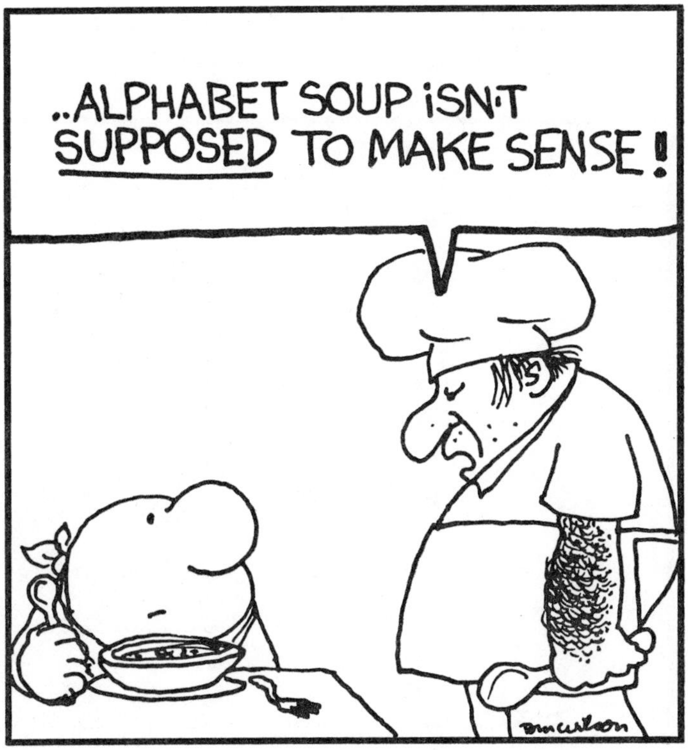
..ALPHABET SOUP ISN'T SUPPOSED TO MAKE SENSE !

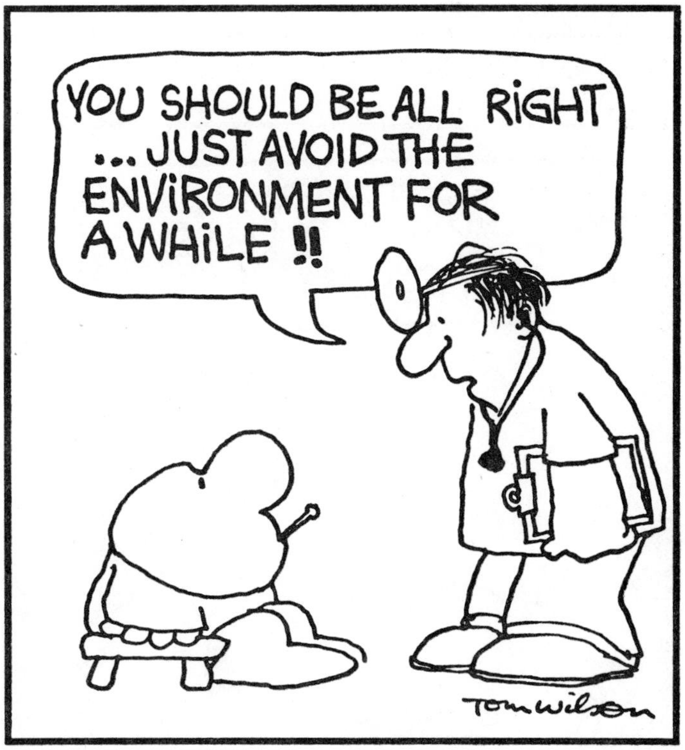
YOU SHOULD BE ALL RIGHT ... JUST AVOID THE ENVIRONMENT FOR A WHILE !!
Tom Wilson

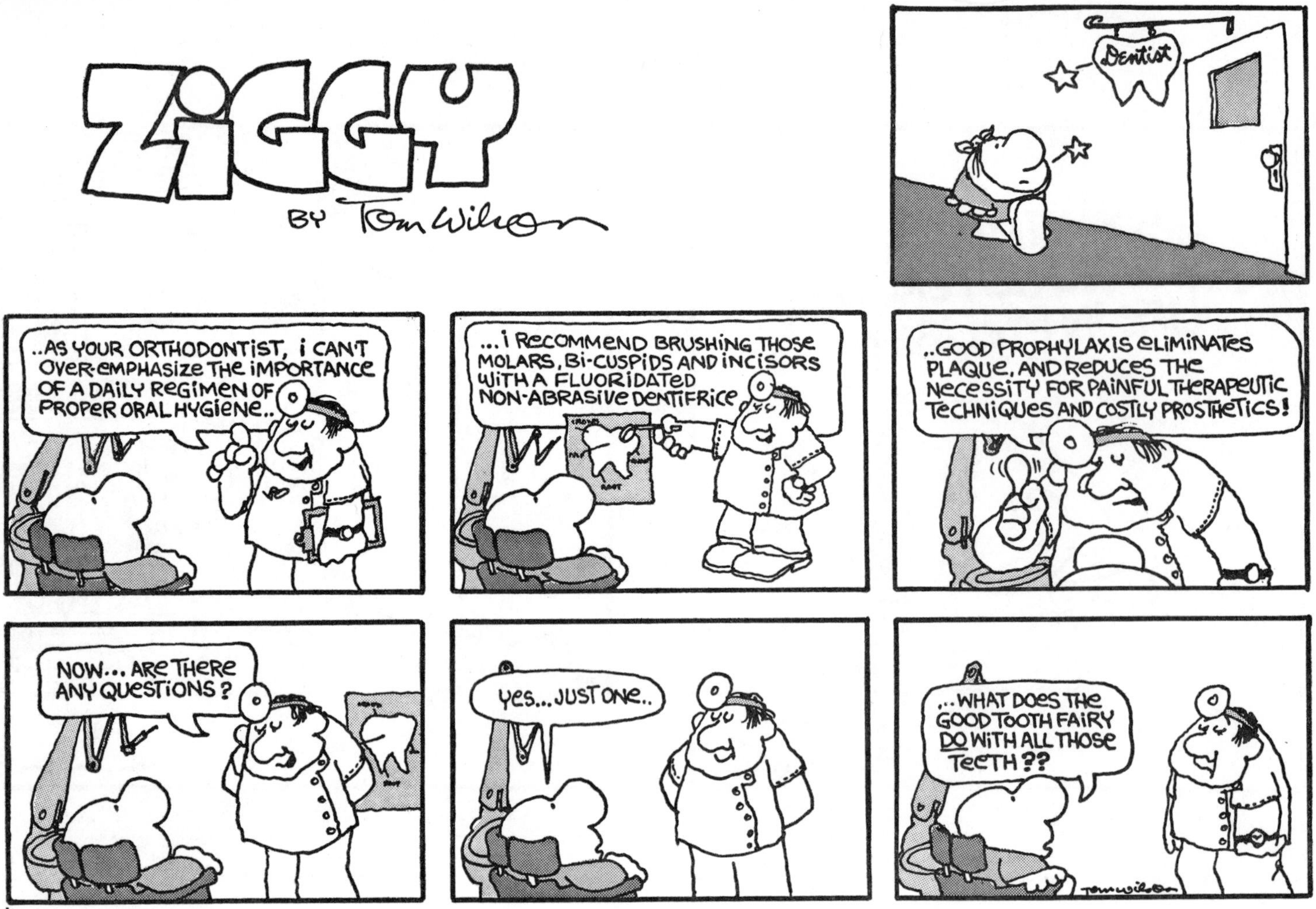
ZiGGY
BY Tom Wilson
Dentist
..AS YOUR ORTHODONTIST, i CAN'T OVER-EMPHASIZE THE iMPORTANCE OF A DAILY REGiMEN OF PROPER ORAL HYGiENE..
...i RECOMMEND BRUSHiNG THOSE MOLARS, Bi-CUSPiDS AND iNCiSORS WiTH A FLUORiDATED NON-ABRASiVE DENTiFRiCE
..GOOD PROPHYLAXIS ELiMiNATES PLAQUE, AND REDUCES THE NECESSiTY FOR PAINFUL THERAPEUTIC TECHNiQUES AND COSTLY PROSTHETICS!
NOW... ARE THERE ANY QUESTIONS?
YES... JUST ONE..
...WHAT DOES THE GOOD TOOTH FAIRY DO WITH ALL THOSE TEETH??
Tom Wilson

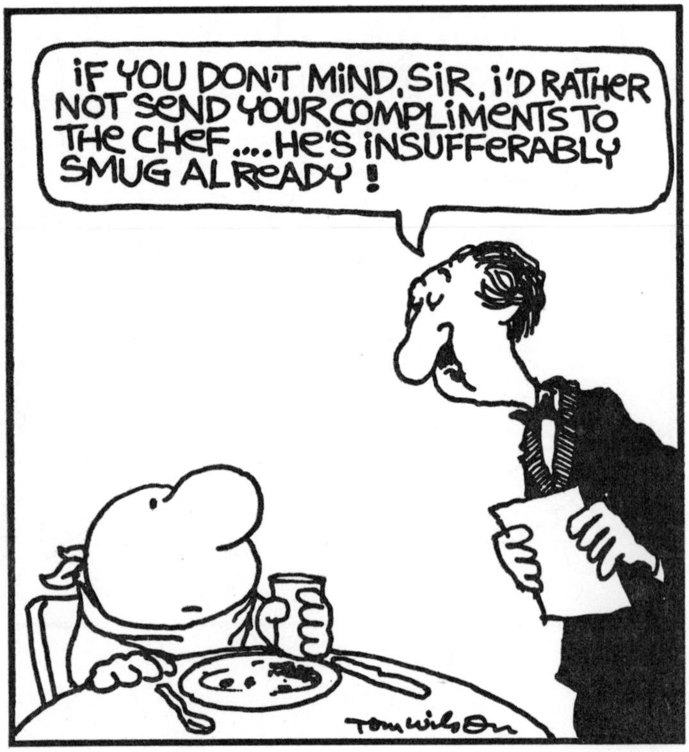
iF YOU DON'T MiND, SiR, i'D RATHER NOT SEND YOUR COMPLiMENTS TO THE CHEF....HE'S iNSUFFERABLY SMUG ALREADY!
Tom Wilson

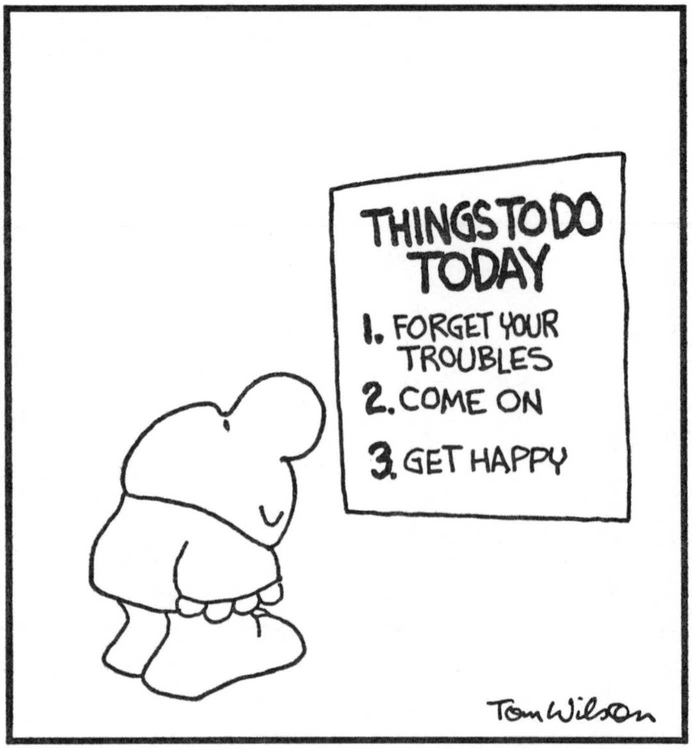
THINGS TO DO TODAY
1. FORGET YOUR TROUBLES
2. COME ON
3. GET HAPPY
Tom Wilson

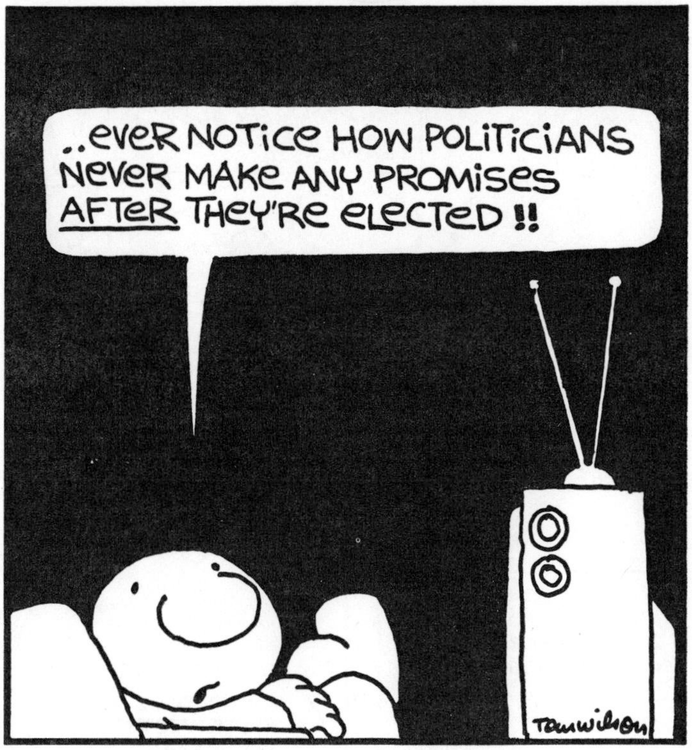
..ever notice how politicians never make any promises AFTER they're elected !!
TomWilson

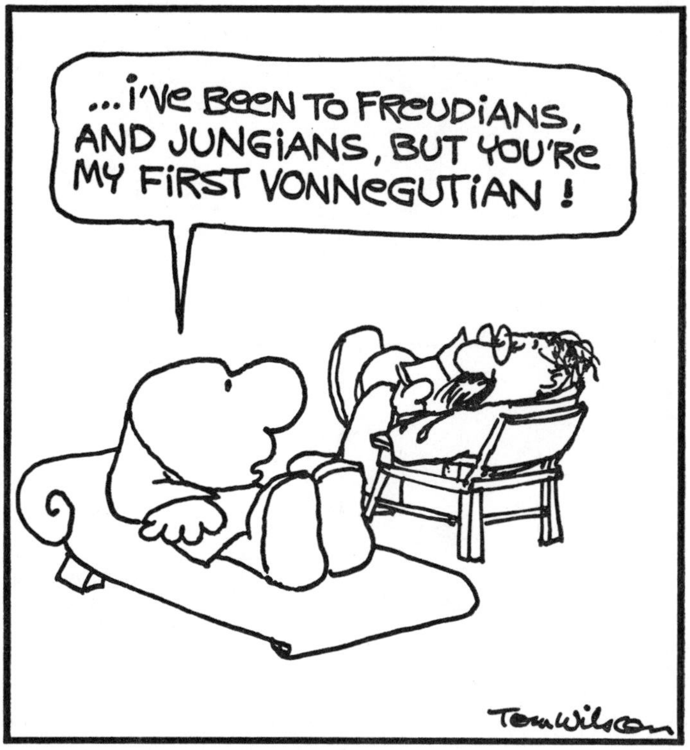
...i've been to Freudians, and Jungians, but you're my first Vonnegutian !
TomWilson

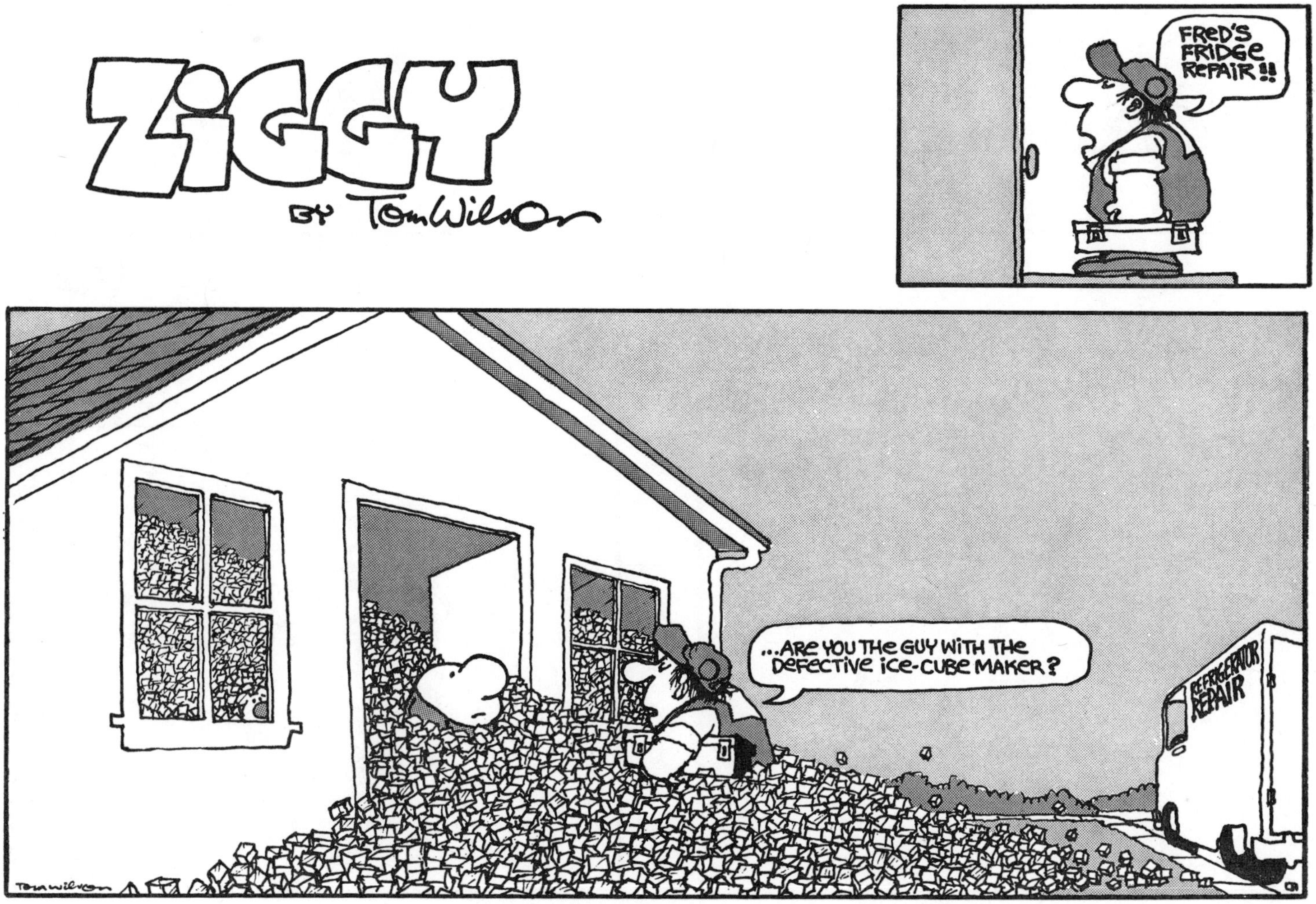
ZIGGY
BY TomWilson
FRED'S FRIDGE REPAIR !!
...ARE YOU THE GUY WITH THE DEFECTIVE ICE-CUBE MAKER?
REFRIGERATOR REPAIR
TomWilson

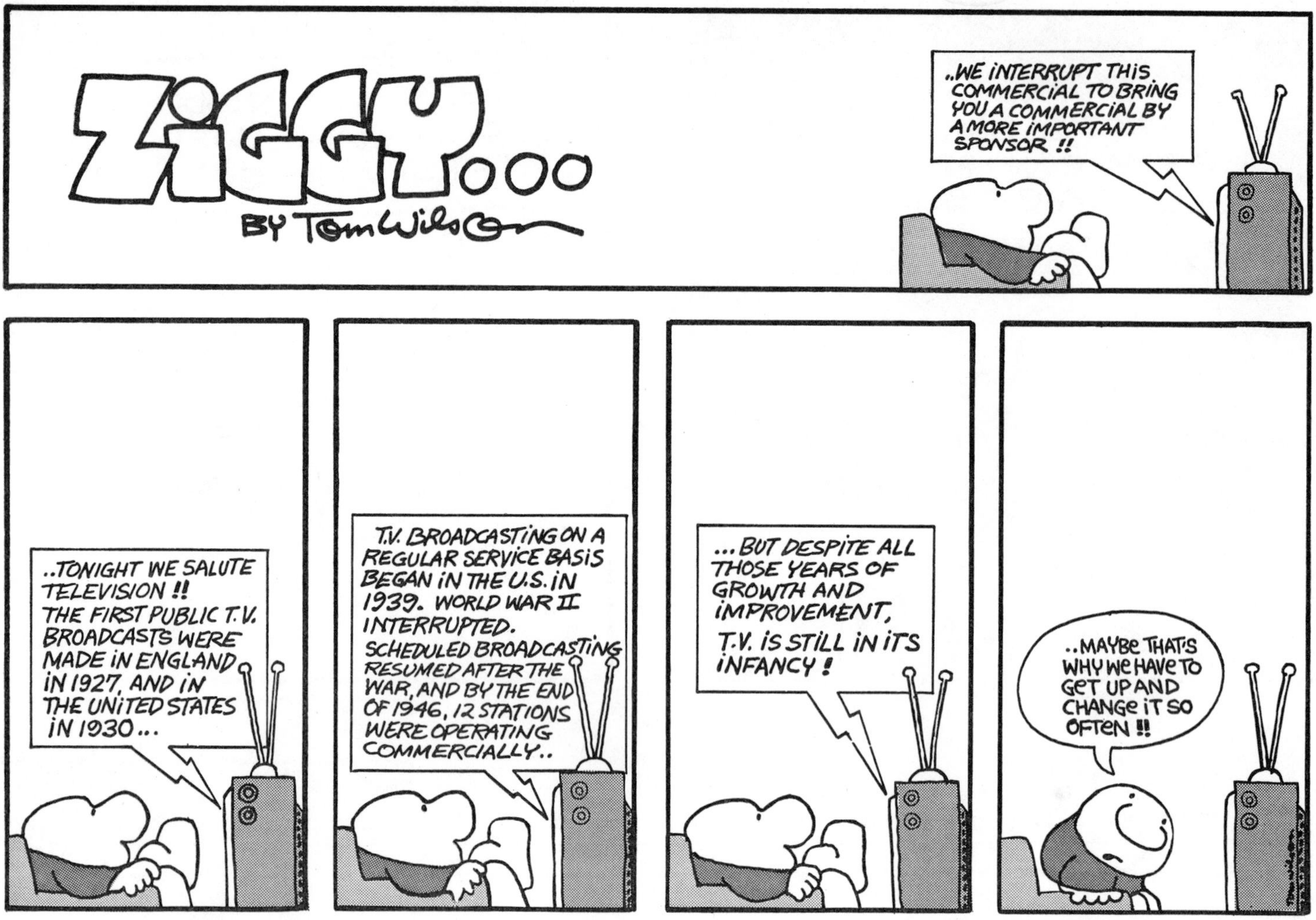
ZiGGY
BY Tom Wilson
..WE INTERRUPT THIS COMMERCIAL TO BRING YOU A COMMERCIAL BY A MORE IMPORTANT SPONSOR !!
..TONIGHT WE SALUTE TELEVISION !! THE FIRST PUBLIC T.V. BROADCASTS WERE MADE IN ENGLAND IN 1927, AND IN THE UNITED STATES IN 1930...
T.V. BROADCASTING ON A REGULAR SERVICE BASIS BEGAN IN THE U.S. IN 1939. WORLD WAR II INTERRUPTED. SCHEDULED BROADCASTING RESUMED AFTER THE WAR, AND BY THE END OF 1946, 12 STATIONS WERE OPERATING COMMERCIALLY..
...BUT DESPITE ALL THOSE YEARS OF GROWTH AND IMPROVEMENT, T.V. IS STILL IN ITS INFANCY !
..MAYBE THAT'S WHY WE HAVE TO GET UP AND CHANGE IT SO OFTEN !!

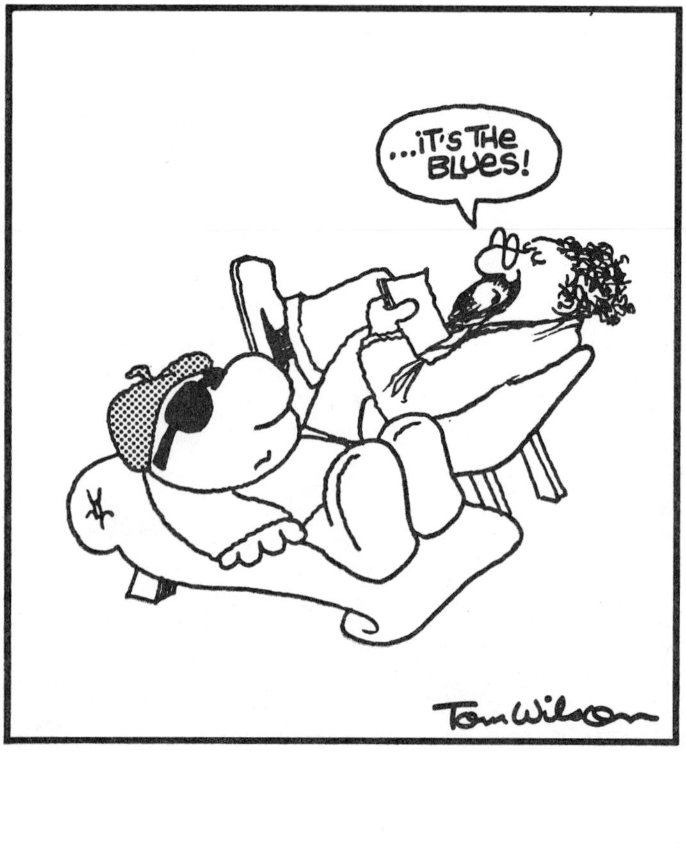
...IT'S THE BLUES!
Tom Wilson

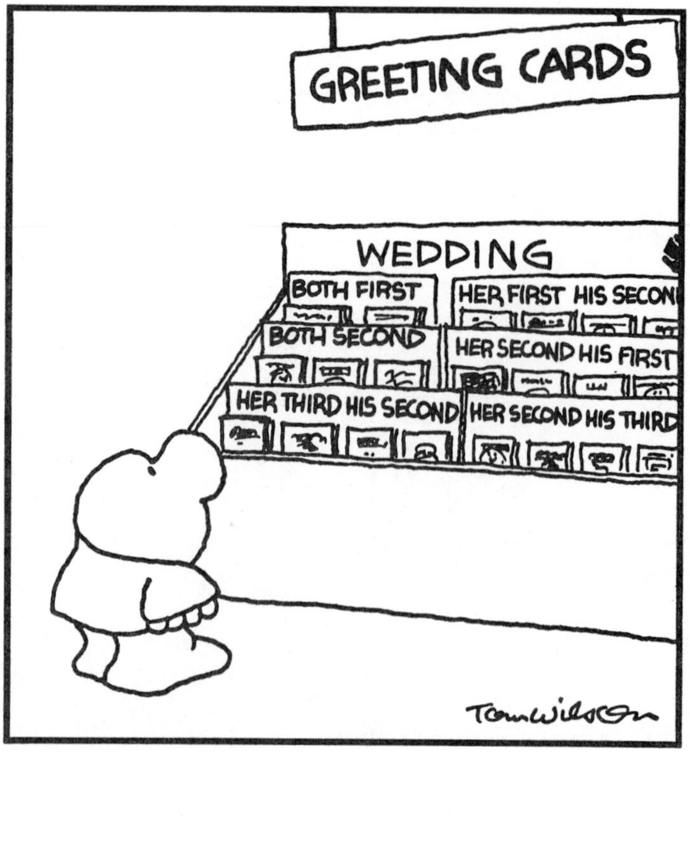
GREETING CARDS
WEDDING
BOTH FIRST
HER FIRST HIS SECON
BOTH SECOND
HER SECOND HIS FIRST
HER THIRD HIS SECOND
HER SECOND HIS THIRD
Tom Wilson

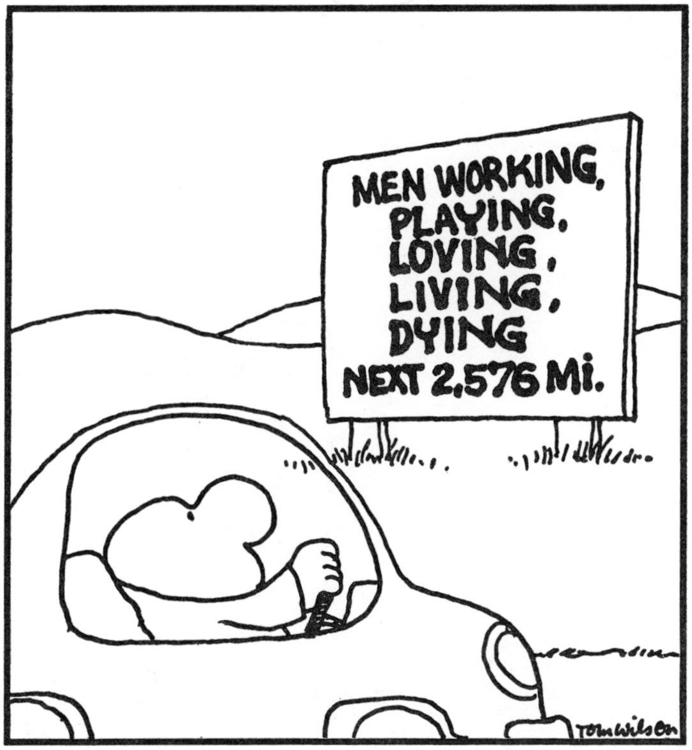
MEN WORKING,
PLAYING,
LOVING,
LIVING,
DYING
NEXT 2,576 Mi.
TOM WILSON

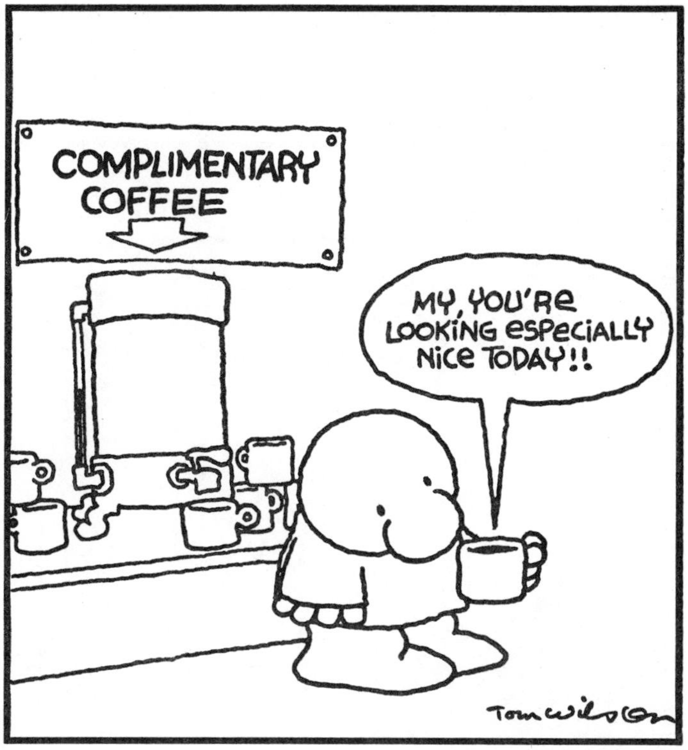
COMPLIMENTARY
COFFEE
MY, YOU'RE LOOKING ESPECIALLY NICE TODAY!!
TOM WILSON

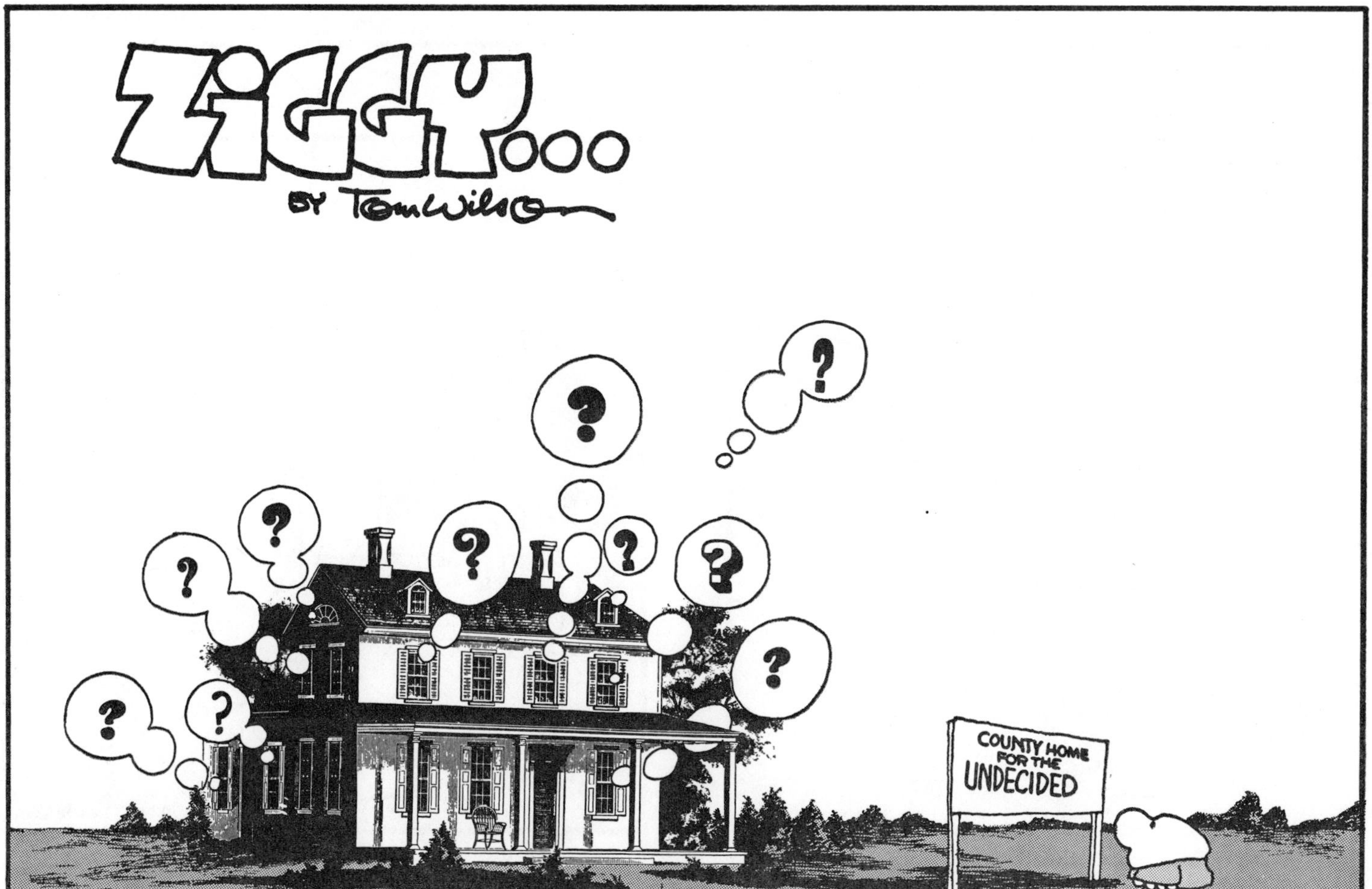
ZIGGY
BY TOM WILSON
COUNTY HOME FOR THE UNDECIDED
TOM WILSON

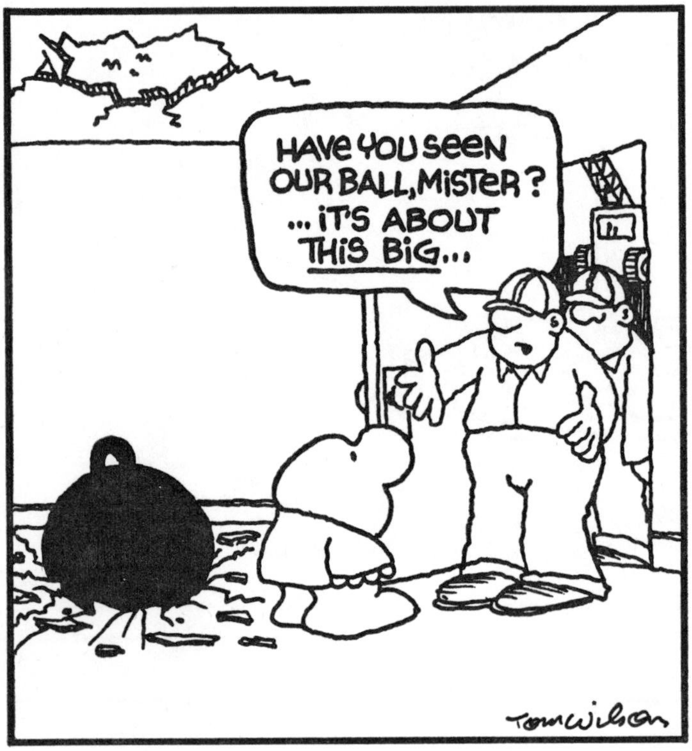
HAVE YOU SEEN OUR BALL, MISTER? ... IT'S ABOUT THIS BIG...
TOM WILSON

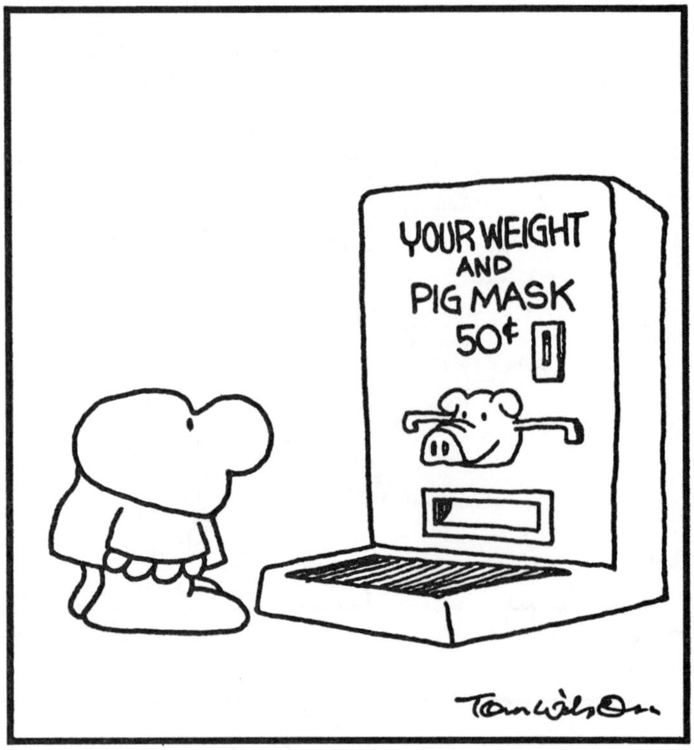
YOUR WEIGHT AND PIG MASK 50¢
TOM WILSON

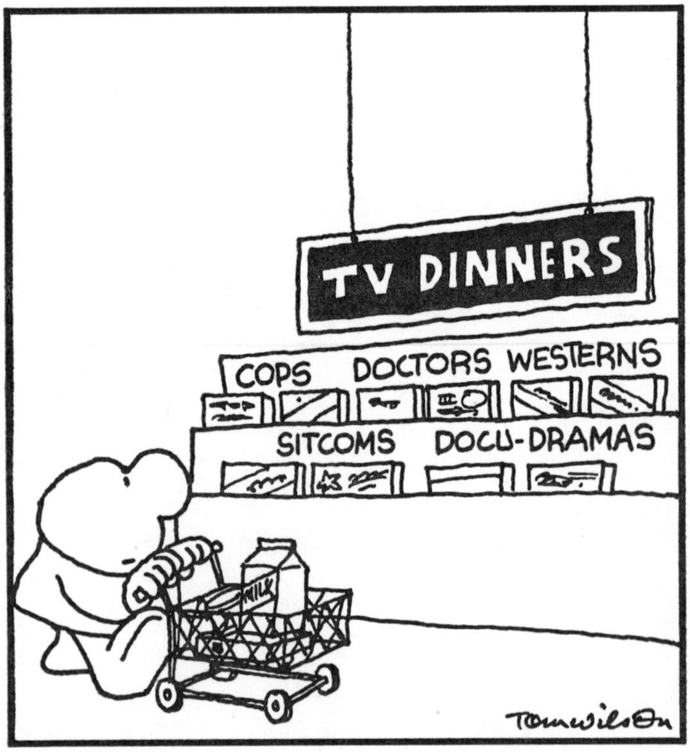
TV DINNERS
COPS
DOCTORS
WESTERNS
SITCOMS
DOCU-DRAMAS
MILK
TOM WILSON

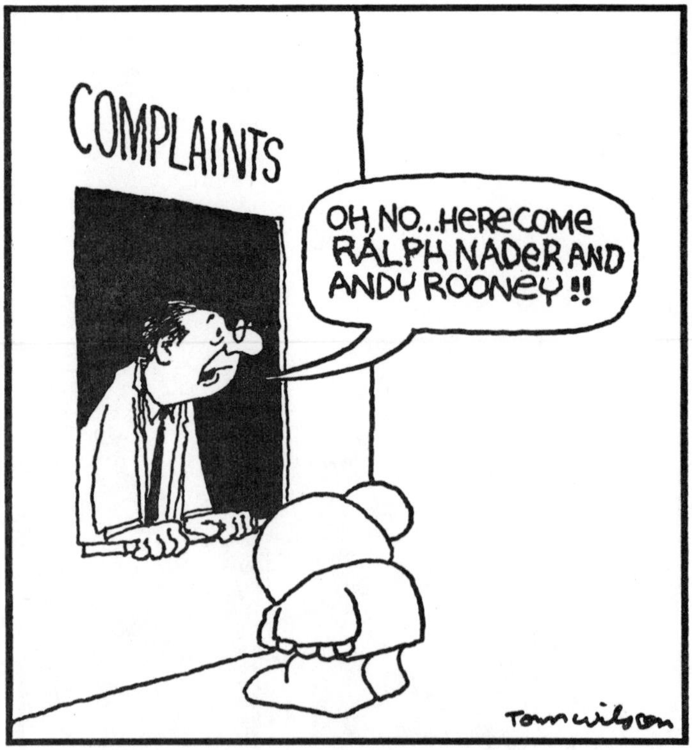
COMPLAINTS
OH, NO...HERE COME RALPH NADER AND ANDY ROONEY!!
TOM WILSON

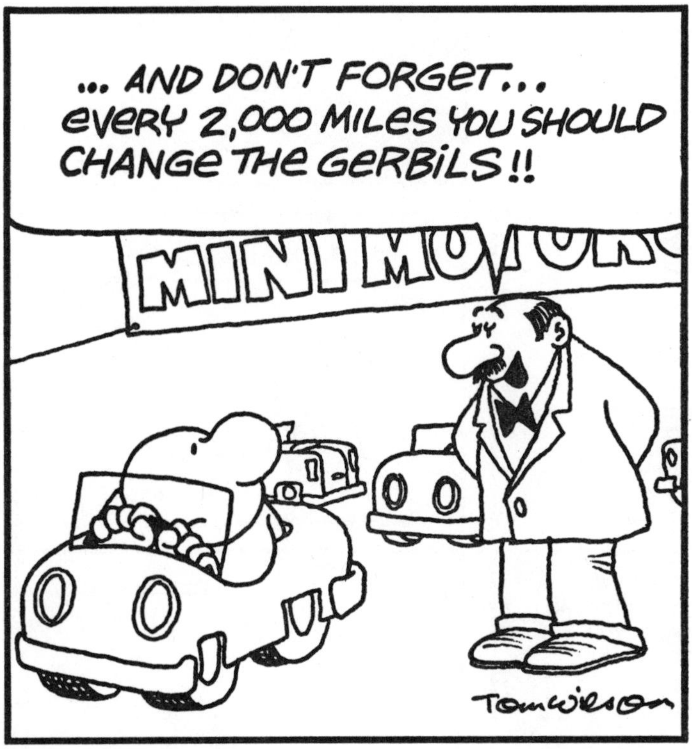
... AND DON'T FORGET...
EVERY 2,000 MILES YOU SHOULD
CHANGE THE GERBILS!!
MINI MO
Tom Wilson

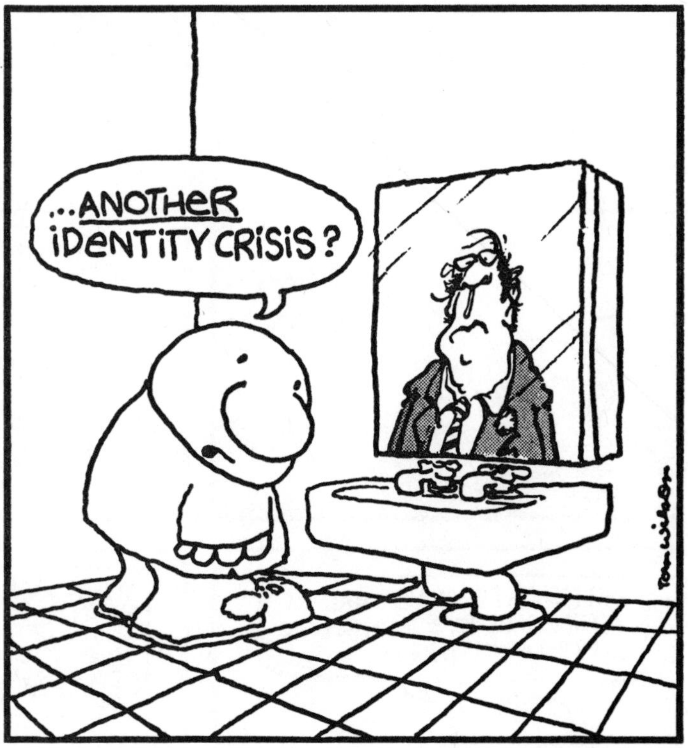
...ANOTHER
IDENTITY CRISIS?
Tom Wilson

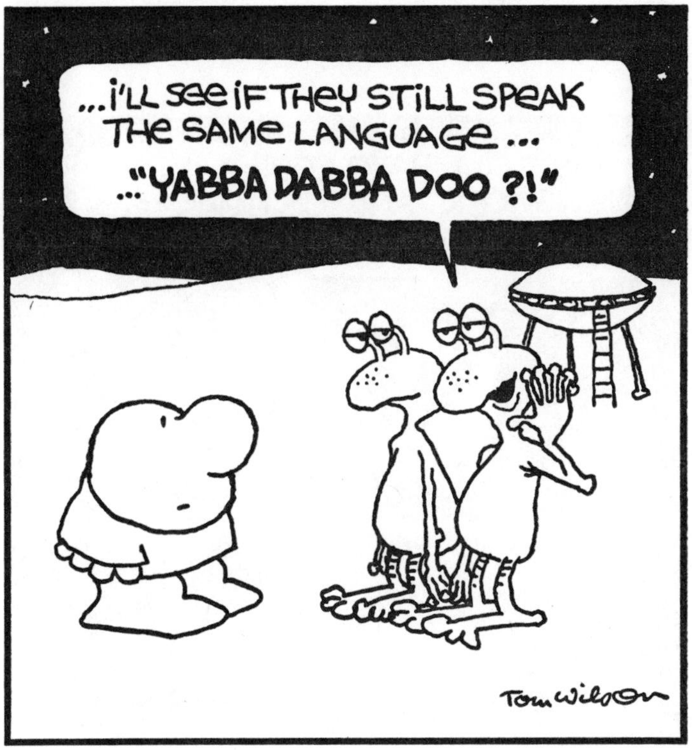
...I'LL SEE IF THEY STILL SPEAK
THE SAME LANGUAGE...
..."YABBA DABBA DOO?!"
Tom Wilson

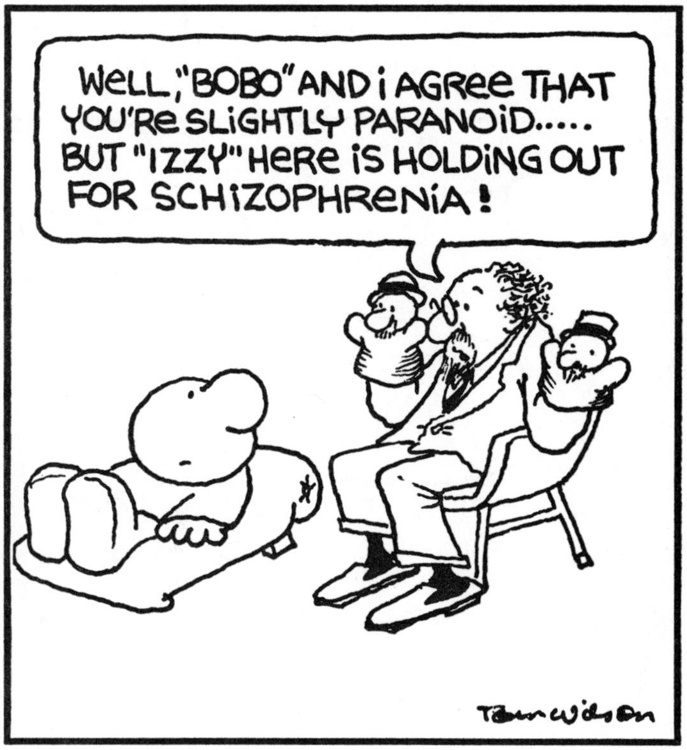
WELL, "BOBO" AND I AGREE THAT
YOU'RE SLIGHTLY PARANOID.....
BUT "IZZY" HERE IS HOLDING OUT
FOR SCHIZOPHRENIA!
Tom Wilson

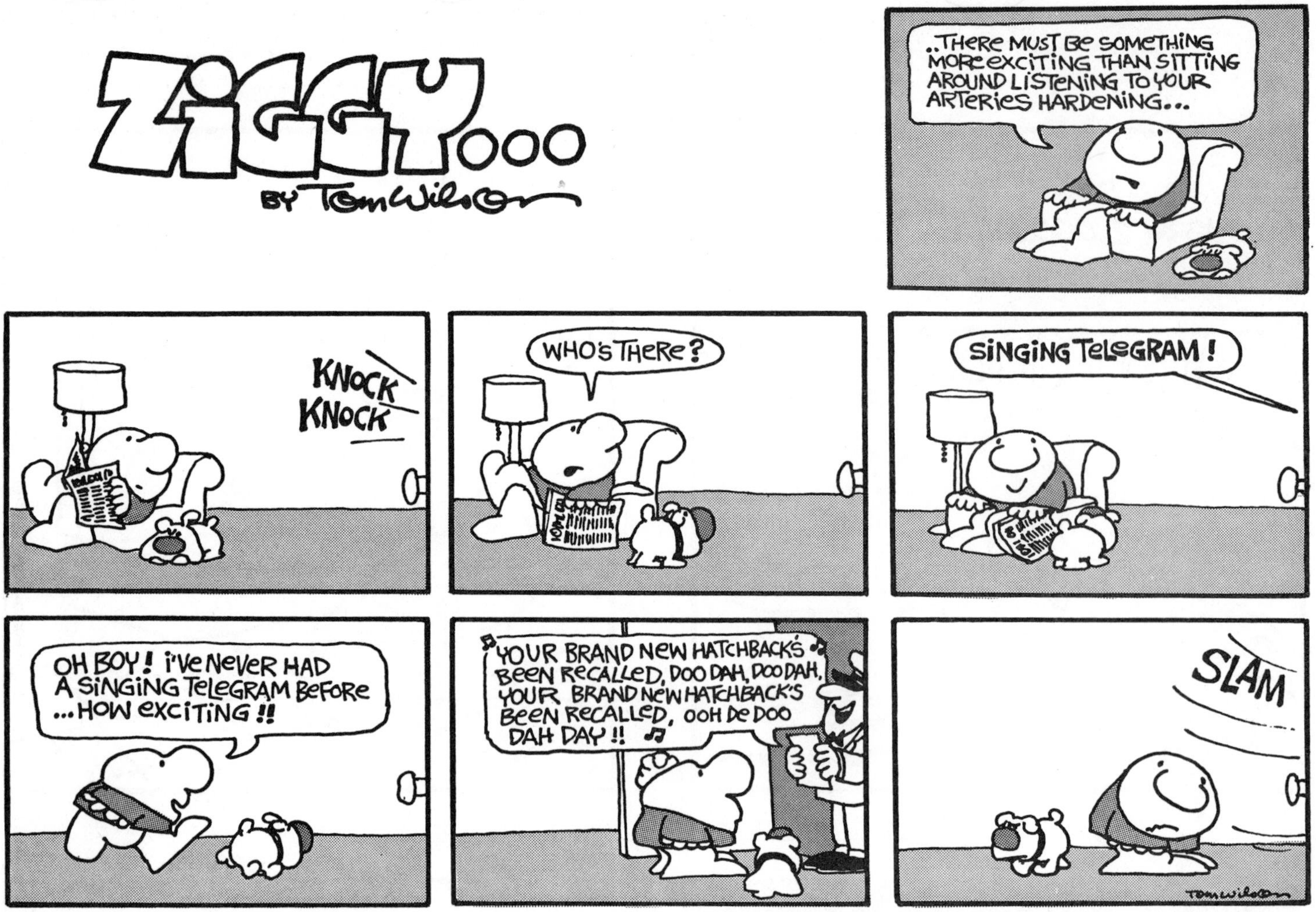
ZIGGY ooo
BY Tom Wilson
..THERE MUST BE SOMETHING MORE EXCITING THAN SITTING AROUND LISTENING TO YOUR ARTERIES HARDENING...
KNOCK KNOCK
WHO'S THERE?
SINGING TELEGRAM!
OH BOY! I'VE NEVER HAD A SINGING TELEGRAM BEFORE ...HOW EXCITING!!
YOUR BRAND NEW HATCHBACK'S BEEN RECALLED, DOO DAH, DOO DAH, YOUR BRAND NEW HATCHBACK'S BEEN RECALLED, OOH DE DOO DAH DAY!!
SLAM
Tom Wilson

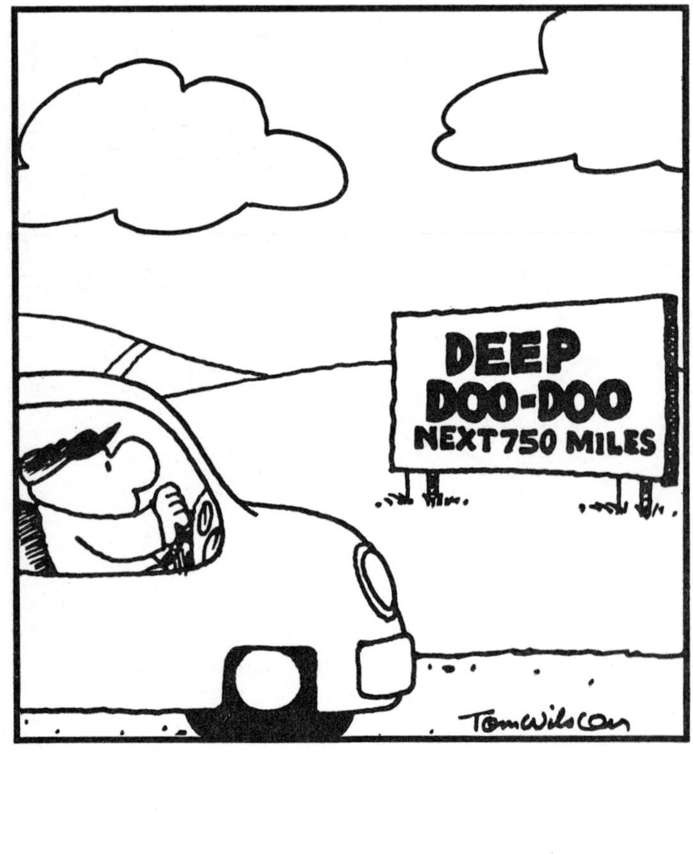
DEEP DOO-DOO NEXT 750 MILES
Tom Wilson

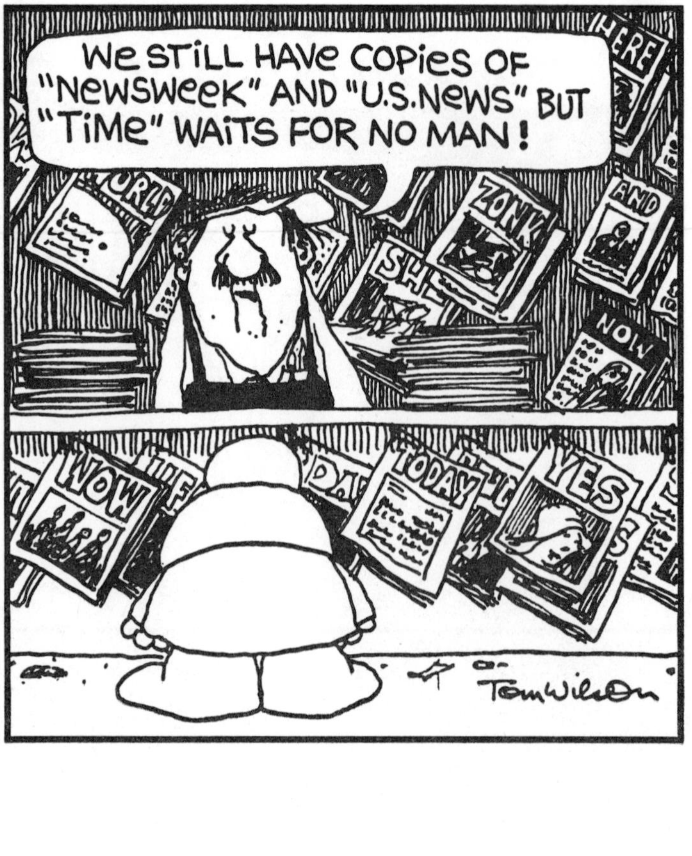
WE STILL HAVE COPIES OF "NEWSWEEK" AND "U.S. NEWS" BUT "TIME" WAITS FOR NO MAN!
ZONK
NOW
TODAY
YES
Tom Wilson

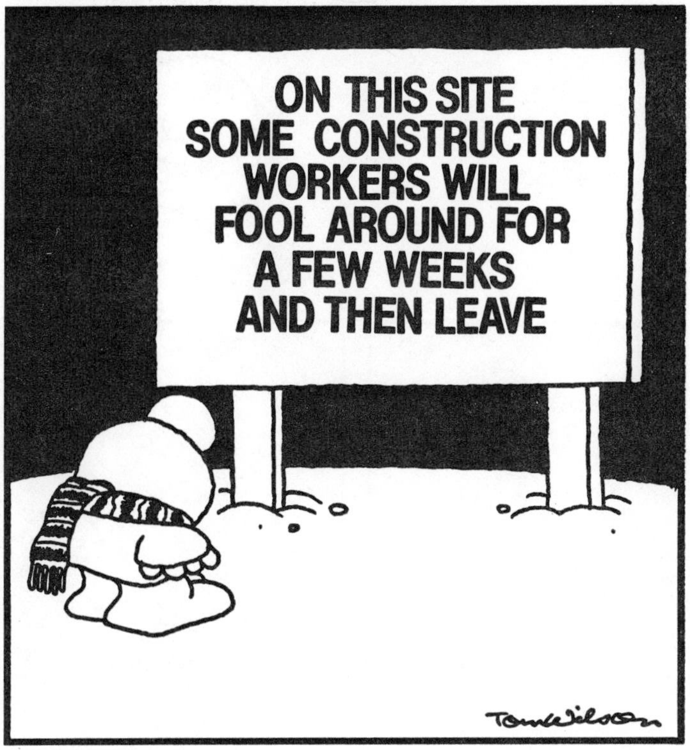
ON THIS SITE SOME CONSTRUCTION WORKERS WILL FOOL AROUND FOR A FEW WEEKS AND THEN LEAVE

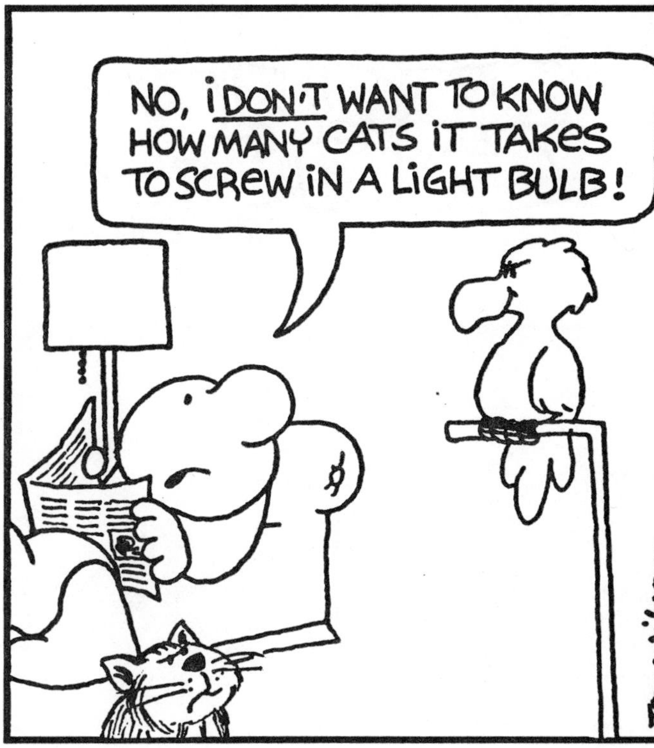
NO, I DON'T WANT TO KNOW HOW MANY CATS IT TAKES TO SCREW IN A LIGHT BULB!

ZIGGY...
BY TOM WILSON

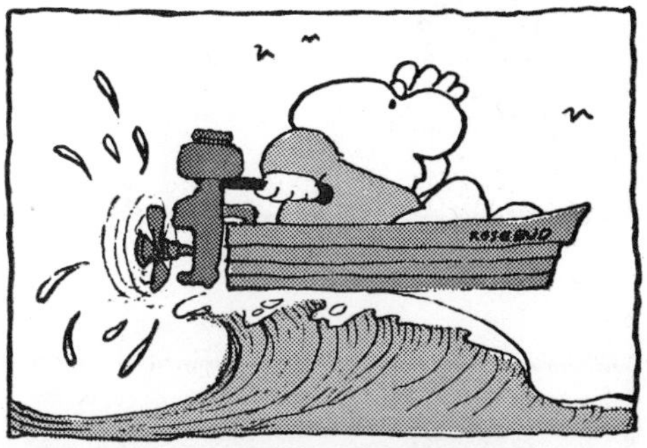

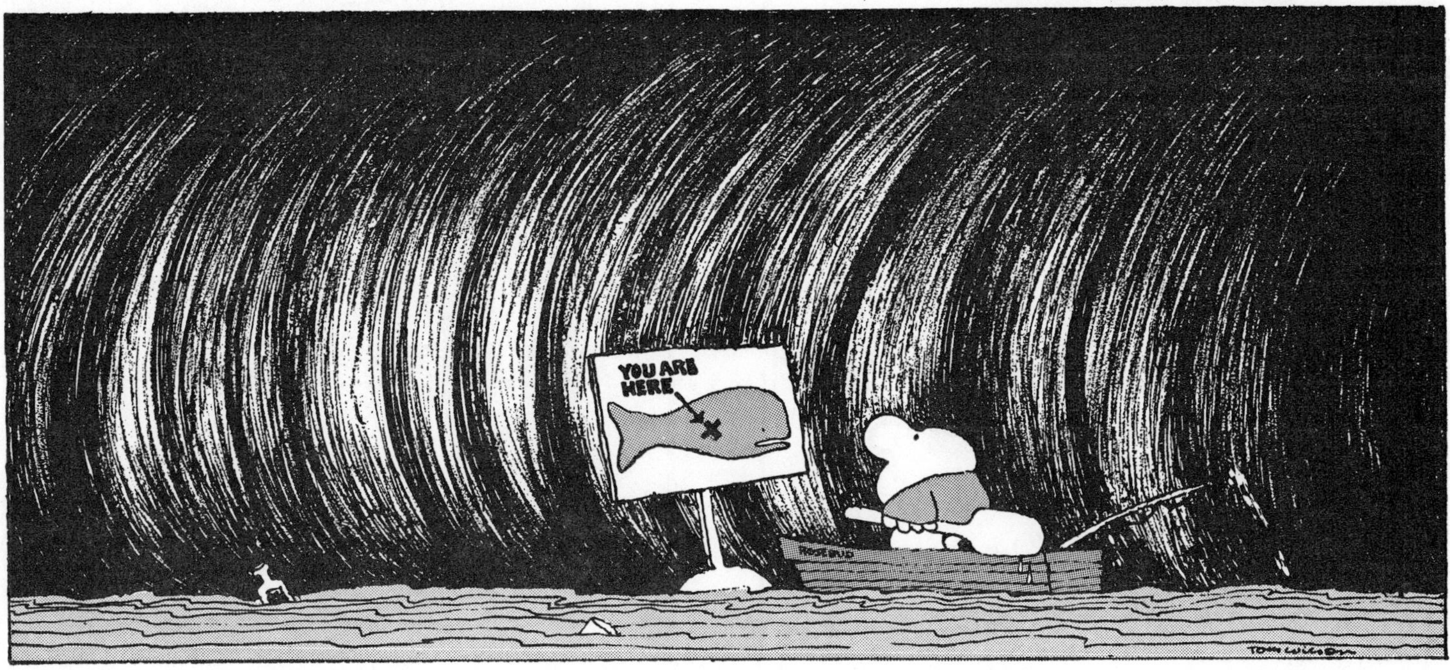
YOU ARE HERE

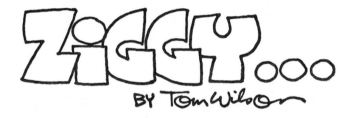

ZIGGY...
BY TOM WILSON

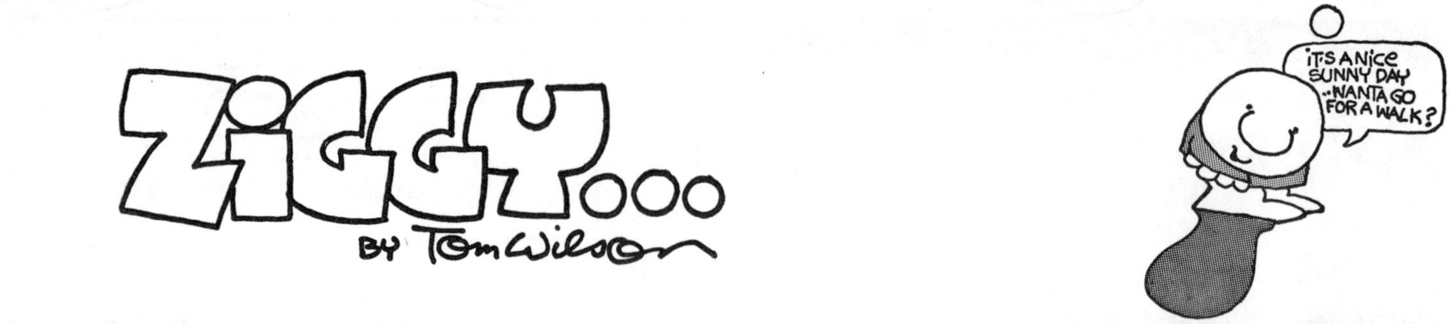
IT'S A NICE SUNNY DAY ..WANTA GO FOR A WALK?

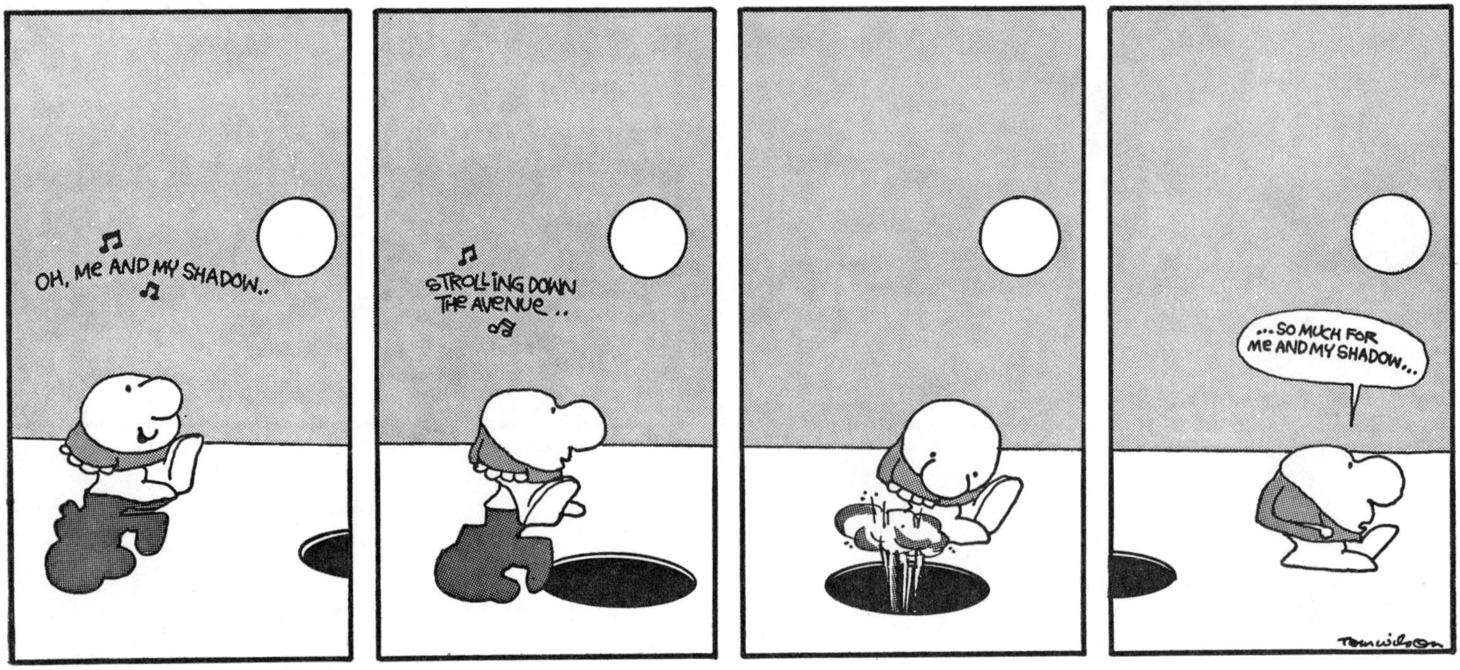
OH, ME AND MY SHADOW..
STROLLING DOWN THE AVENUE..
...SO MUCH FOR ME AND MY SHADOW...
TOM WILSON

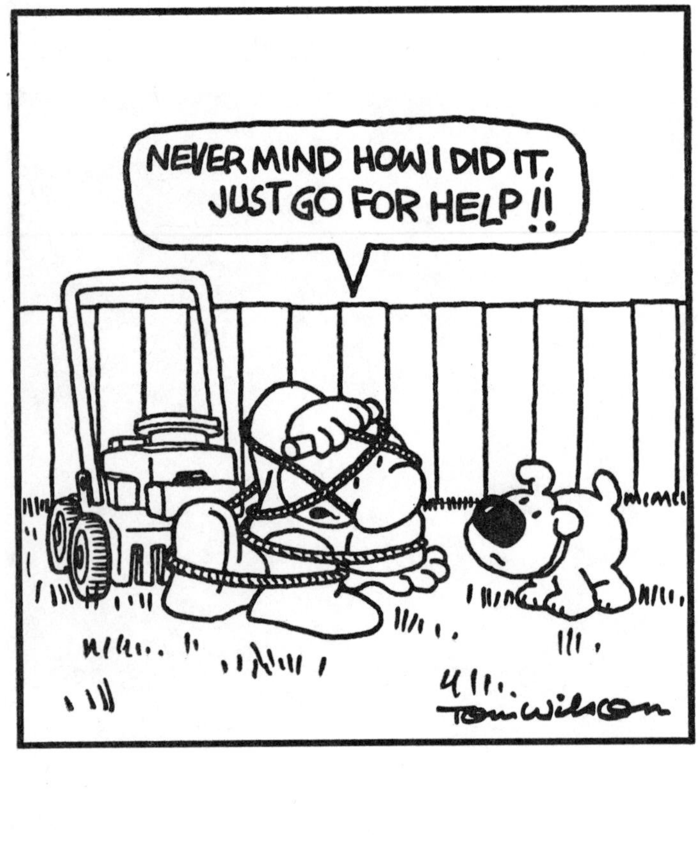
NEVER MIND HOW I DID IT, JUST GO FOR HELP!!
TOM WILSON

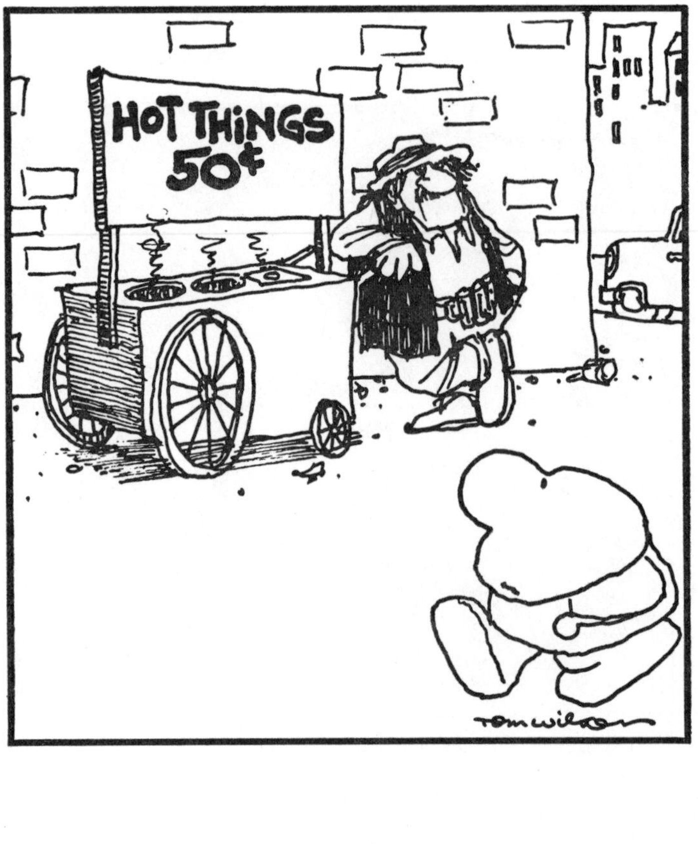
HOT THINGS 50¢
TOM WILSON

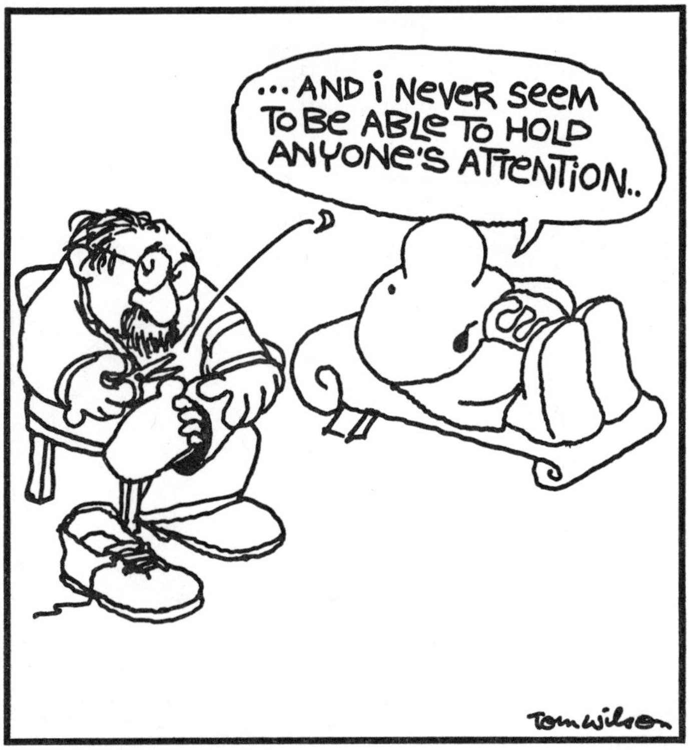
... AND i NEVER SEEM TO BE ABLE TO HOLD ANYONE'S ATTENTION..
TOM WILSON

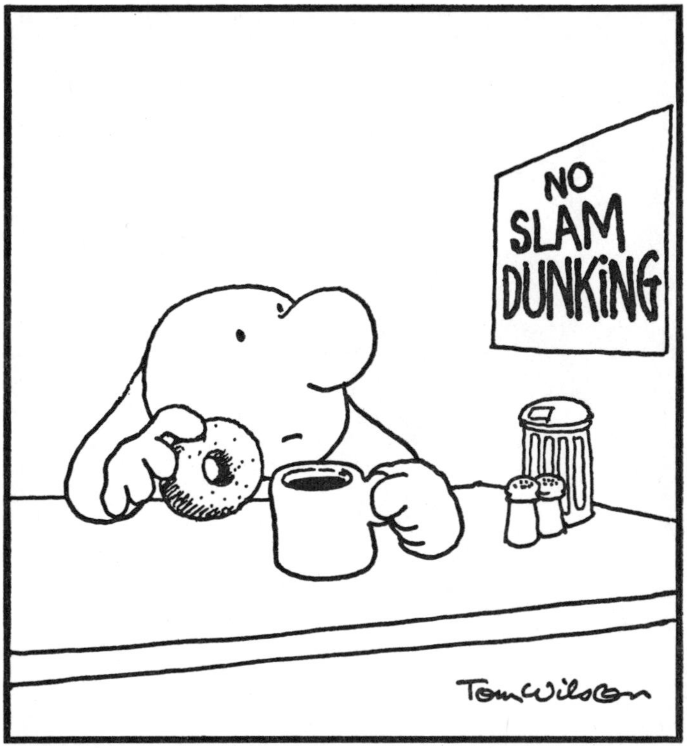
NO SLAM DUNKING
TOM WILSON

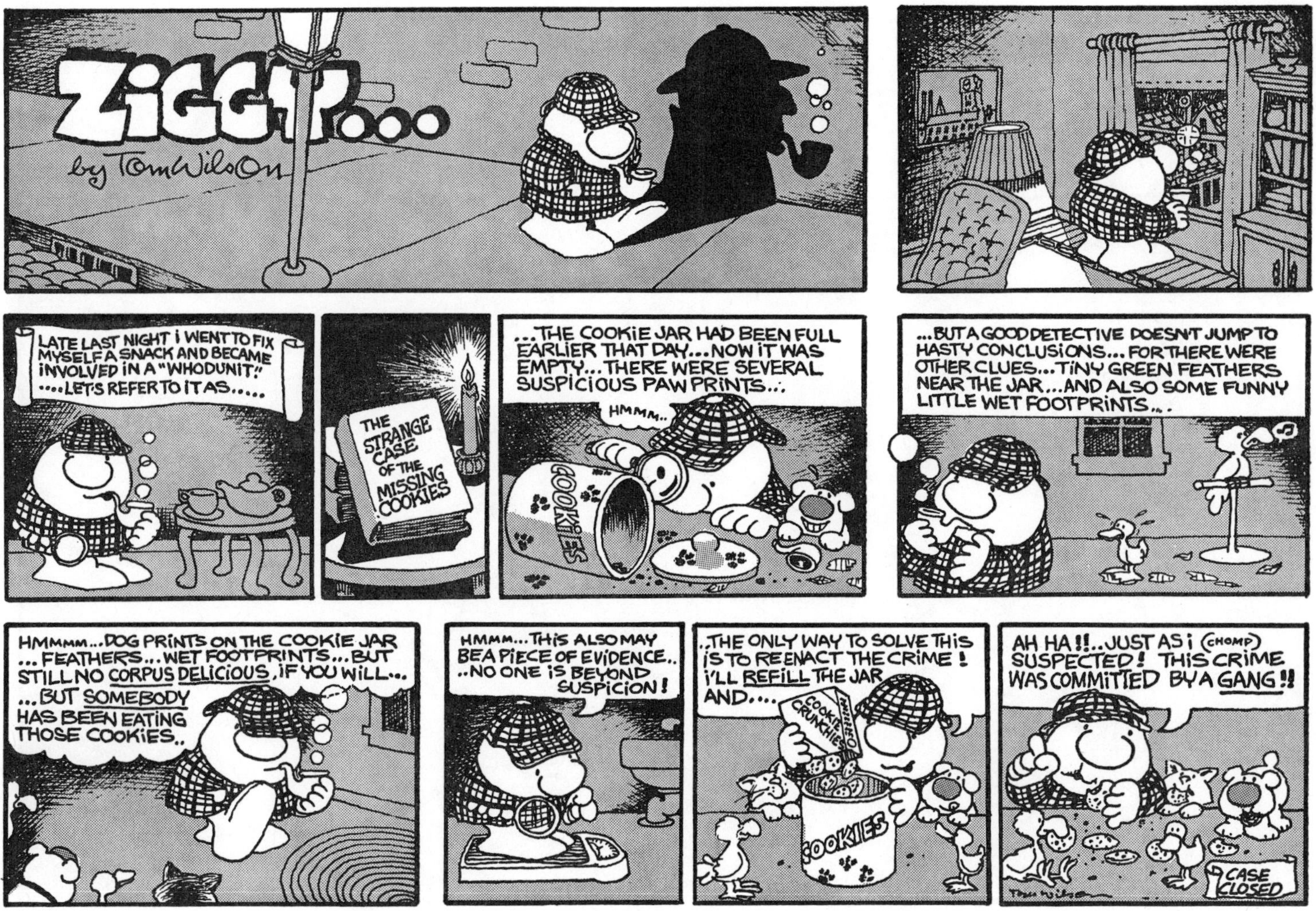
ZIGGY...
by TOM WILSON
LATE LAST NIGHT i WENT TO FIX MYSELF A SNACK AND BECAME INVOLVED IN A "WHODUNIT!" ....LET'S REFER TO IT AS.....
THE STRANGE CASE OF THE MISSING COOKIES
...THE COOKIE JAR HAD BEEN FULL EARLIER THAT DAY... NOW IT WAS EMPTY... THERE WERE SEVERAL SUSPICIOUS PAW PRINTS...
HMMM..
COOKIES
...BUT A GOOD DETECTIVE DOESN'T JUMP TO HASTY CONCLUSIONS... FOR THERE WERE OTHER CLUES... TINY GREEN FEATHERS NEAR THE JAR... AND ALSO SOME FUNNY LITTLE WET FOOTPRINTS...
HMMMM... DOG PRINTS ON THE COOKIE JAR ... FEATHERS... WET FOOTPRINTS... BUT STILL NO CORPUS DELICIOUS, IF YOU WILL... ...BUT SOMEBODY HAS BEEN EATING THOSE COOKIES..
HMMM... THIS ALSO MAY BE A PIECE OF EVIDENCE.. ..NO ONE IS BEYOND SUSPICION!
..THE ONLY WAY TO SOLVE THIS IS TO REENACT THE CRIME! I'LL REFILL THE JAR AND....
COOKIE CRUNCHIES
COOKIES
AH HA!!..JUST AS i (CHOMP) SUSPECTED! THIS CRIME WAS COMMITTED BY A GANG!!
CASE CLOSED
TOM WILSON

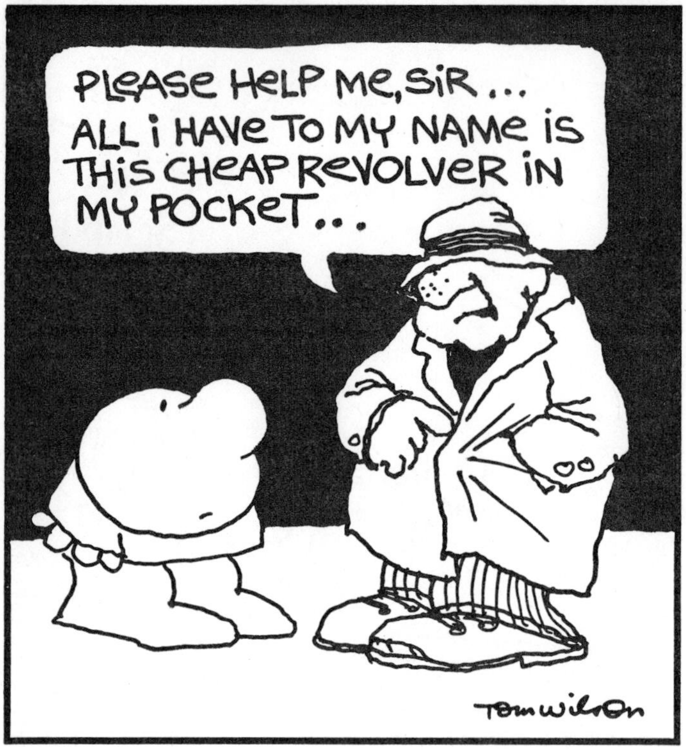
PLEASE HELP ME, SIR ... ALL I HAVE TO MY NAME IS THIS CHEAP REVOLVER IN MY POCKET...
TOM WILSON

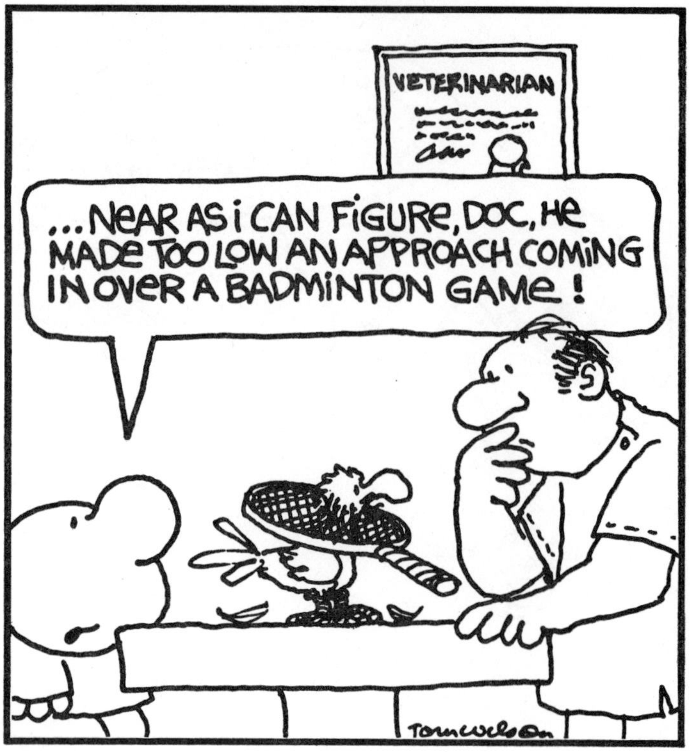
VETERINARIAN
...NEAR AS I CAN FIGURE, DOC, HE MADE TOO LOW AN APPROACH COMING IN OVER A BADMINTON GAME!
TOM WILSON

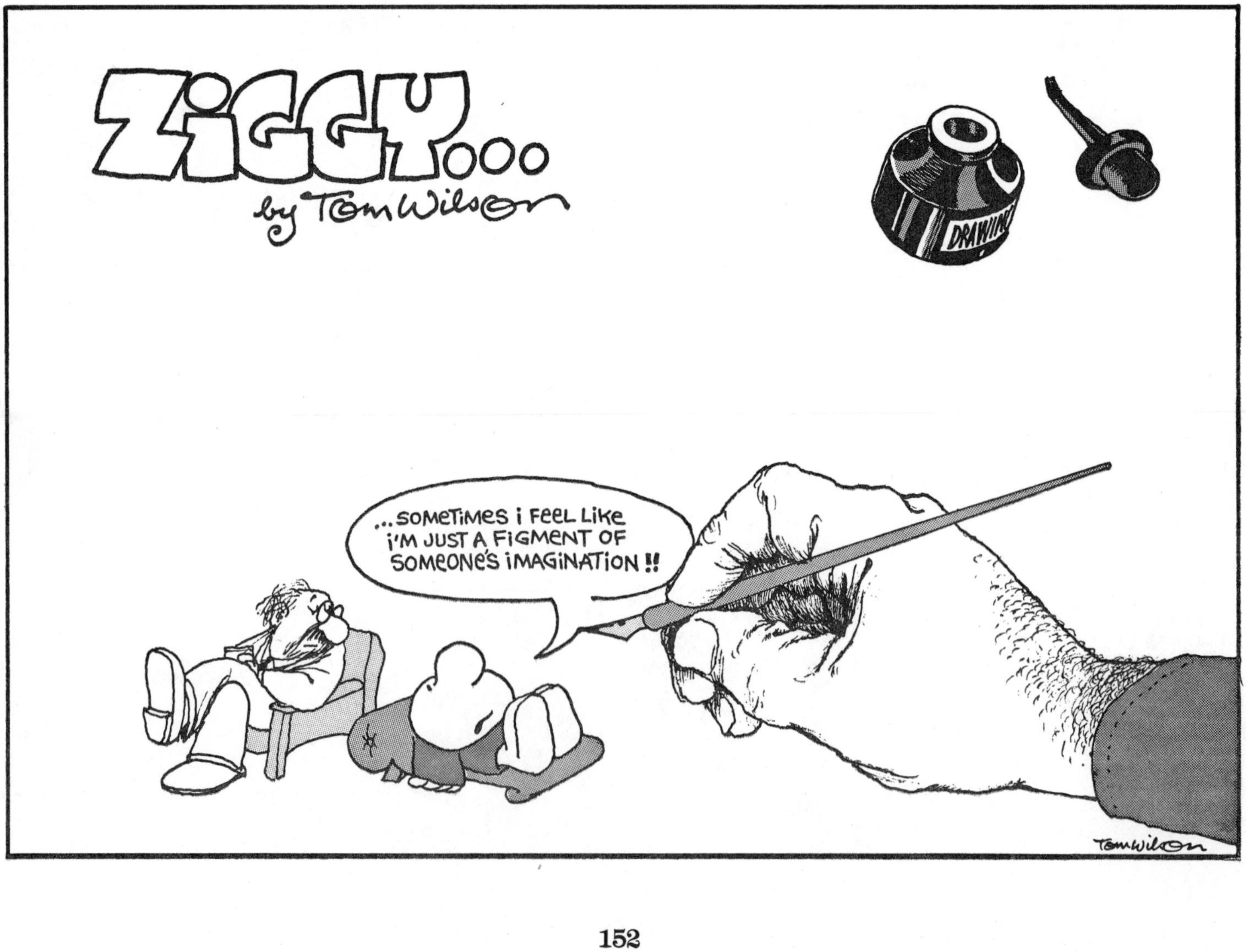
ZIGGY...
by TOM WILSON
DRAWING
...SOMETIMES I FEEL LIKE I'M JUST A FIGMENT OF SOMEONE'S IMAGINATION!!
TOM WILSON